THE *CRATYLUS* OF PLATO

The *Cratylus*, one of Plato's most difficult and intriguing dialogues, explores the relations between a name and the thing it names. The questions that arise lead the characters to face a number of major issues: truth and falsehood, relativism, the possibility of a perfect language, the relation between the investigation of names and that of reality, the Heraclitean flux theory and the Theory of Forms. This is the first full-scale commentary on the *Cratylus* and offers a definitive interpretation of the dialogue. It contains translations of the passages discussed and a line-by-line analysis which deals with textual matters and unravels Plato's dense and subtle arguments, reaching a novel interpretation of some of the dialogue's main themes as well as of many individual passages. The book is intended primarily for graduate students and scholars, both philosophers and classicists, but presupposes no previous acquaintance with the subject and is accessible to undergraduates.

FRANCESCO ADEMOLLO has held postdoctoral research positions at the University of Florence and at the Scuola Normale Superiore in Pisa, and currently teaches Greek and Latin at the Liceo Classico Galileo in Florence. He has published articles on Plato, Aristotle and other topics in ancient philosophy.

THE *CRATYLUS* OF PLATO

A Commentary

FRANCESCO ADEMOLLO

CAMBRIDGE
UNIVERSITY PRESS

University Printing House, Cambridge CB2 8BS, United Kingdom

One Liberty Plaza, 20th Floor, New York, NY 10006, USA

477 Williamstown Road, Port Melbourne, VIC 3207, Australia

314-321, 3rd Floor, Plot 3, Splendor Forum, Jasola District Centre, New Delhi - 110025, India

79 Anson Road, #06-04/06, Singapore 079906

Cambridge University Press is part of the University of Cambridge.

It furthers the University's mission by disseminating knowledge in the pursuit of education, learning and research at the highest international levels of excellence.

www.cambridge.org
Information on this title: www.cambridge.org/9781108458276

© Francesco Ademollo 2011

This publication is in copyright. Subject to statutory exception and to the provisions of relevant collective licensing agreements, no reproduction of any part may take place without the written permission of Cambridge University Press.

First published 2011
First paperback edition 2018

A catalogue record for this publication is available from the British Library

Library of Congress Cataloging in Publication data
Ademollo, Francesco, 1973–
The *Cratylus* of Plato : a commentary / Francesco Ademollo.
p. cm.
ISBN 978-0-521-76347-9 (hardback)
1. Plato. Cratylus. 2. Language and languages–Philosophy. I. Title.
B367.A93 2011
184–dc22
2010045711

ISBN 978-0-521-76347-9 Hardback
ISBN 978-1-108-45827-6 Paperback

Cambridge University Press has no responsibility for the persistence or accuracy of URLs for external or third-party internet websites referred to in this publication, and does not guarantee that any content on such websites is, or will remain, accurate or appropriate.

A Chiara

Die Uhr mag stehn, der Zeiger fallen

Contents

Preface	*page* xiii
Preliminary note	xvi
List of abbreviations	xvii

	Introduction			1
	I.1	Subject and structure of the dialogue		1
		I.1.1	*The correctness of names*	1
		I.1.2	*A map*	6
		I.1.3	*Making sense of etymology*	11
	I.2	The characters		14
		I.2.1	*Cratylus*	14
		I.2.2	*Hermogenes*	18
	I.3	The date		19
		I.3.1	*The dramatic date*	20
		I.3.2	*The relative date*	20
	I.4	The evidence for the text		21
1	Cratylus' naturalism (383a–384c)			23
	1.1	The thesis		23
		1.1.1	*First approach to the thesis (383ab)*	23
		1.1.2	*More details: Hermogenes' name (383b–384c)*	26
		1.1.3	*The origin of natural names*	32
	1.2	Before Cratylus		33
2	Hermogenes' conventionalism (384c–386e)			37
	2.1	Convention and individual decision (384c–385b)		37
		2.1.1	*First statement (384ce)*	37
		2.1.2	*Public and private names (385ab)*	42
	2.2	Truth and falsehood in sentences and names (385bd)		49
		2.2.1	*True and false sentences (385b)*	49
		2.2.2	*The parts of a sentence. True and false names (385cd)*	54
		2.2.3	*Truth values and sentence structure*	59
		2.2.4	*The passage's function in context*	62

		2.2.5	*Authenticity and position of the passage*	68
		2.2.6	*Proclus' testimony*	70
	2.3	Convention and individual decision: further details (385de)		72
	2.4	Hermogenes and Protagoras (385e–386e)		76
		2.4.1	*Man the measure of all things? (385e–386a)*	77
		2.4.2	*The refutation of Protagoras – and of Euthydemus (386ad)*	81
		2.4.3	*Conclusion: objects have a stable being (386de)*	86
	2.5	Before Hermogenes		88
		2.5.1	*Empedoclean and Thucydidean 'conventionalism'*	89
		2.5.2	De natura hominis *and Democritus*	91
3	Naturalism defended (386e–390e)			95
	3.1	First argument: the naturalness of actions (386e–387d)		95
		3.1.1	*The naturalness of actions. Cutting and burning (386e–387b)*	95
		3.1.2	*Speaking (387bc)*	100
		3.1.3	*Naming (387cd)*	103
	3.2	Second argument: the function of names (387d–388c)		107
		3.2.1	*Names as instruments (387d–388c)*	107
		3.2.2	*Aristotle on names as instruments*	114
	3.3	Third argument: enter the namegiver (388c–389a)		115
		3.3.1	*The use and the making of instruments (388cd)*	115
		3.3.2	*The lawgiver as name-maker (388d–389a)*	117
		3.3.3	*Who is the lawgiver?*	121
	3.4	Fourth argument: instruments, names and forms (389a–390e)		125
		3.4.1	*Instruments and forms (389a)*	125
		3.4.2	*Generic and specific forms of tools (389bd)*	129
		3.4.3	*Forms of name (389d–390a)*	132
		3.4.4	*The lawgiver and the dialectician (390bd)*	138
	3.5	Conclusion (390de)		144
4	Naturalism unfolded (390e–394e)			146
	4.1	Searching for a theory (390e–392b)		146
	4.2	The theory discovered. Naturalism and synonymy (392b–394e)		152
		4.2.1	*'Scamandrius' and 'Astyanax' (392bd)*	152
		4.2.2	*'Astyanax' and 'Hector' (392d–393b). The argument previewed*	155
		4.2.3	*A lion begets a lion – and a king a king (393bd)*	159
		4.2.4	*The relative irrelevance of letters and syllables (393de)*	163
		4.2.5	*Synonymical Generation runs wild. The 'power' of names (394ab)*	167
		4.2.6	*'Hector' and 'Astyanax' again (394be)*	172
	4.3	Conclusion (394e–396c)		178
5	Naturalism illustrated: the etymologies of 'secondary' names (394e–421c)			181
	5.1	The arrangement of the etymologies		182
		5.1.1	*Analysis of 394e–421c*	182
		5.1.2	*The systematic character of the etymologies*	189

	5.1.3	*Platonic views in the etymologies (396bc, 399bc, 400ab, 403a–404b, 410b)*	191
5.2		The etymologies and the argument of the *Cratylus*	197
	5.2.1	*Ordinary proper names put aside (397ab)*	197
	5.2.2	*The etymologies as doxography, or the suicide of naturalism (400d–401a)*	199
	5.2.3	*The etymology as doxography (continued): the theory of flux (401d, 402a, 411bc)*	201
5.3		More on the theory of flux	210
	5.3.1	*Locomotion*	210
	5.3.2	*The Penetrating Principle (412–413d)*	215
	5.3.3	*Further evidence about the atomists in the* Cratylus *(412b, 414a, 420d)*	223
	5.3.4	*Atomism in the* Theaetetus	225
	5.3.5	*The Penetrating Principle again (413e–414a, 417bc, 418a–419b)*	227
	5.3.6	*Flux and relativity?*	233
5.4		Meaning in the etymologies	233
5.5		Plato's attitude to the etymologies	237
	5.5.1	*Seriousness in the etymologies (414c–415a, 439bc)*	237
	5.5.2	*The inspiration of Euthyphro (396c–397a)*	241
	5.5.3	*Humour and detachment in the etymologies (398de, 399a, 406bc)*	246
	5.5.4	*The etymologies' epistemological status*	250
6	Naturalism illustrated: the primary names (421c–427e)		257
6.1		From secondary to primary names (421c–422c)	257
	6.1.1	*The postulation of primary names (421c–422c)*	257
	6.1.2	*Intermezzo: the meaning of ῥῆμα (399ab, 421b, e)*	262
6.2		The correctness of primary names (422c–424a)	267
	6.2.1	*Introduction (422ce)*	267
	6.2.2	*Indication by gestural mimesis (422e–423b)*	269
	6.2.3	*Indication by vocal mimesis (423bc)*	271
	6.2.4	*Vocal imitation of the essence (423c–424a)*	274
6.3		The imposition of primary names (424a–425b)	280
	6.3.1	*The etymologies of primary names: false start (424ab)*	280
	6.3.2	*Division of letters (424bc)*	281
	6.3.3	*Division of beings (424d)*	285
	6.3.4	*Matching letters and beings (424d–425a)*	290
	6.3.5	*Intermezzo: names, verbs and speech (425a)*	293
	6.3.6	*First assessment of Socrates' programme*	296
	6.3.7	*How names are and how they should be (425ab)*	298
6.4		The investigation of actual primary names (425b–427d)	302
	6.4.1	*Disclaimers and preliminaries (425b–426b)*	302
	6.4.2	*Letters and primary names: the examples (426c–427c)*	306
	6.4.3	*Conclusion of Socrates' survey (427cd)*	311
	6.4.4	*An assessment of the mimetic survey*	312
	6.4.5	*The discussion with Hermogenes concluded (427de)*	315

7	Naturalism discussed (427e–433b)		317
	7.1 Introduction (427e–429c)		317
		7.1.1 *Preliminary exchanges (427e–428e)*	317
		7.1.2 *Better and worse names? (428e–429b)*	319
		7.1.3 *Hermogenes' name, again (429bc)*	324
	7.2 Naturalism and falsehood (429c–431c)		326
		7.2.1 *Naturalism and the impossibility of false speaking (429cd)*	326
		7.2.2 *Cratylus against false speaking (429d)*	332
		7.2.3 *Cratylus against false speaking, continued*	335
		7.2.4 *Socrates' defence of false speaking (430a–431c)*	338
		7.2.5 *Conclusion*	350
	7.3 Naturalism and imperfect resemblance (431c–433b)		351
		7.3.1 *First round (431ce)*	351
		7.3.2 *Second round: Cratylus' argument from spelling (431e–432a)*	356
		7.3.3 *Second round: Socrates' reply and the 'Two Cratyluses' (432ad)*	359
		7.3.4 *Conclusions on fine and bad names (432d–433b)*	369
8	Naturalism refuted and conventionalism defended (433b–439b)		383
	8.1 Resemblance and convention in names (433b–435d)		383
		8.1.1 *Preliminaries (433b–434b)*	383
		8.1.2 *The* sklerotes *argument: conflicting letters in the same name (434bd)*	390
		8.1.3 *The* sklerotes *argument: understanding, indication, correctness (434e–435b)*	395
		8.1.4 *Convention 'contributes' to correctness (435bc)*	405
		8.1.5 *Conclusions on resemblance and convention in names (435cd)*	413
		8.1.6 *Convention elsewhere in the Platonic corpus*	424
		8.1.7 *The ancient commentators*	425
	8.2 Names and knowledge (435d–439b)		427
		8.2.1 *Cratylus' view that names 'teach' (435d–436a)*	427
		8.2.2 *Names might express false beliefs (436a–437d)*	431
		8.2.3 *Names and the namegiver's knowledge (437d–438d)*	441
		8.2.4 *Knowledge 'without names' (438d–439b)*	444
9	Flux and forms (439b–440e)		449
	9.1 The arguments (439b–440d)		449
		9.1.1 *The lawgivers in a whirl (439bc)*	449
		9.1.2 *Flux and forms: the arguments previewed*	451
		9.1.3 *Enter the forms, exeunt particulars (439cd)*	456
		9.1.4 *The first argument (439d)*	462
		9.1.5 *The first argument and the* Theaetetus	468
		9.1.6 *The second argument (439e)*	473
		9.1.7 *The third argument (439e–440a)*	478
		9.1.8 *The fourth argument (440ab)*	482

9.1.9	*Flux rejected? (440bc)*	483
9.1.10	*Conclusion (440cd)*	485
9.2	Epilogue (440de)	487

Appendix 1:	The text of 437d10–438b8	489
Appendix 2:	Some interpolations and non-mechanical errors in W and δ	496

References	497
I General index	509
II Index of ancient texts	517
III Index of Greek expressions	533
IV Index of words discussed in the Cratylus	536

Preface

This is a commentary on Plato's *Cratylus*. It is a *running* commentary, because it is not organized by lemmata, but rather proceeds by quoting chunks of text (in my own translation) and then going on to explain them in detail. It is, alas, *not a complete* commentary, because there are some parts of the dialogue which I comment on only selectively, as I explain at the beginning of chapter 5. It is primarily a *philosophical* commentary, because what I am chiefly interested in is the purport of the theses advanced in the dialogue and the structure and worth of the arguments for and against them. But it is also a *philological* commentary, because along the way I discuss many matters of textual criticism and interpretation – some relevant to our philosophical understanding of the dialogue, some (usually confined to footnotes) perfectly irrelevant. Actually, I am afraid all I can say about my choice of focus is that as I was writing I tended, almost unwittingly, to imagine myself reading the dialogue in an open-ended seminar free from any sort of schedule, whose sole concern was to discuss anything that might seem interesting about a given portion of text before moving on to the next one. And so it is that, finally, this is a *very long* commentary – something for which I won't apologize.

As a consequence of the last feature, the book has been long (everyone around me says too long) in the writing. During this long span of time I have incurred many debts, both to institutions and to individuals; it is an immense pleasure and relief now to be able to acknowledge them all with heartfelt gratitude.

The Departments of Classics and Philosophy of the University of Florence and the Scuola Normale Superiore in Pisa granted me respectively, and successively, a doctoral fellowship, a four-year junior research fellowship and a two-year post-doctoral one. Each of these institutions allowed me to pursue my research with complete freedom and patiently put up with my seeming unproductivity.

Among individuals it won't be invidious to start by singling out a few especially important names – two sadly before all others.

My first debt of gratitude dates back to almost twenty years ago, to a time when the idea of writing this book was very far from dawning on me. Still a secondary school student, I went to hear John Ackrill deliver two lectures which were to become one of the finest articles ever written on the *Cratylus*. That was my first encounter with the dialogue and my only personal encounter with that most distinguished scholar. I was baffled to see how seriously he took my inept questions and how warmly he encouraged me to keep on studying Plato. This I did in the ensuing years, until I eventually returned to the *Cratylus* as the subject of my degree and Ph.D. theses. I regret that it is now too late to show the finished book to the person who first introduced me to its subject.

Michael Frede read and discussed with me several chapters of an early draft when I spent some time in Oxford in 1999 and 2000. The news of his tragic and untimely death in August 2007, shortly after our last encounter, left me in a state of distraught incredulity. Others have been and will be in a better position than I am to commemorate his exceptional qualities as a scholar and a human being; but I will not refrain from recalling that what most struck me of him, and what perhaps influenced me most deeply, was the distinctive intensity with which he confronted his subject matter – which involved, among other things, a special capacity to communicate to his interlocutors that ancient philosophy was something well worth devoting one's life to.

Myles Burnyeat, whose writings have constituted a model of scholarship for me, sent me a long series of enlightening written comments on a number of issues both before I submitted the book to Cambridge University Press and after, as he volunteered to read it for the Press. I regard our correspondence as one of my happiest intellectual experiences and am profoundly grateful to him for his patient, friendly and stimulating support. Several of his suggestions are recorded in the text. Walter Leszl supervised much of the work I did on the dialogue while I was still a student, kindly enabled me to read his collection of texts concerning ancient atomism before it was published, and sent me wise comments on some bits of the book. Massimo Mugnai mentored, now a fairly long time ago, my first steps in serious philosophy and, in particular, in the interpretation of the *Cratylus*, also drawing my attention to the connections between this dialogue and Leibniz's writings. I have continued to learn from him and to benefit from his friendship over the years. David Sedley, with characteristic generosity, first suggested that I submit the book to

Cambridge University Press, kindly allowed me to read much unpublished material (first and foremost a penultimate draft of his fine book on the *Cratylus*), and discussed some issues with me.

Many other people read and commented on parts of the book or gave advice on individual issues. Thanks are due especially to Fabio Acerbi, Jonathan Barnes, Rachel Barney (who was the other reader for Cambridge University Press), Sergio Bernini, Giuseppe Cambiano, Antonio Carlini, Albio Cassio, Paolo Crivelli, Paolo Fait, Andrea Falcon, Maria Teresa Ademollo Gagliano, Emiliano Gelli, Augusto Guida (who first put the idea of writing a commentary on the *Cratylus* into my head), Katerina Ierodiakonou, Walter Lapini, Alessandro Parenti, Enrico Rebuffat, Laura Venuti. I also thank audiences in Bergamo, Cambridge, Edinburgh, Florence, London, Oxford, Padua and Rome for helpful questions and criticism. In particular, in 2004–2005, when I was in Florence, I gave a seminar on the *Cratylus* which went on for the whole academic year and covered some two thirds of the dialogue; on that occasion I greatly profited from being able to submit my views to the keen scrutiny of Sergio Bernini, Paolo Fait and Walter Leszl.

I am also grateful to Cecilia Conti for allowing me to consult her unpublished thesis on ῥῆμα; to librarians in Florence, Oxford, Venice and Vienna; to Michael Sharp, who as Cambridge University Press's Classics editor first encouraged me to submit my typescript and then gently watched over its transformation into a book along with Elizabeth Hanlon and Jo Breeze; to Linda Woodward, who was an exceptionally meticulous and sympathetic copy-editor and improved the book in many respects; to C. for wholly unrequested help with typing; and to P. for just being there.

My parents, Marco and Maria Teresa, have been giving me all sorts of intellectual, moral and material support over the years. My debt towards them is incalculable.

Finally, my wife Chiara has been by my side through times good and bad, unfailingly believing in me and giving me strength and advice. She also made a substantial contribution to the book's final revision. It is for these reasons, for many others which I shall not recount here, and not least because she is the mother of Caterina and Federico, that the book could only be dedicated to her.

Preliminary note

All translations are my own except when indicated otherwise (although I have often been influenced by existing translations in cases in which it did not seem appropriate to acknowledge direct dependence).

In citing ancient texts I have always followed standard editions and practice; thus I have employed the standard abbreviations of LSJ and *OLD*, seldom replacing them with other, more perspicuous ones drawn from *OCD* (e.g. replacing 'A.' with 'Aesch.' for 'Aeschylus'). In some cases, in order to prevent ambiguities or unclarities, I have specified the edition according to whose numbers of page and line ('Phrynichus, *Praeparatio sophistica* 9.12–17 de Borries') or lemma ('Timaeus, *Lexicon Platonicum* 58 Bonelli') a text is being cited. All Proclus references are to the *in Platonis Cratylum commentaria* (*in Cra.*) unless otherwise noted.

Abbreviations

1 EDITIONS AND TRANSLATIONS OF THE *CRATYLUS* (CITED BY ABBREVIATION)

Aronadio	F. Aronadio (trans. and comm.), *Platone: Cratilo*. Rome and Bari 1996.
Bekker	I. Bekker (ed.), *Platonis Scripta Graece Omnia*, vol. IV. London 1826.
Burnet	J. Burnet (ed.), *Platonis Opera* (5 vols.). Oxford 1900–7.
Cambiano	G. Cambiano (trans.), *Platone: Dialoghi filosofici*, vol. II. Turin 1981.
Dalimier	C. Dalimier (trans. and comm.), *Platon: Cratyle*. Paris 1998.
Ficino	M. Ficino (trans.), *Divus Plato*, 2nd edn. Venice 1491.
Fowler	H. N. Fowler (ed. and trans.), *Plato (vol. VI): Cratylus, Parmenides, Greater and Lesser Hippias*. Cambridge, MA, and London 1926.
Heindorf	L. Fr. Heindorf (ed.), *Platonis Dialogi selecti* (4 vols.). Leipzig 1892–1910.
Hermann	C. F. Hermann (ed.), *Platonis dialogi secundum Thrasylli tetralogias dispositi*, vol. I, Leipzig 1861.
Hirschig	R. B. Hirschig (ed.), *Platonis Opera*, vol. I. Paris 1873.
Jowett	B. Jowett (trans.), *The Dialogues of Plato*, 3rd edn, vol. I. Oxford 1892.
Méridier	L. Méridier (ed. and trans.), *Platon, Oeuvres complètes*, vol. V.2: *Cratyle*. Paris 1931.
Minio-Paluello	[Translation of *Cratylus*, in *Platone, Opere complete*, 2nd edn, vol. II. Rome and Bari 1991.]

OCT	E. A. Duke, W. F. Hicken, W. S. M. Nicoll, D. B. Robinson and J. C. G. Strachan (eds.), *Platonis Opera*, vol. 1. Oxford 1995.
Reeve	C. D. C. Reeve (trans.), *Plato: Cratylus*, Indianapolis, IN, and Cambridge 1998.
Stallbaum	G. Stallbaum (ed. and comm.), *Platonis Opera omnia*, vol. v.ii: *Cratylum*. Gotha and Erfurt 1835 (repr. New York and London 1980).

2 OTHER EDITIONS AND WORKS OF GENERAL REFERENCE (CITED BY ABBREVIATION)

APF	J. K. Davies, *Athenian Propertied Families, 600–300 BC*. Oxford 1971.
Bonelli	M. Bonelli (ed., trans. and comm.), *Timée le Sophiste: Lexique platonicien*. Leiden and Boston 2007.
Buck	C. D. Buck, *The Greek Dialects*. Chicago 1955.
Cooper	G. L. Cooper, III, after K. W. Krüger, *Attic Greek Prose Syntax* (2 vols.). Ann Arbor 1998.
Cufalo	D. Cufalo (ed.), *Scholia Graeca in Platonem, I: Scholia ad Dialogos Tetralogiarum I–VII continens*. Rome 2007.
Daremberg/Saglio	Ch. Daremberg and E. Saglio (eds.), *Dictionnaire des Antiquités grecques et romaines d'après les textes et les monuments* (6 vols.). Paris 1877–1919.
de Borries	J. de Borries (ed.), *Phrynichi sophistae Praeparatio Sophistica*. Leipzig 1911.
DELG	P. Chantraine, *Dictionnaire étymologique de la langue grecque* (2 vols.). Paris 1968–80.
DGE	F. R. Adrados (ed.), *Diccionario Griego-Español*. Madrid 1980–.
DK	H. Diels and W. Kranz, *Die Fragmente der Vorsokratiker*, 6th edn (3 vols.). Berlin 1951–2.
FDS	K. Hülser, *Die Fragmente zur Dialektik der Stoiker* (4 vols.). Stuttgart and Bad Cannstatt 1987.
GP	J. D. Denniston, *The Greek Particles*, 2nd edn. Oxford 1954.

Guarducci	M. Guarducci, *Epigrafia greca* (4 vols.). Rome 1967–78.
Helmreich	G. Helmreich (ed.), *Galeni de elementis ex Hippocratis sententia libri duo*. Erlangen 1878.
IG	*Inscriptiones Graecae* (1873–).
Kern	O. Kern (ed.), *Orphicorum Fragmenta*. Berlin 1922.
KG	R. Kühner and B. Gerth, *Ausführliche Grammatik der Griechischen Sprache: Satzlehre*, 3rd edn (2 vols.). Hannover and Leipzig 1904.
KRS	G. S. Kirk, J. E. Raven and M. Schofield, *The Presocratic Philosophers*, 2nd edn. Cambridge 1983.
Leszl	See Leszl 2009.
Long/Sedley	A. A. Long and D. N. Sedley, *The Hellenistic Philosophers* (2 vols.). Cambridge 1987.
LSAG	L. H. Jeffery, *The Local Scripts of Archaic Greece*, revised edn with a supplement by A. W. Johnston. Oxford 1990.
LSJ	H. G. Liddell, R. Scott and H. Stuart Jones, *A Greek–English Lexicon*, 9th edn. Oxford 1940, with a revised supplement ed. by P. G. W. Glare, with the assistance of A. A. Thompson, 1996.
Nails	D. Nails, *The People of Plato*. Indianapolis, IN, and Cambridge 2002.
OCD	S. Hornblower and A. Spawforth (eds.), *The Oxford Classical Dictionary*, 3rd edn. Oxford and New York 1996.
OLD	*Oxford Latin Dictionary*. Oxford 1968.
PCG	R. Kassel and C. Austin (eds.), *Poetae Comici Graeci*. Berlin and New York 1983–.
PEG	A. Bernabé (ed.), *Poetae Epici Graeci* (2 vols.). Berlin and New York 1996 (2nd edn) 2007.
Pendrick	G. J. Pendrick (ed., trans. and comm.), *Antiphon the Sophist: the Fragments*. Cambridge 2002.
PMG	D. L. Page (ed.), *Poetae Melici Graeci*. Oxford 1962.
SEG	*Supplementum Epigraphicum Graecum*, 1923–.
SSR	G. Giannantoni (ed.), *Socratis et Socraticorum Reliquiae* (4 vols.). Naples 1990.
SVF	I. von Arnim (ed.), *Stoicorum Veterum Fragmenta* (3 vols.). Leipzig 1903–5.

Thesleff	H. Thesleff (ed.), *The Pythagorean Texts of the Hellenistic Period*. Åbo 1965.
Threatte	L. Threatte, *The Grammar of Attic Inscriptions* (2 vols.). Berlin and New York 1980–96.
TrGF	B. Snell, R. Kannicht and S. Radt (eds.), *Tragicorum Graecorum Fragmenta* (5 vols.). Göttingen 1981–2004.
West	M. L. West (ed.), *Iambi et Elegi Graeci ante Alexandrum Cantati*, 2nd edn. Oxford 1992.

Introduction

1.1 SUBJECT AND STRUCTURE OF THE DIALOGUE

1.1.1 *The correctness of names*

Plato's *Cratylus*, the subtitle present in the MSS informs us, is 'about the correctness of names' (περὶ ὀνομάτων ὀρθότητος). More precisely, it is about the question whether the correctness of names is a natural or a conventional matter. But what do the terms 'name' and 'correctness' mean here? This is never spelt out explicitly in the dialogue; the characters just take it for granted from the outset.

As for 'names', the characters take a generous view: they count as ὀνόματα proper and common nouns, adjectives and verbs in infinitive (414ab, 426c) or participle (421c) mood. They do not explicitly include verbs in finite moods, but they seem to be including them implicitly when they say that the ὄνομα is the 'smallest' part of a sentence (385c, see §2.2.2). So it is standard, and doubtless right, to take it that in our dialogue (and elsewhere as well) the term ὄνομα generically applies to any word whose function is not primarily syntactic (hence not to conjunctions and prepositions).[1] Indeed, the term ὄνομα is obviously connected with the verb ὀνομάζειν, 'to name'; and so an ὄνομα is essentially a word that *names* or refers to something.

As for the 'correctness' of such names, on the face of it this is a vague label. Authors like Protagoras and Prodicus appear to have used the same expression, or closely related ones, in connection with questions that have only something in common with what we find in *Cra.* (see §§1.1.2, 4.1). And modern scholars have distinguished several possible ways in which such phrases as 'correctness of names' and 'correct name' could be understood.

---

[1] See Crivelli, forthcoming, §6.1 for a more detailed list of uses of the term in Plato; he points out that the term is also applied to demonstrative pronouns (*Ti.* 50a). For the remark that it is not applied to words of syntactic function see Schofield 1982: 61.

But in fact the label is not vague, and Plato is making his characters discuss a fairly definite issue. We can grasp what that issue is if we pay attention to a basic fact, seldom acknowledged by interpreters, about the way the terms 'correctness' and 'correct' are used. The fact is this: throughout the dialogue all characters express themselves as if there were no difference between being a *correct name* of something and being just a *name* of that thing. They continuously speak as if the phrases 'correct name of *X*' and 'name of *X*' were perfectly interchangeable and equivalent to each other.

This is already evident in the very first lines of the dialogue (383ab). Cratylus is there reported to have claimed that there is a certain natural *correctness of names* (ὀρθότητά τινα τῶν ὀνομάτων) and that a string of sounds which is applied to something only conventionally *is not a name* (οὐ ... εἶναι ὄνομα: he did not say 'is not a correct name'). To clarify this obscure thesis Hermogenes has submitted to Cratylus a few examples, asking whether his *name* is really 'Cratylus' (not 'whether his correct name ...' etc.), whether Socrates' name is really 'Socrates', and so on. When it comes to Hermogenes to set forth his own views (384cd), he wavers in the same way: he starts by claiming that the correctness of names consists in convention and agreement, and that whatever name you impose on something is the *correct* one (τὸ ὀρθόν); but then he goes on to claim, as if offering some sort of explanation, that a name does not *belong* to its object by nature, but rather by custom. Talk of correct names and talk of names *simpliciter* keep on interlacing, e.g., at 385de and at 390d–391a, where Socrates formulates the same interim conclusion in two different ways: first 'names *belong* to the objects by nature' (φύσει τὰ ὀνόματα εἶναι τοῖς πράγμασι), then 'the name has some sort of natural *correctness*' (φύσει ... τινα ὀρθότητα ἔχον εἶναι τὸ ὄνομα). Again, at 422cd we find Socrates claiming that 'the *correctness* of every name ... is one and the same, and ... none of them is different *in respect of its being a name* [τῷ ὄνομα εἶναι]', and that if the correctness of a certain kind of names consists in their indicating what their referent is like, this feature must belong to all kinds of names, 'if they are to be names' (εἴπερ ὀνόματα ἔσται). And the same interlacement is still operating at 433d–435a, where Socrates first assumes that 'the name is a means to indicate the object', then shows that a particular name indicates its object by convention, and hence draws without further ado the conclusion that the *correctness* of that particular name rests on convention.

The examples could be multiplied; but instead of doing so it will be better to venture a few reflections about this way of conceiving of the correctness of names. I shall dub it the 'Redundancy Conception' of correctness and formulate it thus:

(R) '*N*' is a correct name of *X* $=_{df}$ '*N*' is a name of *X*.

On this conception, a correct name of something is not a special name of that thing, distinct from, and superior to, other, incorrect names of the same thing. Rather, a correct name of something is a name which performs successfully the function of a name relative to that thing; it is, quite simply, a name which names that thing. One advantage of this conception is that it provides the speakers with an abstract noun, which they would otherwise lack, that refers to the property of being a name: in the absence of any such Greek term as 'namehood', 'correctness' does duty for it.[2]

The Redundancy Conception of names, as I am calling it, entails two relevant consequences. (i) There are, strictly speaking, *no degrees of correctness*: as one name cannot be more of a name than another, so one name cannot be more correct than another. (ii) There is, strictly speaking, *no such thing as an incorrect name of something*; the expression 'incorrect name of *X*' is, strictly speaking, self-contradictory. For it follows from (R) that, if '*N*' is a name of *X*, then '*N*' is a correct name of *X*, and that, if '*N*' is not a correct name of *X*, then '*N*' is not a name of *X*. That is to say, 'incorrect' here functions as an 'alienating' predicate, like 'fake' in such phrases as 'fake diamond': as a fake diamond is actually not a diamond, so an incorrect name of *X* is actually not a name of *X* at all.

These consequences will perhaps seem startling to some readers; they certainly go against the grain of most *Cra.* scholarship, according to which, while (i) and (ii) form a part of Cratylus' radical views, Socrates rejects one or both of them.[3] But the consequences are there nonetheless; and they harmonize with the fact that only in few, rather marginal passages of the dialogue does someone say something inconsistent with them (e.g. 397ab on incorrect names and 392ad on degrees of correctness). To my mind, such passages are to be dismissed as instances of an innocuous and very understandable *façon de parler*, which is actually devoid of any serious theoretical significance.[4]

---

[2] One author who comes close to recognizing the Redundancy Conception is Bestor (1980: 314), who claims that 'correctness is the same as success'. Bestor, however, thinks it is the analogy between names and tools that allows Plato to conceive of correctness in this way. But that analogy is advanced no sooner than 387d ff., while the Redundancy Conception is in force from the very beginning of the dialogue.

[3] See e.g. Williams 1982: 83.

[4] Note, in particular, that it is almost unavoidable to run foul of (ii) if you hold that there are natural standards which a name must live up to in order to be correct. For then you will be confronted

True, in the course of his discussion with Cratylus (431c–432c, cf. 435cd) Socrates will go out of his way to argue that a name may be made either 'finely' (καλῶς) or 'badly' (κακῶς). The importance of that contention cannot be minimized. But the contention itself is *not* that a name may be either correct or incorrect, or that a name may be more or less correct than another. In my view, the Redundancy Conception of correctness is still in force when Socrates advances his distinction between 'fine' and 'bad' names, as the text indeed confirms (see 432cd, 433ab). The distinction operates *within* the set of correct names, i.e. of names *simpliciter*.

So the issue debated in *Cra.* boils down to this: is the link between a name and the thing it names – its referent – *natural* or *conventional*? The former option, initially held by Cratylus but clarified and developed by Socrates, essentially consists (so we realize as the argument goes on) in the view that a name must somehow reveal, through its etymology, the nature of its referent. So, e.g., the name 'Hermogenes' will be correct only if its bearer really has the nature of an 'offspring of Hermes'; etc. The latter option, initially held by Hermogenes, is fairly clear: it is the view that what something's name is is a matter that depends only on agreement between speakers (and, as a limiting case, on the individual speaker's arbitrary decision).

This issue must not be confused with a different, though not unrelated, one, which concerns the *origin* of names: how did it come about that human beings became equipped with names? How did names originate?[5] The first philosophers who concern themselves explicitly with the latter issue seem to be the Epicureans. They deny that the first names originated out of a deliberate imposition (θέσει), as all previous thinkers took for granted, and maintain instead that they originated from the nature (φύσις) of human beings: they sprang up spontaneously, according to the peculiar feelings and impressions experienced by each tribe (Epicurus, *Ep. Hdt.* 75–6; cf. Lucretius 5.1028–90 and Diogenes of Oenoanda, 12.2.11–5.14 Smith). This issue and the correctness one are obviously different and independent of each other. You may believe that names originated naturally and that, nevertheless, their link with their referents is conventional, in that names may be changed at will. Or you may believe that the first

---

with the question, what about those names – ordinary, conventional names – which do not live up to such standards? And you will have to choose between going against common sense, as Cratylus does by claiming that the names which do not comply with the natural criteria are in fact not names, and going against the Redundancy Conception by saying that they are names, albeit incorrect ones.

[5] On the difference between the two issues see Fehling 1965: 218–29, Barnes 1982: 466–7, Blank 1998: 176–7.

names were the product of a deliberate human imposition and that, nevertheless, there are certain natural standards which any name must satisfy. Thus Epicurus claims that at a further stage each tribe set down some names 'by consensus' (κοινῶς), in order to indicate things less ambiguously and more concisely, and the wise men coined some other names to indicate certain invisible entities they had posited.[6]

There was once a time when scholars, failing to appreciate the difference between these two issues about names – the correctness one and the origin one – commonly claimed that *Cra.* is about the origin of names. This commonplace was false. All the speakers in the dialogue appear to assume that names were set down by someone (who is sometimes referred to as a 'lawgiver': see e.g. 388de, 436bc) and concentrate instead on the nature of the glue that thereafter links name and thing. As Robinson 1955: 110–11 puts it, 'The speakers ... never oppose nature to *positing*, φύσις to θέσις ... The word "θέσις" [390d, 397c, 401b] ... means something compatible with φύσις, not opposed thereto ... You can posit a name either in accordance with nature, or in accordance with an agreement you have made with other men, or in accordance with nothing but your own choice. The assumption of the speakers is that words have to be posited in any case, whether they are natural or not.'

Ancient interpreters of the dialogue, Proclus in the first place, regularly use the expression θέσει, 'by imposition', to refer to the conventionalist thesis in the debate about correctness. On the other hand, θέσει was the very expression used since Epicurus to characterize the idea that names were originally imposed and did not originate naturally. Likewise, the expression φύσει is used to characterize the naturalist side of either debate. This, however, does not mean that the ancient interpreters confuse the two issues. Proclus seems to know that Cratylus and Socrates assign to nature a different role than Epicurus does, and that for Cratylus and Socrates, but not for Epicurus, names have been imposed (XVII, 7.18–8.14). The different senses in which names could be said to be φύσει or θέσει are meticulously distinguished by Ammonius, *in Int.* 34.20–35.23, 36.22–37.13;[7] and

---

[6] On the Epicurean theory of language see Long/Sedley, s. 19, and the commentary at 1.100–1; cf. Sedley 1973. Long/Sedley see in Epicurus some elements of a naturalist theory in Cratylus' sense; according to Sedley 1973: 20, Epicurus' naturalism lies 'in the belief that within a language each name can only be correctly used to denote the one particular class of object with which it was associated in its natural origin'. But the evidence does not seem to license this conclusion, especially as regards a connection with Cratylus; and at least in relation to the *second* stage of language evolution Epicurus clearly acknowledges a role for convention.

[7] But Ammonius, *in Int.* 34.22–32, ascribes to Cratylus the thesis of the natural *origin* of names; and Proclus himself seems to be partially inconsistent on this point. See §1.1.3 n. 15.

the distinction is already present in Alcinous, *Didaskalikos* 160.4–16 (see §8.1.7). The basic point to bear in mind is this. In the debate about correctness, as it is represented in *Cra.*, the conventionalist side and the naturalist side agree that names have been imposed or set down; but while the naturalist believes that a mere act of imposition as such is not sufficient to create a name, because the imposition must conform to a natural criterion if it is to have any value, the conventionalist believes that a name is a name *just in virtue* of its having been imposed. And to that extent he is not misdescribed by the θέσει tag.

I.1.2 A map

Here follows an outline of the whole dialogue. You will see that what is here dubbed part I corresponds to the contents of my chapters 1–2; part II corresponds to the contents of chapters 3–6; part III to the contents of chapters 7–8; and part IV to the contents of chapter 9. Please bear in mind that the outline is, inevitably, opinionated.

I Cratylus' naturalism and Hermogenes' conventionalism

383a–384a	Hermogenes involves Socrates in his discussion with Cratylus. *Cratylus' thesis*: there is a natural correctness of names.
384de	*Hermogenes' theory*: the correctness of names is a matter of convention among speakers and individual decision.
385a–386a	*Clarifications of Hermogenes' theory.*
385bd	There are true and false names as well as true and false sentences.
385e–386a	Hermogenes rejects Protagoras' relativism.
386ae	*Refutation of Protagoras.* There are virtuous and wicked persons, hence wise and unwise persons; therefore it is not the case that everyone's beliefs are true; therefore the objects have a subject-independent being and a nature of their own. (Incidentally, the argument refutes also Euthydemus' view that 'Everything is in the same way for everyone, at the same time and always.')

II Naturalism defended, developed and illustrated

386e–387d	*First argument for naturalism.* Actions too have a nature of their own. Therefore they must be performed in the way in

Subject and structure of the dialogue

which, and with the instrument with which, it is natural to perform them. Examples: cutting, burning, speaking and naming. 'Hence one must also name the objects as it is natural to name them and for them to be named and with that with which it is natural, not as we want.'

387d–388c *Second argument for naturalism.* Every instrument has a function; and as the function of a pin-beater[8] is to separate the weft and the warp, so that of a name is to 'teach and separate being'.

388c–389a *Third argument for naturalism.* Every instrument is made by a craftsman who 'possesses the art'. Names, which are handed down by *nomos* ('custom' / 'law'), are made by the *nomothetes* ('lawgiver'); and not everyone is a lawgiver, but only the one who 'possesses the art'. Thus imposing names is not a matter for everyone.

389a–390e *Fourth argument for naturalism.* Every craftsman who makes an instrument makes it by looking to, and embodying in the relevant material, both the generic form of that instrument (e.g. the form of pin-beater) and the specific form which is naturally appropriate to the specific purpose at hand (e.g. the form of pin-beater for weaving wool). Likewise, the lawgiver makes names by looking to, and embodying in letters and syllables, both the generic form of name and the specific form of name which is naturally appropriate to the object to be named. Furthermore, craftsmen working in different countries with different kinds of the same material can produce equally correct instruments, as long as they carry out the right embodiments; likewise with names from different languages. The work of each craftsman who makes an instrument is supervised and eventually assessed by the instrument's user – in the case of a name, the dialectician. Conclusion: 'Cratylus speaks the truth when he says that names belong to the objects by nature and that not everyone is a craftsman of names.'

390e–392b What does the natural correctness of names consist in? The suggestion that we might try to learn what Protagoras has to say about this is discarded. The suggestion that we might learn something from those cases where Homer

---

[8] See §3.2.1 on 'pin-beater' as a translation of κερκίς.

	distinguishes between a human and a divine name for the same thing is also discarded, because the matter is too difficult for us.
392b–394e	We shall rather try to investigate Homer's distinction between the two names of Hector's son, 'Astyanax' and 'Scamandrius'. Which of the two did Homer regard as the more correct? The former, because, arguably, it was the one used by the Trojan men, whereas the latter was used by the women, and men are, generally speaking, wiser than women.

But why is 'Astyanax' more correct than 'Scamandrius'? Homer says it is because Hector defended Troy. The point is that, generally speaking, father and offspring should be called by the same name, i.e. by names which signify the same: e.g. the lion's offspring should be called 'lion' as well, unless it is a freak, and the king's offspring should be called 'king' as well, unless it is a freak. Thus 'Hector' and 'Astyanax', which signify the same, i.e. that their bearer is a king, are fit for being respectively the name of a king and his son.

394e–396c	An alleged example of Socrates': etymologies of the names in the Atreidae's genealogy.
396c–421c	*Etymologies.*

Socrates, allegedly under Euthyphro's inspiration, sets forth a flow of etymologies, whose purported function is to illustrate the natural correctness of names. He refrains from analysing proper names of humans and heroes and focuses instead on the 'things that always exist by nature':

397c–400c	Preliminaries about the gods (gods, daimones, heroes, humans; soul and body)
400d–408d	Homeric gods
408d–410e	'Natural' gods (objects of natural science)
411a–420e	Names 'concerning virtue'
421ac	'The greatest and finest': logic and ontology.

Many etymologies turn out to presuppose the Heraclitean theory of universal flux.

421c–424a	There must be some names such that other names derive from them but they no longer derive from other names. These are the 'first names', i.e. elementary or simple names. Their correctness, like that of the 'secondary' names which we have been analysing hitherto, must consist in 'indicating

Subject and structure of the dialogue

	what each of the beings is like'. A first name performs this function by being an imitation, by means of letters and syllables, of the referent's essence.
424a–425b	Someone who sets about imposing names must first of all divide up the various kinds of letters, then divide up the various kinds of beings, and finally map the two divisions onto each other, associating letters (both individual letters and groups of letters) with beings according to their mutual resemblance, thus constructing syllables, words and whole speeches. We too must carry out these divisions in order to assess the existing language.
425b–426b	In fact we are unable to carry out the divisions as we should, but we shall try to give an account of the first names as best we can. To the extent that we are ignorant about their correctness, we are also ignorant about that of the secondary ones, which are composed of them.
426b–427d	Tentative account of the mimetic power of Greek letters (and hence of existing Greek first names): ρ imitates movement, ι fineness, λ smoothness, α largeness, etc.

III *Naturalism discussed and conventionalism vindicated*

427d–428d	Socrates begins to discuss with Cratylus (who approves of all that Socrates has been saying so far) and voices his intention to re-examine the whole matter.
428d–429b	Cratylus holds that (a) the correctness of names consists in 'showing what the object named is like'; that, therefore, (b) 'names are said for the sake of teaching'; and that (c) names, which are the products of the namegiving art, cannot, unlike the products of the other arts, be made well or badly and are all (naturally) correct.
429b–430a	Cratylus holds that 'Hermogenes' does not really belong to Hermogenes as his name, but merely seems to. Socrates argues that he is committed to the sophistical view that it is impossible to speak falsely. Cratylus endorses the view.
430a–431c	Socrates refutes the view and shows that in fact it is possible to speak falsely.
431c–433b	As against Cratylus' thesis (c), Socrates shows that a name, like any other image, can be made well or badly.
433b–434b	A new way of stating the contrast between naturalism and conventionalism: they agree that a name is a means

	to indicate an object; but they disagree over the manner in which this is achieved. According to Cratylus, a name indicates an object by being similar to it – and is similar to it by being made up of letters similar to it. According to Hermogenes, instead, a name indicates an object by being a conventional token for it.
434b–435d	On the grounds of some examples (the name σκληρότης, 'hardness'; the names of numbers) Socrates shows that 'agreement and convention have some authority over the correctness of names', although 'perhaps, as far as possible, one would speak most finely when one spoke with elements all of which, or as many as possible, were similar, i.e. appropriate, and one would speak most poorly in the opposite case'. This is presumably meant to refute primarily Cratylus' thesis (a).
435d–436a	Socrates returns to Cratylus' thesis (b). Cratylus holds that the function of names is to teach: that is to say, knowing names (i.e. their etymology) is a way, indeed the only way, of knowing their referents.
436ac	Socrates objects that the namegiver might have encapsulated mistaken views in the names. Cratylus replies that the namegiver had knowledge about the objects named and offers the following argument: the flux etymologies showed that names are concordant with each other.
436c–437d	Socrates refutes Cratylus' reply on two counts: (i) the fact that names are concordant with each other is no guarantee that the views they express are true; (ii) it is actually false that names are so concordant with each other; for other names appear to presuppose, not the view that everything is in flux, but the opposite view that everything is stable.
437d–438b	Socrates points out that Cratylus' thesis (b) that names are the sole source of knowledge about the objects, and his other view that the namegiver had knowledge about the objects named, contradict each other: where did those who imposed the first names get their knowledge from?
438bc	Cratylus tries to find shelter in the claim that the first names were set down by the gods. Socrates, with regard to the conflict between the flux etymologies and the rest ones, responds that a god would not have contradicted himself.

438d–439b	Conclusion: we must learn the truth about the beings not 'from their names' but 'from themselves'.

IV Flux and forms

439bc	Socrates acknowledges that the flux etymologies were correct, i.e. that the first namegivers did believe the flux theory, but suspects that the theory itself is false.
439c–440c	Socrates assumes that the forms exist and are unchanging. He decides to leave aside the issue of the flux of particulars. Then he launches four arguments which show what unpalatable consequences follow from the assumption that everything is in flux. If anything (more specifically, a form) were in flux, it could not be described truly; it would not exist at all; it could not be known; indeed, if everything were in flux, then knowledge itself would not exist.
440ce	Socrates claims that it remains unclear whether or not things are as the flux theory says, but it is certainly unwise to espouse the theory on the basis of etymology. He invites Cratylus to inquire further. Cratylus answers that he will do so, but so far he is much more inclined to agree with Heraclitus.
440e	Socrates parts company with Cratylus and Hermogenes.

I.1.3 Making sense of etymology

It may seem to you that Cratylus' naturalist view of names, and Socrates' initial development of it, are so queer and implausible that there is no philosophical remuneration to be gained by reading a dialogue devoted to rejecting them.

This judgement would be multiply mistaken. For a start, both while trying to establish and illustrate the naturalist theory, and while later arguing against it, Socrates sets forth a number of ideas – about names and their relation to their referents, about truth and falsity, about things having an essence over and above other features, about the construction of a perfect language, about the thesis that everything is always changing and its unpalatable consequences, and so on – which were to prove extremely fertile throughout the subsequent history of philosophy.

Here I won't spell out each of these points in any detail. But I should like to devote a couple of words to the supposed barrenness of Cratylus' thesis itself, as distinct from the suggestions which are advanced in the course of its discussion. What I want to say is that etymology seems to have something to do, both conceptually and historically, with the emergence of the notion of a *meaning or sense* of names. For present purposes I shall allow myself some oversimplification and identify such a notion as that of a certain *informational content which a name conveys or expresses about its referent*. It is not difficult to see that the simplest (though probably not the most interesting) way in which a name may express some information about its referent is through its etymology. And, indeed, the idea that a name expresses some information about its referent is especially likely to be first suggested by consideration of 'transparent' portmanteau names: 'steamboat', 'whirlpool', 'potato-peeler' etc.

We can appreciate the importance of etymology for the emergence of the notion of a meaning or sense of names if we read a famous passage from John Stuart Mill's *System of Logic* (1843, 8th edn 1872), I.ii.5, where Mill argues that proper names denote individuals but are not connotative, i.e. 'they do not indicate or imply any attributes as belonging to those individuals' – in other words, they have no sense at all:

> A man may have been named John, because that was the name of his father; a town may have been named Dartmouth, because it is situated at the mouth of the Dart. But it is no part of the signification of the word John, that the father of the person so called bore the same name; nor even of the word Dartmouth, to be situated at the mouth of the Dart. If sand should choke up the mouth of the river, or an earthquake change its course, and remove it to a distance from the town, the name of the town would not necessarily be changed.

Let us leave aside the 'John' example and focus on the 'Dartmouth' one. Mill cannot apparently think of a better candidate for being connoted by a proper name than what is expressed by its etymology.[9] But even Frege, whose conception of sense as a way of thinking of the name's referent is much more sophisticated, in his seminal essay 'Über Sinn und Bedeutung' (1892) will put it forward, and make the crucial point that two proper names may have the same referent but different senses, by recourse to descriptions like 'The intersection of lines a and b'/'The intersection of lines b and c' and compound names like 'Morning-Star'/'Evening-Star' as his very first examples. Thus you can regard the naturalist thesis that a name must encapsulate a true description of its referent as a remote forerunner of Frege's descriptivist conception of sense.[10]

---

[9] See Sainsbury 2005: 4–6.
[10] It seems to me that, in order to do so, you do not need to ascribe to Frege, as many have done, the view that the sense of a proper name is the same as that of some definite description (e.g. 'Aristotle'/'The pupil of Plato and teacher of Alexander the Great'). See Burge 2005 for some profound inquiries into Frege's notion of sense.

Subject and structure of the dialogue

Let me offer another example. Consider Cratylus' further, even more absurd view that names are the *sole* source of knowledge about their referents (435d–436a). As against this view, Socrates will argue that we must 'learn about the beings without names', i.e. 'themselves through themselves' (438d–439b). Here again we have something with a potential to transcend the limits of the particular debate between Socrates and Cratylus. Read Mill, *System of Logic* 1.i.3:

[T]he signification of names, and the relation generally between names and the things signified by them, must occupy the preliminary stage of the inquiry we are engaged in.

It may be objected that the meaning of names can guide us at most only to the opinions, possibly the foolish and groundless opinions, which mankind have formed concerning things, and that as the object of philosophy is truth, not opinion, the philosopher should dismiss words and look into things themselves, to ascertain what questions can be asked and answered in regard to them. This advice ... is in reality an exhortation to discard the whole fruits of the labours of his predecessors, and conduct himself as if he were the first person who had ever turned an inquiring eye upon nature. What does any one's personal knowledge of Things amount to, after subtracting all which he has acquired by means of the words of other people? ...

... But if we begin with names, and use them as our clue to the things, we bring at once before us all the distinctions which have been recognised, not by a single inquirer, but by all inquirers taken together.

I do not know whether Mill is thinking of our passage (along with those where Socrates claims or suggests that names give us access only to the opinions of their givers, which may be mistaken and in some cases probably are: 400d–401a, 411bc, 436ab, 439bc) and is taking issue with it; but it is tempting to speculate that this is so.[11] Of course, even if my conjecture were right, Mill is no adherent of Cratylus' theory; the study of names which he advocates is something completely different. But he thinks it legitimate to extrapolate from our passage a rejection of *any* view according to which things must be studied via their names – not just of Cratylus' peculiar view. Perhaps Mill is right. And perhaps we could venture an even bolder step, give way to the dangerous charms of anachronism, and look at Cratylus' theory in the light of Dummett's view that metaphysical issues can only be resolved through the theory of *meaning*.[12] Then Plato's reply that the objects can and should be investigated 'without names' will in turn appear to anticipate the position of those philosophers who have

---

[11] On Mill's reading of Plato see Burnyeat 2001b.
[12] See Dummett 1991: 1–19.

rejected Dummett's view and maintained that metaphysical questions 'can only be addressed by independent metaphysical argument, if they can be legitimately addressed at all'[13] – or rather, those philosophers will appear to be standing on Plato's shoulders.

I.2 THE CHARACTERS

In this section I set out and discuss the main information that can be gathered, both from our dialogue and from other sources, about the life and philosophical views of Cratylus and Hermogenes. In doing so I will sometimes refer the reader to my comments on individual passages of *Cra*.

I.2.1 Cratylus

The task of reconstructing the philosophical career of the historical Cratylus from what Plato and Aristotle tell us about him has caused scholars great trouble; for some of the testimonies may seem, at first blush, hard to reconcile with each other. If we heed the chronological indications in the sources, however (as does Sedley 2003: 16–21, with whose fine discussion I largely agree), all the pieces of the Cratylus jigsaw seem to fit together rather well.

I start by considering the evidence from our dialogue.

(1) *Cratylus is an Athenian and is son of a Smicrion*. This can be inferred from Socrates' example of someone's misidentifying Cratylus at 429e: 'Hello, Athenian stranger, son of Smicrion, Hermogenes!', where 'Hermogenes' is likely to be the only misnomer, given that Hermogenes is son of Hipponicus. See §7.2.3.

(2) *Cratylus is still young when the dialogue takes place and is significantly younger than Socrates*. This emerges in two passages: 429d, where Socrates says the sophism Cratylus has just put forward is 'too clever' for him and his age; 440d, where Socrates invites Cratylus to inquire further on the grounds that 'you're still young and in your prime' (see §9.1.10). Of course this is compatible with a spectrum of possibilities; but I think that it wouldn't be far off the mark to conjecture that Cratylus was at least some twenty years younger than Socrates (b. 470–469) and therefore was born not earlier than 450 and possibly later (cf. Nails 106). This is compatible with the fact that the dialogue seems to be set after 421 (see §I.3.1).

[13] Lowe 1998: 8.

(3) *Cratylus holds that names are correct by nature.* Hermogenes reports this at 383a–384a; but Cratylus has not told him much more.[14] In the sequel Socrates plausibly assumes that Cratylus' belief in a natural correctness of names has to do with etymology: roughly, for a name to be correct, it must encapsulate a true description of its referent. At 428bc Cratylus himself approves of Socrates' etymologies.

(4) *Cratylus is becoming a Heraclitean.* At 437a he implies that he endorses the thesis that everything is always in a state of flux; for he avers that those names whose etymology has turned out to presuppose the thesis are (naturally) correct. Indeed, at 440de he expressly claims that he is inclined to believe that 'things are as Heraclitus says'. But the latter passage seems to imply that Cratylus was *not yet* a Heraclitean *before* his conversation with Socrates (see §9.2 and Kirk 1951: 236). That is to say, Cratylus' conversion to Heracliteanism is depicted as taking place in the course of the dialogue, once Socrates' etymologies have brought the theory to his attention, and in spite of the final arguments (439b–440c) whereby Socrates points out the theory's unpalatable consequences.

The Platonic evidence about Cratylus must be supplemented by that of Aristotle; and the supplementation is notoriously delicate.

(5) A first, fundamental Aristotelian report is at *Metaph.* A6.987a29–b7 and is concerned with the origins of Plato's theory of forms.

When he was young, he became acquainted first with Cratylus[15] *and the Heraclitean doctrines that all sensible things are always in flux and there is no knowledge of them. This he believed later too.* But Socrates devoted his inquiries to ethical matters and not at all to nature as a whole, and in those matters sought for the universal and was the first to focus on definitions. Plato accepted his teaching, but for the above sort of reason believed that this concerned different things and not the sensible ones; for he took it to be impossible for the common definition to be of any of the sensible things, given that they are always changing.[16]

The claim that Plato's encounter with Cratylus' views on flux *preceded* his Socratic discipleship[17] entails that Cratylus was a convinced Heraclitean

---

[14] One more thing Cratylus told Hermogenes is that *Hermogenes'* given name is not naturally correct, and hence is not his name at all. In the light of Plato's early association with Cratylus (see (5) below), this leads Sedley 2003: 21–3 to guess that the historical Cratylus was responsible for *Plato's own change of name* from 'Aristocles' to 'Plato' (on which see the testimonies in Riginos 1976: 35–8).

[15] συνήθης ... Κρατύλῳ: not '*pupil of* Cratylus', as the ancient commentators seem to understand this. See Allan 1954: 275–6.

[16] Aristotle tells roughly the same story at M4.1078b12–32 (no mention of Cratylus, but only of the 'Heraclitean accounts'). Cf. also M9.1086a32–b11.

[17] *Pace* Allan 1954: 275 n.2, Aristotle's 'first' (πρῶτον 987a32) is clearly chronological, not logical: see Cherniss 1955. There is, however, an ancient tradition according to which Plato became Cratylus'

'by the decade before 399' (Nails 105), when Socrates died. This is compatible with a conjectural birth date in 450–440, as well as with every other piece of evidence we have been considering so far. It is *possible* that Cratylus was some twenty years younger than Socrates and older than Plato (b. 427); that when he was a young man he first came to believe the nature theory of names and then, during a momentous conversation with Socrates, became a Heraclitean; and that, several years later, he met the young Plato, who was not yet a pupil of Socrates', and convinced him that the sensible world is in a state of perpetual flux. These things might all be true. *Are* they really so? Why, of course not; at the very least, Socrates' role in Cratylus' *Kehre* is plainly fictitious. But we have no particular reason to doubt the rest of Plato's testimony; and so we should cautiously accept it as true. The same basically holds of Aristotle's testimony (5): the burden of proof lies with disbelievers.

It could be objected to Aristotle[18] that those Platonic dialogues which are usually regarded as early are not concerned with the flux of sensible particulars and thus bear no signs of the alleged contact between their author and Cratylus; insofar as those dialogues do at all draw a contrast between the *F* itself and particular *F*s (see *Hp. Ma.* 289ac), this is done on other grounds – i.e. on the grounds that, while the *F* itself is unqualifiedly *F*, particular *F*s are *F* only in some respect or comparison and are not *F* in some other respect or comparison. But the objection can be met; and there are two alternative ways of doing so. On the one hand, Aristotle does not say that Cratylus' influence on the young Plato *manifested* itself immediately; and if his claim that Plato 'believed later too' in the flux of sensible particulars (987a34–b1) implies that Plato believed in flux *both at once and later*, this may be just a natural inference of Aristotle's: from the fact that (i) the young Plato was acquainted with Cratylus' view that the sensible world is in flux and that (ii) the mature Plato himself held a similar view, Aristotle may be just inferring that in fact Plato had been believing in flux all along. On the other hand, Aristotle's words ταῦτα μὲν καὶ ὕστερον οὕτως ὑπέλαβεν, usually translated 'this he believed later too', admit also of a different construal: 'If one takes ... καί ... as "actually",[19] we get the result that Plato was *acquainted* with flux theory from youth, and later actually believed in it' (Myles Burnyeat, personal communication, 2003).

---

pupil *after* Socrates' death: see D. L. 3.6 (on which see §I.2.2), Anon. *Prolegomena* 4.4–7, Olymp. *Vit. Pl.* 192–3 Hermann.

[18] See Kahn 1996: 81 n.20, and more generally 81–3, for the view that what (5) says about Cratylus 'looks like an Aristotelian inference from an over-hasty reading' of *Cra.*

[19] See *GP* 326–7 for καί separated from the word it emphasizes.

The characters

(6) There is another very famous Aristotelian report about Cratylus. At *Metaph.* Γ5.1010a7–9 Aristotle refers to those thinkers who 'saw that all this world of nature is changing and that nothing is said truly of that which is changing – at least, it is not possible to speak truly of that which is changing in every respect and guise [περί γε τὸ πάντῃ πάντως μεταβάλλον οὐκ ἐνδέχεσθαι ἀληθεύειν]'. Then he adds (a10–15):

> This view blossomed into the most extreme of the aforementioned beliefs, that of the professed Heracliteans and of Cratylus, *who in the end* [τὸ τελευταῖον] *thought that one should not say anything but only moved his finger, and criticized Heraclitus for saying that it is impossible to step twice into the same river; for he thought it was not possible to do so even once.*[20]

Aristotle seems to be implying that at some point Cratylus believed that everything is (always) changing in every respect. At that stage, Heraclitus' river dictum seemed too moderate to Cratylus: it is not just that, because the water that flows in the river is always different, the river is no longer the same the second time you step into it; rather, it does not endure even *as* you are stepping into it for the first time. But the main consequence of Cratylus' extremism was that he regarded it as right not to say anything and limited himself to moving his finger – presumably to *point* at things. Of course this was some time after the phase, depicted in *Cra.*, when he would claim that everything has a naturally correct name, and also after the phase, described by Aristotle in (5), when he met the young Plato and told him about flux. It was, Aristotle informs us, '*in the end*' (1010a12) – i.e. at the end of his philosophical career (not necessarily of his life). So, once again, no inconsistency among our testimonies.

What, exactly, was the connection between Cratylus' radical Heracliteanism and his eventual decision to give up speech and limit himself to pointing? According to Sedley (2003: 19), Cratylus reasoned as follows: 'things change so rapidly that you cannot engage with them, either by naming them or by stepping into them, in any way that takes any time at all: during the time taken, however short, they have become something else. So the only way to engage with them is one that is complete at an instant: just point your finger.' But Cratylus' pointing does not seem to be really licensed by this argument; for even the act of pointing is not really 'complete at an instant' and takes *some* time, however short. So I would rather suppose, following Taylor (1960: 76), that for Cratylus the advantage of pointing lay in the fact that *pointing does not commit you to the*

[20] Trans. after Barnes 1984.

identity or nature of the thing pointed at. I want to communicate to you that the water is hot; but uttering the sentence 'The water is hot' would raise distressing philosophical questions: is it, as I am uttering the sentence, still *water*, or the *same water*, given that it is continuously evaporating? Is it still *hot*, given that it is imperceptibly but continuously getting colder? And so on. Thus it will be safest to do no more than just pointing at it – at every instant it is just what it is.

If our testimony (6) is reliable, the discussion of flux both in *Cra.* and in the *Theaetetus* contains several hints at the views of the historical Cratylus. As we shall see in §§9.1.4–5, *Cra.* implicitly assumes, and *Tht.* explicitly argues, that supporters of the apparently moderate thesis that everything is always changing are actually committed to the extreme thesis that everything is always changing *in every respect* – i.e. the thesis which Aristotle seems to be ascribing to him here. Furthermore, both *Cra.* and *Tht.* argue that, if anything is always changing in every respect, then it is impossible to say anything truly about it – which again reminds us of how Cratylus ended up (see §9.2).

(7) I wind up with a final snippet of Aristotelian evidence. At *Rh.* 1417b1–2 we are told that the Socratic writer Aeschines (*SSR* vi a92) reported that Cratylus spoke 'hissing and waving his hands'. Sedley 2003: 20 conjectures that here we have a Cratylus who is on his way towards the eventual abandonment of speech and adoption of gestures as the only means to communicate. He may be right.

I.2.2 Hermogenes

Hermogenes belongs to one of the wealthiest and most powerful families in Athens.[21] He is the son of Hipponicus, an extraordinarily rich man (reportedly the richest in Greece) who was *strategos* in 426 and whose parents were the Callias after whom the peace of 449 with Persia is named and Cimon's sister, Elpinice. Hipponicus had three offspring. By Pericles' former wife he begot Callias, the famous patron of the Sophists, and Hipparete, who married Alcibiades; by some other woman he begot our Hermogenes, who seems to have been an illegitimate, albeit acknowledged, son, because he did not receive a share in Hipponicus' estate, unlike his half-brother Callias (see 391c and §I.3.1), and is described by both Plato

---

[21] The evidence about Hermogenes' family is set forth and discussed in *APF* §7826 and Nails 68–74.

and Xenophon as poor. More precisely, Xenophon describes Hermogenes as poor (X. *Mem.* 2.10: an appalling passage where Socrates suggests that Diodorus buy Hermogenes' friendship by giving him money); what Plato has Socrates say in our dialogue is that Hermogenes 'longs for money but every time misses the mark' (384c) – which fits well with the Xenophontan picture.[22]

Hermogenes was an intimate member of the Socratic circle. At *Phd.* 59b he is mentioned as one of those present at Socrates' death. Xenophon, *Mem.* 1.2.48, refers to him as a 'disciple' (ὁμιλητής) of Socrates along with other well-known characters like Crito, Chaerephon, Simmias and Cebes. At *Ap.* 2–10 he makes it clear that Hermogenes was one of his sources concerning Socrates' trial and reports (as also at *Mem.* 4.8.4–11) a conversation between Hermogenes and Socrates, where the former invites the latter to think about his defence.

Diogenes Laertius, 3.6, claims that Hermogenes was a Parmenidean and was, along with Cratylus, Plato's teacher after Socrates' death. None of this is to be taken seriously (cf. §I.2.1 on Plato's acquaintance with Cratylus, which seems neither to have taken the form of actual discipleship nor to have taken place after Socrates' death). Perhaps Hermogenes is enrolled by Diogenes as a Parmenidean for the simple fact that in *Cra.* his philosophical opponent is Cratylus, a known Heraclitean. But Parmenides might also be considered an influence on Hermogenes' conventionalism in view of his critical remarks on the misguided naming practices of the 'mortals', which presuppose a false conception of reality (28B8.38, 53–4; B9.1; cf. B19 DK).[23]

1.3 THE DATE

We have virtually no evidence as to the dialogue's absolute date, i.e. the year of its composition.[24] But something (admittedly not much) can be said about its dramatic date and relative date.

---

[22] Nails' (162–3) objection that 'Hermogenes' statement on naming beginning, "when we give names to our domestic slaves" (*Cra.* 384d) does not sound like the words of an impoverished man who depends on "charity from his friends" (*pace APF*, citing Xenophon)' is unconvincing.
   Proclus, XXI, 8.26–8 (= *SSR* VI A83), reports that 'in Aeschines Hermogenes is ridiculed as a slave to money. At any rate, he neglected Telauges, who was his companion and a graceful youth'.
[23] See Kahn 1973a: 154–7.
[24] Actually, a piece of evidence to this effect might be hidden in Socrates' murky reference, at 433a, to some Aeginetan decree. But no one has yet offered a satisfactory interpretation of that passage.

I.3.1 The dramatic date

The only indication concerning *Cra.*'s dramatic date comes at 391bc, where Socrates tells Hermogenes that the best way of inquiring into the correctness of names

> is to do so together with those who know, by paying them money and lavishing favours on them. These are the sophists, whom your brother Callias has paid much money, thereby acquiring a reputation for wisdom. But since you aren't master of your father's estate, you must importune your brother and pray him to teach you the correctness about such matters, which he learnt from Protagoras.

Nails 163 comments that 'Hipponicus II († 422/1) [i.e. the father of Callias and Hermogenes] is still alive when Socrates addresses Hermogenes … : "since you haven't yet come into any money of your own" (ἐπειδὴ δὲ οὐκ ἐγκρατὴς εἶ τῶν πατρῴων), implying that Hermogenes had some just expectation of inheriting from his father.' Thus she holds that *Cra.* is set before 422/1, the year of Hipponicus' death. But her 'yet' is *not* in the text, which rather suggests that Hermogenes is not 'master of his father's estate', not because Hipponicus is still alive, but because Hipponicus is dead and Hermogenes has not inherited from him whereas Callias has. Hence the conversation is likely to be set not before but *after* 422/1.

I.3.2 The relative date

The relative chronology of Plato's dialogues is a most controversial subject, and I am unable and unwilling to join the debate. I will just recall that stylometric studies have identified a group of late dialogues (*Sophist, Politicus, Timaeus, Critias, Philebus, Laws*) which share certain stylistic features. *Cra.* does not seem to belong to this group. Many scholars also believe that stylometry has succeeded in identifying a previous, 'transitional' group of dialogues (comprising *Republic, Parmenides, Theaetetus* and *Phaedrus*) and that *Cra.* does not belong to this group either, but rather to an earlier group. Yet I will most cautiously refrain from making this further assumption.[25]

One thing to be considered is that *Cra.* is at home with Platonic forms (389a–390e, 439c–440c: see §§3.4.1–3, 9.1.3) and that it displays an interest in an impressive array of themes (Protagorean relativism, flux, dialectic, division by kinds, the study of letters and their mutual relationships as a

---

[25] Surveys of stylometric studies are offered by Keyser 1992 (who is most pessimistic) and Young 1994.

model for the study of beings, the structure of sentences as basically composed of names and verbs) which will be prominent in dialogues usually assigned to the 'transitional' and 'late' groups – especially the *Phaedrus*, the *Theaetetus* and the *Sophist*. Closest are perhaps the contacts with *Tht.*, which on two distinct occasions offers an improved, more sophisticated version of an argument already contained in our dialogue (the refutation of Protagoras at 385e–386e, cf. *Tht.* 161c–162c, 177c–179c; the first argument against flux at 439d, cf. *Tht.* 181c–183b).[26] This suggests, independently of any stylometric conclusion, that *Cra.* is designed to be read (and presumably was also conceived) before *Tht.*

Another thing to be considered is that readers of *Cra.* in its present shape are expected to be already acquainted with the *Phaedo* in its present shape. The evidence (to be discussed more extensively in §§3.4.1 and 5.1.3) is twofold. (i) At 389b Socrates seems to take for granted the use of the formula ὅ ἐστι *F* as a designation for the forms, whereas at *Phd.* 75d and elsewhere he explicitly recognizes the formula's technical status. (ii) The etymology of Hades' name at 403a–404b appears to presuppose *Phd.*'s conception of death, as set forth especially at 80d–81a, and indeed to criticize and improve on an alternative etymology which is endorsed in the *Phd.* passage.

Thus, to sum up, *Cra.* does not belong to the 'late' dialogues; it is designed to be read after *Phd.* and before *Tht.*; and that's that.[27]

1.4 THE EVIDENCE FOR THE TEXT

In my translations I always use the text of the OCT edition unless otherwise specified; it is mainly from this edition, as well as occasionally from others and from inspection of the main MSS, that I draw my information about textual variants.

On the textual transmission of *Cra.* I have nothing interesting to say.[28] But it may be of some help to the readers if I briefly summarize a few facts, as stated in the preface to the OCT edition (v–xix), and explain the main sigla they are to encounter.

---

[26] On the various subjects mentioned in this paragraph you can see more extensively §§3.4.1–3, 9.1.3 (forms in *Cra.*); 2.4.2 (refutation of Protagoras); 3.2.1, 3.4.4, 6.3.2–4 (dialectic, division, letters); 6.3.5, 7.2.4 (names and verbs); 9.1.4 (argument against flux).

[27] See §2.2.5 for a discussion of Sedley's view that *Cra.* as we read it contains vestiges of *two* distinct redactions, one early and another late (contemporary with the *Sophist* or even later).

[28] Or, at least, nothing that is interesting in the present context. See however Ademollo (in preparation-1) for some considerations on the common source(s) of our MSS. On the transmission of *Cra.* see further Murphy/Nicoll 1993.

The MSS of our dialogue come in three main families. The first is the β family, i.e. the family deriving from a lost common ancestor named β. Members of this family are B (Bodleianus MS E.D. Clarke 39, written for Bishop Arethas by John Calligraphus in AD 895) and D (Venetus gr. 185, twelfth century). The second, most numerous family derives from an extant MS, T (Venetus app. cl. 4.1, tenth century). The third is the δ family, i.e. the family deriving from a lost common ancestor named δ. Its most important member is W (Vindobonesis suppl. gr. 7, eleventh century); but sometimes we shall mention Q (Parisinus gr. 1813, thirteenth century) and B² and T² (i.e. ancient correctors of B and T, which drew their new readings from sources belonging to δ; the former is, and the latter might be, earlier than W).

CHAPTER I

Cratylus' naturalism (383a–384c)

1.1 THE THESIS

1.1.1 First approach to the thesis (383ab)

Our dialogue, like the *Philebus*, opens by bringing us *in medias res*:

HE. So do you want us to let Socrates here join in our discussion?
CR. If you like. (383a1–3)

The situation seems to be the following. Hermogenes and Cratylus are on their way to the countryside (440e) and have been discussing for some time without reaching an agreement. Then they meet Socrates. Hermogenes suggests that they should inform him of the content of their discussion; Cratylus agrees.

But what is the issue Hermogenes and Cratylus were debating just before meeting Socrates? Hermogenes does not explain this in so many words. Rather, he immediately sets forth Cratylus' own view:

HE. Cratylus here, Socrates, says there is a natural correctness of name for each of the beings [ὀνόματος ὀρθότητα εἶναι ἑκάστῳ τῶν ὄντων φύσει πεφυκυῖαν], and what some conventionally agree to call something, uttering a bit of their voice and applying it to the thing, is not a name [καὶ οὐ τοῦτο εἶναι ὄνομα ὃ ἄν τινες συνθέμενοι καλεῖν καλῶσι, τῆς αὑτῶν φωνῆς μόριον ἐπιφθεγγόμενοι]; but there is a natural correctness of names for both Greeks and barbarians, the same for all [ἀλλὰ ὀρθότητά τινα τῶν ὀνομάτων πεφυκέναι καὶ Ἕλλησι καὶ βαρβάροις τὴν αὐτὴν ἅπασιν]. (383a4–b2)

This first part of Hermogenes' exposition is articulated into three coordinate clauses:

(C1) 'There is a natural ... beings' (a4–5),
(C2) 'What some ... not a name' (a5–7),
(C3) 'There is ... same for all' (a7–b2).

(C1) generically announces that there is for each thing a 'natural correctness of name'. The controversy between Hermogenes and Cratylus concerns the following question: What conditions must be met for a word to count as a correct name of something? Here this question receives a very generic answer: a name's correctness is a *natural* matter.

(C2) completes and explains (C1): what some speakers conventionally agree to call[1] something is not a name. Note that (C2) says ' ... is not a name', not '... is not a *correct* name', as we might expect given that (C1) and (C3) are concerned with the *correctness* of names. This suggests that Cratylus is tacitly adopting a certain conception of what it is for a name to be correct, a conception which in fact appears to be shared by Hermogenes and Socrates in many other passages (starting with b2–7, see §1.1.2) and which I call the 'Redundancy Conception' of correctness (cf. §I.1.1). On this conception, 'being a correct name of *X*' and 'being a name of *X*' are equivalent expressions. So the question at issue can be rephrased as follows: What conditions must be met for an expression to count as a *name* of something?

Now, (C2) says that, when some speakers conventionally agree to use a certain string of sounds to refer to something, their agreement is *not sufficient* to make those sounds into a name of that thing. This is precisely because, as (C1) says, the correctness of a name is something natural. Here the question arises whether the speakers' conventional agreement is at least a *necessary* condition for a string of sounds to be the name of something. (C2) does not, strictly speaking, contain an answer to this question. A positive answer will apparently be implied by Socrates at 388d, where he says that names are transmitted to us by custom; but a negative answer is implied by Cratylus at 429c, where he holds that a string of sounds may naturally fit something, and thus be a name of it, even if this is not acknowledged by any convention among speakers (see §7.1.3). Of course nothing prevents a name that bears the required natural relation to its referent from being also conventionally acknowledged as its name, as the text will shortly confirm. But (C2) entails that the factor *in virtue of which* such a name is a name is only its natural relation to its referent.

Finally, let us focus on the Greek phrase which I have translated 'uttering a bit of their voice and applying it to the thing' (a6–7).[2] Many

---

[1] The verb καλέω, 'call' (a6), usually indicates the action of *using* an already established name, and only rarely that of *imposing* a name, as e.g. at 406b, 407bc, 416c. (Verbal aspect plays some role too: the aorist seems to be preferred to express imposition, see Jacquinod 2000.) The latter notion is typically expressed by the verb τίθεμαι: see 384cd and 385d with §2.1.1.

[2] 'And applying it to the thing' aims to render the ἐπι- in ἐπιφθεγγόμενοι: cf. *Phlb.* 18d and the meaning of ἐπί in expressions like ὄνομα καλεῖν ἐπί τινι, 'to apply a name to something' (cf. *Prm.*

interpreters – e.g. Dalimier 193 n.2 – understand φωνή here as 'language' rather than 'voice'. Like Ficino and others, however, I would rather read here an expression of the name's *vocal* nature, which is usually stressed in kindred contexts (*Sph.* 261e, Arist. *Int.* 16a19 etc.). In the present context this also conveys the further suggestion that, on the rival conventionalist account of the correctness of names, a name need not be anything more than a string of sounds associated with something by a convention among speakers.

(C3) picks up (C1) and adds an important point: the correctness of names is universally valid, for Greeks as for barbarians. Cratylus apparently has not clearly spelt out the purport of this statement. But when later Socrates will defend and develop Cratylus' case at length, he will maintain that different languages may contain different, yet equally natural names of one and the same thing (389d–390a). So what is natural and universal is a certain *relation* between name and thing, which can be instantiated by different strings of sounds in different languages, provided that each string satisfies certain conditions for naming a given thing. In this connection it might be significant that Cratylus speaks of a natural correct*ness* of names for each thing, not of a correct name for each thing, thereby focusing on the relation rather than on the items related.

Indeed, nothing so far would prevent even different strings of sounds *within a single language* from bearing the required relation to a given thing. This further possibility is not touched upon in Hermogenes' report, and was perhaps not considered by Cratylus. But it is not incompatible with his claims.[3] Socrates' developments of the theory will not be explicit on this matter. But, at least as far as those developments are concerned, we can extrapolate the point from two clues: first, Socrates' claim that names like 'Hector' and 'Astyanax' reveal an identical nature in different persons (393a–394e); secondly, the fact that later on, in the etymologies, Socrates will have no qualms about the case of a goddess with two names ('Athena' and 'Pallas', 406d–407c). Proclus and Ammonius, we may add, argue that naturalism can countenance 'polyonymy' (see respectively xvi, 7.10–13, and *in Int.* 38.2–17).[4] They are taking for granted Socrates' own version of naturalism; but nothing suggests that they take Cratylus' view of the matter to be any different.

147de). Thus Fowler speaks of 'just a piece of their own voice applied to the thing'; cf. de Vries 1955: 290, Dalimier 193 n.3.
[3] *Pace* Baxter 1992: 9, 135–6, who ascribes to Cratylus the thesis that within every single language there is a biunivocal correspondence between names and things.
[4] Cf. Ademollo 2003: 36–7.

1.1.2 More details: Hermogenes' name (383b–384c)

So far we have seen the bare outline of a naturalist theory of names. For the theory to acquire a definite identity, however, at least two questions need to be answered. First, what does the natural criterion of correctness consist in? Secondly, what is the relation between the names that meet this criterion and the conventionally accepted 'names' in actually spoken languages like Greek?

The latter question is immediately raised in the text, in a passage which will also prove crucial to the former:

> (HE.) So I ask him whether his name is really 'Cratylus'; and he agrees. 'And what is Socrates' name?', I said. '"Socrates"', said he. 'Then the same holds of all the other human beings too? The name we call each person, this is the name for each person? [ὅπερ καλοῦμεν ὄνομα ἕκαστον, τοῦτό ἐστιν ἑκάστῳ ὄνομα;]' And he said, 'Well, at any rate *you* don't bear the name "Hermogenes" [Οὔκουν σοί γε … ὄνομα Ἑρμογένης], not even if all human beings call you so.' (383b2–7)

As Cratylus confirms that the first two examples are naturally correct names, we and Hermogenes are seized by a suspicion: perhaps Cratylus' thesis will leave all current names untouched though boasting to have discovered the ground for their correctness. But when Hermogenes voices this suspicion, Cratylus disappoints him: *he* is the very example of nature and convention's coming apart. Whatever people may say, 'Hermogenes' is not his name.

The passage gives us two relevant pieces of information. First, as in (C2) above, but unlike (C1) and (C3), here there is no talk of correct names, or of the correctness of names; the reported exchange between Hermogenes and Cratylus is couched simply in terms of what someone's name is and whether a particular name 'really' is someone's name. This confirms that Hermogenes and Cratylus are assuming that a correct name is simply a genuine, authentic, bona fide name, and hence are adopting what I have called the 'Redundancy Conception' of correctness.

Secondly, according to Cratylus some current verbal conventions, unlike 'Cratylus' and 'Socrates', do not satisfy the natural criteria; that is to say, some verbal conventions that are believed to be names are not names. Now one would like to know what exactly the status of such conventional pseudo-names is and whether they represent the exception or the rule in ordinary languages like Greek. But first of all, why is 'Hermogenes' not Hermogenes' name?

The thesis

This last question has obviously been asked by Hermogenes himself; but since the results have been discouraging, he now tries to draw Socrates into the discussion:

(HE.) And, though I ask him and am eager to know what on earth he means, he makes nothing clear and deceitfully pretends [εἰρωνεύεται ... πρός με, προσποιούμενος][5] that he, having knowledge about this matter, has something in mind which, if he wished to say it clearly, would make me agree and subscribe to his views. So, if you are somehow able to interpret Cratylus' oracle, I'd gladly listen. Or rather, I'd even more gladly know what *you* think about the correctness of name, if you please. (383b7–384a7)

In the light of the fact that at the end of the dialogue Cratylus will voice a sympathy for Heraclitus' flux theory, and that according to Aristotle's report he even became a radical supporter of this theory (see §I.2.1), his ostentatious mysteriousness should remind us of the characteristic attitude of the Heracliteans described at *Tht*. 179d–180c.

Socrates is going to drop a hint at an interpretation of Cratylus' riddle. But he first protests his ignorance and ironically contrasts it with the knowledge which the sophist Prodicus imparts at a high price:

SO. Hermogenes, son of Hipponicus, there is an ancient proverb that 'fine things are difficult'[6] to know about; and, in particular, knowledge about names happens to be no trivial piece of knowledge. Now, if I'd already listened to Prodicus' fifty-drachma lecture, whose listeners as he says possess a complete education on this subject, then nothing would stop you immediately knowing the truth about the correctness of names. As it is, however, I haven't

---

[5] εἰρωνεύεται ... προσποιούμενος (a1–2) is difficult. It is usually taken to mean 'is ironical ... pretending'; but Lane 2006 argues that in Plato εἰρωνεύομαι never has this meaning and always means 'dissemble, conceal by feigning' instead (cf. *Sph*. 268a, *Lg*. 908e; as regards our passage she agrees with LSJ and Fowler). She suggests that in our passage 'What Cratylus is accused of feigning is not the claim to possess (what he takes to be) knowledge ... It is rather the insinuation that were Cratylus to expound his knowledge, his account would be so compelling that Hermogenes would inevitably and necessarily come to agree. Hermogenes sees this as a feint which conceals the fact that Cratylus may not have such a knock-down proof' (2006: 56–7). It seems, however, that εἰρωνεύομαι can mean just 'feign', as at *Euthd*. 302b, where Dionysodorus is reported to have said something 'after pausing most deceitfully [εἰρωνικῶς πάνυ], as if he were considering some big issue'; and that in our passage the gist of Lane's interpretation fits more naturally with such a construal of the verb.

Yet there is something odd about the idea that Hermogenes is accusing Cratylus of bluff, given that he, though having already discussed the matter with Cratylus in the past (c10–11), is now going to ask Socrates to 'interpret Cratylus' oracle' (a4–5) and to declare himself willing to 'learn' from Cratylus (e1–2). I wonder whether it could not be the case that εἰρωνεύεται does after all mean 'is ironical' (cf. Arist. *Rh*. 1379b31–2, and εἰρωνεία at 1419b7–9) and προσποιούμενος means, not 'pretending', but rather 'making out', 'setting himself up' in a certain way, regardless of whether or not these airs are justified. After all, προσποιέομαι can mean 'claim' (and indeed is so translated here by Fowler; cf. e.g. *Ap*. 23d).

[6] Cf. *Hp. Ma*. 304e; *R*. 435c, 497d. The saying is fathered on Solon: see *sch*. 3 Cufalo.

listened to that lecture, but to the one-drachma one. Hence I don't know how in the world the truth about such matters is. Nonetheless, I'm ready to undertake a common search together with you and Cratylus. (384a8–c3)

Prodicus, of whom Socrates elsewhere declares himself a pupil,[7] notoriously dealt with a subject nominally identical with that of our dialogue: 'First of all, as Prodicus says, one must learn about the correctness of names [περὶ ὀνομάτων ὀρθότητος]' (*Euthd.* 277e). Thereby Prodicus meant his activity of drawing oversubtle semantic distinctions between quasi-synonyms (see e.g. *Chrm.* 163d; *Prt.* 337ac, 340ab; Arist. *Top.* 112b21–6; Stob. 4.20.65), some of which aimed at correcting, rather than expounding, current linguistic practice, and some of which were supported by etymologies (*Prt.* 337c, Gal. *Nat. Fac.* 2.9). Prodicus has often been credited with general theses of some sort, e.g. that there are no synonyms at all, or even that there is a one-to-one correspondence between names and things. But in fact there is no evidence that he went beyond a number of particular distinctions or that he took a stand in the nature/convention debate as it is presented in *Cra.* Thus Socrates' claim that he is ignorant of Prodicus' views and will not take them into account probably has the function to make it clear that, in spite of the common label 'correctness of names', the issue discussed here is different from what Prodicus went in for. Socrates will make a partly similar move with regard to Protagoras at 391bc (see §4.1). In both cases, he simultaneously seizes the opportunity for making fun of the Sophists' greed for money[8] and of the absurd idea that we could learn the truth on a philosophical topic just by buying a ticket and listening to someone's lecture.

Once Prodicus has been put aside, Socrates nonchalantly drops a suggestion about what Cratylus meant:

(SO.) As for the fact that he says 'Hermogenes' is not really your name, I suspect, as it were, that he is mocking you: for perhaps he thinks you long for money but every time miss the mark. However, as I was saying just now, having knowledge of such matters is difficult, but we must put them on the table for a common discussion and examine whether things are as you say or as Cratylus says. (384c3–9)

---

[7] Cf. *Prt.* 341a, *Men.* 96d. On the relations between Socrates and Prodicus see Guthrie 1962–81: III.222–3, 276. Several of the texts cited in this paragraph are collected in # 84 DK.
[8] On the fifty-drachma lecture cf. Arist. *Rh.* 1415b15–17: whenever his hearers began to doze, Prodicus said he interposed a taste of it. Fifty drachma was a considerable sum, if in the late fifth century an unmarried Athenian spent 120 drachma a year for food (60 drachma), clothes, rent and other expenses (Tod 1927: 21–2). Fifty drachma is also half the fine Socrates declares he would be able to pay at *Ap.* 38b. Cf. *La.* 186c, where he claims he cannot afford to pay for the teaching of the Sophists.

According to Socrates, Cratylus was hinting at a contrast between the fact that 'Hermogenes' etymologically means 'offspring of Hermes', Hermes being the patron god of thieves and merchants, of lucky stroke and gain, and the fact that Hermogenes is always frustrated in his economical yearnings.[9] Hermogenes' poverty (on which cf. X. *Mem.* 2.10), together with 391c, where Socrates says that Hermogenes 'is not master of his father's estate' and contrasts his condition with the wealth of his sibling Callias, shows that Hermogenes was an illegitimate, albeit acknowledged, son of rich Hipponicus, and that Callias was actually his half-brother (see §I.2.2).

Although Socrates says that Cratylus was perhaps joking, in fact he does suggest a very serious interpretation of Cratylus' thesis. On this interpretation, the gist of natural correctness is that the *etymology* of a name must somehow express or reveal something true about the referent. Thus 'Hermogenes' is not Hermogenes' name because the description 'offspring of Hermes' is not true of him. As the dialogue will show at length, this interpretation is the right one. Socrates will take it for granted in developing Cratylus' claims and will also try to apply it on a large scale in the etymological sections of the dialogue (394e–427d), where many Greek words are analysed. At 428be Cratylus himself will wholeheartedly approve of the etymological performance and agree that the correctness of names consists in showing 'what the object is like' and that 'names are said for the sake of teaching'. Indeed, as he puts it later on, 'It seems to me that the fine thing they accomplish is teaching ... he who has knowledge of the names has also knowledge of the objects' (435d). Perhaps we cannot be confident that any of these claims can be literally ascribed, not only to the historical Cratylus, but also to the character who was discussing with Hermogenes before Socrates' entrance.[10] Surely, however, these claims capture at least something essential about the views of Cratylus the character. When he said that 'Hermogenes' is not Hermogenes' name, surely he had something of this sort in mind.

We should now ask what the status of the pseudo-names like 'Hermogenes' is. If you take an object, X, and an expression, 'N', which is conventionally regarded as a name of X but in fact fails to live up to naturalist standards, two possibilities are conceivable:

---

[9] See 408b for an alternative explanation of Cratylus' point, of course still in terms of the name's etymology.
[10] But see §8.1.1 for a conjectural attempt to credit the historical Cratylus with the view that the function of names is to 'teach'.

(a) '*N*' is not a name of *X*, but nevertheless does somehow refer to it. A thing can be referred to either by a naturally correct name or by a second-rate, merely conventional designator.
(b) '*N*' does not refer to *X* at all. A thing can be referred to only by a naturally correct name.

Cratylus might hold either (a) or (b); indeed, he seems to waver between the two. Let us reconsider two expressions used by Hermogenes in expounding Cratylus' claims: 'what some conventionally agree to *call* something, uttering a bit of their voice and *applying it to* the thing' (a6–7) and 'not even if all human beings *call* you so' (b7). These expressions suggest that conventional communication does work somehow or other, because they seem to imply that people utter 'Hermogenes' with reference to Hermogenes and thereby understand each other. Indeed, at 427e, 434d Cratylus himself calls Hermogenes 'Hermogenes', as if he took this to be an expression that somehow refers to him.[11] These elements support interpretation (a). So does 429bc, where Cratylus claims that 'Hermogenes' does not even belong to Hermogenes as a name, 'but *seems* to belong to him'. Strictly speaking, this seems to imply that 'Hermogenes' does refer to Hermogenes, albeit in some merely conventional way (see §7.1.3).

In the immediate sequel of that same passage, however, matters begin to look different. Socrates points out that Cratylus must hold that a sentence like 'That is Hermogenes' (where 'that' refers to Hermogenes) is not even false, but impossible to formulate, because Cratylus is committed to the view that it is impossible to speak falsely.[12] Now these lines, taken by themselves, are interpreted most naturally if we suppose that 'Hermogenes' can be nothing but a name. Nothing in the text requires a sophisticated distinction between 'Hermogenes' as a name of someone other than Hermogenes if of anyone at all, and 'Hermogenes' as a mere conventional tag of Hermogenes. No one makes any attempt to save the possibility of meaningfully uttering 'That is Hermogenes.' Indeed, already at 407e and 408b it had been plainly asserted that Hermogenes 'is not Hermogenes'.

In the remainder of the dialogue it is never suggested that Cratylus countenances, or might countenance, a merely conventional kind of reference.

---

[11] 'In both the cases you cite C[ratylus] has been put on the spot. Placatory behaviour?' (Myles Burnyeat, personal communication, 2001). It might be, though the suggestion fits the second passage better than the first.

[12] Socrates seems to be claiming that Cratylus' naturalist thesis *entails* the impossibility of false speaking, while Cratylus for his part does not see this connection and conceives of the two theses as mutually independent. This problem, which I discuss in §7.2.1, has no bearing on our present issue.

Nothing of that sort will be suggested at 433de, where Socrates contrasts the naturalist and the conventionalist thesis in terms of two alternative *ways* in which names can be thought to *indicate* things, either by being similar to them or by being conventional tokens; nor at 434d–435d, where the conclusion that the example σκληρόν indicates its referent by convention and habit, and that more generally convention and habit play a part in the 'indication' of things, is one that Socrates has to force on Cratylus, not one that Cratylus is already prepared to accept.

Now, insofar as (b) is – as most interpreters assume – Cratylus' view, an interesting consequence follows if we also take into account the other Cratylan thesis of the impossibility of false speech,[13] stated at 429b–430a. From the combination of the two theses it follows that it is sheerly impossible to call Hermogenes 'Hermogenes'. For claiming 'That is Hermogenes', or addressing him thus, would amount to saying something false, and hence – since it is not possible to speak falsely – to uttering vacuous sounds. Compare what Cratylus says about the hypothetical case of someone addressing him (Cratylus) as 'Hermogenes': such a person 'would be merely making noise, moving pointlessly, as if one moved a bronze pot by striking it' (430a5–7). We can infer that the same holds when it falls to Hermogenes himself to be addressed as 'Hermogenes', because according to (b) this expression does not refer to him any more than it refers to Cratylus. So, if you tried to utter the statement 'That [referring to Hermogenes] is Hermogenes', the result would merely be the production of meaningless sounds. That this is the upshot of Cratylus' naturalism is clearly asserted by Ammonius, *in Int.* 34.24–30:

Cratylus the Heraclitean, who said that for each thing an appropriate name has been determined by the agency of nature ... and that those who say such a name do really name [ὀνομάζειν μὲν ὄντως], while those who do not say this do not name at all but *merely make noise* [μηδὲ ὀνομάζειν ἀλλὰ ψοφεῖν μόνον].[14]

Cratylus' thesis, in its version (b), is evidently implausible. But we should not be surprised, because Cratylus seems fond of bizarre and paradoxical stances. He supports the sophistical paradox of the impossibility of false speaking and defends it up to the point of holding the absurdities we have just seen, akin to (b) in that they involve a denial of the evidence of communication. And according to Aristotle, *Metaph.* Γ5.1010a7–15, the historical Cratylus eventually came to believe that one should say nothing at all and expressed himself just by moving his finger.

---

[13] Socrates actually seems to infer such a thesis from the very one about names: see n.12.
[14] Wilamowitz 1920: 1.292–3, Grote 1888: III.316, and Baxter 1992: 10–11 all agree with Ammonius.

There is another question which was prompted above by Cratylus' rejection of 'Hermogenes' and which is still awaiting an answer. Does Cratylus think that the Greek language contains more genuine, natural names or more merely conventional pseudo-names? According to Baxter (1992: 11), Cratylus' position is that 'what Greek ought to be is what it (broadly speaking) is ... Some names, like *Hermogenes*, will fail the test, but in general he seems confident that Greek easily satisfies the criteria for a natural language'. In support of this view he adduces 436bc, where Cratylus shows himself convinced that Greek consists of authentic names, which have been bestowed on their referents according to knowledge of their nature. The same lesson can be extracted from 435d, where Cratylus claims that knowledge of names yields knowledge of their referents. Hence Cratylus' theory does not limit itself to defining the criteria of name correctness, but sees these criteria as substantially fulfilled by at least one existing language, the Greek one. Cratylus can thus attain to a sort of reconciliation between convention and nature: as a matter of fact, the existing conventions mostly satisfy the natural criteria.

1.1.3 *The origin of natural names*

A final question one should face in analysing Cratylus' thesis, and one which cannot be easily answered, concerns the *origin* of names. Since, as we have just seen, Cratylus seems to regard Greek as a language substantially embodying the natural criteria, one wonders how this correspondence could have arisen. Who hid into names the truth about their bearers? Unfortunately Hermogenes' report shows that Cratylus has been reticent enough not to go into such details. He will, however, approve of a theory Socrates develops on his behalf. At 388d–389a Socrates argues that names must be the work of a skilled lawgiver (νομοθέτης), and in the etymologies, presented as a practical demonstration of the natural correctness of names, he continuously refers to the lawgiver, or lawgivers, who hid into names their views about things.[15] When Cratylus becomes Socrates' interlocutor, he starts out by praising all Socrates has been saying that far and explicitly acknowledges the lawgivers' role (428c–429a). In the following discussion the legislators reappear here and there; see especially 436bd, where Cratylus claims that surely 'he who imposed the names' had knowledge of the things he was baptizing.

[15] Ammonius, *in Int.* 34.22–32, ascribes to Cratylus the thesis that names are by nature in the sense of being '*products* of nature' (φύσεως ... δημιουργήματα): 'names resemble the natural, not the artificial images of visible things, like shadows and those which usually appear in water or

The assumption that names are artificial products of human activity is consistent with the thesis that they are naturally correct (cf. §I.1.1). The thesis has nothing to say about the circumstances of the name's coming to be; it only claims that between a name and its referent there is necessarily a certain natural fit. Having recourse to an analogy we shall return to in §7.1.3, we may compare Cratylan names to keys.[16] A key is an artificial, human-made tool. But whether or not a particular key, once it has been made, fits a particular lock is a perfectly objective and non-conventional fact, which depends solely on the shape of both key and lock.

At 438bc Cratylus will say that, in his view, 'it was a *more than human* power that imposed the first names on the objects'. This suggestion is immediately countered by Socrates, never to reappear in the dialogue; but some scholars[17] have supposed that it is part of the original stock of views already held by Cratylus at the dialogue's outset (see §8.2.3). This supposition, however, seems unwarranted; it is more natural to think that there Cratylus, pressed by Socrates' arguments, is looking for a way out. His way out is not unattested in contemporary Greek thought, as we shall see in §1.2.

1.2 BEFORE CRATYLUS

The roots of Cratylus' thesis lie in the depths of a popular way of thinking. As in other cultures, so in the Greek one there is a strong consideration of the bond between name and thing. The most part of Greek proper names is constituted by simple or compound names with an immediately recognizable etymological meaning, like Ἀριστοτέλης ('Bestend') or Κάλλιππος ('Finehorse'). These meanings are based on a huge range of concepts, from those relative to the sphere of virtue and fame to the less attractive ones, as the existence of names like Κοπρίων ('Dirty') demonstrates.[18] As is remarked in *Cra.* 397b, the name often expressed a hope for the child's future: see the discussion between Strepsiades and his wife in Aristophanes' *Clouds*, 60–7, where the woman wishes for an aristocratic name like Ξάνθιππος ('Bayhorse'), against which the man sets up his father's name, Φειδωνίδης ('Thrifty').

---

mirrors'. This interpretation is instrumental in contrasting Cratylus and Socrates (cf. 35.1–12), but it is groundless. It also seems to be presupposed by Proclus, LVIII, 25.33–26.3, inconsistently with XVII, 7.18–8.4.

[16] The comparison is Reeve's (xiv), although he makes less of it than I do.
[17] E.g. Goldschmidt 1940: 159–60.
[18] See *OCD* s.v. names, personal, Greek.

Such a situation carries with it a tendency to compare the name with the real nature or fate of its bearer, when this is an adult, in order to ascertain whether the property signified by the name does belong to him. Already Homer often assigns characters names and patronymics describing some of their features, as with the impudent Θερσίτης ('Insolent') or the singer Θερπιάδης ... Φήμιος ('Teller, son of Delight', *Od.* 22.330–1).[19] Sometimes the poet *explicitly* plays with the meaning of the name and hints at its real or supposed relation to the bearer. This happens in the case of Ὀδυσσεύς, derived from ὀδύσσομαι 'hate' (e.g. *Od.* 1.62, 19.406–9), or in the Cyclops episode, where Odysseus shrewdly declares he is called Οὖτις, 'No one' (9.364–70, 407–12).

After Homer, characters with a 'transparent' name, whose etymology accords with their nature or is ironically opposed thereto, remain a constant presence in Greek literature, especially in Hesiod, the tragedians and Aristophanes. Aeschylus often explicitly underlines the tie between name and bearer: e.g. *Th.* 658 'he who strongly deserves his name, I mean Polynices' (Πολυνείκης < πολὺ νεῖκος, 'great strife'). Indeed, in two passages Aeschylus refers to this tie by making use of the very notion of *correctness*, which will also be the core of the debate in our dialogue, obviously in a more specific sense. At *Th.* 829–31 the Chorus mourns the death of Eteocles and Polynices, 'who *in correct accordance with their names* [ὀρθῶς κατ' ἐπωνυμίαν] died rich in glory and strife [<ἐτεοκλειεῖς> καὶ πολυνεικεῖς] because of their impious wishes'. And at *Ag.* 699 the Chorus refers to the union between Paris and Helen as a κῆδος ὀρθώνυμον, a '*correctly-named* κῆδος' (a term which means both 'grief' and 'marriage'), for Troy. In the same tragedy, 681–91, we find the Chorus reflecting upon the mysterious appropriateness of Helen's name:

> Who ever called in such a completely veridical way 'Helen' [Ἑλέναν] her whose spouses had to fight, who was contested between two parts? Maybe someone we do not see, who foreseeing what had been decided by destiny moved his tongue hitting the mark? For suitably [πρεπόντως] as a Hell for ships, a Hell for men, a Hell for cities [ἑλένας ἕλανδρος ἑλέπτολις] she sailed from the delicate, magnificent curtains ...

Here it is also important to note the reference to an indefinite superhuman power who named Helen in accordance with an insight into her destiny. Indeed, Levin 2001: 22–3 suggests that we take seriously the possibility that 'Zeus himself – as Helen's male parent – is envisioned by the poet as having assigned his daughter's *onoma*'. This reference is reminiscent of the notion,

---

[19] For an ample survey of Greek literary etymology, with many examples, see Levin 2001: 13–31.

which occurs both in Plato and elsewhere, that names are bestowed by someone who has some sort of special knowledge of the nature of things. This wise namegiver is sometimes conceived of as a god or a superhuman power (*Lg.* 654a, Diod. Sic. 1.16.1; cf. *Cra.* 397bc, 407e–408b, 438bc), or at least is in close touch with the gods (*Phlb.* 16c–18d; Arist. *Cael.* 279a22–3).

Of course, in the works of the other tragedians too we find a number of reflections of this kind. At *Aj.* 430–2 Ajax discovers a connection between his own name, which he derives from the interjection αἰαῖ, and his misfortunes; at *Ba.* 367 Teiresias expresses the fear that Pentheus (Πενθεύς) may bring mourning (πένθος) to Cadmus' house. In some cases the name turns out to be tragically inappropriate: e.g. *Pr.* 85–6 'By a false name[20] the gods call you Forethinker [Προμηθέα]: for you yourself are in need of a forethinker [προμηθέως], etc.'.

The etymological congruence between name and object eventually becomes a *topos* illustrated through several examples by Aristotle, *Rh.* 2.23. Incidentally, note that one of the examples again makes use of the notion of *correctness*:

> Another *topos* is based on the name, e.g. as Sophocles says 'You certainly are Sidero ['Iron'], and you have a mind in keeping with your name',[21] and as Conon called Thrasybulus *thrasyboulon* ['bold in counsel'], and Herodicus said to Thrasymachus 'You're always *thrasymachos* ['bold in battle']', and said to Polus 'You're always *polos* ['colt']', and said of Draco the lawgiver that his laws were not those of a human being, but of a *drakon* ['dragon'], so harsh they were. So also Euripides' Hecuba says with regard to Aphrodite, 'The goddess' name correctly [ὀρθῶς] begins like that of *aphrosyne* ['folly']',[22] and as Chaeremon says 'Pentheus, named after his forthcoming misfortune'.[23] (1400b16–25)

The *topos* 'based on the name' closes a list of *enthymematic topoi*, which occupies the whole of ch. 2.23. This seems to mean that Aristotle thinks of these etymologies not as mere word-plays, but rather as grounds for some sort of (obviously only rhetorical) *argument*. The passage is all the more interesting as evidence of a rooted way of thinking in that Aristotle is a firm conventionalist.

It is evident how the widespread conception I have briefly illustrated constitutes the basis for Cratylus' doctrine.[24] Some important differences, however, must not be overlooked. To begin with, Cratylus is far more radical than the tradition he depends on, because he has a *general* thesis about

---

[20] Cf. §2.2.4 and n.61.   [21] *TrGF* 658.   [22] Eur. *Tr.* 990.   [23] *TrGF* 71 F4.
[24] Here I am speaking primarily of Cratylus the character of our dialogue, not of the historical Cratylus.

all names, according to which the name of anything can only be a naturally correct one, while the merely conventional pseudo-names are sheer noise, meaningless sounds. The traditional conception, instead, is obviously vaguer and more elastic. It finds expression through a number of individual comparisons between name and thing, which do certainly arise from a sense of what has been called 'the magic of names', but nevertheless do not lead to any *generalization* concerning all names, and allow that a name may provide a false description of its bearer without therefore ceasing to be its name.

It would be of utmost interest to us if we should discover that some other thinker before Cratylus rose above the traditional standpoint and made some progress towards an explicit theorization. But it is very unclear whether this is so. Heraclitus has been a favourite of the attempts at identifying Cratylus' forerunners; but he is not known to have made any general statement about names and their signification. All we can draw from his laconic fragments are some four or five instances (e.g. 22 B114, 48 DK) where he shows adherence to the old, common feeling about names. We shall see in §4.1 that perhaps Protagoras might have taken some steps towards a naturalist account of the correctness of names. According to one interpretation, which on the whole I find plausible, Protagoras seems to have held that the *gender* of names (or of some names) should reflect their male, female or 'neuter' nature. If this is so, then his naturalist account was not based on etymology and hence was of a different brand from that of Cratylus and Socrates. Moreover, there is reason to suspect that Protagoras did not set forth his views about the correctness of names for their own sake, but only insofar as they were subservient to a criticism of Homer.

Another very important feature separating Cratylus from the popular background of his nature-thesis is that he clearly contaminates that background with elements of alien provenance, resulting in a curious and interesting mix of archaic and modern traits. His claims betray a strong sophistic influence. The traditional sense of the 'magic of names' is now cast in terms of the typically sophistic contrast between nature and convention. Cratylus also upholds another sophistic favourite, namely the thesis of the impossibility of false speech, supporting it with a stock argument about saying 'what is not' (429d, see §7.2.2). The picture is further complicated by his Heraclitean sympathies, which begin to emerge at the end of the dialogue and which grew into a radical allegiance at some stage of the philosophical career of the historical Cratylus, as Aristotle reports (see §I.2.1).

CHAPTER 2

Hermogenes' conventionalism (384c–386e)

2.1 CONVENTION AND INDIVIDUAL DECISION (384C–385B)

2.1.1 *First statement (384ce)*

Hermogenes begins to state his own views politely contradicting Cratylus:

HE. Well, Socrates, though I have often discussed both with Cratylus here and with many others, I cannot be persuaded that there is any other correctness of a name than convention and agreement [συνθήκη καὶ ὁμολογία]. For it seems to me that, whatever name one imposes on something, this is its correct name [ὅτι ἄν τίς τῳ θῆται ὄνομα, τοῦτο εἶναι τὸ ὀρθόν]; and that, if one changes it by imposing another one again, and does not call the thing by the former name any more [καὶ ἄν αὖθίς γε ἕτερον μεταθῆται, ἐκεῖνο δὲ μηκέτι καλῇ], the new name is no less correct than the old, as when we change the name of our slaves. For no name belongs by nature to anything [οὐ γὰρ φύσει ἑκάστῳ πεφυκέναι ὄνομα οὐδὲν οὐδενί], but in virtue of the custom and habit of those who made names into habits and those who call things by them [ἀλλὰ νόμῳ καὶ ἔθει τῶν ἐθισάντων τε καὶ καλούντων]. (384c10–e2)

The core of Hermogenes' self-presentation can be divided into three sentences:

(H1) 'I cannot ... agreement' (c11–d2),
(H2) 'It seems to me ... our slaves' (d2–5),
(H3) 'No name ... call things' (d5–7).

Let us examine each sentence more closely.

(H1) asserts that the correctness of the name consists in *convention* (συνθήκη) and *agreement* (ὁμολογία). The meaning of this seems to be the following: what makes a given sequence of sounds into the name of a given thing is just the fact that some speakers somehow agree to call that thing by those sounds. Of course, human agreements are always open to renegotiation, so even before glancing at (H2) we may expect the relation between name and thing to be an unstable one.

The more interesting of the two keywords of (H1) is perhaps συνθήκη. Outside philosophical contexts, συνθήκη or συνθῆκαι means 'treaty', 'contract' or 'arrangement'.[1] In its philosophical use the term seems to be first attested in Plato (besides our dialogue cf. *Cri.* 52de, 54c; *R.* 359a).[2] It is then appropriated by Aristotle, who employs it in his own treatment of the signification of names and sentences (*Int.* 16a19–29, 17a1–2), which is clearly indebted to *Cra.*, and in other connections.[3]

Hermogenes has nothing to say about how his 'convention and agreement' actually works. He says neither how it took place when names were first bestowed on things, nor how it has subsequently been preserved and renewed. As far as the latter point is concerned, however, we may guess that an *implicit* compact takes place every time a speaker adheres to the established linguistic usage.[4] This is confirmed by a comparison with the Laws' speech in the *Crito*. The Laws repeatedly refer to an implicit 'agreement' between them and every citizen, which takes place whenever a citizen decides not to go and live somewhere else, thereby accepting the Athenian laws and pledging himself either to obey or at most to try to persuade them, but never to violate them (51d–52b). See especially 52d (and cf. 52de, 54c), where the Laws mention

> the *conventions* and the *agreements* according to which you covenanted with us to live as a citizen … in deed though not in word [τὰς συνθήκας τε καὶ τὰς ὁμολογίας καθ' ἃς ἡμῖν συνέθου πολιτεύεσθαι … ἔργῳ ἀλλ' οὐ λόγῳ].

Here the wording is clearly reminiscent of (H1), and the compact's implicit nature is openly recognized. Thus Hermogenes' linguistic 'convention and agreement' is likely to keep alive in virtue of the tacit adherence of speakers. Indeed, this might even be how it first took place in the remote beginnings of language; perhaps all that happened then was just that

---

[1] See e.g. Aesch. *Ch.* 555, Th. 8.37.1, Isocr. 4.176, Arist. *Rh.* 1376a33–b31. The *Suda*, Σ 1587 Adler, reports three ways in which an actual συνθήκη could take place: through an oath or a sacrifice or a shaking of hands.

[2] Note that the cognate verb συντίθεμαι had already occurred at 383a6, in Hermogenes' account of Cratylus' claims.

[3] See e.g. *EN* 1133a29, 1134b32, 35.

[4] How many times does this adherence take place? Once in a person's life, or every time one utters a word in accordance with the usage of his community? For a thorough philosophical investigation of convention and other related concepts see Lewis 1969, and Lewis 1983 more specifically on conventions of language.

Convention and individual decision (384c–385b)

the usage of one or more speakers gradually gained consent among a community.[5]

(H2) is introduced by 'for' (d2 γάρ) and is thus presented as a *reason* for the previous statement, or perhaps as an exemplification of it.[6] The correct name for each thing, Hermogenes says, is that which 'one' imposes on it (d2–3), and a name that has been imposed on something can be replaced by another name (d3–5). To illustrate and confirm the fact that in such a case the new name is as correct as the old Hermogenes cites the use of changing the name of slaves (d5).[7] Here Proclus, XXX, 10.23–6, sees an actual argument:

if there is name change, then names are by convention and are conventional tokens of the objects; but the first; therefore also the second.

Two aspects of (H2) are of utmost importance for the ensuing discussion.[8] First, Hermogenes draws a neat distinction between the *imposition* or setting down of a name and its subsequent *use*. This distinction was already implied at 383a, in the account of Cratylus' thesis ('what some *make a convention to call* something ... is not a name'), and will appear again at 385de and elsewhere in the dialogue. Its purport is that the use of a name is correct not in any case, but only provided it conforms to a preceding imposition, which obviously remains valid until it is replaced by another one fixing a new rule for the name's correct use.

---

[5] At 388de Hermogenes has trouble following Socrates' introduction of the figure of the lawgiver, so he is likely not to have such an idea in mind now. Neither is there evidence that he believes that in remote times some sort of assembly made a collective decision (a view which centuries later occurs e.g. in Amm. *in Cat.* 11.11–14, Philop. *in Cat.* 11.34–12.1). With these alternatives we may compare the ancient texts about the rise of social and political life (discussed by Kahn 1981b), where we find several pictures of how the first rules were established. Sometimes it is some clever man who *persuades* other people to accept the introduction of laws and/or religion (Critias 88 B25, Ar. *Nu.* 1421–2, Isocr. 3.6). Sometimes it is people who decide to entrust some lawgivers with the task of choosing a set of laws (Pl. *Lg.* 681cd). Sometimes we have some kind of actual compact: *R.* 358e–359b (featuring the terms συνθήκη and συνθέσθαι), *Lg.* 684ab and perhaps Antiph. fr. 44(a) 1.27–31 Pendrick.

[6] On γάρ introducing instances see *GP* 66–7.

[7] On slaves' names in Greece see Masson 1973, Garlan 1988: 23, Jones 1996: 29, *OCD* s.v. *names, personal, Greek*. The practice of changing the name of a slave (presumably when acquiring them) seems to have had a long-standing fortune if we are to judge by Stallbaum 39–40: 'quemadmodum apud nostrates, qui ab alio *Friedrich* vocatur, apud alium *Iohann* audit'. Diodorus Cronus († c. 284 BC) is known to have rebaptized his slaves by several particles, e.g. ἀλλὰ μήν 'Nonetheless', evidently offering this as a proof of the conventionalist thesis (Amm. *in Int.* 38.17–20, Simpl. *in Cat.* 27.19–21). Cf. Gell. *NA* 11.12.2: Diodorus denied the existence of semantic ambiguity and held that *nec aliud dici videri debet, quam quod se dicere sentit is qui dicit*. An argument from name change to convention is ascribed to Democritus: see §2.5.2.

[8] What I am going to say about (H2) is in almost complete agreement with the excellent remarks of Ackrill 1994: 36, Barney 1997: 148–56, Keller 2000: 286–90, and Sedley 2003: 52–4.

Secondly, Hermogenes' use of the pronoun 'one' (τις) clearly involves a reference to the case of an *individual* speaker.[9] That is to say, (H2) makes the correctness of names dependent (also) upon the individual speaker's arbitrary decision. On the other hand we have seen that (H2) is adduced as a ground or explanation for (H1), where Hermogenes spoke of 'convention and agreement' – two notions which we, instead, intuitively associate with a *plurality* of speakers. Several modern interpreters have found fault with this and claimed that Hermogenes is unduly conflating two very different theses: a moderate one, represented by (H1) and also by (H3), as we are going to see, and an extreme one, represented by (H2).[10] Still, in spite of these criticisms, the connection posited by Hermogenes between (H1) and (H2) is perfectly sound, as already the ancient commentators implicitly assume.[11] If the correctness of names consists in a convention among speakers, then a particular case – the *limiting* case – of this convention will be that where a single speaker makes, as it were, a convention with himself, by deciding to impose a certain name on a certain thing.[12] To appropriate David Lewis's words, 'We might think of the situation as one in which a convention prevails in the population of different time-slices of the same man.'[13] Conversely, if each single speaker has the power to impose a name on a thing arbitrarily, then certainly the same power will belong to a group of speakers, composed of individuals who all make the same decision to bestow one and the same name on a given thing. We shall come back to this question in §2.1.2.

(H3), connected with (H2) by 'for' (ds γάρ), as (H2) was connected with (H1), again presents the thesis from the collective viewpoint. Hermogenes claims that a name belongs to its bearer not by nature but 'in virtue of the custom and habit of those who made names into habits and those who by them call things'. Between this expression and the one employed in (H1), according to which the correctness of names consists in 'convention and

---

[9] *Pace* Kretzmann 1971: 127, Schofield 1972: 246.
[10] Grote 1888: III.285 n.1 went so far as to claim that the two theses contradict each other; Kahn 1973a: 158 writes that 'Hermogenes' statement of the convention-thesis is of course dreadfully confused, since he makes no distinction between the silly Humpty-Dumpty theory of naming ("The name of *x* is whatever I call it") and the more serious view of language as a social institution.' Along the same lines cf. Robinson 1969: 108–9 and Williams 1982: 90.
[11] See Ammonius, *in Int.* 35.13–16 ff., who seems to assume that there cannot be a different brand of conventionalism from Hermogenes'. Cf. Proclus XXXIII, 11.15–23, on which see §2.1.2.
[12] The connection between the conventional νόμος in force and the individual's initiative is ridiculed by Ar. *Nu.* 1421–4 ff.
[13] Lewis (1983: 181–2) was actually concerned with a slightly different issue, i.e. the possibility that 'A man isolated all his life from others might begin – through genius or a miracle – to use language, say to keep a diary.' But the difference is irrelevant for our present purposes.

agreement', there is an evident connection. A lasting convention becomes a custom, and accepting the custom may be the only way of adhering to the convention;[14] on the other hand, a custom which is not grounded in nature is nothing but mere convention. Therefore (H3) asserts, in different terms, the same as (H1); cf. 434e, where Socrates himself maintains that there is no difference between habit and convention. Thus Hermogenes' thesis constitutes a consistent unity, articulated into three sentences which present different features of it but are substantially equivalent to each other, syntactically connected by the two γάρ's in a circular structure. At 385de Hermogenes will again show that he (rightly) conceives of his thesis as a unitary one.

Another aspect of (H3) that is worth remarking is the reappearance of the Redundancy Conception of correctness, which we already encountered in the report of Cratylus' thesis (see §1.1.2). While (H1) and (H2) were concerned with the *correctness* of names, here Hermogenes only talks about the way that a name belongs to its referent, thus apparently assuming that 'being a correct name of *X*' is tantamount to 'being a name of *X*'.[15]

Finally, (H3) poses a couple of problems of translation. Let us take a closer look at the Greek phrase τῶν ἐθισάντων τε καὶ καλούντων (d7). Scholars are divided on how to translate the former participle. Most seem to choose the intransitive use of the verb ἐθίζω, 'get accustomed'. But while the intransitive use is common with the passive, in the active it does not seem to be attested before the first century BC (see LSJ); hence, on the face of it, we had better look for something else. Now ἐθίζω is frequently used in the ditransitive construction, 'to accustom someone to something'. In our case, then, the idea might be that there is a group of people among whom a given name first begins somehow to be used, and who subsequently spread this use among other people by accustoming *them* to it. Alternatively, it seems that ἐθίζω τι may also mean 'make something into a habit';[16] then in our case the object would be 'the name', which is easily understood from d6. This latter solution, presupposed by Fowler's translation 'those ... who established the usage' (cf. Reeve), seems on balance the more natural one in context.

---

[14] Cf. §8.1.1 on 433e τοῖς συνθεμένοις.
[15] Once we appreciate that Hermogenes adheres to the Redundancy Conception, which he shares with Cratylus and Socrates, it becomes pointless to postulate, as Barney 1997: 157 does, that Hermogenes' starting point is an unspoken premiss which she dubs 'conservatism', i.e. the view 'that all our actual or positive names (everything socially recognised as a name) are correct'.
[16] See *Lg.* 793b νόμιμα, ἃ καλῶς μὲν τεθέντα καὶ ἐθισθέντα κτλ. and X. *Cyr.* 8.7.10 παλαιὰ καὶ εἰθισμένα καὶ ἔννομα λέγοντος ἐμοῦ.

We should also capture the nuance conveyed by the different verbal aspect of the two participles, the aorist ἐθισάντων and the present καλούντων. I take it that *two* groups of people are being distinguished, the first included in the second: (a) those who made names into habits, i.e. those who established the habit by introducing the names and persevering in their use; (b) those who use the names in speaking through the course of time, i.e. the first group plus an indefinite number of other people.[17] On this construal (H3) refers not only to the name's first users, but also to all subsequent users.

A final remark on the whole of Hermogenes' thesis is in order before moving on. We should beware of ascribing to Hermogenes the view that names are merely casual aggregates of sounds without etymology, as Rijlaarsdam (1978: 38–9, cf. 23–4) does: nothing suggests that this is what Hermogenes thinks.[18] Rijlaarsdam relies on three passages (397a, 402b, 434a) where it is said that, according to the conventionalist theory, names belong to their bearers 'haphazardly' (ἀπὸ τοῦ αὐτομάτου) and things can be indicated 'with any chance means' (τῷ ἐπιτυχόντι). But what these expressions point to is just the *arbitrariness* of name-giving. They do not mean that Hermogenes denies names any etymological meaning, only that he denies them any *necessarily appropriate* etymological meaning and holds that you are entitled to bestow on anything whatever name you like. No opposition is highlighted in the dialogue between conventionalism and etymology as such; and this is just as well, given that the issue is not how names happen to be made, but rather what the conditions for something to be a name are (cf. Baxter 1992: 20).

2.1.2 *Public and private names (385ab)*

Here is Socrates' first reaction to Hermogenes' claims:

SO. Maybe you've got a point, Hermogenes; but let us see. What, you say, one calls each thing, that is the name for each thing? [ὃ ἄν, φῄς, καλῇ τις ἕκαστον,[19] τοῦθ' ἑκάστῳ ὄνομα;]

HE. So it seems to me. (385a1–3)

---

[17] The fact that καλούντων shares the article of ἐθισάντων is no obstacle and is due to the connection posited between the two groups. See KG 1.611–12, and e.g. Th. 1.1.1 τὸν πόλεμον τῶν Πελοποννησίων καὶ Ἀθηναίων. In particular on cases like ours, with τε after first term, see GP 516, quoting Prt. 355e τὸ 'ἡδύ' τε καὶ 'ἀνιαρόν' and other instances.

[18] The expression νόμῳ, used by Hermogenes at 384d6, has this meaning in the Derveni Papyrus, col. XXII: ἐκλήθη δὲ | Γῆ μὲν νόμωι, Μήτηρ δ' ὅτι ἐκ ταύτης πάντα γ[ίν]εται ('she was called Ge *by custom*; Mother, instead, because everything is born from her'). See §3.3.3 on *PDerv.*, and §6.4.1 on this very passage.

[19] Here the MSS give different readings, which however, through minor corrections, give rise to *two* basic alternatives. One is ὃ ἄν, φῄς, καλῇ τις ἕκαστον (later hand in Ven. app. cl. 4.54, T), chosen

Convention and individual decision (384c–385b)

Thereby Socrates picks up (H2), with the difference that he seems to refer only to the *use* of the name ('What ... one calls each thing'), without mentioning its imposition.[20] Then he goes on:

s o. Both if it is a private citizen who calls, and if it is a city? [Καὶ ἐὰν ἰδιώτης καλῇ καὶ ἐὰν πόλις;]
h e. Yes.
s o. Well then, if I call any of the beings – say, what we now call 'human', if I refer to this as 'horse' [ἐὰν ἐγὼ καλῶ ὁτιοῦν τῶν ὄντων, οἷον ὃ νῦν καλοῦμεν ἄνθρωπον, ἐὰν ἐγὼ τοῦτο ἵππον προσαγορεύω], and to what we now call 'horse' as 'human', then the same thing will be named 'human' publicly and 'horse' privately? [ἔσται δημοσίᾳ μὲν ὄνομα ἄνθρωπος τῷ αὐτῷ, ἰδίᾳ δὲ ἵππος;] And conversely the other thing will be named 'human' privately and 'horse' publicly? Is this what you are saying?
h e. So it seems to me. (385a4–b1)

The crucial point here is obviously Hermogenes' avowal that one and the same thing can have different names on different levels: in our case, a 'public' name, by which the thing is commonly called in a certain linguistic community, and a 'private' one, arbitrarily introduced by an isolated innovator, who is nevertheless a member of that community.

According to some commentators, here Socrates is somehow attacking or criticizing Hermogenes' thesis by arguing that absurd or at least unpalatable consequences follow from it. At xxxiii, 11.15–23 Proclus claims that Socrates refutes Hermogenes' thesis by three arguments, the first of which goes as follows:

If names are by imposition, both a private citizen and a city alike will have authority over the naming of objects, and objects will be called in many different ways and their names will be variously changed ... But the consequent does not hold. Hence neither does the antecedent.

(Note that Proclus, to my mind correctly, presents Socrates' example as a *genuine* consequence of Hermogenes' thesis *as a whole*.) A more moderate interpretation is advanced by Schofield 1972: 251–2, who claims that 'Socrates here does nothing more than present to Hermogenes some considerations which might be expected to discomfort him.' Both Proclus' radical interpretation and Schofield's moderate one are, I think, mistaken: Socrates' considerations about name-reversal have no potential to

---

by Hirschig, Burnet and the OCT editors. The other is ὃ ἂν θῇ καλεῖν τις ἕκαστον (BDWQT²mg.), adopted by Stallbaum, Fowler, Méridier, Barney 1997: 147 and n.13, which should mean 'That by which one *decides to* call each thing', or also 'That which one *imposes to* call each thing'. The first reading is preferable, because it is *difficilior* and is also better connected (through φῇς) to what precedes. The reading with θῇ is judged corrupt also by Dodds 1959: 260.

[20] Cf. Barney 1997: 151. On καλέω see ch. 1 n.1.

refute Hermogenes and are not meant to do so; nor are they more modestly meant to discomfort him.[21]

Let us, for a moment, forget the text and consider the problem in itself. The situation to be assessed is the following: someone (call her 'Neobule') who is a member of a certain linguistic community, more precisely a Greek city, decides, for some reason, to begin to use the name 'human' to refer to horses and the name 'horse' to refer to humans. Thereby she avails herself of the right, which (H2) gives her, to bestow arbitrarily on anything any name she wants. What is peculiar of this situation, and was not explicitly allowed for in (H2), is that the names bestowed are already in use in Neobule's community and that Neobule inverts their reference relative to the community's usage. This may cause misunderstandings if Neobule, when talking to her fellow citizens, uses those names according to her private usage without informing them of what she is doing.[22] The matter would reach Babelic proportions if such a conduct should become widespread. Still, none of this would stop 'human' and 'horse' being the names respectively of horse and human in Neobule's idiolect; in fact it is difficult to see what other status they could have instead.[23]

Furthermore, Neobule need not behave in such a way as to let any misunderstanding arise. When the conversation falls on horses or humans, she can make it explicit that she is following a different convention by saying something like: 'Pay attention: I am going to use the name "human" to refer to what you call "horse" and vice versa.' Or she can just decide to follow the public convention when she is talking to other people (like someone who, being abroad, uses the local idiom) and use her idiolect only when she is talking to herself or keeping her diary. The conventionalist thesis – of which (H2) constitutes an integral part – says only that every individual speaker is free to bestow any arbitrarily chosen name on anything. It is up to the individual to exercise this freedom in a subversive or a judicious way, or rather (as it mostly happens) to forgo exercising it at all and agree to the community's conventions.

---

[21] Thereby I again find myself in agreement with the scholars quoted in n.8.
[22] Which is precisely what Humpty Dumpty does (*Through the Looking Glass* ch. 6, cf. n.10) – although on Alice's request he explains what he has said.
[23] Consider also the following counterexample (cf. Rijlaarsdam 1978: 48–9). Suppose that the decision to invert the reference of 'human' and 'horse' is made by no less than twenty conspirators living in the same city. This is a convention established by a group of speakers, not an individual one; hence no one will doubt that it produces genuine names. Nevertheless this convention too, like Neobule's private one, contradicts the city's usage and may give rise to the same communication problems as soon as one of the twenty happens to be talking to a fellow citizen. (On the misunderstandings arising from the encounter between different conventions cf. August. *De magistro* 43.)

Convention and individual decision (384c–385b)

If now from these considerations we return to the text of *Cra.*, we find evidence that both Hermogenes and Socrates are seeing things roughly in the same way. That Hermogenes conceives of his thesis as compatible with the requirements of communication is shown first of all by the very fact that he is eager for genuine discussion and makes himself no attempt to change the usual meaning of words (Barney 1997: 154). Moreover, in the case of the master who changes the name of his slaves, cited in (H2), it is obvious that the master, in order to have himself understood and obeyed by the slaves, will explain how he wants to call them. A further confirmation comes from 385de, where Hermogenes reasserts his thesis with recourse to a comparison between the (possible) lexical differences among individuals and those among cities and peoples. Of course Greeks and barbarians do not usually understand each other's language; but Greek cities do normally communicate with each other. So Hermogenes does not have in mind – in the first place at least – a Babelic situation at the level of individuals. Accordingly, once the example has been put forward Hermogenes does not look disheartened or appear to think that he has been refuted: he expresses his agreement without putting up any resistance, and a little below (385d2–e3), questioned again by Socrates about his thesis, he will quietly reassert his opinion.[24]

As for Socrates, he only says that, if someone inverts the reference of the names 'human' and 'horse', then the same object will have one name δημοσίᾳ, publicly, and another name ἰδίᾳ, privately. But he does *not* mention the situation of the inverter's talking to other members of the community. Nor does Socrates, once Hermogenes has accepted the example, draw any kind of conclusion; he moves on to another topic and begins to ask questions about truth and falsity. He will return to individual imposition at d2; but again he will draw no conclusion from Hermogenes' answers and will change the subject matter, starting to inquire about the relations between Hermogenes' thesis and that of Protagoras. Neither here nor elsewhere does he accuse conventionalism of undermining the possibility of communication.

We must also observe that the δημοσίᾳ / ἰδίᾳ distinction proposed by Socrates, if rigorously applied, precisely allows to eschew any unfortunate crossing between Neobule's vocabulary and that of his fellow citizens. δημοσίᾳ and ἰδίᾳ do not mean 'pour tout le monde' and 'pour moi', as Méridier translates them, but rather 'publicly' and 'privately'. Hence the δημοσίᾳ / ἰδίᾳ opposition does not straightforwardly set the name-inverter

---

[24] See Baxter 1992: 38 n.34.

against the other speakers. It rather contrasts two *spheres*: the private one (*Neobule's* private sphere), where names have been inverted, and the public one, where they are still as they were before. Now, Neobule is and remains a citizen of the city whose names she has just privately inverted, so she shares in the public sphere as well as in the private one. If she confuses the two spheres, then the communication with her fellow citizens breaks down; if instead she keeps them distinct, then communication can take place.

This interpretation of Hermogenes' thesis and Socrates' reaction to it is borne out at 433e, where Socrates contrasts the two theses with his own words. Hermogenes, he reminds us, holds 'that names are conventional tokens and indicate objects to those who have made the convention ... and that it makes no difference whether one makes a convention like the one which is presently in force or ... makes the convention to call "large" what is presently called "small" and "small" what is presently called "large"'. Here the subject of 'makes a convention' is admittedly the singular 'one' (e6 τις); but it is fairly clear that what is at issue is, primarily at least, a convention among several contractors. Hence Socrates does not give individual imposition a separate mention. The simplest explanation is that he not only sees the unity of Hermogenes' thesis, but also views individual imposition as a secondary and by itself unproblematic facet of the generic assertion of convention. And even Cratylus, in his subsequent reply (434a1–2), does not appear to deem (H2) particularly pernicious.

A little further, at 435a, another passage shows that for Plato the idea of private convention is intimately connected with that of convention in general (Barney 1997: 155, 2001: 136 n.34; cf. §8.1.3). There Socrates says that Cratylus, since he understands 'because of habit' a certain name which does not indicate its referent by nature, has made a *convention with himself*, so that the name's correctness turns out to be conventional. This suggests that the public custom actually is the sum of a plurality of *individual decisions*.

Finally, we must take into account a parallel at *Charmides* 163d.[25] There Socrates answers Critias, who has just established a far-fetched lexical distinction, by stating a general principle:

I allow you to impose each name as you want [ἐγώ σοι τίθεσθαι μὲν τῶν ὀνομάτων δίδωμι ὅπῃ ἂν βούλῃ ἕκαστον]; only make clear to what you apply the name you say [δήλου δὲ μόνον ἐφ' ὅτι ἂν φέρῃς τοὔνομα ὅτι ἂν λέγῃς].

Here Socrates' concession to Critias is formulated in terms which closely recall (H2). The condition set for Critias to take advantage of this concession

[25] Cited by Guthrie 1962–81: v.17.

is that he make it explicit what the names he uses refer to. This is of course the same condition we set on Neobule for the case in which she, talking to other fellow citizens, wanted to use the names 'human' and 'horse' with the inverted reference and nevertheless make herself understood. Hence Plato is aware of this point, and in *Cra.* he must see that individual imposition is compatible with the requirements of communication.

The legitimacy of the individual perspective has also been stressed by other authors. In the *De interpretatione* Aristotle, after echoing (H1) by saying, at 16a19, that a name is a 'spoken sound significant by convention [κατὰ συνθήκην]', at 18a19–20 makes a thought experiment which begins as follows: 'if someone imposed the name "cloak" on horse and human [εἴ τις θεῖτο ὄνομα 'ἱμάτιον' ἵππῳ καὶ ἀνθρώπῳ] …' Here the terminology of name-imposition, the idea of individual arbitrary imposition, and the choice of human and horse as elements of the example clearly derive from *Cra.*[26]

Many centuries later, Locke, *Essay* III.ii.2–8, claims that 'words, in their primary or immediate signification, stand for nothing but the ideas in the mind of him that uses them', and that 'every man has so inviolable a liberty to make words stand for what ideas he pleases, that no one hath the power to make others have the same ideas in their minds that he has, when they use the same words that he does'. At IV.iv.9 Locke considers the case of private name-reversal with reference to two rather different spheres: mathematics and ethics:

Let a Man make to himself the *Idea* of a Figure with three Angles, whereof one is a right one, and call it, if he please, *Equilaterum* or *Trapezium*, or any thing else, the Properties of, and Demonstration about that *Idea*, will be the same, as if he call'd it a *Rectangular-Triangle*. I confess, the change of the Name, by the impropriety of Speech, will at first disturb him, who knows not what *Idea* it stands for: but as soon as the Figure is drawn, the Consequences and Demonstration are plain and clear. Just the same is it in *moral* Knowledge, let a Man have the *Idea* of taking from others, without their Consent, what their honest Industry has possessed them of, and call this *Justice*, if he please. He that takes the Name here without the *Idea* put to it, will be mistaken, by joining another *Idea* of his own to that Name: But strip the *Idea* of that Name, or take it such as it is in the Speaker's Mind, and the same Things will agree to it, as if you call'd it *Injustice*.

Let us take stock. Hermogenes' thesis constitutes a consistent unity, whose various statements follow from each other. It is objectively compatible with the purpose of communication among speakers, but it also remains valid whatever hindrances to communication may arise.

---

[26] Cf. Sedley 2004a (and Ackrill 1963: 130–2 on the meaning of the *Int.* passage).

Hermogenes himself conceives of his thesis in these terms. At 385a1–b1 Socrates does nothing but try to understand this thesis better: first (a2) by reformulating (H2), which constitutes its most problematical feature, then (a6–b1) by illustrating it through an extreme example which clarifies its purport and significance. So far he does not display any polemical attitude.

Hermogenes has also been accused of destroying the possibility of using names incorrectly or making false statements. See e.g. Lorenz/Mittelstrass (1967: 5): 'If, on the other hand, names are correct by convention, any word to be used as a name will be correct (385de). Thus, both cases [Cratylus' and Hermogenes'], taken in their extreme form, do not admit of any incorrect use of names.' [27] This charge, however, is completely unfounded, for at least two reasons. First, Hermogenes does not say that any word we *use* as a name for something is a correct name for that thing. Rather, he repeatedly claims that the correct name for each thing is that which we *impose* on it, all the others being incorrect. This entails that a sentence is not *absolutely* true or false, but true or false *relative to* a particular convention, whether public or private, which determines the meaning of the terms contained in the sentence. So one and the same sentence may bear different truth values on different conventions: e.g. 'Callias is a *horse*' will turn out false for the ordinary Greek speaker and true for Neobule the name-inverter in her idiolect (cf. Barney 1997: 149–56, Richardson 1976: 136–7, Ackrill 1994: 36–7). Secondly, in the immediately following passage (385bd) we find Hermogenes readily acknowledging the distinction between true and false sentences.

Of the two reasons I have just stated, the former is based on compelling textual evidence and is by itself sufficient to prove that Hermogenes is not doing away with the distinction between true and false sentences. The latter reason, instead, is a very controversial one, because 385bd has been interpreted in various conflicting ways. According to one view, in that passage Socrates precisely argues that Hermogenes' theory is incompatible with the distinction between truth and falsity. Others have even supposed the passage to be a foreign element in the present discussion between Socrates and Hermogenes and have transposed or excised it. So it seems that, before using the passage as evidence to confirm our interpretation of Hermogenes' theory, we ought to embark on a thorough discussion of its purport and authenticity. Which is just what we are about to do.

[27] Cf. Fine 1977: 295, Gold 1978: 242–3, Baxter 1992: 18.

2.2 TRUTH AND FALSEHOOD IN SENTENCES AND NAMES (385BD)

A preliminary caveat on the textual question. The view that the passage we are going to discuss cannot stand where all MSS have it, and must be transposed or excised, is becoming a near orthodox one in contemporary scholarship. Nevertheless, texts should not be judged guilty until they are proved to be such. Therefore a sound method requires that we first try to see what sense can be made of the passage on the assumption that it is genuine and is reported by the MSS in its right place. Then, and only then, shall we be in a position to settle the textual issues.

2.2.1 True and false sentences (385b)

According to the MSS text, at 385b2, just after Hermogenes has given his assent to the hypothesis of name-reversal, Socrates abruptly starts questioning him about the possibility and definition of a true and a false sentence:

SO. Come now, tell me: is there anything you call speaking truths and falsehoods?
HE. Yes.
SO. So, among sentences, some are true and others are false? [εἴη ἂν λόγος ἀληθής, ὁ δὲ ψευδής;][28]
HE. Of course.
SO. Now the one which speaks of the things that are as they are is true, while the one which speaks of them as they are not is false? [οὗτος ὃς ἂν τὰ ὄντα λέγῃ ὡς ἔστιν, ἀληθής· ὃς δ' ἂν ὡς οὐκ ἔστιν, ψευδής;]
HE. Yes.
SO. Therefore this is possible, to say with a sentence the things that are and those that are not? [Ἔστιν ἄρα τοῦτο, λόγῳ λέγειν τὰ ὄντα τε καὶ μή;]
HE. Of course. (385b2–11)

These lines raise several questions. Before broaching any of them, however, a word must be said about Socrates' opening phrase, 'Come now' (Φέρε δή b2). This is a fairly common formula for introducing with emphasis a question or command, sometimes marking a turning point in the conversation or situation (e.g. 424b, 430a, b, 436a; *Grg.* 455a; Ar. *Pax* 361, 959). In the

---

[28] Cf. 408c 'the λόγος ... is twofold, true and false', *Sph.* 264a. In place of ἀληθής W reads ὁ μὲν ἀληθής, but ὁ μέν is simply understood: see *GP* 166 and cf. *Prt.* 355d, *R.* 455e–456a, *Phlb.* 36e etc. Alternatively, ἀληθής might be an attribute of λόγος: 'So there is a true sentence and a false one?' (cf. *Ti.* 63a).

first pages of *Cra.*, in particular, it reoccurs at 385e4 as Socrates inquires about Hermogenes' attitude to Protagorean relativism (an inquiry which subsequently grows into an argument for naturalism), then at 387d10 as Socrates starts off another argument for naturalism; and at 389a5 the kindred Ἴθι δή will open the section where the forms are introduced. These formal correspondences might carry some weight when it comes to deciding whether 385bd is to be read where the MSS have it.

I come to the content of our lines. To start with, the λόγος here at issue, which Socrates says is either true or false, is the *declarative sentence* or statement. We may compare 431bc, where Socrates, explaining how it is possible to have a false λόγος, claims that λόγοι are a combination of ὀνόματα and ῥήματα, names and verbs (see §7.2.4). There the obvious interpretation is that he is speaking of true and false declarative sentences and is taking them to be composed of at least one name and one verb (as at *Sph.* 261d–262d). It is reasonable to assume that the same conception is already at work in our passage.

We should now try to understand how Socrates characterizes the sentence's truth and falsity. He actually offers a *double* characterization.

At 385b7–8 he claims that the sentence saying τὰ ὄντα ... ὡς ἔστιν is true, while the sentence saying (τὰ ὄντα) ὡς οὐκ ἔστιν is false. As we are going to see, these formulas can be understood in several ways; at any rate we can safely expect them to constitute a *general* definition of what it is for a sentence – whether affirmative or negative – to be true or false.

Then at b10 Socrates infers that one can say with a sentence τὰ ὄντα τε καὶ μή. Here the participle τὰ ὄντα is a typical occurrence of the verb εἰμί, 'be', with the meaning 'be the case' (so-called *veridical* use): the sentence which says 'the things that are the case' states the facts, describes a situation or state of affairs that does actually obtain, whereas the sentence which says 'the things that are not the case' describes a situation or state of affairs that does not obtain.[29] Hence b7–8 and b10 are clearly meant to pair off in the following way: the sentence which says τὰ ὄντα ὡς ἔστιν is true and says τὰ ὄντα, while the sentence which says τὰ ὄντα ὡς οὐκ ἔστιν is false and says τὰ μὴ ὄντα.

Let us get back to b7–8. On the face of it, here two translations are possible, because ὡς may mean either 'that' or 'as'. Reeve adopts the former view: (A) the sentence which 'says, of the things that are, *that*

---

[29] On 'to be' in Greek see Kahn 1966, 1973b, 1986b; Brown 1994. On the veridical participle see LSJ εἰμί A.III and cf. 429d, *Euthd.* 284a, *R.* 413a, *Tht.* 178b; Hdt. 1.97; Th. 7.8.2; etc.

they are is true, while the sentence which 'says *that* they are not' is false. Most scholars favour instead the latter view: (B) the sentence which 'speaks of'[30] the things that are *as* they are' is true, while the sentence which 'speaks of them *as* they are not' is false. However, these literal translations leave undecided another question, which makes the matter much more complicated, i.e. the use of 'to be' in the two forms τὰ ὄντα and ἔστιν.

The clearly veridical τὰ ὄντα at b10 may suggest that also b7 τὰ ὄντα is an instance of the same use. Hence (A) would actually amount to (A1): the sentence which 'says, of the things that are the case, that they are the case' is true, while the sentence which 'says that they are not the case' (i.e. says, of the things that are the case, that they are not the case) is false.[31] And (B) would actually amount to (B1): the sentence which 'speaks of the things that are the case as they are' is true, while the sentence which 'speaks of them as they are not' is false.

(A1) seems to be supported by several important parallels. Prot. 80 B1 DK: Human beings are the measure of all things, τῶν μὲν ὄντων ὡς ἔστιν, τῶν δὲ οὐκ ὄντων ὡς οὐκ ἔστιν ('of those that are, that they are, and of those that are not, that they are not').[32] Pl. *Sph.* 240d–241a: the false sentence says τά τε ὄντα ... μὴ εἶναι καὶ τὰ μὴ ὄντα εἶναι ('of the things that are, that they are not, and of the things that are not, that they are': ὡς ἔστι is replaced by the unambiguous infinitive εἶναι). Arist. *Metaph.* 1011b26–8: to say τὸ ὂν μὴ εἶναι ἢ τὸ μὴ ὂν εἶναι ('of what is that it is not, or of what is not that it is') is false; to say τὸ ὂν εἶναι καὶ τὸ μὴ ὂν μὴ εἶναι ('of what is that it is, and of what is not that it is not') is true.[33] X. *An.* 4.4.15–16: speaking the truth characterized as saying τὰ ὄντα τε ὡς ὄντα καὶ τὰ μὴ ὄντα ὡς οὐκ ὄντα ('the things that are as things that are and the things that are not as things that are not').[34] From these passages we must keep distinct *Sph.* 263b, which defines the true sentence as the one which says τὰ ὄντα ὡς ἔστιν ('of the things that are, that they are') about something and the false sentence as the one which says τὰ μὴ ὄντ' ... ὡς

---

[30] λέγω + acc. can mean 'speak/say *of* something': see *Euthd.* 300b, *Phd.* 94d, *Smp.* 221e, *Prm.* 137c (quoted by Burnyeat 2002: 53 n.21 on *Euthd.* 284a) and also *Cra.* 434e, Arist. *Rh.* 1406b21 (on which see Kassel 1991: 609).
[31] See Kahn 1973b: 340 n.12.
[32] See Kahn 1973b: 367, 1986b: 13. For a different interpretation see McDowell 1973: 118, Barnes 1982: 544.
[33] See Kahn 1981a: 106.
[34] Here ὡς means 'as', but is followed by a participle in predicative position; and this is, for our concerns, equivalent to ὡς 'that' + indicative.

ὄντα ('the things that are not as things that are'). That is a parallel for (A), i.e. for ὡς = 'that',[35] but not for (A1): for there the 'things that are' and the 'things that are not' are not states of affairs that are or are not the case, but properties that do or do not belong to the subject.[36]

A close inspection of these very parallels, however, reveals a problem for (A1). In all the passages the formula for truth and that for falsity are both *twofold* and account distinctly for the case of the affirmative and the negative sentence. In our argument, instead, there are two simple formulas, of which we should like to give a comprehensive reading, as I said above. A similar situation occurs at *Sph.* 263b, where the two simple formulas are usually taken as comprehensive. However, between *Sph.* 263b and our passage there is a small but significant difference concerning the *false* sentence. According to the Stranger, the false sentence says 'the things that are not as things that are': the formula is very naturally modelled on the case of an *affirmative* sentence (cf. the example 'Theaetetus flies', 263a),[37] although it is presumably meant to cover also the negative case. But in our lines the 'that'-clause which should specify the content of the false sentence is a *negative* one: the false sentence says, of the things that are, 'that they are *not*'. Therefore Socrates would cover the false affirmation and negation with a formula where negation is not very naturally privileged to the disadvantage of affirmation.

This problem inclines me to reject (A1), as well as any other variant of (A), in favour of (B): at 385b7–8 ὡς does not mean 'that', but rather 'as'. (B1), however, is somewhat unpalatable too. For the claim that in speaking falsely one speaks of the things that are, albeit not as they are, is somewhat odd, and requires some speculation if it is to make philosophical sense. For example, assuming that Callias is white, we ought to suppose that the false sentence 'Callias is black' somehow speaks of the fact that Callias is white, though not 'as it is', i.e. not describing it correctly. There may be a parallel at *Euthd.* 284c, where Euthydemus has just said that Dionysodorus, if he speaks at all, 'says the truth and the things that are', and Ctesippus replies: 'he does say the things that are, in a way – not, however, *as* they are' (τὰ ὄντα μὲν τρόπον τινὰ λέγει, οὐ μέντοι ὥς γε ἔχει).[38]

---

[35] See n.34.
[36] See Frede 1992b: 412–23, Crivelli 2008: 235–8, and Crivelli (forthcoming).
[37] At *Phlb.* 38cd too the examples of true and false judgement are both affirmative.
[38] At *R.* 477b, 478a it is said that science knows ὡς ἔστι τὸ ὄν, or τὸ ὄν … ὡς ἔχει ('what is *as* it is'). A veridical construal is offered by Kahn 1981a: 112–14, but it is unclear whether it can be right: see Brown 1994: 220–8 and the text below.

There, however, the oddness could be explained by Ctesippus' need to find a polemical rejoinder.

This brings us to an alternative possibility, (B2): the b7 τὰ ὄντα has nothing to do with the b10 τὰ ὄντα and is *not* veridical, but *existential* instead,[39] while the b7–8 ἔστιν's are *copulative*: the true sentence 'speaks of the things that are as they are', i.e. ascribes to an existent extralinguistic subject features it does have, while the false sentence 'speaks of them as they are not', i.e. ascribes to an existent subject features it does not have.[40] It is very natural to understand that the features in question may be either positive or negative; therefore our formulas, so interpreted, are fit for covering both affirmative and negative sentences.

(B2) is borne out by some textual evidence. There may be parallels at *R.* 477b, 478a and *Euthd.* 284c: these passages, which I have just quoted (above, and n.38) in connection with (B1), can also be interpreted in keeping with (B2). More significant is the evidence internal to *Cra.* The participle τὰ ὄντα has already occurred before our lines, at 383a5 and most recently at 385a6; both passages were concerned with the correctness of the name for 'each of the beings', i.e. each of the things that *exist*. Hence at 385b7–8 Socrates can well use another existential τὰ ὄντα. Thereby he emphasizes the continuity between the previous discussion about names and the present one about truth and falsity. He has just asked Hermogenes whether we can arbitrarily invert the names of the 'beings' (385a6); he now asks whether the true and the false sentence can be defined in terms of how they speak of those very 'beings'.

So I think that (B2) is on balance the likeliest interpretation of our text. It is also an interpretation on which Socrates' definitions accord nicely with *Sph.* 262e, where it is said that every sentence, whether true or false, is 'of something' – which seems to imply that it is about some *existent* subject matter. We ought, however, to keep in mind that what Plato is after here is not a precise definition of truth and falsity in sentences. Rather, for the moment he just wants to make Socrates and Hermogenes agree that *there is* such a thing as truth and falsity in sentences; then he will make them proceed to truth and falsity in *names*.

---

[39] On this interpretation, the repetition of τὰ ὄντα is an instance of the so-called *falsa anaphora*. Cf. §7.3.1 on 431cd, §7.3.4 and n.112 on 432e, and the examples cited by Lapini 1997: 94–5.
[40] Cf. Ficino (f. 107ᵛ), Pfeiffer 1972: 90–1, Kahn 1981a: 131 n.19. (B2) clearly implies a close relationship between the existential and the copulative 'to be', i.e. between a thing's existence and its having certain features. This is just as it should be: see §6.2.4.

2.2.2 *The parts of a sentence. True and false names (385cd)*

Socrates begins his transition from sentences to names by introducing the notion of a true sentence's having *parts*, 'large' and 'small', which are all as true as the sentence itself:

SO. But is the true sentence true as a whole, while its parts are not true? [Ὁ λόγος δ' ἐστὶν ὁ ἀληθὴς πότερον μὲν ὅλος ἀληθής, τὰ μόρια δ' αὐτοῦ οὐκ ἀληθῆ;]
HE. No, the parts too are true.
SO. And are the large parts true, but not the small ones? Or are they all true? [Πότερον δὲ τὰ μὲν μεγάλα μόρια ἀληθῆ, τὰ δὲ σμικρὰ οὔ· ἢ πάντα;]
HE. They're all true, I think. (385c1–6)

What 'parts' is Socrates speaking of? He does not say. However, if he has anything definite in mind (which we may well doubt), he must be thinking either of the *phrases* which may be contained in a sentence or of the component *sentences* which make up a complex sentence.[41] As for the small parts, they must surely include – perhaps, as we are going to see, even coincide with – single *words* like names and verbs.[42]

Whatever the identity of the large and the small parts, the claim that all the parts of a true sentence are true is mistaken. Even if, for the moment, we leave aside the fact that certain parts of a sentence have no truth value at all, and we consider only those parts that do have a truth value, i.e. the sentences of which a complex sentence is composed, the truth of the compound does not entail the truth of its components. Take e.g. a disjunctive sentence ('*P* or *Q*'): for it to be true it is sufficient that only one of the disjuncts be true. In fact, Socrates' and Hermogenes' claim only seems to fit the case of a *conjunctive* sentence ('*P* and *Q*'), whose truth does require the truth of all the conjuncts. In this connection we should be aware that sentential connectives will not become an object of study before post-Aristotelian logic.[43]

Note that it is unclear how exactly the conclusion that all the parts are true is reached. Is Socrates suggesting that the truth of the parts is just a *logical consequence* of the truth of the whole? Then he would commit a fallacy of division (Robinson 1956: 123), because the parts of a whole need not have the same properties as the whole itself. Or is Socrates suggesting that the parts of a true sentence are true for some *specific* reason,

---

[41] Both alternatives can be compared with 432e, where Socrates talks about a λόγος ἐν λόγῳ, i.e. a phrase or sentence contained in a sentence (see §7.3.4).
[42] On the fortune of the topic of the 'parts of λόγος' see Frede 1978: 317–32.
[43] See Kneale/Kneale 1962: 105–6, 146–9, 160–4.

Truth and falsehood in sentences and names (385bd)

which he leaves unspoken, concerning the sentence's structure and its relation to the parts? Then the inference from the whole's truth to the parts' truth would not be direct and fallacious, but indirect and possibly valid, depending on the content of the unspoken premiss(es).[44] The question is less clear cut than it might seem. For Plato may be deliberately using the fallacy of division to force a conclusion which Socrates could also reach otherwise; and in any case, even if the truth of the parts were inferred solely in virtue of a fallacy of division, Socrates would presumably conceive (if only a posteriori) some account of what it is for them to be true.

Be that as it may, Socrates now focuses on that very part of a sentence which is the subject matter of the dialogue:

SO. So is there anything that you say as a smaller part of a sentence than a name?
["Ἔστιν οὖν ὅτι λέγεις λόγου σμικρότερον μόριον ἄλλο ἢ ὄνομα;][45]
HE. No, this is smallest [Οὔκ, ἀλλὰ τοῦτο σμικρότατον]. (385c7–9)

As I said in §2.2.1 above, our dialogue already seems to contain the theory that a sentence minimally consists of a name (ὄνομα) and a verb (ῥῆμα). Here, however, only the name is mentioned as smallest part. This can be explained in two ways. On the one hand, Hermogenes says the name is 'smallest', not '*the* smallest'; and the lack of the article leaves open the possibility that besides the name there are other smallest parts, like the verb. On the other hand, whether or not the lack of the article is significant, ὄνομα here may be used *generically* and include verbs. The latter interpretation, which I find very plausible, is proposed by Ammonius, *in Int.* 60.21– 3.[46] Cf. *Sph.* 261d–262a, where names and verbs are two kinds of ὀνόματα; Arist. *Int.* 16b19–22 'verbs said themselves by themselves are ὀνόματα and signify something', *Po.* 1457b1–10, etc.

In any case Hermogenes' answer that the name is 'small*est*' does not entail that some small parts are less small than the name (e.g. phrases). His use of the superlative, rather than suggesting different degrees of smallness, might just mean that there is *no* smaller part than the name. Then all the small parts would have the same size, i.e. they would all be single words like the name.

---

[44] See §2.2.3 for a discussion of what the unspoken premiss(es) might be as far as the minimal parts of sentences, i.e. names, are concerned.
[45] An alternative translation of c7–8 is: 'Is there anything that you *call* a smaller part of a sentence than a name?' (Fowler, Sedley 2003: 11). But λόγου σμικρότερον μόριον is best taken to be in predicative position, so that λέγειν has the same sense as in c10 and c16. ἄλλο is pleonastic: cf. 433de and see LSJ 11.8.
[46] Cf. Kretzmann 1971: 126 n.1, Schofield 1972: 249 n.2.

Socrates goes on to claim with great emphasis that names too can be true or false:

SO. Then the *name* too, that of the *true* sentence, is said? [Καὶ τὸ ὄνομα ἄρα τὸ τοῦ ἀληθοῦς λόγου λέγεται;]
HE. Yes.
SO. It is said as true [Ἀληθές γε], as you claim.
HE. Yes.
SO. And is the part of the false sentence not false? [Τὸ δὲ τοῦ ψεύδους μόριον οὐ ψεῦδος;]
HE. So I claim.
SO. Therefore it is possible to say a true and a false name, if it is possible to say a true and a false sentence? [Ἔστιν ἄρα ὄνομα ψεῦδος καὶ ἀληθὲς λέγειν, εἴπερ καὶ λόγον;]
HE. Certainly. (385c10–d1)

The single steps of the argument are worth following in detail. To begin with, c10 is puzzling. As my italics are meant to convey, it seems to contain a double stress, first on τὸ ὄνομα, then on ἀληθοῦς: Socrates is inferring something about the *name* and, more precisely, about the name in a *true* sentence. So already Stallbaum 43: 'Ergone etiam *nomen*, quod ad veram orationem pertinet, enuntiatur?'[47] This inference may seem trifling. Perhaps, however, 'is said' (λέγεται) is pregnant and does not just mean 'is uttered'. Perhaps the meaning is rather that the name is somehow uttered with an *assertoric* force: cf. the use of λέγω at *Sph.* 262d, where the Stranger claims that a sentence does not merely name but 'says' something. Now it is far from clear – and it is an issue we shall face in a while – what it is for a name to be uttered with an assertoric force. One thing, however, is already clear: Socrates' question, so interpreted, implies the question whether a name too in a true sentence has a *truth value*. This also suggests a more pregnant reading of 385b10 λόγῳ λέγειν τὰ ὄντα τε καὶ μή: the point now appears to be that one can say or assert 'the things that are and those that are not' *not only* 'with a sentence', *but also* with a name. Again this is Stallbaum's interpretation (recall also his 'enuntiatur').[48]

As Hermogenes' answer to the question is obviously affirmative, Socrates goes on to specify that 'the name[49] contained in a true sentence

---

[47] Cf. Reeve: 'In a true statement, is this smallest part something that's said?'
[48] Cf. Méridier 'on l'énoncé'. Luce 1969a: 224 too speaks of 'stating a name' as parallel to 'stating a sentence'.
[49] τὸ ὄνομα (c10) is the reading of **βδ**, printed by most editors, whereas T has τοῦτο ὄνομα and Par. 1808 has just τοῦτο ('this'), printed by Burnet and defended by de Vries 1955: 293, Luce 1969a: 223–4. But the two readings actually come to the same thing, because τοῦτο would pick up the immediately preceding τοῦτο at c9, which stands in for 'the name', i.e. 'any name'.

has the truth value true: it is said or stated as true (c12). This means that *all* the names of a true sentence are true, especially since at c4–6 it has already been said that all the parts of a true sentence are true.⁵⁰ On the other hand, 'the part' of a false sentence is false (c14). Here too it seems natural to take the definite article with a generalizing force and understand that *all* the parts of a false sentence, hence all its names, are false. We shall see in §2.2.3 that this natural construal has problematic philosophical consequences, which lead some scholars to translate c14 τὸ ... μόριον as '*a* part'.

Finally, Socrates concludes that it is possible to say a true and a false name, if it is possible to say a true and a false sentence (c16–17). Or perhaps his conclusion is rather that it is possible to say a name, and a sentence, *as* true and *as* false: ψεῦδος καὶ ἀληθές may be in predicative position, cf. c12 ἀληθές γε. At any rate, Socrates probably means that *one and the same* name, or sentence, can be true or false depending on certain variable circumstances.⁵¹

Now what are the circumstances in virtue of which a sentence or a name is true or false? In the case of a sentence they should consist in some sort of correspondence, or lack of correspondence, between what the sentence states and the 'things that are' (b7–10). In the case of a name we might suppose that they consist in the mere fact that the name occurs in a true or a false sentence. Such an answer, however, would be poorly explanatory. Furthermore, Socrates' conclusion at c16–17 does not mention the name's being part of a sentence and thus seems to concern names *as such*, regardless of their being inside or outside a sentence (Luce 1969a: 224). In fact Proclus, XXXVI, 11.30–12.3, avers that, according to the conception of truth employed here, which is different from Aristotle's conception of the truth of declarative sentences, (not only sentences, but) 'also names *said by themselves* [καθ' αὑτὰ λεγόμενα] are true'. As Rijlaarsdam 1978: 68 points out, Socrates proceeds analogously at 387cd, where he first introduces naming as a *part* (μόριον) of saying, then makes a point about naming *itself*. Both there and in our present passage, Socrates' move is presumably one from specific to generic: he views the use of names in sentences as a special case of something more general, i.e. the use of names as such.

---

⁵⁰ Strictly speaking, at c4–6 'all the parts' meant primarily 'all *kinds* of part', the large as well as the small ones. But Socrates would not express himself so if he thought that some individual part of a true sentence may not be true.

⁵¹ This suggests that he is speaking of name- and sentence-*types*, not tokens. For the view that sentences can change their truth value cf. Arist. *Cat.* 4a10–b19, *Metaph.* Θ10.1051b1–17 (Crivelli 2004: 72–6, however, argues that for Aristotle the sentences in question are utterances and hence tokens).

So what does a name's truth or falsity consist in? To answer this difficult question we can start from the very generic view, shared by most commentators, that the truth or falsity of names is somehow a matter of their *correctness or incorrectness*. A name is true if and only if it is correct; it is false if and only if it is incorrect. Now correctness and incorrectness are relational matters: a name is correct in relation to something and incorrect in relation to something else. Likewise, if our hypothesis is right, a name is true or false *of* something.[52]

This view is supported by good evidence. Take 429e, where Socrates, discussing Cratylus' paradoxical claim that false speaking is impossible, makes the example of someone meeting him abroad and addressing him as follows: 'Hello, Athenian stranger, son of Smicrion, Hermogenes.' This is actually an example of misnaming, which Socrates in that context presents as a basic and elementary example of false speaking. In the following passage, 430a–431c, Socrates refutes Cratylus' thesis about false speaking, getting him to admit that the distribution or assignment of a name to a given thing is correct (ὀρθή) or true (ἀληθής) if we assign the appropriate and similar name, but is incorrect (οὐκ ὀρθή) or false (ψευδής) if we assign the inappropriate and dissimilar name. Now there is an evident connection between talk of a true or false *distribution* of names and talk of true and false *names*. For, as the correct distribution gives rise to a correct name,[53] so it is reasonable to suppose that the true distribution – which coincides with the correct one – analogously gives rise to a *true* name. Indeed, that argument is especially interesting for our present purposes. For there Socrates argues that, since it is possible to distribute names and verbs incorrectly or falsely, the same holds of λόγοι, sentences, which are composed of names and verbs (431bc, see §7.2.4). This has an obvious bearing on our 385bd passage, where he connects the sentence's truth or falsity to the name's truth or falsity and the latter is (we are supposing) to be construed as the name's being correct or incorrect.

I wind up with a passage external to our dialogue, *Plt.* 281ab:

And the craft which produces warp and weft too, if one calls it the art of weaving [ὑφαντικήν], one says an absurd and *false* [ψεῦδος] name.

---

[52] 'True/false *of*': in Aristotle cf. the expression ἀληθεύεσθαι κατά τινος (whose subject is 'the name' at *Top.* 134a25, b11) and *Metaph.* 1024b27–8: πᾶς λόγος ψευδὴς ἑτέρου ἢ οὗ ἐστὶν ἀληθής, οἷον ὁ τοῦ κύκλου ψευδὴς τριγώνου ('every account is false of something other than what it is true of, e.g. that of the circle is false of a triangle').

[53] This is certainly so, even though Socrates does not use the same adjective in both cases but speaks of 'correct' distribution and 'appropriate' (προσῆκον) name.

There the point is clearly that ὑφαντική is not the name for, and is false of, a certain craft – although it obviously is the name for, and is true of, another craft.

So far so good. Now the question arises what relation there is between the truth or falsity of a sentence and the truth/correctness or falsity/incorrectness of a name. I confront this question in the next section.

2.2.3 Truth values and sentence structure

The problem can be put as follows. Socrates says that both sentences and names are true or false, without suggesting any difference in the way in which they are so or in the sense of the terms 'true' and 'false'. However, sentences and names are *not* homogeneous items. For a sentence (e.g. 'Callias walks') has a structural complexity which is lacking in a name ('Callias'), or a noun phrase ('walking Callias'), or a string of names ('Callias, walking'). We can spell out the sentence's peculiar complexity most conveniently by saying that its function is not the simple one of naming or referring to something; rather, a sentence consists of two parts, one (the subject) which names or refers to what the sentence is about, and another one (the predicate) which says something about it.

This fundamental distinction between subject and predicate is first explicitly set forth by Plato at *Sph.* 261d–263d,[54] though he probably hints at it elsewhere too.[55] In the *Sophist* this distinction coincides with the distinction between names (ὀνόματα) and verbs (ῥήματα). The Eleatic Stranger argues that a mere string of names, or of verbs, does not constitute a sentence: it is only by mixing names and verbs – at least one name and one verb – that you form a sentence, which 'does not merely name but brings something to completion' and 'says' something. Now a sentence has two further features: it is 'of something', i.e. it has a subject, and is 'qualified somehow', i.e. is *true or false*. This suggests that truth and falsity only belong to a sentence, and not to the names and verbs it is composed of. At any rate, this view is a favourite of Aristotle, who says that names and verbs by themselves are 'not yet' true or false and that only the declarative sentence we construct by combining them with each other is so (*Int.* 16a9–18, *Cat.* 2a4–10, etc.). Indeed, seeing that the *De interpretatione* contains other hints at *Cra.* (cf. §§2.1.1–2, 3.2.2) one might even surmise that Aristotle's insistence on this point is partly aimed at our very passage.

---

[54] We shall come back to the *Sph.* passage in §6.3.5.
[55] See ch. 7 n.43.

So the question is: when Socrates claims that both sentences and names can be true or false, is he really going against the *Sophist* and Aristotle? One possible answer is 'No'; for we seem to be already provided with the means to explain away the appearance of any such conflict. We have already established that for Socrates a name is true or false *of something*; but a complete sentence is true or false in a different way, i.e. true or false *simpliciter*. So we can suppose that two distinct (if related) senses of 'true' and 'false' are at stake in our lines, and that Socrates is only guilty of failing to distinguish between them.

Armed with this supposition, we can try out the following account of the relation between the truth or falsity of a sentence and that of the names it is composed of (cf. Kahn 1973a: 160–1, Fine 1977: 295–6, Ackrill 1994: 37). Take a sentence, e.g. 'Callias walks.' This is *true* if and only if 'Callias' is true of something and 'walks' is also true of that thing; it is *false* if and only if 'Callias' is true of something but 'walks' is false of that thing. This account sits very well with the definition of the true sentence as that which 'speaks of the beings as they are' and of the false sentence as that which 'speaks of the beings as they are not'; indeed, it can be seen as making explicit something that was already implicit in that definition. There is, however, a problem. On this account, all the names (i.e. the terms)[56] of a true sentence are true, but not all the names of a false sentence are false, because at least one name, i.e. the subject term, must be true of something. Yet Socrates says that '*the* part' of a false sentence is false (c14); and as we saw in §2.2.2, this is naturally taken to mean that *all* the parts of a false sentence, hence all its names, are false, just as all the parts and all the names of a true sentence are true (c1–11). So we must either abandon this natural construal of c14, and take 'the part' to mean actually '*a* part' (as Fowler and Reeve translate),[57] or look for a different account of the relation between a sentence's and a name's truth and falsity.

A different account could start from the consideration that the sentence 'Callias walks' can be regarded indifferently as the completion of either of two incomplete sentence-frames: 'Callias ...' or ' — walks'. Assuming that 'Callias' is true of something, and that 'walks' is also true of something, it makes no difference whether we say that the sentence is *true* (a) if and only if 'walks' is true of Callias or (b) if and only if 'Callias' is true of something that walks; nor does it make any difference whether we say that the

---

[56] ὄνομα understood generically: see §2.2.2.
[57] For other cases where the import of a definite article is actually indefinite cf. 430c2–7 (§7.2.4) and 432e3.

sentence is *false* (a) if and only if 'walks' is false of Callias or (b) if and only if 'Callias' is false of everything that walks. We could even, redundantly, state the two pairs of equivalent conditions together: 'Callias walks' is *true* if and only if 'walks' is true of Callias and 'Callias' is true of something that walks; 'Callias walks' is *false* if and only if 'walks' is false of Callias and 'Callias' is false of everything that walks. This is what Socrates might have in mind, if his c14 claim that 'the part' of a false sentence is false really means that *all* the parts are.

So far I have been investigating how one, asked whether Socrates is really going against the *Sophist* and Aristotle as he claims that both sentences and names can be true or false, could answer 'No'. This negative answer amounts to what I call the 'Charitable View' of the relationship between Socrates' talk of true and false sentences and his talk of true and false names. What Socrates says elsewhere in the dialogue, however, seems to suggest that the question should rather be answered in the *affirmative* and that we should take what I call the 'Uncharitable View' of the matter, as in fact some scholars do (see Derbolav 1972: 112–15, Denyer 1991: 74, and Sedley 2003: 12–13). Let me illustrate this alternative and, alas, more plausible view.

To do so we must start from the notorious fact that the distinction between the subject and the predicate of a sentence, statement or judgement was by no means obvious in Plato's times. On the contrary, a certain mistaken conception seems to have been rather widespread (and perhaps shared by Plato himself at some stage of his career), according to which sentences were assimilated to names and conceived of as a sort of noun phrases or descriptions. As we shall see in §7.2.2, this misconception lies at the root of some well-known arguments against the possibility of contradiction and false speaking, which are ascribed to philosophers like Prodicus and Antisthenes and which we encounter in several Platonic dialogues, perhaps including *Cra.* itself, if this is a correct construal of 429d. The same misconception seems to inform even Socrates' defence of false speaking at 431bc and his claims at 432d–433b (§§7.2.4, 7.3.4).

So we are entitled to suspect that in our passage Socrates' undifferentiated talk of true or false sentences and true or false names is a symptom that he is mistakenly assimilating the former to the latter and is conceiving of a sentence like 'Callias walks' as essentially equivalent to the phrase 'walking Callias'.[58] Indeed, since at c14 Socrates says that '*the* part' of a

---

[58] The fact that here ὄνομα might have a generic force and include verbs (§2.2.2) is immaterial in this respect. For the distinction between name and verb is *not* the same as the distinction between subject and predicate, although the two coincide in the *Sophist*'s examples. One might recognize

false sentence is false, thereby apparently meaning that *all* the parts are, we are entitled to suspect that he is entertaining a particularly crude version of this misconception: a *holistic* version according to which the sentence is true if and only if all its names are true of its subject matter and the sentence is false if and only if all its names are false of its subject matter – where no room is left for sentences where some names are true and others are false of the subject matter.[59] On the Uncharitable View, as the dialogue goes on Socrates will purge himself of this crude version and put forward other, more refined ones, without ever attaining a completely satisfactory conception of sentence structure.

2.2.4 *The passage's function in context*

Hitherto we have been wrangling our way through 385bd from a mainly internal perspective, without addressing the crucial question of its relation to the immediate context. It is now high time to ask: what could the passage be doing in the position where the MSS report it?

According to most commentators, here Socrates is somehow advancing an argument against Hermogenes. There is, however, no agreement as to what the argument's conclusion should be. Some view it as a *negative* one, contradicting Hermogenes' conventionalist thesis; others as a *positive* one, directly supporting the naturalist thesis. In what follows I examine both alternatives and conclude that neither is acceptable.

Let us begin with the negative version of the story. According to its proponents, the argument aims to refute Hermogenes' 'individualistic' conventionalism, i.e. (H2), as being incompatible with the basic distinction between truth and falsity. E.g. Kretzmann 1971: 127 claims that the argument constitutes the beginning of a '*reductio ad absurdum* aimed at showing that Hermogenes' subjectivism makes it impossible to distinguish between true and false statements'.[60] There are two major stumbling blocks to the acceptance of this interpretation (cf. Richardson 1976: 136–7, Ackrill 1994: 37, Barney 1997: 149–56).

First, Socrates draws no explicit conclusion against Hermogenes; so we should make the rather unpalatable supposition that the argument is a 'truncated' one, whose conclusion is left to be understood. Indeed, it

---

the former distinction while missing the latter and thus understand 'Callias walks' as the structureless string 'Callias, walks' (cf. §6.3.4).

[59] As we saw above, we could also take c14 'the part' to mean 'a part'. But only in the context of the Charitable View is it worthwhile accepting this rather unnatural construal.

[60] Cf. Gold 1978: 242–3, Denyer 1991: 71–5, and see already Horn 1904: 22–3.

seems that the supposed anti-conventionalist conclusion is not just absent from the text, but *incompatible* with it; for the conversation between Socrates and Hermogenes is going to follow a quite different course from the one required by this interpretation. At 385de, immediately after the end of our passage, Socrates asks two further questions about conventionalism, answering which Hermogenes restates his position at some length. That would be the moment for Socrates to denounce a contradiction between these claims of Hermogenes' and his immediately preceding admissions about true and false speaking. Yet he does nothing of that sort; rather, he introduces a new topic, questioning Hermogenes about his attitude to Protagoras (385e–386a). Note that, if Socrates wanted to argue that Hermogenes' theory commits him to denying the possibility of false speaking, he could simply exploit the formulation of 385a, where the conventionalist thesis was presented in terms of how one 'calls' things, with no mention of the imposition which fixes the rule for subsequent usage. Socrates might overinterpret that omission and saddle Hermogenes with the view that any name one uses to call something is correct, independently of any preceding imposition, and that therefore it is impossible to use a name incorrectly and speak falsely. But he makes no such use of the 385a formulation.

Secondly, the supposed refutation would be gravely fallacious. As we saw in §2.1, (H2) cannot be divorced from the rest of Hermogenes' theory, which constitutes an organic whole and is never presented otherwise in the dialogue. According to this theory, what is correct is not any name you *use*, but any name you *impose* on something; hence every sentence is true or false in relation to the particular convention it is based upon (§2.1.2). And the fact that falsehood is fully compatible with convention is unlikely to escape Plato's awareness, especially given that he is going to make Socrates conclude that convention plays at least some part in the correctness of names (434d–439b, see §§8.1.3–5).

Now we had better avoid giving Socrates an argument that is not explicitly set forth in the text, is at odds with the context, and moreover does not work, as Plato himself ought to know. So I reject the view that our passage contains a refutation of Hermogenes.

As we saw above, a different interpretation of our passage has also been advanced, according to which Socrates would take the existence of true and false names to entail directly that the correctness of names is something *natural*. The true name would then be explained as the name which reveals (etymologically) the nature of a given object, the false name as that which does not reveal it.[61] Since Socrates' argument, so interpreted, would positively support naturalism rather than refute conventionalism, perhaps we should characterize this version of the story as 'Pro-naturalist' rather than 'Anti-conventionalist'. A trace of this interpretation can perhaps be detected in Proclus' commentary (see §2.2.6); it is held by Ficino (f. 107ᵛ) and by several modern interpreters, among which Stallbaum 41, Robinson 1956: 123, and Luce 1969a.[62]

This interpretation accords with two passages: 400d (where the 'true' names, used by the gods, are the naturally correct ones) and 425d (where the 'truth' of the primary names seems to be their (natural) correctness).[63] It is, nevertheless, confronted with difficulties analogous to those that ruled out the 'Anti-conventionalist' one. First, the passage would fit in very badly with the context. Indeed, in this case the problem is not only that Socrates does not draw any explicit conclusion in favour of naturalism and does not object, or pretend to expose a contradiction, when at 385de Hermogenes confidently reasserts his thesis; the problem is also that nothing seems to suggest that we should understand the mention of true and false names in connection with the naturalist thesis. Ficino takes Socrates to be arguing that names, besides being true or false as sentences are, are also true or false *in the same way* as sentences are, i.e. by 'speaking of the beings' either 'as they are' or 'as they are not', and to be assuming that this is a matter of their being naturally correct or incorrect: 'et nomina vera sunt illa quae res ita ut sunt potius quam ut placet arbitrio proferunt'. But the assumption that so crucial a step is merely implicit counts as a drawback of his interpretation. Secondly, Socrates' argument would again be a bad one (cf. Schofield 1972: 247–8). For Hermogenes can grant that names are true or false (and even that they are so in the same way as sentences are) without thereby falling into naturalism; nothing in the argument really entails that names are true or false in the sense of being *naturally* correct or incorrect. And Plato himself must be aware of this, as we shall see below.

[61] Cf. also the popular view that a person misdescribed by his own name is ψευδώνυμος, 'bearing a false name', or is so called ψευδωνύμως, 'by a false name': Aesch. *Pr.* 85–6, 717; *Th.* 670; etc. (Luce 1969a: 225).
[62] Cf. Lorenz/Mittelstrass 1967: 5–7. This is also Sedley's (2003: 12 and n.25) interpretation, although he thinks that the passage actually belongs to an earlier edition of the dialogue and hence was originally placed in an at least partly different context: see §2.2.5.
[63] Some consider as parallels also 437d and 438d, where it may seem that the 'true' names are the correct ones and those 'conforming [or 'similar'] to the truth' (ὅμοια τῇ ἀληθείᾳ), i.e. whose etymology expresses the true nature of their referents. But in the former passage it is certain, and in the latter it is probable, that 'true' is not applied to names but to the views they convey: see ch. 8 nn.110 and 113.

So we must reject the view that our passage – read in its present MSS position – contains a refutation of conventionalism or an argument for naturalism. Then what could its function be?

A completely different possibility (first suggested by Richardson 1976: 136–7) is to think that Socrates here has no polemical intent and does not aim to argue Hermogenes into accepting some conclusion, but is just trying to *understand better* Hermogenes' own position. Our passage, so interpreted, appears to be part of a strategy consistently implemented by Socrates in the preceding and following ones.

At 385ab, the passage about name-reversal, Hermogenes had just expounded his thesis, also setting forth its 'individualistic' version, i.e. (H2). Since this point could look paradoxical, it was natural of Socrates to insist on it in order to elucidate its meaning (see §2.1.2). Now someone might fear – as some interpreters have actually done – that (H2) may lead to an argument against the possibility of false speaking, which was a target of frequent sophistic attacks. Hence in our passage Socrates takes care to ascertain Hermogenes' views on truth and falsity. He finds that Hermogenes is so far from approving of those sophistic arguments that he is ready to acknowledge not only the standard distinction between true and false sentences (to which Socrates, tellingly, pays special attention at b2–11), but also an extra distinction between true and false names. Much later in the dialogue, this will turn out to be another issue on which Hermogenes and Cratylus are divided. For at 429cd Socrates will suggest that Cratylus' thesis entails that it is impossible to speak falsely; and Cratylus will confirm his adherence to this outrageous view by recourse to a stock argument according to which it is impossible '*not to say the things that are*' (τὸ μὴ τὰ ὄντα λέγειν) – contrast, here at 385b10, Hermogenes' assent to the question whether it is possible to '*say ... both the things that are and those that are not*' (λέγειν τὰ ὄντα τε καὶ μή). I submit that from the vantage point of Plato, the dialogue's author (though not from that of his character Socrates, who cannot foresee the contents of his conversation with Cratylus), part of our passage's function is also to lay down the first term of this remote and implicit comparison between Hermogenes and Cratylus. The parallel is strengthened by the fact that (as we already saw in §2.2.2) in the discussion of Cratylus' paradox of false speaking at 429d–431c Socrates will establish a connection between the true/false distribution of names and that of sentences – a connection which seems to coincide with that established here between true/false sentences and true/false names.[64]

[64] On the parallel between 385bd and 429c–431c cf. Derbolav 1972: 112–14.

Our passage, as I am tentatively interpreting it, has an interesting parallel in a criticism which Leibniz levels against Hobbes. On Leibniz's interpretation, Hobbes holds an extreme conventionalism which makes truth dependent on human arbitrary decisions, insofar as truth depends on definitions which consist of names and are therefore fully arbitrary (cf. e.g. *De corpore*, 1.3.8). As against this, in the *Dialogus* of 1677 Leibniz argues that, though admittedly names are arbitrary, truth is not, because it depends on something constant underlying the arbitrariness and changeability of names, i.e. the relations between names and things and among names themselves.[65] This general distinction between the arbitrariness of names and the objectivity of truth coincides with what I take to be the implicit moral of our passage.[66]

Back to the passage's context. Since Socrates finds Hermogenes' answers satisfactory, at 385d2 he resumes the previous discussion, which was broken off at b2, and asks two further questions about the conventionalist thesis itself (385de). This is a crucial point, because our passage has been accused precisely of interrupting the discussion of conventionalism which takes place immediately before and after it. There is admittedly something abrupt and untidy about the wording of this resumption, and there is even reason to suspect that something may be wrong with the text (see §2.2.5). But the fact that there is a resumption is by itself unproblematic. Indeed, there might perhaps be a special point in it: by sandwiching the truth/falsity distinction between two avowals of conventionalism on Hermogenes' part, Plato might want to make it especially clear that the distinction has not induced Hermogenes to modify his thesis and that he is ready to hold on to *both*.

Finally, at 385e Socrates will move on to ask Hermogenes whether he endorses Protagorean relativism. It is very natural to take that question too as aiming to explore another possible *liaison dangereuse* of conventionalism, which may be associated with relativism in view of a superficial similarity. This is confirmed by the fact that Hermogenes *immediately* declares his disagreement with Protagoras, before Socrates reinforces this opinion with an anti-relativistic argument to the conclusion that objects have an objective nature (386de). Thereby Plato shows that the two doctrines are independent of each other, at least on the face of it, and makes the picture

---

[65] Leibniz 1923–: A VI, 4A, 24–5 = Ariew/Garber 1989: 271–2.
[66] In the light of several other parallels with *Cra.*, which we shall encounter along our reading of the dialogue, it is even possible to surmise that Leibniz's *Dialogus* was influenced by our passage. On the other hand, Leibniz's answer to Hobbes is firmly placed in the contemporary philosophical debate (see Maat 2004: 332–40). On Leibniz and *Cra.* cf. §6.3.7.

of Hermogenes' views more complex (see §2.4.1). At the same time, the conclusion that objects have an objective nature is also the starting point of Socrates' subsequent refutation of Hermogenes (387a ff.).

So I venture the suggestion that in 385a–386a Socrates carries out three successive inquiries into as many possibly problematic aspects of Hermogenes' views: (i) individual imposition, (ii) the distinction between truth and falsity, and (iii) the connection with relativism. The common purpose of these inquiries is to clarify the meaning and limits of conventionalism; but in the third inquiry this purpose coexists with that of laying down a premiss – 'objects have an objective nature' – which will eventually lead to a refutation of Hermogenes.

On the present interpretation, we should still assume that a true name is a correct one, and a false name is an incorrect one. Clearly, however, the correctness of names must now be understood, not from the naturalist viewpoint, i.e. in terms of their etymology, but rather from the viewpoint *of Hermogenes* – and of most of us.[67]

This is compatible with the evidence cited in §2.2.2 for the equation between a name's truth or falsity and its correctness or incorrectness. At 429e ('Hello, Athenian stranger, son of Smicrion, Hermogenes') the naturalist conception of names is officially still in force, but plays no role in the example and is not referred to at all. At 430a–431c Socrates makes the naturalist assumption that a name is, like a painting, an imitation of its referent, and on the basis of this analogy reaches the conclusion that names can be assigned to things correctly or incorrectly. Nevertheless, it is perfectly legitimate to use 430a–431c to substantiate the present interpretation of the passage, which has nothing to do with naturalism. That argument shows that Plato is able to speak of truth and falsity not only at the level of sentences but also at the level of names, identifying the correct distribution with the true one and the incorrect distribution with the false one. This result has a merely *accidental* connection with the particular theoretical framework within which it is reached. We can use that passage to argue that Plato can speak of a true/false distribution, and hence of true/false names, even within a non-naturalist framework; what is more, Plato himself certainly views this result as a sound one independently of the naturalist framework, which Socrates is ultimately going to reject (Schofield 1972: 247–8). For in the end he will recognize that convention has an important role in the correctness of names and that a name can be

---

[67] Actually, this was already implied by the 'anti-conventionalist' interpretation, according to which the passage aims to catch Hermogenes contradicting *himself* about the problem of falsehood.

correct even though it misdescribes or completely fails to describe its referent (434c–440d, see §§8.1.3–5).

Finally, as for *Plt.* 281ab, nothing there suggests a special concern with the fact that the 'false name' ὑφαντική comes from ὑφαίνω 'weave' and, to that extent, *misdescribes* the craft producing warp and weft. Rather, the point seems to be just that the name ὑφαντική is not that craft's name, is incorrectly applied to (or false of) it, quite independently of etymology.

2.2.5 *Authenticity and position of the passage*

Our discussion of the passage's function brings us to the heart of the textual issue. Schofield 1972: 246–51 argued that the passage (a) cannot stand where the MSS have it, (b) must be transposed between 387c5 and c6. Both proposals are followed by Reeve. The OCT editors accept only (a) and print the whole passage in the usual position but within square brackets; these lines, they write in the apparatus on 387c5, 'nusquam in dialogo qualem nunc habemus convenire videntur'. This might mean either that they regard the passage as an interpolation or that they think it is genuine Plato but actually belongs to a different redaction of the dialogue, earlier than the one we read: cf. 437d–438b, where they controversially suppose an 'author's variant'. This latter possibility is espoused by Sedley (2003: 10–13), who maintains that 'this passage too is an accidental survivor from an earlier edition' and that the passage was excluded from the revised edition because Plato, by the time he wrote the *Sophist*, had come to regard as mistaken the view that the truth or falsity of a sentence can be traced down to the names it is composed of. 'The text', he writes, ' ... underwent enough other alteration for the gap left by this surgical excision to close up seamlessly, so that the passage cannot be satisfactorily reinserted into the text as it has come down to us, and instead has survived by being mechanically copied in at a point where it plainly does not fit. The likely explanation is once again that an early Platonic scholar, coming upon the first edition of the dialogue, copied the offending passage into the margin, presumably as close as he could get it to the part of the dialogue in which it originally occurred, and that, as in the previous case, it got inadvertently copied into the text.'[68]

Schofield's arguments for (a) are the following. The passage interrupts the linear sequence of thought we should have if, instead, 385b1 were immediately followed by d2. Its function is obscure, because it cannot be an

---

[68] On author's variants in general see my Appendix 1 n.5.

argument against Hermogenes. Finally, the question with which Socrates comes back to the conventionalist thesis at 385d2–3, immediately after the passage's conclusion, is suspicious. Socrates asks whether 'what each person says is something's name, that is a name for each person', and he opens his question with ἄρα, a particle whose force is often inferential ('therefore'), as here at 385b10, c10 and c16. Hence Schofield's doubts: 'If 385b2–d1 is in its right place, what is Socrates supposing to license this conclusion? It can hardly be Hermogenes' answer to his previous point ... (385c16–17). And in fact one can find nothing which could possibly support Socrates' conclusion unless one goes back all the way to 385a6–b1, i.e. to just that passage which, according to my proposal, immediately precedes it.'

These arguments can, I think, be resisted. As for the passage's function, in §2.2.4 I have suggested that the passage can be read as an inquiry into Hermogenes' views on truth and falsity, suddenly but relevantly inserted by Socrates into the context of a progressive clarification of the purport and limits of conventionalism. As for d2–3, I grant that there ἄρα is problematic and is probably the symptom that the text requires some sort of emendation; but the emendation required need not concern our lines and need not be as heavy as those that have been proposed (see §2.3).

Furthermore, each of those proposals has some specific drawback. According to Schofield our lines really belong between 387c5 and c6, where Socrates has just claimed that things must be cut, burnt and spoken of according to their nature, and is about to argue that the same holds of naming, which is a part (μόριον) of speaking. But the train of thought of that context would be unnecessarily hampered by the insertion of our passage, whose talk of true and false sentences and names would become pointless.[69] If our lines were instead an interpolation, then we should suppose that early in the transmission of the text (before Proclus: see §2.2.6) someone wrote down in good Platonic Greek a puzzling argument, whose conclusion apparently runs counter to a basic principle of Aristotelian and Stoic logic, and which then somehow found its way into the text at a point where it does not smooth over any difficulty or obscurity, but on the contrary may seem to interrupt the discourse's thread and does not lead to an evident conclusion. Very implausible.

Then what about the view that the passage is a remnant from an earlier edition of the dialogue? Here are some considerations against it. First, whatever we may think of the alleged author's variant at 437d–438b,[70] it

---

[69] Cf. Sedley 2003: 59 n.18. Proclus in his comments on 387c (XLV, 14) gives no sign that he is reading our passage there, nor does he mention it while expounding the argument of 386a–387d (XLVI, 15.1–26).
[70] Like other scholars, I am sceptical: see §8.2.3.

should be emphasized that only there do the MSS actually report different variants. Here the variant is a mere conjecture – which to my mind is not sufficiently justified, because it seems questionable, for the above reasons, whether the passage 'fails to fit structurally into the *Cratylus* as we now have it', as Sedley (2003: 13) claims. Secondly, it is crucial to this view that the presuppositions of the argument in our passage 'unlike anything else in this dialogue, are in direct and overt conflict with the *Sophist*' (2003: 12); but *Cra.* seems to contain other claims that depend on the misconception of the structure of sentences which is exploded in the *Sophist*, as we saw in §2.2.3. Thirdly, generally speaking I find it very hard to believe that Plato could have changed the text of an already published dialogue for doctrinal reasons; and I suspect that it would be possible to find cases in which he did not do so.[71]

So I am inclined to think that, although our passage is briskly introduced and abruptly concluded, and its function is left unusually obscure, it should not be transposed between 387c5 and c6, or excised as an interpolation, or ascribed to an earlier edition of the dialogue. The safest course seems to be to keep it where it stands.

2.2.6 Proclus' testimony

Schofield (1972: 251–2) also tries to show that Proclus did not read the passage where the MSS report it, on the grounds that, if Proclus had read the passage in its present position, he would presumably have interpreted it as an argument against Hermogenes, and that this is not what he does.

Yet there is good evidence that Proclus did read the passage in its present position. At least from XXII, 9 the commentary substantially follows the dialogue's progress from 384a onwards; our passage is dealt with at XXXVI, 11.30–12.17, precisely between the one about name-reversal (385a: XXXIII, 11) and the one about Protagoras (385e–386d: XXXVIII, 12). This is, of course, its position in Plato's MSS and in our editions. In the sequel too the commentary goes on following *Cra.* fairly closely. Hence its order, if it carries any weight, seems to presuppose the present position of 385b2–d1, as the OCT editors recognize in their apparatus.

---

[71] I add a fourth, merely *ad hominem* consideration. Sedley thinks that the passage, in its original context, was subservient to the refutation of Hermogenes; more precisely, he holds a 'Pro-naturalist' view of its function (2003: 12 and n.25; cf. §2.2.4). But then the passage is not 'a complete argument with a beginning, a middle and an end' (2003: 11): the end, the conclusion in favour of naturalism or against conventionalism, is missing. And this increases the cost of Sedley's supposition.

Indeed, there is also a clue that Proclus *did* understand the passage as directed against Hermogenes, and that, more precisely, he held the 'Pro-naturalist' interpretation (cf. §2.2.4). In XXXVI, 12.6–16 he claims that Plato speaks of truth and falsity in four senses, the fourth one being

> in connection with the organs of cognitive life, i.e. sentences, names and letters; for he sees truth and falsity in these too, according to their harmony and appropriateness to the objects [κατὰ τὴν πρὸς τὰ πράγματα ἐφάρμοσιν καὶ συμφωνίαν].

Since Proclus interprets Plato's position in naturalist terms, the 'harmony' he is speaking of is probably something natural (cf. I, 1.7–9; XLVIII, 16.19–23). This is confirmed by the fact that it also concerns *letters*, whose 'harmony' with an object can only be thought to be of a mimetic sort.

This conclusion seems to be at odds with another bit of evidence. At XXXIII, 11.15–17 Proclus claims that Socrates refutes Hermogenes' thesis with three arguments, which he dubs respectively 'abashing' or 'shameful' (ἐντρεπτικόν), 'forcible' (βιαστικόν) and 'cause of most complete persuasion'. The first is the 'human'/'horse' example at 385ab (see §2.1.2),[72] whereas the second and third are not explicitly identified by Proclus. However, at XLVI, 15.1–26 he formulates a chain of seven arguments, reconstructing the discussion from 386a (outset of Protagoras' refutation) to 387d (conclusion that we must name the objects according to nature); this chain he presents as a proof that names are correct by nature. Hence, on the face of it, this should be one of the three arguments against Hermogenes. Then at XLVIII, 16.5–27 Proclus expounds *another* argument, based on the name's being an instrument for teaching and discriminating the essence (388bc); he distinguishes it from a 'previous' one (ἡ πρὸ αὐτῆς) in that it proceeds from the name's very form or species (εἶδος), while the other proceeded from the name's model, i.e. 'the objects'. The 'previous' argument is of course the chain of XLVI. So it seems that the last argument is the third one, 'cause of most complete persuasion'; that the chain in XLVI is the second, 'forcible' one; and that no place is left for our passage in Proclus' list of three arguments against Hermogenes.

Thus we seem to have a conflict between Proclus' comments on our passage and his list of arguments against Hermogenes. This, however, should not cause great worry and should not induce us to withdraw our interpretation of XXXVI. The list's interpretation is largely a matter of conjecture, and we may remark that the term 'forcible' would fit the close brevity

---

[72] And so the name of the first argument refers to the fact that the argument (which Proclus interpreted as an instance of *modus tollens*) 'shames' Hermogenes by showing the absurd consequences of his thesis. Cf. *in Prm.* 866.11, S. E. *PH* 3.135, and Hsch. E 3395 Latte.

of 385bd better than 386a–387d. And, in any case, the vicissitudes which Proclus' text has probably undergone are sufficient to explain any such inconsistency. A parallel case seems to be Proclus' inconsistent interpretation of Cratylus' thesis: see ch. 1 n.15.[73]

2.3 CONVENTION AND INDIVIDUAL DECISION: FURTHER DETAILS (385DE)

At 385d2, after the end of the passage about truth and falsity, Socrates returns (rather abruptly) to Hermogenes' conventionalist thesis:

SO. What each person says is a name for something, this is a name for each person? [Ὃ ἂν ἄρα ἕκαστος φῇ τῳ ὄνομα εἶναι, τοῦτό ἐστιν ἑκάστῳ ὄνομα;]
HE. Yes. (385d2–4)

These lines pose several problems, concerning both the content of Socrates' question and its relation to what precedes it.

I start with the main clause, which admits of two alternative construals. Some scholars[74] take it to mean 'this is a name *for each thing*?', where the dative ἑκάστῳ is neuter and picks up τῳ 'for something' in the previous relative clause. Others[75] instead think it means 'this is a name *for each person*?', where ἑκάστῳ is masculine and expresses relation to the naming subject. On this latter construal, Socrates' point is that (as it follows from the 385bd distinction between 'public' and 'private' names) whatever name an individual imposes on something is a name *for that individual* and not for others; cf. the use of ἑκάστῳ at 385e, where Protagoras' relativism is being presented. In view of the occurrence of ἕκαστος 'each person' in the relative clause, the latter construal seems preferable, because it involves a consistent use of the same pronoun within the same sentence – at the price, however, of some inconsistency with the external context. For in the immediately following question (d5–6) the naming subject is referred to as τις ('one'), while the dative ἑκάστῳ clearly refers to the object named; and if we glance back at 385a2 we see that there Socrates asked 'What, you say, one calls each thing, that is the name for each thing?' (ὃ ἄν, φῇς, καλῇ

---

[73] On Proclus' commentary see van den Berg 2008: 94–5. According to Schofield, the 'forcible' argument is the one 'against Protagoras' (xxxviii, 12.24–7: *Cra.* 386ad). This cannot be so, because Proclus includes that argument in the chain at xlvi, without giving it an autonomous role; and, in fact, at 386a Hermogenes *spontaneously* says he does not agree with relativism. For another attempt, partly different from mine, to identify Proclus' three arguments see Duvick 2007: 123 n.87, 133 n.158, and van den Berg 2008: 112–14.
[74] Minio-Paluello, Schofield 1972: 246, Dalimier.
[75] Fowler, Reeve, Goldschmidt 1940: 52–3 n.2.

Individual decision: further details (385de)

τις ἕκαστον, τοῦθ' ἑκάστῳ ὄνομα;), a question apparently most similar to ours, but where 'one' was the naming subject and 'each thing' the object named.[76]

It is not clear whether 'says is a name for something' refers to the *imposition* or the *use* of a name. Barney (1997: 151), who leans to the latter option, remarks that for Hermogenes 'this should be … only a misleading half-truth: he should stipulate that what one "says" must be in accordance with the relevant baptism to be correct', and surmises that Socrates is trying to draw Hermogenes' attention to the calamitous 'anything goes' variant of his thesis according to which any name you use is correct, independently of a previous baptism. But the phrase might well refer to imposition; and even if it should instead refer to use, it is most natural to think that the reference to imposition is innocently understood, just as at 385a, where Socrates presented Hermogenes' thesis simply in terms of how each speaker can 'call' things.[77]

We can finally turn to the relation between Socrates' question and what precedes it, which should be expressed by the particle ἄρα. Here we have to confront a serious difficulty. On the one hand, it seems natural to take ἄρα to have its typical inferential force ('therefore'), as at b10, c10 and most recently c16;[78] on the other, as Schofield 1972: 248 saw (see §2.2.5), the proposition that Socrates is submitting to Hermogenes cannot be inferred from what immediately precedes it in the MSS text, i.e. the conclusion of the argument about true and false sentences and names (c16–d1). So we are entitled to suspect that the text hides a corruption, and that either ἄρα is itself corrupt or – if ἄρα is both sound and inferential – our lines do not come immediately after d1. Schofield and others choose the latter option and do away with 385b2–d1 somehow or other; but none of those proposals is satisfactory, as I argued in §2.2.5. There are, however, other ways of separating d1 from d2. We could suppose that something has been lost between d1 and d2, perhaps a whole exchange between Socrates and Hermogenes, which provided a justification for the ἄρα. Or we could suppose that the

---

[76] To avoid *both* internal *and* external inconsistency Hirschig corrected ἕκαστος φῇ τῷ into ἑκάστῳ φῇ τις, where the pronouns are distributed exactly as at a2. Such extreme measures are not necessary.

[77] Cf. *Sph.* 220c τοῦτο μὲν ἄρα ἑρκοθηρικὸν τῆς ἄγρας τὸ μέρος φήσομεν ἤ τι τοιοῦτον, where ἑρκοθηρικόν is Plato's coin.

[78] De Vries 1955: 292 suggested that what Socrates says here 'is not a new development, but serves to remind Hermogenes (and the reader) of Hermogenes' former contention. Ἄρα is "according to your theory"'. This use, however, very frequent after ὡς, 'that', introducing reported speech or thought (*GP* 38–9), and attested also in other contexts (*Grg.* 493b; *R.* 598e, 600cd), does not, to my knowledge, occur in questions. Furthermore, it would leave the question without a connecting particle marking Socrates' return to the main topic.

whole of d2–e3 must be transposed between b1 and b2, immediately after the exchange about public and private names and before the argument about true and false sentences and names.[79] Both of these alternative conjectures are cheaper than the various interventions on 385b2–d1 that have been devised so far. And both leave the overall structure of the conversation between Socrates and Hermogenes, as I tentatively analysed it in §2.2.4, essentially untouched: 385b2–d1 can still be read as one stage in a progressive clarification of conventionalism.

I conclude that, if I were to give a critical text of these lines, I would print a *crux* before Ὅ ἂν ἄρα at the beginning of d2 – not as a sign of desperation but to signal that it is uncertain which of the various possible ways of dealing with the difficulties raised by these lines is the right one.

Thereby I take my leave from the nest of problems concerning the whole of 385b2–d4 and move on to the next, less problematic exchange. Socrates points out another consequence of Hermogenes' claims:

SO. And however many names one says belong to each thing, so many will belong to it precisely when he says so? [ὁπόσα ἂν φῇ τις ἑκάστῳ ὀνόματα εἶναι, τοσαῦτα ἔσται καὶ τότε ὁπόταν φῇ·]. (385d5–6)

It is unclear whether Socrates is talking about names which belong to the same thing at the same time, or at different and successive times, or both. The first alternative seems to fit the text more naturally, but I do not think the second is meant to be excluded; in fact Hermogenes is committed to both.

Hermogenes' extensive answer (385d7–e3) falls into two parts. Let us start with the first one:

HE. Yes, Socrates, for I do not know any other correctness of a name than this one: that to me it is possible[80] to call each thing by one name, which I have imposed, and to you it is possible to do so by another name, which you in your turn have imposed [ἐμοὶ μὲν ἕτερον εἶναι καλεῖν ἑκάστῳ ὄνομα, ὃ ἐγὼ ἐθέμην, σοὶ δὲ ἕτερον, ὃ αὖ σύ]. (385d7–9)

This is a restatement of (H2), which has been picked up just now at d2–4. Here, however, Hermogenes explicitly reasserts the distinction between a name's imposition and its subsequent use. He claims that anyone can call anything by the name he has decided to bestow on it. He clearly believes that this claim entails an affirmative answer to Socrates' question – as in fact it does.

---

[79] 385e5 οὕτως 'so' need not be anaphoric and hence presuppose d7–e3 immediately before it: the adverb may also look forward and be answered by e6 ὥσπερ 'as'.
[80] εἶναι (d8) is the infinitive of ἔστι 'it is possible'. Cf. LSJ εἰμί, A.VI.a.

Individual decision: further details (385de)

It is interesting to notice that the characters keep on avoiding any explicit mention of the case of a conversation between two speakers who follow different conventions. True, Hermogenes' example is about himself and Socrates; but, strictly speaking, that does not entail that he is hinting at a contact between them. And should such an encounter take place, Hermogenes' present words – consistently with what we said above – do not entail the Babelic result that each speaker would talk to the other deafly following his own peculiar use.

In the second part of his answer Hermogenes compares the fact that different individuals can call the same thing by different names to the lexical differences among Greek cities and between Greeks and barbarians:

> (HE.) Likewise I see that each city has names of its own for the same things [οὕτω δὲ καὶ ταῖς πόλεσιν ὁρῶ ἰδίᾳ ἑκάσταις ἐπὶ τοῖς αὐτοῖς κείμενα ὀνόματα], both Greeks compared to the other Greeks and Greeks compared to barbarians [καὶ Ἕλλησι παρὰ τοὺς ἄλλους Ἕλληνας, καὶ Ἕλλησι παρὰ βαρβάρους]. (d9–e3)

The textual details of this comparison are problematic. The text given above is found in Q and printed by Heindorf and the OCT. βW read ἰδίᾳ ἑκάσταις ἐνίοις, implausibly preserved by Hirschig; from this reading Burnet drew ἰδίᾳ {ἑκάσταις} ἐνίοις and Buttmann (followed by Bekker, Stallbaum and Méridier) ἰδίᾳ ἑκάσταις ἐνίοτ'. T has only ἰδίᾳ, printed by Fowler. To solve the textual problem it is helpful to grasp the comparison's structure. As many interpreters recognize, the three καί's (καὶ ταῖς πόλεσιν ... καὶ Ἕλλησί ... καὶ Ἕλλησι) are not all on the same level. First Hermogenes somehow says, as a generic and incomplete introduction, that 'the cities', or 'each city', or 'some cities',[81] have peculiar names of their own (e1–2: καί = 'also'). Then he explains *relative to whom* such names are peculiar, distinguishing two cases: lexical differences among Greeks, on the one hand, and between Greeks and barbarians, on the other (e2–3: καί ... καί = 'both ... and', the two Ἕλλησι's picking up ταῖς πόλεσιν with *variatio*). So interpreted, the structure of the comparison suggests that we should delete ει ἐνίοις. For Hermogenes is unlikely to say that 'some' Greek cities (or that Greek cities 'sometimes', with the correction ἐνίοτε) use names different from the barbarian ones. Thus it seems reasonable to have him claim, with Q, that *each* Greek city has peculiar names of its own relative to both the other Greek cities and barbarians. This is

---

[81] ἐνίοις (ει), if correct, would require deletion of ἑκάσταις (as in Burnet) and should be taken as loosely picking up ταῖς πόλεσιν.

compatible with the obvious fact that actually *all* Greek cities share most names as against barbarians.[82]

Two points must be made about the philosophical gist of the comparison, which is independent of the textual matters. First, Hermogenes is once again equating the individual and the collective case, showing that he conceives of his thesis as a unity encompassing both of these aspects. Secondly, it is not really clear whether Hermogenes advances the comparison as some sort of *argument* in favour of his thesis[83] or just as a fact that *agrees* with it. The latter is perhaps more likely as well as more cautious. The former is indirectly suggested by Proclus, XXXI, 11.9–10, and is e.g. the view of Barney 1997: 157, 160. If it were right, then we should say that Hermogenes' argument is countered at 389d–390c by Socrates, who holds that one and the same thing can have different but equally natural names in different languages.

The connection between convention and language variety occurs also in Aristotle, *Int.* 1.16a3–8, where again it is not clear whether we have a full-blown argument. Outright arguments based on the diversity of languages are instead given by Sextus Empiricus (*PH* 2.214; *M.* 1.37–8, 145–9) and then become standard in the subsequent history of conventionalist ideas (Hobbes, *De corpore* 1.2.4; Locke, *Essay* III.ii.1).

2.4 HERMOGENES AND PROTAGORAS (385E–386E)

After Hermogenes' last restatement of conventionalism, in the next section Socrates tackles a new subject matter, i.e. the relation between Hermogenes' conventionalism and Protagoras' relativism. The section plays a twofold role in the structure of the discussion between Socrates and Hermogenes by looking, as it were, backwards and forwards at the same time. On the one hand, it closes the first part of the discussion, where Socrates has mainly tried to understand and clarify Hermogenes' theory. On the other hand, its results will constitute the basis for Socrates' subsequent defence of naturalism and attack on conventionalism (386e ff.).

---

[82] T's text, omitting ἑκάσταις ἐνίοις ('the cities have names of their own for the same things …'), is smoother. For in it the introductory nature of the first καί-clause is clearer, and the somewhat awkward opposition between *each* city and the barbarians has disappeared. Yet it is safer to side with Q, because there is no reason why the other MSS should have inserted *both* ἑκάσταις *and* ἐνίοις. (T's readings always tend to be *breviores*, often rightly so.)

[83] At ει we should then have a case of δέ used 'where the context admits, or even appears to demand, γάρ' (*GP* 169–70).

2.4.1 Man the measure of all things? (385e–386a)

Socrates starts with a direct question. Does Hermogenes, as a parallel to his own theory of linguistic convention, endorse Protagoras' relativist thesis?

so. Come on now, Hermogenes: do the things that are, too, appear to you to be in this condition, that their being is private to each person [πότερον καὶ τὰ ὄντα οὕτως ἔχειν σοι φαίνεται, ἰδίᾳ αὐτῶν ἡ οὐσία εἶναι ἑκάστῳ], as Protagoras said when he said that a human being 'is the measure of all things' – i.e., as he had it, that however the objects appear to me to be, such they are for me, and however they appear to you, such they are for you [οἷα μὲν ἂν ἐμοὶ φαίνηται τὰ πράγματα εἶναι, τοιαῦτα μὲν ἔστιν ἐμοί· οἷα δ' ἂν σοί, τοιαῦτα δὲ σοί]? Or do they seem to you to have some stability of being [βεβαιότητα τῆς οὐσίας] of their own? (385e4–386a4)

Protagoras is credited with the view that things have a nature 'private to each person' (e5–6) and that how they 'appear' to someone, such they are for that one (a1–3), so that they have no 'stability of being' (a3–4).[84] The same thesis is discussed at great length at *Tht.* 151e–179c. Without entering into the details of that discussion, we can say that Protagoras' thesis, in its broad form, denies the existence of a subject-independent way things are, and claims instead that things are just the way they appear to each subject, with regard both to their *perceptual* properties (e.g. being hot or cold) and to *non-perceptual* properties like moral ones (e.g. being just or unjust). All such properties, therefore, turn out to be essentially relative to the perceiving or judging subject; and all the judgements (δόξαι) of each subject on such matters are true for that subject (*Tht.* 161d, 167ad, 172b etc.).[85]

Now in our passage Socrates is precisely speaking of such a broad version of Protagoras' thesis. This is already suggested by his use of the term οὐσία to refer to the way things are, which is private to each of us (385e5, 386a4; cf. 386e). The term here cannot have the typical meaning 'essence', which many interpreters ascribe to it, and which it seems to acquire later on in the discussion (401cd, 423de: see §6.2.4), because Protagoras' thesis is not especially concerned with the *essence* of things. Rather, οὐσία must be a mere nominalization of the copula and stand in for any property, as ascribed by predications of the form ' – is *F*': cf. the occurrences of 'is'

---

[84] On 'stability of being' see §2.4.3.
[85] On Protagoras' thesis see Burnyeat 1979: 71, 77–8. On the relation between perception and judgement, and on the different kinds of predicates the thesis is about, see McDowell 1973: 118–20.

(ἐστίν) and of other forms of the verb 'to be' at 386a2 and 386d.[86] Such properties surely include items like justice or piety, as is confirmed by the fact that Socrates will shortly argue that the very distinction between good and bad, wise and unwise people refutes Protagoras (386ad). So the thesis is here taken in its broad version, extended to moral properties.

Thus Socrates draws a parallel between the two theses of Hermogenes and Protagoras. Between the two there is actually a great formal resemblance. Hermogenes maintains that things have no natural name of their own; that whatever name a speaker decides to impose on a thing, such is that thing's correct name for that speaker;[87] and that, therefore, things may have different names for different speakers. Protagoras maintains that things have no natures of their own; that whatever nature a thing appears to have to a subject, such is its nature for that subject; and that, therefore, things may have different natures for different subjects. The very wording of the two theses is similar. And if we turn again to *Tht.*, then the further bit of resemblance comes out that Protagorean relativism is explicitly concerned with the judgements of both individuals and cities (although Protagoras does not seem to consider the possibility of a contrast between these two spheres, as instead Socrates forced Hermogenes to do). See 168b 'whatever ... seems to each subject, this is the case, both for a private citizen and for a city' (τὸ ... δοκοῦν ἑκάστῳ τοῦτο καὶ εἶναι ἰδιώτῃ τε καὶ πόλει), or 172a:

> In the case of political matters, whatever each city believes fine and foul and just and unjust and pious and impious, and establishes [θῆται] as lawful for itself, that really is so for each city. And in these matters neither is a private citizen any wiser than another, nor a city than another city.

In this passage note also the emphasis on the distinction between the imposition of a rule and the thus established situation, which is parallel to Hermogenes' distinction between imposition and use. Cf. on this last point 177cd:

> Those things which a city establishes to be just because they so seem to it, those are actually just for the establishing city, *as long as they remain valid* [ἃ ἂν θῆται πόλις δόξαντα αὐτῇ, ταῦτα καὶ ἔστι δίκαια τῇ θεμένῃ, ἕωσπερ ἂν κέηται].

Thus Socrates is quite right to observe some kinship between the two theses. Indeed, if we allow ourselves not to take the mention of

---

[86] This construal of οὐσία is suggested by Szaif 1998: 459 n.156. Cf. *Chrm.* 168d; *Tht.* 160c (see Brown 1993: 209), 172b, perhaps 184b–186e (see Kahn 1981a: 119–27), 201e; *Sph.* 239b, perhaps 262c. 'Essence' is instead the interpretation of Ficino, Méridier and Minio-Paluello; Reeve has 'being or essence'.

[87] Note 385d3 ἑκάστῳ (see Goldschmidt 1940: 52–3 and n.2).

Protagoras too strictly, then there are other relativistic pronouncements (whether historical or fictional) about ethics and religion which bear a strong formal resemblance to almost all the features of Hermogenes' thesis – convention, difference among peoples, arbitrary change and temporary validity of what is established. See *Laws* 10.889e–890a, where Plato summarizes the philosophical stance which constitutes his *bête noire*:[88]

These people ... first of all say that the gods are by art, not by nature but by certain laws [τέχνῃ, οὐ φύσει ἀλλά τισιν νόμοις], and that these are different from place to place, according to the way each community agreed to set its own rules [ἄλλους ἄλλῃ, ὅπῃ ἕκαστοι ἑαυτοῖσι συνωμολόγησαν νομοθετούμενοι]. And the fine things are certain ones by nature, but certain others by law, whereas the just things are not by nature at all, but people continuously dispute with each other and always establish new rules on these matters, and whatever new rules they establish and when they establish them, then each one is valid [ἃ δ' ἂν μετάθωνται καὶ ὅταν, τότε κύρια ἕκαστα εἶναι], arising by art and the laws, but not by any sort of nature.

See also Arist. *EN* 1134b18–1135a5 (cf. 1133a29–31), which is particularly interesting because it contains a feature whose presence in Hermogenes' thesis was uncertain: there the existence of different conventions and customs is used as an *argument* for the relative and conventional nature of values (cf. [Pl.] *Min.* 315bd).

That said, however, there is also a great difference between Hermogenes' thesis and that of Protagoras. For the former is merely concerned with names, with the way we *refer to* things, whereas the latter is concerned with the way things *are*. The two theses are logically independent of each other, and in particular linguistic conventionalism does not entail ontological relativism: 'that which we call a rose / by any other word would smell as sweet'. This great difference may be viewed as depending on a little detail: once again, it is the crucial distinction between *imposition* and *use* of a name that makes the difference. If you collapse that distinction, then every use of a word counts as a correct use, and you lose hold of the very notions of error and falsity. And since Protagoras' thesis precisely amounts, in Plato's interpretation, to the claim that all our judgements are true, then the distance between the two theses suddenly becomes much narrower.

So Hermogenes' conventionalism and Protagoras' relativism are two formally similar, yet substantially independent theses. But what is

[88] Cited by Barney 1997: 160–1.

Hermogenes' own position on this issue? Here is his answer to Socrates' question:

HE. Sometime, Socrates, I've been driven by puzzlement [ἀπορῶν] to this very point, i.e. to the very things which Protagoras says; but I don't quite believe that it is so [οὐ πάνυ τι μέντοι μοι δοκεῖ οὕτως ἔχειν]. (386a5–7)

Thus Hermogenes does not endorse Protagorean relativism, although in past moments of puzzlement he has felt attracted to it.

It would be helpful to know whether, in the sentence where Hermogenes expresses his disagreement with Protagoras, οὐ πάνυ τι (a6) means 'not quite', as I have translated it (following Ficino's 'haud satis' and Sedley 1996: 98 and n.43), or rather 'scarcely' or even 'not at all', as translators usually have it.[89] Since Hermogenes is avowing that Protagoras has after all exerted some attraction on him, and since the sense of puzzlement that caused this attraction is not yet likely to have been removed, it is perhaps safer to choose the former meaning, which makes Hermogenes' disagreement less strong. At 391c, however, he will reject Protagoras flatly: 'I *don't at all* accept [ὅλως οὐκ ἀποδέχομαι] Protagoras' *Truth*'.[90] In any event, the fact remains that Hermogenes *disagrees* with Protagoras.

The most interesting thing about Hermogenes' answer is that Socrates will not be content with it, but will advance an argument to refute relativism and establish the conclusion that things have a subject-independent nature (386ae). Now, Plato needs the anti-relativist conclusion because it will constitute the basis for Socrates' subsequent attack on conventionalism; so it is fair of him to have Socrates give an argument for that conclusion. But then what is, from *Plato*'s perspective, the point of Hermogenes' *spontaneous* denial of relativism? Why doesn't Plato have him just answer that he is deeply perplexed and doesn't know what to say? To my mind the answer is twofold. On the one hand, Socrates' argument is not going to be completely satisfactory (see §2.4.3); so perhaps Plato is aware of its limits and, being unwilling or unable to give Socrates a stronger argument, he wants to smooth the way for him by preparing a favourable context. On the other, I believe that Plato precisely wants to give us at least some superficial evidence that conventionalism does not entail relativism. I also believe that one purpose of the dialogue as a whole is to give us more

---

[89] The former meaning is attested at *Euthd.* 286e, *Prt.* 321b and perhaps *La.* 191e, *Ly.* 204d; the latter at *Cra.* 436a, *Tht.* 150d, 176b, *R.* 432d, *Phlb.* 63b and perhaps *Phd.* 57a, *Phlb.* 23b, *Alc.* 2.108e. The ambiguity of οὐ πάνυ τι reflects that of the simpler οὐ πάνυ (on which see LSJ πάνυ, I.3, and Riddell 1867: §139).
[90] See §4.1.1.

conclusive evidence for this major philosophical distinction; for Socrates will in the end espouse at least some form of conventionalism, without thereby resurrecting Protagoras.

It should be clear by now that I firmly disagree (together with Barney 1997: 151–2 and Sedley 2003: 54) with the view that Hermogenes' thesis entails that of Protagoras or that this is what Socrates thinks. Adherents of this view usually suppose that at 385e ff. Socrates argues as follows: *H*[ermogenes] entails *P*[rotagoras], but *P* is wrong, hence *H* is wrong too.[91] Such an argument would be unsound and is not to be found in the text, as we are presently going to see.

2.4.2 *The refutation of Protagoras – and of Euthydemus (386ad)*

Socrates begins his argument against Protagorean relativism:

SO. What about this? Have you sometime been driven to *this* point, i.e. not to believe that any human being is wicked [πονηρόν]?

HE. No, by Zeus; on the contrary, I've often had that experience, so that I believe that some human beings – indeed, a great many – are very wicked.

SO. And have you never come to believe that there are very virtuous [χρηστοί] human beings?

HE. Very few.

SO. But you *did* come to believe there are?

HE. I did.

SO. What's your position on this matter? Is it this, that the very virtuous are very wise [φρονίμους], whereas the very wicked are very unwise [ἄφρονας]?

HE. I believe so. (386a8–c1)

Thus Hermogenes agrees with Socrates that some people (in fact a great many) are wicked and therefore unwise, whereas others (in fact very few) are virtuous and therefore wise.[92] The idea that the wicked are many, whereas the virtuous are few, he draws from traditional morality (cf. Heraclitus 22 B108 DK 'the many are bad, whereas few are good', and Bias 10 ξ 1), thus not accepting the view, put forward by Socrates himself at *Phd.* 90ab, that 'both the very virtuous and the very wicked are few, whereas those in between are most numerous'. But the twofold inference from

---

[91] See e.g. Silverman 1992: 31–4.
[92] According to some scholars, 'I've often had that experience' (b2) means that Hermogenes has often experienced human wickedness; some have even surmised that this has something to do with his financial problems (384c) and with his not being master of his father's estate (391c). Others take αὐτό as proleptic and ὥστε (b3) as epexegetical: the 'experience' in question would then be just that of believing that some people are wicked. But I am unsure whether this is linguistically possible.

being virtuous to being wise, and from being wicked to being unwise, presupposes the well-known Socratic and Platonic tenet that virtue is wisdom or knowledge (cf. e.g. *La.* 192b–199e, *Men.* 86c–89c, *Phd.* 68c–69c; a verbally close parallel at *Cri.* 47a). An intimate member of the Socratic circle, Hermogenes is as familiar with this tenet as he will appear to be with the theory of forms at 389a ff.

The argument goes on by pointing out that the truth of Protagoras' thesis is *incompatible* with the existence of both wise and unwise people:

SO. Then, if Protagoras told the truth and this is the *Truth*, that whatever each person believes, that is the case [τὸ οἷα ἂν δοκῇ ἑκάστῳ τοιαῦτα καὶ εἶναι],[93] is it possible that some of us are wise and some are unwise?

HE. Of course not.

SO. And you also strongly believe this, I think: that since there is wisdom and unwisdom [φρονήσεως οὔσης καὶ ἀφροσύνης] it is not possible at all that Protagoras tell the truth. For one person wouldn't truly be any wiser than another, if what each believes will be true for him [εἴπερ ἃ ἂν ἑκάστῳ δοκῇ ἑκάστῳ ἀληθῆ ἔσται].

HE. That's true. (386c2–d1)

This second part of the argument runs as follows. If Protagoras' doctrine (as set forth in the work entitled *Truth*: cf. *Tht.* 161c, 162a) is true, then there are no wise and unwise people; but there are wise and unwise people (at c6–7 Socrates actually says 'there is wisdom and unwisdom', thereby meaning 'wisdom and unwisdom are *instantiated*', hence 'there are wise and unwise people'); therefore Protagoras' doctrine cannot be true. Writing '*P*' for 'Protagoras' doctrine is true' and '*W*' for 'There are wise and unwise people', we get: 'If *P*, then not-*W*; but *W*; therefore not-*P*.'

That is, uncontroversially, the substance of this part of the argument (cf. Proclus xxxviii, 12.24–7). Whether it is also a paraphrase of what Socrates actually says in the text depends on how we interpret the genitive absolute φρονήσεως οὔσης καὶ ἀφροσύνης (c6–7). If, with most scholars, we took it as equivalent to a conditional clause ('*if* there is wisdom and unwisdom'), then Socrates would not explicitly state the premiss that there is wisdom and unwisdom (i.e. wise and unwise people), and would not explicitly draw the conclusion that Protagoras' doctrine is not true. Rather, Socrates would just claim that, as if Protagoras' doctrine is true then there

---

[93] Two notes on c3–4. (i) Here as in the parallel *Tht.* 152c, I take οἷα and τοιαῦτα as *subjects* respectively of δοκῇ and εἶναι (the latter meaning 'to be true'): cf. c9–d1. On this way of presenting Protagoras' thesis cf. *Tht.* 161c; on the use of οἷα cf. *Tht.* 167c, 172a. All interpreters, instead, take οἷα and τοιαῦτα as *complements*, with an understood 'things' as subject: cf. 386a1–2. Indeed, Heindorf went so far as to insert ἕκαστα after ἑκάστῳ. (ii) The qualification ἑκάστῳ is not repeated in the apodosis, but is clearly left to be understood, as e.g. at *Tht.* 161a.

are no wise and unwise people, so by contraposition if there are wise and unwise people then Protagoras' doctrine is not true: 'If P, then not-W; if W, then not-P.' It would then be left to us to add W as a premiss, in virtue of the previous agreements, and thence conclude that not-P. But that would be an odd way of proceeding on Plato's part. For in what follows Socrates assumes that Protagoras' thesis has been refuted and moves on to reject explicitly also Euthydemus' related thesis (386d3 ff.). Furthermore, why should Socrates at c8–d1, immediately after stating the alleged second conditional, support it by restating the first ('For one person … true for him'), thus actually coming to say 'If P, then not-W; if W, then not-P; for if P, then not-W'? So I think we should take the genitive absolute as equivalent to a *causal* clause: '*since* there is wisdom and unwisdom', which of course entails 'there is wisdom and unwisdom'. This solution (already to be found in the translations by Ficino and Méridier) gives Socrates the required premiss and conclusion and makes the above presentation of the argument into a faithful paraphrase of the text as well.

Now is Socrates' argument valid? The answer to this question depends on how we interpret the predicates 'wicked', 'virtuous', 'wise' and 'unwise'. Clearly Socrates and Hermogenes take these predicates to hold of whatever they hold in an absolute and objective way: by talking about a wise person they mean an *objectively* wise person. Then the argument is obviously valid: for Protagoras' doctrine is actually incompatible with the existence of (objectively) wise and unwise people. The notion of an (objectively) wise person is of course the notion of someone who has knowledge about some subject matter about which others are ignorant, and whose judgement on questions relative to that subject matter is to be authoritative. So, if someone is in this condition with regard to some subject matter (which in the case at issue is ethics), it cannot be the case that, with regard to *that* subject matter, whatever anyone believes is true for him; nor can it be the case, either, that, with regard to *any* subject matter, whatever anyone believes is true for him, as Protagoras claims.

Protagoras, however, would presumably contend that this valid argument is unsound; for he would dispute the premiss that some people are (objectively) virtuous and wise while others are (objectively) wicked and unwise. He would contend that being virtuous and wise, or wicked and unwise, is as subject-relative a matter as being hot or cold: those who seem virtuous and wise to Hermogenes and Socrates are merely so *for* them, but not absolutely or objectively. Then Protagoras would point out that if, on the other hand, the disputed premiss were recast in a form acceptable to him, i.e. as the thesis that *for some subject* some people are virtuous and wise, while others are wicked and unwise, and if the existence of wisdom and unwisdom (c6–7) were understood as the existence of wisdom and unwisdom for some subject, then Socrates' argument would no longer be valid; for it would no longer lead to the conclusion that Protagoras' doctrine is false.

This is the place to remark that the present argument is closely related to a relevant part of the *Theaetetus* discussion about relativism. There Socrates argues that the doctrine is incompatible with Protagoras' own claim to superior wisdom, destroys the possibility of specialist knowledge and dialectic, and equates the wisdom of humans and gods (161c–162c, 169a). Protagoras, in the apology pronounced on his behalf, replies that, although the beliefs of each subject are true for him, some beliefs are 'better' than others, and that the wise man knows how to substitute the better for the worse ones (166d–167d). This position is subsequently made more precise by Socrates: 'Man the Measure' holds as far as one's present perceptual experience and one's beliefs about moral or political matters are concerned, but does not hold for properties like being good for one's health, being advantageous, and in general whatever has to do with the future (171d–172b, 177c–179c).[94] Thus in *Tht.* Plato still holds that relativism has to come to terms with the existence of objective criteria of wisdom and expertise and cannot stand in a completely unrestricted form; only, there he says – more plausibly – that this retreat takes place not in ethics, as in *Cra.*, but in other conceptual areas. As with the theory of universal flux, so here *Cra.* makes a first stab at dealing with a major philosophical issue which will receive deeper, more thorough consideration in *Tht.*[95]

Before drawing a positive conclusion of the argument against Protagoras, Socrates seizes the opportunity of introducing another sophistical view which is somewhat akin to 'Man the Measure' and which Hermogenes ought to reject by the same token:

SO. Yet, I think, you don't either believe, in accordance with Euthydemus, that everything is in the same way for everyone, at the same time and always [πᾶσι πάντα ὁμοίως εἶναι ἅμα καὶ ἀεί]. For so too it wouldn't be the case that some are virtuous and others are wicked, if virtue and vice were always in the same way for everyone [εἰ ὁμοίως ἅπασι καὶ ἀεὶ ἀρετή τε καὶ κακία εἴη].
HE. That's true. (386d3–7)

The Euthydemus here at issue is no doubt the eponymous character of the *Euthydemus*, where he and his brother Dionysodorus are described

---

[94] This account of the *Tht.* discussion is not uncontroversial. See Burnyeat 1990: 19–42.
[95] See §§I.3.2, 9.1.4.

as shameless sophism-mongers.[96] The thesis Socrates is ascribing to him admits of at least two different interpretations.

Many commentators,[97] from Proclus (XLI, 13.13–18) onwards, take the datives πᾶσι and ἅπασι (d4–5), or at least the latter, as expressing *possession*. Then πάντα (d4) should mean 'all properties', and the whole thesis should amount to the following: all properties belong to everything (or perhaps everyone?) in the same way, at the same time and always.[98] I call this the Ontological Hotchpotch interpretation (OH):

(OH) $\forall x \, \forall y \, \forall F \, \forall t \, (x \text{ is } F \text{ at } t \leftrightarrow y \text{ is } F \text{ at } t).$

As a particular case, virtue and vice belong to everything (everyone?) in the same way, at the same time and always (d5–6). Therefore everyone is always simultaneously virtuous and wicked in the same respects and it cannot be the case that some are virtuous while others are wicked.

Others take the datives to express *relation* to a subject, i.e. point of view. Then the thesis is that everything (πάντα, understood quite generally) is *for* everyone (πᾶσι) in the same way at the same time and always. Here the expression 'for everyone' is parallel to Protagoras' 'for each person' (ἑκάστῳ). So, as Stallbaum 46 explains clearly,[99] on this interpretation Socrates is ascribing to Protagoras and Euthydemus two different brands of relativism. Protagoras' relativism is *individual*: for every x, x is F if and only if there is *some* person y such that x is F for y. Euthydemus' relativism is instead *collective*: for every x, x is F if and only if, for *every* person y, x is F for y. I call this the Collective Relativism interpretation: (CR). Here is how it goes more precisely:

(CR) $\forall x \, \forall F \, (x \text{ is } F \leftrightarrow \forall y \, \forall t \, (x \text{ is } F \text{ for } y \text{ at } t)).$

As a particular case, virtue and vice have whatever property they have for everyone and always (d5–6). It follows that everyone always *knows* that virtue and vice have whatever property they have, and hence (thanks to the 'virtue is knowledge' assumption, which was operating at 386b) that everyone is equally virtuous. So it cannot be the case that some people are virtuous while others are wicked.

This interpretation raises several questions. If it is correct, then on what grounds is Socrates ascribing (CR) to Euthydemus? Why does he add the specification 'at the same time and always', which has no parallel in

---

[96] Cf. Arist. *SE* 177b12–13, *Rh*. 1401a27–8, and Nails 152.
[97] Fowler; Reeve; Sprague 1962: 50; Kahn 1973a: 159; Sedley 2003: 55 and n.12; etc.
[98] With (OH) cf. *Dissoi Logoi* 90.5.3–5 DK.
[99] Cf. Dalimier 199 n.29.

Protagoras' case? And need the scope of this 'always' be understood as I have done? After all, the above formulation entails the apparently unpalatable consequence that, e.g., snow is white if and only if in 2009 Callias (who is long dead) knows that snow is white. To answer these questions we must compare *Euthd.* 293b–296d, where Euthydemus and his brother speciously argue that *everyone knows everything* (πάντες … πάντα ἐπίστανται 294a), if they know anything at all, and that Socrates himself *knows everything always and at the same time* (ἀεὶ … ἐπίστασθαι καὶ ἅμα πάντα 296c). It is natural to suppose that in *Cra.* Socrates is actually referring to this thesis, interpreting it in a relativistic sense and recasting it accordingly. The *Euthd.* passage also confirms my construal of the scope of Socrates' 'always': read how Euthydemus goes on at 296cd: 'Hence it's clear that you knew when you were a child and when you were being born and when you were being begotten; and even before you were born, and before heaven and earth came into being, you knew everything, if you always know. And, by Zeus, you will even always know everything, if I want so.'

So we have got two possible interpretations of the thesis here ascribed to Euthydemus: (OH) and (CR). Either way, the thesis turns out to be incompatible with the distinction between virtuous and wicked people and hence is refuted by the assumption that that distinction is sound. But the parallel with Protagoras' thesis and the *Euthd.* passage are not sufficient reasons for believing that (CR) is the correct interpretation. The next passage will provide further confirmation that this is so.

2.4.3 *Conclusion: objects have a stable being (386de)*

Socrates draws a positive conclusion from the refutation of Protagoras and Euthydemus:

SO. Then, if neither everything is for everyone in the same way at the same time and always, nor each thing is privately for each person [εἰ μήτε πᾶσι πάντα ἐστὶν ὁμοίως ἅμα καὶ ἀεί, μήτε ἑκάστῳ ἰδίᾳ ἕκαστον], it is clear that objects have some stable being of their own [αὐτὰ αὑτῶν οὐσίαν ἔχοντά τινα βέβαιόν ἐστι τὰ πράγματα]: they are not relative to us nor dragged up and down by us according to how they appear to us [οὐ πρὸς ἡμᾶς, οὐδὲ ὑφ' ἡμῶν ἑλκόμενα ἄνω καὶ κάτω τῷ ἡμετέρῳ φαντάσματι],[100] but are by themselves, relative to their own being as it is natural for them [ἀλλὰ καθ' αὑτὰ πρὸς τὴν αὑτῶν οὐσίαν ἔχοντα ἧπερ πέφυκεν]. (386d8–e4)

---

[100] ὑφ' ἡμῶν (e2) goes with the immediately following ἑλκόμενα. Fowler and Méridier, instead, print a comma after it and implausibly interpret it as 'caused by us' or 'depending on us' (cf. Dalimier).

In a nutshell, objects have an objective nature of their own. Before commenting on this, however, we must say something on the passage's first line and a half (d8–9), where Socrates again refers to the theses of Euthydemus and Protagoras. Here the parallel between the two expressions πᾶσι ... ὁμοίως and ἑκάστῳ ἰδίᾳ confirms that the former dative does not express possession but *relation*, as the latter does. So it is confirmed that (CR) was the correct interpretation of the thesis ascribed to Euthydemus.

To grasp the purport and scope of d9–e4 we must especially focus on the claim, at d9–e1, that *objects* have some *stable being* of their own. Each of the italicized words deserves some comment.

I start with 'stable'. We must be clear that here the adjective βέβαιος (cf. a4 βεβαιότητα) does not really express stability through time, as it often does (e.g. in the superficially similar context of 411c or at *Phd.* 90c). Here 'stable' is a metaphor for 'subject-independent, objective': cf. 'nor *dragged up and down* by us according to how they appear to us'.[101]

'Objects' (τὰ πράγματα) here is most naturally taken to be equivalent to '*everything*' (cf. d8 πάντα); for it is natural to take the definite article to have a generalizing force and the term πράγματα to be extremely generic, as it so often is. Such seemed to be the meaning of the expression in its previous occurrence at 386a2, within Socrates' presentation of Protagorean relativism, which here is no doubt being echoed; for there τὰ πράγματα picked up 385e4–5 τὰ ὄντα.[102]

The 'being' (οὐσία) of these 'objects', as we saw in §2.4.1, is something much more generic than their essence: it is *the way something is*, as distinct from the way it is perceived or believed to be. Now, however, we should like to know more precisely whether the claim that something has an objective 'being' amounts to the claim that *all* the properties of that thing are objective or to the claim that at least *some* are; and we should need a fine-grained distinction between different kinds of properties. But no such question is answered in the text.

Thus Socrates' conclusion is very general, in virtue of the broad reference to 'objects' and perhaps also of the generic claim that they have an objective 'being' or nature. Socrates' argument, however, was unable to establish so general a conclusion. For the distinction between virtuous and wicked, wise and unwise people proves that *something* has some objective

---

[101] See Burnyeat 1990: 49 n.64 and Ademollo (in preparation-3), and cf. 437a and Hdt. 7.50.2, where βέβαιον means 'certain'.
[102] On τὰ πράγματα as interchangeable with τὰ ὄντα see §3.1.1 n.3. Sedley 2003: 56–8 takes a different view: he understands τὰ πράγματα as '(some, most or all) things', where 'things' do not include, but are contrasted with, actions, which Socrates is going to talk about at e6–9.

properties, but not that *everything* does, let alone that *every* property of *everything* is objective. Presumably Plato here does not want to embark on the difficult task of proving that relativism is false all down the line and lets Socrates take a short cut, taking advantage of the fact that Hermogenes has already distanced himself from Protagoras (386a).

With this conclusion Socrates is now ready to start off a long and complex defence of naturalism. Indeed, the wording of our passage already contains a hint of the course Socrates is going to follow next. This is the expression 'as is *natural*' (e4), prominently placed at the end of the conclusion. It may seem pleonastic; but in fact it is a signal that Socrates is going to side with nature against convention in names.

Before plunging into the ensuing discussion it will be good to have a pause and momentarily leave the text of *Cra.* for some historical considerations about the origins of Hermogenes' conventionalist thesis. This will give us an opportunity to achieve a better grasp of certain distinctive features of the thesis itself.

2.5 BEFORE HERMOGENES

At 433de Socrates says that names might be thought to indicate objects in two ways. One is Cratylus' way; the other is that 'advocated by Hermogenes and *many others*, i.e. that names are conventional tokens'. This is a clear statement that there are 'many other' supporters of Hermogenes' thesis. So it seems convenient to sketch out the development of conventionalist ideas before Plato.

The roots of conventionalism probably lie in common, everyday experience. It is part of this experience to observe that *any* name the parents give their child will remain her name even when she has grown up, whether or not it succeeds in expressing her true nature.[103] As Socrates remarks at 397ab, many proper names of heroes and human beings 'have been set down in accordance with the names of some ancestors, without being appropriate to some of their bearers ... many others are imposed as though to express a wish'. It is also part of everyday experience to observe that people can change their names (or change those of other people, as in the case of slaves, invoked by Hermogenes at 384d); and presumably also to see that what holds of proper names may sometimes hold of other sorts of names as well. Reflection on the existence of languages other than Greek

---

[103] This sort of consciousness is also present in the tragic passages about characters 'bearing a false name' (ψευδώνυμοι): cf. n.61 above.

probably facilitated (though it did not strictly speaking entail: see §2.3) the rise of the idea that between a name and its referent there is no other tie than that established by a convention or custom among speakers.

2.5.1 Empedoclean and Thucydidean 'conventionalism'

Probably the earliest Presocratic philosopher who is known to have maintained something that goes in the direction of the conventionalist thesis is Empedocles, active around the middle of the fifth century BC. Here is fragment 31 B9 DK (= Plu. *Adv. Col.* 1113AB):

> When they [sc. the four roots] come to the air having been mixed in the form of a man, or in the form of the race of wild beasts, or of plants or of birds, then they call this to come into being, and when they are separated apart, this again they call wretched fate. They do not call these things as is right [ἣ θέμις <οὐ> καλέουσι], but I follow the custom and speak thus myself [νόμῳ δ' ἐπίφημι καὶ αὐτός]. (Trans. after KRS)

Here Empedocles says that what we ordinarily refer to as an organism's 'birth' or 'coming into being' should be rightly referred to as a certain 'being mixed together' of parts of the four roots, and what we ordinarily refer to as that organism's 'death' or 'perishing' should be rightly referred to as the 'separation' of those parts. The same point is also made in B8. As comparison with other fragments (B11, 12; Anaxag. 59 B17) makes clear, the reason why our ordinary expressions are not 'right' is that they carry with them the impossible idea of generation from, and destruction back into, what is not, whereas the four roots are eternal. Nevertheless, Empedocles says, 'I follow the custom and speak thus myself': that is to say, 'Provided it is recognized that the terms are not strictly accurate, that birth is really mingling and death separating, the conventional expressions may still be used' (Wright 1981: 176) – as Empedocles himself does at B17.1–13.

Empedocles' claims do entail that, generally speaking, it is possible for an expression to get purchase on its referent in a purely customary and conventional way; in this respect they are obviously relevant to Hermogenes' conventionalist thesis. We must, however, also pay attention to an important difference. Hermogenes' thesis is concerned with different *but synonymous* names imposed by different speakers, or groups of speakers, on one and the same thing. To take a paradigmatic example, cast in modern terms: the meaning which some decide to attach to the word 'human' others can legitimately decide to attach to the word 'horse' instead. So the sentence '*X* is a human' means, in the language of the first group of speakers, the same as the sentence '*X* is a horse' does in the language of the second group. The case considered by Empedocles is different. In his view, the sentence 'an X comes into being' is *not synonymous* with the sentence 'the four roots are mixed together in the form of an X', because the former conveys, while the latter does not, the thought that an X comes into being from what is not; and this is why the former is not 'right' while the latter is – a claim which has no parallel in the various formulations and examples of Hermogenes' thesis. In other words, Empedocles concerns himself with a case where the disagreement between the adherents of two alternative linguistic conventions is not merely linguistic but substantive. This sort of case is relevant to Hermogenes' thesis but does not straightforwardly exemplify it and is not explicitly taken into account in *Cra*.

Similar considerations hold for a famous passage where Thucydides (3.82.4–5), in the course of describing the internal struggles in the Greek cities during the Peloponnesian war, comments that

> People even changed, with their judgement of what was right, the customary assessment of which names were fit to be applied to the things [τὴν εἰωθυῖαν ἀξίωσιν τῶν ὀνομάτων ἐς τὰ ἔργα ἀντήλλαξαν τῇ δικαιώσει].[104] Reckless audacity came to be considered courage devoted to the party; prudent hesitation, fair-seeming cowardice; moderation, a cloak for unmanliness, and ability to understand all aspects of an issue, inaptness to act on any … In sum, one who forestalled another about to commit a crime was praised, as was one who exhorted another to commit a crime which the latter had not thought of.[105]

Here Thucydides seems to be making the following point. A complete upheaval in moral values led people to regard as wrong and blameworthy certain sorts of character or behaviour which are actually, and were previously regarded as, right and praiseworthy, and vice versa. This upheaval was manifested in a drastic change in the use of the terms belonging to the moral sphere: e.g. the adjective 'courageous' came to be applied to items which in fact were *not* courageous and would have been called otherwise within the framework of traditional morality.

Like the fragment of Empedocles which we discussed above, Thucydides' passage bears some relevance to a history of Hermogenes' conventionalist thesis; for it entails, strictly speaking, that names are conventional. If the factional speakers who applied 'courageous' to items which in fact were not courageous could successfully communicate with each other within the new moral and lexical framework, it follows that the term 'courageous' has no

---

[104] On the construal of the text here see Wilson (1982) and Worthington (1982), on whom I am trying to improve on the basis of a comparison with D. H. *Th*. 29.
[105] Translation partly after Crawley.

natural and necessary connection with the set of courageous items and can be made to apply to a different set of items instead, and hence, in the final analysis, that its connection with the set of courageous items is merely conventional. Like the Empedoclean fragment, however, the Thucydidean case differs from Hermogenes' thesis in one important respect. Hermogenes just concerns himself with the possibility of a change in names, i.e. in the linguistic *expression* of our concepts and beliefs, not in the concepts and beliefs expressed; he is interested in the *form* of our sayings, not in their content. If he were to draw examples from moral terminology, he would presumably say that, e.g., by a suitable convention about the meaning of 'right', the sentence 'Treachery is right' could be used to express the belief that treachery is wrong. In the Thucydidean situation, by contrast, the changes in names were the outcome, not of a new linguistic convention, but of changes in people's *beliefs*. It is not that people made the convention to use 'right' in place of 'wrong', 'courage' in place of 'rashness', etc.; they rather *came to believe* that certain items were right instead of wrong, courageous instead of rash, etc.

Plato is of course familiar with the sort of situation described by Thucydides. At *R.* 560c–561a, in describing the corruption of the oligarchic man's son, Socrates says that

> Those boastful discourses ... prevail in the conflict, and naming reverence 'folly' they thrust it out dishonourably as an exile, while calling temperance 'unmanliness' and abusing it they drive it out, and convincing him that measure and moderate expenditure are actually rusticity and illiberality they banish them with the help of many useless desires ... then they recall home insolence and anarchy and prodigality and shamelessness ... extolling them and calling them with fair names – calling violence 'good education', anarchy 'freedom', prodigality 'magnificence' and shamelessness 'courage'.

Strikingly, however, in *Cra.* no reference whatsoever is made to this sort of situation. The reason for this silence is presumably that Plato is alive to the difference between Hermogenes' thesis and the Thucydidean case and wants to avoid any confusion between the two.[106]

2.5.2 De natura hominis *and Democritus*

So far we have not identified a philosopher who can be *exactly* regarded as a supporter of Hermogenes' thesis. In fact, something that does look like a genuine conventionalist pronouncement, albeit limited to a particular

---

[106] *Pace* Barney 2001: 11–13, 36–41, who holds that the Thucydidean case is crucial to understand what, in Plato's view, is wrong about Hermogenes' conventionalism.

case, can be found in a Hippocratic treatise, *De natura hominis* (dated around the second half of the fifth century BC).[107] In ch. 5 the author contrasts the customary distinction among the names of the four humours – blood, phlegm, yellow bile and black bile – with the natural distinction among their characteristics:

> I say, first, that their names are distinct by custom [κατὰ νόμον τὰ οὐνόματα διωρίσθαι] and none of them has the same name as any other; further, that their characteristics are separate by nature [κατὰ φύσιν τὰς ἰδέας κεχωρίσθαι] and neither does phlegm resemble blood at all nor does blood resemble bile nor does bile resemble phlegm.

The reference to the four names' being distinct 'by custom', and not 'by nature', is so brisk and brief that it invites the supposition that when the treatise was written someone had already advanced the view that names are valid only 'by custom', and that here the author is voicing his own endorsement of this view and applying it to the particular case at hand.[108]

Then who was the first advocate of conventionalism in its genuine and general form? A possible candidate is Democritus, the first philosopher to be credited by our sources with a conventionalist thesis proper. Proclus, XVI, 6.20–7.6 (= 68 B26 DK = 129.1 Leszl) reports that

> Democritus said that names are by imposition [θέσει] and established this with four arguments. From homonymy: different objects are called by the same name, therefore the name is not by nature. From polyonymy: if different names will be appropriate to one and the same object, they will also be appropriate to one another, which is impossible [εἰ γὰρ τὰ διάφορα ὀνόματα ἐπὶ τὸ αὐτὸ καὶ ἓν πρᾶγμα ἐφαρμόσουσιν, καὶ ἐπ' ἄλληλα, ὅπερ ἀδύνατον]. Third, from the change of names: why did we change Aristocles' name into 'Plato' and Tyrtamus' into 'Theophrastus', if names are by nature? And from the lack of similar names: why do we say φρονεῖν from φρόνησις, but from δικαιοσύνη we no longer derive anything? Therefore names are by chance and not by nature. Democritus calls the first argument 'polysemic' [πολύσημον], the second 'balance' [ἰσόρροπον], < > and the fourth 'anonymous' [νώνυμον].

This text is too complex and difficult to be dealt with adequately here,[109] so I shall limit myself to a few jottings about the content of Democritus'

---

[107] See Jones 1931: xxvii–viii.
[108] Besides being very brief, the reference to the four names' being distinct 'by custom' is also incidental to the argument, indeed almost gratuitous. Its presence is probably due to the fact that it allows the author to deploy in one go two favourites of the late fifth-century style: the antithesis between what is 'by custom' and what is 'by nature' and the antithesis between what concerns 'names' and what concerns 'things' or 'deeds'. The final statement of *De arte* 2 (see §3.3.3) is similarly gratuitous in its context.
[109] Text and interpretation are discussed in Ademollo 2003, on which I am here improving in some respects.

alleged arguments, their authenticity, and their relation to *Cra*. A general caveat first: Proclus is a generally unreliable doxographer, inclined, in particular, to read full-blown arguments into texts which in fact contain nothing so definite.

The first argument, 'from homonymy', is a powerful one. The name by which Democritus dubbed it according to Proclus, however, is suspect, because the adjective πολύσημος is apparently not attested before the first century AD (Erot. 50.7–8 Klein). The argument has no parallel in our dialogue: interestingly, Plato here pays no attention to 'homonymy' or ambiguity, otherwise than in the *Euthydemus* (275d–278b). The closest he gets to it is at 418e–419a, where Socrates hints at the difference between δέον 'necessary' and δέον 'binding'. At 437a he does claim that the name ἐπιστήμη is ἀμφίβολον, 'ambiguous', because it admits of two possible and incompatible etymologies; but in fact he immediately goes on to claim that one of the two is superior to the other.

The second argument, 'from polyonymy', is hard to understand. The replies reported by Proclus, 7.6–13, and Ammonius, *in Int*. 37.28–38.16, suggest that the point is the following: if different names were naturally appropriate to one and the same object, then they would be the same name – which is impossible *ex hypothesi*. This interpretation, first advanced by Luce 1969b, is strikingly confirmed if we compare Common Notion 7 of the Euclidean *Elements*: τὰ ἐφαρμόζοντα ἐπ' ἄλληλα ἴσα ἀλλήλοις εἰσίν, 'Things that coincide with one another are equal to one another.'[110] At the same time this parallel obviously discredits the argument's authenticity, at least in its present form.

There might, nevertheless, be something authentic at the bottom of the argument; for ἰσόρροπον, its alleged Democritean name, is alien to traditional linguistic terminology[111] and is rather used in physical contexts (*Phd*. 109a) and figuratively (Th. 2.42.2, Arist. *EN* 1164b4). The argument might also have some connection with *Cra*., where Hermogenes refers to the lexical differences between Greek cities and between Greeks and barbarians (385de), and where (as we anticipated in §1.1.1) Socrates will explain how one and the same thing can have different, yet equally natural names in different languages (389d–390a) and will assume that this may

---

[110] Heath's (1926) translation. Heath suspected that Common Notion 7 might be an interpolation. This is not very relevant for my present purposes; the Notion is certainly known to Proclus, *in Euc*. 193.10–14, 196.15–26, although there he quotes it omitting ἐπ' ἄλληλα, hence in a form less similar to the alleged Democritean argument.

[111] Caution, however, is in order, because in some Christian writers ἰσόρροπος, applied to linguistic expressions, does seem to mean 'equivalent': see [Did. Caec.] *De trinitate* 2.5.15 and Epiph. *Ancoratus* 4.5, *Panarion* 69.32.

also hold within a single language ('Athena' / 'Pallas', 406d–407c), as the replies reported by Proclus and Ammonius insist.

The third argument, 'from the change of names', for which Proclus' MSS do not report a Democritean denomination, is again a very strong one. It is reminiscent of Hermogenes' claim that any individual speaker can arbitrarily change the names of things, 'as when we change the name of our slaves' (384d); and you will remember that commenting on that claim Proclus (xxx, 10.23–6) ascribes to Hermogenes essentially the same argument. Strictly speaking, however, neither this coincidence nor the fact that the two examples adduced in the text (the names 'Plato' and 'Theophrastus') must be post-Democritean prove that the argument is a Proclan forgery.

The fourth argument, 'from the lack of similar names', is certainly spurious, because it is shaped by two post-Democritean influences: Aristotle's treatment of paronymy at *Cat.* 8.10a27–b11 and the grammatical debate on analogy in the Hellenistic and Roman age (cf. *Var. L.* 8.54, 57, 61; S. E. *M.* 1.199, 216–17). Nevertheless, the argument's alleged name, νώνυμον, might well be authentic; for it is a pretty rare term, attested only in poetry (e.g. Hom. *Od.* 13.239, Aesch. *Pers.* 1003, Soph. *El.* 1084, *AP* 7.17)[112] and in related exegetical literature, hence not a term which Proclus or another late author would naturally use, let alone ascribe to Democritus. Of course it is difficult to reconstruct the context in which this term originally occurred. Perhaps Democritus made a point about the way in which hitherto nameless things receive a name first: any such thing bears the name that happens to be imposed on it, whatever it is.[113] This might have a connection with Hermogenes' thesis, where (H2) advanced arbitrary (individual) imposition as an argument in support of (H1)'s advocacy of convention and agreement: 384d 'For it seems to me that, whatever name one imposes on something, this is its correct name.'

So there might be an authentic kernel in Proclus' report, spurious though several details may be; and this kernel might have something to do with the nature/convention debate as it is presented in *Cra.* Now it so happens that several passages in the etymologies of *Cra.* appear to presuppose knowledge of Democritean doctrines (see §§5.3.1–3). Such correspondences lend some solid ground to the hypothesis that there might be some relation between Hermogenes and Democritus. But whether this is actually the case, and, if so, what exactly the relation is, remains beyond our ken.

---

[112] Cf. the variant spelling νώνυμνος: e.g. Hom. *Il.* 12.70, Hes. *Op.* 154, Pi. *O.* 10.51.
[113] Cf. Barnes 1982: 168.

CHAPTER 3

Naturalism defended (386e–390e)

In chapter 2 I analysed Socrates' first reactions to Hermogenes' thesis and argued that down to 386d2, where the rejection of Protagoras' relativist doctrine is accomplished, Socrates displays no hostile attitude towards conventionalism. In the sequel, however, what might have seemed just an inquiry into Hermogenes' attitude to Protagoras turns out to have been also, at the same time, the first step of a long and complex defence of naturalism and attack on conventionalism, which will end in 390de with the conclusion that Cratylus is right and Hermogenes is wrong. Our next task is to explore the structure, content and purpose of the arguments which Socrates advances here.

3.1 FIRST ARGUMENT: THE NATURALNESS OF ACTIONS (386E–387D)

3.1.1 *The naturalness of actions. Cutting and burning (386e–387b)*

Socrates' next and crucial step is to argue that *actions* have an objective nature:

SO. Could it then be the case that the objects themselves [αὐτά] have such a nature, while the actions belonging to them [αἱ δὲ πράξεις αὐτῶν] aren't in the same condition? Or aren't these too, I say actions, one kind of beings [ἕν τι εἶδος τῶν ὄντων]?
HE. Of course they are too.
SO. Therefore actions too are performed according to their nature, not according to our judgement [κατὰ τὴν αὐτῶν ἄρα φύσιν καὶ αἱ πράξεις πράττονται, οὐ κατὰ τὴν ἡμετέραν δόξαν]. (386e6–387a2)

Essentially, I take Socrates to be simply arguing, in accordance with the conclusion of Protagoras' refutation (386de), that actions have an objective nature because everything does.[1] But this is compatible with more than one analysis of the inference's details.

Here is a first stab. In the previous lines, according to the interpretation set forth in §2.4.3, Socrates has just ascribed an objective nature to 'the objects' (τὰ πράγματα) quite generally. Now he exploits the ambiguity of the term 'objects' and takes it to mean, specifically, *objects as opposed to actions* (cf. c10 πρᾶξις ... περὶ τὰ πράγματα).[2] So at e6–7 he asks – clearly suggesting a negative answer – whether it could be the case that objects have an objective nature while actions do not. Then, in order to back up the suggestion that actions too have an objective nature, he remarks that actions too, sc. like objects, are 'one kind of beings' (e7–8). Thereby he hints at the following syllogism:

All beings have an objective nature;
Actions are one kind of beings;
Therefore actions have an objective nature.

This talk of 'beings' seems to replace the generic talk of 'objects' at d8–e4,[3] now that the phrase τὰ πράγματα has acquired a specific meaning.[4]

This analysis has left open the question of the phrase αἱ ... πράξεις αὐτῶν (e6–7), for which I have borrowed from Sedley 2003: 56–8 the translation 'the actions belonging to them'. Socrates' treatment of the ensuing examples rules out the apparently obvious interpretation 'their

[1] Cf. Ackrill 1994: 38.
[2] For this contrast between πρᾶγμα and πρᾶξις cf. e.g. *Sph.* 262e.
[3] τὰ πράγματα interchangeable with τὰ ὄντα: 383a4–5 + 390d11–e1, 385e4–5 + 386a2 (most relevant here), 387a2–3 + c1, 411b, 420c, 435d–436b, 438c–439a, 440cd (featuring also τὰ χρήματα); *Phd.* 99de; etc. Those in the know call this sort of phenomenon *Synonymenwechsel*: cf. the examples in Lapini 1997: 81.
[4] Sedley 2003: 56–7 and n.15 proposes a completely different reconstruction. In his view, at e6–7 Socrates' point is not that actions have an objective nature because everything does; the point, to be fully explained by way of example at 387a, is rather that 'if X has its own nature, then any action which is a way of dealing with X has its own nature ... Actions ... get their own nature derivatively from the things *in relation to which* the agent acts'. This interpretation is confronted with three difficulties. (i) The a1–2 conclusion, 'therefore actions too are performed according to their nature, not according to our judgement', does not have conditional form and seems unrestricted. (ii) The cutting example does not take into account the object's nature, which comes into question only with the burning example: see text below. (iii) Sedley's interpretation entails that the e7–8 question, 'Aren't actions too one kind of beings?' does not amount to the minor premiss of the syllogism I have reconstructed in the main text; the point of e7–8 is rather 'to establish that, since actions are ὄντα, "things that there *are*", they have their own "being" (οὐσία), and hence can be included under the description of things with their own nature as having that nature "not relative to us ... but having an intrinsic natural relation *to their own being* (οὐσία)' (cf. Stallbaum 48). Thereby Sedley seems to make e7–8 into *another*, independent argument for the thesis that actions have an objective nature – and a bad argument at that. For from the mere fact that actions are ὄντα it follows that they have an οὐσία, not that they have an *objective* οὐσία: witness 385e, where Socrates asked whether τὰ ὄντα are such that their οὐσία is private to everyone.

The naturalness of actions (386e–387d)

actions', i.e. 'the actions they perform',⁵ and suggests rather that the meaning should be 'the actions concerning them' (cf. c10), i.e. 'the actions performed *on* them'. But the genitive αὐτῶν is a very odd way of expressing this.⁶ So it may be worthwhile to consider an alternative construal, which consists in taking αὐτῶν as a *partitive* genitive: 'those among them which are actions'.⁷ On this construal, Socrates does not trade on the ambiguity of τὰ πράγματα, which still retains its generic meaning, and explicitly presents actions as included among 'objects'. If he also says that actions are 'one kind of beings' (e7–8), this may be just an innocent terminological variation like those cited in n.3, or it may be due to the fact that at 387cd Socrates is in any case going to reserve πράγματα for the objects of the actions.

However that may be, the purport of Socrates' point about actions is rather vague: how exactly is the talk of a 'nature' of actions to be understood? There are certain ambiguities lurking here, which will prove crucial as the argument goes on. For the moment let us read on. Socrates gives the example of the action of cutting something:

(SO.) E.g., if we try to cut some of the beings [ἐάν τι ἐπιχειρήσωμεν ἡμεῖς τῶν ὄντων τέμνειν], shall we cut each one as we want and with that with which we want [ὡς ἂν ἡμεῖς βουλώμεθα καὶ ᾧ ἂν βουληθῶμεν]; or rather, if we want to cut each thing according to the nature of cutting and being cut and with that with which it is natural [ἐὰν μὲν κατὰ τὴν φύσιν βουληθῶμεν ἕκαστον τέμνειν τοῦ τέμνειν τε καὶ τέμνεσθαι καὶ ᾧ πέφυκε], then we'll cut and achieve something [τεμοῦμέν τε καὶ πλέον τι ἡμῖν ἔσται] and do this correctly [ὀρθῶς], whereas if we want to do it against nature [παρὰ φύσιν], then we'll make a mistake and get nothing done [ἐξαμαρτησόμεθά τε καὶ οὐδὲν πράξομεν]?

HE. This is how it seems to me. (387a2–b1)

Socrates here seems to be claiming, quite reasonably, that cutting something is a definite action, different from, say, tearing or breaking something; and that, therefore, for a particular action to count as an instance of cutting something, it must necessarily be performed in a certain way and with a certain kind of tool, which are somehow determined by the nature of the action itself.

---

⁵ *Pace* Méridier 54–5 n.3, in what follows there is no question of actions performed *by* objects: cf. n.11.

⁶ Cf. perhaps Th. 2.79.1 τῇ τῶν Πλαταιῶν ἐπιστρατείᾳ, 'the expedition *against* the Plataeans'.

⁷ Cf. *Tht.* 157a τὸ ποιοῦν ... καὶ τὸ πάσχον αὐτῶν, Th. 4.126.3 τοῖς Μακεδόσιν αὐτῶν, and KG 1.337–8. If neither construal of αὐτῶν seems acceptable we might consider correcting it into αὐτοῖς: 'in the same way *as they are*'.

There are two points which it is important to make about these lines. First, we must be clear that Socrates, insofar as he contrasts the case where 'we'll cut something and achieve something and do this correctly' with the case where 'we'll make a mistake and get nothing done' (a7–9), limits himself to the basic, radical alternative between *succeeding* and *not succeeding* in cutting something. The expression 'we'll do this correctly' (a7–8) means, in this context, 'we'll do this successfully', 'we'll succeed in doing this'; the adverb 'correctly' is, strictly speaking, redundant, exactly like the adjective 'correct' in the phrase 'the correct name of *X*', in accordance with the Redundancy Conception of correctness which is operating in *Cra.* (see §I.1.1). Thus Socrates does not mention (although he does not exclude either) the existence of a scale of *better and worse* ways of cutting something. This idea – with which Plato is obviously familiar[8] – will receive no consideration in any of Socrates' subsequent arguments in favour of naturalism, as we shall see in due course, and will finally surface only much later in the dialogue, in the course of Socrates' discussion with Cratylus (429a).

The second point to be made concerns the level of generality of the conditions of the action's success. Consider Socrates' reference to 'the nature of cutting and being cut' (a5–6). Thereby Socrates seems to refer to the *generic* nature of cutting and being cut, i.e. what it is for *X* to cut *Y* and for *Y* to be cut by *X* quite generally. He is rightly assuming that there is a very close relationship between the two; in effect, it is obvious that the conditions for *X* to cut *Y* are met if and only if the conditions for *Y* to be cut by *X* are also met. Then consider a6–7 'with that with which it is natural', sc. to cut and to be cut. This is how I, like most translators, understand the Greek ᾧ πέφυκε, taking the verb as impersonal.[9] In the present context this construal is required by the previous mention of 'the nature of cutting and being cut'. Theoretically, however, πέφυκε *might* also have a definite subject, i.e. 'each thing' (a4); the meaning would then be 'with that with which it is natural for each thing', sc. to cut and to be cut, and this would introduce into Socrates' claims a new element, i.e. the idea of the nature *of the object involved*. See what happens in the next example:

so. Hence also if we try to burn something, we must not burn it according to any old judgement, but according to the right one; and this is as it is natural

---

[8] Cf. *R.* 352e–353a: although you could cut a vine-branch with a knife and a carver and many other tools, with none would you cut it as finely (οὕτω καλῶς) as with the pruning hook that has been made for this purpose. This is therefore the pruning hook's function: for the function of each thing is what can be done either only or *most finely* (κάλλιστα) with it.

[9] Cf. e.g. *Ti.* 81e, Dem. 14.30, X. *Cyn.* 6.15.

for each thing to be burnt and to burn it, and with that with which it is natural [ᾗ ἐπεφύκει ἕκαστον κάεσθαί τε καὶ κάειν καὶ ᾧ ἐπεφύκει]?[10]

HE. It is so.
SO. Hence this holds of the other cases too?
HE. Certainly. (387b2–7)

Socrates started out with the alternative between cutting something according to the generic nature of cutting something and altogether failing to cut it. But now, as the position of 'each thing' (b4)[11] shows, he has seamlessly moved to the alternative between burning something according to *that thing's* specific nature and altogether failing to burn it. This new formulation seems more complete than the previous one, which identified necessary but not sufficient conditions for the action's success: if you have to cut a tree, using a butter knife will not help, although a butter knife is a tool for cutting and you use it in the appropriate way. So the object's own nature must also be taken into account.

Let me try to bring out more clearly and rigorously the difference between Socrates' treatment of cutting and his treatment of burning. His claims about cutting could be seen as instantiating the following schema:

(A) $\exists R \, \forall x \, \forall y \, (x \text{ performs } \Phi \text{ on } y \rightarrow x \text{ bears } R \text{ to } y)$,

where R is a complex relation which compendiously corresponds to Socrates' reference to the way in which, and the tool with which, it is natural to perform the action Φ. Socrates' claims on burning could instead be seen as instantiating a different schema:

(B) $\forall y \, \exists R \, \forall x \, (x \text{ performs } \Phi \text{ on } y \rightarrow x \text{ bears } R \text{ to } y)$.

A final note on cutting and burning. The association between these two actions can hardly be accidental, given that cutting and burning are two constantly associated surgical practices: see *Grg.* 456b, 479a; *R.* 406d; Heracl. 22 B58 DK; Aesch. *Ag.* 849; etc. Here Socrates is certainly employing both verbs with an eye to their technical use, thereby reinforcing his

---

[10] Here at b4 and at 389a7–8, b10–c1, c6, in place of ἐπεφύκει (literally 'it *was* natural') some editors, with the partial support of some secondary MSS, print πέφυκε ('it *is* natural'), which occurred at a7 and will return at c1 and d4. But ἐπεφύκει is certainly sound and must probably be understood as equivalent to a sort of timeless present: cf. *Tht.* 156a τὸ πᾶν κίνησις ἦν and perhaps also the Aristotelian τὸ τί ἦν εἶναι, and read Alex. Aphr. *in Top.* 42.4–8. De Vries's (1955: 292–3) alternative suggestion that ἐπεφύκει is rather like a retrospective imperfect (like c10 ἦν and perhaps d10–388a2 ἔδει, see n.26), looking back to a7 πέφυκε, is less convincing, because the connection with a7 would be loose and because it seems difficult to explain in the same way the 389ac occurrences.

[11] ἕκαστον is subject of κάεσθαι but *object* of κάειν, not subject of both verbs as some interpreters believe: cf. 387c1–2, d4–5.

claim that an action must be performed in a natural way, and indeed hinting at the notion of *art*, which the argument is to introduce later on. Since, however, in the text the object of 'cutting' and 'burning' is a very generic 'some of the beings' or just 'something' (cf. *Grg.* 476c), the generic meaning of both verbs seems to remain dominant.

3.1.2 Speaking (387bc)

Now Socrates takes an important step in this analogical argument by shifting to the linguistic field:

SO. Speaking [τὸ λέγειν] too is one among actions, isn't it?
HE. Yes.
SO. So will one speak correctly, if one speaks as one thinks one ought to [ᾗ ἂν τῳ δοκῇ λεκτέον εἶναι, ταύτῃ λέγων ὀρθῶς λέξει]? Or rather, if one speaks as it is natural to speak of the objects, and for them to be spoken of, and with that with which it is natural [ᾗ πέφυκε τὰ πράγματα λέγειν τε καὶ λέγεσθαι καὶ ᾧ], then one'll achieve something and speak, otherwise one'll make a mistake and get nothing done [ἐξαμαρτήσεταί τε καὶ οὐδὲν ποιήσει]?
HE. I think it is as you say. (387b8–c5)

What does λέγειν mean here? Since in the 385bd passage about truth and falsity the λόγος was the declarative sentence (see §2.2.1), and λέγειν meant 'speaking' in the very special sense of *stating* or asserting, here the verb is likely to have the same meaning. λέγειν τὰ πράγματα will then mean 'to speak *of* the objects' in the sense of saying or stating something *about* them.[12]

The words 'as it is natural to speak of the objects, and for them to be spoken of, and with that with which it is natural' (c1–2) are crucially ambiguous between two possible interpretations. (a) Socrates may be claiming that, if you are to speak of something quite generally, you must conform to the way in which, and use the tool with which, it is natural to speak of anything; otherwise you will not speak of anything at all. Then he is talking about the *generic* nature of the activity of speaking of something, and his claims, like those about cutting, instantiate schema (A) of the two we distinguished in §3.1.1. (b) Alternatively, Socrates may be claiming that, if you are to speak of something, you must conform to the way in which, and use the tool with which, it is natural to speak of *that* thing; otherwise you will not speak of that thing – and *pro tanto* you will not speak of anything – at all. Then his claims involve a reference to the nature of

---

[12] On λέγειν + acc. meaning 'to speak/say *of* something' see ch. 2 n.30.

each thing spoken of and, like the earlier ones about burning, instantiate schema (B).[13]

It seems clear that we are meant to choose (b) over (a), in the first instance at least, as an interpretation of what Socrates says. For the burning example comes immediately before our lines and is therefore closer than the cutting example; and the reference to the specific nature of the object spoken of makes (b) closer to Cratylus' thesis, which is about to be at stake in the ensuing lines about naming (387cd) and is what Socrates will in the end aver he has demonstrated (390de).

This choice has relevant philosophical consequences. If we adopted (a), Socrates' claims would turn out to be quite reasonable. Speaking, by its very nature, is done with sentences, not knives or drills. Furthermore, there seem some natural constraints upon the ways in which we can put words together to speak of something. E.g., if you want to say something about Callias, expressions like 'Callias is an often' or 'Callias are the' will not do, because they are not grammatical sentences, whereas expressions like 'Callias is white' or 'Callias walks' are all right. And however you may want to spell out this distinction between grammatical and ungrammatical sentences, it seems reasonable to hold that there is something objective and natural at the bottom of it.

By contrast, Socrates' claims are much more problematic on interpretation (b). What should be meant by the claim that to speak of something you must necessarily speak of it in the way and with the tool which are appropriate to *its* own nature, otherwise you will not speak of that thing at all? Here is one likely answer (for which cf. Denyer 1991: 70): you must speak of something by describing it as it really is, ascribing to it features it does possess – in other words, saying something *true* of it. Of course this is utterly mistaken as a philosophical thesis, because it is perfectly possible to speak of something while saying something false of it. Socrates is apparently not alive to the peculiarity of that very special sort of action which is making a statement. More precisely, the difference he seems to miss is the following. Such actions as cutting or burning are, as it were, one-valued, because you either succeed in performing them or altogether fail to perform them; making a statement is instead two-valued, because the success case falls into two subcases, one where the statement is true and another where the statement is false, which belong together as against the failure

---

[13] Either way, Socrates does not say that 'speaking can be done ... well or badly' or that 'speaking can be done naturally and correctly ... or unnaturally and incorrectly' (Sedley 2003: 57, 59). Here as with the other actions, the antithesis is the radical one between success and failure in performing the action; in the latter case the action is *not performed at all*.

case, where you altogether fail to make a statement. Granted, in the case of cutting and burning too the success case admits of a further distinction, as we saw in §3.1.1: the action may be performed better or worse. But this does not make Socrates' present claims any more acceptable. Cutting or burning something well (or badly) comes in a continuous scale of degrees, whereas there are exactly two kinds of statement, the true and the false, as we should know since 385b. Furthermore, what Socrates said of cutting and burning was in fact compatible with there being better and worse ways of cutting and burning, whereas what he is saying now seems incompatible with there being false statements.

So interpretation (b) seems to make Socrates guilty of a serious philosophical confusion between the conditions for speaking of something and the conditions for speaking of it truly. This confusion plays a crucial role in the sophistical arguments designed to prove the thesis that false speaking and contradiction are impossible, which Plato discusses several times in his works.[14] In particular, in our very dialogue Socrates will suggest that Cratylus' linguistic naturalism somehow entails that false speaking is impossible, and after Cratylus has tried to support this consequence by recourse to a stock argument, Socrates will refute him (429b–431c).

What I have been saying so far has a very important consequence. If Socrates is, as a matter of fact, holding that to speak of something you must speak of it truly, and hence that it is impossible to speak falsely, then Plato cannot mean what Socrates says. We must suppose that here Plato is deliberately making Socrates hold a mistaken view, which he will later make him reject. This should cause us no surprise. Bear in mind that we are inside the first of a series of arguments in defence of naturalism, which will eventually lead Socrates to the conclusion that 'Cratylus tells the truth when he says that names belong to the objects by nature' (390de) – a conclusion which Socrates will at least partially reject at the end of the day, when he acknowledges that convention plays a part in the correctness of names (435ac). Therefore on *any* interpretation of the dialogue Plato, the dialogue's author, must know that something is wrong with the arguments for naturalism he has Socrates, the character, put forward. This is all the more so on my own interpretation, on which Plato actually believes that the correctness of names is *entirely* conventional (see §8.1.5).

All this fits in very well with a general way of reading Plato, to which I am sympathetic, according to which Plato exploits the dialogue form to invite his readers to engage actively in the discussion, as if they were

[14] Cf. §§2.2.5, 7.2.2, 7.2.4.

The naturalness of actions (386e–387d)

present to it, by assessing the theses and arguments presented and thinking out for themselves the philosophical problems at stake.[15] To quote Grote's (1888: III.333) words, 'The Platonic dialogues require, in order to produce their effect, a supplementary responsive force, and a strong effective reaction, from the individual reason of the reader.' This strategy can be seen at work in several early dialogues and in works like the *Euthydemus*, the *Parmenides* and the *Theaetetus*. As we read on we shall see how it operates in the remainder of the present argument and of the whole dialogue; for the moment we can suppose that Plato expects us, the readers, to criticize Socrates' claims on speaking as we have just done and to appreciate how different it would be if (a), instead of (b), represented what Socrates means.

3.1.3 Naming (387cd)

Then Socrates moves on from sentences to names. He introduces the action of naming as a 'part' of that of speaking:[16]

SO. Hence naming is a part of speaking [τοῦ λέγειν μόριον τὸ ὀνομάζειν]? For it is, I think, by naming that people speak sentences [ὀνομάζοντες[17] γάρ που λέγουσι τοὺς λόγους].
HE. Of course. (387c6–8)

Socrates' question seems so obscure to Proclus that he dwells at length (XLV, 14.10–30) on its explanation. The construal he suggests first is the right one. We saw already in §3.1.2 that it is reasonable to see a connection between the λέγειν of these lines and the λόγος of 385bd; and surely ὀνομάζειν (naming) is here said to be a μόριον (part) of λέγειν in the same sense in which the ὄνομα (name) was there said to be a μόριον of λόγος. So it is confirmed that λέγειν is speaking in the sense of stating or asserting; and naming is a part of speaking in the sense that 'Speaking is a complex action, one ingredient of which is naming (i.e. using names), since it is by using names as building blocks that people speak sentences.'[18] Indeed, as at 385bd it was tempting to ascribe to Socrates the view that *all* the

---

[15] See e.g. Frede 1992a and Burnyeat 2000b.
[16] According to Schofield 1972, 385b2–d1 should be read exactly here, between 387c5 and c6: see §2.2.5.
[17] ὀνομάζοντες is the reading of βδ, adopted by all editors except Burnet; T has καὶ διονομάζοντες, whence Burnet draws διονομάζοντες, whose meaning however ('to distribute names, distinguish things by names' at *Plt.* 263d) seems not to fit in well with the present context.
[18] Schofield 1972: 249. Cf. Ackrill 1994: 41, Sedley 2003: 59 and n.19. A different, mistaken interpretation, which coincides with the third mentioned by Proclus, is advanced by Fowler and Méridier: 'naming is a part of speaking, for in naming ... people utter speech'.

'smallest' parts of λόγος are ὀνόματα, so here it is tempting to understand that the making of a statement consists *only* of several acts of naming, connected to each other in some way which is not specified.

We can now see how Socrates goes on. First come two resumptive premisses:

SO. Hence naming too is a sort of action, given that speaking too is, as we saw, a sort of action concerning the objects?
HE. Yes.
SO. And actions appeared to us not to be relative to us, but to have some proper nature of their own?
HE. It is so. (387c9–d3)

Then the conclusion:

SO. Hence one must also name the objects as it is natural to name them and for them to be named and with that with which it is natural [ὀνομαστέον ᾗ πέφυκε τὰ πράγματα ὀνομάζειν τε καὶ ὀνομάζεσθαι καὶ ᾧ], not as we want [ἀλλ' οὐχ ᾗ ἂν ἡμεῖς βουληθῶμεν], if there is to be any consistency with our previous agreements? And so we would achieve something and name, otherwise we wouldn't [οὕτω μὲν ἂν πλέον τι ποιοῖμεν καὶ ὀνομάζοιμεν, ἄλλως δὲ οὔ]?
HE. So it seems to me. (387d4–9)

Socrates' claims here present the same ambiguity as the earlier ones about speaking. Socrates might be following schema (A),[19] as in the cutting example and in interpretation (a) of the speaking example, and making just the very general point that, if you are to name something, you must conform to the way in which, and use the kind of tool with which, it is natural to name anything; otherwise you will not name anything at all. E.g., to name something you must produce a string of written marks or vocal sounds, this string must refer to something, and you must produce it with the intention of referring to something; if any of these conditions is not satisfied your act does not count as an instance of your naming something. This would no doubt be a sensible point to make, but it is clearly not what Socrates primarily means here. Clearly the two alternatives he is contrasting are meant to correspond respectively to Cratylus' naturalist thesis about names and to Hermogenes' conventionalist one.[20] Therefore the nature of *each* thing named is in question, and what Socrates primarily means is an instance of schema (B), as in the burning example and in the speaking example, interpretation (b). If you are to name something, you

---

[19] See §3.1.1.   [20] *Pace* Ketchum 1979: 136, Ackrill 1994: 40.

cannot name it 'as you want', as Hermogenes holds; you must name it in the way in which, and with the tool (i.e. the name) with which, it is natural to name *that* thing, as Cratylus holds, otherwise you will not name it – and *pro tanto* you will not name anything – at all.[21]

So interpreted, Socrates' argument is fallacious, because from the true premiss that actions have an objective nature of their own it draws the false Cratylan conclusion that each thing can be named only in accordance with its nature. The fallacy seems to lie in the indiscriminate move from the idea of a generic naturalness of actions to the idea of an object-dependent naturalness: from schema (A) to schema (B). This move is admissible in some cases, like cutting and burning, but not in others, like speaking and naming. You can't *cut* a tree with a butter knife; but you can *call* it 'butter knife' – provided you have previously made the appropriate convention.

So far so good. Things, however, might be more complicated than that. Perhaps it is not just that Socrates, misled by the analogy with cutting and burning, inadvertently slips from schema (A) to schema (B) also as regards stating and naming. For there seems to be some sense in which schema (B) does, after all, apply to naming; and identifying such a sense, or senses, might contribute to explaining why Socrates goes astray or even constitute a positive lesson which we are expected to derive from the argument upon reflection.

To start with, note that at 387d Socrates does not explicitly claim that what is natural about the act of naming has to do with the name's *etymology*. Of course Socrates' 384c guess about what Cratylus might have meant in denying that 'Hermogenes' is Hermogenes' name, and our advance knowledge of the discussion's further developments, press us to assume that this is so; and the assumption may well be right as far as Socrates himself is concerned. But the fact remains that what he says is very generic and might admit of different interpretations.

One alternative interpretation might focus on the relation between a general term (or *common name*, as tradition has it) and each of the particulars it is true of, whose set constitutes its extension – the relation between, say, 'human being' and Callias. Plato does not use different terminology

---

[21] Contrast Baxter (1992: 40): 'Socrates ... is able to accept that bits of speech that refer yet fail to describe adequately or at all are still names; the very analogies he uses, crafts in which there are good, bad and indifferent practitioners, show that a like scale of achievement in naming is to be assumed.' *At this stage* Socrates says nothing like that; throughout the argument (see already §§3.1.1, 3.1.2 and n.13, 3.4.3 and n.103) he concentrates on the radical antithesis between the natural, successful performance and the unnatural, arbitrary, unsuccessful one.

to distinguish between a general term's referring to a certain kind or form ('human being' refers to the human being) and its having a certain extension, i.e. being true of certain particulars ('human being' is true of Callias). He says that a general term is a *name* both of the form it refers to ('human being' *names* the human being) and of the particulars in its extension ('human being' *names* Callias).[22] Now, if you are to 'name' a given particular (e.g. Callias) by means of a general term, obviously you shall succeed only if you use a term (e.g. 'human', 'white', 'Athenian', 'wealthy' etc.) that connotes one of the particular's properties and hence a part of its nature, broadly understood. In this sense it is perfectly right to say that 'one must name as it is natural to name the objects and for them to be named and with that with which it is natural, but not as we want'; and again this is perfectly compatible with Hermogenes' conventionalism.[23]

The relevance of this way of reading Socrates' conclusion is brought out by two later passages. One is 393b–394a, where Socrates claims, among other things, that things must be called by names (general terms) corresponding to the kind they *naturally* belong to: the offspring of a horse must be called 'horse'; but if a horse begets a calf, which is the natural offspring of an ox, it must not be called 'colt' but 'calf'.[24] The other passage is 430a–431c, where Socrates defends the possibility of applying names to things incorrectly or falsely by describing a case in which what is actually at stake is the application of general terms to particular things (in his example, the application either of the term 'man' or of the term 'woman' to an individual man).

Anyway, according to one, superficial level of reading, at 387d we reach the conclusion of a first argument against Hermogenes, which has been unfolding since the discussion of the relations between Hermogenes' and Protagoras' theses at 385e ff. This is clearly what Socrates thinks he is doing; and it is also Proclus' view (XLVI, 15.1–26; cf. XLVIII, 16.25–6). Socrates, however, does not yet claim that Hermogenes' admissions are incompatible with his conventionalist theory; he rather moves on to a new argument. Let us follow him.

---

[22] *Phd.* 78e, *Ti.* 52a: particulars are ὁμώνυμα to (i.e. have the *same name* as) the forms. *Phd.* 102b, *Prm.* 130e: particulars have the ἐπωνυμία of (i.e. are *named after*) the forms they participate in. *R.* 596b: we posit one form περὶ ἕκαστα τὰ πολλά, οἷς ταὐτὸν ὄνομα ἐπιφέρομεν ('for each plurality of things to which we apply the *same name*'; see ch. 9 n.47). *Sph.* 251ab: saying of a particular human being (see Frede 1967: 62 and Crivelli, forthcoming) that he is human, is good, has a certain colour, shape and size, etc., amounts to calling him πολλοῖς ὀνόμασι ('by several *names*').

[23] Cf. Gaiser 1974: 34–5.

[24] Cf. Gold 1978: 240–1.

3.2 SECOND ARGUMENT: THE FUNCTION OF NAMES (387D–388C)

3.2.1 Names as instruments (387d–388c)

Socrates starts off his second argument by questioning Hermogenes about the instrument *with which* each activity is performed:

SO. Come on now [Φέρε δή]:[25] what one has to cut one has to cut, we say, with something [ὃ ἔδει τέμνειν, ἔδει τῳ, φαμέν, τέμνειν]?[26]
HE. Yes.
SO. And what one has to pin-beat [κερκίζειν][27] one has to pin-beat with something? And what one has to drill one has to drill with something?
HE. Of course.
SO. And what one has to name one has to name with something?
HE. It is so.
SO. And what was that with which one has to drill?
HE. A drill.
SO. And what was that with which one has to pin-beat?
HE. A pin-beater [κερκίς].
SO. And what was that with which one has to name?
HE. A name.
SO. Right. Therefore the name too is an instrument [ὄργανον ἄρα τί ἐστι καὶ τὸ ὄνομα]. (387d10–388a8).

Having thus got Hermogenes to agree that the name too is a kind of instrument, Socrates introduces the notion of the *function* of each instrument:

SO. Then if I asked: 'What kind of instrument is the pin-beater?', you would answer: 'That with which we pin-beat', wouldn't you?
HE. Yes.
SO. And what do we do when we pin-beat? We separate [διακρίνομεν] the weft and the warp which are confused, don't we?
HE. Yes.
SO. Then you'll be able to answer in the same way as regards a drill and the other instruments?
HE. Of course. (388a10–b6)

---

[25] Φέρε δή (387d10) confirms that a new argument is beginning. See §2.2.1 on the use of this phrase and ἴθι δή as signposts.
[26] Here at 387d10 and at e1–4, 388a2 the imperfect ἔδει, which I have rendered as if it were a present, is probably retrospective: 'respicit ad superiorem disputationem [387ad], qua docebat unamquamque actionem et rei naturae accommodatam esse debere *et idoneis instrumentis fieri*' (Stallbaum 50–1, my italics).
[27] On my translation of κερκίζειν and κερκίς see below.

The κερκίς is the tool for κερκίζειν. These two terms are usually translated 'shuttle' (Italian 'spola', French 'navette', etc.) and 'to weave' ('tessere', 'tisser' etc.) respectively. But both translations are mistaken, as archaeologists have long been aware and students of Plato are curiously loath to acknowledge. Both here and at *Sph*. 226bc and *Plt*. 282bc[28] Plato says that in κερκίζειν we somehow *separate* threads from each other. This is confirmed by Aristotle, *Ph*. 243b3–9, who claims that the κέρκισις is a kind of 'pushing apart' and of separation (διάκρισις), and also by a couple of Hellenistic epigrams (*AP* 6.288, 174, respectively by Leonidas of Tarentum and Antipater of Sidon). By contrast, at *Plt*. 283ab Plato says that weaving (ὑφαίνειν) consists in *intertwining* warp and weft so as to produce a web. Hence κερκίζειν cannot be weaving, in these texts at least, and the κερκίς cannot be a shuttle, i.e. the tool which carries the weft thread across between the warp threads.[29] Rather, the κερκίς has been identified as a *pin-beater*, i.e. a tool whose sharp tip was used to beat up the weft into place and to separate the warp threads from each other (see Fig. 1).[30]

In my translation I have accepted this view and have done so to the point of rendering κερκίζειν by means of the catachrestic 'pin-beat', in order to mirror the etymological connection with κερκίς. A few doubts, however, remain. (i) Our passage and the other sources agreeing with it do not mention beating up the weft as part of the job of a κερκίς. Indeed, Aristotle *contrasts* the κέρκισις, as a kind of 'pushing apart' and separation, with the σπάθησις, i.e. the action of beating up the weft by means of the σπάθη or 'sword-beater', which is instead a kind of 'pushing together' and

---

[28] In the *Plt*. passage the Stranger claims that τὸ μὲν ξαντικὸν καὶ τὸ τῆς κερκιστικῆς ἥμισυ 'and all those activities that set apart from each other things that are combined' belong to the separating craft (διακριτική) and thus constitute one segment of the wool-working craft. I doubt whether the Greek phrase means 'Carding and one half of the craft of the κερκίς' (so Campbell 1867 and Rowe 1995), which would imply that there is *another*, unmentioned half of the craft of the κερκίς. The meaning, I submit, should rather be '*the half* [i.e. the segment of the wool-working craft] *that contains* carding and the craft of the κερκίς'. Thus the *whole* craft of the κερκίς would be included in the separating craft, as *Cra*. and *Sph*. suggest.

[29] At 388c Socrates is going to claim that the κερκίς is a *weaving* (ὑφαντικόν) tool, used by a weaving expert (ὑφαντικός) or weaver (ὑφάντης). But this need not be an argument for interpreting κερκίζειν as weaving: see §3.3.1.

[30] See Landercy 1933, Crowfoot 1936–7: 44–6 and Barber 1991: 273–4 (and more generally 260–76 on all Greek loom terminology). This identification also agrees with another feature which the sources ascribe to the κερκίς, i.e. its producing a sound (indeed, a melodious sound: Soph. *TrGF* 595, 890; Ar. *Ran*. 1316; *AP* 6.174; etc.). This is hard to reconcile with the view that the κερκίς is the tool which introduces the weft between the warp threads; but it is appropriate to the pin-beater, which can be 'run rapidly along the threads' and thereby produce a 'soft succession of plucking sounds' (Crowfoot 1936–7: 45; she also suggests an explanation of why such sounds are described as melodious).

Fig. 1. Attic black-figure terracotta lekythos (oil flask), attributed to the Amasis Painter, roughly mid sixth century BC. New York, The Metropolitan Museum of Art, Fletcher Fund, 1931 (31.11.10). Image © The Metropolitan Museum of Art.

The woman on the left is beating up into place, by means of a slender rod which is presumably the κερκίς or pin-beater, the weft that has already been passed through the warp. Close to the hand of the woman on the right (whose job is presumably to open among the warp threads the 'shed' where the weft must pass), stuck amidst the warp threads, is the spool or shuttle, which carries the weft across the warp. (See Crowfoot 1936–7: 42–4, von Bothmer 1985: 185–7.)

combination. (ii) In our passage Socrates says that by means of the κερκίς 'we separate *the weft and the warp which are confused*', whereas the scholarly accounts identifying the κερκίς as a pin-beater usually refer only to the job of separating the *warp* threads from each other. Does it make sense to

110 *Naturalism defended (386e–390e)*

suppose that the κερκίς also separates the *weft* threads from each other? Would it make any sense to suppose, instead, that the κερκίς somehow separates *the weft and the warp from each other*?[31]

I leave these questions unanswered and follow Socrates as he moves on from the pin-beater to the name:

SO. Can you, then, answer in the same way about a name too? When we name with the name, which is an instrument, what do we do?
HE. I can't say.
SO. We teach something to each other and separate the objects as they stand,[32] don't we? [Ἆρ᾽ οὖν[33] διδάσκομέν τι ἀλλήλους καὶ τὰ πράγματα διακρίνομεν ᾗ ἔχει;]
HE. Of course.
SO. Therefore a name is an instrument for teaching and for separating being [ὄνομα ἄρα διδασκαλικόν τί ἐστιν ὄργανον καὶ διακριτικὸν τῆς οὐσίας], as a pin-beater is for a web.
HE. Yes. (388b7–c2)

Here Socrates gives us two definitions of the name's function, of which the second (b13–c1) is inferred from the first (b10–11). Both definitions consist of two parts joined together by καί. Let us reread them in parallel: (i) when we name something 'we teach something to each other', hence (i') a name is 'an instrument for teaching'; and (ii) when we name we 'separate the objects as they stand', hence (ii') a name is 'an instrument … for separating being'.

What does 'being' mean in (ii')? It might be supposed that here the term οὐσία is a nominalization of the *existential* εἶναι and thus is a way of picking up collectively (ii)'s plural reference to 'the objects' (τὰ πράγματα).[34] Alternatively, we might think that οὐσία rather derives from the *copulative* εἶναι, that what it picks up in (ii) is 'as they stand' (ᾗ ἔχει), and that therefore it stands in for some feature of the object named. The former construal makes better sense; but it tells in favour of the latter that οὐσία

---

[31] Landercy 1933: 360 (who understands b2 συγκεχυμένους as 'unies ensemble', 359) seems to think that the κερκίς acts also on the weft threads: it '*servira donc à distancer également les fils et à conserver ainsi au tissu largeur et longueur uniformes*'.
[32] By translating ᾗ ἔχει (b11) 'as they stand', not 'as they are' as is usually done, I am trying to mirror the fact that the Greek expression does not contain a form of 'to be'. This might be important when it comes to deciding what οὐσία means at c1: see below. (Cf. ch. 9 n.45 on 439e.)
[33] The ν in Ἆρ᾽ οὖν (MSS) is marked by dots in B. The expression was corrected into Ἆρ᾽ οὐ by Stephanus, followed by Burnet, Fowler, de Vries 293 and the OCT editors. Stallbaum and Méridier retain the transmitted text, which may well be sound: for Ἆρ᾽ οὖν expecting affirmative answer cf. 385b, 389d, *Phd*. 104d, etc.
[34] This is perhaps the view of those who translate οὐσία here as 'reality' (Fowler, Méridier, Dalimier). For this use cf. *Sph*. 261e (names and verbs are means to indicate the οὐσία) and here in *Cra*. perhaps 436e (see ch. 8 n.104).

was at 385e–386e, and will again be at 393d and then 423de, a *feature* of the πράγματα.³⁵ Indeed, the reference to 'separating' (διακρίνειν) the objects may suggest that here the οὐσία is supposed to be some uniquely identifying feature – more precisely, what is specified in the answer to the question 'What is *X*?', i.e. in a definition, as apparently at 401cd, 423de (see §6.2.4) and elsewhere in Plato.³⁶ If this were so, then a translation like 'essence' would be appropriate – and is in fact adopted by several scholars.³⁷ It is, however, more cautious to think that the term οὐσία here refers generically to any feature 'the objects' may have, as it did at 385e–386e (see §2.4.1). This of course leaves open the possibility that the feature in question may, as a matter of fact, be peculiar to the object or even constitute its essence.

Now, it is very natural to take the καί's in both definitions (b10, b13) as explanatory, and hence to understand that (ii) and (ii') somehow explain the import of (i) and (i') respectively, i.e. spell out *what* we teach each other in naming something.³⁸ So the two definitions roughly amount to the following: the function of a name is to *convey information about its referent*, by ascribing certain features to it, and thereby pick out or *distinguish* it from other objects. (NB: 'from other objects' = 'from *some* other objects', not 'from *any* other object'.)

Strictly speaking, none of this yet implies that the name conveys information *through its etymology*. But, as at 387d, it is very natural in context to assume that this is so, and hence to construe Socrates' conclusion as supporting a naturalist conception of the correctness of names (cf. Proclus, XLVIII, 16.5–27). This is no doubt what we are expected to do on reading these lines for the first time and presumably also what Socrates himself does. Indeed, the legitimacy of this interpretation will be confirmed when Cratylus begins, at long last, to speak his mind. At 428e, after Socrates has illustrated the naturalist thesis with a great many etymologies, Cratylus will happily grant him that the correctness of names consists in their 'showing what the object is like' and that, therefore, 'names are said for the sake of *teaching*' (διδασκαλίας … ἕνεκα). Further on, at 435d, Cratylus will spontaneously claim that names have the power to *teach* (διδάσκειν) and that 'he who has knowledge of the names [i.e. of their etymology] has also knowledge of the objects'.³⁹

---

³⁵ The latter construal is implied by Alcinous, *Didaskalikos* 160.29–30 Hermann, who paraphrases τῆς οὐσίας as τῆς ἑκάστου οὐσίας, 'the being *of each thing*'.
³⁶ *Euthphr.* 11ab, *Men.* 72b, *Phd.* 65d, *Phdr.* 237c, 245e, and especially *R.* 534bc (quoted below in §3.4.4), which is also a parallel for the connection οὐσία/discrimination.
³⁷ Ficino, Minio-Paluello and others.
³⁸ Reeve 10 n.13, Ackrill 1994: 41–2, Sedley 2003: 60–1.
³⁹ In §8.1.1 I speculate that it was the historical Cratylus who held that the function of names is to teach.

Now, insofar as this is how we construe Socrates' present conclusion about the function of names, the conclusion is false; and Plato must know that it is false. This is not just for the reason I already adduced in §3.1.2, i.e. that Socrates will eventually argue against naturalism. More specifically, at 433de Socrates will introduce a very different conception of what names are for, which is neutral between naturalism and conventionalism, and according to which names *indicate* the objects.

It seems possible, however, to read Socrates' conclusion also in a different light, according to which it turns out to contain a sensible philosophical point. This is the sort of reinterpretation that should appeal to someone who is reading the dialogue for the second time, after becoming acquainted with the discussion's further developments, and is attempting to understand what went wrong with the arguments for naturalism.

Let us, for a moment, leave aside Socrates' *definiendum* and focus just on his proposed *definiens*: 'teaching something to each other and separating the objects as they stand [i.e. according to their features]'. We have already seen that this could be read as a description of what we do when we define something. More precisely, these words should remind us, as has often been noticed,[40] of the conception of dialectic as the art of dividing up reality into its natural kinds, which Plato sets forth in such dialogues as *Phaedrus, Sophist, Politicus* and *Philebus*,[41] and of which Socrates says at *Phlb.* 16e that 'the gods ... handed down to us this way of inquiring and learning and *teaching each other* [διδάσκειν ἀλλήλους]'.[42] Socrates' words should remind us of this conception of dialectic especially in the light of the fact that he is soon (390cd) going to introduce the figure of the dialectician and (more importantly) that at 424b–425c, in the course of his development of the naturalist thesis, he will sketch out a very complex application of the division method.

We can now return to Socrates' *definiendum* and see how it fits with this reinterpretation of the *definiens* as referring to division by kinds. Strictly speaking, at b7–11 Socrates is defining what we accomplish *on every act of naming* (b7–8 'When we name with the name, which is an instrument, what do we do?'). And so, strictly speaking, our reinterpretation of the *definiens* gives Socrates a false definition: it is not the case that, each and every time we utter a name, we are thereby singling out a kind in the

---

[40] See first of all Levinson 1957: 37–8 and n.33; cf. Kretzmann 1971: 128, 130 and nn.10–11; Gold 1978: 228–9; Barney 2001: 100; Sedley 2003: 60, 66; Crivelli 2008: 225 and nn.17–18.
[41] See in particular *Phdr.* 265d–266c, *Sph.* 253be.
[42] The passage is quoted by Rijlaarsdam 1978: 86 along with *Phdr.* 265d, where however teaching is mentioned in connection with the complementary process of collection.

context of a division. (Here 'we' refers to ordinary speakers; but matters would not change if we instead took it to refer to philosophers.)

Names, however, play an important role in division – not just for the trivial fact that the performance of a division is a linguistic matter, but also, more specifically, because one needs names to *separate* or distinguish each kind from the others. So it is usual to see those engaged in a division asking what the name of each kind they identify is, and sometimes applying an already established name, sometimes coining a new one, sometimes also deciding to leave the kind unnamed (for a sample of how the thing goes see e.g. *Sph.* 219a–221c). Indeed, it could be added that, when the participants in a division coin a new name for an as yet nameless kind, they most often choose a 'portmanteau' denomination which aims at making the object's nature immediately clear: e.g. *Plt.* 261e ἀγελαιοτροφία 'herd-rearing'. Cf. such English terms as 'steamboat', 'whirlpool' or 'trainspotter', and – even more relevantly – the chemist's compound names, e.g. 'paradichlorobenzene'.[43] And in our dialogue it is precisely by focusing on this kind of structure in names that most of Socrates' etymologies (391a–421c; but remember already his early guess, at 384c, about Hermogenes' name) attempt to illustrate the naturalist thesis.

So names (names in general, and 'portmanteau' names in particular) are important for division. Indeed, perhaps one could go further and say that division and definition, too, are important for names, in the sense that the use of names in division and definition is their highest and noblest use; and from a teleological perspective, such as Plato typically adopts, this may be enough to justify the claim that division and definition are the function of names. Sedley (2003: 62) acutely draws our attention to *Timaeus* 46e–47e, where Timaeus makes the bold claim that the eyes' 'highest function for our benefit, in view of which the god has given them to us as a gift' is to enable us to practise astronomy and thence, ultimately, to arrive at philosophy, while the other, lesser benefits do not deserve to be exalted. This is already a nice illustration of Plato's teleological way of thinking; but it is followed (47cd) by other examples, even more relevant to our present concerns:

Again, the same account holds of sound and hearing: they were given as a gift by the gods for the same intent and purpose. For *speech* [λόγος] has been appointed to the same intent, to which it contributes in the largest measure,[44]

---

[43] The importance of this was again seen by Levinson 1957: 38 (from whom I am borrowing the last example); but see already Goldschmidt 1940: 191–4, 202–5. A few examples: *Sph.* 220a πεζοθηρικόν, ἐνυγροθηρικόν, 220c ἑρκοθηρικόν, 222c πιθανουργική, 223b νομισματοπωλική, δοξοπαιδευτική, 224c τεχνοπωλικόν, 267e δοξομιμητική; *Plt.* 264d ὑγροτροφικόν, ξηροτροφικόν.
[44] Translation after Cornford 1937.

and the same goes for music and rhythm. Now, if in *Ti.* speech is for philosophy, in *Cra.* names may well be for division. And although, strictly speaking, this is not yet sufficient to vindicate Socrates' first definition (b7–11) of the name's function, it is sufficient to vindicate the *second* (b13–c1), which does not refer to what we do on every act of naming, but claims just that the name is 'an instrument for teaching and separating being'.[45]

3.2.2 *Aristotle on names as instruments*

A final reflection on this argument is prompted by a passage in Aristotle's *De interpretatione*, 16b33–17a2. In the course of his treatment of the saying (λόγος)[46] in ch. 4, Aristotle avers that

every saying is significant, *not however as an instrument* [οὐχ ὡς ὄργανον δέ], but rather *by convention* [κατὰ συνθήκην], as has been said.

Aristotle's remark is clearly directed against our passage, as is confirmed by his use of the term συνθήκη, which he (not just here, but in *Int.* quite generally) borrows from Hermogenes. That is to say, Aristotle assumes that if a name – and hence a saying – is a sort of instrument or tool, as Socrates argues in our passage, then it follows that it is by nature, not by convention; and he explicitly distances his own conventionalist view of names and sayings from this naturalist view of Socrates.

But why should being a tool entail natural correctness? Of course because the use of a tool is subject to *natural* constraints which depend on the shape and matter both of the tool itself and of the objects it is applied to. By contrast, the link between name and object is wholly conventional and arbitrary. So the assimilation of names to tools is a misleading way of driving us towards the conclusion that the link between names and objects is a natural one. Names are signs rather than tools.

The Aristotelian assumption and his consequent criticism are unobjectionable, if the only tools or instruments we recognize are things like knives and drills. But there seems no reason why we could not broaden our notion of an instrument to include a particular kind constituted by names, which are different from other instruments in that they can perform their function with relation to any object whatsoever. Such instruments could be said to be instruments, say, of linguistic signification.[47]

---

[45] See §3.4.4 for a discussion of how Socrates' present definition of the function of names ties in with his later, equally bold claim that the dialectician is *the* user of names.
[46] On 'saying' as a translation of λόγος in Aristotle see §6.3.5 n.65.
[47] Cf. Grote 1888: III.287 n.3, Keller 2000: 292–3.

If this is right, then the argument's naturalistic turn and its unsoundness do not lie in the *generic* view of the name as a kind of instrument, but rather in the *specific* view of the name as an instrument for teaching and separating the objects' being – indeed, if our considerations in §3.2.1 were right, not even in the specific view as such, but rather in how Socrates implicitly invites us to construe it.

3.3 THIRD ARGUMENT: ENTER THE NAMEGIVER (388C–389A)

3.3.1 The use and the making of instruments (388cd)

Let us resume our reading of the text. Once Hermogenes has accepted that a name is an instrument for teaching and separating being, Socrates does not explicitly claim that, therefore, naturalism is right and conventionalism is wrong. This explicit conclusion he will draw only later, at 390de. For the moment he goes on questioning Hermogenes, apparently without a break, and introduces the notion of the name's *user*. Here the text contains no signpost indicating that a new argument is beginning; but it is convenient to assume that this is so.

SO. Now the pin-beater is a weaving tool? [ὑφαντικὸν δέ γε ἡ κερκίς;]
HE. Of course.
SO. Therefore it is a weaving expert who will use a pin-beater finely – where 'finely' means 'in a way appropriate to weaving' [ὑφαντικὸς μὲν ἄρα κερκίδι καλῶς χρήσεται, καλῶς δ' ἐστὶν ὑφαντικῶς]; and it is a teaching expert who will use a name finely – where 'finely' means 'in a way appropriate to teaching' [διδασκαλικὸς δὲ ὀνόματι, καλῶς δ' ἐστὶ διδασκαλικῶς].
HE. Yes. (388c3–8)

Right at the beginning of this passage (c3) the κερκίς is said to be a *weaving* (ὑφαντικόν) tool – not a κερκιστικόν one, as we might have expected in the light of the use of κερκίζειν at 388ab. This does not conflict with my earlier contention that at 388ab κερκίζειν did not mean 'to weave' (and κερκίς did not mean 'shuttle'). Rather, I take it that Socrates is here referring to weaving, not as a craft that is identical with κερκίζειν, but rather as a craft to which κερκίζειν is *ancillary*: 'a pin-beater is [*ultimately*] a weaving tool'. The reference to the user as a weaver is even easier to explain in this sense, because the one who performs κερκίζειν and the weaver are in any case the same person. Note that all this fits nicely with the teleological reinterpretation of Socrates' definition of the name's function (§3.2.1).

Pay attention as we move on to the tricky lines c5–7. Here it is important to be clear that the emphasis lies on ὑφαντικός and διδασκαλικός. If a pin-beater is a ὑφαντικόν instrument, then it will be a ὑφαντικός person who uses it finely – which is the same as ὑφαντικῶς, in a way appropriate to its being a ὑφαντικόν instrument. The same holds when we substitute διδασκαλικός and διδασκαλικῶς for ὑφαντικός and ὑφαντικῶς.[48]

The claim that it is a 'teaching expert' who uses a name according to its function sounds incredible; but it fits very well with the definition of the name as an instrument for teaching – and can be reinterpreted accordingly. If we, on second thoughts, understand the definition as saying that teaching is the supreme or ultimate function of names (see §3.2.1), then we can, by the same token, understand the present claim as meaning that the teaching expert is the *supreme* user of names, or the user *par excellence*.

At c5–7 notice Socrates' use of the adverb καλῶς, 'finely', which occurs here for the first time in the dialogue. Both here and at 391b, this may be just equivalent to ὀρθῶς, 'correctly'. But later on (431c–433c, 435cd) an important component in Socrates' strategy against Cratylus will be a distinction between the conditions for naming something more or less 'finely' and the conditions for naming it 'correctly' (i.e. for naming it *simpliciter*). So I shall argue in §§7.3.4, 8.1.5.

Now Socrates shifts his attention from the *users* to the *makers* of tools.[49] He will return to the users at 390bc (where the user of names will no longer be introduced as a teaching expert, but rather as 'the dialectician').

In the case of the other activities, such as weaving or drilling, the tool has been produced by someone – a carpenter or a smith – who is no layman but is equipped with the relevant art or craft:

SO. Now whose work will the weaver use finely when he uses the pin-beater? [τῷ τίνος οὖν ἔργῳ ὁ ὑφάντης καλῶς χρήσεται ὅταν τῇ κερκίδι χρῆται;]
HE. The carpenter's.
SO. But is everyone a carpenter or the one who possesses the art? [πᾶς δὲ τέκτων ἢ ὁ τὴν τέχνην ἔχων;]
HE. The one who possesses the art.
SO. And whose work will the driller use finely when he uses the drill?
HE. The smith's.

---

[48] So Dalimier. Other translations fail to lay the appropriate stress on ὑφαντικός and διδασκαλικός, or connect the adverbs ὑφαντικῶς, διδασκαλικῶς to those masculine forms (which refer to the users) rather than to the neuter forms διδασκαλικόν, ὑφαντικόν (which refer to the *tools*). Both faults can be observed e.g. in Reeve: 'So a weaver will use shuttles well; and to use a shuttle well is to use it as a weaver does.'

[49] Cf. Horn 1904: 24–5.

so. Now, is everyone a smith or the one who possesses the art?
he. The one who possesses the art. (388c9–d5)

As in the preceding sections of the discussion, so here you may well feel that Socrates is too rigid. You need not be a professional carpenter in order to construct a pin-beater, or something that will see service as a pin-beater; like many a do-it-yourselfer, you might have only an approximate idea of what is required and manage to construct a crude but not useless tool. Faced with this objection, Socrates might reply that, as long as you want to construct a tool with some definite function, there are at least *some* very basic standards you must respect, or your work will actually be useless. So you must have *some* faint technical knowledge of the matter; and to that extent you are indeed a carpenter.

This is what Socrates *might* reply; but I suspect he would not. Remember the first argument (387ad). There too Socrates claimed that in order to perform a certain activity (cutting or burning something) you must either comply with certain natural constraints or fail altogether; and there too he ignored the intermediate cases. So in our present passage too I suspect that Socrates is drawing a Manichaean contrast between the expert craftsman, who possesses complete skill, and the totally ignorant person, who could never construct the tool in question but by sheer chance.

Socrates has now set the stage for the entrance of the name-maker.

3.3.2 *The lawgiver as name-maker (388d–389a)*

so. So far so good. But whose work will the teaching expert use, when he uses the name?
he. I don't know this either. (388d6–8)

Hermogenes' 'either' refers back to 388b7–9, where 'I can't say' was his answer to Socrates' question about the function of names. Both avowals of ignorance alert the reader to the importance of the point that is being made.

so. Can't you say this either, who hands us down the names we use?
he. No.
so. Doesn't custom [ὁ νόμος] seem to you to be that which hands them down?
he. It seems so.
so. Therefore the teaching expert will use the work of a lawgiver [νομοθέτου] when he uses a name?
he. So it seems to me.
so. But does everyone seem to you to be a lawgiver, or the one who possesses the art? [νομοθέτης δέ σοι δοκεῖ πᾶς εἶναι ἀνήρ ἢ ὁ τὴν τέχνην ἔχων;]
he. The one who possesses the art.
so. Therefore, Hermogenes, imposing a name is not a matter for everyone, but for some sort of name-maker [οὐκ ἄρα παντὸς ἀνδρός ... ὄνομα θέσθαι,

ἀλλά τινος ὀνοματουργοῦ]. And this is, it seems, the lawgiver, who is the rarest of craftsmen to be born among human beings.

HE. It seems so. (388d9–389a4)

So that which hands us down the names we use is νόμος, 'custom', which must have been established by a νομο-θέτης, a νομο-establisher: the name-maker or 'onomaturge', 'the rarest of craftsmen'.

The terms νόμος and νομοθέτης call for some reflection. The former notoriously covers a fairly wide spectrum of meanings, roughly ranging between 'custom' and 'law': 'Νόμος ... signifies an "order" and implies that this order is, or ought to be, generally regarded as valid and binding by the members of the group in which it prevails' (Ostwald 1969: 54). Lack of a neat distinction between the various uses can be observed in *Grg.* 482e–483b, 483e, *Lg.* 889e–890a, the whole of the pseudo-Platonic *Minos*, and Arist. *Rh.* 1373b4–9 (where νόμος is divided into peculiar, ἴδιος, and common, κοινός, the former being either written or unwritten, the latter being the natural one).[50] As for the term νομοθέτης, we are naturally inclined to translate it not as 'custom-giver' but rather as 'legislator' or 'lawgiver'; and it may be helpful to bear in mind that in Socrates' and Plato's Athens the νομοθέται were an actual body of magistrates appointed with the task to examine legislative proposals.[51] But in fact the term νομοθέτης is not free from the same vagueness of νόμος: see *R.* 538d, where no actual *laws* are in play, and *Plt.* 294e–295a, where the νομοθέτης is characterized as 'the one who will direct his herds with regard to what is just and to their contracts with each other' and who will 'set down the νόμος for each one ... whether expressing it in written or in unwritten form, legislating by means of ancestral customs [καὶ ἐν γράμμασιν ἀποδιδοὺς καὶ ἐν ἀγραμμάτοις, πατρίοις δὲ ἔθεσι νομοθετῶν]'.[52]

These things being so, it is hard to devise a translation of the terms νόμος and νομοθέτης in our dialogue that will both sound convincing and mirror the fact that the latter contains the former.[53] I have rendered νόμος as 'custom' and νομοθέτης as 'lawgiver' throughout; but that, strictly speaking, makes Socrates' argument unintelligible.

With this preliminary caveat we can now turn to the argument. One thing that is worth remarking about it is that it incorporates into the

---

[50] See Ostwald 1969: 20–54, Guthrie 1962–81: III.55–7. An attempt at a distinction between custom and law, reserving the term νόμος for *written* prescriptions, is made at *Lg.* 793ad; cf. X. *Mem.* 1.2.42, 4.4.13.
[51] See *OCD* s.v. *nomothetai*.
[52] Rowe's (1995) translation, modified. The passage is cited by Sedley 2003: 70 n.35.
[53] Reeve tries 'rules' for νόμος and 'rule-setter' for νομοθέτης.

Enter the namegiver (388c–389a)

naturalist thesis the conventionalist's appeal to νόμος by ascribing to it a different role. Custom is no longer that *in virtue of which* a name has a certain referent: that is why Socrates does not use the word in the standard causal dative νόμῳ, as instead Hermogenes did at 384d. Rather, custom is merely the *vehicle* for names whose link with their referent is grounded in nature. As Sedley (2003: 68) puts it, 'the opposition underlying the debate, as Socrates constructs it, is not to be understood as one between *nomos* and *physis* as such, but as one between *mere* custom on the one hand, and custom founded on nature on the other'.[54]

The argument's burden is that the lawgiver (both in his newly discovered capacity as name-maker and as the giver of laws in the ordinary sense of the term) is no layman: only 'the one who possesses the art' is a lawgiver (e4–6). And Socrates plainly holds that this goes against Hermogenes' thesis: if the laying down of names is such a technical business, 'not a matter for everyone' (e7), then clearly names are not mere conventions which anyone can create and alter at will. He will insist on this point in his final conclusion at 390de, where he says that 'the imposition of names seems not to be a trivial matter, nor a matter for trivial men, nor for any chance person'.

Socrates has not yet told us what the lawgiver's craft or art (τέχνη) consists in. He is going to do so in the immediate sequel, where he explains that the lawgiver embodies in letters and syllables the form of name specifically appropriate to the nature of each thing. We shall try to understand what that means in §3.4.2. But in any case Socrates' present conclusion seems to be false, or at least misleading. True, no one is a carpenter or any other kind of craftsman unless one is provided with the relevant competence; but the same does not seem to hold for a law- or custom-establisher. Laying down *rules* for oneself or others does not require any particular competence; and the reason is that, while there are objective conditions which must be satisfied for something to count as a certain kind of tool, in the case of rules there are no such objective conditions – except the very generic one that a rule must be established by a subject possessing the appropriate authority. So a rule can be good or bad, wise or stupid, without therefore being more or less of a rule.

What would Socrates say of this criticism? Later on he will come to the conclusion that any namegiver is in danger of making names express his own wrong philosophical ideas (436ab) and that the ancient Greek

---

[54] Sedley (2003: 70–1) also speculates that at 388d9–12 Socrates may be covertly hinting at an etymology of the word ὄνομα from νόμος.

namegivers in particular espoused and encapsulated into names the false theory of universal flux (411b, 439bc). This seems to show that Plato is aware that those particular lawgivers did not, and lawgivers in general need not, 'possess the art'.

But Plato certainly believes that lawgivers *should* be equipped with art. He typically holds that decisions in a city should be taken only by those who have the relevant technical competence, as happens in the other human activities (*Ap.* 20ac, 25ac; *Prt.* 319a–320c; *Men.* 92e–94e, 99bd). The whole *Republic* enterprise – not to speak of the *Laws* – is repeatedly described as an act of 'lawgiving' (νομοθετεῖν: e.g. 403b, 456b, 497d); and we may compare the references to the 'lawgiving art' (τέχνη νομοθετική) at *Grg.* 464b–465c. Thus, *if* we leave aside what Socrates says about the lawgiver as namegiver, to extract from his words a claim about laws and the lawgiver in the ordinary sense of the term, and *if* where Socrates says 'is' we understand 'should be',[55] then behind his conclusion we can discern a plausible thesis, and one that is important for Plato.

Indeed, perhaps there is a way of dispensing with the second 'if'. Suppose you have a naturalist conception of law or νόμος (leaving names aside) that is parallel to Cratylus' naturalist conception of names – a conception according to which either a νόμος lives up to certain natural standards or it is not really a νόμος at all, whatever human authority may have promulgated it. On such a conception, it seems reasonable to hold that one is an establisher of νόμοι, and hence a νομοθέτης, only if one has the ability to grasp the natural standards, and that such an ability is provided by a special art. So it would become possible to extract from Socrates' conclusions a respectable point about νομοθέται in general.

I won't pursue this suggestion in detail here. But I can anticipate that at 429ab Cratylus will deny that the work of some νομοθέται can be better than that of other νομοθέται, i.e. that νόμοι can be better or worse. We shall see there (§7.1.2), on the basis of a number of passages, that the idea that a νόμος as such is something good and beautiful, or is no νόμος at all, is attested both inside and outside Plato's writings. Here, just by way of example, I will only quote [Demosthenes] 25.15–16 (the so-called 'Anonymus περὶ νόμων'),[56] who says that laws aim at what is just, good and convenient, and that every law is the work of *wise* lawgivers:

---

[55] *Pace* Baxter 1992: 41–2, who believes that the 'should be' construal is the *literally* correct one. Socrates, he says, is laying down 'a prescription for a philosophically sound language' and 'is making no claims about whether or not Greek is or is not a natural language'.
[56] On whom see Guthrie 1962–81: III.75–9.

Enter the namegiver (388c–389a)

Every law is a discovery and a gift of the gods and a judgement of wise human beings [πᾶς ἐστι νόμος εὕρημα μὲν καὶ δῶρον θεῶν, δόγμα δ' ἀνθρώπων φρονίμων].

3.3.3 Who is the lawgiver?

The notion of someone who set down our names does not occur only in *Cra*. At *Ti*. 78e Timaeus, after describing the mechanism of breathing, says: 'We say it is on this kind of phenomena that he who imposed the names [τὸν τὰς ἐπωνυμίας θέμενον] imposed the names "inhalation" and "exhalation".[57] Indeed, at *Chrm*. 175b Socrates describes the failure of the search for a definition of temperance thus: 'we can't discover on what of the beings *the lawgiver* [ὁ νομοθέτης] imposed this name, "temperance"'. This abrupt reference to the lawgiver may sound somewhat puzzling, although perhaps it should just show us that the notion of a lawgiver who set names down is one that it is easy for Plato to introduce. Anyway, Plato might conceivably have in mind the Hippocratic tract *De arte*, written around the last quarter of the fifth century BC.[58] In the course of defending the existence of the medical art against its detractors, the author puts forward the following argument (2.3):

For my part I also think that the arts receive their names on account of the forms. For it would be absurd and impossible to hold that forms shoot from names; for names are legislations of nature, whereas forms are not pieces of legislation but offshoots [τὰ μὲν γὰρ ὀνόματα φύσιος νομοθετήματά ἐστιν, τὰ δὲ εἴδεα οὐ νομοθετήματα, ἀλλὰ βλαστήματα].

For present purposes we can take the puzzling expression 'forms' as roughly equivalent to 'kinds' and focus on the final sentence.[59] There the author seems to contrast names and kinds on the following grounds: kinds are a natural affair ('offshoots'), while names are the product of human legislation *on* nature (i.e. they are customary labels attached to the facts of nature), and hence are, so to speak, logically posterior to kinds.[60]

---

[57] Cf. *Lg*. 816b, mentioned in §5.5.

[58] On the date see Jouanna 1988: 190–1, Jori 1996: 43–54. I record the different, tantalizing suggestion by Myles Burnyeat: 'I would be tempted to suspect some reference to the future, malign νομοθέτης Critias himself: contemplate DK 88 B53–73 for his concern with names and his actual title νομοθέτης in B48.17–18.'

[59] In which, following Guthrie 1962–81: III.204 and Jori 1996: 70–1, 71–4 n.3, I take it that φύσιος (i) is sound and must not be excised or transposed after βλαστήματα as some have suggested, (ii) is an *objective* genitive, not a subjective one.

[60] Guthrie 1962–81: III.204 helpfully compares Antiphon fr. 44(a) I.27–II.I Pendrick: 'the laws are agreed upon, not naturally grown, whereas nature is naturally grown, not agreed upon' (τὰ | μὲν | τῶν νό|μω]ν ὁμολογη|θέντ]α οὐ φύν|τα ἐστί]ν, τὰ δὲ | τῆς φύσ]εως φύν|τα οὐχ] ὁμολογη|θ[έ]-ντα). See also II.30–1 'it has been *legislated*' (νε|νο[μο]θ[έ]τηται).

The notion of legislation surely presupposes that of a legislator or legislators; but *De arte* tells us nothing more.

We should now try to determine the status and identity of the lawgiver in our dialogue. Is he conceived of as a historical figure or as a fictional one, and if so, in what sense? To answer this question it will be helpful to keep before our eyes the following survey of Socrates' most relevant claims about, and ways of referring to, the lawgiver.[61]

- There can be lawgivers in barbarian countries as well as in Greece (389d–390a, c).
- The names of some mythical characters (Hector, Orestes etc.) were given by some poet (393a, 394e), or perhaps by chance (τύχη, 394e, 395e).
- Some names were set down by a plurality of people: 'the first men in Greece' 397cd, 'those who named soul' (τοὺς τὴν ψυχὴν ὀνομάσαντας, 399d), 'the Orphics' (400c), 'the first who imposed names' (οἱ πρῶτοι τὰ ὀνόματα τιθέμενοι, 401b; cf. 397cd, 401a, 411b, 418a, 439c).
- On the other hand, singular indeterminate expressions like 'the imposer' (ὁ τιθέμενος) or 'the lawgiver' (ὁ νομοθέτης) occur frequently (397c, 402b, 404c, 406b, 408b, 415b, 417bc, 419a, 426d–427c, 431ce, 436bc, 437c, 438c) or are understood as subject of verbal forms like 'denominated' (ἐπωνόμασεν, 406a, 410b, 414b).
- Sometimes even in the same passage there is a shift from the plural to the singular subject of name-giving or *vice versa* (407ab, 418cd, 438ab).
- At 416c 'that which imposed the names' (τὸ τὰ ὀνόματα θέμενον) is said to be the thought (διάνοια) of 'either gods or humans or both'.
- There is also the suggestion that the *gods*, or some more indeterminate divine force, might be responsible for some names. This is first advanced by Socrates at 397c (perhaps some names were imposed 'by some force more divine than the human one'); it is picked up at 425d; and it is tentatively endorsed by Cratylus at 438bc.

These things being so, clearly Socrates does not want to commit himself to the view that, sometime in the past, one individual of great ingenuity set down all or most of the names we now use. It does not matter to him whether there was one such individual or more; the lawgiver is, so to speak, a species rather than an individual. Indeed, the fact that in the present argument, up to Socrates' final conclusion at 391de, the lawgiver 'is throughout spoken of in the present tense' seems to mean that there are, or may be, still lawgivers around, and that they are responsible for the new

[61] Cf. Rijlaarsdam 1978: 149.

words that are continuously entering every language (Sedley 2003: 68). So the point Socrates wishes to make can be conveniently represented as the conjunction of two distinct theses: (i) the existence of a custom in general, and a name in particular, entails the existence of someone who set it down; (ii) this someone is provided with expert knowledge, which becomes embodied in the custom.[62]

If we understand it literally, (i) is false; for there are other, vaguer ways in which customs in general, and names in particular, gain acceptance among people. But it can be useful as a simplifying hypothesis; and it may well capture all that is essential (at least for our present purposes) about the matter. We know exactly how the noun 'genocide' originated: it was coined by the Polish jurist Raphael Lemkin in his 1944 book *Axis Rule in Occupied Europe*. And we know how the noun 'quality', or rather the Greek ποιότης, originated: it was coined by the Greek philosopher Plato in the dialogue *Theaetetus*, perhaps shortly after 369 BC. Likewise, one may well reason, there must have been *someone* who initiated the custom of calling the turnip 'turnip'. True, most probably that was not originally meant as an authoritative imposition, but this does not matter much. After all, there was *someone* who initiated the custom (or rather the fashion) of adorning men's clothes with cravats, even though that was not originally meant as an authoritative imposition either, and we do know who he was: George Bryan Brummell, better known as Beau Brummell.[63]

The examples of 'genocide' and 'quality' illustrate also thesis (ii): both are cases where a name was made by a knowledgeable namegiver in such a way as to encapsulate a true description of its object. Thus both (along with countless others which we are unable to trace back to an individual establisher: 'steamboat', 'whirlpool', etc.) show that it may be not unreasonable to expect a name like 'turnip' too to have been so devised as to encapsulate some profound truth about the turnip.[64]

Scholars have striven to show that in outlining the figure of the lawgiver Plato was somehow influenced by other thinkers. Goldschmidt (1940: 64–7, 159–61) was impressed by a Pythagorean maxim reported by Iamblichus,

---

[62] On the lawgiver's knowledge see §3.4.4.
[63] Robinson 1955: 104–6 takes a different view: the lawgiver 'is there not as a piece of history but as a mythical device to make it easier to develop an abstract theory ... He is like the constructor of the material world in the *Timaeus*, posited in order to explain better the nature of a world that never was constructed because it has always existed'. But – whether or not this interpretation of the Demiurge is right – names have not 'always existed'; they have been put together somehow or other; therefore someone must have put them together.
[64] Cf. Sedley 2003: 36.

Vita Pythagorae 82 = DK 58 C4 (cf. Procl. *in Cra.* XVI, 5.27–6.19; the maxim is already known to Cicero, *Tusc.* 1.62, and Aelian, *VH* 4.17):

What is the wisest thing? Number; but second, he who imposed names on the objects [ὁ τὰ ὀνόματα τοῖς πράγμασι θέμενος].

Goldschmidt supposed that Cratylus borrowed from the Pythagoreans the notion of a Divine Namegiver, which Plato then modified and integrated within his own conceptual framework. But even if we leave aside the speculation about Cratylus, the supposition is shaky. It is difficult to trust these reports, which might well be derived from *Cra.* itself,[65] especially in the light of the fact that since the Hellenistic period there flourished a rich Pseudopythagorean literature, part of whose aim was to show that Platonic or Aristotelian ideas had been anticipated by Pythagoras or his disciples.[66]

Another suggestion turns on the Derveni Papyrus, a famous roll containing fragments of a commentary on a lost Orphic theogony, mingled with considerations about the Erinyes, initiations and rites of various kinds.[67] The anonymous author subjects Orpheus' poem to an allegorical exegesis which reveals that it actually conveys cosmological doctrines. Among other things, Orpheus' teaching turns out to be encoded in the etymology of the names of the gods mentioned in the poem, some of which he is apparently taken to have coined himself (see cols. XIV, XVII, XXI, XXII),[68] although in at least one case he is said to have just chosen the 'most suitable' (προσφερέστατον) name among those already available (col. XVIII; cf. XIX, XXIII). These things being so, a connection between the Papyrus and the lawgiver of *Cra.* has been suggested by Baxter 1992: 134–8, whose hypothesis is that 'Orpheus is the wise namegiver, and the commentator is the equivalent of Socrates … Socrates can be seen as offering a properly worked-out theory as opposed to the commentator's hasty reasoning.'[69] The possibility of such a connection cannot be denied. But, as a matter of fact, there is no specific evidence in favour of it, and Plato's lawgiver – especially if, as I argued above, he is no single individual – is far

---

[65] As already Steinthal 1890–1: 1.161 thought. Doubts on Iamblichus' report are also voiced by KRS 233 and Baxter 1992: 110.
[66] See Huffman 1993: 18–26.
[67] See the edition and commentary by Kouremenos/Parássoglou/Tsantsanoglou 2006 and the overall interpretation offered by Frede 2007 (who also has some important considerations about the date of the commentary).
[68] This agrees with a late report (Athenagoras *Pro Christianis* 18 = fr. 57 Kern = 1 B13 DK = *PEG* II 41 III) according to which Orpheus 'was the first to invent the names of the gods'.
[69] Cf. Anceschi 2007: 32–5.

away from the Derveni Orpheus. In fact we cannot even be sure that *Cra.* postdates the commentator's work.

3.4 FOURTH ARGUMENT: INSTRUMENTS, NAMES AND FORMS (389A–390E)

3.4.1 *Instruments and forms (389a)*

No sooner is Socrates' third argument brought to a conclusion than a fresh one begins. Unlike the third but like the previous ones, this is introduced by an appropriate signpost.[70] To clarify how the lawgiver imposes names on the objects, Socrates once again starts from the practice of ordinary arts – more precisely, from the making of a pin-beater:

SO. Come on, consider where the lawgiver *looks* as he imposes the names [ποῖ βλέπων ὁ νομοθέτης τὰ ὀνόματα τίθεται]; and consider it on the basis of what we said before. Where does the carpenter look as he makes the pin-beater? To such a thing as is naturally fit for pin-beating [πρὸς τοιοῦτόν τι ὃ ἐπεφύκει κερκίζειν], doesn't he?
HE. Of course.
SO. What about this? If the pin-beater breaks while he is making it, will he make another one by looking to the broken one or to that form [πρὸς ἐκεῖνο τὸ εἶδος], by looking to which he was making also the one he broke?
HE. By looking to that, it seems to me.
SO. Then we might most rightly call that 'the thing itself which is a pin-beater' [αὐτὸ ὅ ἐστιν κερκίς]?
HE. So it seems to me. (389a5–b7)

Both terminology and substance here call for some discussion.

The metaphor of (ἀπο)βλέπειν πρός, 'looking to, keeping one's eye on', by which Socrates here refers to the carpenter's thinking, is very common throughout the dialogues to describe the activity of considering or focusing on something. Fairly often what is said to be 'looked to' is (or includes) a form (or more forms).[71] And sometimes, as in our passage, the person who 'looks to' the form is a craftsman who concentrates on it as on a model to construct something: see *Grg.* 503e, *R.* 596b, *Ti.* 28a. (Two of the last three mentioned passages will receive more detailed consideration below.)

---

[70] Cf. §§2.2.1, 3.2.1, and n.25 above.
[71] See *Euthphr.* 6e, *Men.* 72c, *Hp. Ma.* 299e, *R.* 484c, *Phlb.* 61de.

So in our passage the carpenter is said to look to the form (εἶδος, b3) of pin-beater as a model for constructing a particular, concrete pin-beater. The passage contains two other expressions by which Socrates refers to the form of pin-beater. The first of these is ὃ ἐπεφύκει[72] κερκίζειν, 'such a thing as is naturally fit for pin-beating' (a7–8; cf. *R.* 6. 501b τὸ φύσει δίκαιον καὶ καλὸν καὶ σῶφρον, 'what is by nature just and beautiful and wise'). Clearly this should not be taken to imply that the form of pin-beater has itself a natural disposition to pin-beating or weaving: you cannot use the form to weave a cloak. Rather, the form is the entity corresponding to the notion of something's being naturally fit for pin-beating.[73]

The second expression is αὐτὸ ὅ ἐστιν κερκίς, 'the thing itself which is a pin-beater' or 'what is a pin-beater itself'[74] (b5–6). This is an instance of one version of the formula (αὐτὸ ἐκεῖνο) ὅ ἐστι *F*, '(that itself) which is (an) *F*', which Plato typically uses to designate the form of *F*.[75] Although the formula's syntax is controversial, the controversy has no bearing on our argument, and I will not enter into it. I will merely assume that ὅ is the grammatical subject, ἐστίν is copulative, and '*F*' (here, κερκίς) is its complement.[76] I will also assume that the form of *F* can be referred to as 'that which is *F*' (so interpreted) in that it can be construed as *what it is to be F*, i.e. as the entity corresponding to the notion of something's being (predicatively) *F*. Besides being very natural and being also recommended by other evidence, this interpretation fits well with the previous ὃ ἐπεφύκει κερκίζειν.

The ὅ ἐστι formula is explicitly recognized as technical at *Phd.* 75d, a passage worth quoting in full:

Our argument is not about the equal any more than about the beautiful itself and the good and the just and the pious and ... about all the things upon which we set this seal, 'what is' [οἷς ἐπισφραγιζόμεθα τοῦτο τὸ 'ὅ ἐστι'], both in questions, when we ask questions, and in answers, when we answer.

The formula's technical status is confirmed by 92de ('the being itself which bears the "what is" denomination', ἡ οὐσία ἔχουσα τὴν ἐπωνυμίαν τὴν τοῦ 'ὅ ἐστιν') and *R.* 507b. By contrast, no such indication can be found in

---

[72] On the tense of ἐπεφύκει see n.10 above.
[73] On this see further Ademollo (in preparation-4).
[74] Where 'itself' is meant to intensify 'what is a pin-beater' as a whole, not just 'pin-beater'.
[75] See *Smp.* 211c; *Phd.* 74d, 75b, 78d, 92d; *R.* 532ab, 533b, 597a; *Prm.* 134a; etc.
[76] For some discussion see Kahn 1981a: 127–9, Rowe 1993: 174–5 and Ademollo (in preparation-4). On the accent ὃ ἐστιν (as against ὅ ἔστιν printed in all editions) see Barrett 1964: 425–6, Kahn 1973b: 420–4.

our passage: the formula is not flagged as a special expression as Socrates applies it to the pin-beater case. This suggests that Socrates is assuming that readers are already familiar with it, and hence that *Cra.* presupposes *Phd.* (as another, independent snippet of evidence seems to confirm: see §§I.3.2, 5.1.3).[77]

We can now leave terminological matters behind and turn to something else. Someone may feel like objecting to Socrates that his description of the carpenter's work is false, because carpenters and other craftsmen do not usually spend much time in thinking of the forms; some of them might even be brutal nominalists. But this objection would be seriously misconceived. Socrates does not want to suggest that the work of a craftsman involves the same degree of abstraction as that of a philosopher. What he wants to point out is that in any art or craft there is a (more or less conscious) conceptual component, insofar as the craftsman manufactures his product by having a general idea of the kind of thing he is producing, the proportions it must embody, the purpose it will serve, etc. From Socrates' (and Plato's) vantage point, this conceptual experience is, as a matter of fact, grounded in the existence of the forms; hence his description – a *de re* description – of the craftsman 'looking to' the form. Bear in mind that throughout the dialogues Plato is willing to bring arts and sciences together under the common labels of τέχνη, 'art', or ἐπιστήμη, 'knowledge', associating to the arts such verbs as γιγνώσκω, 'know', or ἐπίσταμαι, 'understand' (although since *Republic* he also tends to recognize a hierarchy among them: see e.g. 533bc). The reason for this high estimate of the arts is, roughly, that there are certain objective rules according to which they are to be performed, so they are not subject to individual arbitrary decision.[78] Notice that this was precisely the main theme of Socrates' first argument against Hermogenes (387ad), which is now being, as it were, translated into the terminology and perspective of the forms.[79]

As I anticipated above, our text is not alone in positing a connection between art and contemplation of the forms. Here is *Gorgias* 503de:

---

[77] Sedley (2007a: 72–3 and n.13) sees it the other way round: the formula's 'first introduction as a technical term appears in fact to have been at *Cratylus* 389b5–6, since there, uniquely, it is introduced to Socrates' interlocutors as an innovation'; hence *Cra.* antedates *Phd.* But while it is obvious that in our passage Socrates is introducing for the first time the κερκίς *instance* of the formula, i.e. ὃ ἔστιν κερκίς, I do not see any evidence that he is also introducing the *general* formula ὃ ἔστιν F, which he does not mention.

[78] Moreover some of them, like carpentry, have a special status in virtue of their strict relation with calculation and mathematics (*Phlb.* 56bc). See Cambiano 1991: 221–34 on the relation between sciences and arts in Plato and on the analogy between craftsman and philosopher. Cf. Murray 1996: 193.

[79] There is also a significant textual link between the two arguments: see §3.4.2.

The good man … will say whatever he says not at random but looking to something [οὐκ εἰκῇ … ἀλλ᾽ ἀποβλέπων πρός τι], won't he? Likewise the other craftsmen, looking to their own product [βλέποντες πρὸς τὸ αὐτῶν ἔργον],[80] each doesn't select and apply the measures he applies at random, but so that what he makes may have a certain *form* [εἶδός τι] … each places each thing that he places into a certain order [εἰς τάξιν τινά], and forces one thing to be suited for and in harmony with another, until the whole object is put together as something orderly and organized.[81]

And this is a famous passage from *Republic* 10, 596b, where Socrates says:

Now, we also are in the habit of saying [εἰώθαμεν λέγειν] that the craftsman who produces either utensil looks to the form [πρὸς τὴν ἰδέαν βλέπων] and so makes in one case the couches and in the other the tables we use, and similarly with the other things?

The close kinship between this and our passage is immediately evident. A difference, however, is that *R.* presents the claim as a *standard*, customary one, while *Cra.* is eager to establish it accurately.[82]

All that I have been saying so far presupposes that the form of pin-beater, or of couch, is a fully genuine form. This is what both our passage (together with the whole argument which contains it and which we have just begun to confront) and *R.* 10 clearly imply. But pin-beaters and couches are *artefacts*; and Aristotle notoriously claims that Academics denied the existence of forms of artefacts (*De ideis* = Alex. Aphr. *in Metaph.* 79.22–80.6; cf. *Metaph.* 991b6–7) and that Plato said that there are forms for, and only for, 'the things that exist by nature' (*Metaph.* 1070a18–19). His reports are at odds not only with our passage and *R.* 10, but also with other texts: *Ti.* 28ab and *Lg.* 965bc, which say that the good craftsman should look to the form; *R.* 510a, where Socrates includes both natural and artificial objects in the second section of the Divided Line, as if there were no ontological difference between them.[83] Therefore I discount Aristotle's report: his claim may well be true of some other Platonist; but it is not true of Plato.[84]

---

[80] Dodds 1959: 328–9 understands βλέποντες πρὸς τὸ αὐτῶν ἔργον (e2) as 'with an eye to their own function' because the object of βλέποντες 'can hardly … be his own product, which is still in the making'. But it seems to me that the ἔργον can be the *form* of the product (cf. e4) – which of course is not itself in the making.

[81] Dodds's (1959) text and Zeyl's translation (in Cooper 1997), modified.

[82] Goldschmidt 1940: 77–9 and Luce 1965, besides noting this, argue that our passage reflects an earlier stage of thought than *Republic* does. But there is no substantive evidence for this (cf. Calvert 1970: 32–3).

[83] See also *Epist.* 7.342de (whose authenticity, however, I doubt: see §8.1.6).

[84] For a judicious discussion see Ross 1953: 171–5 and Leszl 1975: 124–40. On forms of artefacts see also Burnyeat 1999: 245–9. As these authors point out, there is a sense in which Aristotle's report about Plato at *Metaph.* 1070a18–19 may, after all, be accurate; but it is not the sense Aristotle has in mind.

3.4.2 Generic and specific forms of tools (389bd)

Socrates goes on to claim that the making of a pin-beater involves more than just the form of pin-beater. The form of pin-beater is a *generic* form; subordinated to it there are several *specific* forms of pin-beater, each fit for weaving a different kind of garment.

SO. Hence when one must make a pin-beater for a thin or a thick garment, or a linen or woollen one, or for any sort of garment [ἐπειδὰν δέῃ λεπτῷ ἱματίῳ ἢ παχεῖ ἢ λινῷ ἢ ἐρεῷ ἢ ὁποιῳοῦν τινι κερκίδα ποιεῖν], all must have the form of the pin-beater [πάσας μὲν δεῖ τὸ τῆς κερκίδος ἔχειν εἶδος], but the nature which is best for each thing, this one must assign to each product [οἵα δ' ἑκάστῳ καλλίστη ἐπεφύκει, ταύτην ἀποδιδόναι τὴν φύσιν εἰς τὸ ἔργον ἕκαστον].
HE. Yes. (389b8–c2)

A difficult passage. As I understand the Greek, Socrates says that all *particular* pin-beaters (πάσας b9) must 'have', i.e. embody, the form of pin-beater, independently of their specific tasks; but 'to each product', i.e. to each particular pin-beater, one must assign the *kind* of pin-beater which is best for each thing, i.e. for each kind of garment (οἵα δ' ἑκάστῳ καλλίστη ἐπεφύκει, where οἵα anticipates c1 ταύτην ... τὴν φύσιν, while ἑκάστῳ picks up the b8–9 datives).[85]

The 'nature' mentioned in c1 is clearly a *form*: items of the same sort will be designated as ἰδέα and εἶδος at 389e3 and 390a7; and the term φύσις can, generally speaking, refer to forms (*Prm.* 147e, 156de; *Sph.* 257d, 258ab; *Plt.* 306e). So here we have only a linguistic variant, which serves to underline the difference between the generic form and the specific forms. This difference does not involve a difference in ontological status between the two kinds of form.[86] We know since the 'Socratic' dialogues that a form may be *part* of another: the holy is part of the just, courage and justice are parts of virtue (*Euthphr.* 11e–12d; *La.* 190cd, 198a; *Men.* 72c), etc. This notion will be central in the late dialogues' theory and practice of division by kinds (e.g. *Plt.* 262ab); and as I anticipated in §3.2.1, already here in *Cra.* Socrates will show himself thoroughly familiar with division.

---

[85] My interpretation agrees with that of Méridier and Dalimier. Fowler construes διὸ ἑκάστῳ as being picked up by c1 εἰς τὸ ἔργον ἕκαστον: the nature thus becomes the best *for each product* of the carpenter, i.e. for each tool. This makes little sense (cf. c4!). Reeve refers ἑκάστῳ to each particular tool, divorces ἀποδιδόναι from εἰς (unlike c4–5), and translates εἰς τὸ ἔργον ἕκαστον as 'to perform its own work'; none of this is to be commended.

[86] Cf. Gold 1978: 233–8 (*pace* Luce 1965: 24, Calvert 1970: 34; however, Calvert 1970: 26–34 has some sensible remarks on generic and specific forms).

Granted, there is a difference between what Socrates says of the generic form and what he says of the specific one: throughout the argument, both here and in the sequel, only the specific form is said to be embodied by the craftsman in the appropriate material.[87] But that should not be taken to mean that the generic form is only looked to and is not embodied. What it rather means, I submit, is that the embodiment of the generic form *supervenes*, as it were, upon that of a specific form. A carpenter who makes a pin-beater of such-and-such a kind (i.e. a particular instance of a specific form of pin-beater) does not perform *two* distinct acts of embodiment into the same piece of wood, one for the generic form and another for the specific one; rather, by embodying the specific form he simultaneously embodies the generic form as well.[88]

Now let us focus on Socrates' claim that 'one must assign to each product' (c1) the nature or form specifically appropriate to the particular task at issue. The key word here is 'must'. We may happily grant Socrates that the kind of pin-beater that is 'best' or 'finest' (καλλίστη, b10: i.e. most suitable) for manufacturing a linen cloak is not the same as the kind of pin-beater that is 'best' for manufacturing a woollen cloak. But Socrates should in turn acknowledge that within certain limits, which depend on the individual case, it is nonetheless possible to obtain an imperfect but not useless result by means of an imperfectly suitable tool. A good wool-weaver need not be completely hampered by the fact that he has to make do with a pin-beater originally designed for linen. Indeed, Socrates' very reference to the *'finest'* kind of pin-beater for a given purpose implies, strictly speaking, that other kinds of pin-beater can be 'fine', albeit less so, for the same purpose. Does Socrates acknowledge this much or not?

We have already been pursuing this line of thought above, both when talking about the naturalness of actions at 387ad (§§3.1.1–3) and when reflecting on the figure of the lawgiver (§3.3.2). But now we have got a single word to fasten upon; and that word is δεῖ, 'must' (b9, c7), which governs ἔχειν (b10) explicitly and ἀποδιδόναι (c1) implicitly. Very roughly, δεῖ may express either (a) *inevitability* or (b) *need* or *prescription*. Herodotus,

---

[87] One might be tempted to say that there is another difference, i.e. that only the generic form, and not also the specific one, is said to be 'looked to' by the craftsman. But 390e shows that this is not so; and even if it were so, it could hardly have any significance.

[88] This need not (and should not) mean that Socrates would endorse the Aristotelian view that 'the genus absolutely does not exist over and above the species whose genus it is, or does exist but exists as matter' (*Metaph.* Z12.1038a5–6). But perhaps he would sympathize with the milder view that 'we are said to be qualified in virtue of the particular species, because it is these that we possess; for we are said to be knowledgeable in virtue of possessing some particular knowledge' (*Cat.* 8.11a32–4).

2.161.3, uses the verb as in (a) when he says of the pharaoh Apries that οἱ ἔδεε κακῶς γενέσθαι, 'things had to go off badly for him'. Sophocles, *Ph.* 77, uses it as in (b) when he has Odysseus claim 'we must contrive just that [αὐτὸ τοῦτο δεῖ σοφισθῆναι], namely how you'll manage to steal the invincible weapon from him'. Aristotle draws a similar distinction when he remarks (*SE* 165b35–8) that

'What must be' [τὸ δέον] has a double meaning: it means what is inevitable [τό ... ἀναγκαῖον], as is often the case with evils (for some kind of evil is inevitable), while on the other hand we say of good things [τἀγαθά] as well that they must be.

In our lines (b) may seem the most natural interpretation, and is certainly recommended by c8 δέῃ. On this interpretation, what Socrates says is all right: he is just laying down a prescription about how to use pin-beaters best. But if, instead, (a) is the right interpretation of our δεῖ, then Socrates is once again lapsing into the misleading 'all-or-nothing' outlook which already pervaded his first argument (387ad). And, of course, my suggestion is that (a) is literally right and (b) is something we might want to substitute for it on second thoughts.[89]

Next Socrates proceeds to generalize his result and give more concrete examples of it:

SO. And the same holds of the other tools. One must find out the instrument naturally fit for each thing and embody it in that material whence one makes his product [τὸ φύσει ἑκάστῳ πεφυκὸς ὄργανον ἐξευρόντα δεῖ ἀποδοῦναι εἰς ἐκεῖνο ἐξ οὗ ἂν ποιῇ {τὸ ἔργον}[90]] – not such a tool as he wants, but such as is naturally fit [οὐχ οἷον ἂν αὐτὸς βουληθῇ, ἀλλ' οἷον ἐπεφύκει].[91] For it is the drill naturally fit for each thing that one must know how to put into iron [τὸ φύσει γὰρ ἑκάστῳ ... τρύπανον πεφυκὸς εἰς τὸν σίδηρον δεῖ ἐπίστασθαι τιθέναι].

HE. Of course.

SO. And it is the pin-beater naturally fit for each thing that one must know how to put into wood.

HE. That is true.

SO. For each pin-beater belonged by nature to each kind of web [Φύσει γὰρ ἦν ἑκάστῳ εἴδει ὑφάσματος ... ἑκάστη κερκίς], as it seems, and the same for the other cases.

HE. Yes. (389c3–d3)

---

[89] See further §3.4.3 and n.103.
[90] τὸ ἔργον (c5), absent in the usually laconic T, is bracketed by Burnet, deleted by Fowler and the OCT, preserved by Stallbaum and Méridier. Whether a gloss or not, it rightly supplements the sense.
[91] At c5–6 οἷον is the pronoun (cf. b10 οἵα), as Stallbaum, Ficino and Dalimier see. Others take it as the adverb, 'as'. Minio-Paluello refers it to ἐκεῖνο ἐξ οὗ ἂν ποιῇ, i.e. the material; the sequel shows that this is impossible.

As the initial 'And *the same* holds of the other tools' (c3) announces, and d1–2 with its γάρ confirms, the main point of these lines is again the idea that there are a number of specific forms subordinate to a generic form, each fit for a different thing (ἑκάστῳ c6, c10; ἑκάστῳ εἴδει ὑφάσματος d1). Incidentally, Socrates also makes the new point that all the species of a given generic form are to be embodied in the same *material*.[92] Thus each form of drill is to be embodied in iron, each form of pin-beater in wood. But the emphasis still lies on the forms and on the necessity of choosing the one naturally appropriate to each thing.

The expression 'not such a tool as he wants, but such as is naturally fit' (389c5–6) is a close echo of the first argument. Cf. in particular 387a and 387d: 'Hence one must also name *as it is natural* to name the objects and for them to be named and *with that with which it is natural*, but *not as we want.*'

3.4.3 *Forms of name (389d–390a)*

As was to be expected, the case of names is perfectly parallel to that of the other tools:

SO. Then, my excellent friend, also in the case of the name naturally fit for each thing [τὸ ἑκάστῳ φύσει πεφυκὸς ὄνομα] the lawgiver, whom we were talking about, must know how to put it into sounds and syllables, and make and impose all names by looking to that thing itself which is a name [πρὸς αὐτὸ ἐκεῖνο ὅ ἐστιν ὄνομα], if he is to be an authoritative [κύριος] imposer of names – must he not? And if it is not the case that each lawgiver puts the form into the same syllables, one must not fail to recognize this [οὐδὲν δεῖ τοῦτο ἀγνοεῖν].[93] For neither does every smith put the form into the same iron, though he makes the same instrument for the same purpose. But, as long as each embodies the same form, whether in the same iron or in a different one [ἕως ἂν τὴν αὐτὴν ἰδέαν ἀποδιδῷ, ἐάντε ἐν <τῷ αὐτῷ ἐάντε ἐν> ἄλλῳ σιδήρῳ],[94] anyway the instrument is correct, whether one makes it here or among barbarians. Is it not so?

HE. Of course.

---

[92] As Proclus remarks, LIV, 23.26–30; cf. Kahn 1986a: 100.
[93] ἀγνοεῖν (389e1) has been variously emended; Burnet and the OCT editors adopt Peipers's ἀ<μφι>γνοεῖν. But correction seems unnecessary and is rejected by Stallbaum, Shorey 1919 and most other scholars. ἀγνοεῖν here means 'fail to recognize' (Méridier and others: 'forget', less precise); its object τοῦτο is anaphoric rather than proleptic (*pace* Stallbaum, Méridier, Reeve) and refers to the process of embodiment which has just been described: see Shorey 1919.
[94] At 390e1 τῷ αὐτῷ ἐάντε ἐν is Ast's supplement, printed in the OCT; Stallbaum, followed by Méridier, corrected the MSS ἐάντε ἐν into ἐὰν καὶ. The MSS text can hardly stand, *pace* Burnet, Fowler, and de Vries (1955: 293): see *GP* 535–6.

SO. Hence in the same way you will think of the lawgiver, both the one who works here and the one who works among the barbarians, that, as long as he embodies the form of the name appropriate to each thing in syllables of whatever sort [τὸ τοῦ ὀνόματος εἶδος ... τὸ προσῆκον ἑκάστῳ ἐν ὁποιαισοῦν συλλαβαῖς], the one who works here is no worse lawgiver than the one who works anywhere else? (389d8–390a10)

First Socrates suggests (d4–6) that the lawgiver must know how to embody into sounds and syllables the 'name naturally fit for each thing',[95] i.e. the *specific* form of name (cf. c4 'the instrument naturally fit for each thing', 390a6–7 'the form of name appropriate to each thing'). Then he says (d6–8) that the lawgiver must make all names by looking to 'that thing itself which is a name', i.e. the *generic* form of name (cf. b5 'that thing itself which is a pin-beater'). Thus he just presents in reverse order the two stages that were distinguished before. Then Socrates goes on to explain at some length (d8–a9) that one and the same specific form of name can be embodied in different syllables, so that nothing prevents two names from two very different languages from instantiating the same specific form of name. Thereby he evidently aims at showing that, despite what Hermogenes was perhaps suggesting at 385de (see §2.3), the existence of different languages is no argument against naturalism and in favour of conventionalism. In the course of making this point he has recourse (e1–a3) to a further analogy, between the namegiver and the smith.

Let us start with what Socrates says about the forms. The *generic* form of name (d6–7) is unproblematic. Generally speaking, a form is what is specified by a correct definition; we can give a definition of name; so there must be a form of name.

At first glance, the *specific* forms of name (d4–6, d8 ff.) are stranger beasts. But in fact they are perfectly analogous to the specific forms of pin-beater or drill. The fact that different kinds of web require different kinds of pin-beater led us to postulate different specific forms of pin-beater, all subordinate to the generic form: the form of pin-beater for linen, the form of pin-beater for wool, etc. But the objects to be named too can be very different in nature from each other – much more different than any two kinds of web. Then why not postulate specific forms of name too, each appropriate to the nature of a different object? Thus (to supply examples of our own where Socrates, lamentably, gives none) there will be a form of name of the horse, a form of name of justice, etc. A definition of the form of name of the horse will presumably tell us what characteristics a particular name must have (it

[95] More on the significance of this phrase below.

is tempting to say 'how a particular name must be *made*'; see below),[96] if it is to be a correct name of the horse; and a definition of the form of name of justice will tell us what characteristics a particular name must have, if it is to be a correct name of justice.[97] Will there also be such things as a form of name of Callias and a form of name of Coriscus? Socrates does not say. But that would break the analogy with the case of pin-beaters: my wool cloak and yours do not require different kinds of pin-beater.

What sort of characteristics will be mentioned in the definition of a specific form of name? In the light of 388bc it seems clear that such a definition will tell us what the name must 'teach' us about the 'being' or nature of its referent. That is to say, such a definition will tell us what sort of information about the horse any name of the horse must supply. Thereby the definition identifies a general type (a *semantic type*, as opposed to a *phonetic* one, to put it with Kahn 1973a: 164), whose tokens are the horse's various particular names in the various languages, whatever the letters or sounds they are made up of: 'horse', 'cavallo', 'Pferd', etc. (d8–a10). Each of these tokens will instantiate the same type, i.e. the specific form of name of the horse, and supply the same information[98] about the horse.

Now it may seem to us that what Socrates is saying can be translated into more familiar language. Such a translation is offered by Ackrill (1994: 44): 'the ideal name is a *semantically defined* unit not made of sounds or letters. It is in effect the meaning of all the ordinary names in a group of synonyms; and one might well call it the *name-as-concept*, in that what synonyms all express is *the same concept*'. This suggestion is attractive, and in a way illuminating; but at the same time it gives a distorted view of the matter. For nowhere throughout the argument, either in the bit we have been reading so far or in the sequel, does Socrates say that a particular name *expresses*, or signifies, the specific form of name it *instantiates*.[99] He is

---

[96] Actually, I will end by expressing the suspicion that we *should* give way to the temptation. But that is not something we should do unreflectingly.
[97] Of course by 'name of the horse' I mean in fact a name of the *form* of horse, and by 'name of justice' a name of the *form* of justice. But I am conforming to Socrates' silence about what the objects named are.
[98] Why the *same* information? Because, if the form of name of X could be instantiated by names which supply *different* information about X (e.g. Latin *serpens*/Greek δράκων, or Latin *vespertilio*/French 'chauve-souris'), then the form would have to be – rather unpalatably – a repository of all conceivable information about X, something like a Leibnizian complete concept. On the other hand, the fact that the information supplied has to be the same is a serious difficulty for the theory which Socrates is constructing. But I hesitate to press the point, because I doubt whether Plato would have been alive to it. In *Cra.* he does not seem to take theoretical notice of anything like Frege's sense/reference distinction: see §4.2.6 on 394bc.
[99] True, later on, at 394ac, Socrates will introduce the notion of a 'power' (δύναμις) of names; and as we shall see in §4.2.6, that *is* a notion of a meaning or sense of names. But in spite of what Ackrill

attempting to mobilize for his present purposes Plato's favourite conceptual resource, the theory of forms with its 'one over many' strategy; and we should respect the boldness of this attempt.[100]

Nothing so far seems to constitute an argument against Hermogenes; and as Ackrill (1994: 44) saw, the letter of what Socrates says is, strictly speaking, compatible with conventionalism, which is a thesis about the material shape of names – about the sounds and letters they are composed of – not about the semantic types they instantiate or the meanings they express. Yet when Socrates refers to the specific form of name as τὸ ἑκάστῳ φύσει πεφυκὸς ὄνομα (d4–5) he is clearly echoing the clause ὀνόματος ὀρθότητα εἶναι ἑκάστῳ τῶν ὄντων φύσει πεφυκυῖαν, whereby Cratylus' thesis was first introduced (383a); and the very analogy with the tools, the conclusion which Socrates will draw at 390de, and the way he will subsequently develop it at length, all press us to assume something more, i.e. that the information which a name must supply about its referent – its 'teaching' about the referent's 'being' – is a matter of how the name is materially made, hence of its *etymology*. It is *this* assumption that makes the argument into a refutation of conventionalism. On this assumption, the particular names that instantiate the same specific form of name in different languages will all supply the same information about their common referent *through different but analogous etymologies*. Compare the case of the English 'hairdryer' and the French 'sèche-cheveux', or the Italian 'ferrovia' and the German 'Eisenbahn': these are pairs of names which refer to the same thing, and describe it in the same way, despite the fact that they are made up of different sounds and composed of completely different words (not even from the same stem).[101]

There is something more to be said about the specific forms of name; but that will have to wait until we are finished with the whole passage. So let us move on to consider the conditional clause 'if he is to be a κύριος imposer of names' (d8). It is important to realize that the notion of a κύριος namegiver is not just the notion of a *good* namegiver, as opposed

---

seems to believe ('The term *dunamis* … corresponds to *eidos* and *idea* at 389e3 and 390a6'), it would be rash to read those later developments into the present argument, which is never recalled there. See below and §4.2.5.

[100] Gold 1978 compares Socrates' attempt to that of Sellars (1963), who holds that the English 'red', the German 'rot' and the French 'rouge' are all tokens of the same (semantic) type, 'a linguistic kind or sort which is capable of realization or embodiment in different linguistic materials' (1963: 627). The huge difference is that Sellars, unlike Plato, has a thoroughly nominalistic conception of types.

[101] Cf. Leibniz's 1677 *Dialogus*, 1923–: A VI, 4A, 23–4 (= Ariew/Garber 1989: 271) on the analogy between the Latin *lucifer* and the Greek φωσφόρος.

to a bad one. The adjective κύριος ('having authority')[102] rather suggests a stronger interpretation: a κύριος namegiver is a *legitimate*, authentic namegiver, as opposed to an illegitimate one. This suggests that at a8–9, where Socrates says that, on certain conditions, the Greek lawgiver is 'no worse' (οὐδὲν χείρω) than the foreign one, what he really means is that, on those conditions, the Greek lawgiver is not an illegitimate one. And this confirms that δεῖ, both in c3–8 (cf. §3.4.2) and here at d6, is a 'must' of necessity or inevitability, not of prescription. We are not speaking of how names would be made best, but of how they are to be made, if they are to be names at all.[103]

I now wish to make a couple of points about lines d8–a10. My main point is that there is some reason to suppose that, in Socrates' view, the various lawgivers in different countries do not all draw on the same or overlapping stock of sounds, but on completely different ones (see Rijlaarsdam 1978: 109–10, Sedley 2003: 66, 130–1). This supposition may help us save Socrates' consistency later on. When the etymologies arrive at the so-called 'first names', which are names not composed of other names, but directly of sounds (421d ff.), Socrates argues that such names are correct by nature because their sounds (or rather the way they are uttered) *imitate* the object's nature. But it would be embarrassing if one and the same sound should appear to mean one thing in Greece and another, opposite thing in some barbarian language: that would tell heavily against the mimetic account.[104] Socrates would steer clear of this problem from the start, if he were now thinking of foreign languages using completely different sets of sounds. And this is historically quite plausible, if we think not only of what must have been the Greek speaker's reaction to the Semitic languages, but also of how alien another Indo-European language like Persian was likely to sound to Greek ears.

This hypothesis is compatible with the comparison between the namegiver and the smith (e1–a3). Every smith puts the specific form of drill that is fit for a specific task (e.g. the form of drill for drilling marble, as distinct from the form of drill for drilling wood) into the appropriate material, i.e. *iron*. But, Socrates says at e1–2, it is not the case that every smith puts the

---

[102] See in particular the use of κύριος as 'valid', of laws, opinions etc., in contrast with ἄκυρος, 'invalid' (LSJ A.II.2): e.g. *Tht.* 179b, Lys. 18.15, Dem. 24.1.

[103] Contrast Baxter (1992: 44–5): namegiving 'is a τέχνη like any other; this entails that there are good and bad craftsmen, from the true νομοθέτης who produces the best possible names at the top, to the many other lesser craftsmen below him ... Socrates' argument looks towards such an ideal but does not lose sight of the everyday reality'. This is not what Socrates says.

[104] This criticism is suggested by Kretzmann 1971: 136.

same form 'into the same iron' (εἰς τὸν αὐτὸν σίδηρον). This may mean 'into the same *chunk* of iron';[105] but it may also mean 'into the same *kind* of iron', as Rijlaarsdam 1978: 112 saw. That is to say, Socrates may be thinking of the case of different smiths who work in different countries and have *different varieties of iron* at their disposal.[106]

We now have leisure for returning to the specific forms of name. The question which I want to ask is: What are we ultimately expected to do with them? Shall they survive the eventual fall of naturalism?

Many scholars would answer 'Yes'. They believe that, once we sever the merely contingent link between the specific forms of name and etymology, those forms become the argument's most important positive bequest.[107] Indeed, some believe that one main lesson of the dialogue is the following: the specific form of name of *X* is *natural*, while any particular name of *X* which instantiates it is *conventional*.[108]

They may be right; but caution is in order. After the conclusion of the present argument (390de) we shall not hear anything more about the specific forms of name throughout the dialogue. Socrates' silence will be especially striking on two occasions. One is at 394ac, where he puts forward the view that materially different names are actually the same name provided that (and insofar as) they signify the same, or have the same 'power'. Why does he not try to explain this in terms of such names' instantiating the same form? The second occasion is the 424b–425c project of a perfect language. According to this project, we should first divide up the various kinds of letters, then do the same with the various kinds of beings, and then associate letters and beings according to their mutual *resemblance*, thus constructing names that carried, as it were, an analysis of their referent's nature on their face. No mention there of the specific forms of name; names are supposed to be made by someone who turns directly to the forms themselves to be named, not to the forms of their names. And, indeed, you may well think that there is something redundant about the notion of the specific forms of name. If there is any sense at all in referring distributively to them as 'the name naturally fit for each thing' (389d) or 'the name that belongs to each thing in virtue of its nature' (390e), it must

---

[105] Horn 1904: 29–30, Gold 1978: 230.
[106] The Greeks did know of different varieties of iron, extracted from different minerals and places: see Plin. *Nat.* 34.143–5, and cf. Daremberg/Saglio 11.1083–6 and *OCD* s.v. *iron*. An analogous point will perhaps be made with regard to wood at b2 ἐν ὁποιῳοῦν ξύλῳ (see n.109). The problem would not even arise if σίδηρος here did not mean 'iron' but 'metal', as it is sometimes translated. This, however, is linguistically dubious.
[107] See Ackrill 1994: 43–4, 51.
[108] See Kahn 1973a: 173, Gold 1978: 245–6, Barney 2001: 47,

be, as we saw above, that by looking to the form of name of *X* you see what information any particular name of *X* must (somehow or other) supply about *X*'s nature. But then why not get that information by looking directly to the form of *X*?

So I think we should be open to the possibility that the notion of the specific forms of name may be, as a matter of fact, much more tightly connected with the purpose of defending naturalism than is usually supposed. And if my suspicion is right, then what we should do with the notion on second thoughts, after the fall of naturalism, is not to reinterpret it but to junk it.

3.4.4 *The lawgiver and the dialectician (390bd)*

Now Socrates would be ready to reach the conclusion he will in fact draw at 390de, namely that Cratylus is right and Hermogenes wrong. Yet he first prefers to open a digression where he introduces the figure of the dialectician in the context of a distinction between the *production* and *use* of any instrument. His general point is that the work of any craftsman has to be evaluated by someone else: the one who will use it and who is also able to supervise its production.

Here is how it begins:

SO. Now who's the one that will know whether the appropriate form of pin-beater lies in whatever sort of wood [εἰ τὸ προσῆκον εἶδος κερκίδος ἐν ὁποιῳοῦν ξύλῳ κεῖται]?[109] The one who made it, the carpenter, or the one who will use it, the weaver?
HE. He is more likely to be the one who will use it, Socrates.
SO. Then who's the one that will use the lyre-maker's product? Isn't he the person who would know best how to supervise its making [οὗτος ὃς ἐπίσταιτο ἂν ἐργαζομένῳ κάλλιστα ἐπιστατεῖν] and once it has been made would recognize whether it has been well made or not [καὶ εἰργασμένον γνοίη εἴτ' εὖ εἴργασται εἴτε μή]?
HE. Of course.
SO. Who is he?
HE. The citharist.
SO. And who is the one that will use the shipbuilder's product?
HE. The pilot. (390b1–c1)

The point Socrates is making here has a parallel at *R.* 10.601c–602a (remember that our argument already shared with *R.* 10 the form-contemplating craftsman), which is worth considering in detail. There Socrates, within

[109] ἐν ὁποιῳοῦν ξύλῳ (b2): 'in any piece of wood' Fowler (cf. Reeve). On my translation see n.106.

the context of a discussion of poetry as imitation, draws a threefold distinction between *use, production* and *imitation* of something. He states a general principle (601d):

The excellence and fineness and correctness [ἀρετὴ καὶ κάλλος καὶ ὀρθότης] of each tool, living being and action is not related to anything but the use [τὴν χρείαν] for which each has been made or is naturally fit.

And he goes on (601de) to infer that

Necessarily, therefore, the user of each thing is the one who is most expert about it and reports to the maker the good or bad effects in use of the thing he uses. E.g. the flute-player reports to the flute-maker which flutes serve him in flute-playing, and will order what sort must be made, and the other will serve him.

Then Socrates' remarks take on an epistemological hue: he recasts his point (601e–602a) by saying that 'about the fineness or badness of the same tool the maker will have correct opinion … whereas the user will have knowledge'. And then he finally gets at what he had been driving at all along (602a): the imitator has neither knowledge (like the user) nor correct opinion (like the maker) about the goodness or badness of the things he imitates. He is inferior to both.

The parallel is indeed remarkable; but it will prove important[110] to bear a difference in mind. The *R.* distinction is a threefold one between user, maker and imitator; and the ultimate purpose of what is said about the first two is to discredit the third. By contrast, the *Cra.* distinction is merely twofold, and the missing item is precisely the imitator.

Now get back to the text of *Cra.* and see how Socrates applies the maker/user distinction to names:

SO. And who could best supervise the lawgiver's work and judge it when it has been made, both here and among the barbarians? Isn't he the one who will use it?
HE. Yes.
SO. Now this is the one who knows how to ask questions [ὁ ἐρωτᾶν ἐπιστάμενος], isn't he?
HE. Of course.
SO. And the same person also knows how to answer [ἀποκρίνεσθαι]?
HE. Yes.
SO. But the one who knows how to ask and answer questions do you call anything but a dialectician [διαλεκτικόν]?
HE. No, that's how I call him. (390c6–12)

---

[110] See n.116.

Before making any comments it is worthwhile also reading the following lines, which round off the digression about makers and users:

SO. Therefore it is the job of a carpenter to make a rudder under the supervision of a pilot, if the rudder is to be a fine one [εἰ μέλλει καλὸν εἶναι τὸ πηδάλιον].
HE. So it seems.
SO. And it is, as it seems, the job of a lawgiver to make a name, having as supervisor a dialectician, if he is to impose names finely [εἰ μέλλει καλῶς ὀνόματα θήσεσθαι].
HE. That's true. (390d1–8)

At d2 and d6, in the two conditional clauses introduced by εἰ μέλλει, is 'fine' (καλόν) equivalent to 'correct', and 'finely' (καλῶς) to 'correctly'? Or do 'fine' and 'finely' here express something different, i.e. a notion of *excellence* (which may admit of degrees) in the way a tool or a name is made? We were confronted with a similar question at 388c (see §3.3.1). Here as there, the former alternative is probably the right one, at least if we take the text at face value. Here this is suggested by a twofold comparison: on the one hand, with the parallel clause 'if he is to be an *authoritative* giver of names', εἰ μέλλει κύριος εἶναι ὀνομάτων θέτης, at 389d (on which see §3.4.3); on the other hand, with 390a 'anyway the instrument *is correct*', ὅμως ὀρθῶς ἔχει τὸ ὄργανον. But the text is also compatible with the latter construal.

Let me now try to set out all that we learn about dialectic and the dialectician, both explicitly and implicitly, both from the last two chunks of text and from their context.[111]

(i) Here Socrates explicitly recognizes *dialectic as a distinct art*; accordingly, he designates its practitioner by the adjective διαλεκτικός. Outside *Cra.* and those dialogues which contain more advanced theoretical reflections on dialectic (*Republic, Phaedrus, Philebus, Sophist, Politicus*), the adjective and its cognates occur only at *Men.* 75d (the adverb διαλεκτικώτερον, 'more dialectically' or 'more conversationally')[112] and *Euthd.* 290c (a puzzling reference to οἱ διαλεκτικοί which looks like a reference to the *Republic*).[113]

---

[111] See Kahn 1996: 292–328 for a fine survey of Plato's views and terminology regarding dialectic.
[112] 'One must answer more gently, as it were, and διαλεκτικώτερον. And διαλεκτικώτερον means, I think, not just to give the true answer, but also to answer in terms of what the questioner has in addition agreed he knows' (tr. after Sharples 1985).
[113] Cleinias claims that the mathematicians are merely able to discover the objects of their research, but do not know how to use them, so hand them over to 'the dialecticians'. Anticipation of *R.* 6–7 (Kahn 1996: 308–9) or back-reference (Burnyeat 2002: 63 n.46)?

(ii) Socrates claims that the dialectician is the one who has *knowledge of how to ask and answer questions* (this will be recalled at 398d, in the etymology of ἥρως, 'hero', from ἐρωτᾶν, 'to ask': see §5.5.3).[114] Of course we are familiar since the 'Socratic' dialogues with the notion of διαλέγεσθαι as a sort of discussion characterized by question-and-answer and close argument: see *Grg.* 448d, *Prt.* 336bc.

(iii) Although this is not claimed in so many words, I find it hard to deny that the argument clearly suggests a strong *connection between dialectic and the study of the forms*. To say the least, dialectic and the forms stand here in close contextual association with each other.

(iv) Remember the 388bc definition of the function of names as 'teaching something to each other and separating the objects as they stand' (or 'separating being', οὐσία) and the related claim that the one who uses names 'finely', i.e. correctly, is a 'teaching expert' (διδασκαλικός). If we put that earlier passage together with the present one, two consequences follow.

(iv.a) *The aim of dialectic* – what it uses names for – is to *'separate the objects as they stand'*. We saw in §3.2.1 that this has to do with definition and, more precisely, with the method of division, with which Socrates will show himself so familiar at 424b–425c.[115]

(iv.b) *The dialectician is a teaching expert*. This accords with those passages which we encountered in §3.2.1 (*Phlb.* 16e, *Phdr.* 265d), where division and the complementary process of collection, which are the province of the dialectician, are described as methods for teaching something. Another nice passage is *Sph.* 229e–230e, where it is said that one species of the art of verbal *teaching* (τῆς ἐν τοῖς λόγοις διδασκαλικῆς) is the elenchus or examination, which proceeds by *questioning* people about the subjects they pretend to be expert on and showing their opinions to contradict themselves.

---

[114] In fact, as Sedley 2003: 62 rightly emphasizes, here the dialectician is introduced primarily as the one who knows how to *ask* questions (390c6), and only secondarily as the one who also knows how to *answer* them (c8). Cf. 398d, where heroes, ἥρωες, turn out to be dialecticians simply on account of their ability to ask questions, ἐρωτᾶν. Sedley's explanation, 'the thoroughly Socratic notion of interrogative teaching is in the frame', is undoubtedly right.

[115] According to several interpreters (Kretzmann 1971: 127, 130–2; Fine 1977: 296–7; cf. Ackrill 1994: 42, 45–6), one result of Socrates' arguments for naturalism, which is connected with the mention of the dialectician, and which is meant to transcend Socrates' defence of naturalism, is the following: the *lexicon* of ordinary languages like Greek should mirror, as far as possible, the structure of reality. On this view, one aspect of the correctness problem is that a language should not contain names of nonexistent things (e.g. 'phlogiston') or names presupposing a misguided classification of existent things (e.g. 'shorse', a term supposedly true of anything that is either a sheep or a horse). In a sense, this is something which Plato would no doubt endorse (see *Phdr.* 265e–266b, *Plt.* 262a–263d). But it does not seem to be anything that he makes Socrates explicitly concern himself with in *Cra.*, either here or elsewhere.

Apart from the reference to teaching, most of the features mentioned above find parallels elsewhere. At *R.* 534bd Socrates characterizes the dialectician as 'the one who exacts an account of the being of each thing' (τὸν λόγον ἑκάστου λαμβάνοντα τῆς οὐσίας) and who is able to 'define the form of good in discourse by separating it from all other things' (διορίσασθαι τῷ λόγῳ ἀπὸ τῶν ἄλλων πάντων ἀφελὼν τὴν τοῦ ἀγαθοῦ ἰδέαν), 'going through all examinations as in a battle'; and he claims that the most important component in the dialectician's education will be that which will make them 'able to ask and answer questions in the most scientific way'. Cf. the connection between question-and-answer and the investigation of the forms at *Phd.* 75cd (quoted in §3.4.1) and 78d, where, however, dialectic or the dialectician are not mentioned by name.

(v) *The dialectician is the user of names* (390c4 ὅσπερ χρήσεται). At first blush, this is baffling. Don't all sorts of people use names in their everyday business? But of course, as Sedley 2003: 62 has seen (cf. Proclus, LXI, 26.27–27.2), the dialectician is here said to be the user of names in the very same sense in which names were said at 388bc to be instruments for teaching and separating being (see §3.2.1). To be sure, names may be used by other people for other, less sophisticated purposes. But their ultimate purpose, the highest function they can serve, and hence (from a strongly teleological perspective) their function *simpliciter*, is to teach and separate being; and the dialectician is the one who can use them for that purpose.

(vi) *The dialectician is the lawgiver's supervisor.* This is a puzzling claim; and several considerations suggest that it should not be taken at face value – i.e. that Socrates does not really think that the giving of names is, or should be, the result of a cooperation between two distinct figures. To start with, the lawgiver's own art consists, as we have seen, in embodying in letters the form of name specifically appropriate to the nature of each thing to be named; and I do not see how this could fail to involve some sort of knowledge of the nature of the thing to be named – which we should expect to be the dialectician's hallmark.[116] This is confirmed by the fact that Socrates spoke at 388e–389a, and will speak again at 391de, as

---

[116] *Pace* Sedley (2003: 9): 'Nowhere is it so much as hinted by Socrates, on his own behalf, that the early linguistic lawmakers themselves had knowledge of the things they were naming.' You will remember that at *R.* 601e–602a it is argued that the maker has no more than 'correct opinion' about the quality of the tools he makes, whereas knowledge belongs to the user. But as I warned above, that may well be strictly subservient to that passage's specific purpose, which is to discredit the *imitator*.

if the fact that names are made by the lawgiver were *by itself* an argument against Hermogenes' conventionalism.[117]

Furthermore, while throughout *Cra.* we shall continue to hear about the lawgiver(s), nothing more will be said of the dialectician. There are two contexts where Socrates' silence is especially striking. When it turns out (411bc, 439bc) that what the first namegivers really embodied in most Greek names was a mistaken view of the nature of things, that will *not* induce Socrates to conclude that they were not supervised by a dialectician – only that they were confused. And when at 424b–425c Socrates sketches out his bold project of a twofold division of kinds of letters and kinds of beings, followed by the creation of a sort of perfect language, he will *not* refer to any division of labour between lawgiver and dialectician; he will speak throughout as if the same persons ('we') were both to carry out the preliminary divisions and to impose the names by relying on them.

Thus Socrates does not really seem to conceive of namegiving as a joint venture between a lawgiver and a dialectician, despite what he argues at 390cd. Interestingly, however, the rationale behind this seems to be quite different depending on whether we consider the matter from inside the naturalist theory which Socrates is presently constructing or from the outside. Within the theory, namegiving is not really a joint venture because the lawgiver is (I submit) assumed to be himself a dialectician.[118] Outside the theory, namegiving is not really a joint venture because, sadly, at least in most cases the lawgiver is not a dialectician and there is no dialectician to supervise him.

Let me add a word about the former perspective, the one that is internal to the naturalist theory. My suggestion that the lawgiver is assumed to be himself a dialectician may seem open to the objection that the other pairs of makers and users with whom the lawgiver and the dialectician are compared are *real* pairs, formed by really distinct persons (the carpenter and the weaver, the lyre-maker and the citharist, the ship-builder and the pilot). But this is no fatal objection. Compare *Euthd.* 288d–292e (already cited by Goldschmidt 1940: 85). Socrates and Cleinias, given the conception of philosophy as 'possession of knowledge', strive to find out what

---

[117] That would be unjustified if, as Sedley 2003: 73–4 seems to suggest, the lawgiver's peculiar skill, what makes him into 'the rarest of craftsmen', consisted solely in 'the enviable knack of devising words ... which will actually catch on'. (Indeed, I doubt whether this knack plays any role at all in Socrates' account.)
[118] Cf. Horn 1904: 28, Goldschmidt 1940: 85, Baxter 1992: 46.

knowledge it is possession of. Most sciences and arts are concerned with the production or acquisition of something, which must then be handed over to the expert who will use it, whose art is different; thus e.g. lyre-making is much different from the citharist's art. Hence these arts are incomplete and unable to make us happy. What we really need is 'such a science ... in which *making and knowing how to use that which it makes coincide*' (289b), and more generally 'that art which will *itself also know how to use what it acquires* either by making it or by hunting it' (290d). This resembles fairly closely the view I am ascribing to Socrates in *Cra*.

(vii) *The dialectician is the judge of the lawgiver's finished product* (390c3–4). One reason why Socrates says this, and why Plato wants to present the lawgiver as distinct from the dialectician, goes, I submit, as follows: *Socrates is the real dialectician* and the dialogue we are reading will contain a question-and-answer, dialectical examination and assessment of the work of the ancient lawgivers,[119] as Socrates himself states at 425ab.

3.5 CONCLUSION (390DE)

Let us resume our reading of the text. Socrates now returns his final verdict:

so. Therefore, Hermogenes, the imposition of names seems not to be a trivial matter, as you believe, nor a thing for trivial men, nor for any chance person. And Cratylus speaks the truth when he says that names belong to the objects by nature [φύσει τὰ ὀνόματα εἶναι τοῖς πράγμασι] and that not everyone is a craftsman of names, but only that one who looks to the name belonging to each thing in virtue of its nature [ἀλλὰ μόνον ἐκεῖνον τὸν ἀποβλέποντα εἰς τὸ τῇ φύσει ὄνομα ὂν ἑκάστῳ],[120] and who is able to put its form into the letters and syllables [καὶ δυνάμενον αὐτοῦ τὸ εἶδος τιθέναι εἴς τε τὰ γράμματα καὶ τὰς συλλαβάς]. (390d9–e5)

First (d9–11) Socrates picks up the conclusion of the third argument, according to which 'imposing names is not a matter for everyone, but for some sort of namemaker' (388e–389a), and contrasts it with Hermogenes' conventionalist thesis. Then (d11–e5) Socrates claims most explicitly that Cratylus' naturalist thesis is true and presents as part of that thesis *his own*

---

[119] See Anceschi 2007: 35.
[120] τῇ φύσει (e3): 'by *its* nature', not 'by nature', as it is sometimes translated. The article must have a similar force in the phrase εἴς τε τὰ γράμματα καὶ τὰς συλλαβάς (e4–5), which cannot mean just 'into letters and syllables'. The import could be fully spelt out as follows: 'into [letters and syllables which thereby become] *the* letters and syllables of that thing's name'. One might even wonder whether the phrase might fall within the scope of αὐτοῦ (e4).

interpretation and development of it, i.e. the rejection of the 'democratic' stance towards namegiving and the description of the namegiver as looking to the specific form of name of each thing and embodying it into letters and syllables.

Now that we are finished, let me turn back for a brief retrospective remark. Several scholars have found it puzzling that Plato should give Socrates some eight OCT pages of unsound arguments for a theory – linguistic naturalism – against which he will make Socrates launch a devastating attack later on. I for one do not see that there is anything especially puzzling here. True, *Cra.* is alone among Platonic dialogues in having this peculiar structure, where a philosophical thesis is defended elaborately and at great length by a character only to be subsequently smashed by the very same character. But then no Platonic dialogue has exactly the same structure as any other; and this seems to be as good a structure as any can be to catch the readers' attention and give them food for thought. In particular, throughout this chapter I have been striving to show that there is much to be learnt from a careful criticism (and possibly reinterpretation) of Socrates' arguments and that being subjected to such a criticism is precisely part of their intended function.

CHAPTER 4

Naturalism unfolded (390e–394e)

In the previous chapter we saw Socrates advance several arguments to the conclusion that 'Cratylus tells the truth when he says that names belong to the objects by nature.' So far, however, Socrates has not spelt out what it is for a name to belong by nature to its referent, any more than Cratylus did before, in his conversation with Hermogenes. In particular, Socrates has not explicitly claimed that a name's natural correctness has to do with its etymology. This crucial step is to be taken in the next pages of the dialogue.

4.1 SEARCHING FOR A THEORY (390E–392B)

It is Hermogenes, in his response to Socrates' verdict in favour of Cratylus, who says what course the conversation should now follow:

HE. I don't know, Socrates, how one is to counter what you say. Yet perhaps it is not easy to get convinced so suddenly; it seems to me that I would believe you more, if you showed me what you say the natural correctness of a name consists in [ἥντινα φῂς εἶναι τὴν φύσει ὀρθότητα ὀνόματος]. (390e6–391a3)

Predictably, Socrates denies that he already has a definite account ready at hand:

SO. Dear Hermogenes, I'm speaking of no particular correctness. You forgot what I said a while ago, i.e. that I didn't know but would inquire together with you. And now that we are inquiring, I and you, we've reached this view we didn't have before, that the name has some sort of natural correctness and that knowing how to impose a name finely[1] on any object whatsoever is not a matter for every man. Isn't that so?
HE. Of course.

---

[1] καλῶς (b1) is omitted by T, followed by Hirschig and Burnet. T's omissions always deserve serious consideration (cf. ch. 2 n.82); but here it is more cautious to print the adverb.

146

so. Then the next thing to do is to search for what in the world its correctness consists in [ἥτις ποτ' αὖ ἐστιν αὐτοῦ ἡ ὀρθότης], if you wish to know.
he. Of course I do wish to. (391a4–b6)

After the initial disclaimer and the ritual reference to common inquiry (a4–6), he briefly recalls the results of the previous arguments (a6–b2) and picks up and emphasizes Hermogenes' distinction between those results and the next step we must take, i.e. to pin down the natural correctness of names (b4–5).

The distinction between the abstract notion of a natural correctness of names and the concrete account which must now be given of it is an important one. On the one hand, it can be read as confirming that, as I argued in ch. 3, Socrates' arguments for naturalism were intended to be open to various interpretations – not just to the one which is going to become Socrates' official interpretation, according to which natural correctness is a matter of the name's etymology. On the other hand, note how careful Socrates is to avoid claiming that so far he has *proved* anything or that he and Hermogenes have acquired any knowledge about the correctness of names. At a7–8 he introduces his summary of the previous conclusions with the words τοσοῦτον μὲν ἤδη φαίνεται παρὰ τὰ πρότερα, literally 'this much already appears [to us] beyond the things that appeared [to us] before', where the use of the verb 'appear' is very cautious and is compatible with the possibility that our conclusions may later have to be revised.[2]

But how should the new inquiry be carried out?

so. Now inquire.
he. How should one inquire?
so. The most correct way of inquiring, my friend, is to do so together with those who know, by paying them money and lavishing favours on them. These are the Sophists, whom your brother Callias has paid much money, thereby acquiring a reputation for wisdom. But since you aren't master of your father's estate, you must importune your brother and pray him to teach you the correctness about such matters, which he learnt from Protagoras. (391b7–c5)

As at 384bc with Prodicus, Socrates pokes fun at the Sophists' habit of teaching for money – and much money at that. Here the joke allows him a

---

[2] Several translations make Socrates too confident: e.g. Fowler ('we already see one thing we did not know before') and Reeve ('this much is clearer than before'). Méridier adds a further misunderstanding of παρὰ τὰ πρότερα as 'contrairement à la première opinion' (cf. Minio-Paluello), which makes no sense: Socrates' naturalist conclusions do not recant any previous agreement between him and Hermogenes.

reference to the man 'who has paid the Sophists more money than all the others taken together, Callias, the son of Hipponicus' (*Ap.* 20a). And since Callias is (as our passage suggests) Hermogenes' stepbrother, the *legitimate* son of their common father Hipponicus, this in its turn allows Socrates to return to Hermogenes' financial difficulties, which were also mentioned in the passage about Prodicus.[3] Then, at c4–5, comes a more specific reference to the teaching of Protagoras about 'the correctness of such things'. (It is always astonishing to see how many things Plato can do together in a couple of lines.)

What did Protagoras teach Callias? Was it really relevant to the subject matter of *Cra.*? At *Phdr.* 267c it is said that Protagoras dealt with ὀρθοέπεια, 'correct diction';[4] and the context shows that that had to do with rhetoric. But whether in connection with ὀρθοέπεια or in some other connection, Protagoras does seem to have held something which justifies Socrates' present reference to him. We know from Aristotle, *SE* 173b17–174a4, that Protagoras considered the nouns μῆνις ('wrath') and πήληξ ('helmet') as masculine, contrary to common Greek usage, and criticized Homer for saying μῆνιν ... οὐλομένην ('accursed wrath', *Il.* 1.1) instead of μῆνιν ... οὐλόμενον. A plausible way of explaining this is to suppose that Protagoras propounded a natural criterion of the correctness of names, according to which *their gender had to reflect their referent's nature*.[5] This fits well with *Rh.* 1407b7–8, where Aristotle reports that Protagoras distinguished the genders of names into ἄρρενα καὶ θήλεα καὶ σκεύη ('masculine, feminine and *things*') – which suggests that he took the name's gender to express something of the object's nature. It also fits very well with Aristophanes' parody at *Clouds* 658–93, where the idea is pushed to the point of *altering* the ending of words to conform it to the object's natural gender.[6]

So it seems that Protagoras might have taught Callias something relevant to our discussion. But in any case Plato does not want to concern himself with his views and has Hermogenes brush them aside:

---

[3] On the implications of the reference to Hermogenes' not being master of Hipponicus' estate see §I.3.1.
[4] It is unclear whether ὀρθοέπεια is presented as the *title* of a Protagorean work. See de Vries 1969: 225–6.
[5] See e.g. Murray 1946: 177 and Blank 1998: 183–4, 234. Fehling 1965: 212–17 convincingly argues that Protagoras' discussion of gender correctness was probably not put forward for its own sake, but rather in the context of, and as subservient to, a criticism of the *Iliad*'s first lines. Fehling also offers (to my mind, less convincingly) an alternative interpretation of what Protagoras' account consisted in. For a survey of Protagoras' linguistic studies see Pfeiffer 1968: 37–9 and Brancacci 1996.
[6] Gender naturalism will reappear many centuries later: see S. E. *M.* 1.142–53, 184–90; Amm. *in Int.* 35.21–36.21.

HE. My entreaty would be strange indeed, Socrates, if, while I don't at all accept [ὅλως οὐκ ἀποδέχομαι]⁷ Protagoras' *Truth*, I should accept the things said with such a *Truth*⁸ as if they were worth something. (391c6–9)

Hermogenes is referring back to his rejection of Protagorean relativism at 386a. This brisk dismissal is unfair: Protagoras' linguistic views can hardly have been dependent upon his relativism, whether or not they too were advanced in the work entitled *Truth*.⁹

In any case, if Hermogenes is unwilling to learn the modern sophistic wisdom, then the obvious alternative is to revert to Homer, the cornerstone of Greek traditional education:¹⁰

SO. But if, instead, these things do not please you,¹¹ then we must learn from Homer and from the other poets. (391c10–d1)

This is probably also a further dig at Protagoras, whose views on the correctness of names were somehow associated with a criticism of Homer (see n.5).

HE. And what does Homer say on the correctness of names, Socrates, and where?
SO. In many places; but the greatest and finest things he says in those places where he distinguishes between the names by which humans and gods call the same things. Don't you think that in these places he says something great and wonderful about the correctness of names? For clearly the gods call them by those very names that, as regards correctness, are such by nature [οἵ γε θεοὶ αὐτὰ καλοῦσιν πρὸς ὀρθότητα ἅπερ ἔστι φύσει ὀνόματα].¹² Don't you think so?
HE. I know well that they call things correctly, if they call them at all [εἴπερ καλοῦσιν]. But what are these names you are talking about? (391d2–e3)

---

⁷ On ὅλως οὐκ (c7) 'not at all' see LSJ ὅλως III.3. Even if the expression could have a weaker meaning, 'on the whole not' (based on ὅλως 'on the whole', LSJ III.2; cf. §2.4.1 on 386a6 οὐ πάνυ τι), it would probably not have that meaning here, because in that case we should expect μέν to follow ὅλως, not Ἀλήθειαν.
⁸ The usual pun on the title of Protagoras' work (*Tht.* 161c), as already at 386c.
⁹ As Stallbaum 62–3 and others believe; Reeve even translates τὰ δὲ τῇ τοιαύτῃ ἀληθείᾳ ῥηθέντα (c8) as 'the things contained in it'. I for one do not think that the way Hermogenes expresses himself clearly entails this.
¹⁰ Reeve xxiv.
¹¹ Ἀλλ᾽ εἰ μὴ αὖ σε ταῦτα ἀρέσκει (c10): for αὖ 'instead' cf. Th. 6.80.4 εἰ καταστρέψονται ἡμᾶς Ἀθηναῖοι ... καὶ εἰ αὖ ἡμεῖς περιεσόμεθα. Several interpreters, instead, translate as if the meaning were 'if these things do not please you *either*' (e.g. Dalimier 'si ces propos non plus ne te plaisent pas'). But this seems linguistically dubious; and, in any case, before the reference to Protagoras nothing else has failed to 'please' Hermogenes.
¹² αὐτά (d8) may either refer back to ἐπὶ τοῖς αὐτοῖς (d5) or emphasize the following ἅπερ ἔστι φύσει ὀνόματα.

We shall look at Homer's distinctions between divine and human names in a moment. But do not miss, in Hermogenes' final words, the polite shadow of doubt on the very idea of the gods' using names at all (cf. *Euthphr.* 8e εἴπερ ἀμφισβητοῦσιν θεοί, 'if the gods dispute at all').

SO. Don't you know that, of the river in Troy which fought in single combat with Hephaestus, he says 'whom the gods call Xanthus, but men Scamander'?
HE. I do.
SO. Well then, don't you think that this is a grand thing to understand, for what reason[13] it is correct [ὀρθῶς ἔχει] to call that river Xanthus rather than Scamander? Or, if you wish, take the bird which he says 'the gods call *chalkis*, but men *kumindis*': do you regard it as trifling to learn how much more correct [ὀρθότερον] it is for the same bird to be called '*chalkis*' than '*kumindis*'? Or to learn about Batieia and Murine and many other cases both in this poet and in others? (391e4–392b2)

Socrates is referring to *Il.* 20.74, 14.291 and 2.813–14 respectively; the third passage, which he does not quote, speaks of a hill situated in front of Troy, 'which men call Batieia, but immortals tomb of bounding Murine'. Other occurrences of this *topos* can be found at *Il.* 1.403–4 and *Phdr.* 252b (probably Plato's own humorous creation: see §5.5.4).[14]

Socrates' words clearly presuppose the context of contemporary Homeric exegesis in two respects. First, Homeric exegetes (οἱ νῦν περὶ Ὅμηρον δεινοί 407ab) were particularly interested in problem-solving, i.e. in elucidating passages that looked puzzling (see Richardson 1975). It is easy to imagine some of the people who dealt with such matters (like Stesimbrotus of Thasos or Anaximander the younger or perhaps also Antisthenes) speculating about the significance of the same things being called differently by gods and humans, as their modern colleagues have done. In our case this interest in problem-solving coincided with another ancient line of inquiry into Homer's text, i.e. the study of rare words (γλῶσσαι), which was practised by Democritus (68 A33 DK) among others. Indeed, an example of the interest that these Homeric passages may have aroused is offered by Arist. *HA* 519a18–20, who mentions an etymological explanation of Ξάνθος, 'Xanthus', from ξανθός, 'yellow'.[15]

A second aspect of Socrates' appeal to Homer which fits in well with contemporary exegetical practice is the idea that Homer's lines contain elements of some sort of technical knowledge (in our case, about

---

[13] ὅπῃ ποτέ (a2): literally 'in what manner' (Méridier and Dalimier 'en quoi'). Not 'that', as some translate.
[14] Further parallels in West 1966: 387–8. On each of the Homeric passages cited see the comments of Kirk/Edwards/Hainsworth/Janko/Richardson 1985–94. Kirk (1.94) claims that 'No principle [i.e. no *single* principle] to account for these peculiarities of name has been satisfactorily proposed.'
[15] See Goldschmidt 1940: 99. Proclus interprets all three pairs of names in LXXI, 34.13–35.8.

the correctness of names). This idea is operating in Protagoras' claim at *Prt.* 316de that Homer, Hesiod and others of the ancients were disguised Sophists and in the claim, made by Niceratus in Xenophon's *Symposium*, 4.6–7, that Homer can teach us everything.

That said, the pompous tone of Socrates' appeal to Homer (which is going to inform also lines b2–4) strongly suggests that he is being ironical;[16] and when at a6–7 Socrates asks whether Hermogenes regards it as 'trifling' (φαῦλον) to learn about the correctness of *'chalkis'* vs *'kumindis'*, he seems to be implicating precisely that such questions are of meagre importance.[17] This is just as it should be. Remember that at *Protagoras* 347b–348a, at the end of the analysis of Simonides' poem, Socrates writes off the discussion of poetry as pointless and unworthy of an educated person. He compares it to the 'symposia of common, vulgar people', who hire flute-girls and dancers because they are unable to converse with each other, and contrasts it with his own favourite style of conversation: 'we must ... put the poets aside and carry out our conversations with each other drawing only on our own resources, testing the truth and ourselves'.[18]

It has also been thought that in these lines Socrates is beginning to make a very serious point about the notion of correctness, i.e. that correctness 'is a comparative attribute' (Sedley 2003: 78–9). If you glance back at the text you will see that at 392a6 Socrates speaks of learning 'how much *more correct*' (ὅσῳ ὀρθότερον) it is for the same bird to be called *'chalkis'* than *'kumindis'*. Likewise at 392bd he is going to investigate which of the two names of Hector's son was regarded by Homer as 'more correct' and to invoke the general principle that wiser people use names 'more correctly'.

In my view, Sedley's way of interpreting these comparative expressions is not right. For the very notion of degrees of correctness is ruled out by what I call the Redundancy Conception of correctness, which all characters have been holding since the beginning of the dialogue and will continue to hold until the end in all relevant contexts (see §I.1.1). There are only a few occasions on which Socrates speaks of a name as being 'more correct' than another; and they can all, I think, be explained away as cases in which he adopts an innocuous *façon de parler* devoid of any serious theoretical significance. This is confirmed by the fact that even within our lines Socrates and Hermogenes do not express themselves consistently on

---

[16] See e.g. Goldschmidt 1940: 98, de Vries 1955: 293.
[17] Plato's reference to the Homeric distinction between human and divine names was taken very seriously by the Neoplatonics (Procl. LXVIII, 29.6–12; LXXI, 33.7–11: see Linguiti 1988: 340–1).
[18] See Horn 1904: 31.

this score. There is no comparative at 391d7–e3, where Socrates says that the gods clearly use names which are naturally correct and Hermogenes answers that they doubtless call things correctly if they call things at all. And at 392a2–3 Socrates' formulation is ambiguous: 'for what reason *it is correct* [ὀρθῶς ἔχει] to call that river Xanthus *rather than* [μᾶλλον ἤ] Scamander' need not be taken as containing a real comparative.[19]

4.2 THE THEORY DISCOVERED. NATURALISM AND SYNONYMY (392B–394E)

4.2.1 'Scamandrius' and 'Astyanax' (392bd)

Socrates moves on (still with a tone of ironical pomposity) to a different case of double denomination in Homer. This is the case that will, in due course, spark off Socrates' account of the natural correctness of names.

> (SO.) But these things perhaps are too great for me and you to find out. It is, I think, more within human power and easier to investigate 'Scamandrius' and 'Astyanax', the names which he says belong to Hector's son, i.e. to investigate what he says their correctness is. You presumably know the lines where the words I am referring to are to be found.
> HE. Of course. (392b2–8)

Let us make sure that *we* have the Homeric lines clearly in mind. The only Homeric passage mentioning the two names of Hector's son is *Il.* 6.401–3: 'Hector's beloved son, similar to a beautiful star',

τόν ῥ' Ἕκτωρ καλέεσκε Σκαμάνδριον, αὐτὰρ οἱ ἄλλοι
Ἀστυάνακτ'· οἶος γὰρ ἐρύετο Ἴλιον Ἕκτωρ.

whom Hector called Scamandrius, but the others
Astyanax: for Hector alone defended Ilium.

But there is another passage which will turn out to be relevant. It is *Il.* 22.505–7, where Andromache addresses her dead husband as follows: 'He will suffer much, now that he has been deprived of his father,'

Ἀστυάναξ, ὃν Τρῶες ἐπίκλησιν καλέουσιν·
οἶος γάρ σφιν ἔρυσο πύλας καὶ τείχεα μακρά.

Astyanax, as the Trojans call him;
for you alone defended their gates and the long walls.

---

[19] Ficino, Méridier, Dalimier and Reeve do take it so; Fowler and Minio-Paluello do not.

Naturalism and synonymy (392b–394e)

Now look at what Socrates makes of this:

SO. Now which of these two names do you think that Homer regarded as more correct [ὀρθότερον] for the child, 'Astyanax' or 'Scamandrius'?
HE. I can't say.
SO. Look at it this way. If someone asked you whether you think it is those who are wiser or those who are more unwise who use names more correctly – [20]
HE. Clearly I'd say those who are wiser.
SO. Now do the women or the men in the cities seem to you to be wiser, if one is to speak of their whole kind?
HE. The men.
SO. Now you know, don't you, that Homer says Hector's child was called 'Astyanax' by the men of Troy [ὑπὸ τῶν Τρώων] – and clearly 'Scamandrius' by the women, given that the men called him 'Astyanax'?
HE. So it seems.
SO. Now[21] Homer too regarded the men of Troy as wiser than their women?
HE. I think so.
SO. Therefore he thought that 'Astyanax' was more correct a name for the child than 'Scamandrius'?
HE. So it appears. (392b9–d10)

Socrates wants to determine which of the two names Homer considered as *more correct* (b9–11).[22] He kicks off by getting Hermogenes to concede two premisses: first, that the wiser use more-correct names than the less wise do (c2–5); secondly, that the men of a city are, on the whole, wiser than the women (c6–9). The latter is a genuinely Platonic tenet, provided the emphasis lies on 'on the whole': see *R.* 455ce. Then Socrates does something very strange, which we shall have to explain: he claims that Homer says the child was called 'Astyanax' by the 'men of Troy' and infers that, therefore, is was the women who called him 'Scamandrius' (c10–d3). His next step is to secure Hermogenes' agreement to a last premiss, i.e. that Homer too, like Socrates and Hermogenes, regarded men as wiser than women, and hence the Trojan men as wiser than the Trojan women (d5–7). Thus he is finished; and he can draw the conclusion that Homer regarded 'Astyanax', the name used by the men and hence by the wiser speakers, as more correct than 'Scamandrius' (d8–10).

We must now focus on Socrates' strange claim at c10–d3. It seems that, on the one hand, he is taking from *Il.* 6.401–3 the piece of information

---

[20] The sentence seems truncated; I substitute a dash for the question mark usually printed at c4.
[21] οὐκοῦν (c10 and then d5) is not inferential, 'then', but introduces a premiss, 'now': see *GP* 434.
[22] Kirk, in Kirk/Edwards/Hainsworth/Janko/Richardson 1985–94: II.212–13, discusses which of the two names was the child's given name and which was instead a nickname.

that the child was named both 'Scamandrius' and 'Astyanax', but not the further piece of information that it was Hector who used the former name and all the others who used the latter; and that, on the other hand, he is thinking of 22.505–7, where he perversely construes Τρῶες as referring to *male* Trojans as opposed to women. At 392e he will make the confusion between the two Homeric passages complete by offering a quotation that is actually a conflation of the two.

A horrible mess. An *unintentional* one? Like most scholars, I believe the answer is 'No'.[23] This is not because I am assuming that Plato must have known his Homer by heart and that his Homer must have been exactly the same as ours. On several occasions Plato misquotes Homer in a perfectly innocent way, whether this is due to faulty memory or to his being acquainted with a different Homeric text from the one that is printed in our editions.[24] Rather, what I find very suspicious in our particular case is the grossness of Socrates' mistake about *Il.* 6.401–3 (where he does not just misremember a word or two, but completely alters the substance of the passage – and of a most famous passage at that), in conjunction with his absurdly strained interpretation of 22.506. So I believe that Plato is deliberately making Socrates go astray, and that it is probably in order to achieve this purpose that he does not have Socrates quote the Homeric lines. (Or is it *Socrates* himself who pretends he is going astray? It is not easy to tell between author and character here; but 393c will suggest that Socrates can cheat: see §4.2.3.) This hypothesis also allows us to explain another feature of Socrates' discussion, i.e. the fact that he takes for granted, without any justification, that one of the two names 'Scamandrius' and 'Astyanax' must be *more correct than the other*, whereas later on he will make no such assumption about the pair 'Pallas'/'Athena' (406d–407c).[25]

If this is right, the function of Socrates' mistake is twofold. On the one hand, it carries on the parody of current Homeric exegesis that was already at work in the immediately previous references to the verses about divine and human names for the same things. On the other hand, it is a warning for the reader: Socrates' account of the natural correctness of names – which will be inspired by his further reflections on Astyanax's name – is not starting off auspiciously.

---

[23] Cf. Heindorf, Horn 1904: 32, Méridier 16, Labarbe 1949: 334–7, Minio-Paluello 18 n.22, etc. *Contra* see Sedley 2003: 78.
[24] Lohse 1964/1965/1967 discusses all Homeric quotations in Plato (but says nothing about our passage). Before him see Labarbe 1949.
[25] This problem was pointed out to me by Sergio Bernini, who suggested a different explanation. In the pairs formed by one divine and one human name for the same thing, which were dealt with immediately before (391d–392b), Socrates likewise assumed that one name – the divine one – is

4.2.2 'Astyanax' and 'Hector' (392d–393b). The argument previewed

Socrates has concluded that Homer must have regarded 'Astyanax' as more correct than 'Scamandrius' on the (false) grounds that Homer says the former name was used by the Trojan men while the latter was used by the women. But he has not explained what it is about 'Astyanax' that makes it more correct. This question he now goes on to confront.

SO. Well, let us inquire why. But doesn't Homer himself explain the reason to us most admirably? For he says 'for he alone protected their city and the long walls' ['οἶος γάρ σφιν ἔρυτο πόλιν καὶ τείχεα μακρά']. This, it seems, is the reason why it is correct to call the protector's son 'Lord of the town' ['Ἀστυάνακτα] which his father protected, as Homer says.
HE. So it appears to me. (392d11–e5)

Socrates is partly right: at *Il.* 6.403 and 22.507 Homer actually tells us that the name 'Astyanax', which etymologically means 'Town-lord' (ἄστυ-ἄναξ), was given to the child with reference to Hector's role in defending Troy. But obviously Homer does not concern himself with the name's *correctness* at all; he just wants to explain how the name originated. It is Socrates who turns this into an explanation of why the name is correct.

At e1 Socrates quotes *Il.* 22.507,[26] thus continuing to rely on the passage which has allowed him his wayward account of the 'Scamandrius'/'Astyanax' story. But his quotation is imprecise: Homer's text reads ἔρυσο πύλας ('[you] defended the gates') in place of ἔρυτο πόλιν ('[Hector] defended the city'). The mistake is probably significant: ἔρυτο is a reminiscence of 6.403 ἐρύετο, i.e. of the passage Socrates should have been relying on from the start; πόλιν may be a paraphrase of 6.403 Ἴλιον and in any case makes Homer's explanation of 'Astyanax' easier to understand, because it corresponds to the ἄστυ component in Ἀστυάναξ.[27]

Now Homer's explanation needs itself to be explained:

SO. Why on earth?[28] I don't yet myself understand, Hermogenes. Do you understand?
HE. By Zeus, I don't. (392e6–8)

---

more correct than the other; and there he did have some reason to assume this. So perhaps here he is unreflectingly taking for granted that the 'Scamandrius'/'Astyanax' pair will work in the same way, even though here both names are human. (On degrees of correctness see §4.1. Here the problem would be unaffected if Socrates more appropriately assumed that only one of the two names can be correct *simpliciter*.)

[26] For the text of *Il.* 22.505–7 and 6.401–3 see §4.2.1.
[27] See Lohse 1964: 9.
[28] Τί δή ποτε; (e6): cf. *Phlb.* 18a, *Plt.* 283b. The meaning is not 'Indeed?' (Fowler) or 'It does?' (Reeve, picking up e5).

What Socrates does not yet understand is how Homer can adduce the fact that *Hector* defended the city as an explanation of the fact that *his son* was called 'Astyanax', 'Town-lord'. This question may seem silly to you if, reading Homer with an open mind, you recognize that the name 'Astyanax' is said to have been a means to celebrate indirectly Hector's merits. But the question does make sense if you assume, as Socrates is doing, that Homer must be saying something about the name's *natural correctness*, i.e. about the way in which the name is appropriate to the nature of its bearer – hence to the nature *of the child*, not of his father.[29]

Then Socrates begins to see the solution. It will take some time before what he has in mind becomes fully clear, so it will be helpful to get a very sketchy preview of the argument first. It goes as follows:

(1) 'Astyanax' and 'Hector' signify (almost) the same, i.e. both signify that their bearer has the nature of a king. (393ab, 394bc)
(2) It is correct to call a lion's offspring a 'lion', a horse's offspring a 'horse', etc., provided the offspring is not a monster and has the same nature as its parent, as is normally the case. (393bc)
(3) Likewise, it is correct to call a king's offspring a 'king' – or any other name which signifies the same or has the same 'power' – a good man's offspring a 'good' one, etc., provided the offspring is not a monster. (393c–394e)

This is, essentially, the structure of the argument to come. The conclusion is implied: Homer was right to appeal to the kingly nature of Hector, the father, in order to explain the correctness of the name of Astyanax, the son. Homer was right to do so because he had every reason to believe that Astyanax inherited Hector's kingly nature, and the names 'Hector' and 'Astyanax' are equivalent to each other in that both signify that nature.

It should already be evident that there is much that is interesting in this argument – and much that is mistaken. Let us follow Socrates slowly as he takes one step after another, starting with the first statement of (1) (which will be restated at the end of the argument, with a small but important difference):

SO. But, my dear, didn't Homer himself give Hector too his name?
HE. Why?
SO. Because this name seems to me to be somewhat close to 'Astyanax' [παραπλήσιόν τι εἶναι τῷ 'Ἀστυάνακτι'], and these names seem to be

---

[29] Failure to grasp the purport of Socrates' question led Hermann to transpose e6–8 after d10 φαίνεται, i.e. immediately before the quotation of *Il.* 22.507. Stallbaum 67 gives the correct explanation.

Greek. For 'lord' and 'holder' signify roughly the same, i.e. that both names are kingly [ὁ γὰρ 'ἄναξ' καὶ ὁ 'ἕκτωρ' σχεδόν τι ταὐτὸν σημαίνει, βασιλικὰ ἀμφότερα εἶναι τὰ ὀνόματα]; for of that of which one is *lord* one is also *holder*, I think [οὗ γὰρ ἄν τις ἄναξ ᾖ, καὶ ἕκτωρ δήπου ἐστὶν τούτου]; for clearly he rules over it and possesses and *holds* [ἔχει] it. Or does it seem to you that there is nothing in what I am saying, and I am mistaken in thinking[30] that I'm hitting upon a trail, as it were, of Homer's views on the correctness of names?

HE. I don't think so, by Zeus: perhaps you are hitting upon something. (393a1–b6)

This is an important passage, because here Socrates begins to reconstruct Homer's views about the natural correctness of names (b1–6) and thereby to develop his own account of it. It finally turns out that the natural correctness of names (and, we might add, their serving the function of 'teaching and separating being', 388bc) depends on their *etymology* – more precisely, on their etymon supplying a true description of their referent. Socrates' early guess (384c) that Cratylus' rejection of 'Hermogenes' as a correct name of Hermogenes might be due to Hermogenes' failure to be an 'offspring of Hermes' was prophetic.

Socrates starts (a1–5) by pointing out that both Ἀστυάναξ, 'Astyanax' (i.e. 'Town-lord'), and Ἕκτωρ, 'Hector', look like Greek names instead of Trojan ones – which suggests that they were both devised by Homer. Indeed, the two names are 'close', i.e. similar, to each other. Then Socrates goes on (a5–b1) to explain these initial claims. The explanation he offers is that ἄναξ, 'lord', 'signifies roughly the same as' ἕκτωρ, 'holder' (i.e. Ἕκτωρ with a small ε – but remember that Plato wrote both as ΕΚΤΩΡ). And the reason why this in its turn is so is that, if one is ἄναξ of something, then one ἔχει, 'holds', it and hence is ἕκτωρ, 'holder', of it.[31]

The heart of the passage is at lines a5–b1, which contain the first occurrence in *Cra.* of the verb σημαίνω. For the first time in the dialogue we are being told – in a most unemphatic way – that part of the job of names is to *signify* something. But *what* exactly do names signify? What does Socrates mean when he says that ἄναξ and ἕκτωρ 'signify roughly the same' (a6)? Socrates gives us a clue, which has been generally misinterpreted.

Immediately after saying that the two names σχεδόν τι ταὐτὸν σημαίνει Socrates adds an infinitive clause, βασιλικὰ ἀμφότερα εἶναι τὰ ὀνόματα,

---

[30] λανθάνω καὶ ἐμαυτὸν οἰόμενος (b2): see de Vries 1955: 293–4, who cites *Sph.* 234b as a possible parallel.

[31] Socrates' interpretation of Ἕκτωρ as 'Holder', from ἔχειν, is sound. The term is attested as an epithet of Zeus by Hsch. ε 1750 Latte = Sapph. fr. 180 Voigt; Homer himself seems to hint at this etymology in *Il.* 5.472–3, 24.730. The suffix -τωρ is a typical one for *nomina agentis*.

which is clearly epexegetical and has the function of unpacking the reference to 'the same': ἄναξ and ἕκτωρ 'signify roughly the same thing, *i.e. that both names are kingly*', as I translated above. This has seemed problematic to most commentators. 'Haec quin pro corruptis habenda sint, nemo dubitabit', wrote Stallbaum 68; and after reporting attempted corrections by previous editors, he eventually proposed to delete the whole infinitive clause. He was followed by Hirschig, but not by twentieth-century editions; yet the clause has continued to cause trouble, because many translations try (impossibly) to change its syntax: e.g. Minio-Paluello 'e sono ambedue nomi regali';[32] Reeve 'since both are names for a king'. What has seemed problematic is presumably the fact that the infinitive clause, which should specify what both names signify, contains a circular reference *to the names themselves*. But this is hardly a serious problem; and a parallel passage should dispel any lingering doubt. It is 395c3–4, where Socrates sets forth the etymology of the name Πέλοψ, 'Pelops', as 'the one who sees (only) what is near', from the adverb πέλας + the root ὀπ-:

(SO.) This name signifies that the one who sees what is near is worthy of this denomination [σημαίνει γὰρ τοῦτο τὸ ὄνομα τὸν τὰ ἐγγὺς ὁρῶντα ἄξιον εἶναι ταύτης τῆς ἐπωνυμίας].

This passage has suffered an even worse fate than our lines: it was excised by Hermann, followed by Burnet, Méridier, the OCT editors and several translators,[33] while Stallbaum and Fowler preserve it.[34] But it is clear that the two passages support each other and are both sound.[35] Indeed, both receive further support from 413e, where Socrates claims that the name ἀνδρεία 'signifies that courage has been named in battle' (σημαίνει ὡς ἐν μάχῃ ἐπονομαζομένης τῆς ἀνδρείας).[36]

Now, what is really interesting is the fact that Socrates in both passages *specifies what the name signifies by means of a 'that'-clause*. There are many other instances of this in the dialogue: see e.g. 399c 'This name, "human", signifies that [σημαίνει ... ὅτι] the other animals do not investigate anything of what they see ... whereas the human being ...' etc.; and cf. 395ab, 415cd, 419a, 437ab. When this mode of expression is adopted, it suggests

---

[32] Cf. Cambiano and Dalimier. Fowler and Méridier translate correctly.
[33] Minio-Paluello and Reeve. Dalimier mistranslates again: '*Pélops* signifie en effet "celui-qui-ne-voit-pas-bien-loin" et il méritait, me semble-t-il, ce surnom.'
[34] It is funny that most of those who defend 393a7 condemn 395c3–4 and vice versa. Fowler is the exception: full marks to his sound judgement as an editor and translator in both cases.
[35] As argued in Ademollo 2001: 129–31.
[36] Strictly speaking, in this last passage σημαίνω does not govern a 'that'-clause but a clause (ὡς + gen. absolute) which is, in context, essentially equivalent to a 'that'-clause.

Naturalism and synonymy (392b–394e)   159

that Socrates is thinking of what a name signifies not as the name's referent, the thing named, but rather as some sort of *informational content* which the name conveys, through its etymology, *about* its referent – i.e. as something that has to do with the notion of a meaning or *sense* of names. This suggestion becomes explicit in Méridier's translation of our σχεδόν τι ταὐτὸν σημαίνει as 'ont à peu près le même sens'.

Let me quote a passage from a contemporary classic (Kripke 1980: 26) which contains a parallel for all the features of our lines as I am understanding them, i.e. where a name's etymological meaning is expressed by means of a 'that'-clause containing a circular reference to the name itself:

Perhaps we should say that a name such as 'Dartmouth' *does* have a 'connotation' to some people, namely, it *does* connote ... that any place called 'Dartmouth' lies at the mouth of the Dart. But ... it is not part of the *meaning* of the name 'Dartmouth' that the town so named lies at the mouth of the Dart.

Now we must move the spotlight forward to the justification Socrates offers at a7–b1 for his claim that ἄναξ and ἕκτωρ, 'lord' and 'holder', 'signify roughly the same, i.e. that both names are kingly'. With a modicum of paraphrase, the justification is that, if *X* is lord of *Y*, then *X* is holder of *Y*, which presumably means that '*X* is lord of *Y*' entails '*X* is holder of *Y*'. Note that he does not say that *X* is lord of *Y* *if and only if X* is also holder of *Y*, or that the two sentences *entail each other*. And this is just as well, because 'lord' is obviously more specific than 'holder'. This is undoubtedly connected with the fact that the two terms are said to signify *roughly*, not exactly the same – and indeed with the fact that at a4–5 'Astyanax' and 'Hector' were only said to be 'close' to each other.

4.2.3 *A lion begets a lion – and a king a king (393bd)*

We now move on from step (1) of the argument to (2), where Socrates begins to argue that the same terms must be applied to parent and offspring:

SO. It is right, as it seems to me, to call a lion's offspring a 'lion' and a horse's offspring a 'horse' [τὸν λέοντος ἔκγονον λέοντα καλεῖν καὶ τὸν ἵππου ἔκγονον ἵππον]. I am not speaking of the case in which from a horse a monster, as it were, is born, something other than a horse. I am rather speaking of the kind of which it is by its nature an offspring [ἀλλ' οὗ ἂν ᾖ τοῦ γένους ἔκγονον τὴν φύσιν, τοῦτο λέγω]:[37] if, contrary to nature, a horse begets something which

---

[37] At c1 ἀλλ' οὗ ἂν is the reading of βT, substantially confirmed by δ's ἀλλ' οὗ ἐάν and printed by Hirschig, Burnet and the OCT. ἀλλ' οὗ ἂν ᾖ τοῦ γένους = ἀλλὰ τὸ γένος οὗ ἂν ᾖ: for this kind of transposition see Cooper I.537–8, KG II.416–20, and cf. *R.* 402c οὔτε αὐτοὶ οὔτε οὓς φαμεν ἡμῖν

is by nature the offspring of an ox,[38] it must not be called a 'colt' but a 'calf'; nor, I think, if from a human something which is not the human's offspring is born,[39] must the offspring be called a 'human'. Likewise with the trees and with all the other things. Don't you agree?

HE. I agree. (393b7–c7)

Socrates is gesturing, by way of examples, towards a general principle, which I shall call 'Principle of Synonymical Generation' ('PSG' for short). This Principle could be formulated so:

(PSG) If X belongs to kind K, and X begets Y, then in the natural course of events Y too must be called (a) 'K'. If, however, Y is a monster and does not belong to K but to a different kind, say H, as though it had been begotten by an H, then Y must be called (an) 'H', not (a) 'K'.

But how general is this meant to be? What are the admissible substitutions for 'K'? When Socrates says 'Likewise ... with all the other things' (c5), what 'other things' is he talking about? All of the examples he gives in these lines, without exception, concern what we might call *natural kinds* (lion, horse, ox, human, trees); hence it is reasonable to think that PSG must be restricted accordingly, i.e. that the only admissible substitutions for 'K' are terms for natural kinds. Let us dub this the 'Restricted Principle of Synonymical Generation'.

The way in which Socrates introduces the Restricted Principle is strongly reminiscent of the Aristotelian tenet expressed by the slogan ἄνθρωπος ἄνθρωπον γεννᾷ, 'a human generates a human', and sometimes called the 'Synonymy Principle'.[40] According to this Aristotelian tenet, when something comes to be or is produced (whether in natural, artistic or spontaneous generation), a form specifically identical with the product's form

---

παιδευτέον εἶναι τοὺς φύλακας (= οἱ φύλακες οὕς κτλ.), 477c; Soph. OC 907–8 οὕσπερ αὐτὸς τοὺς νόμους εἰσῆλθ' ἔχων, τούτοισι ... ἁρμοσθήσεται (= τοῖς νόμοις οὕσπερ κτλ.), Ant. 404. Ficino translates correctly: 'cuius generis secundum naturam est quod nascitur, hoc dico'. Bekker, Stallbaum and Méridier instead adopt (and most translators translate as if they adopted) ἀλλ' ὃ ἄν, the reading of the fourteenth-century MS Venetus 590, already attested by its coeval antigraph Vindob. Philos. gr. 21 = Y: e.g. Reeve 'I'm not talking about some monster ... but one that is a natural offspring of its kind.' But the former reading is clearly *difficilior*, makes better sense, and is supported by 394de. (In fact the variant is likely to be much more ancient: see Ademollo, in preparation-1, where I also cite more examples supporting my construal of the text.)

[38] Like Hirschig and Méridier, I accept Ast's and Stallbaum's excision of μόσχον (c2), which smells like a gloss.

[39] After c4 γένηται the MSS add some words: ἀλλ' ὃ ἐὰν βW, ἄλλο ἐὰν T, ἀλλ' ἐὰν Q. Despite the efforts of some editors who tried to make something of them, these words are out of place here and were rightly deleted by Peipers. But they suggest something interesting about the origin of the variant ἀλλ' ὃ ἄν at c1: see Ademollo (in preparation-1).

[40] E.g. by Burnyeat 2001a: 33–4 and n.59. See the whole of his 29–38 on *Metaph.* Z7–9, Aristotle's main discussion of the Synonymy Principle.

must pre-exist it, either in nature or in the agent's mind. Read *Metaph.* Z 8.1033b29–1034a2:[41]

In some cases it is even evident that that which generates is such as that which is generated – not, however, the same, nor one in number, but in species, as in natural things (for a human generates a human), unless something comes to be contrary to nature, as e.g. a horse generates a mule [ἂν μή τι παρὰ φύσιν γένηται, οἷον ἵππος ἡμίονον]. And these cases are indeed similar; for what is common to horse and ass, the genus next above them, has not received a name, but it would presumably be both, like a mule.[42]

The similarities between this and our *Cra.* passage are, I think, evident. They even include the reference to a case 'contrary to nature' which, upon reflection, turns out to be no real exception to the rule. (But note the difference between the two examples: while Plato's horse dramatically – and improbably – begets a calf, Aristotle's begets an innocuous mule. There is in fact a rationale behind Plato's choice, as we shall see in due course: see §4.2.6.) Indeed, elsewhere Aristotle too, like Plato, formulates his Principle in the formal mode, i.e. not in terms of what parent and offspring *are* but in terms of what they are *called* – whence the label 'Synonymy Principle'. At Z9.1034a21–3 he claims that 'From what has been said it is also clear that in a way everything comes to be from something which has the same name [ἐξ ὁμωνύμου].' And at Λ3.1070a4–5 he says that 'each substance comes to be from something synonymous [ἐκ συνωνύμου]'.

So far so good. But Aristotle probably jumped on his seat when he first read how Socrates continues:

SO. Rightly said; for you must watch out lest I mislead you somehow [φύλαττε γάρ με μή πῃ παρακρούσωμαί σε]. For by the same reasoning it is also true that, if from a king some offspring is born, he must be called a 'king' [κατὰ γὰρ τὸν αὐτὸν λόγον κἂν ἐκ βασιλέως γίγνηταί τι ἔκγονον, βασιλεὺς κλητέος]. (393c8–d1)

Socrates is extending PSG to the case where *K* = king. This introduces step (3) of the argument (see §4.2.2); and it is a mistake. Of course monarchy is often hereditary; but it is not so in the sense in which being a lion or a human or an oak is. While a lion's offspring is itself a lion for sure, unless it is a freak of nature, a king's offspring need not himself be (or become in due course) a king, or – if kingship be a matter not of actually wearing a

---

[41] In the following lines (1034a2–5) Aristotle wields this against Platonic forms: if all that is needed for the generation of a particular is the pre-existence of a specifically identical Aristotelian form in another particular, then Platonic forms become superfluous.
[42] Translation after Barnes 1984.

crown, but rather of having something like a kingly nature – have such a nature.[43] And when a king's son is still a baby, there is no saying what will be of him. Indeed, Astyanax is a tragic case in point: as Plato doubtless knew very well, the story has it that he did not live enough to be king or manifest a kingly nature.[44]

This is, basically, Socrates' mistake in these lines. He will persist in it later on, at 394a, where he picks up the king case and proceeds to state a completely unrestricted version of the Principle of Synonymical Generation. But another, distinct mistake is looming, although it has not yet been committed; and we should be on our guard against it. This other mistake has to do with the distinction between general terms (or common nouns) and proper names. Socrates is speaking of a king begetting a king; but we know that sooner or later he will be driving at Hector's begetting Astyanax. Yet that is a completely different sort of issue, and PSG, even in those cases in which it works, can be of no help with it. A lion's offspring must be called a 'lion', all right; but it need not be called 'Lion'. And even if it were true that a king's offspring must be called a 'king', it would not yet follow that he must be called 'King'.

That said, I do not think that Aristotle really disapproved of what he read here. Indeed, I surmise that this is one of those occasions on which he found himself in agreement with his teacher. For Aristotle did not read just the words where Socrates effects the illegitimate extension of PSG to the king case, but also the previous ones, which so far I have not commented upon. We shall do well to consider them carefully.

Socrates' very first words in these lines are 'Rightly said' (c8). I suppose he says so because he takes Hermogenes' somewhat emphatic assent at c7 as a sign of reasoned agreement. Then he adds: 'For [γάρ] you must watch out lest I mislead you somehow' (c8–9). That is to say, Hermogenes does well to give a *reasoned* assent, because Socrates might deceive him. This might seem a generic warning. But when Socrates goes on to say '*For* [γάρ] by the same reasoning …' (c8–9), thus introducing the words about kings begetting kings, it becomes clear that he is precisely warning Hermogenes (and the reader) that the analogical extension of PSG from the cases considered at first to the king case is potentially misleading.[45]

---

[43] Hector himself was not the king of Troy; but he certainly had the nature of a king – if there is such a nature at all.

[44] In fact, 397b will suggest that Socrates is perfectly aware of the simple truth about why Astyanax was so called: many names of heroes and human beings 'have been set down in accordance with names of some ancestors, without being appropriate to some of their bearers'.

[45] Socrates' c8–9 warning was taken seriously already by Horn 1904: 33, who however construed it as casting suspicion on PSG as such, not just on its extension. Horn was followed by Méridier 16.

4.2.4 *The relative irrelevance of letters and syllables (393de)*

Socrates continues:

(SO.) And if the name signifies the same [τὸ αὐτὸ σημαίνει] in some syllables or in others, it does not matter. Nor, if some letter is added or subtracted, does this matter either, as long as the object's being, indicated in the name, is dominant [ἕως ἂν ἐγκρατὴς ᾖ ἡ οὐσία τοῦ πράγματος δηλουμένη ἐν τῷ ὀνόματι].
HE. What do you mean?
SO. Nothing complicated. It's as with letters: you know that we utter names for them but not the letters themselves, except in four cases, ε and υ and ο and ω, while the other vowels and consonants we utter while attaching other letters to them and thus making names. But as long as we put the letter's power into the name so that it is indicated, it is correct to call it by that name which will indicate it to us [ἕως ἂν αὐτοῦ δηλουμένην τὴν δύναμιν ἐντιθῶμεν, ὀρθῶς ἔχει ἐκεῖνο τὸ ὄνομα καλεῖν ὃ αὐτὸ ἡμῖν δηλώσει]. Take e.g. βῆτα: you see that the addition of η, τ and α did no harm and did not stop one indicating by the whole name the nature of that letter whose nature the lawgiver wished to indicate [τὴν ἐκείνου τοῦ στοιχείου φύσιν δηλῶσαι ὅλῳ τῷ ὀνόματι οὗ ἐβούλετο ὁ νομοθέτης].[46] So finely did he know how to impose names on the letters.
HE. What you're saying seems to me to be true. (393d1–e10)

At d1–5 Socrates introduces a qualification to the Principle of Synonymical Generation by claiming that the specific letters and syllables of which a name is composed are, within limits, irrelevant. He distinguishes two cases or respects in which this is so; then, at d7–e9, he illustrates the second by recourse to an example.

Let us focus on d1–5 first. The first respect which Socrates distinguishes (d1–2) comes to this: two names may be made up of different syllables and yet signify the same. Hence the formulation of PSG in §4.2.3 must be emended as follows:

(PSG′) If *X* belongs to kind *K*, and *X* begets *Y*, then in the normal course of events *Y* too must be called (a) '*K*', *or any other name that signifies the same*. If, however, *Y* is a monster and does not belong to *K* but to a different kind, say *H*, as though it had been begotten by an *H*, then *Y* must be called (an) '*H*', *or any other name that signifies the same*, not (a) '*K*'.

What Socrates has been saying so far would license us to suppose that he has the following sort of example in mind: a king's son must be called a

---

[46] The clause οὗ ἐβούλετο ὁ νομοθέτης (e7–8) admits of two different construals: (i) = οὗ [sc. τὴν φύσιν δηλῶσαι] ἐβούλετο ὁ νομοθέτης, as in Ficino's translation and in mine; (ii) = ὃ [sc. δηλῶσαι]

'king' himself – or a 'monarch', or a 'crowned head', or … or a 'holder', or a 'town-lord'. But in fact, as I said in §4.2.3, what he is ultimately interested in is a pair of *proper names*, i.e. 'Hector'/'Astyanax'.

The notion that a name can be made up of different syllables is obviously reminiscent of 389d–390a. But there are two differences between that passage and the present one. First, there Socrates spoke of names in *different languages*, whereas here he speaks of names belonging to the *same language*. Secondly (and more importantly), there Socrates spoke of the possibility for two names to *embody the same specific form of name* in different syllables, whereas here he speaks of the possibility for two names to *signify the same* in different syllables.[47] 'Signify the same' here harks back to the 393a claim that the names ἕκτωρ and ἄναξ 'signify roughly the same, i.e. that both names are kingly'; and as we saw in §4.2.2, the formulation of that claim suggested that Socrates was conceiving of the same thing which both names signify as being some sort of informational content or meaning which both names convey.

At 393d3–5 Socrates identifies a second respect in which letters are irrelevant: a name may contain letters which do not contribute to its signification or lack letters which, if present, would contribute to its signification. That this is what Socrates means is shown by the example, which he proceeds to offer at d7–e9, of the names of most letters of the Greek alphabet, which, like βῆτα, contain extra letters besides the one which the name actually signifies. Thereby, however, the discussion of PSG does not seem to make any real progress. The whole of d3–e9 looks like a digression where Socrates anticipates an issue that will become important in the etymological section.

In these lines an important role is played by the clause ἕως ἂν ἐγκρατὴς ᾖ ἡ οὐσία τοῦ πράγματος δηλουμένη ἐν τῷ ὀνόματι (d4–5), which refers to the *limits within which* the particular letters and syllables of which a name is composed are irrelevant. This clause, which I have translated 'as long as the object's being, indicated in the name, is dominant', is clearly picked up inside the letter-names example by e1–2 ἕως ἂν αὐτοῦ δηλουμένην τὴν δύναμιν ἐντιθῶμεν, 'as long as we put the letter's power into the name so that it is indicated'. This is followed by an apodosis (e3–4 'it is correct to

---

ἐβούλετο ὁ νομοθέτης, with attraction of the relative pronoun to the case of its antecedent ἐκείνου τοῦ στοιχείου, as in other translations (e.g. Fowler 'the nature of that letter which the lawgiver wished to designate').

[47] For more on the relationship between the account in terms of embodying the same form and the account in terms of having the same signification see §4.2.5.

call it by that name which will indicate it to us') which makes it clear that only if the condition mentioned in the protasis is satisfied will the name be correct. On the other hand, the former ἕως-clause, the d4–5 one, must have some close connection with d1-2 εἰ … τὸ αὐτὸ σημαίνει, 'if … it signifies the same', which served an analogous function. That is to say, it is not unreasonable to suppose that the following holds:

(4) 'X' and 'Y' signify the same ↔ the same being is δηλουμένη in both 'X' and 'Y' so as to be dominant in both.

This fits nicely with my hypothesis about the meaning of 'signify the same': meaning and connotation, i.e. the expression of the object's features,[48] are often believed to go hand in hand. Yet (4) is still obscure. What exactly is the relation between the parts of either side?

To make some progress let us dissect the d4–5 clause, starting with the participle δηλουμένη. This is the first occurrence in the dialogue of the verb δηλόω, which together with σημαίνω (which has itself just made, at 393a and then d, its first entrance on to the stage) is the main verb used by Plato and Aristotle to refer to the relation between linguistic expressions and what they signify. Both here and in the parallel clause at e3 the participle is usually translated 'shown', 'manifested', 'made clear' or the like;[49] and this is perfectly acceptable if we limit ourselves to these two clauses or to e7, where the object of δηλῶσαι is τὴν ἐκείνου τοῦ στοιχείου φύσιν, 'the *nature* of that letter'. Yet at e4 the verb's object is rather αὐτό, *the letter itself* which is the referent of a particular letter-name; and I doubt whether it makes any sense to say that a name 'shows', 'manifests' or 'makes clear' its referent – unless we suppose that 'to show X' is just short for 'to show X's being or nature'. But that supposition would not be supported by any evidence, and would indeed be contradicted by 433de, where δηλόω (and its derivative noun δήλωμα) is meant to express a name-object relation that is *neutral* between naturalism and conventionalism. Furthermore, in many contexts relevant to our subject, both in *Cra.* and elsewhere, δηλόω appears to be just equivalent to σημαίνω (as we shall see in some detail in §4.2.6). All these considerations constitute the rationale behind

---

[48] I am here using the term 'connotation' in the classic way of, e.g., J.S. Mill, *System of Logic* 1.ii.5.
[49] E.g. Fowler 'made plain', Méridier 'manifestée' (at d4–5). Reeve translates δηλόω as 'express' throughout. But this strikes me as too far from the verb's standard and primary meaning, 'show, make clear' etc. Moreover, although this rendering is appropriate when the grammatical object of the verb is the *being* of the thing named (i.e. when δηλόω has to do with connotation), as here, it becomes awkward when the grammatical object is rather *the thing named itself* (i.e. when δηλόω has to do with denotation), as at e4 and 433de (see §8.1.1 and n.6). Only 'indicate' seems to me as generic as 'signify' and as close to the verb's standard meaning 'show'.

my decision to translate δηλόω as 'indicate' both here (as Sedley 2003: 83 does) and elsewhere.⁵⁰

I move on to 'dominant' (ἐγκρατής). It is unclear what this is supposed to mean; no wonder that Hermogenes asks for some elucidation (d6). To start with, is there any difference at all between (i) the situation in which *X*'s being is indicated by '*X*' and (ii) the situation in which *X*'s being is indicated by '*X*' *and is 'dominant' in it*? The parallel clause at e2–3, where dominance is no longer mentioned, suggests that the answer is 'No': *X*'s being is dominant in '*X*' if and only if it is indicated by '*X*'. So the d4–5 clause, and my (4), are redundant.

That said, the notion of dominance is regrettably vague; and the example of the letter-names, which Socrates offers in response to Hermogenes' request (d7–e9), does little to make it more precise. In the letter-names, which for the most part contain irrelevant letters besides the one referred to,⁵¹ the dominance of the letter referred to consists in the fact that it is the name's *first* letter. E.g. the letter β, which is the referent of the name βῆτα, occupies the first place in it (likewise with ἄλφα, γάμμα, δέλτα etc.). But there are countless other cases to which this account does not apply, i.e. where the initial letter is not the least bit dominant; and Socrates does not tell us what to do with them. Is there anything natural about the fact that βῆτα means β while βῆμα means a step? If we go on arguing along these lines we shall find that convention is ubiquitous, in that even the naturalist needs it to prop up his own account of signification – which of course means that the naturalist's account is just pointless and that convention can do the job by itself. At 434c–435b we shall see Socrates advance an argument roughly to that effect (see §§8.1.1–3).

A word on 'being' before leaving d4–5. The present passage adds nothing to the previous occurrence of the term οὐσία at 388c. Here as there, several interpreters⁵² translate 'essence', while I prefer a more cautious

---

⁵⁰ Translations of ὃ αὐτὸ ἡμῖν δηλώσει (e4): Ficino 'quod nobis significet elementum', Fowler 'that will designate it for us' (the best ones); Reeve 'it will express it for us'; Minio-Paluello 'che ce la mostrerà'; Méridier 'qui le désignera clairement pour nous'; Dalimier 'qui nous la mettra en évidence'.

⁵¹ At d8–9 Socrates mentions four exceptions where the name coincides with the letter itself: ε, υ, ο, ω. In Plato's times these letters were not yet called by the names we still use ('epsilon', 'hypsilon', 'omicron', 'omega'): see LSJ s.vv.

Throughout d7–e9 Socrates uses two terms for 'letter', i.e. γράμμα and στοιχεῖον. The difference between the two seems to lie in the fact that στοιχεῖον (whose original and primary meaning is 'element': cf. 421d–422b) is preferred when a theoretical consideration of letters, or kinds of letters, is somehow in play. As Burkert 1959: 173 put it, 'Was στοιχεῖον von γράμμα unterscheidet, ist eben die Beziehung aufs rationale Analysieren, ist eben die Bedeutung "Element"'; see the whole of his 167–77.

⁵² Ficino, Fowler, Méridier, Minio-Paluello. Cf. §3.2.1.

rendering.⁵³ Many of the etymologies which Socrates is going to set forth cannot be meant to express the *essence* of the name's referent in any reasonable sense; in particular, many names will turn out to encapsulate descriptions which are not *uniquely* true of their referents. This could give rise to an argument in favour of convention: if a name '*N*' encapsulates a description true both of *X* and of *Y*, and yet names *X* but not *Y*, this can only be in virtue of convention. Thus it seems that a thoroughgoing naturalist should really hold that names express some peculiar feature of their referents, if not their essence. But Socrates will not make use of any such argument; and the generic meaning of the term οὐσία here seems to be confirmed by the paraphrase Socrates will adopt at 422d, according to which the correctness of names consists in 'indicating *what* each of the beings is *like*' (δηλοῦν οἷον ἕκαστόν ἐστι τῶν ὄντων). Only at 401cd, and then at 423ce, will the term's meaning be restricted to something like 'essence' or at least 'essential property' (see §6.2.4); and indeed, the 'ideal' names which Socrates goes on to envisage at 424b–425a will presumably be made in such a way as to imitate the essence of their referents.

Something remains to be said about Socrates' second statement, at e2–4, of the limits within which letters and syllables may come and go. This is inside the example about the letter-names; Socrates claims that a name for a letter will be correct as long as we put into it 'its [= the letter's] power so that it is indicated' (αὐτοῦ δηλουμένην τὴν δύναμιν). The reference to the letter's 'power' (δύναμις) may be puzzling. I shall soon argue that the δύναμις of a word, in *Cra.* as elsewhere, has something to do with its *sense*. But this is definitely not the meaning of the term here;⁵⁴ and it would be very odd if it were. Elsewhere in *Cra.* the δύναμις of a letter is something like the way it is articulated or sounds: cf. 412e (the name δίκαιος acquired τὴν τοῦ κάππα δύναμιν for the sake of pronunciation), 424c, 427a, b.⁵⁵ The use of the term in our passage seems to be connected with that. Socrates' point, however, reads somewhat far-fetched: what is included in and indicated by the name is *the letter itself*, not its 'power' (or its 'nature', e6–7).

4.2.5 *Synonymical Generation runs wild. The 'power' of names (394ab)*

Now Socrates returns to the Principle of Synonymical Generation, whose extension to the king case he was discussing at 393cd, before opening the parenthesis on the irrelevance of letters and syllables.

---

⁵³ Cf. Sedley 2003: 83.   ⁵⁴ *Pace* Reeve xxvi.
⁵⁵ Cf. Plb. 10.47.8 and D. H. *Comp.* 12, quoted by LSJ δύναμις iii.b.

so. Then the same reasoning holds of a king as well? For from a king a king will be born at some time, and from a good [man] a good [man], and from a beautiful [man] a beautiful [man], and likewise with all the other cases, from each kind an offspring of the same kind [ἔσται γάρ ποτε ἐκ βασιλέως βασιλεύς, καὶ ἐξ ἀγαθοῦ ἀγαθός, καὶ ἐκ καλοῦ καλός, καὶ τἄλλα πάντα οὕτως, ἐξ ἑκάστου γένους ἕτερον τοιοῦτον ἔκγονον], unless a monster is born. So we must call them by the same names [κλητέον δὴ ταὐτὰ ὀνόματα]. But variation in syllables is possible, so that names which are really the same [τὰ αὐτὰ ὄντα] might seem to the uninitiated to be different from each other – as the physician's drugs, if they are prepared so as to vary in colour and smell, appear different to us even though they are the same, whereas to the physician, who considers the power of drugs, they appear the same, and he is not perplexed by the additives. In the same way, I think, the one who knows about names too considers their power [τὴν δύναμιν αὐτῶν σκοπεῖ] and is not perplexed if some letter is added or transposed or has been subtracted, or even if the name's power [ἡ τοῦ ὀνόματος δύναμις] is embodied in completely different letters. (394a1–b7)

At a1–5 Socrates picks up the king case and adds more examples and a final generalization. He argues that PSG (see §§4.2.2–3) holds true for *K* = king, good, beautiful *or anything else*, i.e. whatever general term we substitute for '*K*' ('and likewise with all the other cases', a3). We may dub this the Unrestricted Principle of Synonymical Generation. Then, at a5–b7, Socrates elaborates on the notion that the letters and syllables of which a name is composed are comparatively irrelevant, and comes (by way of a comparison between names and drugs, a7–b3) to the radical formulation that names which seem to be different, because they are made up of different syllables, may in fact be *the same*, provided they have the same 'power'.

What is striking about the three examples Socrates gives at a2–3 is that they are all homogeneously mistaken. None of them concerns a natural kind; and in none is it actually true that, in a natural course of events, a *K* begets another *K*. By contrast, the examples collected at 393b7–c5 were all about natural kinds; and in all of them PSG did really work. That is to say, we have got two distinct groups of examples (two groups of proposed substitutions for '*K*' in PSG), each consisting of homogeneous items; and while the examples of the first group are all sound, those of the second are all mistaken. Furthermore, since the king example was already anticipated at 393c9–d1, before the digression on letters, what separates the first group from the second is Socrates' 393c8–9 warning: 'Watch out lest I mislead you somehow. For …'

This, to my mind, can only mean one thing: Socrates – or at least Plato – is *perfectly aware of the difference between the two groups of examples* and wishes us to grasp the difference ourselves, identify the argument's faulty step, and consequently hold fast to the Principle of Synonymical Generation only in its Restricted version, while jettisoning the Unrestricted one.

Indeed, there is a further, weighty reason for believing so. Of all possible examples, Socrates' second one turns on a good man begetting a good man 'unless a monster is born'. But it is utterly incredible that Socrates or Plato should regard the case of a good father having a bad son as a monstrosity comparable to the case of a horse begetting a calf. Alas, it is not a monstrosity, but a fairly ordinary fact, which is the basis for the question Socrates raises at *Men.* 93a–94e: how can virtue be teachable if so many fathers, though being themselves good, fail to make their own sons good?[56]

In §4.2.2 we imagined Aristotle's reactions on reading first Socrates' initial statement of his Principle at 393bc and then the introduction of the king case at c9–d1. What would Aristotle say now that the difference between the Restricted and the Unrestricted Principle has become clear? He answers right at the end of *Metaph.* Z9, 1034b16–19:

From these considerations we can grasp a peculiarity of substance, i.e. that it is necessary that there should be present beforehand another substance, actually existing, which produces it [ἀναγκαῖον προϋπάρχειν ἑτέραν οὐσίαν ἐντελεχείᾳ οὖσαν ἣ ποιεῖ], e.g. an animal if an animal comes to be. By contrast, it is not necessary that a qualified or a quantified item should pre-exist other than just potentially [ποιὸν δ' ἣ ποσὸν οὐκ ἀνάγκη ἀλλ' ἣ δυνάμει μόνον].

That is to say: a human begets a human, but it is not the case that a good (human) begets a good (human); all we can say is that a good (human) comes to be from something that is potentially such.[57] Thus Aristotle would explain the difference between Socrates' first and second group of examples as a difference between substances and accidents. How Plato himself would explain it we do not know; I shall offer a modicum of speculation on this score in §6.3.3, while commenting on the division of beings envisaged at 424d.

We can now move on to the second part of our passage, i.e. to lines a5–b7. At a5–7 Socrates picks up his earlier considerations (393de) about the irrelevance of letters and syllables and gives them a twist. Earlier he claimed, or seemed to claim, that names may be different in syllables and

---

[56] Here I am indebted to Myles Burnyeat (personal communication, 2001).
[57] According to Burnyeat 2001a: 36 and n.70, lines 1034b7–19 (of which b16–19 are the conclusion) are 'the climax of Z7–9'.

yet 'signify the same' (τὸ αὐτὸ σημαίνει 393d). Now he makes a bolder claim: names made up of different syllables, which seem different (ἕτερα) to someone who is not an expert about names, may actually be *the same name* (ταὐτὰ ὀνόματα a5, cf. a7). Putting the two claims together we obtain this, as the sequel will confirm:

(5) '*X*' and '*Y*' signify the same ↔ '*X*' and '*Y*' are the same name.

At a7–b3 Socrates begins to explain this startling claim by recourse to a comparison with drugs. The gist of what he says about drugs seems to go as follows: drugs which differ from each other in their outward appearance (colour and smell), and which therefore are regarded as different (ἄλλα) by the non-expert, are actually *the same drug*, and are recognized as such by the physician, if they have *the same 'power'* (δύναμις). The notion of a 'power' of drugs and foods is commonplace in ancient medical literature[58] and is, quite simply, the notion of their being able to produce certain effects when administered to a patient. So it seems reasonable to assume that *X* and *Y* will have the same 'power' if and only if they produce the same effects on any patient *Z* who is in a given physical condition.[59]

Socrates apparently means this: if one and the same substance (e.g. the juice of a certain plant) is the basic ingredient of two preparations, which contain different additives (and hence differ in 'colour and smell') but have the same power, then these two preparations actually count as one and the same drug. Very commonsensical. But note that Socrates' view that the power of drugs is their criterion of identity seems to commit him to a view much more radical, according to which, if two preparations which contain different additives *or even different basic ingredients* have the same power,[60] then they count as one and the same drug.[61]

---

[58] See e.g. Thphr. *HP* 9.19.4 (on which see n.61) on the δύναμις of plants, which were the basic ingredients of most drugs; Dsc. 1 Pr. 1 and *passim* on drugs; Hp. *VM* 3.4, 20.4, *Vict.* 2.39 on foods.

[59] Or, perhaps, *X* and *Y* will have *some* identical power if and only if, for any patient *Z* who is in a given physical condition, *some* of the effects *X* and *Y* produce on *Z* are the same.

[60] The whole of Dioscorides' *De materia medica* (first century AD) will be organized by drug affinities. See e.g. 1.34.1, 37.1, 58.3, 77.3–4 for talk of drugs having the same δύναμις.

[61] Such a view would not be as queer as it might seem at first glance. Theophrastus, *Historia plantarum* 9.19.4, raises a related question: 'Since the natures [φύσεις] of roots, fruits and juices have many powers [δυνάμεις] of all sorts, as regards those which have the same power and cause the same effects [ὅσαι ταὐτὸ δύνανται καὶ τῶν αὐτῶν αἰτίαι], and on the other hand those which cause contrary effects, one might consider a puzzle which perhaps applies to other puzzling cases as well, i.e. whether the items which cause the same effects do so in virtue of one single nature or it is possible for the same effect to come about also from different ones [πότερον ὅσα τῶν αὐτῶν αἴτια κατὰ μίαν τινὰ φύσιν ἐστίν, ἢ καὶ ἀφ' ἑτέρων ἐνδέχεται ταὐτὸ γίνεσθαι].' (In the last quotation φύσιν is my correction for the MSS δύναμιν, which seems to make little sense.)

At b3–7 Socrates rounds off his comparison by returning to names. Like the physician, the connoisseur of names considers only their 'power' (δύναμις again; were it not for the parallel with drugs, the term would perhaps be best translated as 'value')[62] and is not confused by superficial differences in letters and syllables.[63] Thus Socrates finally explains his a5–7 claim that materially different names may actually be the same name in terms of materially different names having the same 'power' or 'value'. Thereby from (5) above we get to this:

(6) '*X*' and '*Y*' signify the same ↔ '*X*' and '*Y*' have the same power ↔ '*X*' and '*Y*' are the same name.

If my hypothesis about 'signify the same' is right, then it seems to follow that the 'power' or 'value' of names is something like their meaning or *sense* (cf. Dalimier 210 n.83: 'la "valeur", c'est-à-dire le sens du mot'), the information they convey about their referent. But before reaching a decision on this issue it will be cautious to wait until we read the crucial next passage, 394b7–d1, and to take into account (what is seldom done) also the main evidence about the use of the term δύναμις in relation to names outside our dialogue. We shall do both things in §4.2.6.

Meanwhile, let me turn to Socrates' startling claim that materially different names are actually *the same name* provided they signify the same or have the same power. This cannot be disposed of as a hyperbole, as interpreters sometimes tend to do. It is a genuine Platonic view that things sharing a common feature or form are *the same* in respect of that feature or form. Thus at *Men*. 72ac Socrates claims that bees, which are many and different from each other, 'do not differ at all but are all the same' (οὐδὲν διαφέρουσιν ἀλλὰ ταὐτόν εἰσιν ἅπασαι) insofar as they are bees. And Aristotle will refine this notion by distinguishing between various kinds of sameness: in number, in species and in genus (*Top*. 1.7). So in our passage Socrates means exactly what he says: materially different names are actually the same name *insofar as* they signify the same, or have the same power. Socrates' talk of sameness between names would be all the

---

[62] 'Vis' Ficino; 'force' Fowler and Reeve; 'valeur' Méridier; 'potere' Minio-Paluello.
[63] Socrates distinguishes (b5–7) between two cases in which two names are materially different from each other: (a) 'some letter' is present in one name but not in the other, or occupies a different position between the two; (b) the two names are made up of 'completely different syllables'. There was a superficially similar distinction at 393d, where Socrates seemed to distinguish between two respects in which letters are irrelevant: (α) two names may be made up of 'different' (not '*completely* different'!) syllables and yet signify the same; (β) a name may contain irrelevant letters and yet be correct, i.e. signify what it should. In fact it seems that the two distinctions do not coincide and that both (a) and (b) illustrate (α).

more pregnant, and the parallel with the *Meno* and Aristotle's notion of sameness in species all the more relevant, if we could read it in the light of the fact that in his refutation of Hermogenes (389d–390e) he put forward the view that for any *X* there is a form of name of *X* which all particular names of *X* instantiate. But Socrates does *not* refer to the earlier passage here. I am inclined to regard this as one sign among others that the notion of a form of name of *X* is superseded by the following developments (cf. §3.4.3). As Kretzmann 1971: 131 (cf. 133) puts it, Socrates 'seems to set aside' the specific form of name 'in favor of "the force" of the actual name, and to replace embodiment with signification'.[64]

4.2.6 'Hector' and 'Astyanax' again (394be)

Now, at long last, Socrates can let Hector and Astyanax (or rather their names) re-enter the scene:

(SO.) It's as in the case we were discussing just now, 'Astyanax' and 'Hector': none of their letters is the same except τ, and yet they signify the same [ταὐτὸν σημαίνει]. And what letter does 'Archepolis' have in common? Yet it indicates the same [δηλοῖ ... τὸ αὐτό]; and there are many other names which signify nothing but a king [οὐδὲν ἀλλ' ἢ βασιλέα σημαίνει]. Others again signify a general [ἄλλα γε αὖ στρατηγόν], like 'Agis' and 'Polemarchus' and 'Eupolemus'. And others are medical [ἰατρικά], 'Iatrocles' and 'Acesimbrotus'; and we could presumably find lots of other names which are discordant in their syllables and letters, but consonant with regard to their power [ταῖς μὲν συλλαβαῖς καὶ τοῖς γράμμασι διαφωνοῦντα, τῇ δὲ δυνάμει ταὐτὸν φθεγγόμενα]. Does it appear to be so or not?
HE. Of course. (394b7–d1)

The Principle of Synonymical Generation has thus reached its most perverted state. It is not just that we must call a king's offspring a 'king'. Much worse than that, we must also call Hector's son 'Astyanax' (or 'Archepolis'), Agis' son 'Polemarchus' (or 'Eupolemus'), etc. And although Socrates does not draw this conclusion explicitly, this is why Homer can explain the correctness of 'Astyanax' with reference to Hector's kingly exploits.

Let us now have a closer look at what Socrates actually does in these lines. He takes three groups of names:

(i) Ἕκτωρ 'Holder', Ἀστυάναξ 'Town-lord', Ἀρχέπολις 'City-ruler';
(ii) Ἆγις 'Leader', Πολέμαρχος 'War-chief', Εὐπόλεμος 'Good-at-war';
(iii) Ἰατροκλῆς 'Famous-for-medicine', Ἀκεσίμβροτος 'Mortal-healer'.

[64] *Pace* Kahn 1973a: 163–4 n.16 and Ackrill 1994: 44 (on whom see already §3.4.3 n.97).

Although Socrates does not employ exactly the same sort of formulation for each of these three groups, it is fair to ascribe to him the following view: the names in each group differ from each other in their letters and syllables, but they all 'signify the same' (ταὐτὸν σημαίνει, c1) or 'indicate the same' (δηλοῖ ... τὸ αὐτό, c2–3).[65]

Here σημαίνειν and δηλοῦν, 'to signify' and 'to indicate', are clearly synonymous, as so often in contexts in which a philosophical reflection on language is at stake.[66] But, once again, what is it for two names to signify or indicate the same thing? In the present context it is not, I submit, to have the same *referent*; for the proper names listed by Socrates as examples are names of different persons. So it must rather be something like having the same (etymological) meaning or *sense* – or, if you prefer, the same (etymological) *connotation* (cf. the 393d mention of 'the object's being, indicated [δηλουμένη] in the name'). My initial hypothesis about 'signify the same', which was advanced on the basis of the formulation at 393a, is thus confirmed; and Socrates' talk of names having the same 'power' will have to be construed in the same way.

It could be (and has been, as we are going to see) objected that in fact each group of examples consists of names whose (etymological) sense is not the same, but only similar.[67] I have two replies. First, the fact that the names in each group differ from each other in sense is, strikingly enough, *not* mentioned by Socrates. Throughout the passage the only difference

---

[65] At c7–9 Socrates also speaks of names which, while ταῖς μὲν συλλαβαῖς καὶ τοῖς γράμμασι διαφωνοῦντα, 'discordant in their syllables and letters', are τῇ δὲ δυνάμει ταὐτὸν φθεγγόμενα. This last expression has been variously translated: 'qui rendent des bruits vocaux de valeur identique' Dalimier; 'qui ... disent, pour ce qui est de la valeur, la même chose' Méridier; 'which ... express the same meaning' Fowler; 'which have the same force or power when spoken' Reeve. What is puzzling here is φθεγγόμενα. Only Dalimier has a chance of being literal here; for φθέγγεσθαι is not exactly 'to say' something, let alone 'to express' a meaning. And yet her translation is somewhat odd: why should Socrates speak of names which 'make the same noise' or 'utter the same sound' with regard to their power, given that he is precisely contrasting difference in sound with sameness of power? I suspect (and have assumed in my translation) that the great Ficino was right to regard ταὐτὸν φθεγγόμενα as carrying on the *musical* metaphor introduced by διαφωνοῦντα: 'syllabis et litteris discordantia, vi autem significationis penitus consonantia'. Of course the expression is pregnant, because names are items one φθέγγεται, utters.
Alternatively, φθεγγόμενα might conceivably be *passive* (cf. *Sph.* 257c ἐπιφθεγγόμενα, and see KG I.120–1 on the passive of deponent verbs) and ταὐτόν predicative: '*uttered as the same name* with regard to their power' (see Ademollo 2009: 37 and n.21). Socrates would then be picking up his earlier point (394ab) that two names are actually the same name provided that, and insofar as, they signify the same.
[66] See *Sph.* 261d–262d (where δηλοῦντα = σημαίνοντα and δήλωμα 'means to indicate' = σημεῖον 'sign'), Arist. *Cat.* 3b10–13 (σημαίνει ~ τὸ δηλούμενον), *Metaph.* 1062a14–15; Diogenes of Babylon, D. L. 7.58 = *FDS* 536 = Long/Sedley 33M.
[67] Ἀστυάναξ and Ἀρχέπολις might be the only exception, if we granted that ἄστυ 'town' is synonymous with πόλις 'city' and ἄναξ 'lord' with ἄρχων 'ruler'.

he mentions, and contrasts with the fact that the names signify the same, concerns their letters and syllables. Secondly, I actually believe that, when Socrates speaks of these names as signifying/indicating *the same*, or as being the same in respect of their power, he is speaking somewhat hyperbolically. He says 'the same', but knows he rather ought to say 'roughly the same'. This is demonstrably so at least in the most important case, i.e. the 'Hector'/'Astyanax' pair. For at 393a Socrates said no more than that these are 'close' to each other. Moreover, he went on to claim that ἕκτωρ 'holder' and ἄναξ 'lord' – i.e. the etymon of the former name and the corresponding part of the etymon of the latter – 'signify *roughly* the same' (σχεδόν τι ταὐτὸν σημαίνει); and the addition of the ἄστυ component to ἄναξ to obtain the compound 'Astyanax' can only increase the difference in sense from 'Hector', because it generates a sense more specific than that of the simple ἄναξ, which was itself more specific than that of ἕκτωρ.

Now consider the phrases οὐδὲν ἀλλ' ἢ βασιλέα σημαίνει and στρατηγόν (σημαίνει), which Socrates uses at c4 to express what the names in groups (i) and (ii) respectively have in common. Above I have translated them 'signify nothing but a king' and 'signify a general' respectively. But what do they mean exactly? On the present interpretation, they do not mean that each of the names in (i) refers to an individual object which is in fact a king, while each of the names in (ii) refers to an individual object which is in fact a general. Nor does Socrates mean (as some have thought: see below) that each of the names in (i) refers to a universal object or kind, the king, while each of the names in (ii) refers to another universal object or kind, the general. This latter construal, besides being incompatible with my interpretation, is in any case unlikely in view of the lack of the article before βασιλέα and στρατηγόν. But then again, I doubt whether the phrases can literally mean that the names in (i) 'mean simply "king"' while those in (ii) 'mean "general"', as Fowler and others translate,[68] although I agree with the spirit of this construal. Rather, I believe the meaning is this: each of the names in (i) signifies an individual object *as a king* – i.e. it signifies *that its referent is a king* – while each of the names in (ii) signifies an individual object *as a general* – i.e. signifies *that its referent is a general*. Socrates expressed himself precisely in the 'that' form at 393a. And in this very passage he picks up that formulation when he says, at c6, that the names in group (iii) are all ἰατρικά, 'medical', i.e. names for a physician: the adjective ἰατρικά is parallel to 393a7 βασιλικά.

[68] Méridier: 'n'ont d'autre sens que celui de "roi" ... signifient "chef d'armée"'; cf. Dalimier. Reeve translates 'signify simply king ... signify general', which fails to make clear what exactly Socrates is claiming.

I now wish to discuss a very different way of reading the present passage, which has been proposed by Heitsch 1985: 58–61 and Sedley 2003: 84–5.[69] They hold that the point which Socrates is making here is not really about proper names (in his exemplification, the proper names Ἕκτωρ 'Holder', Ἀστυάναξ 'Town-lord' etc.), but rather about proper names *construed as general terms*, with small initials as it were (i.e. ἕκτωρ 'holder', *ἀστυάναξ 'town-lord' etc.). The point itself is, in their view, that the terms within each group have different letters and *different (etymological) sense but the same reference*, because they all refer to one and the same kind or type (the king, the general, the physician) through different descriptions. On this interpretation, the δύναμις or power of a term, which is the same for all the terms in each group of examples, is not their sense; for the terms in each group do not in fact have exactly the same sense. Perhaps we might rather take the power to be something like the referen*ce* of a term as distinct from its referen*t*.

It should already be clear from my previous considerations that, to my mind, this 'Fregean' interpretation has four drawbacks: it disregards the 393a clue about 'to signify'; it disregards the 393d reference to 'the object's being, indicated in the name';[70] it adopts a dubious construal of the c4 phrases οὐδὲν ἀλλ' ἢ βασιλέα σημαίνει and στρατηγόν (σημαίνει); and it attaches great importance to an element (the difference in etymological sense between Socrates' examples) which Socrates does not even mention. A fifth drawback is this: the assumption that the proper names offered by Socrates as examples are in fact to be considered as general terms is far-fetched.

If we now take into account the evidence concerning talk of a 'power' of names outside our passage, then we see that it provides a sixth argument against the Heitsch/Sedley view and bears out my interpretation. Let us have a look at this evidence, which so far has received litte attention.

I start with 405e, the only other *Cra.* passage mentioning the δύναμις of names. There Socrates says that some people (cf. Aeschylus, *Ag.* 1080–2) wrongly derive Apollo's name, Ἀπόλλων, from ἀπολῶν, the future participle of ἀπόλλυμι 'destroy',

because they do not examine correctly the name's power [τὴν δύναμιν τοῦ ὀνόματος], and fear it as though it signified some sort of destruction [ὡς σημαῖνον φθοράν τινα]. (405e3–406a1)

---

[69] See also Baxter 1992: 133.
[70] In fact Sedley (2003: 86) lays stress on the 388bc claim that the name of *X* 'separates the being' of *X*. But then he seems to regard 'separating the being of *X*' as equivalent to 'designating *X*' – which I do not understand. The being of *X* is surely something distinct from *X*, especially (though not only) because here 'being', as Sedley himself insists elsewhere, is more generic than 'essence'.

Here what the name signifies is expressed by means of an *abstract* noun ('destruction'), not a concrete one ('destroyer'). Therefore it cannot possibly be the name's referent, not even if the name were considered as a general term. The name's signification, and its power, must have to do with its sense, or meaning, or informational content, or connotation, or what have you.

It is noteworthy that Socrates' 405e reference to the δύναμις of Apollo's name comes both after and before various references to the god's various δυνάμεις, 'powers' (404e, 405a, 406a), as shown by the name's various etymologies. Likewise in our argument Socrates spoke first of a δύναμις of drugs and then went on to use the term in relation to names. It looks as if he feels that this latter use is a still unfamiliar metaphor which has to be made explicit in order to be appreciated. Yet there is at least one pre-Platonic occurrence of the term δύναμις in relation to names, Lysias 10.7. There the speaker is bringing an action for abusive language against a Theomnestus, who publicly claimed that the speaker had killed his (the speaker's) own father. Theomnestus has argued that what the law prohibits is calling someone a 'slayer', *not* saying he has killed someone. The speaker writes off this defence:

I … think we must disagree not about names but about their meanings [οὐ περὶ τῶν ὀνομάτων … ἀλλὰ τῆς τούτων διανοίας], and that you all know that those who are slayers have killed someone.[71] It would have been very difficult for the lawgiver to write in all the names which have the same power [ἅπαντα τὰ ὀνόματα … ὅσα τὴν αὐτὴν δύναμιν ἔχει]; instead, pronouncing himself about one name he gave an indication about all.

What is interesting about this passage from our present point of view is the association between talk of the διάνοια of names, literally their 'meaning' or 'sense', and talk of their δύναμις. This is especially interesting because in the etymologies of our dialogue, as we shall see in §5.4, Socrates will speak of a name's διάνοια (418ab; cf. the use of the related verb νοέω, e.g. at 397e) as something closely connected with the name's signification, if not itself signified by the name, and depending on its etymology.

A related use of the verb δύναμαι is better attested. Herodotus uses it several times to say that a linguistic expression from a foreign language δύναται the corresponding Greek expression (e.g. 2.30.1, 4.110.1, 4.192.3, 6.98.3); I take it that this harmonizes with my interpretation of δύναμις.

[71] Reading ὅσοι ἀνδροφόνοι εἰσί, καὶ ἀπεκτόνασί τινας (MSS) instead of ὅσοι <ἀπεκτόνασί τινας, καὶ ἀνδροφόνοι εἰσί, καὶ ὅσοι> ἀνδροφόνοι εἰσί, καὶ ἀπεκτόνασί τινας (an unnecessary supplement inspired by Auger and accepted by most editors).

Naturalism and synonymy (392b–394e)

And sometimes the verb is used within a claim to the effect that two linguistic expressions δύναται the same: see *PDerveni* coll. x, xi, and especially Arist. *APr.* 49b3–9:

> We must substitute expressions which δύναται the same, names for names and phrases for phrases and name and phrase, and always take the name in place of the phrase; for the setting out of the terms is easier. E.g., if it makes no difference whether we say that the believable is not a genus of the opinable or that the opinable is not a particular kind of believable, because what is signified is the same [ταὐτὸν γὰρ τὸ σημαινόμενον], instead of the phrase mentioned[72] we must take as terms the believable and the opinable.

Here it is pretty clear that 'δύναται the same' means 'have the same sense'. In particular, note that here, as in *Cra.*, having the same δύναμις, or δύνασθαι the same, is treated as equivalent to signifying the same, and that here 'signifying the same' must itself mean something like 'having the same sense'. For Aristotle is saying of two complete sentences that what is signified by them is the same; and he is most unlikely to mean that their *referent* is the same.[73]

Let us now get back to the text and resume our reading. At 394b7–d1, which we have just finished discussing, Socrates has seamlessly (and perversely) extended the Principle of Synonymical Generation to proper names for the natural case in which the offspring belongs to the same kind as the parent. But the Principle also allowed for the possibility of generation 'contrary to nature'; so a corresponding extension must be made for this case as well.

SO. So to those which are born according to nature the same names must be assigned.
HE. Of course.
SO. But what about those which are born contrary to nature, in the form of a monster? E.g., when from a good and God-fearing man an impious son is born, isn't it as in the cases we were considering before, where we saw that, if a horse begets an ox's offspring, the offspring must presumably not have the denomination of its begetter, but that of the kind to which it belongs [οὐ τοῦ τεκόντος δήπου ἔδει τὴν ἐπωνυμίαν ἔχειν, ἀλλὰ τοῦ γένους οὗ εἴη]?
HE. Of course.
SO. Therefore to the impious son which is born of a pious man, too, the kind's name must be assigned.
HE. It is so.

---
[72] I.e. the former.
[73] Cf. Ross 1949: 410, who paraphrases ἃ τὸ αὐτὸ δύναται (49b3) as 'synonymous expressions' and ταὐτὸν ... τὸ σημαινόμενον (b8) in terms of the claim that the two sentences 'mean the same'.

SO. Not 'Theophilus', as it seems, nor 'Mnesitheus', nor any such name, but rather any name which signifies the contrary of these [ἀλλ' ὅτι τἀναντία τούτοις σημαίνει], if the names attain their correctness.
HE. It's undoubtedly so, Socrates. (394d2–e7)

If a pious father begets, 'contrary to nature', an impious son, the son must not be called by any such name as 'Theophilus' (i.e. 'God-beloved') or 'Mnesitheus' (i.e. 'God-remembering'). These names would be appropriate to his father, but not to him, who actually belongs to a different kind and must be named accordingly.

My only comment about these lines is that they help us understand why Socrates, both here (d7–8) and earlier (393bc), chooses a horse begetting a calf as an example of generation 'contrary to nature' instead of Aristotle's much more ordinary example, a horse begetting a *mule*. We can put it as follows. Given the generic situation in which a K begets not a K but an H, Socrates wants to deny that there is any difference between two cases: (a) the case in which K and H are natural kinds, (b) the case in which K and H are not natural kinds.[74] As (a) is a case of generation 'contrary to nature', so is (b). But in fact Socrates' present example (a good, pious father begetting an impious son) suggests that he is especially interested in something more specific than (b), i.e. (b') the case in which K and H are not natural kinds *and are contrary to each other*. Now, if Socrates illustrated case (a) by recourse to the example of a horse begetting a mule, this would weaken the parallel between (a) and (b'). For the mule is a cross-breed, the offspring of a horse and a donkey; as Aristotle says (*Metaph.* Z8.1033b33–1034a2, see §4.2.3), it has a genus in common with both parents. So the example of a horse begetting a calf (i.e. an ox) makes for a sharper contrast between parent and offspring and is fitter to constitute a parallel to the example of a pious man begetting an impious one.

4.3 CONCLUSION (394E–396C)

It is time to take stock of the whole section which we have been discussing in this chapter. The section began at 390e–391a, where Hermogenes asked Socrates – who had just concluded that names are correct by nature – to explain what the natural correctness of names consists in. That purpose

---

[74] Please remember that 'natural kinds' was my own label for Socrates' first group of examples (393bc). One reason for choosing that label was that it was not an overtly Aristotelian one, as e.g. 'substantial kinds' would have been. But what matters is not so much the particular label we adopt as the fact that Socrates recognizes that the examples of his first group have something in common which distinguishes them all from those in the second group (393cd + 394a). See §4.2.5.

Conclusion (394e–396c)

has been achieved: along the way we have indeed learnt that a name's natural correctness consists in the fact that it indicates, through its etymology, the being of its referent – i.e. in the fact that its etymology provides a true description of its referent.

But Socrates has been doing much more than it would have been necessary to achieve this result. Instead of, say, simply hitting upon a number of successfully descriptive names (whether taken from Homer or from some other source), he has been routing the argument through the Principle of Synonymical Generation and its various successive corruptions. Hence a question arises: why do it this way?

This question is all the more pressing because the discussion of the Principle, besides being unnecessary to the achievement of Socrates' purpose, is also strikingly ignored in the immediate sequel. If you have a quick look at how Socrates goes on at 394e–396c, you will see that he etymologizes the names of the genealogy of the Atreidae, proceeding backwards from son to father: Orestes, Agamemnon, Atreus, Pelops, Tantalus, Zeus, Cronus, Uranus. You might think that thereby Socrates is applying the Principle to other pairs of parent and offspring besides the Hector/Astyanax one. But this is not so. If you consider the text in more detail, you see that every name in the series is analysed on its own; that almost no son turns out to have a name ascribing to him the same nature as his father's; and that the Principle is never mentioned explicitly, not even to be rejected.[75] Thus Ὀρέστης derives from ὀρεινόν 'mountainy' (indicating the hero's wild nature); Ἀγαμέμνων from ἀγαστὸς κατὰ τὴν ἐπιμονήν, 'admirable for his steadfastness'; Ἀτρεύς simultaneously from ἀτειρές 'stubborn', ἄτρεστον 'fearless' and ἀτηρόν 'ruinous'; Πέλοψ, literally 'Near-sighted', from πέλας 'near' + the root ὀπ-; Τάνταλος from ταλαντεία,[76] the 'balancing' of the stone which was part of his punishment, and from ταλάντατος 'most wretched'; Ζεύς (together with its heteroclite forms Διός, Διί etc.) from δι' ὃν ζῆν ἀεὶ πᾶσι τοῖς ζῶσιν ὑπάρχει, 'the one *because of whom living* belongs to all living beings'; Κρόνος from κόρος νοῦς, 'pure mind'; Οὐρανός from ὁρῶν τὰ ἄνω, 'looking at the things above'.[77]

So why do it this way? Why does Socrates drag in the Principle of Synonymical Generation? I can think of only one answer: because Plato *is*

---

[75] See Horn 1904: 34–5. *Contra* see Anceschi 2007: 38–9.
[76] Spalding's correction of the MSS ταντάλεια, accepted by most scholars but not by the OCT.
[77] More precisely, it is the adjective οὐρανία, as applied to the 'sight directed to what is above', that is derived from ὁρῶσα τὰ ἄνω (396bc). The Cronus/Uranus pair is perhaps the only one where the Principle could be said to hold: see §5.1.3.

interested in the Principle – and in its various successive corruptions – for its own sake. He wants to stimulate our reflection both on the move from the Restricted to the Unrestricted version of the Principle (a move which he has Socrates flag at 393c) and on the fatal extension to proper names. He wants to do so because he believes that these are philosophically important matters, which can be profitably discussed in the context of an inquiry into the correctness of names.

CHAPTER 5

Naturalism illustrated: the etymologies of 'secondary' names (394e–421c)

With Socrates' analysis of the names in the Atreidae genealogy, from Orestes up to Uranus (394e–396c), the etymologies have begun. The very long section of the dialogue which is devoted to them extends as far as 427d (thus covering 46 pages out of 85 occupied by the whole OCT *Cratylus*) and contains analyses of a great many words, interspersed with moments of theoretical reflection.

As I have already anticipated time and again, in *Cra.* we meet two different kinds of etymology. At a first stage Socrates' analyses follow the pattern established by his discussion of Ἕκτωρ, Ἀστυάναξ etc. in 393a–394e, and already hinted at by his interpretation of Cratylus' 383b claim about Hermogenes' name. According to this pattern – the standard one in Greek etymology before and after Plato – names are more or less disguised *descriptions* of their referents, deriving either from one single word (Ἕκτωρ, Ἆγις) or from more words conflated together in what is actually a compound name (Ἀστυ-άναξ, Ἀρχέ-πολις etc.). Owing to the lapse of time, of course, most names do not bear their etymology on their face any more: some letters must be added or subtracted to recover the original form.

At a second stage (421c ff.)[1] Socrates will face the problem of accounting for those names that cannot be analysed further into other more elementary names. This will call for a different kind of etymologies, based rather on the *mimetic power* of the letters/sounds that constitute a name. Socrates will call such names 'first' or 'primary' (πρῶτα) and those in the former group 'secondary' (ὕστερα).

I devote the present chapter to the former group of etymologies, which are likely to have some connection with Cratylus' own activity. This new subject will require a temporary change of pace on our part. The length of the section to be dealt with makes it impossible for me to translate and

---

[1] There is a second, much shorter series of etymologies of 'secondary' names at 437ac: see §8.2.2.

comment on the whole text. Hence in this chapter (as in a small part of the following one) I shall look at the text from a more distant vantage point than elsewhere, trying to capture what goes on in the etymological section, identifying some strands that run through the whole of it, and discussing in detail a selection of especially relevant passages.

5.1 THE ARRANGEMENT OF THE ETYMOLOGIES

We should first try to get an idea of the contents of the section and how they are arranged. This is no trivial matter, because there are few explicit indications, and the conversation between Socrates and Hermogenes contains several stops, digressions and restarts, which may or may not amount to intended structural joints. My own criterion will be to identify a joint between two groups of etymologies when, and only when, two distinct conditions are satisfied together: (i) there is some sort of explicit interruption in the sequence of etymologies, which separates two groups of names from each other; (ii) the interruption coincides with a recognizable change of subject from the former to the latter group. Whenever my account differs from others (Gaiser 1974: 54–7; Reeve xxvii–ix; Sedley 2003: 89–90, 113–14), this is because I find that one of these two conditions has been neglected.

5.1.1 Analysis of 394e–421c

So at 394e–396c we have the genealogy of the Atreidae, from Orestes back to Uranus; then Socrates apologizes for not pursuing his inquiry even further, according to the line of the Hesiodic theogony. He briefly dwells upon his present etymological 'wisdom', which he attributes to a state of inspiration due to a conversation with Euthyphro (396c–397a). Then Socrates asks where the etymological inquiry is to be started (he should rather say *re*started). He proposes (397ac) to leave aside the names of heroes and human beings; the naturally correct names are rather likely to be found 'concerning the things that always exist by nature' (περὶ τὰ ἀεὶ ὄντα καὶ πεφυκότα: for the moment I defer the question of what such things are).

As a consequence, at 397c Socrates deems it right to begin with the gods (ἀπὸ τῶν θεῶν ἄρχεσθαι), as at a feast, and more precisely with the very name θεοί. Then at 397d–399c it is the turn of the names δαίμων 'daimon', ἥρως 'hero' (two etymologies) and ἄνθρωπος 'human'.

The arrangement of the etymologies

Then, at 399d, Hermogenes says he would like to hear of a matter coming 'next to these' (τούτοις ἑξῆς): the names of the human soul and body, ψυχή and σῶμα (399d–400c: respectively two and three etymologies). This looks like an appendix to the previous group.

At 400d Hermogenes imposes a strong stop: 'These things seem to me to have been adequately [ἱκανῶς] expounded.' He then asks Socrates to inquire into the correctness of the names of the gods (περὶ δὲ τῶν θεῶν τῶν ὀνομάτων) in the same way as he has already done for Zeus's name. Socrates is happy with this proposal, but needs to state a caveat first: we know nothing about the gods and their true names; we shall rather talk about the humans and the opinions that governed their imposition of the gods' names. Hermogenes agrees (400d–401a).

At 401b Socrates actually starts off the series of the Homeric gods' names. The series expressly begins with Hestia, as is customary in sacrifices and prayers (in keeping with Socrates' beginning with the gods at 397c), and goes on until 408d, where the etymology of Pan's name is concluded. Here is a list of the names in this series (with parentheses indicating digressions and numbers indicating that more than one etymology is mentioned for a single name, whether approvingly or not):[2]

Ἑστία 'Hestia', (οὐσία 'being' 2), Ῥέα 'Rhea', Κρόνος 'Cronus', Τηθύς 'Tethys', Ποσειδῶν 'Poseidon' 3, Πλούτων 'Pluto', Ἅιδης 'Hades' 2, Δημήτηρ 'Demeter', Ἥρα 'Hera' 2, Φερρέφαττα/Φερσεφόνη 'Persephone', Ἀπόλλων 'Apollo' 5, Μοῦσαι 'Muses', Λητώ 'Leto' 2, Ἄρτεμις 'Artemis' 3, Διόνυσος 'Dionysus', (οἶνος 'wine'), Ἀφροδίτη 'Aphrodite', Παλλάς 'Pallas', Ἀθηνᾶ 'Athena' 3, Ἥφαιστος 'Hephaestus' 2, Ἄρης 'Ares' 3, Ἑρμῆς 'Hermes' 2, Ἶρις 'Iris',[3] Πάν 'Pan'.

A capital point to remark is that at 401d–402d the etymologies of ὠσία (a Doric variant of οὐσία), Ῥέα and Κρόνος introduce the Heraclitean doctrine of universal flux. The doctrine is hinted at again in the analysis of Φερρέφαττα (404cd) and will later become a dominant theme of the etymologies (see §§5.3.3–4, 5.4).

Socrates makes a first attempt at closing the series of the divine names with 'Ares':

SO. Let us leave off from the gods [Ἐκ μὲν οὖν τῶν θεῶν ... ἀπαλλαγῶμεν], in the name of the gods, because I fear to talk about them; propose to me to talk about whatever else you want. (407d6–8)

---

[2] The name of Zeus has of course been already analysed at 396ab, as 402d recalls. This should hold of Cronus too; yet a fresh etymology is hinted at in 402b.
[3] The Iris etymology (408b) was deleted by Heindorf and all subsequent editors save Stallbaum and Fowler. For a vindication of its authenticity see Ademollo 2001.

Hermogenes, however, still wants to hear about the name 'Hermes'. Having done away with this, and after etymologizing also 'Iris' and 'Pan', Socrates again asks to leave off from the gods (408d4–5 ὅπερ ἐγὼ ἔλεγον … ἀπαλλαγῶμεν ἐκ τῶν θεῶν).

This time Hermogenes indulges him – with a qualification: they will leave off from *such* gods (Τῶν γε τοιούτων 408d6), only to turn to gods of a different sort (περὶ τῶν τοιῶνδε δὲ τί σε κωλύει διελθεῖν … ;). These are the sun, moon and stars, the elements, the seasons and the year (408de): what we might label the objects of natural science.[4] Socrates accepts, and thus we have a new section, which will last until 410e. Here is a list of the terms analysed, with brackets and numbers as above:

ἥλιος 'sun' 3, σελήνη 'moon', μείς 'month', ἄστρα 'stars', ἀστραπή 'lightning', πῦρ 'fire', ὕδωρ 'water', (κύων 'dog'), ἀήρ 'air' 3, αἰθήρ 'aether', γῆ 'earth', ὧραι 'seasons', ἐνιαυτός 'year', ἔτος 'year'.[5]

(More precisely, what Socrates says of the names πῦρ ὕδωρ κύων is that they derive from some barbarian language and hence cannot be etymologized.)

At 411a1–4 Hermogenes expressly introduces another change of topic.

After this kind of names [μετὰ τοῦτο τὸ εἶδος] I should be glad to consider what the correctness of these fine names is, those concerning virtue [τὰ περὶ τὴν ἀρετήν],[6] like 'wisdom' and 'understanding' and 'justice' and all such names.

Socrates remarks that Hermogenes is 'stirring up' no trifling family of names, but consents to embark on this further enterprise, with his lion's skin on. Before actually starting, however, he has something important to say: the names to be presently dealt with confirm his former intuition that the ancient namegivers upheld the theory of universal flux (411bc). After this foreword he shoots out a new stream of etymologies. All of these are related – apart from digressions – to the sphere of intellectual, moral and

---

[4] See *Ap.* 26d on the divinity of sun and moon in common opinion; *Ti.* 40a, *Lg.* 898d–899b for Plato's views on the heavenly bodies. As far as I know, the month, the seasons and the year were not usually regarded as divine (but cf. S. E. *M.* 9.182–4 on Carneades on the divinity of day, month and year).

[5] Sedley 2003: 90 sees a stop after the etymology of ἀστραπή and another one after that of γῆ. But this does not seem to be right. At 408de, where the names in the present section are first announced, they are listed uninterruptedly; and the interruption at 409c10 is certainly, while that at 410c3–4 is probably, irrelevant.

[6] περὶ τὴν ἀρετήν (a3): 'concerning virtue', *not* 'of the virtues' (Reeve, cf. 'virtutum' Ficino). This has an obvious bearing on the section's structure: names like 'pleasure' or 'desire', which we shall meet shortly (419b ff.), may have something *to do with* virtue, but are certainly not names *of* virtues. Thus Reeve's translation implies a neat division between the virtue-names and other names which otherwise might (and indeed should) be included among them.

technical virtues and values, and almost all discover in the analysed word some sort of hint at the flux theory (411d–416d):

φρόνησις 'wisdom' 2, γνώμη 'judgement', νόησις 'intellection', σωφροσύνη 'temperance', ἐπιστήμη 'knowledge', σύνεσις 'understanding', σοφία 'intelligence', ἀγαθόν 'good',[7] δικαιοσύνη 'justice', δίκαιον 'just', ἀδικία 'injustice', ἀνδρεία 'courage', (ἄρρεν 'male' / ἀνήρ 'man', γυνή 'woman', θῆλυ 'female', θηλή 'nipple', θάλλειν 'flourish'), τέχνη 'art', (κάτροπτον 'mirror',[8] Σφίγξ 'Sphinx'), μηχανή 'contrivance', κακία 'badness', δειλία 'cowardice', ἀπορία 'difficulty', ἀρετή 'virtue', κακόν 'bad', αἰσχρόν 'ugly', καλόν 'beautiful'.

Within this group, the discussion of ἀνδρεία causes a digression (414ab), proceeding by several associations of ideas and extending as far as the etymology of θάλλειν. There Socrates remarks that he is going off course, while there are still plenty of names that seem 'important' (σπουδαίων: i.e. names of important *things*) left. One among these, he says, is τέχνη. After the etymology of τέχνη (and after a new digression) we find names that are perfectly homogeneous to those analysed before the 414ab digression. Indeed, at 415a8–9, after etymologizing μηχανή, Socrates says 'we must come *to the height of the names we've said* [ἐπὶ τὴν κορυφὴν ... τῶν εἰρημένων]: for we must search what the names ἀρετή and κακία mean'. He is referring back to his announcement of the virtue-group at 411a; and he says he is reaching the height because he is about to etymologize the very name ἀρετή, 'virtue'. All this shows that the etymologies in 411d–416d form a unitary set, though Socrates' exposition has been momentarily loosened.[9]

At 416e1, after the rather lengthy etymology of καλόν, Socrates asks Hermogenes what is left among *such names* (Τί οὖν ἔτι ἡμῖν λοιπὸν τῶν τοιούτων;). Hermogenes answers mentioning 'these names concerning the good and the beautiful [περὶ τὸ ἀγαθόν τε καὶ καλόν], names of things advantageous and profitable and useful and gainful and their contraries'. Here we do have some sort of a joint, because a new group of names, provided with a reasonable semantic identity, is being announced. But the joint is avowedly a minor one, and we are still firmly in the domain of

---

[7] No recognizable turn in the text before ἀγαθόν, contrary to what is implied by Gaiser's (1974: 56) schema as well as by Sedley's (2003: 113) distinction between a group of 'primarily intellectual virtues' and a group of 'moral virtues'. I do not want to deny that the names from φρόνησις to σοφία do form a strikingly homogeneous group; but, as a matter of fact, this is not a group which Socrates is eager to mark out.

[8] On the spelling κάτροπτον in place of κάτοπτρον see n.129.

[9] *Pace* Gaiser 1974: 56, Sedley 2003: 113 and Reeve xxvii–viii, who mark a stop before τέχνη (the stop is even a major one in Reeve). Gaiser and Sedley, moreover, make τέχνη and μηχανή into a separate subgroup.

the 'names concerning virtue', inaugurated at 411a.[10] Here is this new subgroup, extending from 416e to 419b:

συμφέρον 'advantageous', κερδαλέον 'gainful', κέρδος 'gain', λυσιτελοῦν 'profitable', ὠφέλιμον 'useful', βλαβερόν 'harmful', βλάπτον 'harming', (ἡμέρα 'day' 2, ζυγόν 'yoke'), δέον 'necessary', εὔπορον 'prosperous', ζημιῶδες 'hurtful'.

At 419b5–6 Hermogenes asks Socrates: 'And what about "pleasure" and "pain" and "appetite" and such names?' A new row of names is apparently being introduced; Socrates spits them out in one breath at 419b–420b:

ἡδονή 'pleasure', λύπη 'pain', ἀνία 'sorrow', ἀλγεδών 'distress', ὀδύνη 'grief', ἀχθηδών 'trouble', χαρά 'joy', τέρψις 'delight', τερπνόν 'delightful', εὐφροσύνη 'good cheer', ἐπιθυμία 'appetite', θυμός 'spirit', ἵμερος 'desire', πόθος 'longing', ἔρως 'love'.[11]

These are not virtues or values, but rather emotions and feelings. So they form a group of their own, distinct from the two previous ones (φρόνησις, γνώμη etc. and συμφέρον, κερδαλέον etc.) and presumably constituting a third subgroup of the 'names concerning virtue' of 411a.[12] A carefully organized subgroup: each of the three names that were explicitly mentioned by Hermogenes in his question (ἡδονή, λύπη, ἐπιθυμία) is etymologized together with four closely related others; and each of the three series of five is consecutive, with one exception. The exception is ἡδονή, which is placed at the beginning and is separated from the other pleasure-words: Socrates starts out as if he wanted to pick up the names proposed by Hermogenes one after another, but after λύπη he begins to proceed by semantic affinity.

At 420b6 Hermogenes introduces another row of names, again with a very discreet suggestion that there is some unity among them: 'What do you think about δόξα and *such names* [καὶ τὰ τοιαῦτα]?' In response, Socrates etymologizes the following group of names (420bc):

δόξα 'opinion' 2, οἴησις 'belief', βουλή 'deliberation', βούλεσθαι 'to want', βουλεύεσθαι 'to deliberate', ἀβουλία 'ill-advisedness'.

These are to do with judgement, belief, will and deliberation.[13] Their referents, like those of the former subgroup, are not virtues or values, but rather states or faculties of the soul. But their referents seem to be of a somehow

---

[10] Sedley 2003: 113 ignores the joint and has a single subgroup of 'generic terms of evaluation' stretching from κακία (415a) to ζημιῶδες (419b).
[11] Here I am heavily indebted to Sedley's (2003: 113) excellent translations.
[12] No minor turn before ἐπιθυμία, *pace* Gaiser 1974: 57.
[13] δόξα and οἴησις do not form a subgroup of their own, *pace* Gaiser 1974: 57.

higher rank than those of the former subgroup: intuitively, judgement, will and deliberation have in common a connection with reason which feelings and emotions lack. The text does not allow us to say anything more precise.

At 420d1–2 Hermogenes comments that Socrates' pace has become quicker. The reason, Socrates explains, is that he is running to the end of the race (d3). In any case there are still a few names he wants to discuss, because they are 'next to these' (τούτοις ἑξῆς: the same expression as at 399d).[14] These scraps are discussed in 420de and are the following:

ἑκούσιον 'voluntary', ἀναγκαῖον 'compulsory', ἁμαρτία 'error'.

The notions of will, deliberation and ill-advisedness have evoked those of the voluntary, defined as 'what happens in accordance with will', and its contrary, the necessary or compulsory. This is characterized in its turn as 'what is related to error and ignorance' (τὸ περὶ τὴν ἁμαρτίαν ... καὶ ἀμαθίαν) – which perhaps hints at an etymology of ἁμαρτία from ἀμαθία. These last three names seem to bring us back close to the notion of virtue, whose mention marked a major joint within the etymologies at 411b. So it is confirmed that all the terms we have been examining since then were all more or less strictly 'concerning virtue'.

As he has finished with this tiny group of etymologies, Socrates apparently does not feel like 'running to the end' any more. For he invites Hermogenes to take advantage of his inspired vigour, as long as it is there, and question him further (420e3–5). Hermogenes, without thinking twice, says he is going to question him on 'the greatest and finest' names (τὰ μέγιστα καὶ τὰ κάλλιστα 421a1): the names of truth, falsehood, being, and the very name 'name'. Socrates immediately produces the following sequence of etymologies (421ac):

ὄνομα 'name', ἀλήθεια 'truth', ψεῦδος 'falsehood', ὄν 'what is', οὐσία 'being',[15] οὐκ ὄν 'what is not'.

This group is about logic and ontology. More precisely, as Sedley 2003: 157 remarks, it 'recognisably represents the subject matter of Plato's *Sophist* at the point where it turns to the analysis of propositional truth and falsity in the light of the preceding metaphysical division of the Greatest Kinds (261c–263d)'. And contrary to what Sedley himself says,[16] both content

---

[14] Gaiser 1974: 57 fails to notice the break here.
[15] οὐσία is here derived from ἰουσία (< ἰέναι 'to go'). In 401cd the Doric variant ὠσία had been given a different analysis and still another variant, ἐσσία, had been mentioned: see §5.2.3.
[16] 'Logic and metaphysics are a subdivision of ethics, because they represent the objects and contents of wisdom, a predominantly intellectual virtue which is treated along with the moral virtues. In

and presentation suggest that this group, despite its small size, is a major one, juxtaposed rather than subordinated to the one 'concerning virtue'. As for content, it would be odd to count 'name', 'truth', 'falsehood' and 'being' as falling into the province of ethics, psychology or whatever was the subject of the virtue section. As for presentation, though admittedly the 'greatest and finest' label is not very informative, nonetheless this is one of the few cases where a group of etymologies is introduced with some sort of general description. The other cases are 397b (the 'things that always exist by nature'), 400d and 408d (the gods), 411a (the names 'concerning virtue'). Apart from those passages and the present one, in all the other (minor) joints I have identified in my analysis the section to come was referred to merely by means of a formula like 'Let us talk about "*X*", "*Y*", "*Z*" ...', sometimes adding 'and names *of that sort*': see 399d, 416e–417a, 419b, 420b, 420d.

So the 'greatest and finest' names at 421ac form an autonomous group, on a par with those of the gods (the Homeric and the 'natural' ones) and those 'concerning virtue'. This group rounds off the etymologies of the 'secondary' names. After Socrates' derivation of οὐκ ὄν, 'what is not', from οὐκ ἰόν, 'what does not go', Hermogenes seizes on the very word ἰόν and asks what could be said about the correctness of such names as ἰόν 'what goes', ῥέον 'what flows', δοῦν 'what binds' (421c). This question raises the problem of the existence of elementary names. We shall deal with them in the next chapter.

There is a question which we left pending above and are now in a position to address. It concerns the phrase 'the things that always exist by nature' (τὰ ἀεὶ ὄντα καὶ πεφυκότα) at 397b: understanding what its extension is meant to be would help us understand how the etymologies are arranged. The phrase undoubtedly also introduces, besides the mythological gods, also the following group of the 'natural' gods, i.e. the objects of natural science. But the 'things that always exist by nature' are likely to include also the referents of *all* the other names etymologized by Socrates. The objects of ethics and psychology, logic and ontology, may well be said to 'always exist by nature', especially if you are inclined to think in terms of eternal Platonic forms.[17]

---

short, Plato has an embryonic tripartition of philosophy into physics, ethics and logic, but it is contained within a more basic bipartition ... based on a seminal distinction set out in the *Timaeus* (29b–c) between two kinds of discourse.' With Sedley cf. Goldschmidt 1940: 132–3. Both Gaiser 1974: 57 and Reeve xxviii, instead, view the 'greatest and finest' section as independent.

[17] See Dalimier 219–20 n.120, Reeve xxviii–ix, Sedley 2003: 88.

It is time to take stock. Here is an outline of the whole section 394e–421c:

394e–396c	Prologue: genealogy of the Atreidae
396c–397a	Socrates has been inspired by Euthyphro
397ac	We shall deal with the 'things that always exist by nature'
397c–400c	Preliminaries about the gods (gods, daimones, heroes, humans; soul and body)
400d–408d	Homeric gods
408d–410e	'Natural' gods (objects of natural science)
411a–420e	Names 'concerning virtue':
411a–416d	virtues and values
416e–419b	useful and harmful
419b–420b	emotions and feelings
420bc	rational states or faculties of the soul
420de	voluntary and necessary
421ac	'The greatest and finest ones': logic and ontology.

5.1.2 *The systematic character of the etymologies*

Our discussion so far has brought out the *systematic* character of the etymologies. If you list the names etymologized and the conceptual spheres they belong to, you do not find words common in everyday speech ('house', 'ship', 'fish' …).[18] But you do get a list of the chief directions of Greek thought up to Plato: mythology, physics and cosmology, ethics and psychology, and finally language, logic and ontology. And the list follows a roughly *historical* order, because it roughly matches the development of Greek thought, from Homer and Hesiod to Ionian speculation about nature and then to the tragedians, the Sophists, Socrates, and finally Plato himself.

This feature of the etymologies (which has been emphasized by Baxter 1992: 91–3 and Sedley 2003: 90, 156–7)[19] is confirmed by their many references to other authors. Such references may occur in a number of ways: explicit mentions and more or less transparent allusions, conveyed by the whole of an etymology or some detail of it or just its conceptual

---

[18] Sedley 2003: 90.
[19] The first who highlighted the 'encyclopaedic' character of the etymologies was Goldschmidt 1940: 91–5, 142–3.

content. It is important to notice that only in few cases is what is referred to an actual *etymology* which was advanced by someone before Plato. Since we know nothing of the work of such figures as Euthyphro or Cratylus himself, whose influence on this part of the dialogue is impossible to evaluate, it follows that, as far as we know, the etymologies might well be for the most part Plato's own creation.

Among the authors mentioned by name we can list:[20]

Anaxagoras (400a, cf. 59 B12 DK; 409a, cf. A42 §8; 413c, cf. B12)
Heraclitus (401d; 402ac = 22 B91 DK)
Hesiod (402b, cf. *Th.* 337–70 + 383–403; 406c, cf. *Th.* 195–8)
Homer (402ab, cf. *Il.* 14.201; 408a, 410c, 417c)
Orpheus (400c, 402bc = *PEG* 22F).

Other explicit references are vaguer: the 'sky-watchers' (οἱ μετεωρολόγοι 396c, cf. 401b, 404c), those clever at music and astronomy (405d: Pythagoreans, cf. *R.* 530d), present-day Homeric experts (407ab), etc.

Then there are the authors that are just hinted at. I offer a plausible partial list, laying no claim at all to completeness:

Aeschylus (413a, cf. *Ag.* 1485–6; 404de, cf. *Ag.* 1080–2)
Alcmaeon (399c, cf. 24 B1a DK)
Democritus (412b, cf. 68 A62; 412ce, cf. A101; 414a, cf. B122a; 420d, cf. A66, A58, B83)[21]
Heraclitus (413bc, cf. 22 B16)
Hesiod (413a, cf. *Op.* 2–3; 414d, cf. *Th.* 326)
Hippon (399de, cf. 38 A10)
Homer (403a, cf. e.g. *Il.* 13.43)
Leucippus (412ce, cf. 67 A28)[22]
the Pythagoreans (400c?, cf. *Grg.* 493a, Philol. 44 B14;[23] 401cd, cf. [Archyt.] *ap.* Stob. 1.41.2)
Theagenes (404c, cf. 8 A2, and *Il.* 21.6).

There is a point where Socrates seems to acknowledge – in somewhat puzzling terms – the quantity of his references to other authors. It is at 413d, immediately after the report of his conversations with four physicists, whereby he has been trying to elucidate an etymology:

---

[20] Some of the references listed here are discussed elsewhere in the course of this chapter.
[21] On these and other references to Democritus and Leucippus see §§5.3.1–3.
[22] See n.21.
[23] On the various etymologies of σῶμα and their authorship see the contrasting views of Dodds 1959: 300 and Bernabé 1995.

HE. You seem, Socrates, to have heard these things from someone [ἀκηκοέναι του] and not to be extemporizing.
SO. What about the other things?
HE. Not quite.[24]
SO. Then listen: perhaps also as regards the remaining ones I could deceive you into believing that I don't set them forth as things I've heard. (413d3–8)

It would be interesting to go through these passages, analysing Plato's allusive techniques and discussing the proposed identifications. But that would take more time and space than I can afford.[25] So I prefer to point out that, strictly speaking, the list of the authors hinted at should include *Plato* himself, because some etymologies encapsulate doctrines which he elsewhere endorses or even advances as his own. I shall review the most significant evidence to this effect in §5.1.3. Here I conclude that the ordering criterion of the etymologies is such that, as a matter of fact, they constitute a sort of sketchy historical guide by words to Greek thought up to Plato. To be sure, the sketch is incomplete and objectionable: several important words are missing (e.g. φύσις, γένεσις, κόσμος, πόλις, νόμος), and there is no reference to Parmenides. Nor am I claiming that supplying the sketch is the etymologies' main *purpose*. The etymologies' main purpose or purposes, as I shall tentatively reconstruct them, are substantially independent of their actual arrangement. We have grasped an important feature of the etymologies, but we are still far from understanding them.

5.1.3 Platonic views in the etymologies (396bc, 399bc, 400ab, 403a–404b, 410b)

I have just mentioned that some etymologies appear to encapsulate views which we have reason to consider genuinely Platonic. Let me give a few especially relevant instances of this. My discussion here agrees in several respects with the fine one offered by Sedley (2003: 90–7), who also points out a common thread between the examples: they are all, somehow or other, concerned with the place of intelligence in the world.[26]

---

[24] I.e., 'You don't quite look as if you had heard them too from someone.' My 'Not quite' translates οὐ πάνυ (d6), here usually rendered 'not at all' (cf. §2.4.1 n.89). But since in what precedes several of Socrates' references to other authors were perfectly explicit, Hermogenes cannot now be altogether denying their presence. A milder denial will do.
[25] On that subject you can consult Goldschmidt 1940: 109–42 and Baxter 1992: 99–163, though I often disagree with their treatment of the evidence. Both, in particular, seem to me far too generous in detecting possible connections between *Cra.* and other texts.
[26] In fact, for Sedley this does not hold of the etymology of ψυχή, which he rather takes to illustrate, along with the immediately following one of σῶμα, a distinct theme, i.e. 'the soul-body duality'.

(i) My first instance is at 396bc. Socrates derives the name Κρόνος from κορός νοῦς, 'pure intellect',[27] and then adds:

(SO.) This is the son of Uranus, as the story has it; and it is fine that the sight directed to the things above should be called by this name, οὐρανία ['heavenly'], i.e. ὁρῶσα τὰ ἄνω ['looking at the things above'] – which is precisely where the sky-watchers say the pure intellect comes from, and they say the name for the heavens [τῷ οὐρανῷ][28] has been set down correctly. (396b7–c3)

As Cronus is the son of Uranus, so purity of intellect comes from astronomy. This sounds like a perfectly Platonic doctrine; for elsewhere Plato does hold that contemplation of the heavens leads us to philosophy and purifies our mind (cf. *R.* 527d–528a,[29] *Ti.* 47bc, 90cd).

(ii) A second instance is the 399bc etymology of ἄνθρωπος, 'human' (cf. §6.1.2):

(SO.) This name, ἄνθρωπος, signifies that the other animals do not investigate or calculate or examine [ἀναθρεῖ][30] anything of what they see, whereas the human being has no sooner seen – that is, ὄπωπε – than he examines and calculates about what he has seen. Hence the human being alone among animals was correctly named ἄνθρωπος, 'he who examines what he has seen' [ἀναθρῶν ἃ ὄπωπεν]. (399c1–6)

On the one hand, this seems to echo Alcmaeon, 24 B1a DK = Thphr. *Sens.* 25: 'The human being differs from the other animals because he alone understands [ξυνίησι], whereas the others perceive but do not understand.' On the other hand, it is also reminiscent of *Tht.* 186bc, where Socrates seems to contrast humans with the other animals on the grounds that only humans can attain 'calculations' (ἀναλογίσματα) about their sense-perceptions in respect of being and advantageousness.

(iii) My third instance follows closely upon the second in the text: it is the second etymology of ψυχή, 'soul', at 400ab. After advancing a first

---

But since the ψυχή etymology turns out to presuppose the view that *the soul is the mover of the body* (see text below), I do not see why it should not also contribute to illustrating the intelligence theme, broadly construed.

[27] See Robinson 1995.
[28] I suspect that in place of τῷ οὐρανῷ (c3) we should write τῷ Οὐρανῷ, 'for Uranus', as in Fowler's translation (though not in his text).
[29] *Pace* Sedley 2003: 91, *R.* ceases to be a parallel when Socrates goes on to insist (528e–530c) that astronomy should be practised as a mathematical discipline, not an empirical one, and that hence we should 'leave alone the things in the heavens' (τὰ δ' ἐν τῷ οὐρανῷ ἐάσομεν).
[30] The occurrences of ἀναθρέω in this passage are sometimes translated as if the verb meant 'reconsider, review'. It seems, however, that ἀνα- in this case does not express repetition, but rather intensity. See LSJ ἀνά F.2 (citing ἀνακρίνω as an example), and cf. Eur. *Hec.* 808, Th. 4.87.1.

etymology from ἀναψύχειν, 'to cool' (cf. Hippon 38 A10 DK), Socrates discards it and proposes an alternative one, which, he says, Euthyphro's followers will find more convincing:

SO. What else than soul seems to you to hold and carry along the nature of the whole body so that it lives and moves about?
HE. Nothing else.
SO. And don't you believe Anaxagoras that it is mind and soul that orders and holds the nature of all the other things as well?
HE. I do.
SO. Therefore it would be fine to call this power which carries along and holds nature [ἣ φύσιν ὀχεῖ καὶ ἔχει] by this name, φυσέχην. But it is also possible to pronounce it elegantly as ψυχή. (400a5–b3)

This, as Sedley 2003: 97 puts it, 'points to Plato's highly influential identification of soul with the ultimate source of motion' (for which see *Phdr.* 245c–246a, *Lg.* 10.896a–897b).

(IV) The fourth and perhaps most striking example is the etymology of Ἅιδης, 'Hades', at 403a–404b. Socrates starts out by mentioning that most people believe that this name refers to 'the unseen' (τὸ ἀιδές)[31] and that, fearing the name, they call him Pluto (Πλούτων, the wealth-giver, from πλοῦτος 'wealth': cf. 403a3–5). They are afraid because, once one of us has died, one always stays in his realm, and because the soul goes to him stripped of the body; but they are mistaken (403b). To explain what people's mistake consists in Socrates produces the following exhilarating argument. Many would escape Hades, if he did not bind with the strongest bond those who go there; therefore he binds them not with compulsion but with some sort of desire – indeed, with the greatest of all desires; and no desire is greater than the one you feel when you believe that staying with someone will make you a better person (403cd).

SO. For this reason, therefore, Hermogenes, we shall say that none of those who stay there is willing to go away and come here, not even the Sirens themselves, but they and all the others are overcome by his enchantments. So beautiful, it seems, are the speeches Hades knows how to speak; and this god is (as far as the present argument goes) a perfect sophist[32] and a great benefactor of those who stay with him, who sends up such a great number of good things also to those who live here (so many are his superabundant riches there), and he got the name 'Pluto' after this. On the other hand, as

---

[31] Cf. *Grg.* 493b, Hom. *Il.* 5.844–5, Soph. *Aj.* 606–7 (Anceschi 2007: 91); and note that Hades' name can also be spelt without the initial aspiration and the diphthong, i.e. Ἀΐδης or *Ἄϊς (gen. Ἀΐδος, dat. Ἀΐδι). See LSJ.
[32] σοφιστής here means 'sage': cf. *Smp.* 203d, *R.* 596d.

regards the fact that he doesn't want to associate with humans when they have their bodies, but begins to do so only when the soul is pure of all the evils and desires which are to do with the body [ἐπειδὰν ἡ ψυχὴ καθαρὰ ᾖ πάντων τῶν περὶ τὸ σῶμα κακῶν καὶ ἐπιθυμιῶν], doesn't it seem to you that he is a philosopher and someone who has well reflected[33] that thus he could restrain them, binding them with the desire for virtue, while as long as they have the body's agitation and folly not even his father Cronus could keep them with him binding them with his famous bonds?[34]

HE. Perhaps you've got a point, Socrates.

SO. And the name Ἅιδης, Hermogenes, is far from having been given after the unseen [ἀπὸ τοῦ ἀιδοῦς]; it was rather after his always knowing all things fine [ἀπὸ τοῦ πάντα τὰ καλὰ <ἀεὶ> εἰδέναι][35] that he was called Ἅιδης by the namegiver. (403d7–404b4)

Here every reader will be reminded of the *Phaedo*'s views about death and the afterworld. We should especially compare *Phd.* 80d–81a, where Socrates also *endorses* the etymology of Ἅιδης from ἀιδές which he here rejects. There he speaks of the soul as

the unseen, which goes to such a place, noble and pure and unseen [ἀιδῆ], quite literally to the realm of Ἅιδης, into the presence of the good and wise god;

and he says that the soul who leaves the body in a pure condition

departs for what is similar to it, the unseen [τὸ ἀιδές], which is godly and immortal and wise, where, once it has arrived, it is its lot to be happy, having freed itself from error and folly and fears and wild loves and the other human evils.

This is an especially striking case of an etymology encapsulating a view which in another dialogue is set forth as an important Platonic truth. But there is actually more to it. It is fairly clear that our passage does not anticipate the *Phaedo*, but rather *presupposes* it (and indeed criticizes and

---

[33] At a2–3 I retain the MSS reading οὐ φιλόσοφον δοκεῖ σοι εἶναι καὶ εὖ ἐντεθυμημένον, taking δοκεῖ as impersonal (cf. KG II.34, quoting among others Hdt. 3.124, Th. 4.3.3) and τὸ αὖ μὴ ἐθέλειν ... ἀλλὰ τότε συγγίγνεσθαι (e7–a1) either as accusatives of relation or as *nominativi pendentes* (cf. our 403a5–6, 404c, *Prm.* 128b and the other examples cited by KG I.47 and Riddell 1867: §271.b). All twentieth-century editions instead accept Heusde's twofold correction φιλοσόφου ... ἐντεθυμημένου, which makes τὸ αὖ μὴ ἐθέλειν ... ἀλλὰ τότε συγγίγνεσθαι into the subject of δοκεῖ: 'the fact that he doesn't want ... but only associates with them ... doesn't this seem to you to befit a philosopher and someone who has well reflected that ...'

[34] Cf. *Il.* 14.203–4.

[35] At b3 I accept Hermann's supplement ἀεί, which enables Socrates to account for the Ἀ- in Ἅιδης. On an alternative view (Sedley 2003: 95 n.34, cf. Dalimier 234–5 n.193), Socrates might be thinking that the Ἀ- means 'together'. He does in fact dwell on this meaning of ἁ- later, at 405cd, without mentioning our passage. But this tells against Sedley's view: if it were right, Socrates should either give his elucidations on ἁ- already in the present passage or refer back to it in the later one.

improves on it, as far as the etymology of Ἅιδης is concerned).³⁶ This harmonizes with an earlier clue (the use of the ὅ ἐστι formula at 389b, see §3.4.1). See further §I.3.2.

(v) I wind up with a negative example, i.e. an etymology which has been thought to contain a Platonic nugget, like the previous ones, but to my mind does not. At 409d–410c Socrates discusses one after another the words πῦρ 'fire', ὕδωρ 'water', ἀήρ 'air', αἰθήρ 'aether' and γῆ 'earth'. The first two are taken to be loans from some barbarian language. The last is derived from γεννήτειρα, 'begetter'. ἀήρ receives no less than three alternative analyses: it may be so called because it αἴρει, 'lifts', things from the earth,³⁷ or because it ἀεὶ ῥεῖ, 'is always flowing', or because wind arises from its flow and the word actually derives from ἀητόρρους, 'gale-flow'. As for αἰθήρ,

(SO.) since it is always flowing and running round the air [ἀεὶ θεῖ περὶ τὸν ἀέρα ῥέων], it would be rightly called ἀειθεήρ. (410b6–7)

Sedley 2003: 14–15 contends that in this passage Socrates is acknowledging *aether as a fifth element* besides the four Empedoclean elements; and since in the *Timaeus* the elements are four, aether being just the purest kind of air (58d), he supposes that we are in the presence of a late, post-*Timaeus* addition made by Plato to the original redaction of *Cra.*³⁸ To back up this hypothesis Sedley invokes three pieces of evidence: (i) Xenocrates' testimony (frr. 264–6 Isnardi Parente = 53 Heinze = Simpl. *in Ph.* 1165.33–9, *in Cael.* 12.21–7, 87.20–6) that Plato regarded aether as a distinct element; (ii) the pseudo-Platonic *Epinomis*, probably written by Plato's secretary Philip of Opus, where (981c) the elements are five, including aether; (iii) Aristotle's *De caelo*, which postulates 'aether as an element with an eternal, because naturally circular, motion' and at 270b16–25 (cf. *Mete.* 339b16–30) endorses something close to our etymology:

It seems that its name has been transmitted from the ancients until the present time, and that they held the same view as we are now stating; for we must believe that the same opinions have come down to us not just once or twice but infinitely many times. Therefore, believing that the first body was a different one over and above earth, fire, air and water, they named the highest region αἰθήρ, imposing this denomination on it because it always runs [ἀπὸ τοῦ θεῖν ἀεί] for an everlasting time. Anaxagoras misapplies this name: he uses the name αἰθήρ in place of 'fire'.

---

³⁶ *Pace* Boyancé 1941: 162–5; cf. instead Fowler 4.
³⁷ αἴρω is the Attic form of a verb often spelt as ἀείρω in poetry, which makes it even closer to ἀήρ.
³⁸ Sedley (along with others) supposes the presence of author's variants, due to the existence of two different redactions of *Cra.*, also at 385bd and 437d–438b: see §§2.2.5 and Appendix 1.

Indeed, Sedley goes so far as to take seriously the possibility that the *Cra.* etymology of αἰθήρ 'shows the influence of the young Aristotle'.

These hypotheses are intriguing; but I doubt that they withstand close examination. To start with, Sedley is trying to keep together things which are in fact quite distinct. The aether of the *Epinomis* (and apparently also of Xenocrates' testimony about Plato) has little to do with the aether of *Cra.* and with Aristotle's element, because it is *not* characterized in terms of its motion and is *not* said to be the stuff of the heavens. Rather, it is introduced in the context of a classification of different kinds of living beings according to the stuff of which their bodies are mainly made up: in this classification, the stars are (for the most part) fiery, while aether is the element of which the body of *daimones* is (for the most part) made up.[39]

Thus, of the texts cited above, only Aristotle's *De caelo* might possibly be relevant to the view that in our passage Socrates is acknowledging aether as a distinct element. But then other difficulties arise. The conjecture that our passage might have been influenced by the young Aristotle I find implausible, if only because in fact Aristotle (unlike the later tradition) *never* uses the term 'aether' to refer to the special element which he posits as the stuff of the heavens (he calls it 'first element' or 'first body').[40] Hence the only option that remains open is to suppose that Socrates is here *anticipating* Aristotle's doctrine. But it is much more economic to think that in our passage, as in the *Timaeus*, the term αἰθήρ designates just a kind of air, the purest and highest one. On this view, when Socrates says that aether runs 'round the ἀήρ', he is letting the term ἀήρ denote not only air in general, but also specifically the lower air as distinct from the upper one which is αἰθήρ. The distinction between ἀήρ as the lower air and αἰθήρ as the upper, brighter one may be sufficient to account for *Phd.* 109bc, 111b (where the αἰθήρ is 'the pure heaven in which the stars are', is placed above the ἀήρ and is said to be to ἀήρ as ἀήρ is to water in respect of purity); it was mistakenly ascribed to Homer by Aristarchus, mainly on the grounds of a couple of passages (*Il.* 14.288, a tree 'reached through the ἀήρ to the αἰθήρ'; 2.458, a gleam 'reached through the αἰθήρ to heaven').[41] That Socrates should etymologize only the name of *this* particular kind

---

[39] See Falcon 2001: 174–83, 2005: 77–83. Falcon also points out that in *Epin.* (and, we may add, in Xenocrates' testimony) the rationale behind the postulation of a fifth element seems to be that the association, made by Plato in *Ti.*, between elements and regular polyhedra left one regular polyhedron, the dodecahedron, without a corresponding element; and that this motivation is incompatible with Aristotle's physical theory (and, we may add, is apparently extraneous to *Cra.*).

[40] See Falcon 2005: 113–21. Contrast [Arist.] *De mundo* 392a5–9.

[41] Aristarchus' comments, as reported by Aristonicus, can be read in sch. A *ad Il.* 2.458, 14.288.

of an element, apparently on a par with the names of the four elements, is only natural. For in Homer and in poetic tradition down to the fifth century, including Empedocles himself, αἰθήρ was the chief designation for air (not just for the upper and brighter air), ἀήρ meaning rather 'mist' or 'haze'.[42] No term for any kind of fire, water or earth had a comparable pedigree.

'But', it could be objected, 'the *Cra.* etymology of αἰθήρ refers to aether's being always in motion; and this surely anticipates Aristotle's doctrine, if it is not influenced by it.' I answer that the etymology need not be meant to identify everlasting motion as a *distinctive* characteristic of aether at all. As we saw above, the second etymology of the word ἀήρ (410b1–5) derives it from ἀεὶ ῥεῖ, 'is always flowing', and the third too contains a reference to air's 'flowing'.[43] So I suspect that all that is meant to be distinctive of aether here is its being located above, or rather round, the ἀήρ in the specific sense of this term. But there is nothing specifically Aristotelian in this view.

5.2 THE ETYMOLOGIES AND THE ARGUMENT OF THE *CRATYLUS*

The etymologies interact with the course of the whole dialogue's argument in a number of ways. These interactions must, I submit, form at least part of the *raison d'être* of the etymologies themselves.

5.2.1 *Ordinary proper names put aside (397ab)*

We start in 397ab. Socrates has completed the etymologies of Atreus' genealogy up to Uranus (394e–396c) and claimed that he has been inspired by Euthyphro (396d–397a). Then he pauses to decide from what sort of names to start, in order to show that 'each name has not been set down merely by chance, but has some [sc. natural] correctness' (μὴ πάνυ ἀπὸ τοῦ αὐτομάτου οὕτως ἕκαστα κεῖσθαι, ἀλλ' ἔχειν τινὰ ὀρθότητα).[44] His

---

[42] See Kahn 1960: 140–8; Schmidt 1976: 75–6; Kingsley 1995: 15–18, 24–9, 35.
[43] Sedley 2003: 106 claims that 'Air merely "flows", an essentially unstructured or chaotic form of motion, while aether "runs", namely, we are told, round the outer perimeter of the air.' But this goes against the evidence. Sedley says that Socrates, like Aristotle, derives αἰθήρ from ἀεὶ θεῖ, whereas in fact Socrates derives αἰθήρ from ἀεὶ θεῖ περὶ τὸν ἀέρα ῥέων (> ἀειθεήρ). That is to say, aether *both* 'runs' *and* 'flows'. Hence there is no reason to believe that 'flowing' is, by itself, a chaotic sort of motion – only that it is a *generic* sort of motion.
[44] As Barney 2001: 27 n.7 notes, 'naturalism can ... be rephrased as simply the thesis that there *is* such a thing as the correctness of names, and conventionalism as the denial of it'. Cf. 427d, 429b.

proposal is to leave the proper names of heroes and humans out of the etymological inquiry as eschewing natural criteria of correctness:

The names that are used to refer to heroes and humans [τὰ μὲν οὖν τῶν ἡρώων καὶ ἀνθρώπων λεγόμενα ὀνόματα] might perhaps deceive us. For many of them have been set down in accordance with names of ancestors, without being appropriate at all to some of their bearers [πολλὰ μὲν γὰρ αὐτῶν κεῖται κατὰ προγόνων ἐπωνυμίας, οὐδὲν προσῆκον ἐνίοις], as we were saying at the outset; many others people impose as though expressing a wish [ὥσπερ εὐχόμενοι τίθενται], like 'Euthychides' [= 'Fortunate'], 'Sosias' [= 'Saviour'] and 'Theophilus' [= 'God-beloved']. Such names must, I think, be left alone: we are most likely to find the correct ones in the realm of the things that always exist by nature [περὶ τὰ ἀεὶ ὄντα καὶ πεφυκότα]. (397a9–b8)

I have already dwelt upon several features of this passage. At the end of §5.1.1 I addressed the question of what the 'things that always exist by nature' are. In §4.2.3 n.44 I remarked that Socrates' remark on well-wishing names perfectly fits the case of Astyanax and thus helps us to spot a flaw in the argument of 393a–394e. More generally, in §4.2 we discussed the difference (which was obliterated by Socrates in that argument) between proper names and general terms – between 'lion' and 'Lion', or 'king' and 'King'. Here I wish to add something about this last point.

Here Socrates seems to be committing himself to the view that many proper names are not naturally correct but are nonetheless names and name their nominata in virtue of something other than natural appropriateness – something easily identified with convention. This is, as Goldschmidt 1940: 105 said, 'le premier échec de la thèse naturaliste'.[45] There is, however, some unclarity as to what the scope of this setback exactly is. It might seem that here Socrates is acknowledging that some names are not naturally correct and hence, with regard to those names, is divorcing naming (no longer regarded as a natural affair) from correctness (still regarded as a natural affair). But this would be inconsistent with the fact that in the sequel Socrates appears to hold on to the Redundancy Conception of correctness (according to which being a name of X is the same as being a correct name of X: see §1.1.1). Therefore we must consider the possibility that Socrates' real point is different and goes like this: 'For many proper names, it is not the case that they belong to their bearers by nature. Hence the only move that is left for a naturalist to make, *if he is to count as a naturalist*, is to withdraw Redundancy and claim that these

[45] Proclus too seems to be impressed by our passage and to base on it his theory that (for the most part at least) the names of corruptible things, unlike those of eternal ones, are conventional: see x, 4.11–16; XIX, 8.21–3; XXX, 11.1–4; LI, 18.20–6. Cf. Amm. *in Int.* 37.1–13, quoted in §8.1.7.

are genuine names but are incorrect by the natural standards.' The implication would then be that natural correctness, once it were thus divorced from the name-relation, would be in danger of being reduced to a merely subsidiary feature of names, which is a higher price than the naturalist ought to pay; and that so we had better hold on to Redundancy and conclude that many proper names are such that no form of naturalism is true of them.

Someone might object to my interpretation on the grounds of the expression τὰ … τῶν ἡρώων καὶ ἀνθρώπων λεγόμενα ὀνόματα (a9–b1). If the meaning of this were 'the *so-called* names of heroes and men' ('les prétendus noms', Dalimier), then one could argue that here Socrates, far from divorcing naming from correctness, is keeping the two together up to the point of rejecting as pseudo-names those alleged names which are not naturally correct. This would obviously be in tune with Cratylus' own paradoxical claim that 'Hermogenes' is not Hermogenes' name. It would, however, be odd if Socrates were so nonchalantly condemning *many* of the proper names we use every day as pseudo-names. Furthermore, Socrates' use, at b2–4, of the expressions '*have been set down*' (κεῖται) and '(people) *impose*' (τίθενται) suggests that the naturally incorrect proper names at issue are meant to be names after all: contrast 429c, where Cratylus will claim that 'Hermogenes' has not even been set down (οὐδὲ κεῖσθαι) as a name for Hermogenes, i.e. does not even belong to Hermogenes as a name. Thus other interpreters ignore λεγόμενα (Ficino, Fowler) or choose different renderings: Méridier 'Les noms donnés aux héros et aux hommes', Minio-Paluello 'i nomi che si dicono degli eroi e degli uomini', Reeve 'the names that heroes and men are said to have'. The last is the course I have followed in my own translation.

So I trust that the objection can be disposed of and that my interpretation of the passage is correct. The next section should, among other things, also lend it further indirect confirmation.

5.2.2 *The etymologies as doxography, or the suicide of naturalism (400d–401a)*

We now jump to 400d. After the etymology of σῶμα (cf. §5.1.1) Hermogenes asks Socrates to move on to the proper names of the individual gods:

HE. These things seem to me to have been adequately expounded, Socrates. But regarding the names of the gods, as e.g. you were saying just now about 'Zeus', could we perhaps investigate in the same manner [κατὰ τὸν αὐτὸν τρόπον] according to what sort of correctness their names have been set down [κατὰ τίνα ποτὲ ὀρθότητα αὐτῶν τὰ ὀνόματα κεῖται]? (400d1–5)

Socrates' answer is extremely interesting.

SO. Yes, by Zeus, we could, if we had good sense,[46] in one manner which is the best [ἕνα μὲν τὸν κάλλιστον τρόπον], saying that we know nothing about the gods [περὶ θεῶν οὐδὲν ἴσμεν], either about their very nature or about the names they themselves call each other, whatever these may be – for they clearly use the true ones. (400d6–e1)

Socrates says, in a mildly ironical tone, that the best way of inquiring[47] would actually consist or result in acknowledging our ignorance about the gods. (Do not miss the echo of Protagoras 80 B2 DK: 'About the gods I am unable to know either that they are or that they are not or what their shape is,' etc.) Then, in the following lines, the best way is contrasted with a second-best way:

(SO.) A second manner of correctness [δεύτερος δ' αὖ τρόπος ὀρθότητος] is that, as we are accustomed to do when we pray in our prayers, by whatever name and whencesoever the gods be pleased to be called, thus we too call them, as people who know nothing else. For that seems to me a fine custom. So, if you wish,[48] let's inquire after, as it were, preliminarily saying to the gods that we won't investigate anything about *them* [περὶ αὐτῶν], as we don't think we are able to, but rather about the humans, i.e. holding what opinion they imposed their names on them [ἀλλὰ περὶ τῶν ἀνθρώπων, ἥν ποτέ τινα δόξαν ἔχοντες ἐτίθεντο αὐτοῖς τὰ ὀνόματα]. For this is secure from the gods' wrath. (400e1–401a6)

The second-best way is introduced as a second manner *of correctness* (e1). The idea is that different sorts of inquiry discover different sorts of correctness. If we had been able to carry out seriously the former sort of inquiry, we should have grasped the correctness of the true names of the gods. But, unable as we are to do this, we shall stay content with etymologizing the *human* names of the gods, instead of the divine ones (e1–a2),[49] and concerning ourselves with the *opinion* (δόξα) of the namegivers about the gods, instead of the truth (a2–6).

---

[46] At d6–7 I, like most editors, keep the MSS εἴπερ γε νοῦν ἔχοιμεν. The OCT prints Heindorf's ἔχομεν.

[47] ἕνα μὲν introduces the contrast between this best way of inquiring and the second-best way of e1 ff. (LSJ εἷς, 3.), while at the same time stressing the best way's uniqueness (LSJ 1.b).

[48] At a2 I accept Τδ's *lectio difficilior* εἰ βούλει οὖν (see *GP* 427 on οὖν third in a sentence) as against the β reading εἰ οὖν βούλει, adopted by Burnet and many others. The OCT editors print Jordan's superfluous {εἰ} βούλει οὖν.

[49] At e1–3 Socrates explicitly refers to a typical pattern of the ancient hymns, where the god is invoked with one or more names and epithets, followed by some formula extending the invocation to any

It is not difficult to see the relevance of this to the whole dialogue's argument (Kahn 1973a: 157 speaks of a 'decisive shift'; cf. Schofield 1982: 63). According to the theory to which Socrates is allegedly giving practical application, the name of an object is naturally appropriate to it and expresses its 'being'. Now we learn that, as far as the names of the gods are concerned, Socrates will be content with recovering the namegivers' opinion rather than the truth about the gods, while on the other hand continuing to characterize his inquiry as being about 'correctness' in some secondary sense. Socrates thus shifts from philosophy to doxography. He renounces showing that names convey the truth about their referents, and instead accepts as names expressions that might convey something false of their referents, since opinions (as Plato tirelessly insists in the dialogues and will insist even here at 436ab) can be true as well as false.[50] Thus the names of the gods turn out to be no different from those of the heroes and humans, contrary to what Socrates said at 397ab; and the conventionalist implications of that passage are confirmed. The twist is a momentous one, although it is not emphasized, and amounts to nothing less than the suicide of naturalism.

5.2.3 *The etymologies as doxography (continued): the theory of flux (401d, 402a, 411bc)*

The philosophical significance of Socrates' turn is strengthened by the fact that it is not limited to the names of the gods, but characterizes pervasively the etymologies of the 'secondary' names. From a certain point onwards, as I have already mentioned, the etymologies begin to be organized around a main theme, namely the Heraclitean theory of universal flux, which turns out to be presupposed by the majority of names.

Its first occurrence is at 401d, less than a page after the doxographical turn. But before looking at it, let me supply some context.

Socrates is discussing the name of the goddess Hestia and remarks that

50. Probably, my good Hermogenes, the first ones who imposed names were no trifling people, but rather some sort of sky-watchers and chatterers [μετεωρολόγοι τινές καὶ ἀδολέσχαι]. (401b7–9)

---

other way the god may be pleased or require to be called: see the passages quoted by Norden 1913: 143 ff., and in Plato (who loves such formulas, often in ironical contexts) *Prt.* 358a, *Euthd.* 288ab, *Smp.* 212c, *Phdr.* 273c and especially *Phlb.* 12bc.

[50] *Pace* Sedley (2003: 92): 'While Socrates does not keep pointing out that the etymologies are uncovering philosophical truths, he does speak throughout the cosmological section as if he is *assuming* that the decoded messages are true ones.'

'Sky-watchers and chatterers' is ambiguous. It is the sort of expression that was used in Socrates' and Plato's times to convey the common man's contempt towards whatever appeared as idle speculation, whether or not about genuinely physical subjects.[51] Plato seems to appropriate such expressions with pride and ironical defiance at *Tht.* 175d, 195bc, and also at *Phdr.* 269e–270a, where Socrates says something that can be literally translated thus: 'All the great arts require chatter and sky-talking [ἀδολεσχίας καὶ μετεωρολογίας] about nature.' But there Socrates goes on to indicate Anaxagoras as a model of sky-talking and as someone who led his pupil Pericles to the nature 'of mind *and mindlessness*' (νοῦ τε καὶ ἀνοίας). This should make us suspect that his words also contain some more complicated irony, i.e. that he is also suggesting that as far as figures like Anaxagoras were concerned the popular jibe was not completely unjustified.[52] In our lines too we are left in doubt about what Socrates' judgement on the namegivers' philosophical interests exactly is;[53] and this ambiguity is, I take it, deliberate.

Next Socrates claims that 'if one examines the foreign names, one finds out as well what each means' (401c1–2). Then he identifies two dialectal variants of the Attic word οὐσία:

(SO.) For example, in the case of what we call οὐσία, there are some who call it ἐσσία and yet others who call it ὠσία. (401c3–4)

Never mind whether these forms were really existing in Plato's times or he is making them up.[54] At 401c4–d3 Socrates argues that the name 'Hestia', Ἑστία, derives from ἐσσία and thus actually refers, or rather originally referred, to 'the essence of all things' (τὴν πάντων οὐσίαν: see §6.2.4). Then he comes to ὠσία, on which he makes what might at first seem an incidental remark:

(SO.) As for those who called the essence of all things ὠσία, these would probably believe, in agreement with Heraclitus, that all the beings are on the go

---

[51] See Ar. *Nub.* 333 (and cf. 228, 360–1), 1485, *Pax* 92; Eupolis *PCG* fr. 386; Pl. *Phd.* 70c, *R.* 488e–489a, 489c, *Prm.* 135d, *Plt.* 299b.

[52] See Rowe 1986: 204–5. This is, however, a controversial matter.

[53] Remember that at 396c οἱ μετεωρολόγοι were credited with the view, which Plato endorses, that 'pure intellect' (or 'pure *mind*': νοῦν) comes from astronomy. See §5.1.3. On the other hand, at 404c Socrates will suppose that the namegiver μετεωρολογῶν applied the name Ἥρα to ἀήρ (cf. perhaps Theagenes, 8 A2 DK, and *Il.* 21.6).

[54] Both forms are linguistically plausible: see *DELG* II.840, Buck 129. ἐσσία is apparently unattested; it is sometimes said to occur in Stob. 1 *Prooem. coroll.* 3 = Philol. 44 B11 DK, where however it is an arbitrary correction of the MSS οὐσία. As for ὠσία, it is attested in late pseudo-Pythagorean forgeries: Ocellus *ap.* Stob. 1.20.3 (p. 129.15 Thesleff) and the pseudo-Archytas (pp. 19, 23.18, 24.18, 26.21, 27.16 Thesleff). Philolaus, 44 B6 DK, has the phrase ἁ ἐστώ τῶν πραγμάτων.

and nothing is at rest [τὰ ὄντα ἰέναι τε πάντα καὶ μένειν οὐδέν]. Hence, in their opinion, their cause and principle is that which pushes [τὸ οὖν αἴτιον καὶ τὸ ἀρχηγὸν αὐτῶν εἶναι τὸ ὠθοῦν], for which reason it has finely been called ὠσία. (401d3–7)

So it is that the name ὠσία appears to presuppose a kind of Heraclitean flux theory. Later on (§5.3.1) I shall have something more to say about Socrates' apparently odd talk of a 'pushing' principle; but for now, let me go on tracking his various references to flux.

After the conclusion of his treatment of ὠσία Socrates would like to go on to the names of Rhea and Cronus. 'Cronus' name, however,' he says, 'we've already discussed' (401e2–3). He is referring back to 396b. But then he corrects himself, because a new etymology of 'Cronus' is arriving:

(SO.) But perhaps I am talking nonsense.
HE. Why, Socrates?
SO. My good friend, a swarm of wisdom has come into my mind.
HE. What is it?
SO. It sounds absolutely ludicrous, and yet I think it has a certain plausibility [Γελοῖον μὲν πάνυ εἰπεῖν, οἶμαι μέντοι τινὰ πιθανότητα ἔχον].
HE. What is this plausibility?
SO. I seem to see Heraclitus saying some ancient wise things, i.e. precisely those concerning Cronus and Rhea[55] which Homer too said.
HE. What do you mean?
SO. Heraclitus says, I think, that 'All things move and nothing is at rest [πάντα χωρεῖ καὶ οὐδὲν μένει]', and, likening the beings to the stream of a river, that 'You could not step twice into the same river [δὶς ἐς τὸν αὐτὸν ποταμὸν οὐκ ἂν ἐμβαίης]'.
HE. It is so. (401e3–402a11)

This very famous passage might constitute an actual quotation from some point of Heraclitus' work.[56] It has two close parallels: Arist. *Metaph.* 1010a10–15 and Plu. *De E* 392B. The former is especially relevant for us because Aristotle says that Cratylus 'criticized Heraclitus for saying that it is impossible to step twice into the same river [ὅτι δὶς τῷ αὐτῷ ποταμῷ οὐκ ἔστιν ἐμβῆναι]; for he thought it was not possible to do so even once'. The authenticity of these reports about Heraclitus is a vexed question. Several

---

[55] ἀτεχνῶς τὰ ἐπὶ Κρόνου καὶ Ῥέας (a5): I tentatively follow Dalimier as against the standard construal, 'precisely those things which are as old as the days of Cronus and Rhea' (cf. LSJ ἐπί II), which reads somewhat awkwardly.
[56] The quotation marks printed in the text by Burnet, the OCT editors, and other editors of *Cra.* are generally removed by editors of Heraclitus, presumably as a sign of caution. If που (a8) meant 'somewhere', as some believe, it would encourage us to view the passage as a real quotation. But the meaning need not be one of place (see LSJ, and e.g. 386c).

scholars[57] reject them as spurious and somehow dependent on another famous river-fragment, 22 B12 DK (= Eus. *PE* xv 20.2–3: ποταμοῖσι τοῖσιν αὐτοῖσιν ἐμβαίνουσιν ἕτερα καὶ ἕτερα ὕδατα ἐπιρρεῖ, 'upon those who step into the same rivers different and different waters flow'). Others instead defend them and accept, in particular, Plutarch's version as authentic on a par with B12.[58]

However that may be, at 402b1 Socrates picks up the thread of the etymologies. He who imposed the names Ῥέα and Κρόνος, he says, agreed with Heraclitus and deliberately gave the two gods 'names of streams' (the implied derivations are Ῥέα < ῥέω and Κρόνος < κρουνός, 'spring').[59] The same conception was shared by Homer, Hesiod and Orpheus. The mention of Homer and Orpheus is substantiated by quotations: *Il.* 14.201 = 302 'Ocean the begetter of the gods, and their mother Tethys' and *PEG* 22F on the primeval wedding between 'beautiful-streamed Ocean' and Tethys.[60]

Socrates' reference to Hesiod is not explained. But we can grasp what he has in mind, and gain a better understanding of the passage, if we allow ourselves a brief digression and take into account a notable parallel at Arist. *Metaph.* 983b27–33, in the context of a discussion of Thales' thesis that water is the principle:

Some believe that this thesis about nature was held also by the very ancient people who lived much before the present generation and were the first to speculate on theology. For they made Ocean and Tethys the fathers of generation, and they said that what the gods swear by is water, i.e. what they called Styx. For what is oldest is most valuable, and what one swears by is the oldest.

The parallel between this passage and the *Cra.* one is clear, if we realize that Aristotle's 'some' quoted the same Homeric verse and that their ancient theologians cannot have failed to include Orpheus. But, indeed, the parallel becomes perfect – and Plato's reference to Hesiod is explained – if we see the lucubration about Styx as a reference to *Th.* 337–70 and 383–403, where we read that Oceanus and Tethys begot the rivers and the Oceanids, Styx being the most eminent and the one who became what the gods swear by. The parallel between Plato and Aristotle was first noted by Snell 1944, who plausibly argued that they have a common source, namely a chrestomathy by Hippias (see Clem. *Strom.* 6.15 = 86 B6 DK and cf. D. L. 1.24). On a reasonable hypothesis, Hippias quoted

---

[57] E.g. Marcovich 1978: 147–8, KRS 195–7.
[58] Thus DK (where Plutarch's report constitutes fragment B91), Kahn 1979: 168–9, Tarán 1999, Sedley 2003: 104 n.12.
[59] See Anceschi 2007: 75–6 for some evidence connecting Cronus with water.
[60] On the genealogies implied by these verses see Janko, in Kirk/Edwards/Hainsworth/Janko/Richardson 1985–94: iv.180–2.

passages relating to the role of water in early poetry and cosmology, perhaps including Heraclitus' river-fragment.[61] In Plato's hands, Heraclitus becomes central and the other texts become precedents of *his* thesis rather than Thales'.

In any event, these texts – Socrates says – are concordant with each other and all point towards Heraclitus' doctrine (402c2–3 καὶ ἀλλήλοις συμφωνεῖ καὶ πρὸς τὰ τοῦ Ἡρακλείτου πάντα τείνει). After this outburst the flux theme is still vital in the etymology of Tethys' name (402cd). Then it disappears from the scene, which gets crowded with the names of other gods. At 404cd it peeps out again in the etymology of Φερρέφαττα, a name of Persephone derived from Φερέπαφα, 'because of her wisdom and *touching of what is in movement* [ἐπαφὴν τοῦ φερομένου]'. Then another long interval, stretching through the rest of the godly names and all the names concerning natural science. To be sure, the cosmological etymologies contain a number of references to change. For example, the second etymology of ἥλιος (409a) supposes that the sun is so called 'because it always revolves going [ἀεὶ εἰλεῖν ἰών] around the earth'; μείς ('month') is derived from μειοῦσθαι ('decreasing', 409c); the etymologies of ἀήρ and αἰθήρ (410b) contain references to air's and aether's 'flowing' and 'running', as we saw in §5.1.3; γῆ, or rather γαῖα (410bc), derives from the same root as the epic perfect γεγάασιν ('they have been generated') and thus etymologically means 'begetter'. But none of these etymologies adverts to, or implies, the *general* flux theory: you don't have to be a flux theorist to etymologize 'earth' from 'begetter'. Indeed, at 410cd the final etymologies of ὧραι ('seasons') from ὁρίζω ('bound') and ἐνιαυτός/ἔτος ('year') from ἐν ἑαυτῷ ἐτάζον ('inspects within itself', sc. the plants and animals it brings to light) make no explicit reference to flux.[62]

The flux theory comes up again at the opening of the section 'concerning virtue' (cf. §5.1.1):

SO. Well, by the dog, I think I was not prophesying badly what I realized just now,[63] that the very ancient men who imposed names were absolutely like most present-day wise men who, by continually turning around and around searching how the beings are, get dizzy [εἰλιγγιῶσιν], and then the objects

---

[61] According to Snell, Plato just took Hippias' quotations and jestingly substituted Heraclitus for Thales. That Heraclitus was already quoted by Hippias was suggested by Mansfeld 1983.

[62] Therefore I am reluctant to agree with Sedley 2003: 106–7 either that flux 'dominate[s]' the cosmic etymologies or that the final pair 'emphasises the ultimate importance of order and measure in cosmic change'.

[63] At 411b4 μαντεύεσθαι is *infinitus imperfecti* (see KG 1.194); the back-reference is to 401e–402c, cf. ἐνενόησα with 401e ἐννενόηκα. Since I take the ὃ immediately following μαντεύεσθαι as the verb's object, I would follow Hirschig and Méridier in printing μαντεύεσθαι ὃ without any comma.

seem to them to be moving around and moving in all ways [περιφέρεσθαι τὰ πράγματα καὶ πάντως φέρεσθαι]. And they don't hold responsible for this opinion what has happened inside them, but allege the objects themselves to have such a nature that none of them is steady or stable, but they all flow and move and are always full of every sort of movement and coming-to-be [ῥεῖν καὶ φέρεσθαι καὶ μεστὰ εἶναι πάσης φορᾶς καὶ γενέσεως ἀεί]. (411b3–c5)

From *this* point onwards, the connection with the flux theory becomes a *structural* feature of the etymologies of the secondary names. In various guises, which we shall analyse in detail later on, almost all convey a reference to the thesis that everything 'flows' or 'is in motion' – whatever that may exactly mean. Read how Socrates goes on:

(SO.) I say this because I thought of it in relation to all the names mentioned just now.
HE. What do you mean, Socrates?
SO. Perhaps you didn't notice that the names mentioned a moment ago have been definitely imposed on the objects on the assumption that they are moving and flowing and coming to be [ὡς φερομένοις τε καὶ ῥέουσι καὶ γιγνομένοις τοῖς πράγμασι … ἐπίκειται].
HE. I had not thought of it at all.
SO. Well, first of all, this one which we mentioned first encapsulates the assumption that the things are such.[64]
HE. Which name?
SO. φρόνησις ['wisdom']: it is the 'intellection of movement and flux' [φορᾶς … καὶ ῥοῦ νόησις]. It would also be possible to understand it as 'benefit of movement' [ὄνησιν … φορᾶς]; in any case, it has to do with moving. (411c5–d6)

Then Socrates etymologizes along the same lines the words γνώμη, νόησις, σωφροσύνη, and so on (see §5.1.1). For example,

(SO.) As for ἐπιστήμη, it expresses that the soul worth mention follows the objects, which are in movement [ὡς φερομένοις τοῖς πράγμασιν ἑπομένης τῆς ψυχῆς τῆς ἀξίας λόγου], without being left behind or running ahead: therefore we must insert the *h* and name it ἐπιστήμη.[65] (412a1–4)

Now let us get back to 411bc. What is important for our present purposes is that there, at the beginning of the section of the etymologies devoted to

---

[64] What does ὡς ἐπὶ τοιούτων ἐστίν (d2) mean *literally*? Perhaps 'is as if it were about such things'; or perhaps there is a connection with such turns of phrase as κεκλῆσθαι ἐπί τινος, 'to be called after something' (see LSJ ἐπί A.III.2). The translations of Fowler ('is subject to such assumptions'), Ficino ('ad aliquid huius generis attinet'), Dalimier ('s'applique … à des telles choses'), Reeve ('is … like this') all look more or less imprecise. Hirschig corrected τοιούτων into τοιούτοις, which should yield the literal meaning 'is as if it had been *imposed on* such things' (LSJ B.III.5).
[65] On the text of a3–4 see §8.2.2 n.105.

it, the flux theory is definitely presented in an *unfavourable* light. The picture of the ancient and modern sages' dizziness, and of their failure to recognize its causes, is drily ironical; significantly, it closely recalls another dry picture, that of the misologists at *Phd.* 90bc.

But what, exactly, is wrong with the flux theory? Barney 2001: 73 suggests that 'the etymologies point to the truth *en bloc* through their general message that things are in flux, as indeed Plato believes the things around us to be', but they are mistaken insofar as they fail to consider the existence of unchanging non-sensible objects, the forms. More precisely, according to Sedley 2003: 108–9, the fact that the picture of the namegivers' dizziness occurs right here, 'at the watershed between the cosmic and the ethical etymologies', suggests that Plato endorses the references to flux contained in the former, but rejects those in the latter: the flux theory is all right as far as the sensible world is concerned, but it is mistaken in relation to values (and presumably to any other sort of abstract objects).

Now, it is certainly true that Plato does in some sense believe that the sensible world is in flux (see §9.1.3); but here I am doubtful. For at 411bc Socrates presents the flux theorists, ancient and modern, in an *unqualifiedly* unfavourable light, without suggesting that they might be partly right. He does not say 'Seeing that *sensible* things are in flux, they get dizzy and come to believe falsely that *values* too are.' Nor does he say 'Seeing that *some* things are in flux, they get dizzy and come to believe falsely that *all* things are.' He rather says something like this: 'By dint of turning around searching how *the beings* [τὰ ὄντα b7; τὰ πράγματα b8, c2] are, they get dizzy and come to believe falsely that the beings are in flux.' Socrates just speaks of 'the beings' or 'the objects' throughout, as if the flux theorists' mistake consisted in ascribing flux to *whatever* kind of beings or objects. Again, Socrates does not ascribe the flux theorists' dizziness to their focusing only on sensible things (contrast *Phd.* 79c). Instead, he ironically says that they get dizzy 'by continually turning around' in their inquiries (b6–7); and a few lines below he claims that they should blame their dizziness on their own *internal* experience, not on 'the objects themselves' (c1–3). Thus Socrates does not seem to be saying or implying that flux theorists are right about sensible things though wrong about values. He rather seems to be saying that flux theorists are, at least in some sense, wrong across the board. True, he realizes this in connection with the names 'concerning virtue'. But, as I argued above, those names, besides concerning virtue, also have another peculiar feature: they are the first group of names whose etymologies turn out to presuppose *systematically* the *general* flux theory. What came before, apart from the anticipation at 401d–402d, were the 'cosmological' names, some of whose etymologies (though not all) at most implied the view that *something*, typically the name's referent, is in a state of becoming or flux (e.g. 410b ἀήρ 'air' < ἀεὶ ῥεῖ 'always flows'). Thus Socrates draws no contrast between the flux theory as applied to the sensible world and the flux theory as applied to values. Strictly speaking, he considers the theory only once, in connection with names for values.

The unfavourable light cast on the flux theory at 411bc leads the reader to see *the whole* of the etymologies as characterized by a constant feature, i.e. the switch from philosophy to doxography (cf. §5.2.2), which shows up with increasing strength. This feature made its first occurrence at 397ab, when the proper names of heroes and humans were put aside as being, for the most part, ways either of honouring ancestors or of expressing wishes. It was reaffirmed at 400d–401a, in the foreword about the gods' names, which were said to reflect human opinion, which *can* be false. It is still present now, in connection with the names 'concerning virtue', which *do* presuppose a false doctrine, as our passage suggests.

So we end up with a host of names which, Socrates claims, do not give us access to the truth (as naturalism requires) but just to someone else's opinion, which may turn out to be false and in some cases does. This is the process I have called 'the suicide of naturalism'. That it does really take place in the dialogue, and is part of Plato's deliberate strategy, is confirmed by the final discussion between Socrates and Cratylus. There against Cratylus' claim, that the analysis of names yields knowledge of their referents, Socrates will argue that names merely incorporate the namegiver's beliefs, which will deceive us if they happen to be mistaken (436ad), and that in fact the flux theory is false (439b–440c). There can be little doubt that the etymologies anticipate those later arguments (cf. Schofield 1982: 68). Indeed, it seems very reasonable to suppose that the anticipation, given its recurrent and pervasive character, constitutes one of their purposes. That is to say, at least part of the etymologies' function is to contribute to the argument of the dialogue by undermining naturalism while pretending to put it into practice.

So far so good. Obviously, however, the theory of flux cannot be just another example of the fact that etymology reveals nothing more than the (possibly false) namegiver's beliefs. For the theory of flux is not any old philosophical theory; it is a main theme in Plato's metaphysical thought, continuously recurring in the dialogues in several guises, sometimes strongly opposed, sometimes partly endorsed. As we shall see in more detail in §§5.3.4 and 9.1.4, at *Tht.* 152de Socrates claims that almost all Greek philosophers and poets have been supporters of a particular version of flux theory; and the claim about Homer is there substantiated by the same quotation about Ocean and Tethys as at *Cra.* 402b. Plato's historical picture, both in *Cra.* and in *Tht.*, probably involves some degree of irony, as many readers have suspected;[66] but there is also something serious to it. Plato is perhaps unlikely to regard, e.g., Empedocles as a genuine flux *theorist*; but he may well mean that flux is something to which Empedocles' views commit him, as a matter of fact.

The etymologies of *Cra.* demonstrate something even stronger, i.e. that the flux theory enjoyed favour since the very first namegivers; and they show how pervasive its influence was by detecting its presence in the etymon of a great many names. As a result, when at the end of the dialogue (439b ff.) Socrates argues against the theory on the assumption of the existence of the forms, what we shall witness is an epoch-making philosophical clash: Plato's metaphysics is contrasted with the whole of Greek thought since its very origins. Notice how ascribing this function to the etymologies enables us to account for their extraordinary length (cf. Schofield 1982: 63): the clash is all the more impressive once we have realized that the flux theory is everywhere.

This brings us to another, even more basic function of the flux etymologies: they *introduce the flux theory* as a topic for philosophical discussion. This point requires that we pay some attention to the dialogue's structure. Let me sketch it out as follows. There is a debate about the correctness of names (383a–385e). Socrates argues in favour of the nature-theory (385e–394e) and then puts it into practice in the etymologies – or so he claims (394e–427d). The etymologies find out that many names consistently presuppose a certain metaphysical doctrine, the flux theory. Then Socrates refutes the nature-theory (428a–439b), eventually concluding that reality must be studied directly rather than through the analysis of names, and then argues against the flux theory (439b–440c). The conclusion is that the flux theory must be examined further (440ce).

Now consider the succession of the topics as it emerges from this sketch. The discussion about names brings to light a metaphysical doctrine about the nature of things; then the discussion about names ends with the moral that, if we want to know the nature of things, we ought to study the things themselves rather than their names. At this point the focus briefly shifts on that very metaphysical doctrine which had been presented before. Thus

---

[66] We can imagine some supporters of flux, like Cratylus himself (cf. *Tht.* 179d–180c), trying to find traces of their favourite theory in the ancient poets (a widespread practice), and hence being parodied by Plato. This is probably the case at *Tht.* 153cd, where an allegorical interpretation of Homer's 'golden cord' (*Il.* 8.18–27) appears among several ludicrous 'arguments' for flux.

the overall progress of the dialogue proceeds from names to things and, as it were, *mimes* (on a larger scale) the conclusion about names, i.e. that we ought to study the things rather than their names. In this development the etymologies are the essential joint, because they constitute the connection between the inquiry about names and the one about things.

5.3 MORE ON THE THEORY OF FLUX

The theory of flux presented in *Cra.*, apart from its role in the structure of the etymologies and of the whole dialogue, is a most interesting subject in itself. I devote this section to an analysis of its main features.

5.3.1 Locomotion

If we want to get a clearer idea of the theory's content, the first passages to consult are those where it is first introduced. We saw them in §5.2.3: 401d (ὠσία), 402ac (the 'swarm of wisdom': Heraclitus, Homer etc.), 404cd (Φερρέφαττα), and 411bc ff. (introduction to the names 'concerning virtue'). Here I should like to highlight one striking feature they all share, which so far seems to have passed unnoticed: the preponderance of *verbs of motion* to refer to change. 401d presents the namegivers as holding, in agreement with Heraclitus, 'that all the beings are on the go [ἰέναι] and nothing is at rest [μένειν]'. 402ac ascribed to Heraclitus the thesis that 'All things move [χωρεῖ] and nothing is at rest [μένει].' 404cd refers to the flux theory with the clause ἅτε ... φερομένων τῶν πραγμάτων, 'since the objects are in movement' (literally 'are carried about', 'are transported'). Finally, 411bc says that to the dizzy wise men 'the objects seem to be moving around and moving in all ways' (περιφέρεσθαι τὰ πράγματα καὶ πάντως φέρεσθαι); that they react believing that the objects' nature is such that 'none of them is steady or stable, but they all flow and move [ῥεῖν καὶ φέρεσθαι] and are always full of every sort of movement and coming-to-be [πάσης φορᾶς καὶ γενέσεως]'; and that the names 'concerning virtue' have been imposed on the objects 'on the assumption that they are moving and flowing and coming to be' (ὡς φερομένοις τε καὶ ῥέουσι καὶ γιγνομένοις). The examples could be multiplied.

Now one might try to play down these references to spatial motion by holding that they are just metaphors for change in general. This may be true of the verb ῥέω, in view of the clearly metaphorical significance of Heraclitus' river image, and is certainly true of the noun κίνησις, 'motion', which normally refers to *spatial* motion but is standardly adopted by Plato

More on the theory of flux 211

and Aristotle as a generic term for change. But the references to spatial motion are too many, and conveyed by means of too many different terms, for it to be possible to explain them away. Furthermore, the terms φέρομαι and φορά resist such a treatment in a special way, because elsewhere they are specifically used to pick out spatial motion as a kind of change distinct from, e.g., qualitative change: see *Tht.* 181cd, distinguishing ἀλλοίωσις (alteration) and φορά as two kinds of κίνησις, and cf. *Prm.* 138bc and Aristotle, *Ph.* 226a32–b1, 243a35–40.

Indeed, the text itself contains unmistakable signs that *Cra.*'s insistence on spatial motion (henceforth = 'movement') must be taken seriously. Consider again the etymology of ὠσία at 401d: since all things are in movement, 'their cause and principle is *that which pushes* [τὸ ὠθοῦν]'. This talk of a 'pushing' principle is hard to be explained away as figurative and strongly suggests that Socrates is thinking of an actual state of movement in things.

Another significant passage which gives us evidence to the same effect occurs at 412c. It is Socrates' analysis of the adjective ἀγαθόν, 'good':

(SO.) This name wishes to belong to the admirable component of nature as a whole [τῆς φύσεως πάσης τῷ ἀγαστῷ]. For since the beings travel [πορεύεται τὰ ὄντα], there is both quickness and slowness in them [ἔνι μὲν ἄρ' αὐτοῖς τάχος, ἔνι δὲ βραδυτής]. So the quick is not the whole, but an admirable part of it [ἔστιν οὖν οὐ πᾶν τὸ ταχὺ ἀλλά τι αὐτοῦ ἀγαστόν]. So to this admirable and fleet component [τούτῳ οὖν δὴ τῷ ἀγαστῷ <καὶ θοῷ>] this name belongs, τἀγαθόν.[67] (412c1–6)

---

[67] The *constitutio textus* of c4–5 is difficult. The MSS read ἔστιν οὖν οὐ πᾶν τὸ ταχὺ ἀλλά τι αὐτοῦ ἀγαστὸν τοῦτο· οὗ δὴ τῷ ἀγαστῷ [τῶν ἀγαστῶν **δ**]. 422a shows that ἀγαθόν must be derived from ἀγαστόν, 'admirable', + θοόν, 'fleet'. One way of obtaining this is that which I have adopted and translated above, adapting a suggestion of Heindorf: correction of the MSS τοῦτο· οὗ into τούτῳ οὖν and insertion of καὶ θοῷ after τῷ ἀγαστῷ. Another partly different but equivalent solution is Stallbaum's, endorsed by Méridier: ἔστιν οὖν οὐ πᾶν {τὸ ταχύ} ἀλλά τι αὐτοῦ ἀγαστόν <τὸ θοόν>. τούτῳ οὖν δὴ τῷ ἀγαστῷ ('So the fleet is not the whole, but an admirable part of it. So to this admirable component …'), where καὶ θοῷ is not added, but rather τὸ ταχὺ is deleted as a gloss and τὸ θοόν is inserted as the expression originally glossed and ousted by the gloss.

Burnet, Fowler and the OCT editors accept Baiter's simpler correction of ἀγαστόν τοῦτο· οὗ (c5) into ἀγαστόν. τοῦ θοοῦ. But what does the text mean with this correction? Fowler and Minio-Paluello (cf. Sedley 2003: 114) take it to mean 'Now not the whole of the quick [οὐ πᾶν τὸ ταχύ], but a part of it, is admirable. So to the fleet's admirable part [τοῦ θοοῦ … τῷ ἀγαστῷ] this name belongs, τἀγαθόν.' But this cannot be right, because the etymologies insist on the distinction between a quicker and a slower component in flux, as we shall shortly see, but know nothing of a *further* distinction between the quick's admirable part and the rest of it; indeed, Socrates has just claimed that 'this name wishes to belong to the admirable component *of nature as a whole*' (c1–2). Alternatively, one might construe τοῦ θοοῦ … τῷ ἀγαστῷ as 'the admirable*ness* of the fleet'. Cf. Reeve: 'So what moves quickly is not all there is, but the admirable part of it. Hence this name "*tagathon*" … is applied to what is admirable (*agaston*) about the fast (*thoon*).' But then the snag is that at c2, c5 (τὸ) ἀγαστόν means '(the) admirable *part*', not 'admirableness'.

In §5.3.2 we shall be able to say more both about this distinction between a quick and a slow component amidst the universal flux and about the distinction, suggested by the previous passage, between a 'pushing' component and another that is pushed. For the moment it is enough to remark that the present distinction, along with the very use of the verb πορεύομαι (whose concreteness, and resistance to a figurative construal, I have tried to render in my translation), is strong evidence that the references to movement are to be taken literally.

Now, it may seem obviously false to say that all things are always moving. Things often seem to undergo some sort of change without moving (see Arist. *Cat.* 14): a still bowl of soup becomes cold from hot; a white person's skin becomes brown in virtue of a stationary exposure to sunlight. So why should the flux theory be represented as claiming that all things are always moving and even stressing the role played by their movement at the expense of other sorts of change?

I submit that the answer is this: Plato believes that all or most of the thinkers to whom he is ascribing the flux theory are somehow committed to the view that *movement is the basic kind of change*, to which all the other kinds of change can be reduced.

More precisely, part of what Plato thinks might be that many, if not all, natural philosophers tried to account for kinds of change apparently other than movement (qualitative change, generation and destruction) by taking them to consist in the combination and separation of certain basic constituents of reality – combination and separation being forms of movement. And if this were what Plato thinks, he would agree with Aristotle, who holds himself, and ascribes to his predecessors, the view that movement is the primary kind of motion or change. Read *Ph.* 8.9.265b17–32 (cf. 8.7.260b8–15):

> That movement in respect of place is primary among motions is testified by all those who have made mention of motion; for they assign the principles of motion to the things which impart this sort of motion. For separation and combination are motions in respect of place, and this is how Love and Strife move: one of them separates and the other combines. Anaxagoras too says that Mind, which was the first to move, separates ... The same goes also for those who hold that generation and corruption are caused by density and rarity; for they order these things by means of combination and separation.

Here Aristotle is referring to the doctrines of Empedocles, Anaxagoras and Anaximenes respectively.

You will notice that I have omitted, and replaced with dots, part of the Aristotelian passage. This is not because I consider it irrelevant to our discussion. Quite the contrary, I want to put forward the hypothesis that the words which I have omitted, and which we shall read in due course, are especially relevant to *Cra.*'s references to flux. The omitted words are about the atomists, Leucippus and Democritus; and my hypothesis is that in setting forth the flux theory Plato is chiefly – though not exclusively – thinking of those philosophers.

To see the relevance of this hypothesis you must first recall a few facts. The atomists notoriously held that the basic elements of reality are atoms and the void, and that everything else besides atoms and void is mere appearance. The objects in the sensible world are aggregates of atoms, while the qualities usually ascribed to the objects are just the result of the encounter between their atoms and our senses. Hence the atomists claimed that (in a way) only atoms and void exist: see S. E. *M.* 7.135 (68 B9 DK = 60.1 Leszl); Alex. Aphr. *in Metaph.* 303.31–2 (13.3 Leszl); and other texts we shall shortly see.

Now, according to the atomists, atoms are *always in movement* through the void, colliding with each other and thus forming more or less stable aggregates. Among many sources for this you can read e.g. Aristotle, *Cael.* 300b8–11 (67 A16 = 64.1 Leszl), who reports that Leucippus and Democritus claimed that 'the primary bodies are always moving in the infinite void' (ἀεὶ κινεῖσθαι τὰ πρῶτα σώματα ἐν τῷ κενῷ καὶ τῷ ἀπείρῳ). Cf. *Metaph.* 1071b32–4 (67 A18 = 42.3 Leszl) 'they say there is always motion' (ἀεὶ γὰρ εἶναί φασι κίνησιν), and Hippol. *Haer.* 1.12.1 (67 A10 = 4.4 Leszl), who reports that Leucippus said that the beings 'are infinite and always moving, and coming-to-be and change are continuous' (ἄπειρα εἶναι καὶ ἀεὶ κινούμενα καὶ γένεσιν καὶ μεταβολὴν συνεχῶς οὖσαν).

This everlasting movement of the atoms and their being, together with void, the only true reality are instructively associated by two major witnesses: Plutarch *Adversus Coloten* 1110E5–1111F1 (68 A57 = 8.1 Leszl) and Galen *De elementis ex Hippocrate* 1.2 = 3.2–5.9 Helmreich (A49 = 8.3 Leszl). I quote excerpts from Plutarch:[68]

[Colotes] says that the claim that 'by custom is colour, by custom is sweet, by custom all combination, while what really exists is void and the atoms [νόμῳ χροιὴν εἶναι καὶ νόμῳ γλυκὺ καὶ νόμῳ σύγκρισιν <ἅπασαν, ἐτεῇ δὲ τὸ κενὸν καὶ> τὰς ἀτόμους]' has been advanced by Democritus against the perceptions. (1110E7–10)

What does Democritus say? That substances infinite in number, indivisible and incorruptible, and also unqualified and impassive, move scattered about in the void [ἐν τῷ κενῷ φέρεσθαι διεσπαρμένας]. And when they approach each other,

---

[68] I translate Leszl's (forthcoming) text, which differs from Einarson/de Lacy's on minor details.

or meet or intertwine, then of the aggregates one appears to be water, another fire, another a plant and another a human being, but actually all there is is what he calls 'indivisible forms' and nothing else [εἶναι δὲ πάντα τὰς ἀτόμους ἰδέας ὑπ' αὐτοῦ καλουμένας, ἕτερον δὲ μηδέν] ... Neither does colour exist originating from colourless elements, nor nature or soul from unqualified and impassive elements. (1110F4–1111A8)

> They [sc. atoms] are struck and strike each other all the time and cannot produce from themselves, not only an animal or a soul or nature, but even a common multiplicity or a single heap, since they are *always quivering and separating from each other* [παλλομένων ἀεὶ καὶ διισταμένων]. (1111E8–11)

Plutarch's account is no doubt influenced by his own polemical intent against the Epicurean Colotes; but its substance is confirmed by many other sources, like Galen mentioned above or Aristotle *On Democritus, ap.* Simpl. *in Cael.* 294.33–295.20 (68 A37 = 7.1 Leszl). Let me insist on one point which is clearly implied by these reports: according to the atomist doctrine, the movement of the atoms accounts for *all* the other kinds of change seemingly taking place in ordinary objects, like qualitative change. We can now, at long last, fill in the gap in my initial quotation from Aristotle's *Physics* 8.9, reading lines 265b25–9 (19.2 Leszl), where we are told that the atomists too

> say that nature's motion is motion in respect of place [τὴν κατὰ τόπον κίνησιν κινεῖσθαι τὴν φύσιν] ... of the other kinds of motion they think that none belongs to the primary items [τοῖς πρώτοις], but to the things deriving from these [τοῖς ἐκ τούτων]: for they say things increase and decrease and alter in virtue of the indivisible bodies combining and separating [αὐξάνεσθαι γὰρ καὶ φθίνειν καὶ ἀλλοιοῦσθαι συγκρινομένων καὶ διακρινομένων τῶν ἀτόμων σωμάτων].

Here the atomists would seem to accord some limited legitimacy to talk of other kinds of change, though only in relation to compounds. A more drastic version is offered by Simplicius, *in Ph.* 1320.16–19 (19.4 Leszl):

> Democritus and his followers acknowledged only motion in respect of place [μόνην τὴν κατὰ τόπον κίνησιν ἔλεγον]. For they said that also things subject to alteration are in motion with respect to place [καὶ γὰρ τὰ ἀλλοιούμενα κατὰ τόπον ἔλεγον κινεῖσθαι], but this escapes notice because the thing changes place not as a whole but in its parts.

These things being so, the hypothesis that Plato has the atomists especially in mind when he sets forth the flux doctrine in *Cra.* would easily explain Socrates' talk of a theory according to which things are constantly in movement and in which the role of movement is stressed at the expense of other sorts of change. 'The objects', or 'the beings', are always in movement because their basic constituents, i.e. atoms, are – or, if you prefer,

More on the theory of flux

because for the atomists the expressions τὰ πράγματα and τὰ ὄντα primarily refer to the atoms themselves, which are always in movement, and only secondarily to the compound things of ordinary experience.

5.3.2 The Penetrating Principle (412c–413d)

Now back to the text of *Cra*. Reading on will provide further evidence in favour of my atomist hypothesis as well as further important details about the flux theory itself.

We left the text at 412c, where the etymology of ἀγαθόν introduced us to the presence of two components, the quick and the slow one, within the universal flux. This intriguing distinction gets immediately expanded in the subsequent etymology of the word δίκαιον. To be precise, after ἀγαθόν Socrates turns first to δικαιοσύνη, 'justice'. But this appears at once to derive from δικαίου σύνεσις, 'understanding of what is just' (412c7–8), whilst its component word δίκαιον, 'just', is difficult to analyse: many seem to agree about it up to a certain point, but beyond that disagreement arises (c8–d1). For

so. Those who believe that all there is is in the act of travelling [τὸ πᾶν εἶναι ἐν πορείᾳ] think that most of it is such as to do nothing else than moving [οὐδὲν ἄλλο ἢ χωρεῖν], but that there is something passing through all this [διὰ δὲ τούτου παντὸς εἶναί τι διεξιόν], through whose action all that comes to be comes to be [δι' οὗ πάντα τὰ γιγνόμενα γίγνεσθαι]. This second component, they think, is very quick and fine [τάχιστον ... καὶ λεπτότατον]. For otherwise it could not go through all there is, if it were not very fine, so that nothing was impervious to it [ὥστε αὐτὸ μηδὲν στέγειν], and very quick, so as to treat the other things as if they were standing still. And so, since it governs all the other things by going through them [ἐπιτροπεύει τὰ ἄλλα πάντα διαϊόν], it was correctly called by this name, δίκαιον, acquiring the power of κ for the sake of euphony. (412d2–e3)

Thus from δι(κ)αϊόν, 'passing through', comes δίκαιον. According to the flux theorists, there is a duality of principles or elements in the universal 'travel' of things. Most of what there is has an unqualified natural disposition to *moving* (χωρεῖν).[69] The other principle has an *active* role. It runs through the former, preponderant one thanks to its fineness, which enables it to penetrate everywhere, and to its quickness; and somehow or

---

[69] Stressing the passivity of this main element of reality, Fowler translates χωρεῖν here as 'to be a ... receptacle' (LSJ III), Reeve as 'give way' (LSJ I, the primitive meaning). The verb, however, must mean 'to move' (LSJ II), as in 402a πάντα χωρεῖ καὶ οὐδὲν μένει, a passage obviously relevant to the present one, and as most interpreters take it (including Minio-Paluello and Ficino, who, however, apparently fail to recognize the *consecutive* τοιοῦτον ... οἷον at d3).

other it causes and governs all that comes to be (d4–5, e1).[70] This distinction evidently coincides with the two distinctions which we encountered earlier: the one which singled out a 'pushing' component in flux as the 'cause and principle' of the beings (401d) and the one between a slow and a quick component in flux (412c).

This doctrine is interesting in the extreme. It is also strongly reminiscent of no less than three other doctrines: (i) the atomist theory of the soul, (ii) the conception of fire set forth in the *Timaeus*, and (iii) Stoic theology. Let me say something on each in turn.

(i) The atomist theory of the soul is expounded in Aristotle's *De anima*, I.2, and in several passages from the ancient commentators. Here is 403b31–404a9 (67 A28 DK = 101.1 Leszl), with emphasis added here and there:

Democritus says that it [sc. soul] is a sort of *fire and heat* [πῦρ τι καὶ θερμόν]. For, since the figures and the atoms are infinite, the spherical ones he says to be fire and soul ... because such 'figures' are especially able to *penetrate through everything* and *move the other things, being themselves in motion* [διὰ τὸ μάλιστα διὰ παντὸς δύνασθαι διαδύνειν τοὺς τοιούτους 'ῥυσμοὺς' καὶ κινεῖν τὰ λοιπά, κινούμενα καὶ αὐτά] – for they took soul to be that which supplies living beings with motion.

And here is 405a5–13 (68 A101 = 102.1 Leszl): soul

seemed to some to be *fire*: for this is made up of the *finest particles* and is the most incorporeal of the elements [λεπτομερέστατόν τε καὶ μάλιστα τῶν στοιχείων ἀσώματον], and moreover it is moved and moves the other things primarily [κινεῖταί τε καὶ κινεῖ τὰ ἄλλα πρώτως]. Democritus has expressed himself even more neatly ... he said that soul is the same as mind, and this is made of the first and indivisible bodies and *causes motion* because of the *smallness of its parts* and because of its shape [κινητικὸν δὲ διὰ μικρομέρειαν[71] καὶ τὸ σχῆμα]; and among shapes he says that the spherical one is *most mobile*, and such are mind and fire [τῶν δὲ σχημάτων εὐκινητότατον τὸ σφαιροειδὲς λέγει· τοιοῦτον δ' εἶναι τόν τε νοῦν καὶ τὸ πῦρ].

---

[70] At d4 you may well be disappointed with the sequence διὰ δὲ τούτου παντός ... δι' οὗ, which does not mean 'through all this ... through which', with δι' οὗ answering διὰ δὲ τούτου as one would naturally expect: δι' οὗ must instead mean '*by means of* which', being independent of διὰ δὲ τούτου and having instrumental rather than local meaning. (My translation of δι' οὗ = 'through whose action' aims to mirror this ambiguity.) The problem disappears if instead of δι' οὗ we write δι' ὅ, which is the reading of MS Par. 1812 and was independently conjectured by Hirschig. This may be meant to suggest, by way of a refinement, that in διαϊόν δια- means *both* 'through' *and* 'because of'. See n.77 for a further reason in favour of the correction; and notice that corruption of δι' ὅ into δι' οὗ is easily justified also because Plato probably wrote both in the same way, i.e. as ΔΙΟ (see §5.5.3 n.142 and Ademollo, in preparation-1 and in preparation-5).

[71] μικρομέρειαν: *v.l.* λεπτομέρειαν. Editors are divided.

At 405a5–7 Aristotle seems to say that someone else before Democritus identified soul and fire on account of fire's fineness, incorporeity, motive power and mobility. It would be very interesting to know whether this is actually so, and who these people were. Anyway, Democritus is the major character Aristotle has in mind here; and the correspondences between his theory of the soul and the *Cra.* passage are impressive. Democritus' spherical soul-atoms have many of the features of our Penetrating Principle: penetrating everywhere, being very fine, being very quick, being endowed with some sort of causal power. (Admittedly, Democritus does not seem to assign any sort of *cosmic* function to the soul-atoms or claim that the world as a whole has a soul which pervades it; in these respects the Stoics are a better parallel, see below.) Indeed, further on in the text we shall encounter a clue to the effect that the Penetrating Principle is fiery, like Democritus' soul-atoms. And finally, the action of Democritus' spherical atoms, and of *Cra.*'s principle, takes place in a world constantly in movement. This point is not emphasized in the *De anima* passages, but is widely attested elsewhere, as we saw in §5.3.1, where I first made the hypothesis that the atomists play an important role in the theory of flux. That hypothesis is now receiving ample confirmation.

But then why does Socrates never mention Democritus or Leucippus by name? I take it that this silence is eloquent and deliberate, and that it was Plato's second-best course of action once he was persuaded not to burn Democritus' treatises, as he would have wished to do (D. L. 9.40).

(ii) Next comes the *Timaeus*. When that dialogue describes the structure of the four primary bodies as made up of regular polyhedra, it claims, at 56ab, that fire is constituted by tetrahedra on the grounds that among regular polyhedra the tetrahedron is the 'fittest for cutting and sharpest' (τμητικότατόν τε καὶ ὀξύτατον), the 'most mobile' (εὐκινητότατον), the 'smallest' (σμικρότατον) and the 'lightest' (ἐλαφρότατον). Later on, at 58b and 78a (cf. 61e), Timaeus explains that fire 'has gone through everything, reaching everywhere most of all' (εἰς ἅπαντα διελήλυθε μάλιστα), in virtue of its 'fineness' (λεπτότης), and that 'of all kinds, fire has the smallest parts [σμικρομερέστατον] and hence passes through [διαχωρεῖ] water, earth, air and whatever is composed of these, and nothing is impervious to it [στέγειν οὐδὲν αὐτὸ δύναται]'. This account of fire has points of contact *both* with our passage, 412de, *and* with Aristotle's account of Democritus' fiery atoms. I take these points of contact as lending some indirect confirmation to the connection between our passage and Democritus.

(iii) Finally, the connection with Stoic theology. It is well known that the Stoics posited two principles, one passive, i.e. matter, and another one active, i.e. God, which pervades matter and constructs or shapes everything.[72] Some ancient sources claim that the Stoics derived at least part of this doctrine from Plato and the Academy.[73] They seem to have been especially influenced by the *Timaeus* and its early Academic interpretations;[74] but I find it plausible that our passage, with its notion of an active and ordering principle penetrating everywhere, also played some role in the formation of the Stoic doctrine. This hypothesis is particularly reasonable given that the Stoics were certainly influenced by our dialogue in other respects, i.e. with regard to the etymologies and the theory of the mimetic primary names.[75]

Let us resume our reading of the text. So far the flux theorists have told a single story. But from this point onwards, Socrates says, disagreement begins:

(SO.) Up to this point, as I was saying just now, many agree that this is the just. But since I am stubborn on this point, Hermogenes – all these things I have thoroughly learnt in secret, i.e. that this is the just and the cause [τοῦτό ἐστι τὸ δίκαιον καὶ τὸ αἴτιον][76] (for that 'because of which' something comes to be, that is the cause [δι' ὃ γὰρ γίγνεταί <τι>, τοῦτ' ἔστι τὸ αἴτιον];[77] and someone said it was correct to call it 'Zeus' [Δία[78]] for this reason). But when, in spite of hearing this, I nonetheless gently question them again: 'Then what *is* just [Τί οὖν ποτ' ἔστιν ... δίκαιον], my dear, if these things are so?', then I seem to be asking beyond what is proper and leaping too far. For they say I have learnt enough and then try each to say different things, trying to satisfy me, and they don't agree any more. (412e3–413b3)

---

[72] See D. L. 7.134, S. E. *M.* 9.75–6, Alex. Aphr. *Mixt.* 224.32–225.2, Aet. 1.7.33 (= *SVF* II.300, 311, 310, 1027).

[73] Calcidius, *in Ti.* CCXCIV; Cic. *Ac.* 1.35, 39–43.

[74] See Sedley 2002 on Cic. *Ac.* 1.24–9.

[75] See §6.1.1 and Long 2005: 36–9. The connection between our passage and Stoic metaphysics is discussed in more detail in Ademollo (in preparation-5).

[76] At a3 we must keep the MSS τοῦτο, which refers back to the Penetrating Principle mentioned in the previous lines (exactly as at a1), instead of accepting Buttmann's superfluous correction ταὐτό, as the OCT editors do. NB: The whole clause means 'This is the just and the cause', *not* 'this just is also the cause' (Stallbaum, Méridier, Dalimier).

[77] Here some have seen a hint at a new etymology of δίκαιον, or rather a refinement on the etymology from διαϊόν. However, it seems to me that this would be inappropriate in the present, recapitulative context, especially if we keep a3 τοῦτο (see n.76). I rather suggest that these words explain Socrates' sudden use of the phrase τὸ αἴτιον (thus also allowing the digression about Δία < διά) and *recall* something *previously* said. This in turn confirms that at 412d4 δι' ὃ was to be read in place of δι' οὗ (see n.70).

[78] Hermann's acute correction of βTW's ἰδίᾳ (defended by Stallbaum 136–7, Méridier, Dalimier) and Q's δι' ἅ. The name Ζεύς was etymologized, with a role for διά, at 396ab; parallels for the Δία/διά connection in §5.1.2.

Mind your μέν's and δέ's here. At e3–a1 Socrates starts by recapitulating what he has been saying so far (μέχρι μὲν οὖν ἐνταῦθα ... τοῦτο εἶναι τὸ δίκαιον, 'Up to this point ... that this is the just'). Then, at a2, he begins to move on (ἐγὼ δέ ... περὶ αὐτοῦ, 'But since I am stubborn on this point'). But at a2–6, as I see it, he momentarily interrupts this change of subject and picks up his previous recapitulation (ταῦτα μὲν πάντα διαπέπυσμαι ἐν ἀπορρήτοις ... διὰ ταῦτα, 'all these things I have thoroughly learnt in secret ... for this reason'). Only at a6 is he really ready to move on (ἐπειδὰν δ' ἠρέμα αὐτοὺς ἐπανερωτῶ ... ἄλλεσθαι, '*but* when, in spite of hearing ... leaping too far').[79]

Thus Socrates draws a neat distinction between what the flux theorists agree and what they disagree upon – a distinction which most translations blur. They agree upon the answer to the question, *what the δίκαιον is* (see 413a1 τοῦτο εἶναι τὸ δίκαιον, cf. a3); that is to say, they share both the identification 'The δίκαιον is the διαϊόν' (i.e. the etymology δίκαιον < διαϊόν) and the general account of the Penetrating Principle's activities which we have been given so far. Socrates says that this part of the story he has learnt 'in secret' (a3), which I take as an indication that in fact no one ever connected this doctrine with an etymology of the word δίκαιον.[80]

The flux theorists instead disagree upon the answer to the question, *what is δίκαιον* (without the article: a7 Τί οὖν ποτ' ἔστιν ... δίκαιον ... ;).[81] In the present context, this seems to mean that they disagree upon how to identify concretely the Penetrating Principle. Let us read their competing answers (the sun - fire - heat - Mind), which are ordered from the most concrete to the most abstract:

(SO.) One says that this is just, the sun [τοῦτο εἶναι δίκαιον, τὸν ἥλιον], because only it governs the beings, going through and burning them [τοῦτον γὰρ μόνον διαϊόντα καὶ καίοντα ἐπιτροπεύειν τὰ ὄντα].[82] Now, when I report

---

[79] For Sedley 2003: 116, instead, a2–3 ταῦτα μὲν πάντα διαπέπυσμαι ἐν ἀπορρήτοις looks forward and introduces all the developments to come (413ad). But in the light of the contrast with a6 ἐπειδὰν δ' it seems that ταῦτα ... πάντα can only be all the *previous* things, not all the *following* ones.

[80] Alternatively, one might take it as an indication that in fact no one ever held this doctrine. But if I was right above, then someone *did* hold at least most of it, namely Democritus. Contrast *Tht.*'s Secret Doctrine (152ce), which is clearly called 'secret' because the historical Protagoras, to whom it is fictionally ascribed, in fact never taught it.

[81] The article τό is spuriously inserted in a7, and then again in b3, by the MSS of the δ family. Many translate as though they read it. It reappears at c5, 9, and that is no harm: its lack is significant only in the context of a distinction between the two questions.

[82] At 413b4 I read καίοντα, the standard form in Attic inscriptions, not the MSS κάοντα, printed in all editions (see Dalimier 252 n.280, Sedley 2003: 38). This obviously makes the etymology better. Note also that διαϊόντα καὶ καίοντα improves on the original etymology, δίκαιον < διαϊόν, because it accounts better for the κ.

this to someone, glad as though I had heard something fine, as soon as he hears this he laughs at me and asks whether I think that there is nothing just among humans when the sun has set. So, since I persist in asking him what he, in his turn, says it is, he says it is fire.[83] This however is not easy to know. Another one says it is not fire itself [οὐκ αὐτὸ τὸ πῦρ], but the heat itself that is present in fire [αὐτὸ τὸ θερμὸν τὸ ἐν τῷ πυρὶ ἐνόν]. Another one says he laughs at all these accounts: the just is what Anaxagoras says it is, Mind [νοῦν]: he says that, self-ruling [αὐτοκράτορα] and mixed with nothing [οὐδενὶ μεμειγμένον], it orders all things going through them all [πάντα ... κοσμεῖν τὰ πράγματα διὰ πάντων ἰόντα]. At this point, my dear, I am much more perplexed than before trying to learn about what the just is. Anyway, as regards the purpose of our inquiry, this name, at least, appears to belong to it for these reasons. (413b3–d2)

This extraordinary piece of quasi-doxography is thick with references to other thinkers, ranging from allusion to actual quotation, as Hermogenes and Socrates themselves acknowledge in the following lines (413d3–8), which we read in §5.1.2. It will be helpful to assign letters – respectively A, B, C and D – to Socrates' anonymous interlocutors.

We start with A, the weirdest of the lot. It is not clear in what sense he can maintain (b3–5) that the *sun* is something 'going through', διαϊόν. The obvious answer – because it crosses the sky – would be hardly pertinent to the matter at issue, but still is probably the right one. This answer receives support from *Tht.* 153cd, where one of the dubious 'arguments' in favour of the flux theory is Homer's famous 'golden cord' passage (*Il.* 8.18–27), interpreted allegorically as if it were actually speaking of the sun's motion and its importance for the preservation of everything. Moreover, if we do not lose sight of the present lexical meaning of δίκαιον, 'just', then it is surely relevant that the Sun was traditionally regarded as the watchman of justice (cf. Hes. *Op.* 267–9 with *Il.* 3.277, etc.). Thus, somehow or other, A's view fits in – rather awkwardly – with the context.

Next come B, who says the Penetrating Principle is fire (b5–c2), and C, who says it is rather fire's heat (c3–4). There need not be a strong opposition between the two; actually the first of the *Theaetetus* 'arguments' for flux (153a) refers together to '*heat and fire*, which begets and governs the other things too' (τὸ ... θερμόν τε καὶ πῦρ, ὃ δὴ καὶ τἆλλα γεννᾷ καὶ ἐπιτροπεύει). Remember also that according to Aristotle's report in *De an.* 403b31–404a1, which we read above, Democritus conceived of the soul as

---

[83] There is a problem of punctuation at c2: ὅτι αὖ ἐκεῖνος λέγει αὐτό, τὸ πῦρ φησιν (Burnet, Fowler, Minio-Paluello, Reeve) or ὅτι αὖ ἐκεῖνος λέγει, αὐτὸ τὸ πῦρ φησιν (Stallbaum, Hirschig, Méridier, OCT, Dalimier, Sedley 2003: 117)? I choose the former, in order to preserve the force of αὐτὸ τὸ πῦρ at c3 and to avoid having as many as three αὐτό's = *ipse* in just two lines (c2–3).

'a sort of fire and heat' (πῦρ τι καὶ θερμόν). On the other hand, and quite compatibly, B and C also seem to hint at distinct individual thinkers, as we are going to see.

B enters the stage (413b5–c1) sneering at A's appeal to the sun: what happens to justice after sunset? The quip confirms that the lexical meaning of δίκαιον as 'just' was relevant to understand A's view. Moreover, it is a neat quotation from Heraclitus 22 B16 τὸ μὴ δῦνόν ποτε πῶς ἄν τις λάθοι; 'How could one escape the notice of that which never sets?' Thereby Heraclitus obviously means that we need a more reliable candidate than the sun for watchmanship over justice. And his own candidate would be precisely *fire*, as is suggested by Hippolytus, *Haer.* 9.10.7–8 (containing B64–6):

He says that a judgement of the universe and all the things inside it takes place by means of fire, saying thus: 'Thunderbolt steers all things' … by 'thunderbolt' meaning the everlasting fire. He says that this fire has intelligence and is the cause of the government of the whole of things [τῆς διοικήσεως τῶν ὅλων αἴτιον] … 'For', he says, 'fire will judge and condemn everything suddenly coming upon it.'

This and other Heraclitean texts about fire as the fundamental element of reality (B30, 31, 90), together with the allusion to the sun fragment, license the conclusion that B represents Heraclitus.[84] On a number of important counts, however, Socrates' initial account of the Penetrating Principle at 412d2–e3 cannot be confidently laid at Heraclitus' door. For Heraclitus does not say that fire is quicker or finer than any other element; indeed, he does not say that it is quick or fine at all. Nor does he seem to say that fire penetrates or passes through anything else, but rather that fire *turns* into other elements.[85]

At 413c2 Socrates winds up his report on B with the comment 'But this is not easy to know [εἰδέναι].' This is obscure. I tentatively endorse Sedley's (2003: 117) suggestion that thereby Socrates might be 'referring to the lack of empirical support for any view which gives fire itself a governing role throughout nature'; but I would try to improve on it by deleting 'empirical'.

---

[84] See Guthrie 1962–81: 1.456, Kahn 1979: 274–5 and others.
[85] Admittedly, universal penetration could be read into B41 = 85 Marcovich: γνώμην †ὁτέη κυβερνῆσαι† πάντα διὰ πάντων, which might be taken to mean 'the intelligence which pilots all things *through all*' (Mondolfo 1972: 93 n.135). Kahn 1979: 275 suggests that penetration through everything may be meant in B66 πάντα … τὸ πῦρ ἐπελθὸν κρινεῖ καὶ καταλήψεται (see above in the text). Finally, I add that the pseudo-Hippocratic *De victu* 1, a pastiche imitating especially Heraclitus among other philosophers, says that fire 'can move all things always' (1.3) and 'pilots all things always … without ever keeping still' (1.10) – where 'always' is διὰ παντός, literally *'through all'*. The report of Aetius 1.28.1 (A8) is under heavy Stoic influence.

As for C (413c3–4), I shall only remark that the role ascribed to τὸ θερμόν is vaguely reminiscent of Hp. *De carnibus* 2: 'What we call heat seems to me to be immortal and to think of everything and to see, hear and know everything, both the things that are and those that will be.'[86] But, again, the author of the Hippocratic tract does not seem to hold that heat is fine or quick or penetrates everywhere.

Finally, D. What he says about Anaxagoras' Mind at c4–8 is included by DK in 59 A55 and is, in part, a close quotation from B12 (Simpl. *in Ph.* 164.24–5 + 156.13–157.4), where we read that

Mind is infinite and self-ruled [αὐτοκρατές] and is mixed with nothing [μέμεικται οὐδενὶ χρήματι].

D adds that Mind also 'orders all things going through them all' (c7–8). In our Anaxagorean testimonies the ordering of reality is widely attested as Mind's activity; but strictly speaking we hear nothing of its *going through everything*.[87] Indeed, B11 (Simpl. *in Ph.* 164.23–4) avers that there are things where Mind is *not* present. Universal penetration could, however, be read into B14 (*ibid.* 157.7–9), which says that Mind is 'where all the other things are too'. Mind is also 'the *finest* [λεπτότατον] and purest of all things', says B12 shortly after the sentence quoted above, and thus it has another of the generic features ascribed to the Penetrating Principle by all flux theorists (412d5–7).

If now we turn back and reconsider the whole of 412c–413d, which we have just finished analysing, we see that Socrates has succeeded in first outlining a generic theory of two principles of a world in flux (412ce) and then setting forth the views of various philosophers – most notably Heraclitus and Anaxagoras – as more or less plausible candidates for being particular versions of the generic outline (413ad). He might have referred to other philosophers as well: Diogenes of Apollonia, who in 64 B5 DK says that Air 'has reached everything and disposes all things and is present in everything' (ἐπὶ πᾶν ἀφῖχθαι καὶ πάντα διατιθέναι καὶ ἐν παντὶ ἐνεῖναι); or Empedocles, who in 31 B134 speaks of a 'holy mind' which 'darts through all the universe with swift thoughts' (φροντίσι κόσμον ἅπαντα καταΐσσουσα θοῇσιν).[88] But in many respects the generic outline fits none

---

[86] See Sedley 2003: 118 for another suggestion, concerning Socrates' teacher Archelaus.
[87] The pseudo-report πάντα φησὶν αὐτὸν κοσμεῖν τὰ πράγματα διὰ πάντων ἰόντα (c7–8) might perhaps be meant to receive support from a tendentious interpretation of Anaxagoras' verb for the ordering effected by Mind, i.e. δια-κοσμεῖν. Cf. 419a τὸ διακοσμοῦν καὶ διϊόν.
[88] For some speculation about the identity and role of this divinity see Guthrie 1962–81: II.257–63. I shirk questions about the legitimacy of claiming that Anaxagoras' or Empedocles' Mind is material.

of these better than Democritus, whom Socrates does not mention at all, with his theory of the soul.

5.3.3 Further evidence about the atomists in the Cratylus (412b, 414a, 420d)

There is in fact no reason to resist the suggestion that the atomists have a role in the etymologies, because *some* role they seem to have anyway, quite independently of my hypotheses. References to Democritus and ancient atomism have been detected by scholars in three passages.

The first passage is at 412b and immediately precedes the etymology of ἀγαθόν, which we saw in §5.3.1. The name here at issue is σοφία, 'intelligence', which Socrates derives from φορᾶς ἐφάπτεσθαι, 'to touch movement':

> (so.) This is rather obscure and foreign; but we must recall from the poets that in many places they say, of whatever of the things beginning to advance quickly, 'it rushed' [ἐσύθη]. And the name of a Laconian among the highly reputed ones was precisely 'Sous' (Σοῦς): for this is how Lacedaemonians call the quick dash [τὴν ... ταχεῖαν ὁρμήν]. Therefore σοφία signifies touching of this movement [ταύτης ... τῆς φορᾶς ἐπαφήν], on the assumption that the beings are in movement. (412b2–8)

Thus σοφία < σοῦ (ἐπ)αφή. Now, that, as Socrates says, there was a famous Spartan called Σοῦς is true: Plutarch mentions a Σόος as a famous ancestor of Lycurgus (*Lyc.* 1.4–2.1).[89] What looks suspicious is rather the claim that σοῦς is the Spartan name of the quick dash. This is all the more suspicious once you realize that σοῦς was something of a technical term in Democritus' physics. Read Arist. *Cael.* 313b4–6 (68 A62 DK = 69.1 Leszl): Democritus

> says that the 'rush' does not dash in one direction [οὐκ εἰς ἓν ὁρμᾶν τὸν σοῦν], calling 'rush' the motion of the atoms which move upwards.

The parallel between *Cra.* and Aristotle's testimony is noticed by Baxter 1992: 156–7. We may add that it does not involve just the word σοῦς, but also its connection with ὁρμή ('dash')/ὁρμᾶν ('to dash'). Indeed, the fact that this etymology, like that of Φερρέφαττα/Φερέπαφα at 404cd, speaks of our cognition of the world in flux in terms of ἐπαφή, 'touching', might be a further point of contact with Democritus: cf. Arist. *Sens.* 442a29–b1 = 68 A119 = 120.1 Leszl,

---

[89] See Dalimier 250–1 n.274.

Democritus and most natural philosophers ... make all objects of sense into objects of touch [ἁπτά]. Yet, if this is so, clearly it also is the case that each of the other senses is a kind of touch [ἁφή τις].[90]

It seems evident to me that Plato is making Socrates hint at Democritus' doctrine and, at the same time, creating a sort of comical smokescreen with his reference to the historical Σοῦς and to a fictitious Laconic term.

Another reference to Democritus is the etymology of γυνή ('woman') from γονή ('childbirth', 'womb') at 414a, half a page after the conclusion of the δίκαιον passage:

(SO.) γυνή, it seems to me, wants to be γονή. (414a3–4)

This has a very close parallel in Democritus, 68 B122a DK = 191.2 Leszl (see *Et. Gud.* 325.25, 326.25–6 de Stefani):

γυνή: as Democritus says, a sort of γονή.[91]

Finally, the third reference to Democritus has been identified in the etymology of ἑκούσιον ('voluntary') at 420d, towards the end of the etymologies of the secondary names:

(SO.) As for ἑκούσιον, what yields and does not resist [τὸ εἶκον καὶ μὴ ἀντιτυποῦν] but, as I am saying, yields to the going [εἶκον τῷ ἰόντι] has been indicated by this name, i.e. by what happens in accordance with the will.[92] Instead the 'compulsory' and resistant [τὸ δὲ 'ἀναγκαῖον' καὶ ἀντίτυπον], being against the will, is what concerns error and ignorance [τὸ περὶ τὴν ἁμαρτίαν ἂν εἴη καὶ ἀμαθίαν], and has been likened to the progress down the ravines [τῇ κατὰ τὰ ἄγκη πορείᾳ], because they, being difficult to pass through, rugged and bushy, keep from proceeding. Thence perhaps it was called ἀναγκαῖον, being likened to the progress through the ravine. (420d5–e3)

---

[90] On this last point see Goldschmidt 1940: 135 and Leszl 2009: *Presentazione dei testi*, §15. Translation after Barnes 1984.

[91] The parallel is noted by DK *ad loc.* and by Leszl 2009: 430 n.1317. DK, however, doubt whether the Democritus in question is the atomist or Bolus of Mendes (third century BC), a writer in magic and pharmacology one of whose works was falsely ascribed to Democritus. But the parallel, together with the others, tells in favour of genuine Democritean authorship.
  NB: Neither the text I translate nor the sources I quote are the same as in DK: see Ademollo (in preparation-2).

[92] τῷ κατὰ τὴν βούλησιν γιγνομένῳ (d7) is most naturally connected with the immediately preceding δεδηλωμένον ἂν εἴη τούτῳ τῷ ὀνόματι; presumably the meaning of 'this name' is now being specified, with the usual indifference towards use/mention distinctions. Thus we also obtain a neat parallel with the following τὸ δὲ 'ἀναγκαῖον' ... παρὰ τὴν βούλησιν ὄν. This is the way Stallbaum and Minio-Paluello understand the text. Others instead take τῷ κατὰ τὴν βούλησιν γιγνομένῳ to pick up τῷ ἰόντι (d6): 'yields to what is going, that which occurs in accordance with the will'.

As Sambursky 1959 pointed out, the phrase εἶκον καὶ μὴ ἀντιτυποῦν (d5) has a striking parallel in Simpl. *in Ph.* 1318.35–1319.1 (68 A58 = 19.3 Leszl), who says that atoms διὰ τοῦ κενοῦ εἴκοντος καὶ μὴ ἀντιτυποῦντος κατὰ τόπον κινεῖσθαι ('move in respect of place through the void which *yields and does not resist*'). Simplicius' phrase is exactly the same as Socrates'; hence it is reasonable to suppose that 'Plato in his etymology is alluding to an original Democritean expression' and Simplicius is quoting Democritus directly or indirectly.[93]

I wonder whether we can take a further step, focusing on the phrase τὸ περὶ τὴν ἁμαρτίαν ἂν εἴη καὶ ἀμαθίαν (d8–9). This connects the compulsory with 'error and ignorance' and possibly suggests, with a wordplay, some etymological relation between ἁμαρτία and ἀμαθία. In any case it does not correspond to anything that has been said about the voluntary and seems to be a rather gratuitous addition. So what is its purpose?

Sambursky 1959 compared it to Pythagorean maxims saying that learning must come about voluntarily (ἑκουσίως), i.e. from the will of both teacher and pupil, if it is to be correct and reach its goal, whereas involuntary (ἀκούσιος) learning is bad and ineffective (Iamb. *VP* 183, Stob. 2.31.119). This might be right; but it would make it hard to see what the passage's unity consists in. So I will chance a different conjecture. Socrates' reference to ἁμαρτία and ἀμαθία might allude to a maxim included in the so-called *Sayings of Democrates* and ascribed to Democritus in DK together with most of the others (B35–115).[94] The maxim goes as follows (B83 = 161.1 Leszl): ἁμαρτίης αἰτίη ἡ ἀμαθίη τοῦ κρέσσονος, '*ignorance* of what is better is cause of *error*'. The two terms tied together in a wordplay are the same as in *Cra.*, where Democritus has just been hinted at in the etymology of ἑκούσιον. This is, I submit, no coincidence: the function of the ἁμαρτία-ἀμαθία phrase in *Cra.* might be to stress the previous allusion to Democritus.

5.3.4 Atomism in the Theaetetus

This is not the place to pursue the question of the relations between Democritus and Plato for its own sake. But it will be good to say something about the *Theaetetus*, which has several impressive points of contact with *Cra.*[95]

---

[93] The positive association between ἀναγκαῖον ('compulsory', but also 'necessary') and resistance has some chances of being Democritean too. Cf. Aet. 1.26.2 (68 A66 = 77.1 Leszl): Democritus by ἀνάγκη meant 'the *resistance* and movement and impact of matter' (τὴν ἀντιτυπίαν καὶ φορὰν καὶ πληγὴν τῆς ὕλης).

[94] See Diels' note at II.153–4. On the question of the authenticity of the 'Democrates' fragments see Warren 2002: 30–1.

[95] For a recent discussion of the question with regard to the *Timaeus* see Morel 2002.

At *Tht.* 152ce, as I have already anticipated, Socrates introduces a certain doctrine which, he says, was secretly taught by Protagoras to his pupils and was endorsed by almost all Greek wise men from Homer onwards, with the exception of Parmenides (roughly the same pedigree as is ascribed to the flux theory in *Cra.* 402ac and 411bc).[96] The function of this Secret Doctrine is, at the very least, to depict a world in which two theses would turn out to be true: (i) Theaetetus' thesis that knowledge is perception, (ii) Protagoras' relativist thesis that things are for anyone the way they appear to him.[97] We shall read the Secret Doctrine's first statement in §9.1.5. What is important for our present purposes is the fact that at *Tht.* 153d–157c the Doctrine unfolds into a very sophisticated account of perception. On this account, what we would ordinarily describe as the perceptual encounter between an external object having a certain quality and a sense-organ perceiving it (e.g. a white stone and an eye that sees it) is actually the encounter between two 'slow motions' (stone and eye) which produce as their twin offspring a pair of 'quick motions', a perceived quality and a perception of it (whiteness and sight), which travel between them and do not exist outside each individual encounter.

Here we can already point out another parallel between *Cra.* and *Tht.* Both dialogues tell us of a theory of flux involving a distinction between a quick and a slow motion. In *Cra.* the distinction is between the bulk of the moving reality (slow) and the Penetrating Principle (quick); in *Tht.* the distinction is between the subject and the object of perception (slow) and their perception and perceived quality (quick). So the two dialogues initially offer the same distinction, though they develop it quite differently. The common distinction is all the more interesting because it is introduced in very similar terms:

Since the beings travel, there is both quickness and slowness in them [ἐπειδὴ ... πορεύεται τὰ ὄντα, ἔνι μὲν ἄρ' αὐτοῖς τάχος, ἔνι δὲ βραδυτής]. (*Cra.* 412c)

All these things ... are in motion, but there is quickness and slowness in their motion [ταῦτα πάντα μὲν ... κινεῖται, τάχος δὲ καὶ βραδυτὴς ἔνι τῇ κινήσει αὐτῶν]. (*Tht.* 156c)

I take it that the *Tht.* distinction is, like that of *Cra.*, a distinction between properties of, or things in, *spatial* movement.[98] Several scholars,[99]

---

[96] The claim that Protagoras taught this doctrine *secretly* is of course tantamount to an admission that the historical Protagoras did not teach it at all (cf. n.80).
[97] The relations between Theaetetus' thesis, Protagoras' thesis and the Secret Doctrine are very controversial. I follow Lee 2005: 77–92 (to my mind the most convincing interpretation; see also 93–117 on the Docrine's development and eventual refutation); for a different view see Burnyeat 1982: 3–11 and 1990: 8–10, 42–52.
[98] See Dancy 1987: 83 and n.63.
[99] See especially McDowell 1973: 138. The issue is discussed by Lee 2005: 105–6.

instead, understand it in the light of the distinction, which Socrates draws later on in the same dialogue (181cd), between spatial movement and alteration, i.e. qualitative change: on their view, the quick motion is spatial movement and the slow one is alteration. But this interpretation is far from natural for anyone who is reading the dialogue for the first time; and the very parallel with *Cra.* tells against it.[100]

Now let me get back to the Secret Doctrine's account of perception. Some aspects of it, especially the ontological status of the physical objects, are notoriously controversial.[101] But I think it is open to anyone's interpretation to recognize that the account of perception owes something to the atomists (as already noted by Guthrie 1962–81: v.78).[102] We saw in §5.3.1 that, as Plutarch and other sources attest, Democritus held *both* that physical objects are constituted by ever-moving atoms *and* that sensible qualities are subjective and 'customary'. Thus he could be legitimately regarded as embodying the very convergence of flux and relativism that characterizes the *Theaetetus*' theory. A further, remarkable parallel is that, according to Democritus' theory of vision – as set forth by Theophr. *De sensu* 50 (68 A135 = 117.1 Leszl) – both the seeing subject and the object seen emit an effluence that contracts and moulds the air *between* them, forming an image which enters the subject's eye.[103]

Thus *Cra.* and *Tht.* state two different flux theories which seem to have this in common: while being ascribed to almost all Greek thinkers save Parmenides, in fact both draw inspiration especially from different aspects of Democritus' atomist doctrine. We shall see in due course (§9.1.5) that the two dialogues also share part of their criticism of either theory.

5.3.5 *The Penetrating Principle again (413e–414a, 417bc, 418a–419b)*

I devote this section to the scrutiny of other etymologies which, like those of ἀγαθόν and δίκαιον at 412c–413d, turn on the theory of the Penetrating Principle.

---

[100] Here I cannot offer a detailed discussion of the *Tht.* passage; I hope to be able to do so on another occasion. Let me just point out that it does not seem to me mandatory to take 156d3 αὐτῶν as referring back to δι τὰ ... γεννώμενα, as most scholars seem to assume.

[101] See Burnyeat 1990: 7–65 (esp. 7–19) and Brown 1993: 203–16.

[102] Guthrie's view seems to have been mostly ignored by subsequent scholars. The *Tht.* passages are, however, included in Leszl's (2009) collection, 54.3–5.

[103] Democritus' theory of vision and that of *Tht.* are to be compared with two other doctrines, the relations between these four accounts of vision being far from clear. One might be the theory of Empedocles, who perhaps claimed that vision involves both the emission of light from the eye and an effluence from the object (see 31 B84 with Arist. *De sensu* 437b23–5 + 438a4–5, and Guthrie 1962–81: II.234–7; however see also *Meno* 76c, Thphr. *De sensu* 7, with KRS 310 n.1). The

228   *The etymologies of 'secondary' names (394e–421c)*

We start at 413e–414a with ἀνδρεία, 'courage':

(SO.) ἀνδρεία signifies that courage is named in battle – and a battle in what is, if it flows, is nothing but the contrary flux [τὴν ἐναντίαν ῥοήν]. So, if one removes the δ from the name ἀνδρεία, the name ἀνρεία itself expresses this fact. Clearly, then, ἀνδρεία is the flow contrary, not to any flow, but to the one flowing against the just [παρὰ τὸ δίκαιον]. Otherwise courage would not be praised. (413e1–414a2)

I won't enter into the details of this quaint etymology, which I don't really understand.[104] What is important for our present purposes is Socrates' mention, at a1, of a flow which goes 'against the just'. Since at 412c–413d Socrates has just derived δίκαιον from διαϊόν, part of what he means here is no doubt παρὰ τὸ διαϊόν, 'against the going-through' – i.e. against the Penetrating Principle. But I take it that Socrates is not just using the term δίκαιον in place of its original form.[105] To see what else he might mean, jump to 417bc and read the etymologies of κέρδος, 'gain', and λυσιτελοῦν, 'profitable':

(SO.) κέρδος indicates what it means [δηλοῖ ὃ βούλεται] to someone who puts into the name a ν instead of the δ: for he names the good in another way [τὸ γὰρ ἀγαθὸν κατ' ἄλλον τρόπον ὀνομάζει].[106] For since it gets mixed with everything by passing through and reaching everything [κεράννυται ἐς πάντα διεξιόν],[107] he imposed the name by denominating this capacity; and inserting a δ instead of the ν he uttered κέρδος.
HE. And what about λυσιτελοῦν?
SO. It seems, Hermogenes – he doesn't seem to me to say λυσιτελοῦν as retailers use this name, if something repays the expense.[108] He seems to call the good [ἐπιφημίσαι τὸ ἀγαθόν] λυσιτελοῦν in the sense that, being the quickest part of being, it does not let the objects stand still, nor does it let movement come to an end of its moving and stop and pause, but it always does away with [λύει] any end [τέλος] of movement which is attempted, and renders

---

other account is offered at *Ti.* 45bd, 67cd: from the eye there flows a sort of fire, akin to the one constituting daylight and coalescing with it to form a single body. This body reaches and touches the object seen – or rather the fiery stream of particles emitted from the object and constituting its colour – and transmits the object's motions to the subject's soul.

[104] In particular, it is obscure to me how the form ἀνρεία makes the relation of ἀνδρεία to ἡ ἐναντία ῥοή plain. According to Méridier 96 n.2, Ἀνρεία 'est espliqué par Socrate comme formé de ἀν(ά): *en sens contraire* (ou peut-être ἄνω: *vers le haut*; cf. plus bas [414a: ἀνήρ 'man' < ἄνω ῥοή, 'upward flow']), et de ῥεῖν (*couler*). But ἀνά does not mean 'contrariwise'; and I fail to understand why the 'good' flow should go upwards and the 'bad' one downwards.

[105] In what follows I am indebted to a crucial suggestion by Sergio Bernini.

[106] The subject of ὀνομάζει (b3) is an understood 'the namegiver'.

[107] Reeve's translation, 'Because the good penetrates everything, it has the power to regulate (*kerannutai*) everything', is multiply mistaken.

[108] That is to say, λυσιτελοῦν does not derive (as it actually does, see LSJ) from λύειν τέλη, literally 'to indemnify for expenses incurred'.

movement unceasing and immortal. For he called λυσιτελοῦν what does away with the end of movement. (417b1–c7)

It turns out that both κέρδος and λυσιτελοῦν were originally *descriptions of the Penetrating Principle*. Among other things, Socrates says of either name that by means of it the namegiver 'names the good in another way' (b2–3) or 'calls the good' (c5–6). Part of what he means thereby is just that either name is a telescoped description of that very thing of which the name ἀγαθόν is a telescoped description, i.e. the Penetrating Principle (cf. 412bc and §5.3.2). But it seems clear that Socrates also means that *the Penetrating Principle is the good*, and that, likewise, at 414a he also meant that *the Penetrating Principle is the just*. I suppose that this, in turn, means that the Penetrating Principle is *the principle of (cosmic) goodness and justice*, or perhaps that it is *what is supremely good and just*.

Let me try to spell out this point more clearly. The terms ἀγαθόν, δίκαιον, κέρδος and λυσιτελοῦν have two features in common. On the one hand, they are all value-terms. On the other hand, etymology reveals that they are all telescoped descriptions of the same physical principle, which causes and governs everything by virtue of its being most fine and quick and penetrating everywhere. We could cast this as a contrast between the *present lexical meaning* of such terms and their *etymological meaning*; and we could ask what relationship there is between the two – how exactly, e.g., διαϊόν 'going through', besides altering to δίκαιον, acquired its present lexical meaning 'just'. Socrates' remark, in our passage, that the namegiver coined κέρδος and λυσιτελοῦν as names for τὸ ἀγαθόν, 'the good', suggests an answer to this question. It suggests that in fact the terms at issue were value-terms from the start, i.e. that *their present lexical meaning was already their original lexical meaning*. Thus ἀγαθόν, besides having the etymological meaning 'admirably quick' (or something like that), also had the lexical meaning 'good' from the very beginning; διαϊόν, besides having the etymological meaning 'going through', had the lexical meaning 'just'; and so on. The reason why these terms immediately acquired such a lexical meaning is, I suppose, that the Penetrating Principle, which governs everything, was regarded by the namegiver as the quintessence of goodness, justice and profitability.[109]

---

[109] Note that ἀγαθόν is special in this respect, because it is the only one among these terms whose etymological meaning already had some *prescriptive* force. So in the case of ἀγαθόν the distance between etymological and lexical meaning is shorter than in the other cases.
  What about ἀνδρεία? Did the namegivers regard the Penetrating Principle as the quintessence of courage too? Well, strictly speaking at 413e–414a Socrates did *not* say that ἀνδρεία or ἀνρεία

A complicated story. But besides being suggested by what Socrates says in the passages we have just read, it is, to say the least, perfectly compatible with what he said in the discussion of δίκαιον (412c–413d), where the term's lexical meaning 'just' seemed to play a role (see §5.3.2).

The whole discussion we have been engaging in so far has prepared us for the analysis of δέον, 'necessary' or 'needful', which Socrates sets forth at 418a–419b. At 418a Hermogenes questions Socrates on the adjective ζημιῶδες, 'hurtful'. Socrates' answer introduces δέον as a similar case:

(SO.) Look, Hermogenes, how true my words are when I say that by adding and subtracting letters people greatly alter the senses of names [τὰς τῶν ὀνομάτων διανοίας], so that, by introducing very small changes, they sometimes make them signify the contrary [τἀναντία ... σημαίνειν]. It is so with δέον: for I thought and was reminded of it just now[110] from what I was about to tell you, i.e. that this fine modern language of ours twisted around δέον and ζημιῶδες to express quite the contrary [καὶ τοὐναντίον περιέτρεψε μηνύειν], obliterating what their sense is [ἀφανίζουσα ὅτι νοεῖ], while the ancient language indicates what either name means [ἡ δὲ παλαιὰ ἀμφότερον δηλοῖ ὃ βούλεται τοὔνομα]. (418a5–b6)

Socrates' point is that the *etymological meaning* of some names alters (or rather: becomes difficult to recognize) as the name's shape changes, until the original meaning disappears (or rather: is no longer recognizable) and is (apparently) replaced by a different and even contrary one. What he has in mind in the case of δέον and ζημιῶδες will become apparent shortly. For the moment he goes on to explain that 'the ancients' made large use of the letters ι and δ, which the moderns tend to replace with the more grandiose ε / η and ζ respectively. Then, at 418b8–e4, he discusses by way of example the etymology of ἡμέρα 'day' (from ἱμείρω 'desire', sc. daylight) and ζυγόν 'yoke' (from *δυαγόν, in turn from δύω 'two' + ἄγω 'carry'). Then he comes back to δέον:

SO. So, in the same way, first of all δέον, in its present shape, signifies the contrary of all the names concerning the good [τοὐναντίον σημαίνει πᾶσι τοῖς περὶ τὸ ἀγαθὸν ὀνόμασιν]. For the δέον, which is a kind of good [ἀγαθοῦ γὰρ ἰδέα οὖσα], seems to be a bond [δεσμός] and hindrance to movement, as though it were akin to the βλαβερόν ['harmful'].
HE. It does exactly seem so, Socrates. (418e5–10)

In ordinary Greek δέον – the present participle of the impersonal δεῖ, which is a form of the verb δέω 'need' – means 'necessary' or 'needful': a

---

was a name for the Penetrating Principle, but only for that which runs counter to what opposes the Penetrating Principle. And in any case I think we should not be too fussy over such details.

[110] Apparently a back-reference to 414d.

positive notion, indeed 'a kind of good', as Socrates says (e7).[111] Now it may be natural to associate this word with another, virtually indistinguishable one, i.e. δέον, contr. δοῦν, which is the present participle of *another* verb δέω meaning 'bind'. But for the flux theory, with its obsession for universal motion, the notion of a bond or shackle is a negative one; as such it plays a role in the etymologies of terms like αἰσχρόν, 'ugly' (from ἀεὶ ἴσχον τὸν ῥοῦν, 'always restraining flux', 416ab), and βλαβερόν, 'harmful' (from βουλόμενον ἅπτειν ῥοῦν, 'wanting to fasten flux', 417de), which Socrates recalls at e8–9. Therefore δέον 'necessary', in its present shape (e5–6), is at variance with the other names of positive values, whose etymology contained a reference to something flowing, going through etc. But the inconsistency is wiped out by etymology:

 so. But not if you use the ancient name, which is much more likely to be correct than the present one: it will agree with the previous names of good things [ὁμολογήσει τοῖς πρόσθεν ἀγαθοῖς], if for the ε you substitute the ι, as it was in old times. For once more διόν ['going through'],[112] not δέον, signifies the good, which is precisely what he praises. Thus he who imposed the names doesn't contradict himself, but δέον, ὠφέλιμον, λυσιτελοῦν, κερδαλέον, ἀγαθόν, συμφέρον and εὔπορον appear to be the same, signifying by different names what orders and goes through, which has been extolled throughout, whereas what restrains and binds is blamed [τὸ αὐτὸ φαίνεται, ἑτέροις ὀνόμασι σημαῖνον τὸ διακοσμοῦν καὶ διϊὸν πανταχοῦ ἐγκεκωμιασμένον, τὸ δὲ ἴσχον καὶ δοῦν ψεγόμενον].[113] And in fact ζημιῶδες, if according to the ancient language you substitute δ for ζ, will appear to you to belong to that

---

[111] For ἰδέα = 'kind, sort' cf. *R.* 544c, *Phdr.* 238a, *Tht.* 187c; Th. 3.81.5; etc.

[112] διόν (a3) is T's reading (διάιον β, δαίον δ), accepted by Stallbaum, Fowler, Méridier, Reeve. Burnet, Minio-Paluello, the OCT and Dalimier instead adopt Heindorf's emendation διϊόν. Only with διόν, however, does Socrates really give effect to his a2–3 suggestion to replace the -ε- in δέον with -ι-. To be sure, διόν is not a correctly formed participle of δίειμι 'go through', whereas διϊόν is. I regard it as an *intermediate* stage between δέον and its alleged etymon διϊόν: cf. e.g. βουλαπτεροῦν, intermediate between the adjective βλαβερόν and the original phrase βουλόμενον ἅπτειν ῥοῦν (417e).

[113] τὸ αὐτὸ ... ψεγόμενον (a7–b2) is thorny. (i) At a7–8 I adopt the standard punctuation, with comma after φαίνεται, instead of the OCT's, with comma after σημαῖνον. The latter punctuation would invite a construal where τὸ αὐτό is the object of σημαῖνον, not the subject of φαίνεται; but that would seem to require σημαῖνον<τα>. (ii) At a8 I accept W's reading διϊόν, printed in the OCT and translated by Ficino and Dalimier; βT read ὄν, corrected by Bekker into ἰόν with the approval of most scholars. (iii) Among those who read ἰόν at a8, Hirschig and Minio-Paluello construe ἰόν πανταχοῦ together, 'going everywhere'; but πανταχοῦ cannot be attached to verbs of motion and must qualify bi ἐγκεκωμιασμένον instead: cf. 417e2–3. (iv) As regards the participles ἐγκεκωμιασμένον and ψεγόμενον (b1–2), my translation agrees with that of Fowler and Reeve. Alternatively we might, like Méridier and Minio-Paluello, take both participles as object complements with σημαῖνον: 'signifying by different names *that* what orders and goes through has been extolled throughout, while what restrains and binds is blamed'. The snag is that the names in question do not *directly* signify anything about 'what restrains and binds'.

which binds the going [ἐπὶ τῷ δοῦντι τὸ ἰόν] and to have been given as δημιῶδες. (418e11–419b4)

Here Socrates' main point is clear, although several details are difficult. The correct etymology of δέον 'necessary' has nothing to do with δέω 'bind': δέον rather derives from διϊόν 'going through'.[114] This of course is yet another description of the Penetrating Principle; as Socrates says, it *signifies the good* (a3–4 σημαίνει … τἀγαθόν).[115] Thereby he makes the same sort of point as at 417b2–3 and c5–6 about κέρδος and λυσιτελοῦν (which he recalls a couple of lines below, at a6). And the good, Socrates says, is what the namegiver 'praises' (a4). That is to say, the hypothesis that διϊόν, the etymon of δέον, is a description of the Penetrating Principle and hence of 'the good' harmonizes with the fact that the *lexical meaning* of δέον (not just the *present* lexical meaning, on my interpretation) is a positive one. The 'necessary' or 'needful' is *'a kind of good'*, Socrates said at e7. Thus δέον agrees with 'the previous names of good things' (a1–2: cf. e6–7 'all the names concerning the good').[116] All these names, of which Socrates here gives an incomplete list, agree (indeed, 'appear to be the same', a7–8) insofar as they all refer to the Penetrating Principle, which orders and goes through everything, and convey praise about it by having a positive lexical meaning, whereas those names which derive from descriptions of something which opposes the universal flux have a negative lexical meaning (a8–b1).

In this section we have raised – in connection with names whose etymon contains a reference to the Penetrating Principle – the question of the relation between etymological and lexical meaning. Among other things, we have also read Socrates' considerations, in the course of his analysis of δέον, about how a name's etymological meaning may be perverted in time, until it even comes to conflict (or rather to seem to conflict) with the name's lexical meaning. Thus it seems not inappropriate to insert here a brief survey of some of the various ways in which Socrates in the etymologies refers to the (etymological) meaning or sense of names.

---

[114] As Dalimier 257 n.321 remarks, in some Greek dialects there are cases of -ιο- where Attic has -εο-: e.g. ριοντος for ῥέοντος, ιοντος for ἐόντος (Lejeune 1972: 239). 'Il n'est donc pas exclu qu'on ait vraiment eu une forme dialectale *dion = déon* que Socrate croyait antérieure à la forme attique.' This is not impossible, especially in view of the reading διὸν at 419a3 (cf. n.112). Socrates, however, is usually explicit in his appeals to dialectal evidence.

[115] 'The good' (a4), not 'a good' (Reeve).

[116] τοῖς πρόσθεν ἀγαθοῖς (a2): literally 'with the previous good [names]': cf. Reeve. Fowler translates 'with the previous words for "good"', which is mistaken, because the previous words did not *mean* 'good'.

Before doing that, however, let me briefly draw one further moral of our discussion of flux in the etymologies.

5.3.6 Flux and relativity?

Several scholars (inspired, in the last analysis, by Irwin 1977) think that flux in Plato is more often a matter of the same thing simultaneously having opposite features in different respects or comparisons – that is to say, a matter of relativity – than a matter of genuine change through time. This view has been applied to the flux theory of our dialogue too. Thus Sedley 2003: 112 avers that 'What the value etymologies profess to expose' is how *relativist* assumptions are endemic in Greek culture.

Although I have strong reservations about this view, here I will not discuss it in its full generality.[117] At least as far as *Cra.* is concerned, however, our findings so far show that it cannot be right. The flux theory conveyed by the etymologies is a robustly physical theory according to which everything is engaged in *spatial* change, i.e. locomotion, and reality consists of two material principles, one quick and active, the other slow and passive, of which the former pervades the latter. This theory has nothing to do with relativity.

5.4 MEANING IN THE ETYMOLOGIES

In §§4.2.2 and 4.2.6 we met several expressions which are used by Socrates to refer to the (etymological) meaning or sense of names and to its expression: the verbs δηλόω, 'indicate', and σημαίνω, 'signify' (in some contexts, though not in others); the noun δύναμις, 'power', and its cognate verb δύναμαι. However, there I anticipated that other expressions are used in *Cra.* to the same effect. Here I review the relevant evidence (which is partly set out by Rijlaarsdam 1978: 146).

I have identified three other groups of expressions apparently referring to the (etymological) meaning or sense of a name, each belonging to a different semantic sphere: roughly, (A) will, (B) communication and (C) thought.

(A) The first group consists of the verb βούλομαι, occurring in phrases like ὅτι βούλεται τὸ ὄνομα, and the noun βούλησις. The normal meaning of these expressions would be respectively 'want', 'what the name wants', and

---

[117] For such a discussion see Ademollo (in preparation-3).

'will'; but in fact they are equivalent to 'mean', 'meaning' etc., and so they are often translated in *Cra.* (cf. LSJ βούλομαι, III.; a theoretically nice, if hardly feasible, set of translations would be 'intend', 'what the name intends', and 'intention').[118] The shift from 'want' to 'mean' may be due to an ellipse, fuller expressions being sometimes attested: 412c τοῦτο … βούλεται τὸ ὄνομα ἐπικεῖσθαι ('this name wants *to belong*'); 414b 'τέχνην' ἰδεῖν ὅτι ποτὲ βούλεται εἶναι (literally 'seeing the name τέχνη, what in the world it wants *to be*'; cf. 414a, 426c, d, 436b); *Tht.* 156c τί … βούλεται οὗτος ὁ μῦθος … ; … βούλεται … λέγειν ὡς … (literally 'What … does this story want …? It wants *to say* that …').[119]

Here is a selection of occurrences of the items in this group:

(so.) The name's form [ἡ … τοῦ ὀνόματος ἐπωνυμία][120] is slightly altered and has been shrouded, so that it does not indicate the hero's nature to everyone [ὥστε μὴ πᾶσι δηλοῦν τὴν φύσιν τοῦ ἀνδρός]; but to connoisseurs about names it adequately *indicates what the name* 'Atreus' *means* [ἱκανῶς δηλοῖ ὃ βούλεται ὁ 'Ἀτρεύς']. (395b5–8; cf. 417b, 418b)

(so.) The name γῆ *signifies what it means* more effectively [μᾶλλον σημαίνει ὃ βούλεται], if one uses the name γαῖα. (410b7–c1)

(so.) Throwing many letters into the first names, at last they bring it about that no one among humans could *understand what in the world the name means* [συνεῖναι ὅτι ποτὲ βούλεται τὸ ὄνομα]: as e.g. they call even the Sphinx σφίγξ istead of φίξ. (414d1–4; cf. 401c, 402c, 418d)

(so.) We must search for *what* the names ἀρετή and κακία *mean* ['ἀρετὴ' … καὶ 'κακία' ὅτι βούλεται τὰ ὀνόματα ζητητέα]. (415a9–b1)

(so.) The addition of ψ conceals the name's *meaning* [ἐπικρύπτει τὴν βούλησιν τοῦ ὀνόματος]. (421b6–7)

These texts give us three pieces of information. The 'meaning' of a name is something the name *indicates* or *signifies*; it depends on the name's *etymology*; and it is something that may or may not be *understood* by the speakers, depending on the etymology's transparency.

A further point emerges from other texts: the same terminology concerning a name's (etymological) 'meaning' may also be applied to the person who imposes the name. Thus at 393e we saw that the legislator wanted (ἐβούλετο) to show the nature of a certain letter by means of a name; and

---

[118] 'Intention' is the historically correct form of the nowadays current 'intension'. See Geach 1962: 157 n.6.
[119] See also Arist. *EN* 1110b30 (cf. 1119b34, 1125b33). Cf. also the Italian 'voler dire' and its Romance equivalents.
[120] Literally 'the name's denomination'; in any case not 'the meaning of his name' (Reeve).

at 423b we read of someone wanting (ἐβούλετο again) to indicate something by his body. To be sure, the application of the verb 'to want' to a human subject is, by itself, trifling. What is perhaps less trifling is the sameness between expressions about persons and expressions about names. This suggests that there is a close connection between the 'meaning' of a name and what the imposer meant by it.[121]

(B) I come to the second group of expressions, the one concerning *communication*. Here the main entry is the verb μηνύω, which may have one of the following meanings: 'reveal, make known' (*Ap.* 24d, *R.* 366b, *Phlb.* 14b; Eur. *Ba.* 1029); 'signify, indicate' (*Phd.* 95c; Th. 2.42.2); 'inform against' someone (*Lg.* 730d; And. 1.20); 'claim' (*Ti.* 55d). At *Sph.* 257b μηνύω is used in relation to a kind of linguistic signification, i.e. the fact that the negations μή and οὐ prefixed to a name μηνύει something different from the name's referent. I have chosen to translate the verb as 'express'. Here is a selection of occurrences:

(s o.)   As for the name Φερρέφαττα, many fear both this name and the name Ἀπόλλων ... but it *expresses* that the goddess is wise [μηνύει σοφὴν εἶναι τὴν θεόν] ... the same holds of Apollo, as I am saying: many have been scared about the god's name, as though it *expressed* something terrible [ὥς τι δεινὸν μηνύοντος]. (404c5–e2; cf. 418b, 437b)

(s o.)   As for ἐπιστήμη, it *expresses* that the worthy soul follows the objects, which are in movement [μηνύει ὡς φερομένοις τοῖς πράγμασιν ἑπομένης τῆς ψυχῆς τῆς ἀξίας λόγου]. (412a1–2)

(s o.)   ἀνδρεία signifies that courage is named in battle ... So, if one removes the δ from the name ἀνδρεία, the name ἀνρεία itself *expresses* this fact [αὐτὸ μηνύει τὸ ἔργον τὸ ὄνομα ἡ 'ἀνρεία']. (413e1–414a2)

The information we extract from these texts tallies with our findings about the former group. What a name 'expresses' depends on its *etymology*; and if the etymology is misleading, then speakers may believe the name to express something else than it actually does – that is, they may misunderstand what the name expresses. Moreover, as the verb βούλομαι, so μηνύω too can have as a subject the person who imposes the name besides the name itself:

(s o.)   νόησις itself is a longing for the new [τοῦ νέου ... ἕσις] ... he who imposed the name νεόεσις *expresses* [μηνύει] that this is what the soul longs for. (411d8–e2)

Apart from μηνύω, the same group *might* also include some occurrences of λέγω, 'say' (402e, 410b, 412ab, 417de, 421a). In these passages Socrates apparently claims that a certain name λέγει something (its etymological

---

[121] Cf. Geach (1962: 157 n.6): 'the intention of a term, i.e., what we intend by it'.

meaning). But an alternative construal is also possible, according to which the subject of λέγω in these passages is not the name but the namegiver. Cf. 407b, where the namegiver is explicitly mentioned; but he can always be the understood subject of a verb, see 406a ἐπωνόμασεν, 414b μεμίμηται ... συναρμόσας, 417b, etc. Translators mostly adopt the former construal. Some, however, supply 'the poet' as a subject in 410b; and Stallbaum 141, 152 seems to see that at 417de λέγει is suspiciously close to a ψέγει ('blames') whose subject can only be the namegiver. Actually the only passage where the former construal *must* be correct, hence the only certain occurrence in *Cra.* of λέγω for etymological meaning, seems to be this:

(SO.) The word συνιέναι *says* that the soul travels together with the objects [συμπορεύεσθαι ... λέγει τὴν ψυχὴν τοῖς πράγμασι]. (412a7–b1)[122]

(C) The third group of expressions pertains to the semantic sphere of *thought*. It consists of the verb νοέω, occurring in phrases like ὅτι τὸ ὄνομα νοεῖ, and the noun διάνοια.[123] Having already reserved the translations 'mean' and 'meaning' for group (A), here I will translate in terms of 'sense'. Here is a typical occurrence, with parallels:

(SO.) What in the world might the *sense* of the name δαίμονες be? [τί ἄν ποτε νοοῖ τὸ ὄνομα οἱ 'δαίμονες';] (397e2–3; cf. 407e, 416ab, 418b)

Moreover, if you return to 418ab, which we read in §5.3.5, you will see that those lines contain not only another occurrence of the verb νοέω, but also, more interestingly, one of the noun διάνοια. This is when Socrates said that

adding and subtracting letters people greatly alter the *senses* of names [τὰς τῶν ὀνομάτων διανοίας], so that, by introducing very small changes, they sometimes make them signify the contrary [τἀναντία ... σημαίνειν]. (418a6–b1)

The whole of 418a5–b6 is especially interesting, because it contains expressions from *all* three groups which I have distinguished in this section.

---

[122] LSJ λέγω III.9 report occurrences of λέγω 'mean'. The only one allegedly having a linguistic expression as a subject is Ar. *Eq.* 1059 τί τοῦτο λέγει, 'πρὸ Πύλοιο'. In context, however, this may well mean 'what does *the oracle* mean by πρὸ Πύλοιο?' rather than 'what does πρὸ Πύλοιο mean?'

[123] See LSJ νοέω IV, νόος III, διάνοια IV. Arist. *SE* 10 discusses a distinction between arguments πρὸς τοὔνομα ('relative to the name') and arguments πρὸς τὴν διάνοιαν ('relative to the meaning'). The definition of 'not πρὸς τὴν διάνοιαν' is the following: 'when one does not use the name with reference to the thing which the answerer believed to be the object of the question as he granted the premiss', 170b16–17). See Bonitz 1870 on other occurrences of διάνοια 'meaning' in Arist.; and cf. also D. L. 9.52 on Protagoras: τὴν διάνοιαν ἀφεὶς πρὸς τοὔνομα διελέχθη ('neglecting the *meaning* of words, he discussed employing verbal snares').

Taking stock of the evidence for group (C), once again we find that there is something to the signification of a name, i.e. its διάνοια, which depends on the etymology and may be more or less clearly intelligible to ordinary speakers. And once again, Socrates employs the very same terms describing the namegiver's activity. He talks about what the namegiver *thought* in giving certain names (νοεῖν 399d, 401d, 402b; διανοεῖσθαι 407b); he even refers to what imposes names as 'the διάνοια of gods or humans or both' (416c).

5.5 PLATO'S ATTITUDE TO THE ETYMOLOGIES

Read without prejudices of any sort, the etymologies *qua* etymologies may well strike you as delirious. Socrates goes on for a disproportionate amount of pages to offer utterly implausible analyses, reaching bewildering results by reckless methodological anarchy. To the many examples we have already met I will only add the worst of the lot: the terrible, 'dithyrambic' etymology of σελήνη ('moon'), or rather the Doric variant σελαναία (409ac), which Socrates derives from *Σελαεννεοάεια because σέλας νέον τε καὶ ἕνον ἔχει ἀεί ('it always has a light both new and old').[124]

Thus many interpreters have not only found the etymologies ridiculous, but also believed that they are *meant* to be so. But is this true? And if so, in what sense? That is the subject of this section.

5.5.1 Seriousness in the etymologies (414c–415a, 439bc)

Those scholars who have considered the etymologies as purposely ridiculous have been naturally led to the view that they constitute a parody of someone or something and are set forth 'ludibrii tantum et irrisionis gratia', as Stallbaum 4 put it. The most interesting version of the parodical interpretation[125] is due to Baxter 1992: 86–8, 94–9, 162–3; let him tell us whom Plato should be parodying and why. 'Plato ... sees a culture-wide fallacy afoot, that of interpreting language ... as if it were transparently "natural", offering easy access to the essences of things' (87). 'Etymology is an unreliable tool in seeking knowledge about things. This is the major positive result from the etymological inquiry, and it is here that one

---

[124] The phrase σέλας νέον τε καὶ ἕνον ἔχει ἀεί (409b12) hints at ἕνη καὶ νέα, the Athenian name – reportedly coined by Solon – for the last day of the month (Polansky *ap*. Sedley 2003: 107 n.18): see Ar. *Nub*. 1134, Lys. 23.6, Plu. *Sol*. 25.4, D. L. 1.58.
[125] I leave aside the unfortunate attempts to identify an individual historical target of the parody, like Antisthenes or Heraclides Ponticus.

should seek the unifying feature of the etymologies ... So many theories and thinkers are represented because the use of etymology to "prove" a point was an unthought assumption of poets and philosophers from Homer to the Sophists. This assumption amounts to a version of Cratylus' error' (96). Moreover, 'Not only had many people made the error of overvaluing names, but to refute them properly (or indeed to prove the point that Greek was a natural language) a thorough survey of names had to be undertaken ... all kinds of names of all kinds of things must be laid open to scrutiny' (98).

This interpretation is very likely mistaken; for there are various weighty reasons (which have been pointed out mainly by Grote 1888: III.299–312 and Sedley 1998: 141–7, 2003: 25–50) for believing that Socrates regards the etymologies as sound. Let me set them out.

(i) One simple and powerful argument is based on the enormous length of the etymological section. Even if we discount the etymology of the primary names (426c–427d) and the theory these are based upon (421c–426b), still the result is some thirty-eight OCT pages. This seems really too much for *any* reasonable sort of polemic or parody, even one whose target is as broad as Baxter supposes, especially in the case of such an original writer as Plato. It would be much better if we could show that the etymologies are there to fulfil some positive and independent design of their author.

(ii) A second argument is based on 439c, near the end of the dialogue, at the beginning of Socrates' attack on the theory of flux:[126]

> SO. Again, let us investigate this further point, in order that these many names which point in the same direction do not deceive [ἐξαπατᾷ] us, if those that imposed them did impose them believing that all things are always moving and flowing – for *it does seem to me that they too had this belief* [φαίνονται γὰρ ἔμοιγε καὶ αὐτοὶ οὕτω διανοηθῆναι] – whereas this is perhaps not so. (439b10–c4)

Socrates' hypothesis is twofold: on the one hand, the namegivers did really impose many names in the belief that everything is always moving and flowing; on the other hand, their belief was false. This amounts to a recognition that the etymologies were, as Sedley 2003: 28 puts it, 'exegetically correct' (i.e. they correctly reconstructed the namegivers' thought), but not 'philosophically correct'. The passage is not easily explained away

---

[126] For more on this passage, and in particular for a textual note on 439c3 καὶ αὐτοί, 'they *too*', see §9.1.1 and n.1.

as ironical or unserious; hence it constitutes first-hand evidence that both Plato and Socrates endorse a great part of the etymologies.

(iii) Outside *Cra.* Plato sometimes has recourse to etymology in contexts where no one could possibly suspect irony. See *Ti.* 90c εὐδαίμων 'happy' < εὖ κεκοσμημένος δαίμων 'well-ordered daimon'; *Lg.* 654a χορός 'dance' < χαρά 'joy'; 714a νόμος 'law' < νοῦ διανομή 'distribution of intellect'. At *Lg.* 816b two etymologies, respectively of ἐμμέλεια and πυρρίχη (names of two kinds of dance) from ἐμμελῶς 'harmoniously' and πῦρ 'fire', are associated with the claim that many ancient names must be praised as 'having been set down well and according to nature' (εὖ καὶ κατὰ φύσιν κείμενα).

(iv) No ancient interpreter of the dialogue seems to have raised doubts about its etymologies: 'If Plato was joking, the joke flopped' (Sedley 2003: 39). Apart from Proclus' commentary, you can look up D. H. *Comp.* 95–6, who refers to Plato as the first who introduced the discussion of etymology; Alcinous, *Didask.* 159.44–5, who says that Plato expounds the whole topic of etymology; Plu. *De Is. et Os.* 375CD, who – between his own etymologies of the names Ἶσις and Ὄσιρις – approves of the etymologies concerning flux; etc.

(v) It makes no sense to judge the *Cra.* etymologies by the standards of modern scientific etymology, which did not develop before the nineteenth century. On average they are not wilder, or more ridiculous, than those of a great many other ancient writers on the subject, even those whose purposes are certainly serious.[127] Aristotle is one of them: see e.g. *EN* 1132a30–2, 1152b7, and especially *Mete.* 339b16–30, *Cael.* 270b16–25, where Aristotle derives the name αἰθήρ ἀπὸ τοῦ θεῖν ἀεί, 'from its always running' (cf. *Cra.* 410b and §5.1.3), thereby finding the ancients in agreement with his own conception of the first element, and reproaches Anaxagoras for wrongly using the term αἰθήρ to mean fire. As Simpl. *in Cael.* 119.2–4 explains, Aristotle is rejecting not only Anaxagoras' theory of aether, but also, implicitly, his alternative etymology of αἰθήρ from αἴθειν, 'to burn'. Thus Aristotle seems to assume that the right theory was also the ancients' theory, running together a philosophical issue (the nature of aether) and

---

[127] Few ancient authors voiced doubts on etymology. In Cic. *Nat.* 3.62–3 the Academic Cotta scoffs at the Stoic etymologies of divine names (cf. 2.62–9): 'What a dangerous practice; for with many names you'll get stuck ... though since you think Neptune was so called after *nare* ['to swim'], there will be no name whose derivation you could not explain by fastening on just one letter.' His criticism is taken over by Augustine, *De dialectica* vi. See esp. 9: 'in my opinion this is more a matter of curiosity than necessity ... Even though it were a great help to explicate the origin of a word, it would be useless to start on a task whose prosecution would go on indefinitely. For who could be able to discover why anything has been called what it has been called? Add that the judgement on the origin of words, like that on the interpretation of dreams, depends on each man's ingenuity' (tr. after Jackson/Pinborg 1975). See also Quint. *Inst.* 1.6.32–8.

an exegetical one (the etymology of αἰθήρ): a move much in the spirit of *Cra*. Also telling is his comment on the etymology of αἰών 'eternity' from αἰεὶ ὄν 'always being' at *Cael*. 279a22–8: 'this name has been uttered by the ancients *in a state of divine inspiration* [θείως]'.

(vi) On the face of it Socrates is actually confident that his analyses are sound: he does recognize the danger of unruly etymology, but denies that he is falling victim of it. To see this we must read 414c–415a. The context of that passage is the following: Socrates has just offered a strained analysis of τέχνη ('art') as ἐχονόη = ἕξις νοῦ ('possession of mind'), as Hermogenes remarks.[128] Socrates replies with a complaint:

SO. My dear, you don't know that the names which were imposed first [τὰ πρῶτα ὀνόματα τεθέντα] have been buried by those who wanted to make them high-sounding, attaching and subtracting letters for the sake of euphony and effecting a complete distortion, generated both by embellishments and by the action of time [καὶ ὑπὸ καλλωπισμοῦ καὶ ὑπὸ χρόνου]. For doesn't it seem absurd to you that ρ has been thrown into κάτροπτον?[129] Such things are the work of those who do not care about truth but are only interested in taking affected positions with their mouths. Thus in the end, by dint of putting letters into the original names, they bring it about that nobody could recognize what in the world the name means. One example is that they call the Sphynx σφίγξ instead of φίξ,[130] and there are many others.

HE. These things are so, Socrates. (414c4–d6)

Socrates continues:

SO. On the other hand, if one will allow the insertion and subtraction of any letter one may wish [εἰ δ' αὖ τις ἐάσει καὶ ἐντιθέναι καὶ ἐξαιρεῖν ἅττ' ἂν βούληταί τις εἰς τὰ ὀνόματα], there will be great leeway [εὐπορία] and anyone could make any name fit any object whatsoever.

HE. What you say is true.

SO. True indeed. But, I think, it's up to you, my wise overseer, to preserve moderation and plausibility [τὸ μέτριον ... δεῖ φυλάττειν καὶ τὸ εἰκὸς σὲ τὸν σοφὸν ἐπιστάτην].

HE. I should want to do so.

SO. And I want it together with you. But don't be too exact [μὴ λίαν ... ἀκριβολογοῦ], my dear, 'lest thou deprive me of my might'.[131] (414d7–415a2)

We might think that at d7–9, as in the previous lines, Socrates is still speaking of how names are altered in time. But the way he proceeds, at

---

[128] On Socrates' analysis of τέχνη and Hermogenes' reply (414bc) see §8.1.5.
[129] At 414c8 all MSS and editions have κατόπτρῳ, the dative of κάτοπτρον 'mirror'. On the Attic orthography κατρόπτῳ see LSJ, Dalimier 253 n.292 and West 2002.
[130] Cf. Hes. *Th*. 326 and see West 1966: 256–7.
[131] Socrates is quoting *Il*. 6.265.

e2–a2 ('But, I think, it's up to you …'), to refer to his own etymological performance suggests[132] that already at d7–9 he was actually speaking of the etymological recovery of the names' original form, which is the *reverse* of the hitherto described process of alteration, and that αὖ (d7) had the function to mark the transition from talk of arbitrary *alteration* to talk of arbitrary *reconstruction*.

Thus Socrates is claiming awareness of the pitfalls of etymology, which may lead to methodological anarchy; but he does not seem to be much worried as far as he himself is concerned. What moral should we draw from this? Taken by itself, the passage might be construed as ironical and designed precisely to make us realize that moderation and plausibility are standards the etymologies fail to live up to. But if we consider it in the light of the previous arguments, then it is much more plausible to suppose that Socrates is speaking with a straight face and is committing himself to the plausibility of the whole etymological edifice (Sedley 2003: 43).

If these arguments are sound, as I believe they are, then the etymologies are unlikely to be an enormous send-up or anything else of that sort. They are not primarily directed against anyone; and Socrates and Plato regard at least most of them as plausible reconstructions of the original form of the words analysed.

5.5.2 *The inspiration of Euthyphro (396c–397a)*

And yet there is more than this to the etymologies. Let me focus on Socrates' repeated claim that he is in a state of inspiration, due to a conversation with Euthyphro. At 396cd, after etymologizing Uranus' name and thus completing the genealogy of the Atreidae, Socrates claims that, if he could remember the names of the earlier ancestors of the gods in Hesiod's *Theogony*, he wouldn't stop explaining how correctly their names have been set down,

(so.) until I had tested this wisdom which now has suddenly come upon me I don't know whence, to see what it will do, whether it will fail or not.
he. Indeed, Socrates, you really seem to me to utter prophecies suddenly like those who are possessed by a god [ὥσπερ οἱ ἐνθουσιῶντες ἐξαίφνης χρησμῳδεῖν]. (396c6–d3)

Socrates, however, does have an idea of his wisdom's origin: it must have been a long conversation with Euthyphro, early this morning.

---

[132] See Horn 1904: 37, Rijlaarsdam 1978: 143.

so. And I do allege, Hermogenes, that it has mainly come upon me from Euthyphro the Prospaltian. For this morning at dawn I spent much time with him and gave ear to him. So, possessed as he was [ἐνθουσιῶν], he is likely, not only to have filled my ears with his divine wisdom, but also to have got hold of my soul. (396d4–8)

The inspiration theme returns time and again in the etymologies, sometimes along with references to Euthyphro:

(so.) I've got some swarm of wisdom in my mind. (401e5)

(so.) 'So that you may see what Euthyphro's horses are like'.[133] (407d8–9).

(so.) Probably, either Euthyphro's Muse has abandoned me, or this is something most difficult. (409d1–3)

(so.) Don't be too exact, my dear, 'lest thou deprive me of my might'.[134] (415a1–2)

(so.) As long as my vigour is present, let us not release it. (420e3–4)

(Add 428c, on which see below.)

In some of these passages Socrates compares his performance to a chariot-race – an image which is connected with Parmenides' and Pindar's representation of themselves as driven by a chariot (Parm. 28 B1 DK; Pi. O. 9.81, P. 10.65, I. 2.2, 8.61; see Barney 1998: 77, 92). The chariot image is the link allowing us to bring under the heading of the inspiration motif passages which do not refer directly to inspiration:

(so.) You don't watch over me as I am, so to speak, driven off the course when I reach smooth ground.[135] (414b2–4)

so. I am running towards the end. (420d3)

Now it is very reasonable to identify the Euthyphro who is responsible for Socrates' inspiration with the eponymous character of the *Euthyphro*.[136] This is a rather dull-minded soothsayer, ridiculously sure he has exceptional knowledge about things divine. This 'knowledge' involves acritical acceptance of the myths about the gods' fights against each other (*Euthphr.* 4e–5a, 5e–6c). In particular he refers to Zeus's fettering Cronus and Cronus' castrating Uranus; and in *Cra.*, significantly, his name comes

---

[133] Socrates is quoting *Il.* 5.221–2 etc.
[134] Cf. n.131.
[135] The metaphorical use of this expression is attested elsewhere too (Aesch. *Pr.* 883, and perhaps also *Ag.* 1245, *Ch.* 514). Here, however, it is pregnant.
[136] It is, by contrast, unreasonable (*pace* several scholars) to identify the conversation between Socrates and Euthyphro which Socrates refers to here with the one that takes place in the *Euthyphro*, which has nothing to do with etymology. Cf. Owen *ap.* Baxter 1992: 28 n.73 and Sedley 2003: 3 n.5.

out just after the mention of these gods.[137] He is usually laughed at when he foretells the future in the assembly (3bc) and is treated ironically by Socrates too (5c, 15d–16a).

These things being so, it seems very reasonable to think that in *Cra.* the claim that Socrates has been inspired by Euthyphro is not seriously meant. That is to say, Socrates does not really believe that the claim is true. Indeed, at 428c Cratylus himself will politely cast doubts on it:

(CR.) You appear to prophesy much according to my mind, whether you were inspired by Euthyphro or some other Muse had long been dwelling in you without your knowing about it. (428c6–8)

The phrase 'some other Muse' (c8) alludes to the originality of Socrates' performance.

But if the claim that Socrates has been inspired by Euthyphro is not meant as a literally true one, then what is its purpose? Various different answers are available. Anyone can agree with Sedley (2003: 41) that 'the motif of Socrates acting under inspiration is a device by which Plato acknowledges that etymology was not the kind of enterprise that his teacher Socrates actually went in for'. But Sedley (2003: 40–1) also supposes that the inspiration claim is meant to convey 'the typical self-deflation involved in pretending that his [sc. Socrates'] superior etymological skill is inspired by, and therefore derivative from, what is in reality the inferior skill of Euthyphro'. This latter hypothesis is much more debatable than the former. For we could instead suppose, as many have done, that the claim's purpose is to relieve Socrates of the full paternity of what he says, create some distance between him and his own performance, and thus arouse some sort of suspicion about the etymologies.

The text so far is too indeterminate to allow us to opt between these alternative possibilities. We must read on and see whether the sequel will shed some retrospective light on the present lines. Socrates has a strange proposal to make:

(SO.) So it seems to me that we must do so: for the present day make use of this wisdom and pursue what is left of the inquiry into names; but tomorrow, if you agree, we shall conjure it away and purify ourselves [ἀποδιοπομπησόμεθά τε αὐτὴν καὶ καθαρούμεθα], after finding the person who is skilful at this sort of purifications, either one of the priests or one of the sophists. (396d8–397a2)

Here the promise of a purification is the crucial point; and the key to its interpretation is provided by the phrase ἀποδιοπομπησόμεθα …

---

[137] See Burnet 1924: 5, Baxter 1992: 108.

αὐτήν (e3–4). The verb (ἀπο)διοπομπέομαι, and the cognate noun (ἀπο)διοπόμπησις, always refer to conjuring away or expelling something *bad*, either in genuine religious contexts or metaphorically. This is so since the earliest occurrences: Pl. *Lg.* 854b, 877e, 900b; [Lys.] 6.53. For example, at *Lg.* 854b we are told that the person caught by a perverse desire for temple-robbery, due to the influence of some ancestral and non-purified sin, should reject such a thought and go 'to the ἀποδιοπομπήσεις' as well as 'to sacred rites of evil-averting gods'. Our terms are given explanations of this sort in several lexica of the imperial age: see Aelius Dionysius α *158; Phrynichus, *Praeparatio sophistica* 9.12–17 de Borries; Timaeus, *Lexicon Platonicum* 58 Bonelli; and cf. Pollux, *Onomasticon* 1.33.5. Their definitions are inherited by the scholia *ad loc.* (23 Cufalo). Here is Phrynichus (already quoted by Stallbaum):

ἀποδιοπομπεῖσθαι καὶ διοπομπεῖσθαι. This means 'to dismiss and clear away causes of pollution [ἀποπέμπεσθαι καὶ ἀποκαθαίρεσθαι μύση]'. The name is composed of δῖον, which is the skin of the victim sacrificed to Zeus, standing on which they purified themselves ... and from πέμπεσθαι.

And here is Timaeus:

Ἀποδιοπομπεῖσθαι. To dismiss and push away the guilts [ἀποπέμπεσθαι καὶ διωθεῖσθαι τὰ ἁμαρτήματα] availing oneself of Zeus's assistance [συμπράκτορι χρώμενος τῷ Διΐ].[138]

Thus Socrates' project of a purification seems to amount to some sort of warning against the etymologies. But this ties in with the latter of the two alternative ways of interpreting the 396d inspiration claim which I distinguished above. That interpretation is now confirmed: throughout 396d–397a Socrates is consistently telling us to be on our guard, because the etymologies will contain something misleading, if not mistaken.

In this connection it may be helpful to add a few words about the identity of the purifier-to-be, εἴτε τῶν ἱερέων τις εἴτε τῶν σοφιστῶν (397a1–2). Here some translate σοφιστής as 'wise man', as at 403e; the σοφιστής, so interpreted, might even be related to the σοφία, 'wisdom', which has suddenly come upon Socrates (396c7). Nevertheless, as I read the text I find it quite difficult to keep clear of the meaning 'sophist' (Fowler, Méridier).

---

[138] Timaeus is suggesting that the διο- component in (ἀπο)διοπομπέομαι derives from Zeus's name; we have just seen that Phrynichus gives a different explanation. The meaning stated as the original one of the whole verb by LSJ ('escort out of the city the δῖον κώδιον' – the κώδιον being a sacred ram's fleece) seems to have been somehow reconstructed on the basis of Phrynichus and Eustathius, *in Od.* 1935.9–13; but I have not found it directly attested anywhere. See the apparatus *ad sch.* 23 in Cufalo's (2007) edition for more on ἀποδιοπομπέομαι.

Now, if we allow σοφιστής here to be at least ambiguous, and the meaning 'sophist' to play at least some role (as I think we should), then the reference to the sophist would conclude the promise of a purification revealing some irony or playfulness in Socrates' words, as a sort of *fulmen in clausula*. Why a sophist? Perhaps it is just another dig at the category, which was last teased in 391bc; or perhaps it is a hint that there will be something sophistical in the etymological performance, or that the etymologies would be liable to be refuted by a sophist.[139] In any case, the reference to a sophist seems to harmonize with our findings about the purport of the purification project.

But *what*, exactly, is the problem with the etymologies? What, exactly, is Socrates warning us against? Someone might suppose that the problem is the theoretical background of the etymologies, i.e. the naturalist thesis which they aim to illustrate. This thesis will become a target of Socrates' criticism later on; and it will be explicitly suggested that this implies a sort of palinode on Socrates' part. After the etymologies have come to an end, and at the very beginning of the discussion with Cratylus, who has just said he agrees with Socrates' inspiration whatever its source (428bc, quoted above), Socrates says:

(SO.) I myself have long been marvelling at my own wisdom, and I distrust it [θαυμάζω καὶ αὐτὸς πάλαι τὴν ἐμαυτοῦ σοφίαν καὶ ἀπιστῶ]. So it seems to me that we must re-examine what I am saying. For being deceived [ἐξαπατᾶσθαι] by oneself is the most terrible thing of all: when the deceiver is not absent even for a little while, but is always there, how could that not be fearful? Hence one must, as it seems, frequently turn around to what has been said before, and try, as that famous poet has it, to look 'forward and backward at the same time'.[140] (428d1–8)

'This suggests', Reeve writes (xxxv), 'that it is dialectical examination that will provide the needed exorcism, an exorcism that is indeed begun … in the discussion with Cratylus.' For the subsequent discussion will precisely show, among other things, how deceitful (cf. the occurrences of the verb ἐξαπατάω at 436b and 439c) it is to trust etymology as a guide to the knowledge of things.

Reeve's suggestion, however, is unconvincing. To start with, the naturalist thesis was *not* defended under Euthyphro's alleged inspiration. Moreover, Socrates at 396e has promised a purification for the *following*

---

[139] I would not make much of the fact that at *Sph.* 230a–231b sophistry is defined as the art of purifying people by refuting them and freeing them from wrong opinions. The connection between purification and the sophist in *Cra.* may well be entirely *ad hoc*.

[140] See §7.1.1 for a couple of notes on this passage.

day, while the refutation of Cratylus will take place immediately; indeed, the etymologies themselves already anticipate, to some extent, the later rebuttal of the naturalist thesis (see §5.2.2). Therefore it seems better – and it is in any case much more natural – to take Socrates' references to inspiration as concerning the etymological performance *as such*. At the end of the dialogue the purification is, at best, still incomplete; we have, so to speak, to act as Socrates' purifiers, finding out what is wrong with the etymologies and assessing their real worth.

Thereby we are still left with our question: what, exactly, is wrong with the etymologies? The arguments we reviewed in §5.5.1 show that they are unlikely to be a parody, a joke, a prank, a send-up, or whatever. I shall try to find out in §5.5.4 what they might be instead.

In the meantime, Socrates' inspiration claim, as I have been construing it so far, can be helpfully compared with his first speech in the *Phaedrus*. That speech is allegedly pronounced under an inspiration due to Sappho and Anacreon (235cd) or rather to the Nymphs and other local deities (238cd, 241e, 262d, 263d). But it soon turns out to be 'silly and somewhat impious', such as to require a purification and a retraction (242b–243e). Only after the conclusion of the second, reparative speech will Socrates manage to find some role for the first one too, then presenting it as justly directed against the wrong sort of love (265a–266b) – something that had not been really suggested before. Thus, as Barney 1998: 72–3 holds, the *Phaedrus* supplies an example of inspiration used as a device to distance Socrates from his speech, which is going to prove either wrong or, at least, requiring robust qualifications to become acceptable.

5.5.3 Humour and detachment in the etymologies (398de, 399a, 406bc)

Our first step towards an accomplished purification of Socrates consists in leaving Euthyphro behind us and turning to a few clues that not everything is serious in the etymologies. In what follows I list some piecemeal evidence to this effect, leaving completely aside as irrelevant (in accordance with what I said in §5.5.1) any individual word-analysis that just sounds ridiculous or far-fetched to our own ears. Please remember that, for the moment, no general moral should be drawn from my comments on each point.

(A) We begin with a genuinely funny invention: the second etymology of ἥρως ('hero'). After deriving ἥρως from ἔρως ('love') at 398cd, Socrates says with reference to the lawgiver that:

(SO.) Either this is what he says about the heroes, or that they were wise and skilful orators and dialecticians, competent to question and speak [ἐρωτᾶν ἱκανοὶ ὄντες <καὶ εἴρειν>]:[141] for εἴρειν is λέγειν. Thus if you call them, as we were saying just now, in the Attic language,[142] the heroes turn out as a sort of orators and questioners [ῥήτορές τινες καὶ ἐρωτητικοί], so that the heroic race becomes a kin of orators and sophists. (398d5–e3)

'Aliam profert nominis etymologiam eamque admodum festivam et iocularem', comments Stallbaum 86. In fact, the idea that the Homeric heroes turn out to be orators and sophists versed in question-and-answer dialectic is almost irresistible. As Goldschmidt (1940: 113–14) suggests, it has a parallel at *Phdr.* 261bd, where Socrates mentions certain rhetorical writings of Nestor, Odysseus and Palamedes (heroes famous for eloquence and ingenuity), 'which they composed at Troy when they had time'. Phaedrus conjectures that Socrates is representing Gorgias as Nestor, and Thrasymachus or Theodorus as Odysseus; then it becomes clear that Palamedes is meant to be the Eleatic Zeno. The irony of this passage from the *Phaedrus* is complex and subtle. There is the 'humorous trait of archaic heroes, spending their leisure from warfare composing rhetorical treatises'.[143] But there is also a jibe at the fictitious pieces of rhetoric whose speaking characters are precisely those heroes: Gorgias' *Apology of Palamedes* (82 BIIa DK), Hippias' *Troikos* (apparently a dialogue between Nestor and Neoptolemus: Philostr. *VS* I.11.4 = 86 A2, *Hp. Ma.* 286ab = A9), or the speeches of Ajax and Odysseus for Achilles' weapons, made up by Antisthenes (V A 53–4 *SSR*).[144] We may wonder whether Socrates also has in mind certain Euripidean tragedies whose heroic characters betray, in their speeches, the influence of sophistry.[145]

Our etymology in *Cra.* is likely to contain the same sort of humour as the *Phaedrus* exchange. On the one hand, there is irony towards the appropriation of Homeric characters and contexts for rhetorical purposes; in particular, the reference to the heroes' being skilled questioners might hint at Hippias' *Troikos*, which began with Neoptolemus asking Nestor a

[141] H. Schmidt added καὶ εἴρειν after d7 ἐρωτᾶν (accepted by Méridier only); after ὄντες it looks slightly more suitable for the purpose of explaining the omission. Stallbaum 87 inserted καὶ λέγειν in this position; cf. Ficino 'ad interrogandum disserendumque promptissimi'.
[142] In the ancient Attic orthography, prior to the introduction of the Ionic alphabet featuring H and Ω as signs for long open *e* and *o* (403/402, see Threatte I.26–51) and to the adoption of EI and OY as signs for long close *e* and *o* (end of fifth century BC – mid fourth century BC, see Threatte I.172–90, 238–58), the words ἥρως, ἐρωτᾶν and εἴρειν were written ΗΕΡΟΣ, ΕΡΟΤΑΝ and ΕΠΕΝ. Socrates' talk of 'language' (φωνή) loosely refers to this fact, as at d2–3 immediately above, which he here recalls at d8. Cf. 410c with Leroy's (1967) comments and Ademollo (in preparation-I).
[143] de Vries 1969: 204.
[144] Antisthenes also seems to have written a *Defence of Orestes* (D. L. 6.15).
[145] Socrates might perhaps rely on a tendentious interpretation of *Il.* 9.442–3, where Phoinix recalls that Peleus entrusted him with teaching young Achilles μύθων τε ῥητῆρ' ἔμεναι πρηκτῆρά τε ἔργων.

question and perhaps went on as a dialogue. On the other hand, there is also, most simply, the intrinsically comic picture of the epic heroes practising dialectic and questioning each other under the walls of Troy.

(B) Sometimes Socrates seems to describe what he is doing by means of self-ironical expressions. See the preliminaries of the etymology of ἄνθρωπος, 'human':

SO. You trust Euthyphro's inspiration, as it seems.
HE. Evidently.
SO. And rightly so: for even now I seem to have had a clever idea [κομψῶς ἐννενοηκέναι], and, if I am not careful, I shall risk becoming wiser than I should [σοφώτερος τοῦ δέοντος] before the day is over. (399a1–5)

Plato's use of the adjective κομψός, 'clever', and cognate words is very often ironical (429d, *Hp. Ma.* 288d, etc.), though there are exceptions to this (e.g. *R.* 525d). Here how can we tell the tone of the occurrence of the adverb κομψῶς (a4)? The ironical construal is supported by an element which was already emphasized by Stallbaum 89: Socrates' reference to the danger of becoming *wiser than he should* before the day is over – hence before the purification planned for tomorrow. 'Becoming wiser than he should' probably amounts to transgressing some boundary he should not transgress. This again sheds a somewhat unfavourable light on the performance.

(C) In one passage Socrates perhaps *acknowledges* that a playful dimension has some role in a specific etymology. Consider the etymologies of Dionysus and Aphrodite's names at 406b7–d2. 'What about Διόνυσος and Ἀφροδίτη?', Hermogenes asks. 'You're asking a big question, son of Hipponicus,' are the first words of Socrates' answer. Here is how it goes on in the Greek:

ἀλλὰ ἔστι γὰρ καὶ σπουδαίως εἰρημένος ὁ τρόπος τῶν ὀνομάτων τούτοις τοῖς θεοῖς καὶ παιδικῶς. (406b8–c1)

What does this mean? Two notes of interpretation are in order. First, ὁ τρόπος τῶν ὀνομάτων (literally 'the manner of the names'). It is a fair guess that this is closely related to, or identical with, the name's *etymon*: cf. 409d ἔχοις ἂν εἰπεῖν πῦρ κατὰ τίνα τρόπον καλεῖται; (literally 'could you say *in what manner* is fire called?'), where the *etymology* of πῦρ is being asked for. Secondly, ἔστι … εἰρημένος. I take this to express the etymon's being *explained* or spelt out. The expression is unlikely to be a periphrastic perfect (= εἴρηται); I would rather construe it as consisting of existential ἔστι + predicative εἰρημένος: 'there is the etymology as explained' = 'there is an explanation of the etymology' (cf. KG 1.39–40). So I offer the following translation of the whole clause:

But that doesn't matter, because[146] the etymology of the names for these gods can be explained both seriously and playfully,

which agrees with Fowler's ('There is both a serious and a facetious account of the form of the name of these deities'; cf. Minio-Paluello and Reeve). And if this construal is correct, then Socrates is confessing to a playful attitude towards this etymology, and the passage constitutes evidence for the general thesis that here and there in the section Socrates appears, in some sense, to be joking.[147]

Let us read a bit further into the text:

(SO.) So for the serious one you have to ask someone else, but nothing prevents us from setting forth the playful one, because the gods too love play [φιλοπαίσμονες γὰρ καὶ οἱ θεοί]. Dionysus might be the giver of wine [ὁ διδοὺς τὸν οἶνον], playfully [ἐν παιδιᾷ] called Διδοίνυσος. (406c1–4)

Socrates again insists on the concept of play. At c3 καί ('too') suggests that *someone else* besides the gods loves play: this might be humans in general – or Socrates himself.

(D) The last piece of evidence does not belong to *Cra.*, but to another dialogue. Hence all it shows is that Plato *can* have a playful approach to etymology, not that he *does* have such an approach in *Cra.*

The other dialogue is the *Phaedrus*, at the point where Socrates, describing the different kinds of madness, dwells on the prophetical one. At 244bc he derives μαντική ('divination') from μανική ('madness'), which is identified as the name given by the ancient namegivers (τῶν παλαιῶν οἱ τὰ ὀνόματα τιθέμενοι). Everything here appears to be very much in the spirit of *Cra.*; so it is interesting to remark that Socrates attributes the insertion of τ to coarse-tasted contemporaries, apparently without remembering that the word μάντις occurs already in Homer.

In the passage's sequel (244cd) Socrates contrasts prophetic madness with the 'artful' sort of divination based on the interpretation of signs like the flight of birds. On this art practised by sane men the ancients bestowed the name οἰονοϊστική, since they rationally provided understanding and information (νοῦν τε καὶ ἱστορίαν) for human opinion (ἀνθρωπίνῃ

---

[146] On ἀλλά ... γάρ see *GP* 100–3.
[147] Caution is in place, however, because there is an alternative, albeit less natural, construal: 'the etymology of the names for these gods has been *imparted* both seriously and playfully' (cf. Ficino, Méridier, Dalimier). On this construal, Socrates is not contrasting two *accounts* of the etymology of these names, but two *etymologies*, the serious and the playful, both original and dating back to the namegivers (for multiple original etymologies cf. 395bc, 404e–406a, b). Clearly, if this were the meaning of the sentence, then Socrates would be ascribing a playful mood not to himself but to the namegivers.

οἰήσει): hence the present name οἰωνιστική, from οἴησις + νοῦς + ἱστορία, the long vowel ω being due to the moderns' eagerness to exalt its gravity. Once again, all this is entirely in line with *Cra.*, where the changes undergone by the form of names are ascribed to some people's will to make them sound 'tragic', i.e. high-sounding (414c). So far so good; but one wonders whether Plato could reasonably fail to be aware of the correct and obvious derivation of οἰωνιστική from οἰωνός, 'bird', plus the ending -ιστική, one of the standard ones for names of arts in Greek. Sedley (2003: 35–6) supposes that he did *not* fail and that he may have thought either that it was οἰωνός which derived from οἰωνιστική or that οἰωνιστική was a name combining two coexistent etyma, as those at *Cra.* 395bc, 404e–406a, b. But in fact Socrates here says nothing like that: the connection with οἰωνός is not even mentioned. And yet the *Phdr.* passage remarks, in the very same lines, that οἰωνιστική works 'by means of *birds* [ὀρνίθων] and the other signs' (244c6–7)!

These considerations (some already sketched by Hackforth 1952: 59) prompt the conclusion that, at the very least, the passage cannot be entirely serious. Later on I shall return to the peculiar tone of *Phdr.*, suggesting that it may yield a key to the spirit of our *Cra.* etymologies.

5.5.4 *The etymologies' epistemological status*

An interpretation which aims at keeping together all the threads I have been unwinding so far has been offered by Barney 1998: 75–84, who construes the etymologies as an 'agonistic display', i.e. an instance of a genre which (as she convincingy argues, following a suggestion of Proclus, *in Prm.* 631–3) is well attested in Plato's dialogues, and whose central feature is that Socrates 'succeeds in competition on the home ground of the non-philosophical claimant to knowledge'. Other instances of the same genre are Socrates' first speech in the *Phaedrus*, explicitly competing with that of Lysias; the funeral oration in the *Menexenus*, arising from a criticism of the standard ones; and the interpretation of Simonides' poem in the *Protagoras*, where Socrates' wrestle with Protagoras culminates.

The dialogues Barney takes into account have several points of contact with *Cra.* First, in the *Phaedrus* and *Menexenus* Socrates' speech is ascribed to someone else (respectively Sappho etc., *Phdr.* 235cd, and Aspasia, *Menex.* 236ac), thus relieving Socrates of its paternity – although these excuses fail to convince the interlocutor completely (*Phdr.* 235d, *Menex.* 236c, 249e). In *Cra.* this obviously corresponds to Euthyphro's alleged inspiration, doubted by Cratylus at 428c. Secondly, in the *Phaedrus* and *Protagoras* the speech is somehow or other rejected after its conclusion (respectively by means of Socrates' palinode, *Phdr.* 242b–243e, and his judgement that the interpretation of poets should be banished from discussion, *Prt.* 347b–348a). Thirdly, Protagoras' strategy of transferring the philosophical discussion to the exegesis of the poets (*Prt.* 338e–339a) can be viewed as parallel to the strategy of scrutinizing names to find the truth about reality.

According to Barney, the point of the agonistic genre lies in the fact that, in a context of 'methodological anarchy', where rhetoric, literary interpretation and etymology contend to dialectic the role of privileged access to philosophical knowledge, Socrates can dismiss them authoritatively only after he has shown his prowess at them and his superiority to the opponent. Thus in the *Protagoras* it is only after the long discussion of Simonides, and the subsequent dismissal of literary interpretation, that Socrates can make Protagoras face the problem of virtue in dialectical terms. 'Likewise in the *Cratylus*, Socrates' ability to offer a successful etymological display puts him in a position to transcend the etymological method and eventually to dismiss it' (1998: 84).

Barney (1998: 77–8) finds the main evidence for her view in Socrates' description of his *tour de force* as a chariot-race (see §5.5.2). The chariot image reminds her of the very agonistic race in *Iliad* 23. She also quotes Socrates' pronouncement at 421d: 'The contest [ἀγών] does not seem to me to allow of excuses.' But isn't that too scanty? The *Cra.* connection between chariot-race and inspiration (on which see again §5.5.2) does not make the references to the latter into an argument for the presence of agonism, despite what Barney seems to think. Furthermore, in *Cra.* I miss an explicit contrast between Socrates' performance and someone else's practice. Such a contrast is very evident in the 'agonistic' dialogues: Lysias' speech, the orators in the *Menexenus* and Protagoras are acknowledged as Socrates' competitors in the *agon*. In *Cra.*, instead, we find nothing comparable. True, on several occasions Socrates offers and contrasts different etymologies of the same word (he 'makes a point of outdoing himself', as Barney 1998: 77 puts it); sometimes he also refers to other people's etymologizing. But that is really not much, and in any case not enough. Barney may well grasp a real feature of the etymologies; but I strongly doubt that this is 'the central and organizing fact about them', as she maintains.

To reach an alternative account it will be helpful to start by recapitulating what we have learned so far.

On the one hand, the etymologies have several serious philosophical purposes. They sketch a historical and systematic picture of the development of Greek thought from Homer to Plato; they attempt to put into practice the naturalist theory of names, thus helping us to understand better how it works, and then bring it to suicide, anticipating some of Socrates' final arguments against it; they also introduce the theory of flux, finding it enshrined in the original form of names, and bequeath it to a further autonomous discussion to be pursued after the debate about names has come to an end. If I am right, they even give the theory of flux a very definite shape by associating it with a leading character, Democritus, some of whose doctrines are hinted at.

Note that these serious philosophical purposes do not require that the etymologies be 'exegetically correct', i.e. faithful analyses of the original form and meaning of words. Indeed, a number of signs (Euthyphro's alleged inspiration, the promise of a purification, and various witticisms and disclaimers) indicates that Plato wants to keep himself at a distance from the etymological performance as such. But, on the other hand, there is also strong evidence (basically, Socrates' claim at 439c plus several historical considerations) that most etymologies are presented with a straight face as 'exegetically correct' reconstructions of the namegivers' thought.

These things being so, the only possible way of keeping together the various strands consists, as far as I can see, in stressing the *literary* nature of Socrates' performance. What I mean is that I see a crucial feature of the etymologies in their being a 'virtuoso performance' (Sedley 2003: 40) where Plato takes sheer delight in an outburst of verbal creativeness, quite apart from any other purpose – doxographical, philological or whatever. It is precisely such an internal, autonomous moving principle of the etymologies that gives Plato considerable freedom in pursuing his other purposes. Thus he advances most etymologies as genuine ('exegetically correct') and brings to light the namegivers' opinions, including especially the theory of flux. But he also takes the occasion for stressing the importance of atomism in this last connection, though probably not believing that the first namegivers really anticipated Democritus' specific doctrines. He has great fun throughout and sometimes deliberately makes Socrates propose a facetious etymology (e.g. ἥρως, see §5.5.3). That some etymologies seem to Plato less plausible than others *qua* etymologies is perfectly reasonable, although he obviously has no *real* criterion to tell a sound from a bad one, and although his judgements on that score would perhaps not coincide with ours.

What we have said so far about the complex purposes of the etymologies implies consequences as to their epistemological status. They are not only meant to say something true or plausible about the development of

Plato's attitude to the etymologies 253

Greek thought, the namegivers' opinions etc.: pleasure and amusement are part of the goal as well. Now this peculiar epistemological status may require certain caveats to help the reader view the etymological performance in the right perspective. Thus, when Socrates' fun merges into irony, and when he ascribes his prowess to a dubious inspiration to be conjured away the day after, perhaps his purpose is precisely to supply such epistemological caveats.

Let me appeal, following a suggestion of Grote,[148] to what seems to me an analogous case. Think of Plato's *myths*. A first, extrinsical similarity between the myths and the etymologies is this: a typical Platonic myth is, like our etymological section, a long section which suspends, and gives readers some relief from, the dense argument of a Platonic dialogue. But, I submit, there is more than that to the analogy; and this is best brought out if we recall some crucial features of Plato's myths.

Surely Plato's myths have a profound philosophical function, which typically (though not exclusively) consists in supplying a fair guess about the nature of what lies beyond our rational capacities – e.g. the soul's fate after death. On the other hand, the myths contain many descriptions and narratives which cannot be accounted for as serving the same philosophical function. Their function rather seems to be to add details, enrich the story, and give free rein to Plato's talent as a writer. How should we read the description of the four subterranean rivers, and their role in the souls' afterlife, at *Phd.* 111c–114c? What about the virtuoso description of the Spindle of Necessity at *R.* 616b–617d, or the minute picture of the regrowing of the soul's wings at *Phdr.* 251ae? A myth, we might very roughly say, consists of a kernel, endowed with philosophical significance, plus a setting which presents the kernel in a literarily attractive form. The border between these two components is vague, and it is difficult or impossible to tell them sharply from each other. But in principle they are distinct, as is proved by the fact that sometimes the same kernel is presented in different, not strictly compatible ways (as is the case in the afterlife myths). Now, the difference between kernel and setting results in a different epistemological status between the two. The epistemological status of the myth's kernel is difficult to grasp, but has to do – roughly speaking – with such notions as

---

[148] 'I believe that he intended his etymologies as *bona fide* guesses, more or less probable (like the developments in the Timaeus, which he repeatedly designates as εἰκότα, and nothing beyond): some certain, some doubtful, some merely novel and ingenious ... when he gives particular consequences as flowing from' his general views, like the naturalist theory, 'his belief graduates down through all the stages between full certainty and the lowest probability, until in some cases it becomes little more than a fanciful illustration – like the mythes which he so often invents to expand and enliven these same general views' (1888: III. 309–10).

persuasion and plausibility as opposed to knowledge and certainty. On the other hand, the status of the kernel's setting seems to be something even more indeterminate, such as to threaten the meaningfulness of questions about Plato's belief in it. E.g., part of the kernel of several afterlife myths is the idea that our disembodied souls are rewarded and punished after death until they are reincarnated. Plato believes this and finds it reasonable and plausible. But should we say the same of the Spindle of Necessity as Er describes it? To my mind, this would be as inappropriate as to suggest that Plato definitely believes that the Spindle story is false. Belief and disbelief are somewhat inadequate alternatives in this sort of matters.[149]

This account accords with the partial disclaimers Socrates sometimes adds to his myths to qualify his commitment. Recall *Phd.* 114d:

> Asserting with confidence that these things are as I have expounded is not appropriate for a man of sense. But that *either these things or things of this sort are true about our souls and their dwellings* … this seems to me both appropriate to assert and worth the risk for someone who thinks that it is so, because this risk is a fine one; and one must, as it were, sing such stories as enchantments to oneself.

Here, as already elsewhere, the *Phaedrus* myth offers some especially interesting parallels. Remember that Socrates' alleged inspiration in *Phdr.* helped us understand his analogous claim in *Cra.*; later on the etymologies at *Phdr.* 244bd constituted exhibit (D) in my search for playful elements in the etymologies (§5.5.3). Then a moment ago, speaking of the 'setting' of a myth as distinct from its philosophical kernel, I cited the regrowing of the soul's wings at 251ae. That passage is a bravura piece wonderfully mixing wild imagination with exact description and lexical richness; perhaps, however, its relevance to *Cra.* goes even further. While we are reading of the soul's itch and irritation, due to the regrowth of the wings' stem, we encounter the *Cra.*-style etymology of the word ἵμερος, 'desire': looking at a beautiful boy the soul receives 'particles coming and flowing [μέρη ἐπιόντα καὶ ῥέοντ'], which for this reason are called ἵμερος' (251c6–7).[150] Then, a little below, Socrates winds up his description of the symptoms of love as follows (252bc):

> This experience … human beings term 'love', but hearing how the gods call it you will probably laugh because of your young age. I think some of the Homeridae recite two verses in praise of Eros from the unpublished ones, of which the second is absolutely outrageous and not completely metrical. They sing of him

---

[149] For some general considerations along the same lines, using the *Protagoras* myth as an example, see Sedley 2007b: 100.
[150] A different etymology at *Cra.* 419e–420a.

Plato's attitude to the etymologies 255

thus: 'Him mortals call winged Eros, immortals Pteros, because of his wing-generating compulsion.' Now, one may either believe this or not [τούτοις δὴ ἔξεστι μὲν πείθεσθαι, ἔξεστιν δὲ μή]; nonetheless the cause of the lovers' experience happens to be exactly this.

Socrates allegedly quotes from the repertory of the Homeridae[151] two verses about Eros, following the Homeric *topos* (ironically evoked at *Cra.* 391d–392b) of the distinction between human and divine names. The second verse is clumsy and unmetrical, as Socrates himself points out. In view of this fact, of the general tone of the passage, and of Socrates' final comment that we may or may not believe the story, several scholars have suspected that both verses are actually a humorous creation of Socrates' and that he is inviting us to recognize it as such.[152] If this is true (as I think it is), then it is a lighthearted piece of humour, of a vaguely surrealistic variety, studiedly inserted within the myth and highlighting its literary aspect as a telltale sign.

There is one more passage from *Phdr.* which I wish to consider. It is where Socrates introduces dialectic as the art of division by kinds, somehow exemplified by the conjunction of his two speeches. At 265bc he refers back to the second speech with a characteristic disclaimer, much in the spirit of *Phd.* 114d quoted above, though somewhat more distancing:

Representing I don't know how the experience of love by means of a comparison, perhaps grasping something true, but perhaps also being driven astray [ἴσως μὲν ἀληθοῦς τινος ἐφαπτόμενοι, τάχα δ' ἂν καὶ ἄλλοσε παραφερόμενοι], mixing together a not wholly implausible speech [οὐ παντάπασιν ἀπίθανον λόγον], we sang a mythical hymn, respectful of moderation and piety, in praise of my master and yours, Eros.

Just a bit further he identifies the dialectical component as the only serious element in the speeches, contrasting it with all the rest, which, he says, seems to have really been 'playfully done, by way of amusement' (τῷ ὄντι παιδιᾷ πεπαῖσθαι, 265c).[153] In relation to many things of utmost importance that were contained in the myth, this judgement is deliberately exaggerated; no doubt, however, it also refers to all that was actually playful or literary, and hence is also Plato's genuine recognition of that feature. Now, in *Cra.* Socrates' spirit might be roughly the same when, at 402a, he announces an etymological 'swarm of wisdom' and terms it 'quite ludicrous to say, but nonetheless, I think, possessing some plausibility' (Γελοῖον μὲν πάνυ εἰπεῖν, οἶμαι μέντοι τινὰ πιθανότητα

---
[151] A guild of rhapsodes in Chios, who recited Homer's poems.
[152] See e.g. de Vries 1969: 159–60, Rowe 1986: 185.   [153] Rowe's (1986) translation.

ἔχον). Recall also the 'playful' (παιδικόν) etymology of Dionysus' name at 406bc (exhibit (C) in §5.5.3 above). This seems to confirm that there is some sort of affinity between the two dialogues and that *Phdr.* may help us gain a clearer picture of Socrates' ambiguous attitude towards his *Cra.* etymologies.[154]

[154] On play and seriousness in Plato, and on some relevant uses of παιδιά and related terms, you may want to consult Morgan 2000: 164–79.

CHAPTER 6

Naturalism illustrated: the primary names (421c–427e)

6.1 FROM SECONDARY TO PRIMARY NAMES (421C–422C)

6.1.1 The postulation of primary names (421c–422c)

We now resume our reading of the text from 421c3, at the end of the etymologies of the 'greatest and finest' names. Socrates has just derived ὄν and οὐκ ὄν, 'being' and 'not being', from ἰόν and οὐκ ἰόν, 'going' and 'not going'. Hermogenes is very satisfied, but asks a question which will prove difficult to answer and will set the agenda of the discussion for the next pages:

HE. These names you seem to me to have broken up most bravely, Socrates. But if one were to ask you about this ἰόν and ῥέον and δοῦν, what correctness these names have ...
SO. '... What should we answer him?' This is what you say, isn't it?
HE. Definitely. (421c3–8)

Thus Hermogenes asks Socrates about the very word from which ὄν was derived in the last etymology, i.e. ἰόν. His point is clearly that so short a word seems difficult to analyse further. The same holds of the other two examples advanced, ῥέον ('flowing') and δοῦν ('binding'). Both are very short words and both occurred earlier in some etymologies: see 410b, 415d, 419b.

Socrates' first reaction consists in identifying, and then discarding, two possible loopholes:

SO. Well, just now, at some point, we procured one way of seeming to answer something sensible.
HE. What do you mean?
SO. Saying, of whatever we don't understand, that it is some sort of barbarian name. Perhaps some of them might really be of that very kind; it also might be that the first names [τὰ πρῶτα τῶν ὀνομάτων] are impossible to recover because of their antiquity. For given that names have been twisted in all

257

ways, it would be no surprise if the ancient language, relative to the present one, were no different from a barbarian language.

HE. You say nothing unreasonable. (421c12–d6)

Faced with a name we are unable to etymologize, we can say either that it is of barbarian provenance (cf. 409de, 416a) or that it derives from one of the 'first' (i.e. most ancient) names, so that its etymology has become impossible to discover (cf. 414c). In fact, Socrates remarks, these two moves are substantially equivalent, because the ancient language is perhaps as different from the present one as a barbarian language is (cf. 425e–426a).[1]

Socrates overtly presents these possible answers as dodges; in the earlier passages he is now referring to, the idea of barbarian loans was already termed a 'contrivance' (μηχανή) for solving difficult cases. So we may well suspect that Hermogenes' d6 assent is over hasty. Indeed, in the following lines Socrates does just what we could expect of him: far from being satisfied with his clever device, he embarks on a thorough inquiry.

SO. Yes, what I say is plausible. Nonetheless, a contest doesn't, I think, allow for excuses:[2] we must be eager to examine these names. Let us reflect upon this: if on any occasion one will ask about those expressions through which the name is said [δι' ὧν ἂν λέγηται τὸ ὄνομα, ἐκεῖνα ἀνερήσεται τὰ ῥήματα],[3] and then again will inquire about those through which those expressions are said [δι' ὧν ἂν τὰ ῥήματα λεχθῇ, ἐκεῖνα πεύσεται], and if he won't stop doing this, then isn't it necessary that the answerer will eventually give up?

HE. So it seems to me. (421d7–e5)

Thus the discussion rises from the particular cases submitted by Hermogenes to a general and abstract problem, i.e. the necessity of finite etymological analysis. These lines are best commented on along with the following ones, where Socrates makes his point more clearly:

SO. So when would he who gives up have to give up, if he is to stop at the right point? It is when he arrives at those names which are, as it were, elements of the other sentences and names [ἃ ὡσπερεὶ στοιχεῖα τῶν ἄλλων ἐστὶ καὶ λόγων καὶ ὀνομάτων], isn't it? For it is no longer right, it seems, that these should appear to be composed of other names [ἐξ ἄλλων ὀνομάτων συγκείμενα], if this is their condition. E.g., we said just now that ἀγαθόν is composed of ἀγαστόν and θοόν; we might perhaps say that θοόν is

---

[1] The clause οὐδὲν θαυμαστὸν ἂν εἴη εἰ ἡ παλαιὰ φωνὴ πρὸς τὴν νυνὶ βαρβαρικῆς μηδὲν διαφέρει (d4–5) is sometimes curiously mistranslated: 'it wouldn't be surprising if the ancient Greek word was the same as the modern foreign one' (Reeve, cf. Fowler).
[2] Cf. *Lg.* 751d, Ar. *Ach.* 392, fr. 349 *PCG*. Some take d8 ἀγών as 'trial' rather than 'contest'.
[3] 'Those expressions through which the name is said' (d9–e1) = 'Those expressions of which the name is composed and which (or whose remains, present in the name) must be uttered for the whole name to be uttered'.

composed of other names, and those of still other ones. But if we ever get hold of a name which is no longer composed of any other name [ὃ οὐκέτι ἔκ τινων ἑτέρων σύγκειται ὀνομάτων], we should rightly say that then we had reached an element [ἐπὶ στοιχείῳ τε ἤδη εἶναι][4] and that this must no longer be traced back to other names.

HE. What you say seems to me to be right. (422a1–b5)

Sooner or later, Socrates argues, the answerer will give up satisfying the questioner's demands for further etymologies, and the analysis will thus come to a stop. But not any stop is the right stop. The analysis stops at the right point only if it has reached something *elementary*, i.e. names not further composed of other names.

Socrates' talk of names that are the 'elements' (στοιχεῖα 422a3, cf. b2–3) of the other names and sentences has sometimes been misunderstood. According to some scholars (perhaps influenced by the fact that the term στοιχεῖον can also mean 'letter', and indeed will do so at 424b ff.), the elementary names envisaged here are not words in the ordinary sense, but are the very letters or sounds of which words are composed.[5] But in fact both our passage and the following ones make it very clear that the elementary names are perfectly ordinary names, made up of letters and syllables, like the trio ἰόν ῥέον δοῦν (see especially 422b6–7, 423e–424b, 424e–425a; cf. Kretzmann 1971: 135–6). They are elementary, not because they are not analysable into anything at all, but just because they are not analysable into other *names*, i.e. they are *atomic* or anhomoeomerous.

A point which deserves some comment is Socrates' reference to the components of a name as ῥήματα (421e1–2), 'expressions'. But since discussion of this point will require a digression on the controversial meaning of ῥῆμα, I will postpone it until the next subsection. Here I would rather add a couple of remarks from a broader, historical perspective.

First, the problem of infinite etymological analysis returns in later authors. S. E., *M*. 1.241–5, wields it against the use of etymology to establish that a given word is pure Greek. If one wants to prove the 'Hellenism' of a given word by means of etymology, Sextus argues, then one should prove in the same way the purity of its components, and so on to infinity, or the analysis must stop at some non-etymologizable word, whose purity is just a matter of customary usage – which entails that the purity of the initial word too was a matter of customary usage. Sextus does not seem

---

[4] ἐπὶ στοιχείῳ ... εἶναι (b2), literally 'be *at* an element': cf. *Phdr*. 274e, *Plt*. 274b. But note that ἐπί + dat. can also mean 'in possession of' (LSJ B.III.7), which would tie in with b1 λάβωμεν 'get hold of'.
[5] See Annas 1982: 106–10, Baxter 1992: 76–8.

to consider the possibility of mimetic etymology. But Augustine, *De dialectica* VI 9–10, reports that the Stoics avoided the etymological regress by postulating *mimetic* elementary names: 'you must search until you arrive at the point where the thing is concordant with the word's sound in virtue of some similarity [*ut res cum sono verbi aliqua similitudine concinat*]'. This is roughly going to be Socrates' solution, which the Stoics endorse.[6]

From an even broader point of view, our argument can be seen as a miniature model of all those arguments which prove that a certain process cannot go on endlessly but must eventually come to a stop. Note especially the expression ἀνάγκη ... ἀπειπεῖν, 'it is necessary to give up' (421e3), which also occurs in a similar context at *Ly.* 219c,[7] and which is reminiscent of Aristotle's typical turn of phrase ἀνάγκη στῆναι or ἵστασθαι, 'it is necessary to stop' (*APo.* 81b30–7, *Ph.* 256a29, *Metaph.* 1070a4 etc.).

At 412c Socrates' back-reference to the etymology of ἀγαθόν serves the twofold function of giving a concrete example of his claims about elementary names and bringing him back to Hermogenes' original question, which was also about concrete instances, i.e. ἰόν, ῥέον and δοῦν. To these he now returns, supposing that they are elementary:

SO. Hence, in this case too,[8] the names you're asking about happen to be elements [στοιχεῖα], and at this point we must investigate in some other manner what their correctness consists in [δεῖ αὐτῶν ἄλλῳ τινὶ τρόπῳ ἤδη τὴν ὀρθότητα ἐπισκέψασθαι ἥτις ἐστίν]?
HE. It is reasonable.
SO. Reasonable indeed, Hermogenes; at any rate, all the previous names appear to have gone back to these. And if this is so, as I think it is, come and inquire together with me again [αὖ], lest I should rave explaining what the correctness of the first names must be like [οἵαν δεῖ τὴν τῶν πρώτων ὀνομάτων ὀρθότητα εἶναι].
HE. Just speak – within the limits of my capacities I shall inquire together with you. (422b6–c6)

---

[6] Cf. Orig. *Cels.* 1.24 (= *SVF* 11.146 = *FDS* 643, where the text is mistranslated): the Stoics held that names are by nature, 'because the first sounds imitate the objects, of which names are said' (μιμουμένων τῶν πρώτων φωνῶν τὰ πράγματα, καθ' ὧν τὰ ὀνόματα). Note that here the adjective πρῶτος is not applied to the atomic names, as it is going to be in Socrates' argument, but to the letters of which they are composed.
[7] In *Ly.* 'giving up' may seem to be *alternative* to arriving at something primary: Burnet's text is ἀνάγκη ἀπειπεῖν ... ἢ ἀφικέσθαι ἐπί τινα ἀρχήν ('it is necessary to give up ... *or* to arrive at some principle'). But ἢ is Schanz's correction of the MSS καί, which can and should be retained (cf. Dancy 2004: 200 n.24).
[8] In καὶ νῦν ἃ γ' ἐρωτᾷς τὰ ὀνόματα (b6) Stallbaum 167–8 and many translators join νῦν with ἐρωτᾷς: 'the names you're now asking about too'. This strikes me as much less natural than the construal I adopt in the text.

The supposition that the three names submitted by Hermogenes are elementary ones is only likely, after all, given that they are so short and that no etymology is apparent. Socrates, however, also offers a sort of partial argument, i.e. that all the previous names have 'gone back' to these (εἰς ταῦτα ἀνεληλυθέναι, c1). This claim is actually false as far as many previous etymologies are concerned, although many others did contain at least a cognate of ἰόν and ῥέον (e.g. the infinitives ἰέναι and ῥεῖν, or the noun ῥοῦς). We may allow Socrates some exaggeration – unless perhaps ταῦτα is to be corrected into τ<οι>αῦτα to obtain the meaning 'all the previous names appear to have gone back to names *like these*'.

In any case, besides claiming that ἰόν, ῥέον and δοῦν are elementary Socrates makes a further, important step. The correctness of such names, he says, must be inquired into 'in some other manner' (b7). When it comes to the elementary or atomic level, the sort of analysis we have seen at work so far must be replaced by some other kind of analysis. That is to say, Socrates is announcing that his developments of the naturalist thesis must now make a fresh start. This is confirmed by several textual signals. The new inquiry will be one into 'what' the correctness of such names 'consists in' (ἥτις ἐστίν, b8) or 'must be like' (οἵαν δεῖ ... εἶναι, c3–4): this echoes 391ab, where Socrates and Hermogenes undertook to search 'what' the natural correctness of names 'consists in' (ἥτις ... ἐστιν, 391b5, cf. a3). The idea of a fresh start is also conveyed by the adverb αὖ, 'again' (422c2).

The names that are going to be scrutinized have been introduced at 422ab as 'elements'. At c3, however, Socrates presents the forthcoming inquiry as one into the correctness 'of the first names'. What does this mean? The meaning of the phrase τὰ πρῶτα ὀνόματα (or τὰ πρῶτα τῶν ὀνομάτων) was at 414c and 421d, and will again be at 438ac, 'the *earliest* names'. 421d seems especially relevant, because it is placed in the preliminaries of the present argument, where Socrates, trying to escape Hermogenes' question about ἰόν, ῥέον and δοῦν, mentioned the antiquity of 'the first names' as a possible cause of their inscrutability. This may predispose us to interpret the present occurrence too in a chronological sense, as do Fowler and Méridier ('les noms primitifs'). Yet the 'first names' here are initially introduced as 'elements'; and here as well as in the sequel (422ce) they are clearly identified on the basis of their simplicity, not their ancientness. Hence their priority must be *logical* rather than chronological (cf. Reeve 66 n.120). To mirror the ambiguity of the Greek phrase I translate it 'the first names' everywhere; but in my comments I shall sometimes refer to the logically first names as the *primary* names.[9]

What relation is there between the two meanings of the phrase 'the first names'? On the one hand, there seems no reason why some elementary, logically first (i.e. primary) names could not be coined later than some complex, logically secondary names. On the other, the creation of any complex name presupposes the existence of at least one elementary name from which it is derived. So there is, after all, some connection between logical and chronological priority. Indeed, Socrates might be assuming that, as a matter of fact, most (if not all) of the earliest names were elementary names and vice versa; and then the two kinds of priority would be broadly (if not completely) equivalent in extension. It is, however, unclear whether he does make this assumption: see §8.2.3.

6.1.2 *Intermezzo: the meaning of* ῥῆμα *(399ab, 421b, e)*

Before following Socrates' fresh start on the correctness of the primary names, there is a question whose discussion was postponed above and must now be accomplished. It is Socrates' claim, at 421e1–2, that a name is constituted by ῥήματα. The meaning of this term in Plato and Aristotle is debated; but the debate seldom takes into account the evidence (especially the pre-Platonic one) for the term's usage. Hence I shall give the present digression a rather wide scope, largely drawing on Conti's (1977–8) unpublished work. Further discussion on ῥῆμα, with special reference to its grammatical usage, will follow in §§6.3.5 and 7.2.4.

ῥῆμα derives from the same Indo-European stem as the Latin *verbum* and the English 'word'. It belongs to a Greek lexical family among whose members we may list the verb εἴρω 'say', the nouns ῥῆσις 'speech', ῥήτρα 'covenant, law', ῥήτωρ 'speaker', and the verbal adj. ῥητός 'enunciated/enunciable'. The meaning of the Greek stem behind these words is spelt out by Conti 1977–8: 21 as follows: 'dire consapevolmente qualcosa di importante in cui è coinvolto colui che parla e coloro che ascoltano'. And ῥῆμα, as Conti shows, usually indicates a *brief but efficacious or relevant linguistic expression*. Here is a selection of occurrences: Archil. 109 West;

---

[9] There are presumably several reasons that lead Socrates to substitute talk of 'first names' for talk of 'elements'. Being an adjective, 'first' is more easily associated with 'name' than 'element' is; moreover, it allows a convenient reference to the complex names as 'secondary'. Most of all, Socrates is going to account for the correctness of these names in terms of their letters, and given that στοιχεῖον also means 'letter', it might create some confusion. In fact, στοιχεῖον will reappear at 424b with the meaning 'letter' and keep it to the end of the dialogue.

Sim. *PMG* 543.19; Pi. *N.* 4.94; Soph. *Aj.* 243; Hdt. 3.153.2, 6.65.4; Ar. *Ran.* 97, 924–9, 1155; *PDerveni* XXIII; Aeschin. 1.17, 3.166–7; Dem. 19.13–14, 209; Pl. *Prt.* 341e, *Euthd.* 287c, *Tht.* 190c, *Sph.* 265c, *Lg.* 783c, 838b. Often a ῥῆμα is even a famous *saying* or maxim: Isocr. 15.166; Pl. *Prt.* 343ab, *R.* 336a. In several cases, however, all that is relevant to the meaning of ῥῆμα is just the reference to a *linguistic* expression, because the sphere of language must be somehow contrasted with another sphere (reality, thought, or music): Soph. *OC* 873; Ar. *Ran.* 1059; Th. 5.111.3; Antiph. 5.5; Pl. *Ion* 536c, *Grg.* 489bc, *Euthd.* 305a, *Phd.* 102b, *Phdr.* 228d.

The size of a ῥῆμα is variable, as becomes clear when we are able to check the expression at issue. It may be an autonomous *sentence*, as in many of the examples above; but it may also be a *phrase*. Examples (with distinct ῥήματα separated by commas): Ar. *Ran.* 97–102 αἰθέρα Διὸς δωμάτιον, χρόνου πόδα, and a third one covering two verses; Pl. *Sph.* 257b μὴ μέγα. Even a *single word*: Ar. *Pax* 929–31 Ὀΐ; Aeschin. 2.40 κέρκωψ, παιπάλημα, παλίμβολον; Pl. *R.* 462c ἐμόν, οὐκ ἐμόν; *Ti.* 49e τόδε, τοῦτο; *Sph.* 237d τι.

Often, especially in Plato, in contexts devoid of recognizable grammatical interest ῥῆμα is joined with ὄνομα to form the pair ὀνόματα καὶ ῥήματα. Thus e.g. Aeschin. 3.72; Pl. *Ap.* 17bc 'speeches embellished ... with ῥήματα and ὀνόματα', *Smp.* 198b, 199b, 221e '[Socrates' speeches] are externally clothed in such ὀνόματα and ῥήματα', *R.* 601a, *Tht.* 168bc 'you will examine ... but not, as before, on the basis of the customary usage of ῥήματα and ὀνόματα', 184c, 206d. In such cases the two terms are usually translated respectively 'words' and 'expressions' or 'phrases'. In fact, this interpretation can be proved right in two cases. Aeschines 3.72 says:

He said we must not (I even remember the ῥῆμα whereby he expressed himself, because of the unpleasantness of both the speaker and the ὄνομα) 'break the alliance away from peace' [ἀπορρῆξαι τῆς εἰρήνης τὴν συμμαχίαν],

where 'the ῥῆμα is the whole expression, the ὄνομα is ἀπορρῆξαι' (Riddell 1867: 36). The second passage is *Smp.* 198b, where Socrates is commenting on Agathon's speech: 'But, in the conclusive part, who wasn't astounded hearing the beauty of those ὀνόματα and ῥήματα?' Now, the last section of Agathon's speech (197de) 'consists of a chain of laudatory phrases organised in pairs or series, with a high degree of symmetry, rhyme and assonance ... nearly all the thirty-one members (or "cola") into which the passage can be articulated ... are recognisable ... as metrical units familiar in Greek lyric poetry' (Dover 1980: 123–4). Thus, given the usual meaning of ῥῆμα, at 198b the term is very likely to refer to these *cola*, while ὀνόματα refers to the individual, well-chosen, sometimes even poetical words occurring in Agathon's bravura piece.[10]

So Aeschines and the *Symposium* confirm that, where ὀνόματα and ῥήματα are mentioned together in non-grammatical contexts, 'names and phrases', or even more generally 'names and expressions', is generally a suitable translation.

We can now turn to some passages from *Cra*. The first occurrence has carried much weight in the scholarly debate on ῥῆμα:

> SO. First of all ... we must consider this point about names, that often we throw in some letters and subtract others, using the name differently from what we mean, and we change the accents. Take e.g. Διὶ φίλος: for this to become a name instead of a ῥῆμα [ἵνα ἀντὶ ῥήματος ὄνομα ἡμῖν γένηται], we subtracted the second ι and began to pronounce the middle syllable as grave instead of acute. (399a6–b3)

After this preliminary remark on the proper name Δίφιλος coming from Διὶ φίλος, 'dear to Zeus',[11] a few lines below Socrates faces the case of the term ἄνθρωπος, 'human' (cf. §5.1.3):

> SO. Now the name of humans too has experienced one of these changes ... For from a ῥῆμα it has become a name [ἐκ γὰρ ῥήματος ὄνομα γέγονεν], as one letter, the α, was subtracted and the final syllable became grave ... Hence the human being alone among animals was correctly named ἄνθρωπος, 'he who examines what he has seen' [ἀναθρῶν ἃ ὄπωπε]. (399b6–c6)

So we have got two cases of an ὄνομα deriving from a ῥῆμα: Δίφιλος < Διὶ φίλος and ἄνθρωπος < ἀναθρῶν ἃ ὄπωπε. What does ῥῆμα mean here?

Several scholars take the point to be a *syntactic* one and construe ῥῆμα as 'predicate': see e.g. Guthrie 1962–81: III.220–1 ('literally *rhēma* means only a "thing said", and a name or noun is contrasted with it as that of which things are said') and Luce 1969a: 226 (names 'have turned out to be compressed or abbreviated phrases describing ... the nature of their nominates. As phrases they clearly predicate qualities of the individuals they denote ... ῥῆμα is used in its basic sense of "something stated", i.e. predicate. In so far as names are constituted by ῥήματα

---

[10] A little sample: 197d1–5 οὗτος δὲ ἡμᾶς ἀλλοτριότητος μὲν κενοῖ, οἰκειότητος δὲ πληροῖ ['he empties us of estrangement and fills us with intimacy'] ... πραότητα μὲν πορίζων, ἀγριότητα δ' ἐξορίζων ['providing gentleness and banishing fierceness']· φιλόδωρος εὐμενείας, ἄδωρος δυσμενείας ['bountiful of favour, bountiless of disfavour'].

[11] To understand what Socrates says here you must bear in mind that the acute accent was used to indicate a higher pitch on a given syllable, whereas the grave accent merely indicated the lack of such an accentuation (see [Dion. Thr.] 3). Thus in Διὶ φίλος the -ι- of φίλος has an acute accent, which becomes grave in Δίφιλος.

they say something about their nominates').[12] But a syntactical perspective would be decidedly incongruous in the present context, which is centred on the *material* features of names (letters, accents etc.) and the changes they may undergo. Therefore, if ῥῆμα ever means anything like 'predicate',[13] it is unlikely to do so here. What 399ab rather says is that, in the case of both Δίφιλος and ἄνθρωπος, a *single word* (ὄνομα) is derived from a *phrase* or (compound) expression (ῥῆμα). This construal, which fits in very well with the context and with the uses of ῥῆμα reviewed above, is adopted by LSJ 1.2, Riddell 1867: 36, Lutoslawski 1897: 430, and others: cf. Fowler and Reeve 'phrase', Minio-Paluello 'locuzione', Cambiano 'espressione', etc.

This construal of 399ab is confirmed when we get to the subsequent occurrence of ῥῆμα in *Cra*. It is at 421b, near the end of the etymologies and the beginning of the discussion of primary names:

SO. As for ἀλήθεια ['truth'], this too resembles the other names.[14] For the divine movement of being seems to have been called by this ῥῆμα, i.e. ἀλήθεια, as if it were a 'divine roaming' [θεία ἄλη]. (421b2–3)

Here the term ῥῆμα is applied to the very name to be etymologized instead of the phrase it comes from. Shall we think[15] that Socrates is especially interested in the possible use of the name 'truth' as a predicate and therefore introduces it as such out of the blue? This is hardly credible – also on account of the fact that the following, correlative name ψεῦδος, 'falsity', is going to be called an ὄνομα (421b7). Much more probably, here ῥῆμα means 'expression', in accordance with its commonest use reviewed above (cf. again Minio-Paluello and Cambiano). Indeed, here, as in the previous passage, the use of ῥῆμα might even have something to do with the name's deriving from a phrase: introducing a name as a ῥῆμα may suggest, in advance of the etymological analysis, that it actually ought to be viewed as

[12] Cf. Stallbaum 89, Méridier 74 n.1, Pfeiffer 1968: 59–60, Dalimier 224 n.142, Sedley 2003: 163 ('description').

[13] In fact, I believe this is *never* the case in Plato or Aristotle: see §6.3.5. But my conclusions about what the term means here are independent of this.

[14] At b1–2 the MSS read καὶ τοῦτο τοῖς ἄλλοις ἔοικε συγκεκροτῆσθαι, which cannot stand: ἔοικε cannot mean both 'resembles', with τοῖς ἄλλοις, and 'appears', with συγκεκροτῆσθαι (*pace* several scholars, e.g. Méridier '*Alêtheïa* ..., à son tour, ressemble aux autres noms, et paraît être un composé'). Editors who see this either (a) correct καὶ τοῦτο into κατὰ ταὐτὰ with Heindorf ('ἀλήθεια seems to have been welded together *in the same way as* the others') or (b) delete συγκεκροτῆσθαι with Hermann ('As for ἀλήθεια, this too resembles the others'). The OCT editors, immoderately, do both things. I opt for (b), along with Burnet and Fowler, because (a) makes little sense, while (b) means that ἀλήθεια is like the other names which pointed to the flux theory. συγκεκροτῆσθαι is likely to be a gloss by someone who did not understand τοῖς ἄλλοις and tried to create a connection with the previous etymology (cf. a7).

[15] As Luce 1969a: 226 appears to do; cf. Dalimier.

a contracted phrase (Conti 1977–8: 208). Plato might have a special reason for stressing this feature precisely here: the phrase ἄλη θεία is a particular case, because it coalesces into ἀλήθεια without *any* change in letters, so ἀλήθεια seems a fully transparent compound, like 'steamboat'.

Thus we finally reach our argument on primary names: more precisely, lines 421e1–2. Here it is noteworthy that Socrates envisages, at least as a possibility, the analysis of *one* name into *several* constituent ῥήματα. This fact, independently of the previous considerations, is enough to ensure that the term here does not mean anything like 'predicates'.[16] A name may conceivably be said to derive from a predicate (though I for one find it difficult to understand what this might mean, given that names need not belong to a different grammatical category from the expressions they derive from – witness ἀλήθεια < ἄλη θεία); but it would be very odd to say that a name derives from *several* predicates. Hence ῥήματα must mean generically 'expressions' (thus Cambiano; cf. Barney 2001: 82 n.2) and apply to *any* sort of possible components of an etymology, phrases as well as single words (though many translations would restrict it to the latter). When at 422a2–5 Socrates says the analysis will eventually reach *names* (ὀνόματα) not further composed of other names, these names are meant to be a particular case of the ῥήματα of the previous lines. Cf. the a5–b3 example: ἀγαθόν consists of ἀγαστόν and θοόν, which in the sketch provided above would be the ῥήματα.

Actually, this last passage suggests a refinement to our earlier conclusions about ῥῆμα as 'phrase' both at 399ab and elsewhere. We are entitled to suppose that the original, primary meaning of ῥῆμα in the contrast with ὄνομα is something like 'non-ὄνομα', i.e. that ῥῆμα is essentially meant to refer to a linguistic expression which is not (or insofar as it is not) an ὄνομα, it being left to the context to determine what kind of expression it actually is – whether it is a phrase, or a name viewed just as a component of the ὄνομα under discussion, or something else.[17] And since one possible contrast you may want to draw is between the ὄνομα and the *verb*, this hypothesis might easily explain why at some point ῥῆμα acquired the further, specific meaning 'verb'. That is to say, perhaps ῥῆμα originally came to refer to the verb by characterizing it, not as something which 'gets said' of the ὄνομα (as is often supposed), but more modestly as the 'other part' of a sentence besides the ὄνομα.

---

[16] Or 'descriptions', as Sedley 2003: 123, 163 translates it.
[17] Cf. Barney 2001: 185 n.8 and (partly) Hoekstra/Scheppers 2003: 59.

The correctness of primary names (422c–424a) 267

Be that as it may, we shall return to ῥῆμα in §§6.3.5 and 7.2.4. It is now high time to read on.

6.2 THE CORRECTNESS OF PRIMARY NAMES (422C–424A)

6.2.1 Introduction (422ce)

After the interlude on ῥῆμα we resume our continuous reading of the dialogue. We left Socrates announcing, at 422c, an inquiry into the correctness of primary names. Now he sets the ball rolling with some important preliminary remarks:

SO. Now, I think you agree that the correctness of every name, whether first or ultimate, is one and the same [μία γέ τις ἡ ὀρθότης παντὸς ὀνόματος καὶ πρώτου καὶ ὑστάτου], and that none of them is different in respect of its being a name [τῷ ὄνομα εἶναι].
HE. Of course. (422c7–10)

Socrates thus sets a condition upon the forthcoming inquiry. All names, from the simplest to the most complex, are indistinguishable *qua* names. Hence their correctness must be basically one and the same, over and above the different specific accounts appropriate to different kinds of names. That is to say, the primary names, for all their peculiarity, must have something basic in common with the secondary ones. (Note how freely Socrates switches from talk of correctness to talk of names *qua* names. The 'Redundancy Conception' of correctness is in force: see §I.1.1.)

Socrates' talk of 'ultimate' (ὑστάτου, c8) names calls for some comment. Here for the first time he uses a term correlative to 'first'; this, however, is a superlative, whereas in the following he will usually refer to derivative names with the comparative ὕστερα (d6 etc.), 'secondary'. Probably ὕστατον is used here because Socrates is envisaging a scale of increasing complexity in names, with the 'primary' ones, i.e. those not composed of other names, at one extreme, and the 'ultimate' ones, i.e. those not constituting part of other names, at the opposite extreme.

Socrates next proceeds to recall how the correctness of secondary names was defined:

SO. But the correctness of the names we've been going through now aimed at being such as to indicate what each of the beings is like [δηλοῦν οἷον ἕκαστόν ἐστι τῶν ὄντων].
HE. Certainly. (422d1–4)

The central notion expressed in these lines has been familiar to us at least since 393de, where we read that a name must indicate (δηλοῦν)[18] the object's being (οὐσία) or nature (φύσις).[19] Socrates assumes without further ado that this is the required generic account of correctness, applying to primary as well as secondary names:

SO. Therefore this feature must be possessed by the first no less than by the secondary ones, if they are to be names [εἴπερ ὀνόματα ἔσται].
HE. Of course.
SO. But the secondary ones, it seems, were able to accomplish this through the prior ones [διὰ τῶν προτέρων].
HE. So it seems.
SO. Very good. But the first ones, which no others yet underlie, in what manner [τίνι τρόπῳ] will they make the beings as manifest [φανερά] as possible to us, if they are to be names? (422d5–e1)

Thus Socrates confidently claims that any name whatsoever must 'indicate what each of the beings is like' (d5–6). This much is common ground between primary and secondary names; henceforth the two kinds part company. Secondary names perform their function 'through the prior ones' of which they are composed (d8–9). Once more, as at c8 on 'ultimate' names, we can appreciate Socrates' exactness in suggesting a scale of complexity: here he speaks of the *'prior'* (cf. 433d), not the primary names, because a secondary name need not be directly composed of primary ones, only of names closer to the primary ones, i.e. *simpler* than it is.[20] The primary names themselves, on the other hand, require a different explanation. They must perform the same function – reformulated at d12–e1 as 'making manifest' the objects – in a different 'manner' (τρόπος, cf. 422b7).[21]

---

[18] As usual, interpreters here translate the verb δηλοῦν (d2) in a variety of ways: e.g. Fowler 'showing', Méridier 'faire voir', Minio-Paluello and Cambiano 'manifestare', Reeve 'expressing', Barney 2001: 88 'disclose'. In the present passage, all of these would be more or less acceptable. For my own choice, 'to indicate' (cf. Ficino), see §§4.2.4, 4.2.6.

[19] In our lines, however, there is a certain confusion between talk of the correctness of names and talk of names themselves. Strictly speaking it is names, rather than their correctness, that should be said to 'aim at' being such as to 'to indicate' something. So the text could be paraphrased as follows: 'The correctness of the names we've been going through now *is* such that *names* aimed at indicating ... etc.' (cf. 428e for a similar formulation).

[20] Socrates' precision is obscured by translations of διὰ τῶν προτέρων as 'by means of the primary ones' or the like. Fowler and Minio-Paluello get it right – although the former employs chronological language ('later' and 'earlier').

[21] So it is not the case that, as Sedley 2003: 125 has it, for Socrates 'whatever relation obtains at the secondary level ... must also apply at the primary level'. This entails that, when Socrates assumes (e.g. 427cd) that not only primary names, but also secondary names are *imitations* of their referents, this generalization is not a trivial consequence of his earlier assumptions about the relation between primary and secondary names (as Sedley 2003:126 thinks), but is instead unwarranted.

6.2.2 Indication by gestural mimesis (422e–423b)

But what is this different manner? Socrates, as usual, chooses a roundabout approach:

(SO.) Answer me on this point: if we had no voice or tongue, but wanted to indicate the objects to each other [δηλοῦν ἀλλήλοις τὰ πράγματα], then wouldn't we, as dumb people actually do, try to make signs with our hands and our head and the rest of the body?
HE. How could we do otherwise, Socrates?
SO. If we wanted to indicate what is aloft and what is light, then, I think, we would raise our hand towards the sky, imitating the object's very nature [μιμούμενοι αὐτὴν τὴν φύσιν τοῦ πράγματος]; if instead we wanted to indicate the things beneath and the heavy ones, then we would turn our hand towards the earth. And if we wanted to indicate a horse in the act of running [ἵππον θέοντα], or any other animal, you know that we would make our own bodily postures as similar as possible to those things.
HE. It seems to me that it must necessarily be as you say.
SO. So, I think, there would come to be a means to indicate something with the body [ἄν ... δήλωμά του τῷ σώματι ἐγίγνετο]:[22] if our body, as it seems, imitated that which one wanted to indicate [μιμησαμένου ... τοῦ σώματος ἐκεῖνο ὃ ἐβούλετο δηλῶσαι].[23]
HE. Yes. (422e1–423b3)

Thus Socrates momentously introduces the notion of an *imitation* of the objects – or rather of their *nature* (a3). This notion will turn out to be the key to the correctness of the primary names. It is also, more generally, a central topic in Plato's reflection on reality and art.

Once again, for the reasons set out in §§4.2.4 and 4.2.6, I have translated δηλοῦν as 'to indicate' (e3, a2, a5; cf. Cambiano 'indicare') and discarded more loaded translations like Méridier's 'représenter'.[24] So the passage's point, summarized by Socrates himself at a8–b2, turns out to be the following: if you are to *indicate* something by gestures, you must *imitate* it or its nature.

The summary contains the noun δήλωμα (a8), a derivative of δηλόω, which occurs here for the first time in extant Greek literature and might

---

[22] At a8 του τῷ σώματι is Heindorf's correction (accepted by Stallbaum, Hirschig, Méridier, the OCT, Dalimier, and Reeve) of δ's τούτου τῷ σώματι. βT read τοῦ σώματος, emended by Schanz (followed by Burnet, Fowler and Minio-Paluello) into του {σώματος}, 'of something'.
[23] The subject of b2 ἐβούλετο is not 'the body', as it might seem and as many translate, but an understood τις (Ficino, Reeve). Cf. e.g. *Ap.* 29b and see KG 1.35–6.
[24] Bestor 1980: 312–13 and n.4 translates δηλοῦν as 'to communicate'. Many translations offer no single consistent rendering of the verb, either relative to d2 or within this very passage. Reeve, however, renders it as 'to express' everywhere (see §4.2.4 n.49). On δηλοῦν here see further n.27.

even be Plato's coin. Two alternative translations suggest themselves: the abstract 'indica*tion*' ('indicazione' Cambiano) and the concrete 'indica*tor*' (or, less barbarously, 'means to indicate').[25] The latter is clearly mandatory where the name is said to be a δήλωμα, as at 433d, *Sph.* 261d–262a (where δήλωμα seems equivalent to σημεῖον 'sign', as δηλόω to σημαίνω) and other places like *Lg.* 792a. This creates a presumption in favour of a concrete rendering in our line and elsewhere as well.

Thus Socrates claims that *gestural indication entails gestural imitation*. Is he right? Two objections could be raised, because he seems to disregard two alternative forms of gestural indication: (i) indicating things by *pointing* at them, (ii) indicating things by means of non-mimetic, purely *conventional* gestures. The former objection would misfire. For even granting, for the sake of argument, that you can indicate ordinary objects like horses or stones by simply pointing at them, without any further specification of what the pointing is meant to indicate, still there are clearly many cases where pointing is *not* a viable option: indicating an absent object, or an object together with some of its properties (note that a4 θέοντα is probably predicative: not 'indicating a running horse', but 'indicating a horse *as running*').[26] The latter objection, instead, is successful. Option (ii) is a real one: indeed, today the standard language used by dumb persons contains many signs whose mimetic power is unrecognizable or nonexistent. Socrates, therefore, ought to recognize that gestures may be significant without being imitations. His failure to recognize this can, however, be explained and partly excused. Option (ii) is after all rather outlandish, since as a matter of fact most gestures used in everyday life do have a certain mimetic power. And of course Socrates' disregard for this possibility is dictated by the very purpose of his argument. He aims to account for the primary names in naturalist terms and, more precisely, in terms of imitation of the names' referents; so, if he acknowledged that gestures may indicate by convention, he would wreck the argument, and he might as well conclude that names too are conventional. In fact, when a little below it finally comes to names, he will commit a perfectly analogous fallacy, inferring that names imitate from the fact that they indicate (see §6.2.3).[27]

---

[25] Some nouns in -μα, though probably they were once *nomina actionis*, have a concrete meaning and indicate objects which accomplish (or are *means* to accomplish) certain actions: e.g. ὄμμα 'eye'. Cf. Bolelli 1953: 54–9, Risch 1974: 49–50. Neither Bolelli nor Chantraine 1933: 175–90 discuss δήλωμα.

[26] Indeed, more accurately we should say that mere pointing is *always* ambiguous. See Quine 1960: 52–3.

[27] The latter objection might be redirected against my own translation of δηλοῦν. All problems would seem to vanish if δηλοῦν had a stronger meaning than 'to indicate', perhaps like Méridier's

6.2.3 Indication by vocal mimesis (423bc)

We can now follow Socrates' next step. As you might expect, he proceeds to export his conclusions concerning gestures to the *vocal* sphere:

SO. But since we want to indicate with voice, tongue and mouth, the product of these organs will be a means to indicate each thing then [τότε ἑκάστου δήλωμα ἡμῖν ἔσται τὸ ἀπὸ τούτων γιγνόμενον], when an imitation concerning a thing whatsoever comes to be through them [ὅταν μίμημα γένηται διὰ τούτων περὶ ὁτιοῦν] – won't it?
HE. Necessarily, it seems to me. (423b4–8)

Socrates' main point here is clear: *vocal* indication too, like gestural indication, consists in the imitation of an object. Note that, while the claims about gestural indication were presented in counterfactual form ('if we had no voice ...': 422e–423b), now we have a causal sentence, describing the actual situation ('but since we want ...').[28] As a matter of fact, Socrates and his friends are *not* dumb and do not communicate by gestures.

The analogy between gestures and spoken sounds is of course objectionable. Gestural signs do mostly follow mimetic patterns of some sort, though strictly speaking they need not do so. But the same does not hold of vocal signs, which both need not be and in fact *are not*, for the most part, governed by any such criterion. Nevertheless, we shall give Socrates his faulty analogy.

The analogy is put forward in a Cratylan spirit. The sounds issuing from our mouth, Socrates says, constitute 'for us' (ἡμῖν: ethical dative, not translated above) a 'means to indicate' just when (τότε ... ὅταν) they constitute an imitation of something. Otherwise – it is implied – our sounds indicate nothing at all. Here we can recognize a version of Cratylus' initial thesis, taken in its radical form (see §1.1.3): if our sounds do not conform to a natural criterion, then they are not names and do not indicate anything at all.

Now for a subtle point. A few lines above, mimetic gestures were introduced as a means to *indicate the objects* (δηλοῦν ... τὰ πράγματα, 422e3)

'représenter' or Dalimier's 'faire voir': if we assume that we want to *represent* things, then it does follow that we should *imitate* them. Cf. Robinson (1969: 133): 'From the account of the name as a description or revelation or δήλωμα, the speakers are led to conceive it as an imitation or μίμημα.' Nonetheless, I hope what I said in §§4.2.4, 4.2.6 is enough to show that we should not translate δηλοῦν otherwise. I add that a strong translation risks making Socrates' claim into something even *too* obvious, almost a tautology – which it had better not be.

[28] The causal translation of ἐπειδή (b4) is adopted by Méridier and Cambiano. Others have 'when' or 'if', but then we should probably have ἐπειδάν + subjunctive.

in the world: what is light or heavy, animals, etc. Therefore, when at 423b5 Socrates speaks of 'indicating' (δηλοῦν) with the voice, without specifying *what* we should indicate, it is natural to understand 'indicating [the objects]' again. This is confirmed by the immediately following expression ἑκάστου δήλωμα, 'a means to indicate each thing' (b5). Thus Socrates here seems to be assuming that the function of spoken sounds, as of gestures, consists – at least partly – in indicating things or objects. This is different from what we have been told so far and will be told again elsewhere, i.e. that names *indicate the objects' being* or nature (393de), or what each thing is like (422d, cf. 428e). Generally speaking, indicating something is not the same as, and does not entail, indicating its properties.

What is interesting about the difference between the two notions is that the former is, whereas the latter is not, neutral in the debate between nature and convention in names. For the moment the inconsistency is eased by the fact that at 422e–423b Socrates appeared to be speaking (also) of indicating things *along with their properties*, or things *as qualified somehow* (see §6.2.2). But at 433d–434a Socrates will end up claiming unqualifiedly that names indicate objects and presenting this as common ground between conventionalism and naturalism. The identification of this common ground will then play a decisive role in Socrates' subsequent argument in favour of convention (434b–435d).

None of the questions we have just discussed – in particular, not the faultiness of Socrates' analogy – seems to occur to Hermogenes, whose critical-mindedness is nodding in this phase of the dialogue. Thus nothing stops Socrates from reaching a tongue-twisting definition:

SO. Therefore a name is, as it seems, a vocal imitation of that which it imitates [μίμημα φωνῇ ἐκείνου ὃ μιμεῖται], and he who imitates with his voice names whatever he imitates [καὶ ὀνομάζει ὁ μιμούμενος τῇ φωνῇ ὃ ἂν μιμῆται].
HE. So it seems to me. (423b9–12)

Quite understandably, some interpreters have been stunned by this rigmarole. My own perplexities concern μιμεῖται (b10). Since what Socrates has just said is that vocal indication consists in vocal imitation, now I would expect him to conclude that a name is a vocal imitation of what it *indicates* – not of what it *imitates*. So I would write δηλοῖ in place of μιμεῖται, which could have easily ousted it in this context (cf. especially the following ὃ ἂν μιμῆται).

However that may be, the gist of the definition is that a name is a vocal imitation of its referent. The generality of this claim is noteworthy. 'A name' ought to mean 'all names'; but what we are after, as 422cd has made clear, is

The correctness of primary names (422c–424a)

rather an account of *one* specific kind of names, i.e. primary names, which are different from secondary ones. That is to say, Socrates here seems to speak as if primary names were the only kind of names. He will do the same on several other occasions (425a, 430ab, 431d, 434ab); and yet he will continue to assert the primary/secondary distinction (425b, 426ab). The explanation is, I take it, that Socrates has a certain strong conception of the priority of primary names, according to which, insofar as they are the elements of all other names, they are the *most fundamental* names, while the others are merely derived from them by combination and hence are, in a sense, parasitical upon them. That this is so is confirmed by 427cd, where Socrates explicitly avers that secondary names too are *imitations* of their referents. Thus *secondary names are assimilated to primary ones*. We shall return to this issue in §§6.3.4 and 6.4.3 (where I argue that the assimilation is actually unwarranted).

Socrates, however, is discontented with his definition, though not for the reason we have just discussed. Thus he replies to Hermogenes' b12 formula of assent:

SO. But, by Zeus, *to me* it doesn't yet seem to be a fine thing to say, my friend.
HE. Why?
SO. We would be forced to grant that these people who imitate sheep and cocks and the other animals name these things which they imitate.
HE. That's true.
SO. So does this seem to you to be fine?
HE. Not to me. But, Socrates, what sort of imitation should the name be? [τίς ἂν … μίμησις εἴη τὸ ὄνομα;] (423c1–10)

Generally speaking, the imitation of an animal's cry does not constitute a name of that animal. This, however, does not lead Socrates and Hermogenes to reject the idea that a (primary) name is a vocal imitation of something. Rather, it remains to find out what *specific* sort of vocal imitation a name is.

Before seeing how Socrates completes the definition, it would be nice to understand better his reference to the people who imitate animal cries. According to Stallbaum 171, the reference is very generic: 'istos homines de plebe vel pueros, quicunque demum sunt'. This is certainly part of what Socrates has in mind, but, I think, not the whole of it. For one thing, Socrates might be thinking, more precisely, of performances of *mimes*: Arist. *Aud.* 800a25–9 speaks of people who imitate the cries of 'almost all animals', and Plutarch, *Quomodo adul.* 18c, mentions a Parmeno and a Theodorus who were good at imitating a pig and a pulley respectively. For another thing, Socrates might be (indeed, probably *is*, as the following lines will suggest) thinking also of something to do with poetry and its performance. Animal cries occur time and again in Aristophanes' comedies (e.g. *Av.* 227–8, 237, 260–2; *Ra.* 209–68); at *Pl.* 290–5 a character urges the chorus to 'bleat songs of sheep and smelly goats'. Furthermore, our passage is reminiscent of *Republic* 3, where Socrates decries the imitation of 'horses neighing and bulls lowing and rivers roaring and sea resounding and thunders' (396b) and of 'thunders and noises of winds and hails, and of axles and pulleys, and sounds of trumpets, flutes, panpipes and all instruments, and moreover cries of dogs, sheep, and birds' (397a). There, as in the parallel *Lg.* 669cd, the *poets*' use of onomatopoeia is at stake (along with their use of programme music and sound effects).[29]

6.2.4 Vocal imitation of the essence (423c–424a)

Socrates and Hermogenes have to round off the definition of what a (primary) name is. Socrates tackles this new stage of the inquiry by first insisting on what a name is *not*:

SO. It seems to me that we shall not be naming, first, if we imitate the objects as [καθάπερ] we imitate them in music – although then too we imitate them with the voice – and secondly, if we imitate the very items which [ἅπερ] music imitates. (423c11–d4)

This sudden introduction of 'music' into the argument as a kind of *vocal* imitation may at first seem surprising. But it can be explained, if we suppose that the term μουσική here has its broad sense, covering poetry as well as music proper (see 406a; *Phd.* 60e–61a; *R.* 373b, 376e, 398b; *Lg.* 669b), and that poets were included among the imitators of the previous passage, as I anticipated above (§6.2.3).

Socrates' claim is that 'musical' imitation is different from naming in the twofold respect of (a) *how* the imitation comes about, (b) *what* gets imitated. In what follows he illustrates first and foremost (b):

(SO.) What do I mean thereby? Do the objects have each a sound and a shape, and many of them a colour as well? [ἔστι τοῖς πράγμασι φωνὴ καὶ σχῆμα ἑκάστῳ, καὶ χρῶμά γε πολλοῖς;]
HE. Of course.
SO. It seems, then, that the onomastic art is not involved if one imitates these features, and does not concern these imitations. For the arts involved therein are respectively music and painting, aren't they?
HE. Yes. (423d4–10)

---

[29] On the *R.* passages see Stanford 1973 and Burnyeat 1999: 270–1.

The correctness of primary names (422c–424a)

This passage falls into two parts. In the first one (d4–6) Socrates gets Hermogenes to agree that each object has a sound[30] and a shape, and many have a colour. The 'objects' he is talking about may be either *particular* material objects (whether animate or inanimate) or *kinds* thereof. The latter possibility is perhaps preferable, because all the instances of primary names in the dialogue are general terms, not proper names (421c, 426d–427c), and because the cases of imitation which have been compared with naming also seemed to concern kinds (a running horse, 423a; a sheep, 423c; etc.) rather than particulars. In any case, Socrates seems to imply that many *but not all* of the objects having sound and shape also have colour; that is, there are some sounding and shaped but colourless objects. The reference is probably to stretches of water, although it is not impossible that Socrates may have glass in mind.[31]

In the passage's second part (d7–10) Socrates and Hermogenes agree that the onomastic art, i.e. the art whose practitioner is the lawgiver or 'onomaturge' (cf. 388e–389a), is not concerned with the imitation of such features of an object as its sound, shape and colour. That is to say, names do not imitate such features, which rather fall within the province of music (sound) and painting (shape and colour). Thereby the passage begins to explain the previous claim that names do not imitate the same *items* as music does (d2–4), while at the same time enlarging the perspective to consider painting too.

The explanation Socrates offers, however, is unsatisfactory, precisely as far as his reference to imitation of sound is concerned. Although at c4–6 he was certainly right in distinguishing names from the mere imitation of animal cries (or, for that matter, of any other sound), now he seems to overlook the fact that many genuine names do, after all, have an onomatopoeic value. Note also that Socrates seems to suggest that sound is the *only* feature of an object that music imitates – surely an implausibly restrictive characterization of the scope of music. In fact, Plato is forcing the discussion towards a definite thesis, which begins to surface in the next lines.

---

[30] While at 423b and d2 φωνή means 'voice', here at d4 its meaning must be as generic as possible: Socrates is generalizing from the case of vocal imitation of animal cries to the case of vocal imitation of any *sound* whatsoever. Cf. *Chrm.* 168d, *R.* 507c, *Tht.* 156c, 185a, *Ti.* 67b, and see Ax 1986: 107–8.

[31] Colourless glass is usually said to have been rare in Greece before the discovery of glass-blowing (probably first century BC). But it seems to have been available in Asia Minor since the eighth–seventh century BC (see Stern 2007: 346–7).

so. And what about this? Doesn't it seem to you that each thing also has an essence [οὐ καὶ οὐσία δοκεῖ σοι εἶναι ἑκάστῳ] as well as a colour and the features we were saying just now? Don't, in the first place, colour itself and sound each have an essence [πρῶτον αὐτῷ τῷ χρώματι καὶ τῇ φωνῇ οὐκ ἔστιν οὐσία τις ἑκατέρῳ αὐτῶν], and so all the other things which deserve this appellation, 'to be' [καὶ τοῖς ἄλλοις πᾶσιν ὅσα ἠξίωται ταύτης τῆς προσρήσεως, τοῦ εἶναι]?

he. So it seems to me. (423e1–6)

The notions and distinctions introduced in these lines are extremely interesting in themselves, quite apart from their immediate context: as Barney 2001: 88 puts it, 'Socrates now gently advances the ontological subplot of the dialogue.' This subplot started at 385e–386e, with the discussion of Protagoras' thesis and the conclusion that the objects have a subject-independent being, and has further developed with the introduction of the theory of forms, the Principle of Synonymical Generation and the theory of flux.

In the first sentence (e1–2) Socrates contrasts properties like sound, shape and colour with the οὐσία of each thing. Here the term οὐσία cannot be as generic as it was at 388c or 393d (see §§3.2.1, 4.2.4), where it was a mere nominalization of the copula and stood in for *any* property, as ascribed in a predication of the form '... is *F*'. Therefore we are entitled to suppose that it is equivalent to something like 'essence' (i.e. what each thing really is, what is specified in a correct definition) or at least 'essential feature' (i.e. any component in something's essence, like *animal* in *biped animal*). In any event, 'essence' is the translation I adopt.[32]

This construal is borne out a few lines below by the occurrence of the quasi-technical phrase 'what each thing is' (ἕκαστον ὅ ἐστιν, e9). Indeed, οὐσία probably began to mean 'essence' as early as 401cd, in the course of the etymology of Ἑστία (see §5.2.3), where Socrates derived Ἑστία from ἐσσία, allegedly a dialectal variant of οὐσία, and said that Ἑστία/ἐσσία refers to ἡ τῶν πραγμάτων οὐσία ('the οὐσία *of the objects*') or τὴν πάντων οὐσίαν ('the οὐσία *of all things*'). Those expressions would be odd, if οὐσία meant 'being' in the most generic sense; but they are perfectly natural, if the term is instead used to refer to something like the nature or essence of all things. And that this is so is confirmed by the following etymology of ὠσία, the other alleged dialectal variant of οὐσία, from ὠθοῦν, 'pushing',

---

[32] Cf. Crivelli 2008: 227. I have considered sticking to 'being' throughout. But this would make it difficult to render the 424b distinction between ὄν and οὐσία.

referring to the active principle of change. That too suggests that the οὐσία is meant to be something like the true nature of all things.

At e2–5 Socrates proceeds to expand on his initial statement. He starts (e2–4) by remarking that the other features themselves have an οὐσία. To put it in Aristotelian terms, in relation to a given subject we can distinguish the essence from the accidents, but then the accidents themselves have their own essence. Our lines are especially reminiscent of *Top.* 1.9, where Aristotle first distinguishes the essential question τί ἐστι; ('what is it?') from other questions ('how much?', 'how qualified?' etc.) which can be asked about a given subject, then says that τί ἐστι; can be asked about entities of *any* kind, substances as well as qualities, quantities etc.[33]

Possession of an οὐσία is next (e4–5) further extended from colour and sound to 'all the other things which deserve this appellation, "to be" [εἶναι]'. This step requires some comment. Here εἶναι could presumably be (and in fact is sometimes) translated as 'to exist'. Therefore essence is being extended from colour and sound to all the other things that can be said[34] to exist. This is likely to be meant as a most inclusive label; the passage's train of thought, however, suggests that Socrates has primarily universals in mind rather than particulars.[35] Essence was first attributed to 'objects' which seemed to be *kinds* rather than particulars (d4, see above); then we have moved on to *properties* of these objects, like sound, shape and colour; now we shift further to whatever else exists, presumably keeping on the same level of generality.

Thus at e3–5 Socrates holds that

(1) X ἐστί → X has an οὐσία,

that is to say,

(1*) X exists → X has an essence.

The paraphrase, however, conceals the close etymological relation between οὐσία and εἶναι. Socrates is perhaps stressing this relation when he introduces εἶναι as '*this* appellation', which may involve a back-reference to

---

[33] On τί ἐστι in *Top.* 1.9 see Frede 1981: 36–9. The parallel with *Cra.* is noted by Sedley 2003: 84 and n.15.
[34] The term πρόσρησις (e5) means no more than 'appellation' (Méridier), 'denomination' or the like: cf. *Plt.* 258a, 306e, and πρόσρημα *Phdr.* 238b, προσρητέος *R.* 428b, 431d. Those who translate 'predicate' (Minio-Paluello, Sedley 2003: 61 n.24, cf. Dalimier) go too far.
[35] In any case, particulars need not be excluded. The fact that they are sometimes said to 'be' to a lesser degree than the forms is irrelevant: cf. *Phd.* 79a etc.

οὐσία in the previous line. (1*) might prove controversial; but (1) sounds, and is certainly meant to sound, almost as a truism.

This brings us to the heart of complex issues about the use of the verb 'to be' in ancient Greek philosophy. Roughly and briefly, Plato, as well as Aristotle, seems to recognize no sharp distinction between the complete use of εἶναι to mean 'to exist' and the incomplete use where εἶναι expresses predication or identity. For both Plato and Aristotle, to quote Owen's slogan, 'to be is always to be something or other'. Plato seems to see between two sentences like 'Callias is' and 'Callias is just' a relation analogous to the one obtaining between 'Jane is teaching' and 'Jane is teaching French': '*X is* (complete use) entails *X is something* and *X is F* entails *X is*. *X is not* (complete use) is equivalent to *X is not anything at all*.'[36] Aristotle's own view of the matter is partly different from Plato's: Aristotle seems to think that '*X is F*' entails '*X is*' not for any substitution of '*F*', but only for those substitutions which are *essential* predicates of *X*. Thus for Callias to be is to be a substance of some kind, whereas for whiteness to be is to be a quality of some kind, etc.[37] Now it is in Aristotle's direction, rather than in Plato's standard one, that our *Cra.* passage seems to go at first glance, with its close connection between something's εἶναι and its having an οὐσία. But perhaps we need not suppose that Plato here is assuming such a direct tie between a thing's existence and its essence. Perhaps his idea here is rather the following. If *X is* (= exists), then *X is* variously characterized; and if *X is* variously characterized, then there must also be something which *X is* in a special and fundamental way, something which makes it into the very thing it *is*. So whatever *is* (= exists) also has an *essence*. Thus the tie between existence and essence is not direct, as in Aristotle, but merely indirect.

So far so good. Socrates' brief remarks about οὐσία, however, exciting as they may be for us, are firmly placed in the context of his argument. Hence we must not lose sight of what he is driving at. In the following lines he begins to show his hand:

SO. What then? If one were able to imitate this very feature of each thing, its essence [τὴν οὐσίαν], with letters and syllables [γράμμασί τε καὶ συλλαβαῖς], he would indicate what each thing is, wouldn't he? [ἆρ' οὐκ ἂν δηλοῖ ἕκαστον ὅ ἐστιν;]
HE. Certainly. (423e7–424a1)

These lines contain several very important points. To appreciate the first two you must bear in mind Socrates' earlier claim that naming differs

---

[36] Brown 1999: 477. Cf. Brown 1994 and Burnyeat 2003.
[37] See Owen 1965: 264–78, Kahn 1978: 259–61, Dancy 1986: 49–59.

from music and painting with respect both to *how* and to *what* we imitate (423cd).

(i) After introducing essence as a special feature of each thing, distinct from other features like sound, shape and colour (imitated by music and painting), Socrates now explicitly envisages the possibility of *imitating the essence* of something. That is to say, essence too is something that can be imitated.

(ii) Socrates specifies that he is thinking of imitation by means of 'letters and syllables' (e8). This probably hints at the question of the *mode* of imitation, which so far the argument had left untouched. The use of letters and syllables constitutes, I think, the mode of the new kind of imitation; as such it is being implicitly contrasted with the mode distinctive of music and painting. The difference from painting need not detain us; Socrates himself had explicitly contrasted naming and painting only in terms of their objects (423d). With music the matter is more interesting. Musical notes are obviously unlike letters and syllables. But what about imitations of animal cries, which Socrates seemed to include in 'music' (423cd)? Perhaps Socrates thinks that animal cries, and hence also their realistic imitations, consist of inarticulate sounds and do not contain letters and syllables. Aristotle might object that some animals are able to articulate letters, γράμματα, with their tongue (*HA* 504b1–3, *PA* 660a14–b2), though he also says that animal sounds are not στοιχεῖα because they do not combine to form syllables (*Po.* 1456b22–37). Another counterexample to Socrates' claim is constituted by onomatopoeic words like the Aristophanic βρεκεκεκὲξ κοὰξ κοὰξ, which are made of letters and syllables and which, in the discussion above, as well as in §6.2.3, seemed to us to be part of what Socrates had in mind.

(iii) Socrates says that he who could imitate the essence with letters and syllables 'would indicate what each thing is' (e9). Thereby he is recalling 422d, where he stated that what every name does is 'to indicate what each of the beings is like' (δηλοῦν οἷον ἕκαστόν ἐστι τῶν ὄντων) and then set about inquiring how this generic function was performed by primary names. Now Socrates is eager to stress that imitation of essence with letters and syllables meets that initial requirement. The fact that we are back where we began is a clear signal that the inquiry into the primary names has achieved its goal.

This becomes explicit in the next lines:

SO.   And what would you call the man who is able to do this? The previous ones you called musician and painter respectively; what would you call this one?

HE. To me, Socrates, he seems to be this thing we were searching for a while ago: it seems to me that this would be the onomast [ὁ ὀνομαστικός]. (424a2–6)

So this is the conclusion: the 'onomast', i.e. the namegiver or lawgiver who was introduced at 388e–389a, is able to imitate the essence of each thing with letters and syllables. A corresponding definition of names is clearly implied: names – or perhaps, more precisely, *primary* names – are imitations, in letters and syllables, of the essence of things.

6.3 THE IMPOSITION OF PRIMARY NAMES (424A–425B)

6.3.1 The etymologies of primary names: false start (424ab)

Now that we have got an account of the correctness of primary names, it would seem natural to return to the question which first sparked off the search for it. This is just what Socrates does:

SO. If this is true, therefore, it seems that we must next inquire into those names you asked me about, ῥοή and ἰέναι and σχέσις, whether or not with their letters and syllables they lay hold of their being [εἰ τοῖς γράμμασι καὶ ταῖς συλλαβαῖς τοῦ ὄντος ἐπιλαμβάνεται αὐτῶν] so as to imitate their essence [ὥστε ἀπομιμεῖσθαι τὴν οὐσίαν].
HE. Certainly. (424a7–b3)

Actually, for the moment Socrates will not manage to present any etymologies of primary names; other concerns are going to distract him until 426c. Anyway the passage, apart from its promissory role, is a tricky one. I shall first examine its difficulties on the assumption that the text goes as the main editions print it, then try out a different approach.

(a) Hermogenes' original question at 421c was about the names ἰόν 'going', ῥέον 'flowing', δοῦν 'binding'. But here Socrates rather seems to say that it was about ῥοή 'flux', ἰέναι 'to go' and σχέσις 'restraint'. This seeming inaccuracy has not greatly worried interpreters: after all, elsewhere Plato has Socrates maintain that too much care in the use of words is 'unworthy of a free man' (*Tht.* 184c). Barney 2001: 83 n.3 also plausibly suggests that primary names 'include all roots not susceptible to etymology, which we can pick out by whatever cognate we please'. Note, however, that – unlike ἰέναι and ῥοή – the word σχέσις has *no* extrinsic connection with the corresponding item in Hermogenes' question, i.e. δοῦν. The only connection between σχέσις and δοῦν is a *semantic* one. Hence all we can say is perhaps that Plato is inaccurately substituting ῥοή for ῥέον and ἰέναι for ἰόν, and mistakenly substituting σχέσις for δοῦν.

The imposition of primary names (424a–425b) 281

(b) Consider the phrase 'lay hold of their being' (b1). The verb's grammatical subject is not 'the onomast' from a6, as is generally assumed, but 'those names which you asked me about' (a8), as Ficino saw. The problem is that 'their' (αὐτῶν) should not refer to the names ῥοή ἰέναι σχέσις, as might seem natural, but to their *referents*.[38] What we must examine is whether the names in question express with their letters and syllables what *their referents* are 'so as to imitate their essence'. (In this last consecutive clause we may perhaps suppose that the terms 'imitate' and 'essence' are *specifications* of the more generic 'lay hold of' and 'being' respectively.)

So far we have made acceptable sense of the passage as editors print it. I shall now illustrate a partly different way of reading the text, which may deserve discussion. To start with, note an interesting relation between the two trios ἰόν ῥέον δοῦν and ῥοή ἰέναι σχέσις. To each of the participles in the former trio there corresponds, in the latter trio, either a *noun* from the same root (ῥέον ~ ῥοή) or something which may do duty for it: a semantically equivalent noun from another root (δοῦν ~ σχέσις) or the infinitive of the same verb (ἰόν ~ ἰέναι). So I submit that by the terms ῥοή, ἰέναι and σχέσις Socrates might be referring, not to the *names* which were the object of Hermogenes' question, but rather to the *things* (flux, going, restraint) *signified* by those names. That is to say, the three terms ought to be printed without quotation marks. This proposal clears Socrates' back-reference of sloppiness and has also a further advantage: now the things to which b1 αὐτῶν must refer are actually there in the text to be referred to. So the sense would be:

we must next inquire into those names you asked me about, [i.e.] inquire into flux and going and restraint, whether they [sc. those names] with their letters and syllables lay hold of *their* being [= the being of flux, going and restraint].

6.3.2 *Division of letters (424bc)*

We shall now see what new concerns keep Socrates, as I anticipated above, from immediately reverting to Hermogenes' question about ἰόν, ῥέον and δοῦν. In the next subsections we are going to speak of division by kinds, the project of a perfect language, the difference between imposing names and reconstructing the work of previous imposers, and yet other topics.

Rather than answering the question, with a characteristic move Socrates first reacts by widening his perspective:

---

[38] So Fowler and Reeve. Méridier, Minio-Paluello and Dalimier take αὐτῶν to refer to the *names*.

so. Come on, let us see whether among the first names there are only these or there are many others.
he. For my part, I think there are others too.
so. Yes, that's likely. But what should be the procedure of the division whence the imitator begins to imitate? [τίς ἂν εἴη ὁ τρόπος τῆς διαιρέσεως ὅθεν ἄρχεται μιμεῖσθαι ὁ μιμούμενος;][39] (424b4–8)

This, however, is too long a step. Socrates is taking for granted that the person who imposes the primary names ('the imitator') must begin with a division of some sort. This very point, however, is far from obvious and needs to be established. Socrates probably realizes this at once, because he reformulates his question in a more satisfactory way:

(so.) Given that the imitation of the essence happens to proceed by means of syllables and letters, isn't it most correct to divide up first of all the letters [διελέσθαι τὰ στοιχεῖα πρῶτον], as those who set to work on rhythms first divide up the powers [τὰς δυνάμεις] of letters, then those of syllables, and thus at that point come to examine rhythms, not before?
he. Yes. (424b8–c5)

The new question opens with a positive proposal about the imitator's division: first of all he ought to divide up the letters. Then Socrates does not directly proceed to submit to Hermogenes further stages of the imitator's work; he rather switches to a comparison with students of rhythms. This comparison supports the initial proposal about names and also anticipates its following stages. Students of rhythms, it is said, first divide the 'powers' of letters, then those of syllables, and only after doing this do they undertake the examination of rhythms. This already suggests that, in the same way, the maker of primary names will first divide letters, then syllables, and only after accomplishing these divisions will he be able to deal with full-blown names.

The study of rhythms here at issue, and the divisions which must precede it, coincide partly with our *metrics* and *prosody* respectively. The preliminary divisions will presumably distinguish various sorts of letters/sounds on the grounds of their articulation (which Socrates seems to refer to by the term δύναμις, c2; cf. §4.2.4), as we are going to see, and identify their contribution to the quantity of each syllable. As for the study of rhythm, it will then concern the combination of long and short syllables to form feet, metres and verses, as at *R*. 399e–400c, where Socrates illustrates this discipline mentioning dactyls, iambs, trochees and other metrical units.

---

[39] Not: 'how are we to divide off *the ones* with which the imitator begins his imitation?' (Reeve, with my italics; cf. Stallbaum 174, Méridier).

Socrates' ascription of the classification of letters to experts in rhythm fits well with Aristotle's claim (*Po.* 1456b31–8, cf. *PA* 660a7–8) that *metrics* deals with differences in articulation, aspiration, quantity and accent among letters, as well as with the various kinds of syllables. Generally speaking, ancient reflection on language seems to have originated from the study of poetry: Protagoras' distinctions of the grammatical genera and of four kinds of clause were apparently set forth within a discussion of the *Iliad*'s first line.[40] Such inquiries can be associated with some definite figures. In the *R.* passage Socrates mentions Damon as his expert on matters of rhythm;[41] but Socrates' reference to the preliminary prosodic divisions has no correspondence in the reports about Damon's activities. Rather, they perfectly match a passage in the description of Hippias' multifarious competences at *Hp. Ma.* 285cd (cf. *Hp. Mi.* 368d), where Socrates refers to 'those things which you are able to *divide* [διαιρεῖν] most precisely amongst men, about the *power of letters and syllables* and about *rhythms* and harmonies [περί τε γραμμάτων δυνάμεως καὶ συλλαβῶν καὶ ῥυθμῶν καὶ ἁρμονιῶν]'. We should also bear in mind that Democritus is reported by D.L. 9.47–8 (68 A33 = 0.6.1 Leszl) to have written works entitled *Explanations about Sounds, On Rhythms and Harmony* and *On Euphonious and Cacophonous Letters*.[42]

In the following lines Socrates returns to the making of primary, mimetic names:

SO. So mustn't we too, in the same way, first divide the vowels [πρῶτον μὲν τὰ φωνήεντα διελέσθαι], then of the others, according to their kinds, the voiceless and soundless [ἔπειτα τῶν ἑτέρων κατὰ εἴδη τά τε ἄφωνα καὶ ἄφθογγα] – this, I think, is how the experts on these matters express themselves – and then those which aren't vowels but aren't soundless either [καὶ τὰ αὖ φωνήεντα μὲν οὔ, οὐ μέντοι γε ἄφθογγα]? And divide, among vowels themselves, all their mutually different kinds [καὶ αὐτῶν τῶν φωνηέντων ὅσα διάφορα εἴδη ἔχει ἀλλήλων]?[43] (424c6–d1)

---

[40] Cf. Arist. *Rh.* 1407b7–8 = 80 A27 DK with *SE* 173b17–22 = A28 (both texts are cited in §4.1); D. L. 9.53–4 = A1 with Arist. *Po.* 1456b15–1 = A29; and see Fehling 1965: 212–14.
[41] On Damon see 37 DK. On his relations with Socrates see especially *La.* 180cd, 197d.
[42] On this whole matter see Burkert 1959: 178–9. Following Belardi 1985: 41–2 n.25, we may also mention Archinus, who advocated the introduction of the Ionic alphabet in Athens in 403–2, and to whom Alex. Aphr. *in Metaph.* 834.5–11 ascribes analyses of the articulation of some sounds.
[43] ὅσα (c10) goes with διάφορα εἴδη and is the *object* of ἔχει: we must divide up all the different specific forms that the kind of vowel embraces. Minio-Paluello instead takes ὅσα as the *subject* of ἔχει: 'dei vocali stessi quanti hanno specie diverse fra loro' (cf. Reeve 'those that differ in kind from one another').

The suggested procedure, in the order in which Socrates illustrates it, seems to go as follows: (i) isolate ('divide', sc. from the rest) the *vowels*; (ii) among the *other* letters, distinguish the voiceless and soundless from the voiceless (he says 'not vowels') but not soundless, and distinguish their various kinds; (iii) distinguish also the various kinds of vowels. That is to say:

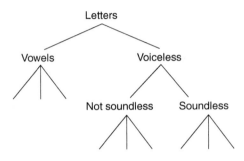

Thus we have a tripartition of letters within a more basic *bipartition* between vowels and 'voiceless' = consonants, which was mentioned in 393e and is also attested in Euripides, *TrGF* 578. The same scheme is presupposed in *Tht.* 203b, where we are given examples: σ is 'one of the voiceless ones, a mere sound' (τῶν ἀφώνων ἐστί, ψόφος τις μόνον), while β 'has neither voice nor sound' (οὔτε φωνὴ οὔτε ψόφος), like most other letters. On the other hand, a neatly tripartite scheme is offered at *Phlb.* 18bc as an instance of the division method; the voiceless but sounded (= not soundless) letters are there said to be 'intermediate' (μέσα) between the other two kinds. The tripartition returns, with other examples and different terminology, in Arist. *Po.* 20.1456b25–31:[44] 'The species of letters are vowel, semivowel [ἡμίφωνον] and voiceless. A vowel is pronounced without contact [sc. of tongue and palate or teeth, or between lips: *PA* 660a4–7] and has audible voice; a semivowel is pronounced with contact and has audible voice, like σ and ρ; a voiceless is pronounced with contact and by itself has no audible voice, but together with those which have some voice becomes audible, like γ and δ'. Thus Plato's distinction between two kinds of 'voiceless', and Aristotle's distinction between semivowel and voiceless, seem

---

[44] On Aristotle see the discussion in Belardi 1985: 68–86. The Platonic and Aristotelian accounts may be compared with that of [Dion. Thr.] 6.

roughly equivalent to our distinction between *continuous* and *momentary* (or stop, or *mute*) consonants.

The historical and linguistic details we have been considering so far should not distract us from a basic fact. Division by kinds or forms, i.e. the division of a kind into subkinds and species, down to the smallest ones, is regarded by Plato in several dialogues as a fundamental method of philosophical inquiry, and as a task, if not *the* task, of dialectic.[45] He sketches a number of directions to this effect in *Phdr.* 265e–266b, 277b, and *Phlb.* 16c–18d (where, as we have said, the method is exemplified precisely in relation to letters). In the *Sophist* (on which see further §6.3.3) and *Politicus* he gives lengthy concrete examples of divisions, insisting on the worth of the method itself. *Cra.* is often ignored in accounts of Platonic division, but in fact it seems to occupy a significant place in its history. Here division is not directly linked with dialectic; but there is an indirect connection between the figure of the dialectician and the task of 'separating the objects as they stand', which *is* germane to division (see 388bc, 390cd, and §§3.2.1, 3.4.4; cf. Barney 2001: 100).

The significance of *Cra.* for Platonic division becomes even more evident in the next passage. So far Socrates has been referring to current distinctions about sounds and letters; but now he goes on to apply division to ontology, the study of the things that are.

6.3.3 Division of beings (424d)

We are now entering what is perhaps the textually most difficult and obscure passage of the whole dialogue, whose analysis will detain us for quite a while. It will be convenient to begin with the Greek text, namely that of Méridier and the OCT, which I take to be correct, along with a brief, selective apparatus.

(ΣΩ.) καὶ ἐπειδὰν ταῦτα διελώμεθα, τὰ ὄντα εὖ πάντα αὖ οἷς δεῖ ὀνόματα ἐπιθεῖναι, εἰ ἔστιν εἰς ἃ ἀναφέρεται πάντα ὥσπερ τὰ στοιχεῖα, ἐξ ὧν ἔστιν ἰδεῖν αὐτά τε καὶ εἰ ἐν αὐτοῖς ἔνεστιν εἴδη κατὰ τὸν αὐτὸν τρόπον ὥσπερ ἐν τοῖς στοιχείοις· (424d1–5)

d1   ταῦτα   T δ: πάντα β | τὰ ὄντα del. Beck (prob. Burnet et Fowler) ‖   d2   αὖ οἷς Badham: αὖθις MSS

The context of this pericope already gives us an idea of what its content must be like. At c6–d1 we have just encountered the project of a division

---

[45] On division see Ackrill 1970: 93–109.

of letters; at d5 ff. we are going to read that we must proceed to match letters and beings and thus form names. Therefore it is reasonable to expect this pericope to say, somehow or other, that to the division of letters there must correspond a division of beings (τὰ ὄντα, d1). With this in mind I shall tackle the text with a piecemeal approach.

(i) καὶ ἐπειδὰν ... ἐπιθεῖναι (d1–2). If here we read αὖθις with the MSS, as Stewart 1975 would have us do, then we get the apodosis εὖ πάντα αὖθις δεῖ ὀνόματα ἐπιθεῖναι ('we must in turn impose all names well'). This must be preceded by the protasis ἐπειδὰν πάντα διελώμεθα τὰ ὄντα ('when we have divided *all* beings', reading β's πάντα instead of Tδ's ταῦτα: Socrates cannot say 'when we have divided *these* beings', because the beings have not been mentioned yet). But thereby the whole sentence would appear to be out of place. At this point it is too early to speak of the imposition of names, which is not touched on before 425a1–2; it is the preliminary ontological division that should be at issue here, rather than being quickly assumed by the protasis. Therefore we should accept Badham's economical conjecture,[46] which gives us the phrase τὰ ὄντα ... πάντα αὖ οἷς δεῖ ὀνόματα ἐπιθεῖναι ('in turn all the beings on which we must impose names'), preceded by the protasis ἐπειδὰν ταῦτα διελώμεθα ('when we have divided these', sc. *the letters*). We still lack the verb qualified by εὖ in the apodosis. But from διελώμεθα in the protasis, and from c6–7 δεῖ ... διελέσθαι, we can supply δεῖ διελέσθαι: 'and when we have divided these letters, then in turn [we must divide] well all the beings on which we must impose names' (cf. Méridier, Dalimier, Sedley 2003: 128). Thus Socrates says exactly what he should be saying here.[47]

Admittedly, τὰ ὄντα εὖ πάντα αὖ sounds awkward,[48] as Stewart 1975: 169–70 points out; hence we might consider the possibility of further refinements. For one thing, we might transpose εὖ πάντα into the protasis, either after διελώμεθα (Hermann) or after ταῦτα (Robinson): 'and when we have *well* divided *all* these letters, then in turn [we must divide] the beings on which we must impose names' (cf. d5 ταῦτα πάντα καλῶς διαθεασαμένους). For another thing, we might insert into the text

---

[46] In capital script AYOIΣ is easily mistaken for AYΘIΣ.
[47] Fowler makes a different use of Badham's conjecture. He deletes τὰ ὄντα with Beck and translates: 'And when we have made all these divisions properly [ἐπειδὰν ταῦτα διελώμεθα {τὰ ὄντα} εὖ πάντα], we must in turn give names to the things which ought to have them [αὖ οἷς δεῖ ὀνόματα ἐπιθεῖναι, sc. δεῖ].' The imposition of names is again announced too early, while the division of beings does not receive a clear and distinct mention; moreover, αὖ is first in a sentence, which is not Greek (see LSJ αὖ).
[48] Not, however, because εὖ and αὖ are so close to each other: cf. R. 421a, Ar. fr. 113 *PCG*.

the lacking δεῖ διελέσθαι, e.g. after ἐπιθεῖναι (Robinson). Actually it would suffice to insert just διελέσθαι, either after διελώμεθα or after ἐπιθεῖναι.

(ii) εἰ ἔστιν ... στοιχεῖα (d2–3): literally 'if there are some which all [sc. beings] are referred to like the letters'. If my account of (i) is correct, then 'some' and 'all' mean 'some beings' and 'all beings' respectively. Hence, according to Socrates, one must inquire whether some beings are such that all the others 'are referred to' them. This sounds pretty obscure, but receives some light from the comparison with letters. On a natural reading, ὥσπερ τὰ στοιχεῖα hangs on ἀναφέρεται πάντα: the question is whether there are some beings which all beings are referred to *as letters are*, i.e. as there are some letters which all other letters are referred to.[49] Thus Socrates is recalling the previous division of letters in vowels and voiceless, illustrated at c6 ff.; 'are referred to' actually means 'are brought under';[50] and the beings which all beings 'are referred to' are the *most general kinds* of beings (Méridier: 'en cherchant s'il est des catégories auxquelles ils se ramènent tous, comme les éléments', cf. Stallbaum 176, Sedley 2003: 128). Hereafter I will call such kinds *categories* for brevity.

Socrates does not try to identify these categories, and we should respect his reserve. However, there is reason to suppose that the categories are meant to be just two; for the envisaged division of beings ought to run parallel to a basically *bipartite* division of letters (§6.3.2). And if this is so, we may tentatively recall a bipartite division of beings which seems to have been current in the ancient Academy and is indeed ascribed to Plato himself – who in fact might be mentioning it at *Sph.* 255cd. According to this division, τὰ ὄντα are either 'themselves by themselves' (αὐτὰ καθ' αὑτά: e.g. human being, horse) or 'relative to something' (πρός τι or πρὸς ἕτερα: e.g. larger, double, knowledge, good).[51] We might also be tempted to suspect some sort of connection between these divisions and the distinction, suggested at 393b–394a (see §§4.2.3, 4.2.5), between two classes of

---

[49] Less naturally, ὥσπερ τὰ στοιχεῖα might hang on εἰ ἔστιν εἰς ἃ (d2): the beings which all beings are referred to would then be said to be *like letters*. 'Are referred to' would then mean 'consist of', and the comparison would be with the relation between names and their letters, not between letters and their kinds. Cf. Reeve 'if there are some things to which they can all be carried back, as names are to the letters'. On a closely related construal, ὥσπερ τὰ στοιχεῖα = ὥσπερ πρὸς τὰ στοιχεῖα: 'Plato ... speaks of the basic elements "to which all things are referred as to their στοιχεῖα"' (Kahn 1973a: 166 n.19, cf. Heindorf, Dalimier 'comme à des éléments', Stewart 1975: 171). But it seems to me that this would require ὥσπερ στοιχεῖα, without the article.
[50] On ἀναφέρω cf. *Phd.* 75b, 76d; *R.* 484c; *Phdr.* 237d.
[51] See *Divisiones Aristoteleae* pp. 39–41 Mutschmann (= D. L. 3.108–9 + *Codex Marcianus* 257); Hermodorus *ap.* Simpl. *in Ph.* 248.2–5; Simpl. *in Cat.* 63.22–4; and Dancy 1999. The *Sph.* passage is very controversial: for discussion see Crivelli (forthcoming).

kinds, those of which it holds and those of which it does not hold that 'a *K* begets another *K*'.[52]

(iii) ἐξ ὧν ... στοιχείοις (d3–5): literally 'from which it is possible to see both them and whether there are kinds in them in the same way as in letters'. We can start with ἐξ ὧν. Scholars usually take it to be linked with d2 εἰς ἅ. But its antecedent may also be the immediately preceding τὰ στοιχεῖα, as Barney 2001: 94 n.15 believes.

Consider the former construal. On almost any interpretation, εἰς ἅ refers to a class of beings which are somehow *fundamental* relative to the others (on my interpretation, are categories); then so should ἐξ ὧν too. This is, indeed, the view of Stallbaum 176 and Méridier ('s'il est des catégories auxquelles ... et d'après lesquelles on peut à la fois les voir eux-mêmes et reconnaître s'il existe en eux des espèces comme dans les éléments').[53] Here it is unclear whether the 'them's (αὐτά, ἐν αὐτοῖς) should refer generically to beings or specifically to the categories. Thus Socrates may be saying one of two things: (a) on the basis of (or starting from) the categories, we can 'see' both the beings themselves and whether there are kinds among them; (b) on the basis of (or starting from) the categories, we can see both the categories themselves and whether there are kinds in them. Either way, I doubt that the former conjunct makes good sense. That is to say, I doubt that this construal accounts satisfactorily for the clause ἐξ ὧν ἔστιν ἰδεῖν αὐτά (d3).

On the latter construal, which I prefer, instead, Socrates says that, *on the basis of the parallel with letters* (ἐξ ὧν), we can see both 'them' (αὐτά) and whether there are kinds 'in them' (ἐν αὐτοῖς) as in letters. 'Them' I take to refer to the *categories* of beings mentioned in (ii), at d2 εἰς ἅ: the comparison with letters enables us to 'see', i.e. identify,[54] both those categories and

---

[52] The connection might not be identity. The old Academic division between absolute and relative beings might be more general than the distinction suggested at 393b–394a; in particular, the class of absolute beings might be broader than that of the items of which it holds that a *K* begets another *K*. For while the examples of absolute beings supplied by Hermodorus are 'human being and horse', and those of D. L. 3.108 are 'human beings, horse and the other animals', the *Codex Marcianus* gives the list 'human being, *house, cloak, gold-piece*' (cf. S. E. *M.* 10.263).

[53] Sedley 2003: 128–9 and n.12 takes a partly different view. He would write a comma after εἴδη (d4), a comma after στοιχείοις (d5) where all editions place a colon, and make τε καί (d4) join, not αὐτά (d3) and εἰ ... στοιχείοις (d4–5) as both governed by ἰδεῖν (d3), but rather ἰδεῖν and ἐπίστασθαι (d6) as both governed by ἔστιν (d3). Here is the result: 'proceeding from which we can view them in their own right, and, if they contain species, survey all these, just as we did with the letters, and have a science of applying each one [i.e. each letter] on the basis of likeness'. In addition to the objection I advance in the text, I notice that this involves a strained construal of τε καί (d4; though see *GP* 517 on postponed τε). Also strained is the lack of any pause to take breath at d5, before Socrates introduces the crucial stage where the two divisions are mapped onto each other.

[54] Some favour a very pregnant construal of ἰδεῖν αὐτά. Thus Fowler translates 'see what their nature is' and Barney 2001: 94 n.15 explains that 'Plato is touching on a point made more explicitly later: the letters had better be akin to the elements of things, and so able to reveal them.' But

The imposition of primary names (424a–425b) 289

whether they contain further *more specific kinds* (εἴδη). A parallel prescription was set forth in the case of letters at c6–d1: letters 'other' than vowels (i.e. the voiceless) had to be divided κατ' εἴδη, 'according to their *kinds*', into soundless and sounded; vowels in turn had to be divided into their εἴδη.

Two further notes on this interpretation. First, note the difference in length and emphasis between the two conjuncts '*both* those categories *and* whether they contain further more specific kinds'. Since the categories have already been introduced in (ii), here they receive a merely resumptive mention (αὐτά), only to enable Socrates to move on to their species, which constitute the novelty in (iii) and deserve more space. We could translate: 'to see *not only* [τε] the categories themselves, *but also* [καί] whether there are kinds in them ... etc.' Secondly, 'in the same way as in letters' is redundant; but this is excusable, especially at the end of so long and complex a sentence.[55]

I can now offer a continuous translation of this exceptionally difficult passage:

(SO.) And when we have divided these letters, then in turn [we must divide] well all the beings on which we must impose names, if there are some which all are referred to as letters are, on whose basis it is possible to see not only those beings themselves, but also whether there are kinds in them in the same way as in letters. (424d1–5)

Thereby we are finally in a position to note that this text is importantly reminiscent of another programmatic passage, *Sophist* 253ae.[56] The bare bones of that passage are the following. Among letters some 'harmonize' with each other, some do not, and vowels in particular have the function of connecting the other letters; it is the task of grammar to know which letters combine with which. Analogously, among kinds some mix with each other, some do not. Knowing which mix with which, and what kinds are responsible for the mixing and the division of all the others, is the task of the philosopher-dialectician: he is expert at dividing by kinds, and this

---

the meaning of ἰδεῖν seems plainer, especially because it also governs the following 'whether ...' (In fact Barney seems to sever d4 εἰ from ἰδεῖν, coordinating it with d2 εἰ: εἰ ἔστιν εἰς ἃ ... καὶ εἰ ἐν αὐτοῖς. But the unity of αὐτά τε καὶ εἰ ἐν αὐτοῖς is secured by the τε.)

[55] Cf. e.g. 439b and *Lg.* 793c, where τῶν ἀρχαίων ὑποπεσόντων, which closes the period, is strictly speaking superfluous. In our lines the redundancy would be removed – at the price of a looser connection with what precedes – if ἐξ ὧν were linked to nothing in particular, but picked up more generically what precedes: '*in virtue of all this* it is possible to see not only the categories themselves, but also whether there are kinds in them etc.'

[56] The analogy between things, on the one hand, and letters and syllables, on the other, is exploited elsewhere too: *Tht.* 201e–208b, *Plt.* 277e–278d, *Phlb.* 16c–18d, etc. See *Intr.*, §I.3.2.

amounts to 'knowing how to discern, kind by kind, how things can combine with each other and how they cannot'. That passage and ours share two crucial notions: (a) the structure of the alphabetic/phonetic system is a *model* for understanding the structure of reality, (b) this structure is revealed, at least to a relevant extent, by division by kinds. Of course *Sph.* has a more complex perspective, revealed by the emphasis – which has no parallel in *Cra.* or in the other dialogues concerning division – on the role of vowels and of those kinds (= being and difference) which run through the others, causing their mixing or division. These mutual relations among kinds, which *Sph.* is interested in and partially explores with the sample inquiry into five 'greatest kinds', may cut across vertical divisions.

6.3.4 Matching letters and beings (424d–425a)

Once we have divided letters, on the one hand, and beings, on the other, the next step is to map the two divisions onto each other, matching letters and beings according to their mutual resemblances. Thus we shall construct words whose composition mirrors the nature of their referents.

Before plunging into this long stretch of text, note how sophisticated, and interesting for a history of Platonic division, this strategy is. In the dialogues it seems to have a parallel in the project sketched at *Phdr.* 271a–272a, 277bc (Grote 1888: III.313 n.3): a division of kinds of souls and one of kinds of speeches, which should be brought together to see what kind of soul is persuaded by what kind of speech.[57]

> (SO.) And when we have well examined all these things, we [must] know how to apply each item according to its resemblance [ἐπιφέρειν ἕκαστον κατὰ τὴν ὁμοιότητα], whether we must apply one to one, or many, mixing them together, to one [ἐάντε ἓν ἑνὶ δέῃ ἐπιφέρειν, ἐάντε συγκεραννύντα πολλὰ ἑνί], as painters when they want to imitate something sometimes apply only purple, sometimes any other dye, but sometimes mixing many dyes together, e.g. when they prepare a flesh-coloured pigment[58] or something else of that sort, as each image seems to require each dye, I think – in the same way we too shall apply letters to the objects [τὰ στοιχεῖα ἐπὶ τὰ πράγματα ἐποίσομεν], both one to one, where it seems to be required, and many together [καὶ ἓν ἐπὶ ἕν, οὗ ἂν δοκῇ δεῖν, καὶ σύμπολλα], making what

---

[57] Actually the *Phdr.* project is more complicated: we should also be able to tell *for what reason* a certain kind of soul is persuaded by a certain kind of speech, and also *what kind of opinion* it is persuaded to hold. But the twofold division seems to be the central point.
[58] On ἀνδρείκελον (e2) cf. X. *Oec.* 10.5–6, Arist. *GA* 725a26, and the ancient lexica (Poll. 7.129.6, Tim. 50 Bonelli, Hsch. α 4741). Some translate 'a picture of a man' *vel sim.*, a meaning LSJ attests only in late texts.

The imposition of primary names (424a–425b)

they call syllables, and then in turn combining syllables, of which names and verbs are composed [ἐξ ὧν τά τε ὀνόματα καὶ τὰ ῥήματα συντίθενται]. And again from names and verbs we shall finally construct something great and beautiful and whole: as in the former case the picture[59] with the art of painting, so in this case speech [τὸν λόγον] with onomastic or rhetoric or whatever the art is. (424d5–425a5)

At d5–7 Socrates introduces the new topic of the association of letters and beings. Then at d8–e3 he switches to a long and elaborate comparison with the use of various dyes in painting. At e4 Socrates breaks off the comparison, with a slight anacoluthon (a main verb is lacking, but 'apply' is easily understood from d9), to reimport its content on to his original topic. Thus, at e4–425a5, he illustrates the construction of a series of language-units of increasing largeness: syllables, words (names and verbs), and finally – in a crescendo of emphasis – speech. (Here I assume that ῥήματα and λόγος are respectively 'verbs' and 'speech'; I defend this interpretation in §6.3.5.)

The basic idea here is that one must impose names by bringing together the two initial divisions (letters and beings) and establishing a correspondence between them according to the criterion of *resemblance* (d6). This criterion dictates a complex correspondence. For to one thing we must sometimes 'apply' one letter, sometimes several, i.e. a syllable or a whole word (d7, e5–a2). It is not clear whether speech (a2–5) too is regarded as a linguistic unit that can be made to correspond to some single item in the division of beings.[60]

Socrates' instructions are extremely abstract, and for the moment are not accompanied by examples. Later on (426c–427c) he does give a sample analysis of some Greek letters and names, which however is preceded by strong disclaimers (425b–426b), so that it need not be, and probably is not, completely faithful to the present programme. In the meantime, trying to understand how the correspondence between letters and beings is really supposed to work requires a bit of speculation. Some role, as also the comparison with dyes suggests, must be played by the greater or lesser complexity of each object. Thus, if the letter α resembles and is applied to *A*, and the letter β resembles and is applied to *B*, then the syllable βα will presumably resemble and be applied to the compound *BA*. It is important to be clear that the sort of composition here at issue is not – primarily at

---

[59] On ζῷον (a3) = 'picture' see LSJ II; cf. 429a and *Plt.* 277c, quoted in n.65. Some translate 'the living being', which makes no sense.
[60] The move from names and verbs to speeches is also a move from the *imposition* of names and verbs to their *use*. 'Each act of name use is, like namegiving, an assignment of name to object; and both kinds of act are to be judged by the same standard, resemblance' (Barney 2001: 97, cf. 99).

least – the one whereby a material object is composed of material parts. Rather, it must be the sort of composition whereby various kinds or properties combine to make up a thing's nature, and of which the ontological division announced at 424d should constitute an analysis.[61]

We can try to make this still somewhat vague account more precise by supposing that letters resemble a certain number of *basic, though not ultimate, elements* of reality (i.e. kinds or properties), and that syllables and names, which consist of letters, resemble the compound nature of the items which consist of those elements. I say 'basic, though not ultimate', because the ultimate elements of reality will presumably have to be the categories of 424d; and these cannot be resembled by any specific letter.[62] It cannot be the case either that every letter resembles a distinct category (because the categories are unlikely to be as many as twenty-four) or that only some letters do (because this would create an asymmetry among letters). Rather, the parallel between the two divisions envisaged by Socrates seems to require that the categories correspond, not to specific letters, but to *kinds* of letter: more precisely, to the two *summa genera* of letters, i.e. vowel and voiceless. In §6.3.3 I recalled that the ancient Academy knew of a bipartite categorial distinction between beings 'themselves by themselves' and beings 'relative to others'.

This brings me to another problematic facet of Socrates' project. Consider the case of a letter of the 'voiceless and soundless' kind which is included in the name of a certain compound object because it resembles an element of the object's nature. E.g. suppose that κ is included in the name λύκος because it resembles an element of the complex nature of a wolf. Then what is the name of *that* very element, seeing that κ cannot be pronounced alone? I surmise that the answer is the following: if a letter cannot be pronounced alone, then the name of the very item it resembles consists of that letter *plus other supporting ones*, whose function is merely to help pronunciation. This supposition will be borne out when Socrates finally gives examples (426c–427c, see §6.4.2).[63] In the meantime, remember 393de: to refer to most letters we use, not the letter itself, but a name composed of the letter in question plus other ones – e.g. βῆτα, where only β is significant.[64]

---

[61] Cf. Arist. *Metaph.* 1023b23–5 on the sense in which a genus can be said to be a part of its species.
[62] Of course 'letter' in the present discussion always means 'letter-*type*'.
[63] *Contra* see Baxter 1992: 78: it is 'reasonable to assume that Plato must mean all the elements in a correct name to have some mimetic force'.
[64] Of course at 393de Socrates is speaking of the *existing* names of letters, whereas our passage is about perfect names to come. But seeing that some letters *cannot* be pronounced in isolation, their names cannot fail to contain extra supporting letters.

The imposition of primary names (424a–425b) 293

We still have to face a final question. When Socrates says that names and verbs are composed of syllables, and speech of names and verbs (425a1–4), he seems to be speaking of *all* names and verbs. What is the place of those names which are composed of other names, i.e. *secondary* names? Socrates has not forgotten them, because he is shortly going to refer to them (425b2). We already encountered the same problem at 423b, commenting on which I suggested (§6.2.3) that Socrates was viewing primary names as the fundamental kind of names and assimilating secondary names to them. In our passage, however, there is a further reason for his silence on secondary names. As soon as from syllables we get complete words, i.e. primary names and verbs, then we already have all the essential components for constructing speeches, even if those primary names and verbs have not yet been assembled to form secondary ones. Secondary names and verbs greatly enrich our lexicon, but do not constitute a step in the sequence which Socrates is interested in, i.e. letters – syllables – names/verbs – speech.

6.3.5 *Intermezzo: names, verbs and speech (425a)*

We shall have more to say about the relation between primary and secondary names. Now, however, we need to discuss a point which so far I have been leaving aside. This is the identity of the linguistic items called ῥήματα and λόγος (425a1–5).

First, λόγος. This is probably not 'language' (Fowler), but a concrete language-unit of some sort, consisting of both ὀνόματα and ῥήματα: cf. 431bc, where λόγοι are said to be the *combination* (σύνθεσις) of ὀνόματα and ῥήματα. So the right translation might be 'sentence' (Reeve), which however does not seem to fit very well with the description of the λόγος as 'a great and beautiful whole'. This rather suggests 'speech' (Méridier 'discours'), conceived of as something which may be a simple sentence, or a whole period, or something even greater and more complex.[65]

---

[65] Barnes 2007: 204 translates our λόγος as 'saying' and contends that here, as in Arist. *Int.* 4–5 and *Po.* 20.1457a23–30, a λόγος is 'any expression whatever which is more complex than a single name or verb', including phrases like 'biped animal' (cf. 2007: 180). But our passage suggests, and 431bc confirms, that a λόγος must contain *at least one name and one verb*, as in the *Sophist* (see below). Cf. §7.2.4 (and §7.3.4, especially n.112, on λόγος referring to phrases).
For the λόγος as 'something great and beautiful and whole' (425a2–3) cf. *Phdr.* 264c 'each λόγος must be composed like a living being, having a body of its own, in such a way as not to be without head or feet, but have both middle parts and extremities, written so as to suit each other and the whole'. For the comparison between λόγοι and pictures (a3–4) cf. *Plt.* 277c 'it seems that our λόγος like a picture [ζῷον] has an adequate external profile, but has not yet acquired, as it were, the vividness due to the dyes and the mixture of colours'.

Secondly, ῥήματα. These are the units that are combined with names to form speech. Now here at 425a some suppose ῥήματα to be 'phrases', i.e. intermediate units between names and sentences or speeches;[66] we saw in §6.1.2 that the term has this meaning in several texts, including *Cra.* 399ab. Here, however, this cannot be so. For Socrates says, at 425a1–2, that both names and ῥήματα are composed of syllables. This entails (as Barney 2001: 186 sees) that ῥήματα lie *at the same level* of composition as names, i.e. are *single words composed of syllables*, not phrases composed of words. And this requirement is satisfied if ῥήματα means 'verbs' – as in fact it is usually understood.

Now, to grasp the real purport of this distinction between names and verbs we cannot but turn to *Sph.* 261d–263d,[67] where the Eleatic Stranger distinguishes two kinds of 'vocal means to indicate concerning reality': the ῥῆμα, defined as the means to indicate 'applied to actions' (ἐπὶ ταῖς πράξεσιν), and the ὄνομα, defined as the vocal sign imposed 'on the things themselves that perform those actions' (ἐπ' αὐτοῖς τοῖς ἐκείνας πράττουσι). The ῥῆμα is exemplified by no less than five verbs in third person singular, the ὄνομα by common and proper nouns. The 'first and smallest' sentence arises from the union of an ὄνομα and a ῥῆμα: e.g. ἄνθρωπος μανθάνει, '(a) human being learns'.

Thus it seems clear that in *Sph.* ὄνομα and ῥῆμα mean respectively 'name' and 'verb' and specify two distinct *word-classes*, the former of which includes proper names, common nouns, and presumably also adjectives.[68] However, *Sph.* also identifies a *syntactic* difference between names and verbs. This surfaces first in the definition of names. While the definition of verbs as signs of actions is based on the kind of object signified, the definition of names as signs *of agents* somehow points to the name's

---

[66] See Lutoslawski (1897: 431): the passage contains 'a succession of increasing units, beginning with a single letter, progressing to a syllable, a word, a phrase, and a speech. The parallelism of ὀνομαστική and ὄνομα, ῥητορική and ῥῆμα confirms this.' Cf. Denyer 1991: 149–50. Barney 2001: 96 too has 'phrases'.

Others think of the ῥῆμα here as something like a *predicate*: Horn 1904: 44 ('Aussagewort'), Dalimier 265 n.365 (ῥῆμα 'désigne la formule prédicative qui peut se réduire au verbe seul'), Sedley 2003: 128–9 ('descriptions', cf. 162–4). This construal, like the previous one, is ruled out by the argument I go on to offer in the text. Furthermore, such a syntactic perspective would be out of place in the present context: it would be odd of Socrates to say 'with letters you can make up syllables, with syllables you can make up names *and predicates*'.

[67] The *Sph.* passage was already touched upon in §2.2.3. With the following outline cf. Frede 1992b: 412–23, Szaif 1998: 457–62.

[68] The meaning of ὄνομα and ῥῆμα is the same in Aristotle, *Po.* 1457a10–18 and (I take it, although the matter is somewhat controversial) *Int.* 1–3. See Whitaker 1996: 52–61, 148–9. Cf. the *Art* ascribed to Dionysius Thrax, 12–13, where ὄνομα includes proper nouns, common nouns and adjectives, and is distinguished from ῥῆμα 'verb'.

function as subject of a sentence and thus introduces a syntactic perspective. This perspective becomes more evident in 262e–263d, where it comes out that each sentence contains two parts, one (the subject) which refers to what the sentence is about and another one (the predicate) which says something about it. In the examples 'Theaetetus sits' and 'Theaetetus flies' these two parts coincide respectively with the name and the verb, whose syntactic function is thus clarified.

So we have a double distinction: between *name and verb*, on the one hand, and between *subject and predicate*, on the other. The two distinctions coincide in the examples of the *Sophist*, which are sentences of the 'first and smallest' sort, composed of a name and a verb only.[69] But they do not coincide in general: the class of predicates is broader than the class of verbs and includes also predicates formed by the copula + a complement ('is (a) man', 'is white').[70] What is more, you may recognize the former distinction without yet recognizing the latter. You may realize that there are two distinct word-classes, which contain words with different features (e.g. verbs have tense, names do not), without yet connecting this distinction with the syntactic one between subject and predicate.[71] You may even realize that a sentence minimally consists of a name and a verb without yet being really aware of their distinct contribution to the sentence's syntactic structure.

Now *Sph.*, despite what is sometimes said, does not introduce the name–verb distinction as a completely new one. Theaetetus' perplexity at 261e–262a need not imply that the distinction is something previously unknown, only that Plato wants to stress its importance and perhaps that his definitions are partially new. Indeed, a couple of textual details suggests that the meanings 'name' and 'verb' for ὄνομα and ῥῆμα are already established: 262a1 κληθέν ('one kind called names, the other verbs'), a4 λέγομεν ('the means to indicate applied to actions we call verb': not λέγωμεν, 'let us call').[72] Therefore ὄνομα and ῥῆμα may well be 'name' and 'verb' already at *Cra.* 425a, as I have argued above.[73] This, however, does not mean that our passage also contains the *syntactic* distinction between

---

[69] As Barnes 2007: 107–8 points out, this is exactly the view of several ancient commentators: see Gal. *Inst. log.* 2.2.3, Apul. *Int.* 4, Mart. Cap. 4.393.
[70] The Stranger might have such predicates in mind at *Sph.* 262c2–3.
[71] Cf. Arist. *Po.* 1457a14–18, where verbs are distinguished from names only in virtue of their signifying time. Contrast *Int.* 16b6–10: verbs both signify time and are signs of what is predicated.
[72] See Szaif 1998: 461 n.427.
[73] In 426e six *infinitives* are referred to as ῥήματα. There the term is perhaps likely to mean 'verbs', although we cannot exclude that the meaning is just 'expressions' (see §6.1.2). A little above, 426c, the infinitive κίειν was called an ὄνομα.

subject and predicate. Whether the latter distinction too is drawn in *Cra.* is a question we shall ask in §§7.2.4 and 7.3.4.

If Socrates in our passage appears to presuppose the meaning of ῥῆμα as 'verb', we are entitled to ask where he gets it. Here we may quote Cornford (1935: 307): 'At *Cratylus* 425a the notion that speech or statement … consists of names and verbs is taken as familiar, without explanation. It was probably due to the grammarians, for the previous context refers to their classification of letters.' If we take this hypothesis seriously, we must recall that at 424c the division of letters was ascribed to experts in rhythms, and record that Democritus reportedly wrote, not only works on sounds, letters and rhythms (see §6.3.2), but also a treatise Περὶ ῥημάτων, whose content is unknown (D.L. 9.48 = 68 A33 DK = 0.6.1 Leszl). This brings me to the further (and final) conjecture that Democritus was the first, or one of the first, who identified the verb and called it ῥῆμα.[74]

6.3.6 First assessment of Socrates' programme

Before moving on to the conclusion of Socrates' speech a provisional assessment of what we have been reading so far is in order. Our assessment depends, of course, on what we take to be the programme's purpose. If – as we have been led to expect – the purpose is to supply an authentically naturalist theory of how primary names must be imposed to be correct, then the programme is open to serious criticism and is probably bound to be unsuccessful, because it seems unable to do without an element of convention. Let me briefly specify some of the problems, partly following Barney 2001: 95, 105–6 and n.31, 120 and n.12.

First, it is far from clear how letters or sounds could imitate the nature of very abstract entities like justice or equality. We can suppose that the imitation would have to be essentially *metaphorical*. It seems, however, that assigning such a basic role to metaphor would introduce an element of convention. In particular, there would seem to be no natural way to determine whether a word, uttered in a certain context, had literal or metaphorical meaning.

A second group of problems is related to the fact that Socrates says nothing about *syntax*. Could what he says be consistently extended to the flexion of nouns and verbs? Moreover, is a primary name just an unstructured

---

[74] Momigliano 1969: 157–8 n.4 thought that in Democritus' lost work 'ῥῆμα vada inteso nel senso di locuzione verbale secondo la distinzione già platonica in *Cratyl.*, 425a'. For a different view see Conti 1977–8: 200–2.

collection of letters, or does it have an internal structure, matching the relations among the object's various features? A consistent naturalism would seem to require the latter; yet only convention seems able to discriminate between groups of letters containing the same elements in different order (e.g. αβ and βα).

Thirdly, ordinary speakers, faced with a complex group of sounds, will not be immediately able to analyse it into its elements, discerning the exact value of each and its contribution to the whole. Learning the meaning of such expressions, and then understanding them in use, will inevitably be a matter of convention. The role of convention is especially evident in the case of those names which contain extra supporting letters (see §6.3.4): only convention can tell the extra letters from the mimetic ones. And as for the names of letters (the most conspicuous case, as we saw, of names containing extra supporting letters, and the only one Socrates acknowledges), how could Socrates explain in naturalist terms that the name βῆτα names the letter β instead of the kind or property resembled by the letter?[75]

More generally, any element of imperfection contained in a name, however little, imports a corresponding element of convention that is required to neutralize it and enable speakers to interpret the whole name correctly. As Barney says, 'there is … no natural partial degree of resemblance which suggests itself as a threshold for representational adequacy. Any such partial degree has the potential to mislead … it is only because imperfect representational correctness tends to be backed by quite elaborate conventional codes and assumptions about relevance that it does not invariably mislead us.'

Fourthly, there is a problem about the relation between primary and secondary names. Here, however, we must be very careful. According to many scholars,[76] Socrates' mimetic programme conflicts with his earlier claim that different namegivers can embody the same specific form of name in different letters and syllables (389a–390a), or with the claim that the etymology of secondary names often requires the addition or subtraction of some letters (393d–394b, 399ab, 414cd). I do not believe there is a real conflict on these points. The mimetic programme does *not* rule out that different sounds resemble the same thing, either in the same language (cf. 427ab) or in different ones – provided that different languages are assumed to use different sets of sounds (see §3.4.3). Hence there may be semantically equivalent primary names both in the same language and in

---

[75] Cf. Williams 1982: 85.
[76] E.g. Goldschmidt 1940: 151 n.1, Schofield 1982: 64–5.

different ones, and the mimetic programme does not conflict with 389a–390a. As for added and subtracted letters, again there is no conflict, if we assume that primary names too may contain extra letters (see §6.3.4). As long as a secondary name preserves the significant letters of its primary components, the extra letters may be freely added or subtracted. That is to say, extra letters *are* a problem – but not a problem that concerns the relation between primary and secondary names.

So the conflict is not the one scholars generally identify. Rather, the problem is simply that primary and secondary names have meaning in two very different ways. In particular, a secondary name cannot be directly analysed into its letters. Let us take, e.g., the compound name καρπο-φόρος, 'fruit-bearing', and assume that both its components are primary names which mean respectively 'fruit' and 'bearing'. If you just analysed the name into its letters, you might as well form the belief that it meant 'fruit that bears', or indeed something even more different. What natural fact can allow you to recognize whether a particular name is primary or secondary and, in the latter case, what kind of analysis is appropriate to it? Once again, it seems that only convention can tell.

Socrates' programme, if we read it as a genuine naturalist enterprise, founders on these difficulties – and perhaps on still other ones, which we shall see in due course. But is this the only possible way of reading it? Let us go back to the text.

6.3.7 How names are and how they should be (425ab)

At 425a5 Socrates rouses himself: he realizes that his train of thought has undergone a shift of perspective. At 424b7–8 he began to examine the procedure followed by 'the imitator', thus speaking of the namegiver with the same detachment he had been adopting throughout. But no later than c6, after a comparison with students of rhythms, returning to the imposition of names he shifted to the first person plural: 'So mustn't *we* [ἡμᾶς] too, in the same way, first divide vowels … etc.' Since then he has been sticking to the first person all through his speech: d1 'when *we* have divided', e4–5 '*we* too shall apply', and most recently 425a2–3 '*we* shall finally construct a great and beautiful whole'. Thereby Socrates has been gradually taking on the namegiver's point of view, as if it were 'our' business to build up and impose the primary names. It is from this identification that he now rouses himself:

(SO.) Or rather not *we* – in speaking I was carried away. For it was the ancients who composed these items as they are now composed [συνέθεσαν … οὕτως

The imposition of primary names (424a–425b) 299

ἥπερ σύγκειται], whereas we must, if we are going to know how to examine all these matters expertly, divide in this way [οὕτω διελομένους] and in this way see whether the first names and the secondary ones have been set down appropriately or not [εἴτε κατὰ τρόπον τά τε πρῶτα ὀνόματα κεῖται καὶ τὰ ὕστερα εἴτε μή]. But stringing these items together differently is, I fear, faulty and unmethodical [ἄλλως δὲ συνείρειν μὴ φαῦλον ᾖ καὶ οὐ καθ' ὁδόν], dear Hermogenes.

HE. By Zeus, Socrates, perhaps it is so. (425a5–b5)

Our task, Socrates says in a nutshell, is to examine the existing language, not to create a new one. It is the ancients who 'put together' or 'composed' the existing language-units (a6 συνέθεσαν has no object expressed, and we must supply a very generic one);[77] what *we* must do is different. First, we must 'divide in this way' (b1). This seems to mean that we must divide letters and beings as Socrates has just been recommending; he is not withdrawing those directions, but only the idea that we should use them for imposing names.[78] Second, in the same way (note b1–3 οὕτω … οὕτω), i.e. in the light of those very divisions, using them as a yardstick, we must assess the correctness of the existing primary and secondary names.

Socrates adds a final, rather obscure remark on the faultiness of ἄλλως … συνείρειν (b3). What does this mean? συνείρειν literally means 'to string together' (e.g. a λόγος or λόγοι: *Plt.* 267a, Arist. *EN* 1147a21). Hence it probably refers to the composition of language-units, like a6 συνέθεσαν, with which it also shares the lack of an expressed object and the need for a very generic one (unless we should supply 'names' from b2 as some[79] do). As for ἄλλως, it suggests a contrast with the preceding οὕτω's: 'differently', sc. from how it has been recommended, i.e. without performing the preliminary divisions.[80] Having just claimed that we must assess the correctness of names in the light of the recommended divisions, Socrates supports this claim with the remark that composing names not in accordance with them would be faulty.

---

[77] συνέθεσαν … οὕτως ἥπερ σύγκειται (a6): note that συνέθεσαν, 'composed', is the form which corresponds in the active to the middle συνέθεντο, 'made a convention', while σύγκειται, 'are composed', could itself mean 'a convention has been made' (cf. 433e ἐάντε τις συνθῆται ὥσπερ νῦν σύγκειται!). An oblique hint, in advance of the appropriate discussion, that names were actually at the time of their imposition, and are still now, a matter of convention?

[78] Fowler translates οὕτω διελομένους as 'take it [sc. language] to pieces as they put it together' (cf. Reeve). Thereby he takes οὕτω to refer not to Socrates' directions about division, but to the nearer οὕτως ἥπερ σύγκειται (a6). He also implausibly takes διελομένους to mean 'taking to pieces', rather than 'dividing' like the other forms of διαιροῦμαι in 424bd.

[79] See Horn 1904: 45, Fowler and Minio-Paluello. LSJ interpret συνείρειν here as '*connect* them [sc. names] with their roots'. Reeve: 'any other way of connecting names to things'. Dalimier: 'suivre un autre ordre' (cf. Sedley 2003: 42: 'to proceed in any other way'). Barney (2001: 97): 'to discourse in any other way' (see LSJ II.2).

[80] But it might also mean 'at haphazard' (Fowler): cf. LSJ II.3.

Let us try to grasp the significance of these lines. If Socrates, the character, gets 'carried away' and then suddenly rouses himself, this is because Plato, the author, deliberately has him do so. This may be just a touch of realism; or, more interestingly, it may be a stage-direction to the reader. The stage-direction must somehow concern the contrast between what Socrates was doing, i.e. sketching the project of a rational nomenclature based on natural criteria, and what he says he should rather do, i.e. to investigate an actual language. In my view the point is twofold and concerns both horns of the contrast. On the one hand, Plato is hinting that actual languages like Greek do not live up to the high standards of Socrates' project. On the other hand, he is laying stress on the project itself and inviting us to regard it, not as a momentary slip, but as a positive result of this section of the dialogue.

But how can the project be presented as a positive outcome? Of course, Socrates might find it irreproachable and seriously envisage an ideal language which would (in his opinion) live up to naturalist standards of correctness. Then he also ought to maintain that actual names, insofar as they do not live up to those standards, are not correct. This, however, is not what he is going to maintain. For, as I have anticipated time and again, Socrates will not leave the dialogue as a naturalist; in the end he will reject Cratylus' theory and embrace some form of conventionalism. He will, however, insist that names tend to resemble their referents with their letters and that those names which actually do so are *finer* than the others. (So I interpret the difficult 434c–435d: see §§8.1.2–5.)

In accordance with those forthcoming conclusions, the project sketched in our passage admits of a more modest interpretation, as a sketch of how names *would best* be made for philosophical purposes. So understood, the passage does not aim at offering a strictly naturalist account of correctness, and does not challenge the ordinary names' claims on reference to things. This interpretation fits well with the fact that Socrates, before correcting himself, explicitly speaks in the first person and concerns himself with names *to come*.

Now for a linguistic remark. At b1–4 Socrates says that our task is to see whether or not the existing names have been set down 'appropriately' (κατὰ τρόπον), and that assembling names or other language-units differently than has been said is 'faulty and unmethodical' (φαῦλον … καὶ οὐ καθ' ὁδόν). These expressions may be equivalent respectively to 'correctly' and 'not correct'. But I find it striking that here Socrates, gathering up the threads of his long speech since 424c, does not use the key terms 'correctness' and 'correct', and has instead recourse to other expressions, two of which (i.e. the first and the third) occur nowhere else in the dialogue. Indeed, talk of 'correctness' is absent from the whole of 424b–425b (with the not very significant exception of 424b10 'isn't it most correct to divide first of all the letters ...'), and will reappear only at 425d. So we should consider the possibility that Plato here is *deliberately* avoiding expressions concerning correctness and making Socrates employ weaker expressions instead. This is perfectly in order, if Plato is eventually going to make Socrates (a) settle the question of correctness in favour of conventionalism, but at the same time (b) specify how names would *best* be made, and if our passage serves to illustrate the *latter* point.[81]

The fact that Plato makes Socrates sketch the project of a perfect language does not imply that he seriously entertains the idea of a linguistic reform; indeed, he shows no interest (either here or elsewhere) in any practical matter involved in a realization of such a project. So the point seems to be a different one. As at the earlier stages of the discussion, Plato wants to extract from the naturalist thesis all the good it can yield, before finally refuting it. The project of a perfect, 'philosophical' language, considered from a purely *theoretical* point of view, is one very interesting idea we can extract. Its interest also lies in the fact that it gives Plato the opportunity to carry on the dialogue's 'ontological subplot', reflecting on the division of reality into kinds and on the analogy between beings and letters.

Here I cannot dwell on the great historical relevance of Socrates' project; but I cannot help mentioning how reminiscent it is of those envisaged by several philosophers writing in the 1660s and afterwards, like Comenius, Dalgarno, Wilkins and Leibniz.[82] I do not know to what extent, if at all, these authors actually drew inspiration from our dialogue. At least Comenius and Leibniz seem to have read it; in particular, Leibniz was certainly very impressed by the etymologies of actual primary names which Socrates offers at 426c–427d, so much so as to quote the whole passage in his unfinished and unpublished *Epistolica de historia etymologica dissertatio* (written around 1712), §18.[83]

---

[81] Goldschmidt 1940: 144–5, 152, sees the passage as a mere dialectical move: 'Platon, tout en restant dans les vues de Cratyle, montre comment celui-ci, s'il veut être logique avec lui-même, devrait concevoir son système.' This is to throw away the impressive theoretical machinery deployed in this passage.

[82] See Baxter 1992: 68–72 on Comenius and Maat 2004 on Dalgarno, Wilkins and Leibniz. Among these authors only Comenius seems to share Socrates' view that, in the ideal language, letters must be applied to beings on the basis of *resemblance*.

[83] The *Dissertatio* has been provisionally edited by Gensini 1991: 191–271. For another possible connection between Leibniz and the *Cratylus* on primary names see §6.4.2 and n.104.

6.4 THE INVESTIGATION OF ACTUAL PRIMARY NAMES (425B–427D)

6.4.1 Disclaimers and preliminaries (425b–426b)

Socrates should now – according to what he has just said – proceed in two steps: first make the required divisions of letters and beings and establish the required correspondences, then check whether the existing primary names have been imposed in accordance with such divisions and correspondences. But the task turns out to be out of reach. As so often, Plato's Socrates has told us what we ought to do, but is not really going to do it.

SO. What then? Do you trust you'd be able to divide these things in this way [ταῦτα οὕτω διελέσθαι]? I don't.
HE. Then so much the less do I.
SO. Shall we therefore give up? Or do you want us to try as we can, even if we should be able to discern little of these matters? And, as we premissed a short while ago to the gods that though we knew nothing of the truth we were guessing at the humans' opinions about them, so now too should we proceed after saying to ourselves that, if these things had to be divided expertly [εἰ μέν τεχνικῶς ἔδει αὐτά διελέσθαι],[84] whether by us or by anyone else, this was the way they had to be divided [οὕτως ἔδει αὐτά διαιρεῖσθαι], but now we'll have to deal with them, as they say, 'according to our capacity'?[85] Do you think so, or what else do you say?
HE. I most emphatically think so. (425b6–c8)

The wearisome syntax of Socrates' very long sentence (which I have divided for clarity) does not obscure the main point. On the one hand, the previously recommended divisions are necessary for a thorough examination of names; on the other hand, *we* are not able to perform them. So we shall do what we can, offering a second-best inquiry in place of the thorough one. Here Socrates is recalling 400d–401a, where he renounced examining the names the gods call themselves and contented himself with an inquiry into the names they are called by humans.

Before embarking on the second-best inquiry, however, Socrates has first to express, then to silence, a qualm:

---

[84] At c4 the MSS read εἰ μέν τι χρηστόν ἔδει, preserved by Hirschig; he reprints Ficino's translation 'si quam optime distinguenda haec fuissent', which seems impossible. εἰ μέν τεχνικῶς ἔδει is the text printed by the OCT editors (who slightly modify an earlier emendation by Reinhard; an alternative is Duke's εἰ μέν τι χρησιμώτερον ἔδει), perhaps on the grounds that Plato never uses the adverb χρηστῶς (which at first glance would seem to be the most obvious way of emending χρηστόν. Burnet, Fowler, Méridier adopt Ast's εἰ μέν τι χρῆν, followed by deletion of ἔδει.
[85] Cf. *Hp. Ma.* 301b.

The investigation of primary names (425b–427d) 303

so. I think, Hermogenes, that the objects will appear ridiculous when it becomes manifest that they have been imitated with letters and syllables [Γελοῖα μὲν οἶμαι φανεῖσθαι ... γράμμασι καὶ συλλαβαῖς τὰ πράγματα μεμιμημένα κατάδηλα γιγνόμενα].[86] And yet it is necessary. For we don't have anything better to refer to about the truth of the first names [περὶ ἀληθείας τῶν πρώτων ὀνομάτων][87] – unless perhaps, as tragedians when they are at a loss resort to the machines lifting gods in the air, you want us too to get off in the same way, saying that the first names were imposed by the gods and for this reason are correct [τὰ πρῶτα ὀνόματα οἱ θεοὶ ἔθεσαν καὶ διὰ ταῦτα ὀρθῶς ἔχει]. Is this the strongest account for us too? Or perhaps that one, that we have received them from some barbarians, and barbarians are more ancient than us? Or that it is impossible, owing to their antiquity, to investigate them, like barbarian names? All these would be very clever dodges for the person who is unwilling to give an account of how the first names have been correctly set down [λόγον διδόναι περὶ τῶν πρώτων ὀνομάτων ὡς ὀρθῶς κεῖται]. (425d1–426a4)

Is what Socrates fears will appear 'ridiculous' (d1) the abstract theory which has just been stated or the forthcoming analysis of actual primary names? Several commentators believe it is the former.[88] I rather believe the latter, as is suggested by the whole train of thought from 425b6 onwards, by the future 'will appear' and by the parallel with another unequivocal 'ridiculous' at 426b6. Yet it must be acknowledged that the theory itself, or at least its basic idea of names as imitations, seems to be presented at d3–4 as something we accept *faute de mieux*.

I shall have more to say on Socrates' fear of ridicule later on. For the moment, however, we can already point out that at this stage he seems to be guided mainly by methodological considerations, i.e. by the view that somehow or other we must account for the correctness of the primary names, if we do not want to fall back on such unsatisfactory loopholes as were already suggested and rejected at 421cd, which Socrates now recalls. (Note that the first of the three possible ways out mentioned here, namely invoking a *deus ex machina*, was not considered before; it is a desperate move Cratylus will make at 438bc.)

---

[86] This clause (d1–3) is usually understood as 'it will appear ridiculous that things are *made manifest* by being imitated with letters and syllables'. Thus κατάδηλα (d2) would refer to the *disclosure* of the objects' nature in names. But the other occurrences of the adjective in *Cra.* (408e κατάδηλον γενόμενον, 415b, 416a) do not suggest this pregnant construal and have rather to do with the *perspicuity* of an etymology. For my own construal cf. *Ap.* 23d κατάδηλοι γίγνονται προσποιούμενοι μὲν εἰδέναι, εἰδότες δὲ οὐδέν: 'it becomes manifest that they claim to know, but know nothing'.
[87] 'The truth of the primary names' (d4–5): the truth *about* them? Or the fact that *they* are true, i.e. truthful, i.e. correct (cf. 385c and §2.2.4)? I incline towards the latter.
[88] Goldschmidt 1940: 144–5 n.1, Schofield 1982: 65, Barney 2001: 90 and n.9.

Socrates' mainly methodological perspective becomes more evident in the next lines:

(SO.) And yet to the extent that one does not know the correctness of the first names [ὅτῳ τις τρόπῳ τῶν πρώτων ὀνομάτων τὴν ὀρθότητα μὴ οἶδεν], it is impossible for him, I think, to know that of the secondary ones [ἀδύνατόν που τῶν γε ὑστέρων εἰδέναι], which must necessarily be cleared up on the basis of those [ἃ ἐξ ἐκείνων ἀνάγκη δηλοῦσθαι][89] which he knows nothing about. But evidently he who claims to have expert knowledge on these matters must be able to give a demonstration [ἀποδεῖξαι][90] above all and most clearly about the first names; or he must know well that he'll talk nonsense as far as the secondary ones are concerned. Or do you think otherwise?
HE. Not at all, Socrates. (426a4–b4)

Knowledge about the correctness of secondary names presupposes knowledge about the correctness of primary ones, of which the former are composed. Conversely, lack of knowledge about the correctness of primary names turns any account of the correctness of secondary names into nonsense.

The point can be put as follows. As we have (or should have) done in the etymologies of secondary names, showing the correctness of a name like 'ABCDEFG' amounts to showing that it reveals the nature of its referent by being composed of 'ABC' + 'DEFG'. Let us suppose that 'ABC' and 'DEFG' are primary names. If we do not show how they too reveal the nature of their referents (e.g., if we declare them to be inscrutable barbarian loans), then our whole analysis of 'ABCDEFG' is invalidated; for we have not really shown that it has a natural link with its referent. As far as we know, its primary uninvestigated components – or at least some of them – might even bear their meanings just by convention. But then the conventionality of the primary level would infect the further ones: a secondary name containing a conventional primary name is itself conventional, even if it happens to describe its referent's nature truly.

---

[89] This is probably the only place in *Cra.* where δηλόω expresses something done *to* names, not *by* them. (See §7.1.3 n.18 on 429c6.) Most interpreters take the point to be that secondary names are 'made evident', or even 'explained', on the basis of primary ones. δηλόω, however, usually does not have this meaning, at least when the grammatical object – or, in the passive, the subject – is a noun or pronoun; it usually means 'show', 'indicate' (see §4.2.4). On the other hand, Reeve's translation of δηλοῦσθαι as 'to express something' would only fit the active. I have hesitantly followed the former interpretation. Could the meaning instead be 'which must necessarily *be shown to be composed of those*', or perhaps 'which must necessarily *be shown to be [correct]* on the basis of those'?

[90] ἀποδεῖξαι here is often translated 'explain'. With Dalimier, I stick to the literal meaning; as a matter of fact, however, the verb seems to be used as a variant on 'give an account' (a3).

The *Derveni Papyrus*, col. XXII, supplies a concrete example of the danger we ought to avoid. The author says that one and the same goddess is called Γῆ 'Earth', '*by convention*' (νόμῳ); Μήτηρ 'Mother', 'because everything is born from her'; and Δημήτηρ 'Demeter', from Γῆ Μήτηρ. We might say that Δημήτηρ is a secondary name, which provides a true description of its referent's nature, but one of whose components, i.e. Γῆ, is declared to have no etymological explanation. This would deprive the whole secondary name Δημήτηρ of natural correctness. Therefore, if Socrates exploited some of the ways out which have just been mentioned, thus leaving primary names unexplained, he would invalidate whatever efforts he previously made to give a naturalist account of secondary names. On the other hand, a successful account of primary names would provide those previous efforts with firm foundations.[91]

The point made in our passage is a particular instance of a general principle which emerges from the refutation of the 'Dream' theory at *Tht.* 201e–206b: knowledge of a compound presupposes knowledge of its elements. Even more generally, 'Knowledge must be based on knowledge.'[92] Indeed, according to Kahn 1973a: 167–8 a major purpose of the whole discussion of secondary and primary names is precisely that of pointing to the general thesis: 'Plato was here concerned to work out a serious ideal for systematic knowledge.' It is perhaps difficult to be sure that Plato was so *concerned*; for he does not make Socrates explicitly advert to any general principle.[93] But I take it that, at the very least, he cannot fail to see that Socrates' point can have wide application.[94]

Socrates rounds off his preliminaries to the 'primary' etymologies with some final disclaimers:

SO. Well, what I have realized[95] about first names seems to me absolutely outrageous and ridiculous [πάνυ μοι δοκεῖ ὑβριστικὰ εἶναι καὶ γελοῖα]. So I'll share it with you, if you want; but if you're able to draw something better from some other source, try to share it with me in turn.

HE. I'll do so. Come on, don't be afraid and tell me. (426b5–9)

---

[91] Thus I fail to see here any 'obliquely critical comment on the etymologies' (Schofield 1982: 64, cf. Horn 1904: 38). Of course, in the etymologies Socrates was still unaware of the problem of primary names. All this implies, however, is that their value as confirmation of the naturalist thesis is conditional upon the analysis of primary names.
[92] The formulation of this more general principle comes from Fine 1979.
[93] *Pace* Sedley 2003: 125 (cf. 127).
[94] *Pace* Annas (1982: 111–12): 'The *Theaetetus*, reflecting upon the concept of knowledge rather than uncritically using it, generalises the result that the *Cratylus* has unwittingly attained.'
[95] ἃ ... ἐγὼ ᾔσθημαι (b5): 'my notions' Fowler, 'mes impressions personnelles' Méridier, etc. My translation seems to me more literal (cf. LSJ αἰσθάνομαι I.2, II.), but it actually boils down to the same thing, because Socrates is leaving open the possibility that his forthcoming account may be outdone by a better one.

The main point in these lines is the phrase 'absolutely outrageous and ridiculous' (b6). The latter term was already used at 425d1, where Socrates said the outcomes of the inquiry would be γελοῖα. Both terms refer to the seeming extravagancy of the mimetic analyses that Socrates is going to offer. There is a nice parallel at *Phdr.* 252b: before quoting the two alleged verses of the Homeridae (see §5.5.4), Socrates says that Phaedrus will perhaps laugh (γελάσῃ) on hearing them, and that the second verse is 'absolutely outrageous' (ὑβριστικὸν πάνυ) and unmetrical – where the outrageousness presumably lies in its clumsiness and its very unmetricality.

In our passage these derogatory terms create some sort of distance between Socrates and the forthcoming mimetic analyses. But are they meant to throw complete discredit on them? Are those analyses just a *divertissement*, as the Homeridae verses probably are? These questions are very similar to those raised by the secondary etymologies; hence we may expect the answers to be similar too. I shall deal with this issue in §6.4.4. For the moment, read on.

6.4.2 *Letters and primary names: the examples (426c–427c)*

We are now ready for Socrates' exemplification of what he has been holding so far. This is presented in a single, continuous speech, from 426c1 to 427c6. Socrates takes into account a series of Greek letters (or rather, as we should say instead, the corresponding sounds), with no systematic order and no attempt to follow his own earlier recommendations about the need for preliminary divisions. He explains what each letter has been used to imitate, citing names where it occurs. Thus he gives us, as a matter of fact, a series of etymologies of primary names, although this procedure is the reverse of the one he followed with secondary names. There the starting point was the names to be analysed, and Socrates moved from one to the other according to various semantic associations; as a result, the same component might occur in different etymologies. Here, instead, Socrates starts from the letters and says in what names each is contained.

Socrates' survey can be divided into nine headings. Here follows a paraphrase, interspersed with some comments of mine.

426c1-e6. Socrates starts with ρ (i.e. the sound /r/, as he should rather say). ρ seems to him 'to be an instrument, as it were, [expressive] of every sort of motion' (ὥσπερ ὄργανον εἶναι πάσης τῆς κινήσεως). This prompts a somewhat garbled digression (c2–d3) on the very term κίνησις, 'motion', which is derived from κίειν 'to go' + ἴεσις 'going',[96] and then on its contrary στάσις, 'rest', interpreted as a 'negation of going' (ἀπόφασις τοῦ ἰέναι) which has been altered by an 'embellishment'.[97] At the end of the digression Socrates resumes what he was saying about the power of ρ, which is used by the namegiver to *imitate movement* (d5 πρὸς τὸ ἀφομοιοῦν τῇ φορᾷ, cf. d7 διὰ τούτου τοῦ γράμματος τὴν φορὰν μιμεῖται). Then he gives several examples of words which contain ρ and whose meaning is related to movement (d6–e4): ῥεῖν 'to flow'; ῥοή 'stream'; τρόμος 'trembling'; τρέχειν 'to run'; κρούειν 'to strike'; θραύειν 'to fracture'; ἐρείκειν 'to rend'; θρύπτειν 'to break'; κερματίζειν 'to crumble'; ῥυμβεῖν 'to whirl'. Socrates also explains why the namegiver employed precisely this letter to imitate movement: 'He saw, I think, that the tongue in pronouncing this letter is least at rest and most agitated' (e4–5).

Here Socrates' account raises a twofold difficulty. On the one hand, some of the examples ('fracture', 'break', 'crumble') actually seem to have little to do with movement and hence not to suit his account of ρ. On the other, at 434c Socrates will refer to this passage as if it said that ρ resembles 'movement and motion and *hardness* [σκληρότητι]', whereas our lines assign to ρ the sole function of resembling movement and do not mention hardness at all. In fact, these two difficulties might be two sides of a single coin; for the examples which have little to do with movement might perhaps have more to do with hardness.[98] The picture is further complicated by a textual problem. Among the examples, τρέχειν (e1) is the reading, or perhaps the conjecture, of Q = Par. gr. 1813, while the other MSS read τραχεῖ, 'harsh'. Almost all editors print τρέχειν, but some preserve τραχεῖ in view of 434c.[99] This reading, however, would give Socrates an example intolerably extraneous to the notion of movement. How can we sort out this mess? We might suppose that the passage is corrupt and that in its original form

---

[96] At c3, 7 I, like most scholars, accept DTQ's reading ἴεσις (cf. W ἴεσσις), a *hapax* from εἶμι. B reads ἴεσις ('rushing', from ἵημι, adopted by Dalimier 265 n.371). Burnet, followed by the OCT, conjectured ἔσις (again from ἵημι), which already occurred at 411d, 420a.

[97] Scholars seem to think that στάσις must contain a privative α: e.g. Méridier 115 n.3 'la vraie forme serait ἀ-ίεσις'. The OCT adopts Duke's correction of στάσις (d1) to στάεσις, presumably suggesting a derivation from *ἀ-έσις. Hence στ- would be part of the 'embellishment'. Yet 427a8–b2 suggests that the τ in στάσις might express rest. Could Socrates be anticipating this? 'Negation of going' would then mean that στάσις contains τ, for rest, + ἴεσις 'motion': something like 'rest from motion' (cf. Dalimier 266 n.373).

[98] Cf. Barney 2001: 124 n.17, Sedley 2003: 139.

[99] Thus Ficino, Méridier, Belardi 1985: 28 n.8 and Dalimier. According to Belardi, τραχεῖ is also indirectly supported by later texts which mention the harshness of ρ: e.g. D. H. *Comp.* 80. But this need not derive from our passage.

it did claim that ρ resembles movement as well as hardness. But the corruption would have to be a very complex one; for the text as it stands goes very smoothly and repeats several times that the function of ρ is to resemble movement. Alternatively, we may resign ourselves to allowing that the passage is inconsistent, both internally and possibly also with 434c. This latter policy could perhaps attract adherents of the view that our text of *Cra.* preserves traces of two distinct editions (see §2.2.5 and Appendix 1).

426e6–427a2. Next comes ι, employed 'for all the fine things, those which should most go through everything' (πρὸς τὰ λεπτὰ πάντα, ἃ δὴ μάλιστα διὰ πάντων ἴοι ἄν: note the abundance of iotas). Socrates is obviously recalling the Penetrating Principle which had an important role in the flux theory (412c–413d); that is why λεπτά here must mean 'fine', not 'light' as some translate it. As examples Socrates mentions ἰέναι, 'to go', and ἵεσθαι, 'to rush'.

427a2–8. φ ψ σ ζ are 'breathy' (πνευματώδη) letters. Socrates gives a list of things these letters are used to imitate, thus simultaneously listing examples of names containing those letters: ψυχρόν 'cold', ζέον 'seething', σείεσθαι 'to be shaken', σεισμός 'shock'.[100] Then, giving a general characterization of such things, and at the same time adding a further example, he concludes that the namegiver mostly seems to use such letters when he imitates τὸ φυσῶδες, 'what is blowy'.

a8–b2. δ τ, whose pronunciation involves the 'compression' and 'leaning' of the tongue (sc. on the teeth),[101] are useful to imitate δεσμός 'bond' and στάσις 'rest'. (On στάσις see n.97.) Again Socrates exploits the use/mention ambiguity both to tell us what *things* the letters in question imitate and to exemplify the *names* where they occur.

b2–5. λ, in whose pronunciation the tongue 'glides most of all' (ὀλισθάνει μάλιστα), is used by the namegiver in the names λεῖον 'smooth', ὀλισθάνειν itself, λιπαρόν 'oily', κολλῶδες 'gluey', 'and in all such names'.

b5–7. Since γ[102] 'lays hold of the gliding of the tongue', the combination γλ (the only one considered in this passage) is used in γλίσχρον 'viscous', γλυκύ 'sweet', γλοιῶδες 'glutinous'.

---

[100] The OCT adopts Heindorf's correction of σεισμόν (a5) to σισμόν 'hissing'. His point was that the immediately preceding ὅλως announces a generalization, whereas σεισμός is not more general than σείεσθαι. But is σισμός?
[101] Socrates literally speaks of 'the δύναμις of δ and τ's compression and leaning of the tongue'. Cf. b6, 393e, 412e, 424c, and see §4.2.4.
[102] More literally, 'the δύναμις of γ' (b6): see §4.2.4.

c1–3. Because of the 'internal' (εἴσω) nature of the sound of ν, the namegiver used it to form the words ἔνδον 'inside' and ἐντός 'within', imitating the things with the letters (ὡς ἀφομοιῶν τοῖς γράμμασι τὰ ἔργα).

c3–4. α and η were assigned respectively to largeness and length, because they are 'large' (μεγάλα) letters. Thereby Socrates refers to the opening of the mouth in pronouncing them (see Belardi 1985: 33 and n.11).

c4–6. To name what is 'round' (γογγύλον) the namegiver needed the letter (Socrates says 'the sign') ο. Therefore he 'mixed very much [πλεῖστον] of this letter' in the round's name.[103] Socrates does not make it explicit, but his point here is obviously that in pronouncing ο the mouth takes on a round shape.

End of the paraphrase of 426c1–427c6. Now, before going on and seeing how Socrates rounds off his speech, we can begin to advance some overall remarks on the method and contents of Socrates' survey.

To start with, as far as we know the survey is thoroughly original. Of course we cannot rule out the possibility that someone before Plato – perhaps the historical Cratylus – put forward some etymologies of this sort. But the fact is that we know nothing of any such antecedent to Socrates' survey, as we know of no antecedent to his abstract treatment of primary names.

Secondly, how shall we define the sort of analysis of the power of letters which Socrates carries out here? It is not an *onomatopoeic* analysis, because onomatopoeia consists in something he rejected at 423ce, i.e. the imitation of something's sound by the sounds of its name. According to Socrates' theory, what ought to be imitated is rather the essence of things. It may then be tempting to speak of a *sound-symbolic* analysis. Even this term, however, may prove misleading. Sound-symbolism is sometimes conceived of as the imitation of certain features of things by the sounds of words. But throughout our passage, as Belardi 1985: 33–43 and Baxter 1992: 62–3 insist, Socrates concerns himself with the way each letter or sound is *articulated* rather than with the letter or sound itself. The imitation is performed by the movements and positions of the tongue, the lips

---

[103] πλεῖστον (c5) should not mean 'most', because γογγύλον contains more γ's than ο's. I follow Minio-Paluello and Reeve ('abbondantemente', 'lots of it'). Fowler and Méridier have instead recourse to the vague notion of ο as the 'chief' or 'dominant' letter in γογγύλον, though this does not seem to be what πλεῖστον means.

NB: In place of γογγύλον Ficino read the synonymous but more common στρογγύλον. The reading is already in the Greek MS he kept before him in translating (Laurentianus 85.9, fourteenth century: see Carlini 1999) and in its antigraph (Laurentianus 59.1, same century). Even if it were correct (as it certainly is not), πλεῖστον could hardly mean 'most', because στρογγύλον contains *as many* γ's as ο's.

and all the phonatory apparatus; indeed, at 423b Socrates already spoke of indicating something 'with voice, tongue and mouth'. To be sure, there is a correspondence between such movements and positions, on the one hand, and the resulting sounds, on the other. The sounds, however, do not constitute the factor that is responsible for the imitation; they are rather an epiphenomenon. So, strictly speaking, we should say that Socrates is interested in a sort of *articulatory mimesis*.[104]

The rationale for this approach lies in Socrates' very theory of primary names. If he contented himself with just claiming that the letters of words imitate the features of things, then it would be difficult for him to account for the various particular associations between sounds and features. These associations would then probably turn out to rest on unaccountable intuitions, or even to be merely subjective. But this would presumably not satisfy Socrates' request for an 'account', or a 'demonstration', about primary names (426ab). A theory of primary names such as the one he has been sketching and should now put into practice should require that the associations rest on some firm, objective ground. Bringing articulation into the picture provides exactly such a ground – or so it may seem. For the articulatory facts admit of an objective description. Once we have supplied such an objective description we may hope to be able to establish a correlation, based on equally objective resemblances, between the articulation of sounds and the features of things.

Probably there is also another reason for Socrates' focus on articulation. When at 423e he defined names as imitations of each thing's essence with letters and syllables, he seemed to regard the use of letters and syllables as a special mode of vocal imitation, which distinguishes names from, e.g., mimicry of animal cries (cf. §6.2.4). Now in our passage Socrates had to give concrete examples of that conception of names. So he may very naturally translate his earlier appreciation of the role of letters and syllables into a focus on their articulation. If names, unlike other vocal imitations, are composed of letters and syllables,[105] and if what distinguishes letters and syllables from other vocal sounds is their being articulated, then it is only natural to view the imitation performed by them precisely from the perspective of their articulation.

Another point deserving some comment is that our passage confirms a previous hypothesis about Socrates' theory. In §6.3.4 I supposed that,

---

[104] Cf. Leibniz, *Nouveaux essais*, III.ii.1: 'il y a quelque chose de naturel dans l'origine des mots, qui marque un rapport entre les choses et les sons et mouvements des organes de la voix'.
[105] This assumption is actually questionable: see §6.2.4.

The investigation of primary names (425b–427d) 311

for Socrates, the association of a single letter with a being (424d) should normally take place *inside* a full-blown name which also contains other letters. That is to say, normally a single letter, resembling a certain being, should occur together with other letters both in the name of the very being it resembles and (*a fortiori*) in the names of other, more complex beings. Now this is borne out by the examples in our passage. Here no letter is treated as being in itself a name of what it resembles; letters always occur within words.

So much is enough for the reconstruction of the details of Socrates' survey. We must now read its conclusion and then go on to raise more general questions about its merits and demerits and its place in the argument of the *Cratylus*.

6.4.3 Conclusion of Socrates' survey (427cd)

Socrates will not pursue the topic of primary names any further. What he has been saying so far is enough:

(SO.) And in the same way the lawgiver appears to have been bringing the other things into accordance with letters and syllables [τἆλλα οὕτω φαίνεται προσβιβάζειν καὶ κατὰ γράμματα καὶ κατὰ συλλαβάς],[106] making a sign and a name for each of the beings [ἑκάστῳ τῶν ὄντων σημεῖόν τε καὶ ὄνομα ποιῶν]. Then from these and by means of these very ones he composed the rest by imitation [ἐκ δὲ τούτων τὰ λοιπὰ ἤδη αὐτοῖς τούτοις συντιθέναι ἀπομιμούμενος]. (427c6–d1)

Socrates first generalizes the outcomes of his sample survey: in the same way as we have been seeing so far the legislator made up a sign, i.e. a name (c8 τε καί is explanatory), for *each* of the beings. This generalization is probably hyperbolical. For we know that some beings bear *secondary* names, which are not directly composed of letters and syllables, but rather of other names. And it seems clear that in the following sentence, 'Then from these and by means of these very ones he put together *the rest* by imitation' (c8–d1), 'these' refers to all primary names, whereas 'the rest', put together by means of them, are precisely secondary names.

---

[106] On προσβιβάζειν τι κατά τι cf. *Phdr.* 229e; τἆλλα are the other things to be named by means of letters and syllables (LSJ II.2, Stallbaum, Méridier). 'Bringing into accordance' does not, of course, mean that the lawgiver *arbitrarily* associates things and letters; he rather recognizes and exploits objective resemblances between the two realms. Scholars have generally been puzzled by this sentence and have understood προσβιβάζειν (and, accordingly, τἆλλα) in various ways: e.g. 'apply' Fowler, 'accommodare' Ficino (cf. perhaps *Tht.* 153c).

This very same sentence, however, besides showing that Socrates has not lost sight of secondary names, also shows that he is once more giving primary importance to primary names (cf. §§6.2.3, 6.3.4). For he avers that also in the case of *secondary* names the lawgiver proceeds 'by imitation'. Thereby Socrates is perhaps assuming that secondary names are mimetic insofar as (i) they are composed of mimetic primary names, (ii) their composition somehow mirrors the structure of their referent's nature. With (ii) we can compare 438d, where those secondary names whose etymology encapsulates a right outlook on the world are termed ὅμοια τῇ ἀληθείᾳ, 'similar to the truth'.[107] Cf. also *Sph*. 221c, where the noun ἀσπαλιευτική 'angling', derived from ἀνασπάω 'draw upward' + ἁλιευτική 'fishing', is said to be '*copied* [ἀφομοιωθέν] from the action itself'.[108]

Socrates' claim is questionable. A secondary name – whose composition involves syntax, as we have seen – cannot imitate its referent by means of letters and syllables *in the same way* as a primary name does; either it is no imitation at all or it is a much more complicated sort of imitation, about which nothing has been said so far.

6.4.4 An assessment of the mimetic survey

Socrates' mimetic survey raises a host of problems. To start with, his sample names contain a number of letters whose mimetic power has nothing to do – or is even in conflict – with the meaning of the whole name (cf. §6.3.6). What is the function of ο in ῥοή, of τ in τρόμος and τρέχειν, of σ in δεσμός? What single job does ε perform in words with so different meanings as ἐρείκειν, ἰέναι, δεσμός and ἔνδον? Or take γογγύλον. Socrates

---

[107] But see §8.2.4 and n.114.
[108] In fact the lexicon of imitation occurs also in the etymologies of some secondary names (see Rijlaarsdam 1978: 165). E.g., Socrates says that a name 'represents' (ἀπεικάζειν 414a) something, or 'has been made similar' (ἀπείκασται 420d, 421b, cf. 419cd, 420e) to something, and hence is a 'representation' (ἀπείκασμα 402d, 420c) of it. He also says that the lawgiver 'has imitated' (μεμίμηται 414b) something with a name, which therefore is an 'imitation' (μίμημα 437a). But all these expressions (with the possible exception of 419c and 437a) actually seem to refer to the fact that the etymologies at issue describe the object's nature *metaphorically*, implicitly likening it to something else (cf. LSJ ἀπεικάζω 1.2–3). Hence they are hardly relevant to our passage's claim that secondary names are imitations.

For the notion of a structural resemblance between secondary or compound names and their objects cf. Leibniz's 1677 *Dialogus*: 'the compound *lucifer* bears to the words *lux* and *ferens* a relation corresponding to the relation which the thing signified by *lucifer* bears to the thing signified by the words *lux* and *ferens*' (1923–: A VI, 4A, 23; Ariew/Garber 1989: 271). Note that in the same passage it is also said that the 'primary elements' (*prima elementa*), among which *lux* and *ferens* seem to be reckoned, need *not* resemble their referents at all.

says it contains a great deal of o; but it contains even more γ. So what natural fact makes o, rather than γ, the relevant letter in γογγύλον?

It is also unclear how one should account for the differences in meaning among names containing the same letter. E.g. ρ occurs in several terms, somehow connected with the notion of movement, whose meanings are obviously different. To give a thoroughly naturalist account of them, Socrates ought to show that their differences in meaning are due to the presence of other significant letters besides ρ. He does not do so and probably could never manage to do so.

In sum, Socrates' sample names would not live up to thorough naturalist standards. Yet they apparently ought to. For Socrates, both immediately before the mimetic survey (426a) and immediately after (427d), explicitly connects it with the issue of the correctness of names – i.e. with the naturalist solution to that issue. Therefore Socrates' analysis does not achieve its purpose and fails. On the other hand, Plato can hardly be unaware of this failure. For when, some pages later, Socrates turns to arguing against Cratylus (434b–435d), his argument for convention will precisely hinge on the compresence of conflicting letters in a single name. So what is Plato's strategy here?

One possible answer is that the mimetic survey has a purely dialectical function within an overall strategy aiming at the refutation of the naturalist theory. On this interpretation, Plato wants to push the theory to its extreme consequences, stress the unescapableness of those consequences (425d–426b), and then show them to be untenable, thus refuting the whole theory. Supporters of this line[109] emphasize Socrates' disclaimers, especially his claims that the inquiry is going to yield 'absolutely outrageous and ridiculous' outcomes, and read them as stage-directions to the reader, signalling that the forthcoming inquiry is going to be unsound. There is an evident connection between this interpretation and the reading of the secondary etymologies as a parody or a joke: in both cases it is supposed that Plato disbelieves the analyses he makes Socrates advance.

This answer is, I think, mistaken. One weighty reason for thinking so is precisely the parallel with the secondary etymologies. Taken as a practical demonstration of the naturalist theory (which is how they were officially presented), those etymologies were a flop, and were meant to be so. Moreover, Socrates kept his distance from them in a number of ways: he ascribed them to a dubious Euthyphronic inspiration and on several occasions appeared to adopt a playful or even ironical stance towards them.

[109] See e.g. Belardi 1985: 39–41.

On the other hand, both Socrates and Plato seem to endorse most of those etymologies as 'exegetically correct' reconstructions of the original form of words and of the namegivers' thought. To account for this peculiar mixture of humour and seriousness I stressed the virtuosic nature of those etymologies and compared their ambiguous epistemological status with the one of Platonic myths (see §5.5.4). Now it is from the secondary etymologies that the whole mimetic enterprise arises, with the function of completing their job. Hence there is a strong presumption that it should be interpreted at least partially along the same lines.

Another reason for taking the etymologies of primary names seriously is that Socrates' analyses of the mimetic power of letters, if we take them apart from their role in a naturalist theory, contain nothing that Plato could not believe. Indeed, in the course of time other thinkers have advanced similar considerations in all seriousness. To see this you only have to read Augustine's report of Stoic views in *De dialectica* VI, 9–12, or Leibniz, *Nouveaux essais* III.ii.1; the remarks of both on 'r' and 'l' are especially close to those of Socrates.

Of course, as we have seen, fatal difficulties arise if we assume that the mimetic survey is really meant to constitute a naturalist inquiry (in the very specific sense of *Cra.*) into letters and primary names. But suppose that we free the survey from the too ambitious task of confirming the naturalist theory of names, and we read it as just an inquiry into the mimetic powers of Greek letters and their role in the meaning of names. If that were the purpose, then Socrates might legitimately believe he has achieved it. He might legitimately think that his survey shows the following two points: (i) Greek letters resemble, in virtue of their articulation, certain features of things; (ii) some of the letters included in Greek primary names are included therein precisely on account of their mimetic power.

These conclusions have nothing to do with the correctness of names, at least as that matter is conceived of in our dialogue. In particular, you might endorse them and yet deny that names are correct by nature. You might hold that the mimetic tie between letters and things, however real, is too vague and weak to ground the meaning of names, and that it could even be disregarded by a conventional stipulation among speakers. You can take the name ῥοή and make it mean 'rest' instead of 'stream'; the resemblance between ρ and movement would then not correspond to the name's meaning. This sort of stance is, I believe, close to the one Socrates is actually going to adopt. In particular, at 435c he seems to claim *both* that most names are, as a matter of fact, similar to their referents *and* that convention plays an important role in the correctness of names.

Then what about Socrates' repeated assertion that his views are 'ridiculous'? To my mind, this is not a sheer disavowal of the mimetic survey. It is rather an indication that Socrates is aware that the survey will strike most readers as something new and surprising;[110] that he is not claiming certainty about its details; and that he acknowledges that it, like the secondary etymologies before it, contains a component of playfulness and virtuosity.

6.4.5 *The discussion with Hermogenes concluded (427de)*

It is time for Socrates to gather the thread of his whole discussion with Hermogenes:

(SO.) This, Hermogenes, appears to me to be the meaning of the correctness of names [αὕτη μοι φαίνεται … βούλεσθαι εἶναι ἡ τῶν ὀνομάτων ὀρθότης], unless Cratylus here has something different to say. (427d1–3)

Remember when Hermogenes, at the very outset of the dialogue, said he would be glad to know what Socrates thought about the correctness of names (384a). Remember also when, later on, he asked for an explanation of 'what you say the natural correctness of a name consists in' (391a). Socrates is now finally claiming he has answered those original questions and winding up his long conversation with Hermogenes. One part of the dialogue is over. In fact, these are the last words Socrates directly addresses to Hermogenes; Cratylus is about to become his interlocutor.

The transition from one part of the dialogue to the next, however, requires further preparation:

HE. In fact, Socrates, Cratylus often causes me a lot of trouble, as I said at the beginning, claiming that there is a correctness of names, but saying nothing clear as to what it consists in [ἥτις δ' ἐστίν]. As a consequence, I'm not able to know whether each time he pronounces himself so unclearly on these matters intentionally or unintentionally. So now, Cratylus, tell me in the presence of Socrates whether you like what Socrates says about names or you have something different and finer to say. And if so, then tell it to us, so that you may either learn from Socrates or teach us both. (427d4–e4)

---

[110] Cf. Sedley 2003: 76. He compares *R*. 473c, where 'the innovative but vitally serious proposal that philosophers should be kings is introduced with the same admission that it will incur ridicule'. Note, however, that here in *Cra.* Socrates makes it clear that *he himself* regards his views as ridiculous, whereas in *R*. it is not so clear that the ridicule is more than just the scorn of the unphilosophical ones (cf. 452ae).

These carefully constructed lines divide into two parts of almost equal length. The first part (d4–8) is addressed to Socrates and recalls the dialogue's opening, where Hermogenes complained of Cratylus' obscurity (383b–384a) and said he had 'often' been discussing these matters with him and others (384c). In a sort of ring-composition, this has the effect of stressing that a first part of the dialogue has come to an end. (Notice Hermogenes' mention of the possibility that Cratylus' obscurity may be 'unintentional': a malicious suggestion that he might just be confused.) The second part of these lines (d8–e4) is addressed to Cratylus and contains an invitation, or rather a challenge, to take a stand in the discussion. (Note that Hermogenes has been won over by Socrates' arguments: conventionalism does not seem to constitute a viable option any more.) As we are going to see in the next chapter, Cratylus takes up the challenge.

CHAPTER 7

Naturalism discussed (427e–433b)

7.1 INTRODUCTION (427E–429C)

7.1.1 *Preliminary exchanges (427e–428e)*

We are now going to hear Cratylus' first words since his laconic 'if you like' of 383a3, whereby he allowed Hermogenes to involve Socrates in the discussion. In a few lines he is to become Socrates' only interlocutor down to the end of the dialogue, while Hermogenes remains silent.

CR. But, Hermogenes, do you regard it as easy to learn and teach any subject that quickly, let alone such a weighty one, which seems to be of the utmost importance? (427e5–7)

A very cautious opening. Hermogenes patiently tries to overcome Cratylus' resistance:

HE. By Zeus, I don't. But Hesiod's saying seems to me fine, that it is helpful 'even if one should store little upon little'.[1] So, if you're able to bring us even little progress, don't shirk the trouble, but be kind to Socrates here – you owe it to him – and myself.[2] (428a1–5)

These are the last words we shall hear from him in the dialogue. Socrates adds a very diplomatic invitation, full of Attic courtesy:

SO. Furthermore, Cratylus, I myself for my part wouldn't confidently maintain any of the things I've said [οὐδὲν ἂν ἰσχυρισαίμην ὧν εἴρηκα]; I just inquired together with Hermogenes following what seemed right to me. So, as far as this problem is concerned, don't be afraid and speak, if you've got something better to say: be assured that I'll accept it. And if you've got something finer than these things to say, I wouldn't be surprised. For you seem to me to have both thoroughly examined such matters by yourself and learnt them

---

[1] Hes. *Op.* 361–2.
[2] With a different punctuation the text would mean 'be kind to Socrates here – and you owe the same to me'. But cf. *Grg.* 461d.

from others. So, if you say something finer, enrol me too as one of your pupils on the correctness of names. (428a6–b5)

Taken at face value, these words are especially aimed at the possibility that Cratylus might feel embarrassed by Socrates' own account of the correctness of names. However, Socrates' disclaimer concerning his conversation with Hermogenes (a6–8)[3] is not merely a polite understatement, nor just a generic profession of Socratic ignorance, like his initial one at 384ac. As is shortly going to become clearer, Plato makes Socrates distance himself from his earlier conclusions also in order to prepare the forthcoming discussion with Cratylus, where some of those conclusions will be questioned and finally rejected.

It would be unsafe to infer from Socrates' words that Cratylus does have some pupils on the subject of the correctness of names, or that he has in turn been influenced by some definite thinker, whom Socrates is now referring to. Cratylus probably has *no* pupils at all – otherwise we might expect him not to have been so reticent at the outset.[4] The reference to his having 'learnt from others' is probably not seriously meant either: since Cratylus has not said anything yet, Socrates has no evidence for such a claim. Socrates is just generically praising the thoroughness of Cratylus' knowledge on the basis of the commonplace that you come to know something either by discovering it yourself or by learning it from others (cf. 436a, 438ab; *La.* 186c–187a).

Socrates' *captatio benevolentiae* produces the desired effect. For a moment it becomes clear that Cratylus' self-consideration has been tickled, though he immediately retreats to his previous attitude:

CR. Yes, Socrates, as you say, I have certainly been engaged in these matters, and perhaps I might make you into a pupil of mine. Nonetheless I fear it is quite the contrary, because I somehow feel like addressing to you Achilles' words, those he says to Ajax in the *Prayers*.[5] He says: 'Ajax, offspring of Zeus, son of Telamon, lord of peoples, thou seemed to say everything after my heart.' And to me, Socrates, you appear to prophesy much according to *my* mind, whether you were inspired by Euthyphro or some other Muse had long been dwelling in you without your knowing about it. (428b6–c8)[6]

---

[3] The disclaimer is echoed at 440c in a recantation of the naturalist approach to the etymologies.
[4] Cf. *Tht.* 180bc on the Heracliteans' failure to have pupils. A passage in Aristotle has sometimes been taken to report that *Plato* was Cratylus' pupil, but this is not so: see §I.2.1, (5).
[5] *Il.* 9.644–5. The division of the Homeric poems into books seems to date back to Alexandrian scholarship; in the classical period reference was made to episodes bearing a title, as here.
[6] On c7–8, 'whether ... about it', see §5.5.2.

Introduction (427e–429c)

In any case, Cratylus has finally been led to take a stand. By means of Achilles' words he approves the *whole* of Socrates' exposition (though c6 'much' somehow weakens the approval's force), presumably referring both to its theoretical parts and to the etymologies and mimetic analyses. Of course it does not follow that the whole of Socrates' exposition reflects the views of the historical Cratylus, or the views held by Cratylus the Platonic character before meeting Socrates. In particular, Cratylus' approval gives us no reason to believe that the historical Cratylus conceived a theory like the mimetic one. He is, however, likely (as Socrates already guessed at 384c) to have drawn a connection between natural correctness and etymology.

In his reply Socrates makes his purposes clearer. This is a crucial point:

> SO. My good Cratylus, I myself have long been marvelling at my own wisdom, and I distrust it [θαυμάζω καὶ αὐτὸς πάλαι τὴν ἐμαυτοῦ σοφίαν καὶ ἀπιστῶ]. So it seems to me that we must re-examine what I am saying. For being deceived [ἐξαπατᾶσθαι] by oneself is the most terrible thing of all: when the deceiver is not absent even for a little while, but is always there, how couldn't that be fearful? Thus one must, as it seems, frequently turn around to what has been said before, and try, as that famous poet has it, to look 'forward and backward at the same time'.[7] So now let us see what we have said. (428d1–e1)

Socrates had already shown himself amazed at his etymological 'wisdom', which he had received from Euthyphro (396cd). Here, however, the 'wisdom' he is talking about has a broader scope: it covers all that Socrates has achieved so far and Cratylus has just approved. Now, Socrates' attitude towards this 'wisdom' is importantly new. He does not just declare himself amazed; he also says something stronger, namely that he 'distrusts' or disbelieves it (d2).[8] Accordingly, he goes on to illustrate the danger of self-deception and announce a re-examination of his earlier claims. This is as explicit a stage-direction as any can be. The suggestion is plainly that there was something wrong in Socrates' discussion with Hermogenes and that we must now find out what it was.

7.1.2 Better and worse names? (428e–429b)

Thus the actual discussion between Socrates and Cratylus begins. Socrates kicks off recalling his own earlier definition of natural correctness as

---

[7] *Il.* 1.343, 3.109 (cf. 18.250, *Od.* 24.452).
[8] It is unclear whether πάλαι (d1) goes with *both* θαυμάζω *and* ἀπιστῶ (Méridier, Reeve) or only with θαυμάζω (Fowler). In the former case, Socrates would be saying 'I've long been marvelling and distrusting'. Since so far he has given no unambiguous sign of distrust in his own performance, I prefer the latter.

'indicating what each of the beings is like' (δηλοῦν οἷον ἕκαστόν ἐστι τῶν ὄντων 422d, cf. 393de):

(so.) The correctness of a name, we say, consists in showing what the object is like [ὀνόματος ... ὀρθότης ἐστὶν αὕτη, ἥτις ἐνδείξεται οἷόν ἐστι τὸ πρᾶγμα].[9] Shall we say this is a satisfactory claim?
cr. To me it seems most satisfactory, Socrates. (428e1–4)

Then Socrates recalls another claim advanced in the course of his argument against Hermogenes:

so. Therefore names are said for the sake of teaching? [Διδασκαλίας ἄρα ἕνεκα τὰ ὀνόματα λέγεται;]
cr. Of course. (428e5–6)

Socrates is referring to his definition of the name as an instrument by which we 'teach something to each other and separate the objects as they stand' (388bc). There is, however, a difference, apart from the obvious one that he is now leaving separation aside. In 388bc the thesis about teaching constituted an argument for, not a consequence of, natural correctness. Here it is the other way round: he seems (e5 'Therefore') to hold that his definition of natural correctness entails the thesis about teaching.

As at 388bc, Socrates' question about the function of names is formulated with reference to the *use*, not the imposition of names. This is revealed by a5 λέγεται,[10] which means 'are said, spoken', not 'are given' or 'are made' as it is sometimes translated. And yet in what follows we suddenly switch from use to imposition:

so. So shall we say that this is an art and there are craftsmen of it [καὶ ταύτην τέχνην εἶναι καὶ δημιουργοὺς αὐτῆς]?[11]
cr. Of course.
so. Who are they?
cr. The very ones you were speaking of at the outset, the lawgivers [τοὺς νομοθέτας]. (428e7–429a1)

In the light of what precedes, 'this is an art' (e7) apparently ought to refer to the art of teaching. This seems to bring about a conflict with the fact that at 388bc names, as instruments for teaching, were said to fall within the

---

[9] Literally 'the correctness of a name is that which will show what the object is like': cf. 422d.
[10] See Kretzmann 1971: 137 and n.30.
[11] Note that here the *copulative* εἶναι in the first clause (ταύτην τέχνην εἶναι) enables an *existential* εἶναι to be understood in the second clause (δημιουργοὺς αὐτῆς). Right the same happens in Arist. *APo.* 90b25–6; another similar passage (but with the implicit existential verb in the first clause and the explicit copulative in the second) is *Prm.* 137c. The two uses of εἶναι are closely connected: see §6.2.4 and Brown 1994, 1999 (and cf. further the passages cited by Bumyeat 2003: 13 and n.43).

Introduction (427e–429c)

competence of the *teacher* – not, as Cratylus now answers, the lawgiver,[12] who was rather said to *make* the names the teacher *uses* (388de). The lawgiver and the teacher, however, are or can be one and the same person (see §3.4.4). Hence Cratylus may be implicitly presupposing their identity in his answer; or (what is perhaps more likely) Socrates' 'this is an art' may already be an elliptical reference to imposition.[13]

However that may be, these lines bring the makers and the making of names back to the fore. Cratylus has evidently assimilated Socrates' earlier claims on the lawgiver(s); but the subject is now going to appear much less straightforward than before. Socrates at once seizes on a point he had neglected in his discussion with Hermogenes:

SO. So shall we say that this art too arises amongst humans like the others, or not? I mean something like this. Some painters are, I suppose, worse [χείρους] and some are better [ἀμείνους], aren't they?
CR. Of course.
SO. Then the better ones make their works, namely the paintings, finer [καλλίω], while the others make them inferior [φαυλότερα]? And likewise with builders: the houses made by some of them are finer, those made by others poorer [αἰσχίους]?
CR. Yes. (429a2–11)

Earlier on Socrates had failed to recognize the existence of better and worse ways of accomplishing the same task or performing the same action. He had rather presented several radical contrasts: between doing things in the natural way (and thus succeeding) and doing them in an entirely arbitrary way (and thus failing altogether), between the skilled craftsman and the ignorant uninitiated (386e–387d, 388c–389a; see §§3.1.1, 3.1.2 and n.13, 3.1.3 and n.21, 3.4.3 and n.103).[14] Now he seems to waive that radical approach in favour of a more tolerant one. But look what happens when he tries to extend the tolerant approach to the spheres directly involved in the present discussion:

SO. Is it, then, the same with lawgivers? Do some make their works finer, while others make them poorer?
CR. Now I no longer agree.
SO. So you don't think that some laws are better and some are inferior? [Οὐκ ἄρα δοκοῦσί σοι νόμοι οἱ μὲν βελτίους, οἱ δὲ φαυλότεροι εἶναι;]
CR. I don't.

---

[12] To be precise, Cratylus says 'the lawgive*rs*', in the plural. He may be thinking of several lawgivers for a single language or of several languages, each with one lawgiver (or more) of its own.
[13] Reeve translates ταύτην τέχνην εἶναι as 'Is there a craft *for that*' (my italics), probably in order to make clear both the reference to imposition and its connection with teaching.
[14] Cf. Grote 1888: III.317 n.4.

so. Then, as it seems, neither do you think that one name has been set down worse and another one better? [κεῖσθαι τὸ μὲν χεῖρον, τὸ δὲ ἄμεινον;]
CR. I don't. (429b1–9)

When it comes to νόμοι (more generic than either 'laws' or 'customs', see §3.3.2), and then to names, which are a kind of νόμοι, Cratylus wants the radical approach to retain its full force. He has an all-or-nothing view of what it is to be a νόμος, or a name.

Let us, for the moment, leave νόμοι aside and concentrate on names instead. Here Cratylus' all-or-nothing view is likely to depend on his naturalist thesis. The point is probably his allegiance to what in §1.1.1 I dubbed (C2), i.e. to the thesis that convention among speakers is not sufficient to make a string of sounds into the name of an object (383a); that, in other words, verbal conventions are either *naturally* correct names or no names at all. If now Cratylus granted that names can be more or less finely made, then Socrates could argue that mere verbal conventions, rather than being no names at all, are just badly manufactured names. To be sure, Cratylus might then specify that the distinction between better and worse, or finer and poorer, operates only *within* the set of naturally correct names, leaving out mere verbal conventions. (This is, in effect, the view he will be painfully forced to accept later on, at 431c–433c.) But this distinction would be threatened by problems of vagueness: where should we draw the boundary between the poorest natural names and the mere verbal conventions? The all-or-nothing stance is Cratylus' attempt – a doomed one – to steer clear of these difficulties.

We are shortly going to see how this interpretation of what is at stake in our lines is borne out by Socrates' next question. Before that, however, let me say a word about Cratylus' previous and more general claim that νόμοι cannot be better or worse (b4–6). As I see it, there is no reason to suppose that he has a general thesis about lawgivers and νόμοι, and it is best to suppose that his generic claims on this score are merely designed to back up the specific claim about names. But, in any case, if we try to reconstruct an assumption about νόμοι (in the sense of 'laws') that corresponds to (C2) about names, then we get the thesis that a law is not just whatever a city enacts, because laws that do not satisfy certain natural criteria (wrong laws) are no laws at all. This thesis occurs elsewhere in Plato's dialogues, where it is regarded with sympathy: *Hp. Ma.* 284b–285b, *Lg.* 715ab, [*Min.*] 314c–315a; cf. *Plt.* 293ce (on constitutions), X. *Mem.* 3.9.10.[15] The kinship

---

[15] Grote 1888: II.88–90 and nn., III.317 n.1; cf. below n.19. Some have also compared Thrasymachus' thesis that rulers *qua* rulers never make mistakes (*R.* 340d–341a), which, however, is derived differently.

between this thesis and Cratylus' one on names (which lies in the fact that laws and names are two kinds of νόμοι) might contribute to explaining Plato's interest in the latter thesis.

Now let us proceed to Socrates' next question:

SO. Therefore all names have been set down correctly? [Πάντα ἄρα τὰ ὀνόματα ὀρθῶς κεῖται;]
CR. Those that are names at all ["Ὅσα γε ὀνόματά ἐστιν]. (429b10–11)

This exchange is puzzling. So far all characters have been sharing what I have called the 'Redundancy Conception' of correctness, according to which all genuine names are, by definition, correct names, and being a name of *X* is the same as being a correct name of *X* (see §I.1.1). Therefore Socrates' question may seem superfluous; or it may arouse the suspicion that he has abandoned the Redundancy Conception in favour of the view that 'incorrect' means just 'poorly made' and that a name may be an incorrect name of *X* while still being a name of *X*. However, I do not think that we really have to ascribe to Socrates such a sudden change of mind, which would also be contradicted by what he says later on (432a–433b: see §§7.3.3–4). Socrates may well be implicitly adopting Cratylus' specific point of view, according to which names are correct *by nature*. Or he may be viewing matters as at 397a, where he framed naturalism simply as the thesis that *there is* a correctness of names,[16] presenting conventionalism as the thesis that names belong to their bearers 'haphazardly'. Either way, Socrates' question is actually equivalent to: 'Therefore all names are *naturally* correct?' (cf. Schofield 1982: 69). In other words: 'So you stick to your earlier claim that mere verbal conventions, being no naturally correct names, are no names at all?' Accordingly, Cratylus' answer amounts to: 'Yes, a string of sounds is either a naturally correct name or no name at all' – which boils down to the same as (C2).

Thus lines b10–11, if rightly interpreted, confirm that in b7–9 a concern with Cratylus' (C2) lay both behind Socrates' question whether νόμοι and names may be better or worse and behind Cratylus' negative answer. Thereby, however, the status of the mere verbal conventions like 'Hermogenes' is still far from being clarified; hence in the next lines Socrates is going to inquire more specifically about this issue. Cratylus' following answer will then lead to a discussion of the problem of false speech (429c–431c). Only at the end of that discussion shall we come back to better and worse names.

---

[16] Cf. 427d and Barney 2001: 27 n.7.

7.1.3 Hermogenes' name, again (429bc)

Cratylus' curt restatement of (C2) in b11 is hardly satisfactory. Socrates tries to take a concrete case into account:

SO. What then? Let us come back to what we were saying just now: shall we say that this doesn't even belong to Hermogenes here as a name ['Ερμογένει τῷδε πότερον μηδὲ ὄνομα τοῦτο κεῖσθαι φῶμεν],[17] unless he has something to do with Hermes' lineage, or that it does belong to him, only not correctly? [ἢ κεῖσθαι μέν, οὐ μέντοι ὀρθῶς γε;]

CR. I think, Socrates, that it doesn't even belong to him, but *seems* to belong to him [Οὐδὲ κεῖσθαι ... ἀλλὰ δοκεῖν κεῖσθαι], and that this name really is of someone else, the very one who has the required nature [εἶναι δὲ ἑτέρου τοῦτο τοὔνομα, οὗπερ καὶ ἡ φύσις].[18] (429b12–c6)

In these crucial lines Cratylus is faced with a dilemma: is the expression 'Hermogenes' *not a name* of Hermogenes at all, or is it an *incorrect name* of Hermogenes? Cratylus, who has just claimed that all names belong correctly to their bearers, obviously chooses the former alternative. His answer consists of two claims.

First, 'Hermogenes' is not, but merely *seems* or *is believed* to be, Hermogenes' name (c4–5).[19] This claim seems, strictly speaking, to imply that 'Hermogenes', though not being a *name* of Hermogenes, does after all conventionally refer to him (this possibility I dubbed '(a)' in §1.1.2). For the claim apparently implies that people use 'Hermogenes' as a name of Hermogenes when they utter and understand sentences like 'Hermogenes does so-and-so'; and this in turn implies that 'Hermogenes' does refer to Hermogenes, albeit in some merely conventional way. Thus Cratylus is here, as a matter of fact, granting convention a role (cf. Reeve xlii, Smith 2008: 136). His admission, however, is remarkably tortuous and unexplicit,

---

[17] I take it that τοῦτο (c1) is the subject of κεῖσθαι, while ὄνομα is in predicative position (see KG I.628–30, and cf. Dalimier). Some instead translate ὄνομα τοῦτο as 'this name': cf. *R.* 399c, *Ti.* 52d, *Phlb.* 16c, quoted by Riddell 1867: §37f.

[18] After φύσις (c6) the MSS read ἡ τὸ ὄνομα δηλοῦσα ('that indicates the name'), accepted by Fowler, the OCT and Dalimier. This is rather puzzling, because elsewhere in *Cra.* (393de, 395b, 396a, 422d) it is the name that 'indicates' the nature, not the other way round. Hence I, along with Burnet and Méridier, accept Schanz's deletion of the phrase. (Heindorf, inspired by Ficino's and Cornarius' translations, and followed by Hirschig, wrote ἣν τὸ ὄνομα δηλοῖ, 'which the name indicates'.)

[19] Here we can appreciate another parallel from the *Minos* (cf. §7.1.2), quoted by Grote 1888: III.317 n.1. After arguing that there is no such thing as a bad law (νόμος) and defining law as 'discovery of what is', at 317c Socrates claims that, among the treatises about the government of the city, 'the *correct* [ὀρθόν] one is a royal law, whereas the incorrect one is not, but *seems* [δοκεῖ] to be a law to those who don't know: for it is unlawful'.

Introduction (427e–429c)

and indeed is soon going to be dropped. To understand why we must turn to the second part of his answer.

Cratylus' second claim is that 'Hermogenes' is the name *of someone other* than Hermogenes, i.e. of the person whose nature is described by the name's etymology (c5–6). As we saw in §1.1.1, at 383a Cratylus' (C2) strictly speaking left open the possibility that convention might be a *necessary*, though not a sufficient, condition for a string of sounds to be the name of something. Now we learn that this is not so. A name – Cratylus is now implying – once it has been coined, names the object whose nature its etymology expresses and only that object, regardless of whatever speakers may believe or establish (cf. Williams 1982: 84).[20] This thesis importantly complements the three theses ascribed to Cratylus by Hermogenes' initial report of 383ab. In particular it can be viewed as an expansion of (C2); hence I shall dub it (C2*).

(C2*) is a perfectly consistent development of (C2). For if the view that the relation between a name and its referent is a natural one is to be taken seriously, then there is no reason why the beliefs and decisions of speakers should bear any relevance to that relation. Recall the comparison between Cratylan names and keys, which we introduced in §1.1.3. Once a key has got out of the smith's mould, then whether or not it fits some particular lock, and, if so, what lock it fits, is a completely objective matter, which hinges on the shape of the key and the lock and is independent of any human belief or decision thereabout. So, if the key fits one particular lock and does not fit another one, this fact is untouched by our believing or legislating that it fits the latter and not the former. Likewise it is perfectly consistent of Cratylus, who has a naturalist view of names, to hold that 'Hermogenes' is the name of the person (the key for the lock) with the appropriate nature, independently of human beliefs and decisions.[21]

It is, however, unclear how this stance can be reconciled with the view that names are νόμοι, advanced by Socrates at 388de and now picked up in his conversation with Cratylus at 429ab. Radical and uncompromising

---

[20] You might think of adding: 'if there is one and only one such thing'. But throughout the dialogue Cratylus and Socrates alike display no interest either in the existence or in the uniqueness of the referent. The latter omission is especially unfortunate, since the availability of names whose etymology fits more than one thing constitutes an argument for conventionalism.

[21] Smith 2008: 135 argues that 'Because a baptism has no effect on establishing a name's reference on the mimetic account, it cannot be considered to be a distinct speech act over and above ordinary name use ... apparent baptisms are assimilated to ordinary cases of name use.' But a baptism does have some effect *on the name's having a reference* (though not on its having the reference it does), by bringing the name into existence. And making a key surely counts as a distinct kind of act from using it.

as Cratylus' conception of νόμοι may be (§7.1.2), in any case the view that names are νόμοι seems to imply an acknowledgement of their being *social* institutions. But it is unclear how this social character may belong to a name whose relation to the referent is totally independent of speakers' beliefs, decisions and practices.

A consequence of (C2*) seems to be that sentences containing the name 'Hermogenes' are true or false depending on facts, not about Hermogenes, but about the real referent of 'Hermogenes', i.e. the person satisfying the description 'offspring of Hermes', whoever he may be. For example, the sentence 'Hermogenes is walking' is true or false depending on whether this unknown person is walking. This consequence gives rise to two sorts of difficulties. For one thing, it is intrinsically bewildering and counter-intuitive. For another, it conflicts with what Cratylus has just implied, i.e. that 'Hermogenes' does conventionally refer to Hermogenes though not being his name (see above). For, if this were the case, then there would also be a sense in which 'Hermogenes is walking' is true or false depending on whether Hermogenes is walking. Then sentences containing the term 'Hermogenes' would be systematically ambiguous and would admit of two interpretations, one where 'Hermogenes' is a name whose referent is the real 'offspring of Hermes', the other where 'Hermogenes' is a conventional designator whose referent is Hermogenes. This outcome is of course untenable, and this may explain why Cratylus is so reluctant to acknowledge the role of convention. Indeed, now that (C2*) has been asserted Cratylus will give no further signs that might be read as support to the possibility of conventional designators. The rest of the discussion will strongly suggest that, on Cratylus' view, a thing can be referred to only by a naturally correct name, conventional designators being altogether ruled out (version (b) of Cratylus' thesis in §1.1.2).

7.2 NATURALISM AND FALSEHOOD (429C–431C)

7.2.1 *Naturalism and the impossibility of false speaking (429cd)*

So far we have been going on the apparently pacific assumption that, on Cratylus' view, a sentence can be true as well as false. But is this really so? We are in for a shock:

so. One doesn't even speak falsely when one asserts that he is Hermogenes [οὐδὲ ψεύδεται ὅταν τις φῇ Ἑρμογένη αὐτὸν εἶναι], does one? For I fear that not

Naturalism and falsehood (429c–431c)

even this is possible, to assert that this is Hermogenes, if he isn't [μὴ γὰρ οὐδὲ τοῦτο αὖ ᾖ, τὸ τοῦτον φάναι Ἑρμογένη εἶναι, εἰ μὴ ἔστιν].[22]

CR. What do you mean?

SO. That speaking falsehoods is altogether impossible, isn't this what your theory entails? [Ἆρα ὅτι ψευδῆ λέγειν τὸ παράπαν οὐκ ἔστιν, ἆρα τοῦτό σοι δύναται ὁ λόγος;] For, my dear Cratylus, those who say so are quite numerous, both nowadays and in the past. (429c7–d3)

Think of someone pointing to Hermogenes and saying 'This is Hermogenes' (or of someone just saying, without pointing, 'The person who is discussing with Socrates is Hermogenes'). We would normally say that thereby the speaker has *truly* asserted of this person that he is Hermogenes. But Cratylus holds that 'Hermogenes' is not this person's name and this person 'is not Hermogenes' (407e, 408b). Therefore he is apparently committed to holding that such an assertion is *false*. (If he regarded 'Hermogenes' as a conventional designator of this person – version (a) of his theory, see §7.1.3 – then he should grant that one can also, in a sense, *truly* assert of this person that he is Hermogenes. But Socrates here seems to ignore this possibility and assume that Cratylus holds version (b), according to which there are no conventional designators, and 'Hermogenes' does not refer to this person at all.)

Socrates, however, suspects that matters are even worse. Perhaps, on Cratylus' view, it is *not* even the case that one who asserts of this person that he is Hermogenes is speaking falsely (c7–8). For perhaps, on Cratylus' view, it is even *impossible* to assert of someone who is not Hermogenes, i.e. whose name is not 'Hermogenes', that he is Hermogenes (c8–9). Cratylus does not immediately understand this conjecture and asks for an explanation (c10). Socrates explains that he suspects that Cratylus is committed to the *general* view that false speaking is impossible (d1–2): a view that has many adherents, present and past (d2–3).

Thus, putting aside secondary details, we can view our lines as containing essentially the following argument, formulated by Socrates on Cratylus' behalf:

If you assert of this person that he is Hermogenes, then you speak falsely;
It is impossible to speak falsely;
Therefore it is impossible to assert of this person that he is Hermogenes.

---

[22] I remove the question mark that editors usually print after ἔστιν (c9). See KG I.224 and LSJ μή A.2.b, μὴ οὐ I.2.

But why does Socrates think that Cratylus is committed to the argument's second premiss, i.e. to the thesis that it is impossible to speak falsely? To answer this question we must start from a detailed analysis of d1–3.

To begin with, Socrates speaks of Cratylus' λόγος (d2). It is usually thought that this means just 'what you are saying' and refers to Cratylus' last answers (b7–c6); I prefer to think that the λόγος here is rather Cratylus' whole *theory* of names, of course with special reference to what he has just said. Now Socrates establishes a connection between Cratylus' theory and the general thesis that 'It is impossible to speak falsely' (hereafter 'ISF' for brevity). He expresses this connection asking ἆρα τοῦτό σοι δύναται ὁ λόγος; (d2). Here δύναται is usually translated 'means';[23] but this translation is potentially misleading. Socrates cannot reasonably suppose that Cratylus' theory of names literally *means* ISF. He might perhaps suppose that the former *implicates* the latter, i.e. that ISF is what Cratylus conveys, though not what he strictly and literally says;[24] but, again, I do not see what should license such a supposition. Rather, as Burnyeat 2002: 40 n.1 recognizes,[25] Socrates is probably supposing that Cratylus' theory *entails* ISF. This meaning of δύναμαι is not recorded by LSJ, but can be derived both from the very meaning 'mean' and from the meaning 'have the power to produce' (405b, *Phlb.* 23d; Eur. *Med.* 128).[26] Furthermore, this interpretation perfectly suits another text, which constitutes a striking parallel to our passage. At *Euthd.* 286c Socrates asks Dionysodorus, who has just argued that contradiction is impossible: 'Speaking falsehoods is impossible [ψευδῆ λέγειν οὐκ ἔστιν] – for *this is what the argument entails* [τοῦτο γὰρ δύναται ὁ λόγος], isn't it – and the speaker must either speak the truth or not speak at all?' There too Socrates' point is not that the argument for the impossibility of contradiction means or implicates ISF; he is rather suggesting that the former *entails* the latter.[27]

So, to return to our passage, in lines 429d1–2 Socrates suggests that Cratylus' theory somehow entails the paradoxical thesis ISF. This thesis

---

[23] On δύνασθαί τι = 'to mean something' see §4.2.6. The 'meaning' at issue need not be a linguistic one: see *Prt.* 324a, Th. 6.36.2, Ar. *Pl.* 842.
[24] See Denyer (1991: 72): 'is the implication of your argument that …'
[25] But cf. already Schofield 1982: 69 and Aronadio's translation 'implica'.
[26] Indeed, the very English verb 'to mean' can be used as equivalent to 'to entail'. That is why I regard the translation of d2 δύναται as 'means' as potentially misleading, but not necessarily mistaken.

δύνασθαί τι may also mean 'to be *equivalent* to something' (Th. 6.40.2; Hdt. 2.142.2, 6.86.γ; X. *An.* 1.5.6). Hence Socrates might also be claiming that Cratylus' theory and ISF are logically equivalent. But I do not see how so strong a claim could be justified.
[27] 'Questo è infatti ciò che il ragionamento implica' is Decleva Caizzi's (1996) translation.

constitutes a premiss in an argument to the conclusion that it is impossible to assert of their friend that he is Hermogenes. Quite interestingly, when Socrates first states the conclusion Cratylus is puzzled and asks for an explanation (c10), thus prompting Socrates to set out his second premiss. Cratylus' puzzlement seems to mean that he has not previously thought of the point Socrates is making. In fact, as his next answer (d4–6, see §7.2.2) shows, he does endorse the general thesis ISF, only on grounds that are *independent* of the naturalist theory of names. This may explain why he does not see that ISF applies to Hermogenes' case. (On this way of reading our lines cf. Burnyeat 2002: 40 n.1.)

Now it is difficult to see *how* Cratylus' theory of names can entail ISF. On the face of it, although Cratylus has a peculiar conception of names and of what may or may not count as a name of something, there is no reason why he should deny that a statement where a name is misattributed to something is a *false* statement. For example, we take it that, since 'Callias' is not the name of Coriscus, one who says of Coriscus that he is Callias makes a false statement. Then why should Cratylus not take it that, since 'Hermogenes' is not the name of his friend, one who says of his friend that he is Hermogenes makes a false statement?

Perhaps there is an argument showing that Socrates' suggestion in d1–2 is correct.[28] Consider the following:

(1) If it is possible to speak falsely, then names are by convention.

By contraposition this is equivalent to the following:

(2) If names are not by convention, then it is not possible to speak falsely.

And since, if names are by nature, then they are not by convention, it follows that

(3) If names are by nature, then it is not possible to speak falsely.

---

[28] On any interpretation, Socrates should think that ISF is a consequence of Cratylus' theory, not of Cratylus' theory *plus* other controversial premisses, or other premisses which actually are by themselves sufficient to derive ISF. Consider Smith's (2008: 148) suggestion: 'the mimetic theory of names *entails*, that there is no difference in function between a predicate and a referring term: both pick out their objects by being *like* them. And since the ὀνόματα imitate their objects, a sentence, as a complex of ὀνόματα which pick out their objects by imitation, will pick out its complex of objects by imitating them. So the mimetic theory leaves us with two possible outcomes for a sentence – either it imitates (is like) a complex set of objects (or state of affairs) and picks out that state of affairs, or it does not imitate a complex set of objects and does not pick them out.' Here the real culprit would seem to be *not* the naturalist assumption that names are like their referents, but rather the assumption that a sentence is nothing more than a list of names and that making a statement is nothing more than naming (see §7.2.2, (C)). This assumption is *by itself* sufficient to derive ISF, with or without the naturalist assumption.

Now, (3) is a very reasonable construal of Socrates' suggestion in d1–2. So I propose to focus on (1), show in what sense it can be regarded as true, and thereby vindicate the truth of (2), of (3) and ultimately of Socrates' claim.

Now suppose that two persons see someone who is taking a bath at some distance. The man they see is Coriscus, but they mistake him for Callias, who is actually sleeping at home. The first person asks: 'What is Callias doing?', and the second answers: 'Callias is taking a bath.' In the language common to both speakers 'Callias' is the name of Callias, not of Coriscus; so the second speaker has made a *false* statement. On the other hand, in some sense both speakers have referred to Coriscus, and the second speaker has said something *true* of him. Here, according to Kripke's analysis (1979: 13–15, cf. 1980: 25–6 and n.3), we should distinguish between the *semantic referent* of a name, i.e. its nominatum (Callias), and the *speaker's referent*, i.e. 'that object which the speaker wishes to talk about, on a given occasion, and believes fulfills the conditions for being the semantic referent' (Coriscus). Generally speaking, the semantic referent and the speaker's referent of a name may not coincide; and at least some false statements are such that their falsity depends on such a divergence – i.e. on the fact that a name is being used to refer to an object other than its nominatum.

Now, the nature of the distinction between semantic reference and speaker's reference is such that the speaker's referent might actually *become* the semantic referent under appropriate conditions. 'What was originally a mere speaker's reference may, if it becomes habitual in a community, evolve into a semantic reference' (Kripke 1979: 22).[29] That is to say, the speakers' false beliefs about the referent may, in the long run, take the place of a new baptism. In our example, the fact that 'Callias' can be used to refer to Coriscus seems to imply that there is no incompatibility between 'Callias' and Coriscus and that Coriscus *might* be or become – though he presently is not – the nominatum of 'Callias'. Therefore semantic reference is a conventional matter; and names (at least *proper* names; but, arguably, the point could be extended to any other kind of names) are conventional.

This line of reasoning could, I submit, be used by someone who wanted to establish (1) – hence also (2), (3) and Socrates' claim at 429d1–2, which seems equivalent to (3). Is it *Socrates'* own line of reasoning? To my mind, the argument contains nothing that it would be substantially anachronistic

---

[29] Cf. the well-known case of the name 'Madagascar' (Kripke 1980: 163).

to ascribe to Plato;[30] but since in comparison with the extreme brevity of what Socrates says it is rather complicated, I doubt that it may be exactly what he has in mind. However, I suspect that in any case Socrates must have in mind something less definite than an actual argument – something rather like an intuition, which my argument may successfully unpack and spell out. My suspicion accords with two pieces of evidence.

First, in 430a–431c Socrates will refute ISF, but then will *not* turn this refutation against Cratylus' theory of names and claim to have constructed a *reductio* of the theory. Socrates' failure to do so may suggest that he is not really sure that Cratylus is committed to ISF. (But it may also be just due to the course taken by the discussion. The refutation will uninterruptedly develop into a resumption of the issue of better and worse names, which was pending since 429b, and this will further lead to a frontal attack on Cratylus' theory of names at 434c–435d.)

Secondly, consider d2–3, which so far we have been neglecting: 'For [γάρ] ... those who say so are quite numerous, both nowadays and in the past.' Here 'for' seems to mean that the diffusion of the thesis about false speaking confirms its ascription to Cratylus: 'Doesn't your theory entail that false speaking is altogether impossible? [*I wouldn't be surprised if this were your view,*] for ...'[31] This fits well with my suspicion that Socrates' ascription of ISF to Cratylus is more of a conjecture than an inference proper.

But who are 'those who say so', i.e. the past and contemporary supporters of ISF? So far as contemporaries are concerned, there are plenty to choose from, as we are going to see in §7.2.2: both the thesis itself and other related theses, from which it can be easily derived, are well attested in Socrates' and Plato's age. As for the past supporters, Socrates is very likely thinking of Parmenides' anathema on 'what is not', which was echoed and exploited in many arguments against false speaking, including the very one which Cratylus is about to advance at 429d4–6. Parmenides himself, however, seems to conceive of 'what is not' as what does not exist and is nothing at all, rather than as a false proposition or a state of affairs that is not the case.[32] Furthermore, far from deeming false speaking impossible, he seems to hold that most human beliefs are utterly mistaken (28 B1.28–30, 8.50–2 DK). So, in spite of the use to which his anathema was subsequently put,

---

[30] In particular, Plato is able to conceive of what *we* should describe as a divergence between speaker's reference and semantic reference: see *Phdr.* 260bc.
[31] See *GP* 61–2 on γάρ presupposing an ellipse.
[32] *Pace* Kahn 1986b: 14–18. See KRS 245–6, Brown 1994: 217–20.

Parmenides cannot be counted among the supporters of the impossibility of false speaking. Socrates' hint is ultimately misguided.[33]

7.2.2 Cratylus against false speaking (429d)

Let us, at long last, resume our reading of the dialogue. We left Socrates asking Cratylus whether his theory entails that false speaking is impossible and adding a remark on this view's broad diffusion. Here is Cratylus' answer:

> CR. Yes, Socrates. For how could one, saying that which he says, not say what is? [Πῶς γὰρ ἄν ... λέγων γέ τις τοῦτο ὃ λέγει, μὴ τὸ ὂν λέγοι;] Saying falsehoods is just this, i.e. not to say the things that are, isn't it? [ἢ οὐ τοῦτό ἐστιν τὸ ψευδῆ λέγειν, τὸ μὴ τὰ ὄντα λέγειν;][34] (429d4–6)

This argument admits of several, not mutually exclusive construals, which follow from different ways of understanding the phrase λέγων ... τοῦτο ὃ λέγει (d4–5). Note that within this phrase, whatever its exact meaning, τοῦτο ὃ λέγει could be replaced without loss by 'something'. This replacement allows us to formulate the argument more clearly. It also enables us to recognize the parallel with an argument ascribed by Proclus to Antisthenes: 'Every sentence is true: for he who speaks says something [ὁ γὰρ λέγων τὶ λέγει], and he who says something says what is [ὁ δέ τι λέγων τὸ ὂν λέγει]; and he who says what is speaks truly' (XXXVII, 12.18–23 = Antisth. V A 155 SSR). Proclus says that Antisthenes used his argument to show that contradiction is impossible; but I suspect that he is just giving his interpretation of Cratylus' argument and ascribing it to Antisthenes.

Now let us come to the various possible construals of Cratylus' argument.

(A) According to the simplest construal – which I have adopted in my translation – λέγων τοῦτο ὃ λέγει means 'saying that which one says', where 'that which one says' refers to the *content* of a sentence, the proposition it expresses. For example, if one utters the sentence 'Theaetetus flies', what one says is *that* Theaetetus flies. Then the argument can be reconstructed as follows: if one says that which one says, one says something;

---

[33] We should not get upset if Socrates' interpretation of Parmenides seems to diverge from ours. There is a parallel case. At *Sph.* 241d, 258ce the Eleatic Stranger – no stranger to Eleatic philosophy – suggests that Parmenides' ban on speaking of what is not includes a ban on negative predications of the form '*X* is not *Y*': a view that is rightly rejected by most modern interpreters (Brown 1994: 219, 230–1).

[34] τὸ μὴ τὰ ὄντα λέγειν (d6) is '*not* to say the things that are', as ἄν ... μὴ τὸ ὂν λέγοι (d5) is 'could ... *not* say what is'. Some inexactly translate 'say the things that are not', 'say what is not'.

and if one says something, one says 'what is'. Here 'what is' ought to mean 'what exists', but Cratylus exploits its ambiguity and takes it to mean 'what is the case'. So, if one says what one says, one says what is the case, and false speaking is impossible.

There is nothing banally wrong with this argument except the final equivocation on the meaning of 'what is'. In particular, the view that 'something' entails existence, which is explicit in my reconstruction and in Antisthenes' alleged argument (cf. *R.* 478bc, *Prm.* 132bc, *Sph.* 237bc), is a perfectly legitimate one to hold. We may compare the nowadays standard view that the quantifier '∃' expresses existence. Some supporters of this view would acknowledge that 'Callias says something' can be regimented as '(∃x) Callias says x' and asserts the existence of something that Callias says, namely a proposition.[35] But, of course, nobody thinks that the existence of a proposition – whatever it may be for a proposition to exist – entails its truth. That is basically the point where Cratylus' argument goes astray.

(B) On another construal, λέγων τοῦτο ὃ λέγει means 'speaking of that of which he speaks'.[36] Then Cratylus' argument runs as follows: if one speaks of that of which one speaks, one speaks of something; and if one speaks of something, one speaks of 'what is'. Again 'what is' is crucially ambiguous as between 'what exists' (the meaning required by the argument) and 'what is the case' (the meaning Cratylus needs). More precisely, the whole expression τὸ ὄν λέγειν is ambiguous as between 'to speak of what exists' and 'to say what is the case'. And again the argument contains no trivial mistake except this crucial equivocation. Indeed, many philosophers would agree that only what exists can be a proper subject matter of discourse: for we cannot refer to what is not there to be referred to. In particular, Parmenides deemed it impossible to speak of what is not (see especially 28 B2.7–8, 6.1 DK). This may be important in our present connection, since Parmenides seems to have just been hinted at by Socrates at d2–3.

(C) On a third possible construal Cratylus' argument does not hinge on a mere equivocation, but on a substantive philosophical mistake. Recall the conception, which we had to take into account in §2.2.3, of a (declarative) sentence as a sort of noun phrase. According to this conception the sentence 'Callias is white' as a whole names or refers to Callias, or perhaps

---

[35] The view that 'something' entails existence was denied by the Stoics (see Sen. *Ep.* 58.15, Alex. Aphr. *in Top.* 301.19–25, with Long/Sedley 1.163–4). Its present-day counterpart has its opponents too (see McGinn 2000: 15–51, Orenstein 2002).
[36] See ch. 2 n.30 on λέγω + accusative = 'speak *of* something'.

white Callias.[37] This view notoriously threatens to make false speaking impossible. For a name can either name (refer to) something or fail to be a name at all; and in uttering a supposed name you can either successfully name (refer to) something or fail to name anything at all – in which case you fail to perform an act of naming. Likewise, if sentences are akin to names, a sentence can either refer to something or fail to be a sentence at all; and in uttering a sentence to make a statement you can either successfully refer to something or fail to refer to anything at all – in which case you fail to perform an act of stating. In other words, stating, like naming, is either completely successful or abortive. Therefore, if sentences are akin to names, no room seems to be left for the possibility of false sentences or false speaking.[38]

The view we have just illustrated might be at work in Cratylus' argument. To make this explicit we might translate τοῦτο ὃ λέγει 'that which he *speaks*' and reconstruct the following argument: if one speaks that which one speaks, one speaks something; and if one speaks something, one speaks 'what is'. Here perhaps there is no longer any reason to decry the fallacious equivocation on the meaning of 'what is', i.e. 'what exists'/'what is the case', which infected both (A) and (B). Once stating is assimilated to naming, nothing more is required for a sentence to be true than the existence of its referent.

Each of the above construals is supported by significant parallels. (A) matches Proclus' first objection against 'Antisthenes' (xxxvII, 12.21–3): 'Falsehood too exists [ἔστιν καὶ τὸ ψεῦδος] and nothing prevents the one who says what is [τὸν τὸ ὂν λέγοντα] from saying something false.' (B) may have a very close parallel in the argument at *Euthd.* 283e–284a, where we can discern a progress from λέγειν τὸ πρᾶγμα περὶ οὗ ἂν ὁ λόγος ᾖ 'speaking of the object which the sentence is about' to λέγειν τὸ ὄν 'speaking of what is' and, finally and fallaciously, to τἀληθῆ λέγειν 'speaking truths'.[39] (C) matches Proclus' second objection against 'Antisthenes' (12.23): 'he who speaks speaks *of something* and does not

---

[37] Or the *fact* that Callias is white. This specific version of the story, according to which a sentence names or refers to a fact, is reconstructed by Denyer 1991 behind several ancient arguments against contradiction and false speaking, including Cratylus' own (where its presence had already been supposed by Ackrill 1997: 53, Fine 1977: 299). To my mind, however, this is no natural way of construing the texts at issue.

[38] This criticism, often repeated in present-day literature on the subject, stems from Russell 1956: 187–8 (whose target was the version according to which a sentence is the name of a fact). NB: From all the above variants of the assimilation of sentences to names we must carefully distinguish Frege's doctrine that all true sentences name the True and all false sentences name the False. See Denyer 1991: 19–21.

[39] On (B) in *Euthd.* see Sprague 1962: 15.

speak *something* [περί τινος λέγει, καὶ οὐχὶ τὶ λέγει]'. The argument at *Euthd.* 283e–284a can also be read thus; in the same dialogue, the assimilation of sentences to names informs the argument against the possibility of contradiction at 285e–286b.[40] *Tht.* 188d–189b contains a related argument about false judgement.[41] Finally, this seems to be the point of Antisthenes' denial of the possibility of contradiction, as reported by Arist. *Metaph.* 1024b26–1025a1.[42]

7.2.3 *Cratylus against false speaking, continued*

We can now turn to Socrates' reaction to Cratylus' argument.

SO. The argument is too clever for me and for my age, my dear friend. Nevertheless tell me this much: do you think that it is not possible to speak falsehoods but it is possible to assert them? [λέγειν μὲν οὐ δοκεῖ σοι εἶναι ψευδῆ, φάναι δέ;]
CR. I don't think it's possible to assert them either.
SO. Nor to say them, nor to address them to anyone? [Οὐδὲ εἰπεῖν οὐδὲ προσειπεῖν;] (429d7–e3)

Socrates is not going to challenge Cratylus' argument directly, showing why it is fallacious: with a characteristically self-deprecatory move, he declares himself unable to discuss it. This may (but need not) mean that Plato himself finds it difficult to spot what is wrong with the argument. This interpretation would be especially likely if what is wrong with the argument were a mistaken conception of the structure of sentences (see (C) in §7.2.2). For the dialogue contains other signs that may suggest some unclarity upon this issue (see §§2.2.3, 7.2.4, 7.3.4). In fact, according to a widespread scholarly opinion, for a long time Plato was at a loss to solve the sophistical puzzles generated by such misconceptions, until he finally provided the correct solution in the *Sophist*.[43]

In any case, Socrates goes for a different approach and tries to grasp the real purport of Cratylus' claim that false speaking is impossible. He wants to make it clear that the issue is not merely terminological: what Cratylus is rejecting is not the description of a certain phenomenon as 'false speaking', but the very *existence* or possibility of that phenomenon, however

---

[40] On (C) in *Euthd.* see Frede 1992b: 414–15.
[41] See Burnyeat 2002: 43–50.
[42] On Antisthenes see Denyer 1991: 27–33.
[43] The solution is already hinted at in *Tht.* 188d–189b, as Burnyeat (1990: 77–9, 2002: 40–50) shows. Burnyeat's (2002: 50–66) further contention, that hints in the same direction are also present in the *Euthydemus*, I find less convincing (cf. n.114).

described. Thereby, of course, Socrates also underlines the absurdity of Cratylus' position. To bring this out more effectively, he has recourse to a fictional example:

(SO.) For example, if someone, meeting you abroad,[44] should seize your hand and say: 'Hello, Athenian foreigner, son of Smicrion, Hermogenes', would this person speak these things or assert them or say them [λέξειεν ἂν ταῦτα ἢ φαίη ἂν ταῦτα ἢ εἴποι ἂν ταῦτα]? Or would he address thus not you, but Hermogenes here? Or no one? [ἢ προσείποι ἂν οὕτω σὲ μὲν οὔ, Ἑρμογένη δὲ τόνδε; ἢ οὐδένα;] (429e3–7)

The envisaged situation is basically clear: someone, greeting Cratylus, misnames him. The details of the example, however, deserve close examination.

The greeting addressed to Cratylus is a complex expression, composed of three simpler ones: 'Athenian foreigner', 'son of Smicrion', 'Hermogenes'. The first of these is correct: Cratylus would be truly described, in the given situation, as an Athenian foreigner. The third expression is obviously incorrect: on anyone's view, 'Hermogenes' is not Cratylus' name. What of the second expression? Who is Smicrion? Since we know that Hermogenes is son of Hipponicus (384a), it seems reasonable to guess that 'Smicrion' is the actual name of Cratylus' father and that the description 'son of Smicrion' is true of Cratylus.[45] According to this conjecture, 'Hermogenes' is the only misnomer in the greeting. Therefore the essential kernel of the example seems to consist in *someone's addressing Cratylus as 'Hermogenes'*. The other two expressions (together with 'Hello' and the extralinguistic device of seizing the hand) have the function of confirming what Socrates suggests at e5–7: the interlocutor would actually utter the whole complex expression and address Cratylus by means of it. He would neither address Hermogenes (i.e. the person conventionally called thus) nor fail to address anyone at all. Nor, we may add, would he address the supposed natural referent of 'Hermogenes', the man with the appropriate nature, if there is one (cf. c5–6).

It is important to be clear about the nature of the items whose truth or falsehood is being discussed. In c7–9 Socrates seemed to be interested in the falsehood of whole sentences and statements: 'when one asserts *that* he is Hermogenes … to assert *that* this is Hermogenes'. The present example, however, does not concern a sentence, but something syntactically more elementary, i.e. the misattribution of a *name*, which Socrates apparently

[44] ἐπὶ ξενίας (e4): 'abroad' (cf. Antiph. 2.2.9), not 'in hospitable fashion' as some translate.
[45] See DK 65 A1 n. and Kirk 1951: 225 n.1.

Naturalism and falsehood (429c–431c)

regards as a case of false speaking.[46] This view is consistent with 385bd, where he maintained that names can be true or false as well as sentences. But it is actually imprecise: misattributing a name can perhaps constitute a necessary condition for someone to be speaking falsely, but it does not seem to constitute a sufficient condition. In particular in Socrates' example we should say that the mistaken greeting *implies* a certain false belief, not that it is itself false.

So much for Socrates' example. Cratylus brazens it out:

CR. To me, Socrates, it seems that he would utter these sounds in vain [ἄλλως]. (429e8–9)

To describe the act performed by his imaginary interlocutor Cratylus discards the verbs suggested by Socrates and resorts to the non-committal φθέγγομαι, 'utter', instead.[47] The adverb ἄλλως, 'in vain', makes his position clear: the poor chap would utter mere sounds and say nothing significant.[48] So he would not manage to address anyone with the words 'Hello, Athenian stranger' etc. As a matter of fact Cratylus is choosing the last of the alternative assessments of the situation suggested by Socrates at e5–7.

But Socrates does not give up and tries to get something out of this unpromising answer. Ignoring the qualification 'in vain', he clings to Cratylus' use of the verb 'utter':

SO. I am happy with this too. Would he who uttered these sounds utter them as true or as false? Or one part of them as true and another part as false? Even this would be enough. (430a1–4)

Of course, if Cratylus should grant that one may *utter* something true or false, then his scandalous thesis, that false speaking is impossible, would be reduced to an innocuous linguistic prescription: what is ordinarily described as 'false speaking' should be redescribed as 'false uttering'. That is why Socrates says he is happy with talk of 'uttering'.

Note that the possibility that the utterance is part true, part false (a2–3) is not mentioned just for the sake of completeness, as a merely theoretical possibility. Rather, its mention points to the fact that one part of the complex expression addressed to Cratylus ('Athenian foreigner', and probably

---

[46] This is why I have rendered φαίη ἄν (e6) as 'would *assert*', in line with c7, c8, e1. Cf. Dalimier, who translates φάναι as 'affirmer' throughout 429ce (268 n.387).
[47] Cf. 383a, where ἐπιφθεγγόμενοι, a compound from the same verb, occurred in Cratylus' characterization (reported by Hermogenes) of the conventionalist view.
[48] On ἄλλως see LSJ II.3. Reeve's translation, 'he is not articulating them as he should', is misleading.

also 'son of Smicrion', see above) does apply to him, while another part ('Hermogenes') does not.

In spite of Socrates' efforts, however, Cratylus stubbornly goes his own way and states his position as clearly as possible:

CR. For my part I'd say that such a person was just making noise [ψοφεῖν], moving pointlessly [μάτην], as if one moved a copper vessel striking it. (430a5–7)

So what we would ordinarily describe as a case of misnaming is no more significant than someone's beating a pot.[49] The same would presumably hold when *Hermogenes* himself is addressed or referred to as 'Hermogenes'. For, according to Cratylus' view, 'Hermogenes' is a (naturally correct) name neither of Cratylus nor of Hermogenes. And although there is actually a very important difference between these two cases, in that 'Hermogenes' has no relation at all to Cratylus, whereas it is the conventional name of Hermogenes, Cratylus seems prone to obliterate this difference (cf. §§1.1.2, 7.1.3, 7.2.1).

7.2.4 Socrates' defence of false speaking (430a–431c)

Since he has not managed to persuade Cratylus to come to terms, Socrates now can only refute him. He begins by making two preliminary moves. He recalls the thesis, which he established at 422d–424a in the course of developing the naturalist theory, that a name is an *imitation* of an object; and he establishes an analogy between names and paintings as two kinds of imitations.

SO. Come on, Cratylus, let's see if we can be reconciled somehow. Wouldn't you maintain that the name is one thing and that which the name belongs to is another?
CR. Yes.
SO. And you also agree that the name is an imitation of the object [τὸ ὄνομα ... μίμημά τι εἶναι τοῦ πράγματος]?[50]
CR. Definitely.
SO. And you say that paintings [τὰ ζωγραφήματα] too are, in some different way, imitations of certain objects?
CR. Yes. (430a8–b5)

---

[49] On the sonority of a χαλκίον cf. *Prt.* 329ab, where the focus is on the *length* of the orators' answers, but their vacuity is also hinted at, as Dalimier 269 n.393 notes.
[50] We could also write μίμημά τι εἶναί του πράγματος, 'an imitation of *some* object': cf. b4 μιμήματα ... πραγμάτων τινῶν.

Then Socrates makes the point that both kinds of imitations, names and paintings, can be *distributed* or *applied* to the things of which they are imitations:

SO. Well, then – for perhaps I don't understand what in the world you're saying, and what you're saying might be right – is it possible to distribute and apply [διανεῖμαι καὶ προσενεγκεῖν] both of these imitations, i.e. both paintings and names, to the objects of which they are imitations, or not?
CR. It is. (430b6–c1)

Socrates does not yet explain what it means to 'distribute' or 'apply' an imitation to the object of which it is an imitation. For the moment it seems reasonable to take this notion in a very broad sense: we distribute an imitation *X* to an object *Y* if and only if we perform an act that *implies the belief* that *X* is an imitation of *Y*.

SO. Now consider this first. One could assign the man's image to the man and the woman's image to the woman [ἆρ' ἄν τις τὴν μὲν τοῦ ἀνδρὸς εἰκόνα τῷ ἀνδρὶ ἀποδοίη, τὴν δὲ τῆς γυναικὸς τῇ γυναικί], and so on, couldn't one?
CR. Certainly.
SO. And also, vice versa, the man's image to the woman, and the woman's image to the man?
CR. This too is possible.
SO. Now, are both of these distributions [διανομαί] correct, or only one of the two?
CR. Only one of the two.
SO. The one, I think, that assigns to each thing what is appropriate and similar ["Ἦ ἂν ἑκάστῳ ... τὸ προσῆκόν τε καὶ τὸ ὅμοιον ἀποδιδῷ].
CR. So it seems to me. (430c2–14)

Before doing anything else, let me clarify a terminological issue. At 430ab Socrates has just been distinguishing two kinds of μιμήματα ('imitations'): names and ζωγραφήματα ('paintings'). Now he begins to speak of an εἰκών ('image') without explaining whether this new term is roughly equivalent to the generic μίμημα or to the specific ζωγράφημα. The rest of the argument, however, will show that the latter is the case. Indeed, in 430de two further equivalents are introduced: ζῷον (again 'painting', etymologically linked with ζωγράφημα) and γράμμα ('picture'). So one and the same item can be indifferently called a ζωγράφημα or ζῷον or an εἰκών or a γράμμα. But of course this is no fixed terminology: later on εἰκών will include names (431d etc.).

We can now turn to the content of these lines. Generally speaking, Socrates here wants to establish that an image, which represents a certain object, can be assigned or distributed either to the object it does represent or to some other object instead. The former sort of distribution is correct, the latter incorrect. But, in any case, the image remains an image of what it represents, even if on a particular occasion it happens not to be distributed to it.

The example Socrates gives is not very clear. We might expect it to concern the possibility of assigning to a particular person either their own image or someone else's. But this is made unlikely by the fact that all seems to hinge on the person's *gender* and by Socrates' consistent use of the definite article: he speaks of assigning the image of 'the' man, or 'the' woman, to 'the' man, or 'the' woman.[51] If we take the text at face value, the example seems to have the two following features. First, the image at issue is the image of a *generic* object, i.e. an image that aims to represent, not a definite particular man or woman (e.g. Coriscus or Aspasia), but rather the whole class of men or women, by displaying some relevant and typical traits of its members.[52] Such are, e.g., the pictures used in textbooks to illustrate male and female anatomy. Secondly, the object to which the image is assigned is also a generic one. Think of someone who points to the picture of a female blackbird in a zoology text and claims that this is what male blackbirds look like: she is assigning to the (generic) male the picture of the (generic) female. It is, however, difficult to imagine a plausible analogous example concerning human beings.

On the face of it, this is how Socrates' example should be understood. Fortunately, however, we shall shortly see that 430e–431a suggests a partly different interpretation, according to which the example does concern the image of a generic man or woman, but this is supposed to be assigned to a *particular* man or woman instead of a generic one. This means that not all the definite articles in our lines must be taken at face value: those in the dative case are actually equivalent to indefinite ones (c3, c6–7: 'to *a* man', 'to *a* woman').[53] Of course, assigning the image of a generic man or woman to a particular man or woman is tantamount to holding that he or she is a man or a woman.

Now we are ready for Socrates' next step, where he turns to his advantage the analogy between paintings and names:

SO. Well, in order that you and I, who are friends, don't have a quarrelsome discussion, accept what I am saying. Such a distribution I call *correct* in the case of both imitations, paintings and names, but in the case of names besides

---

[51] Reeve translates none of the articles: e.g. c2–4 'Can we assign a likeness of a man to a man and that of a woman to a woman, and so on?'
[52] Cf. Williams 1982: 88.   [53] Cf. the analogous case of the article at 385c14 (§2.2.3).

calling it correct I also call it *true* [ἐπὶ δὲ τοῖς ὀνόμασι πρὸς τῷ ὀρθὴν καὶ ἀληθῆ]. The other distribution, the giving and application of what is dissimilar [τὴν τοῦ ἀνομοίου δόσιν τε καὶ ἐπιφοράν], I call *incorrect*, and also *false* in the case of names [οὐκ ὀρθήν, καὶ ψευδῆ ὅταν ἐπ' ὀνόμασιν ᾖ]. (430d1–7)

Here Socrates is simultaneously making two distinct points. (i) The distribution of names to things can be either correct or incorrect, like the distribution of images or paintings, insofar as both names and paintings are imitations. (ii) In the case of names, but not in the case of paintings, the correct distribution of names can also be called 'true', the incorrect distribution 'false'.

Following Denyer 1991: 79–80, (i) can be more fully stated as follows. A name, which imitates and thus names a certain object, can be assigned or distributed either to the object it does name or to some other object instead. The former sort of distribution is correct, the latter is incorrect. But, in any case, the name remains a correct name of what it imitates, even if on a particular occasion it happens to be distributed to something else instead. Thus Socrates is actually vindicating the possibility of incorrectly distributing a name that is in itself perfectly correct, hence of using an expression that is false but significant, contrary to what Cratylus argued in 429d–430a. This is reminiscent of the *Sophist*'s doctrine that a false sentence attributes to the subject features which are perfectly real in themselves but are different from whatever feature the subject does possess (263bd).[54]

(ii) contradicts Cratylus' claim that it is impossible to speak falsely or address someone falsely. It also asserts an asymmetry between the distribution of paintings, which can only be said to be correct or incorrect, and the distribution of names, which can also be said to be true or false. Socrates gives no reason for this asymmetry, and discussion of this issue must be deferred until we come to his own examples at 430e–431a. But I can anticipate that, in my view, the reason is that names are *linguistic* items, whereas paintings are not, and that the notions of truth and falsehood have a connection with the sphere of language which they do not have with the sphere of paintings, pictures, images and the like.

In any event, Socrates' former point, i.e. that the distribution of names, like that of paintings, can be either correct or incorrect, is already too much for Cratylus:

CR. But, Socrates, I suspect that in the case of paintings this is possible, I mean to distribute them incorrectly, whereas in the case of names it isn't, but it is necessary always to distribute them correctly. (430d8–e2)

---

[54] Cf. Frede 1992b: 412–23, Crivelli 2008: 235–9, and Crivelli (forthcoming).

His tone, however, is significantly softer than before. Socrates responds by pressing the analogy and describing in more detail what happens when the distribution takes place:

SO. What do you mean? What is the difference between the two cases? Isn't it possible to go to a man, say 'This is your picture' [εἰπεῖν ὅτι 'Τουτί ἐστι σὸν γράμμα'] and show him either, if it so happens, an image of himself or, if it so happens, one of a woman [δεῖξαι αὐτῷ, ἂν μὲν τύχῃ, ἐκείνου εἰκόνα, ἂν δὲ τύχῃ, γυναικός]? By 'show' I mean bring to the sense of eyesight.
CR. Of course.
SO. Well, isn't it possible to go to this very man again and say 'This is your name' [εἰπεῖν ὅτι 'Τουτί ἐστιν σὸν ὄνομα']? For the name too is an imitation, like the painting, it seems. So this is what I am saying: Shouldn't it be possible to say to him 'This is your name' and after that bring, in turn, to his sense of hearing either, if it so happens, the imitation of himself, saying 'man' [τὸ ἐκείνου μίμημα, εἰπόντα ὅτι 'ἀνήρ'], or, if it so happens, that of the female of the human kind, saying 'woman' [τὸ τοῦ θήλεος τοῦ ἀνθρωπίνου γένους, εἰπόντα ὅτι 'γυνή']?[55] Don't you think that this is possible and does sometimes happen?
CR. I want to come to terms with you, Socrates; let it be so. (430e3–431a7)

This stretch of text falls into two parallel parts, which describe respectively the distribution of pictures (430e3–8) and of names (430e9–431a7). Both descriptions follow a common pattern consisting of three successive stages. (I) You step up to a man. (II) You utter the sentence 'This is your picture/name.' (III) You let the man see or hear an imitation, which in the picture case may be either 'an image of himself' or an image of a woman, whereas in the name case it may be either 'the imitation of himself', i.e. the name 'man', or the imitation of 'the female of the human kind', i.e. the name 'woman'.

As far as stage (I) is concerned, we ought to remark that the man we step up to and address is clearly a *particular* man, despite what might have been suggested by a literal reading of 430c (see above), where Socrates spoke of assigning an image to 'the man' or 'the woman'.

Let us move on to stage (II) and to the sentences 'This is your picture' and 'This is your name.' Each constitutes a *preamble* to the distribution proper, a preamble whose function is presumably to identify the person we are addressing and make clear what is about to happen. I surmise, however, that the preamble need not necessarily involve the utterance of a *sentence*, although here it happens to do so. For one thing, the same basic purpose could also, and more naturally, be served by an appropriate

---

[55] On the inclusion of ἀνήρ and γυνή (a3–4) within quotation marks see below.

gesture or a whole pragmatic context: recall the example in 429e, where the interlocutor uttered no sentence, but his seizing Cratylus' hand and his saying 'Hello, Athenian stranger, son of Smicrion' roughly played the preamble role relative to the distribution of the name 'Hermogenes'. (In fact, in a way our very stepping up to the man in question can be viewed as already part of the preamble; perhaps stages (I) and (II) must not be sharply separated from each other.)[56] Furthermore, Socrates' claim that the distribution of names differs from that of pictures in being true or false as well as correct or incorrect (430d) would lose plausibility, if both kinds of distribution necessarily involved a sentential preamble like 'This is your picture/name'. For then both sorts of distribution would involve at least one proper truth bearer (Williams 1982: 88).

Stage (III) raises several questions. One concerns the imitation's content. In the picture case, Socrates says at e5–6, we show the man either 'an image of himself' (ἐκείνου εἰκόνα) or 'one of a woman'. These expressions would seem to suggest that, just as the man we are addressing is a particular man, so the picture is the picture of a *particular* person, i.e. either the man himself or a particular woman. Yet, as already at 430c, this alternative seems odd; it would rather be natural to contrast the man's picture with the picture of another particular person, no matter whether a man or a woman. Now the analogy with the name case comes to our aid. For there (e9–a7) what is distributed is clearly not a proper name but a *general* term, i.e. either ἀνήρ 'man' or γυνή 'woman'.[57] This shows that, likewise, the distributed picture is meant to be one of a *generic* man or woman, as 430c had already suggested and as Williams 1982: 88 sees. In particular, the expression τὸ ἐκείνου μίμημα, 'the imitation of himself' (a2–3), which in context must refer to the general term 'man', shows that the parallel ἐκείνου εἰκόνα, 'an image of himself' (e5), can and probably does refer to the picture of a generic man, although at first glance neither would seem a natural construal.

Socrates' choice of the names ἀνήρ and γυνή as examples is interesting for another reason besides their being general terms. At 414a both

---

[56] Indeed, Sedley (2003: 133, 135) goes so far as to claim that 'telling you that such and such is your name is how Socrates characterises the very same speech act that I perform when, in greeting you, I address you in the vocative' – and that the vocative itself need not be that of the very nouns 'man' and 'woman' (see stage (III)), but just a masculine or feminine vocative. This is perhaps too distant from what Socrates literally says. It is, I submit, in order to foreclose any possible way out which Cratylus might be willing to take that Socrates is trying to depict a situation as unambiguous and explicit as possible, at the price of a certain unnaturalness.
[57] *Pace* Ficino and Reeve, who translate a3 τοῦ θήλεος as 'feminae cuiusdam', 'a female'.

names were etymologized as *secondary* ones. Yet they are now presented as examples of names' being imitations of their referents, as *primary* names are. This ought not to disconcert us, since throughout the section on primary names Socrates tended to assimilate secondary to primary names, until he even claimed that secondary names too are a product of imitation (427cd, see §6.4.3).

My last point about stage (III) concerns what happens after the preamble. Since in the picture case we are just supposed to show the picture, i.e. 'bring it to the sense of eyesight', in the name case the parallel act of 'bringing' the name 'to the sense of hearing' must consist in just *uttering* the name. Yet it is not clear how we should understand the expressions printed in all editions as εἰπόντα ὅτι ἀνήρ ... εἰπόντα ὅτι γυνή (a3–4). On the one hand, ὅτι may be *pleonastic* and introduce a piece of direct speech, as in all its other occurrences in the passage (e4, e9, a1).[58] Hence a3–4 can be translated 'saying "man" ... saying "woman"', as I did above together with Méridier and Reeve. This construal requires doing something no editor does, i.e. printing ἀνήρ and γυνή within quotation marks (εἰπόντα ὅτι 'ἀνήρ' ... εἰπόντα ὅτι 'γυνή'), exactly like the sentences Τουτί ἐστι σὸν γράμμα / ὄνομα, which follow the other pleonastic ὅτι's. On the other hand, printed without quotation marks the text invites us to take the ὅτι's as genuine conjunctions, introducing 'that'-clauses with omitted copula, and to translate 'saying that [he is] a man ... saying that [he is] a woman'.[59] This should be understood as follows: (we utter the name 'man' or 'woman' and *thereby, as a matter of fact,*) say that the person is a man or a woman. The 'that'-clauses should not be meant to specify the *form* of our utterance (for we are not supposed to utter a sentence but a simple name), but rather what the utterance actually amounts to. This is best brought out by Dalimier's translation 'en lui disant qu'il est "homme" ... en lui disant qu'il est "femme"'.

Let us sum up. In Socrates' example, the subject matter (what the name or picture is distributed to) is supposed to be a particular thing. Each of the two distributions consists in a preamble followed respectively by the ostension of a picture and the utterance of a name. The preamble has the function of identifying the subject matter; in the example it takes the form of a sentence, but generally speaking it need not do so. The ostended

---

[58] On pleonastic ὅτι see LSJ II.1, who claim it is attested 'even where the quotation consists of one word', citing *Prt.* 330c, *Men.* 74b, c. These passages, however, present the same ambiguity as ours, and an omitted copula cannot be ruled out.

[59] See Fowler, Minio-Paluello, Sedley 2003: 134–5. Another possibility is 'saying that [the name is] "man" ... saying that [the name is] "woman"'.

Naturalism and falsehood (429c–431c)

picture represents a generic object; the uttered name is a general term. The basic point is the following: we can apply to a given thing either a name that does name it (i.e. to whose extension it does belong) or a name that does not. This point is of course not limited to general terms; clearly Socrates' example is also meant to vindicate the possibility of maldistributing a proper name (e.g. 'Hermogenes' to Cratylus, cf. 429e), which would be analogous to maldistributing the picture of a particular person.

Thus Socrates draws a neat distinction between the act of identifying something and the act of applying a name to it.[60] As several interpreters have rightly stressed,[61] this can be viewed as a first approximation to the fundamental distinction (first set forth at *Sph.* 261d–263d) between two parts of a sentence: the subject, whose function is to identify or refer to what the sentence is about, and the predicate, whose function is to say something about it. However, it is important to be clear that *Cra.*'s distinction concerns the application of an isolated name, not the *internal* structure of a sentence; it is a distinction between two acts which does not imply a corresponding syntactic distinction. In fact, it is far from clear whether in *Cra.* Socrates deploys a sound conception of the structure of sentences. We already had to face this doubt with regard to 385bd (§2.2.3), where it seemed likely that Socrates was assimilating sentences to names and failing to appreciate the former's structural complexity; here the following lines will shortly give us the opportunity for a supplement of discussion. What the *Sophist* recognizes, instead, is precisely that a single sentence can perform both functions by dividing them between its two parts.

Let us resume our reading of the text. We are reaching the denouement: Socrates drives home the conclusion he already announced at 430d, i.e. that the distribution of names can be either true or false.

s o. You do well, my dear, if this is how the matter stands; now we must not fight about it at all. So, if in this case too there is such a distribution [εἰ δ' οὖν ἔστι τοιαύτη τις διανομὴ καὶ ἐνταῦθα], we want to call one of these two situations 'speaking truly' [ἀληθεύειν], the other 'speaking falsely' [ψεύδεσθαι]. (431a8–b3)

---

[60] According to some commentators (Smith 2008: 145–50, Crivelli 2008: 228–9, and apparently already Crombie 1963: 482–3), Socrates' point is that a name can be used to refer successfully to something it does not (etymologically) describe or imitate, as in Donnellan's (1966) theory of the referential use of definite descriptions. I do not see how this could be right. In the hypothetical situation Socrates is considering, the reference is carried out (successfully) by the preamble, not by the maldistributed name 'man' or 'woman'; Socrates does not argue that the maldistributed name successfully *refers* to the addressee, but that it is successfully *applied* or ascribed to him. For this interpretation to be sound Socrates would have to consider a different kind of situation: e.g. you want to tell someone, whom you mistakenly take to be a woman, that she is so-and-so; then you step up to that person and say '*Woman*, you are so-and-so.'

[61] See Ackrill 1997: 53–4, McDowell 1973: 236, Owen 1986: 120 n.41.

If 'in this case too' (i.e. in the case of names, as compared to that of pictures) both a successful and an unsuccessful distribution are possible, then – Socrates says – let us call them respectively 'speaking truly' and 'speaking falsely'. This of course means that the true or false distribution of names is *a case* of true or false speaking, actually the simplest and most basic case, which is already sufficient to refute Cratylus' claim that false speaking is impossible. As Kahn 1973a: 161 puts it, 'Plato is not yet prepared to attack the larger problem of false statement, but he wishes to insist on the existence of falsehood as such, in the simplest case of applying the wrong ὄνομα to a given object.'

According to the interpretation I offered above, the picture distribution and the name distribution are neatly parallel to each other. But, then, why can only the latter be said to be true or false, whereas both can be said to be correct or incorrect (430d)? To my mind, this asymmetry simply depends on the fact that names are *linguistic* items, whereas pictures are not (cf. Sedley 2003: 133 n.17). The idea is presumably that the notions of truth and falsehood, unlike the broader notions of correctness and incorrectness, apply to the relation between language and the world but not to the relation between pictures and pictured things. As a generic idea this is of course right. But one might reply that even within the linguistic sphere the notions of correctness and incorrectness have a broader extension than the notions of truth and falsehood, and that the mere assignment of a name to a thing is precisely one of those cases where talk of truth or falsehood is inappropriate.[62]

---

[62] Williams 1982: 88 advances a different interpretation. In his view, for the asymmetry to be explained the distribution should be 'an activity which, when done with a name, yields a *logos*, something that can be true, and when done with a picture, does not. We can imagine a wordless *dianome* of a picture – handing it to the subject, for instance; and we can imagine a partly worded one, in the form of someone's saying, for instance, "You are ... " and presenting a picture. The analogy to this in the case of names would be saying "You are ... " and presenting a name. But ... saying "You are ... ", followed by presenting "*N*", comes to saying "You are *N*", which, unlike its picture analogue, can be true as well as correct.' Now Williams' interpretation may seem to fit the text very well: if we understand 431a3–4 εἰπόντα ὅτι ἀνήρ ... εἰπόντα ὅτι γυνή as 'saying that [he is] a man ... saying that [he is] a woman' (see above), and furthermore we take this at face value, as specifying the utterance's actual form, then Socrates' account of name distribution may seem to assign a crucial role to a sentence like 'You are a man/woman', which has no parallel in the picture case. Nevertheless, Williams' interpretation is open to several objections. (1) A sentence like 'You are a man/woman' is not necessary for the assignment to come off: after the preamble it must be possible simply to *utter* the name, as in the picture case we simply show the picture. Indeed, Socrates, unlike Williams, does not even consider the possibility of a 'partly worded' picture assignment. And in his example, where the *preamble* happens to take sentential form, it seems redundant to suppose that after 'This is your name' one should necessarily add 'You are a man/woman', rather than just uttering the promised name. (2) When the topic of falsehood was introduced at 429ce, Socrates switched freely from examples in sentential form ('This is Hermogenes')

Naturalism and falsehood (429c–431c)

Now we can read how Socrates rounds off his refutation of Cratylus:

(SO.) And if this is so, and it is possible to distribute names incorrectly and not to assign to each thing the appropriate ones [μὴ ὀρθῶς διανέμειν τὰ ὀνόματα μηδὲ ἀποδιδόναι τὰ προσήκοντα ἑκάστῳ], but sometimes the inappropriate ones, then it should be possible to do this same thing to verbs too [εἴη ἂν καὶ ῥήματα ταὐτὸν τοῦτο ποιεῖν]. And if it is possible to consider so verbs and names, necessarily it is possible to consider so sentences too [εἰ δὲ ῥήματα καὶ ὀνόματα ἔστιν οὕτω τιθέναι, ἀνάγκη καὶ λόγους]. For it is to sentences that the combination of these elements amounts [λόγοι ... ἡ τούτων σύνθεσίς ἐστιν], I think. Or what do you say, Cratylus?
CR. I say so: it seems to me you're right. (431b3–c3)

Socrates argues that, if names can be incorrectly distributed, then so can ῥήματα (b3–6); and if names and ῥήματα, then also λόγοι, which are composed of both (b6–c2). That much is beyond question; but the meaning of the terms which here I have left untranslated, the way in which the distribution of the items they refer to takes place, and several other points, are a matter for discussion.

First of all, a note on the translation of οὕτω τιθέναι (b6). This is unlikely to mean 'assign so' (Fowler, Méridier, Reeve), as we might expect, because in the dialogue τίθημι is always used in connection with the imposition of names, as distinct from their use. But then again, the meaning cannot be 'impose so' (Dalimier, Barney 2001: 181, Sedley 2003: 135), because imposition is not in question here. I suggest the meaning is *'consider* so' (see LSJ B.II), where 'so' stands in for 'as capable of being distributed correctly or incorrectly' (cf. b3–5).

ῥήματα must mean 'verbs', as most interpreters translate it, rather than 'phrases' as at 399ab and elsewhere (see §6.1.2).[63] There are two reasons for believing so. First, 'verbs' appeared to be the meaning in 425a, a passage significantly parallel to ours, where Socrates spoke of constructing the λόγος from ὀνόματα and ῥήματα (see §6.3.5). Secondly,

---

to an example concerning the mere attribution of a name ('Hello ... Hermogenes'); therefore he cannot now conceive of name distribution as necessarily involving a sentence. (3) In 431bc Socrates is going to argue that, if names can be incorrectly distributed, so can verbs, and if names and verbs, then also sentences. If the false name distribution already involved a false sentence, then the reasoning would be circular.

[63] 'Phrases' is the construal of Lutoslawski 1897: 430–1 and Denyer 1991: 149–50, who interpreted 425a in the same way. Others take ῥήματα here as 'predicates' (Oehler 1962: 59 n.1, Sedley 2003: 135). But, to my mind, while ῥῆμα does mean 'phrase' in at least some other passages of *Cra.*, it does not mean 'predicate' anywhere else in the dialogue (or, for that matter, anywhere at all in Plato or Aristotle): see §§6.1.2, 6.3.5. In any case, here this meaning would fit in badly with the context. If ῥήματα meant 'predicates', why should the general terms 'man' and 'woman' count as ὀνόματα, 'names', rather than ῥήματα?

Socrates' claim that λόγοι are a combination (σύνθεσις) of ὀνόματα and ῥήματα strongly suggests that ὀνόματα and ῥήματα are *heterogeneous* kinds of items, which are equally necessary to make up a λόγος.[64] This would not be so if ῥήματα were phrases, which normally *contain* names; but it is obviously so if they are verbs. In fact this is exactly the point at *Sph.* 263d, where a λόγος ('sentence') is termed a σύνθεσις ἔκ τε ῥημάτων γιγνομένη καὶ ὀνομάτων, a 'combination arising from verbs and names'.

Socrates does not say what the distribution of a verb consists in. By analogy with the name case we may suppose that it would consist in the specification of a subject matter followed by an utterance of the verb. For example, we might point to someone who is sitting and then utter either (correctly and truly) the verb 'sits' or (incorrectly and falsely) the verb 'flies'. Still, it is unclear *what* exactly the verb is distributed *to*. In the terminology of *Sph.* 262b, it could be either the action or the agent; in our example, either the person's sitting or the sitting person.

Now let us move on to the λόγοι. We can safely assume that these are (declarative) *sentences* and that the incorrectly assigned λόγοι are *false* sentences. Socrates' move from names, via verbs, to sentences is the reverse of the one implied by 429ce, where he passed from the false sentence 'That is Hermogenes' to the mistaken greeting 'Hello ... Hermogenes'. Thus the discussion of false speaking comes full circle and the refutation of Cratylus is rounded off.

Socrates' claim that sentences are a combination of names and verbs clearly seems to imply that, as in the *Sophist* (cf. especially 263d, quoted above), the minimal sentence consists of a name and a verb: e.g. 'Theaetetus sits'. Socrates need not believe that *all* the names and verbs in an incorrectly distributed sentence are incorrectly distributed; he may just mean that every incorrectly distributed sentence, i.e. every false sentence, contains either an incorrect name ('Theaetetus is a *dog*') or an incorrect verb ('Theaetetus *flies*'). But remember 385bd, where Socrates' claim that 'the part' of a false sentence is false apparently meant that *all* the parts are false (see §2.2.3). Furthermore, doubts about this point will be raised by a related claim Socrates will make at 432de: see §7.3.4.

As in the case of verbs, so in the case of sentences Socrates does not say what they are distributed to. However, it seems natural to think that a sentence is distributed or assigned to what it is about, and that this is

---

[64] Cf. Barney 2001: 182.

what the sentence's subject-term refers to. So it seems natural to think that 'Theaetetus sits' is distributed to Theaetetus.[65]

Socrates does not say what the distribution of sentences consists in either. This is actually a very delicate question. As Derbolav (1972: 113–14) and McDowell (1973: 236) note, what Socrates says seems to suggest that the distribution of sentences is analogous to the distribution of names, and that therefore sentences themselves are basically akin to names. If we take this suggestion seriously, then we must ascribe to Socrates the view that a sentence, like a name, can only be assigned to something independently *given*, and that the utterance of a sentence, like that of a name, must be preceded by the identification of a subject matter. So, e.g., to assign the sentence 'Theaetetus sits' we should first make it clear that we are going to say something about Theaetetus (either by means of gestures or by approaching Theaetetus and saying something like 'This is your sentence') and then utter the whole sentence, which may be either true or false.

So, according to this interpretation, Socrates' defence of the possibility of false speaking shares with some of the arguments *against* it the mistaken assumption that sentences are basically akin to names.[66] However, those arguments coupled that assumption with the parallel one that stating (the act we perform in uttering a sentence) is basically akin to naming. From this twofold confusion it followed that making a false statement is as impossible as naming something that is not there to be named. Socrates, instead, here tries to divorce the two assumptions and to accept the former while rejecting the latter; for he holds that stating is not like naming, but rather like applying a name to a *given* thing. Of course this compromise solution is far from satisfactory. For it misrepresents the actual use of sentences, and contrasts with the *Sophist*'s distinction, according to which a complete sentence – unlike a name or verb – is by itself able to perform the twofold function of referring to a subject matter and saying something about it. In particular, note that a sentence, unlike a name, cannot be maldistributed to something while referring to something else instead; for a false sentence as a whole refers to nothing at all (Denyer 1991: 80).

This diagnosis of what Socrates is assuming in our passage fits well with his insistence (which we criticized above) on the claim that the

---

[65] Alternatively we could think that a sentence is distributed to a *fact* (see Sedley 2003: 164). But this more sophisticated hypothesis is not supported by the very little that Socrates says here. It is also confronted with a specific problem: to what fact is a *false* sentence distributed?

[66] Such might be the very argument which Cratylus advanced at 429d and which Socrates declared himself unable to discuss: see §7.2.2.

assignment of a simple name can already be said to be either true or false. For, if sentences are assimilated to names with respect to their structure, at the same time names (or rather their assignment) can be assimilated to sentences with respect to the bearing of a truth-value.[67] This situation strongly reminds us of 385bd, where Socrates' extension of truth and falsehood from sentences to names made us suspect that he was mistakenly assimilating sentences to names (§2.2.3). In fact, between the two passages there is a sort of specular correspondence: there Socrates moved from the truth or falsehood of sentences to that of names; here he is making the reverse move from names to sentences.[68] To be sure, neither passage provides more than circumstantial evidence of Socrates' misconception, and neither rules out that he may, after all, be aware of the peculiar nature of sentences.[69] But the same suspicion will be aroused again by 432de (see §7.3.4), whereas no clear indication to the contrary will emerge. So we seem to be justified in taking an uncharitable stance towards Socrates on this score.

7.2.5 Conclusion

Be that as it may, Socrates has finally forced Cratylus to acknowledge that it is possible to speak falsely. His argument for this conclusion has exploited the naturalist assumption that names are imitations of things. But that assumption is not really essential to the argument or to the conclusion, nor is it conceived as such by Plato. 'It is the mere *fact* that a name is correctly applied to one thing, incorrectly to another, which is the condition of the possibility of a name's being true or false, not the explanation of this fact by the theory of natural appropriateness accepted by Cratylus. In so far as Socrates' argument is made to depend on the acceptance of this explanation it is merely *ad hominem* against Cratylus. And this must surely be recognized by Plato, since at the end of the day ... Socrates rejects Cratylus' theory' (Schofield 1972: 247–8). In other words, Plato ought to realize, and presumably does realize, that Socrates' defence of false speaking should, in its essentials, survive the eventual fall of naturalism.

---

[67] Here is Derbolav's (1972: 113–14) diagnosis: 'Sokrates geht also vom Wort linear zum Satz über, indem er das Zuordnungsschema vom Teil auf das Ganze überträgt, was nur dadurch verschleiert wird, daß er gleichzeitig den grammatischen Topos vom Satz als Haupt-Zeitwort-Gefüge verwendet. Die Bezeichnung "wahr" für die richtige Ding-Wort-Zuordnung ist also gleichsam von der Wahrheit des Ganzen her erborgt, während das Zuordnungsschema umgekehrt vom Wort auf den Satz übertragen ist.'
[68] Cf. ch. 2 n.64.   [69] See Fine 1977: 294 n.12.

7.3 NATURALISM AND IMPERFECT RESEMBLANCE (431C–433B)

Recall the context in which the discussion about false speaking originated. At 429a Socrates got Cratylus to agree that there are better and worse painters; that the paintings made by the better ones are finer, while those made by the worse ones are inferior; and that likewise architects make finer or poorer houses according to their capacity. But when, at 429b, Socrates asked whether the same holds of lawgivers (νομοθέται) and their products, i.e. whether νόμοι and names can be better (or finer) or poorer (or inferior, or worse), then Cratylus did not agree any longer and claimed that all names are (naturally) correct. Then a question about the status of the name 'Hermogenes' (429b12–c3) sparked off the discussion about false speaking. That discussion is now over, and Socrates punctually reverts to the previous subject. He is now going to argue that the name of a given thing can be better or worse.

The debate on this point occupies the text from 431c to 433b and can be divided into two rounds. In the first round (431ce) Socrates argues for his thesis simply on the basis of the analogy between names and pictures. But when we might think he has attained his objective, a fresh argument advanced by Cratylus starts a second round of the debate (431e–433b), where Socrates first neutralizes Cratylus' argument and then goes on to set forth at length his views on better and worse names.

7.3.1 First round (431ce)

Socrates' return to better and worse names is abrupt and unemphatic:

SO. Now if, again, we compare the first names with pictures [Οὐκοῦν εἰ γράμμασιν αὖ τὰ πρῶτα ὀνόματα ἀπεικάζομεν], is it as with paintings?[70] In paintings it is possible both to include all the appropriate colours and shapes [πάντα τὰ προσήκοντα χρώματά τε καὶ σχήματα ἀποδοῦναι] and also not to include them all, but to leave some out and add some others, so that they may be too many and too large [καὶ μὴ πάντα αὖ, ἀλλ' ἔνια ἐλλείπειν, ἔνια δὲ καὶ προστιθέναι, καὶ πλείω καὶ μείζω]. Or is it not possible?
CR. It is.
SO. Then he who includes them all renders the pictures and the images fine [ὁ μὲν ἀποδιδοὺς πάντα καλὰ τὰ γράμματά τε καὶ τὰς εἰκόνας ἀποδίδωσιν],

---

[70] Here (c5) the Greek text contains an anacoluthon. Socrates starts off as if he were making a point about names through a comparison with paintings, but then his point is actually about paintings themselves; only at d3–4 will he come to names.

whereas he who adds or subtracts does produce pictures and images too, but bad ones? [γράμματα μὲν καὶ εἰκόνας ἐργάζεται καὶ οὗτος, ἀλλὰ πονηράς;] CR. Yes. (431c4–d1)

Socrates is elaborating on something Cratylus already granted at 429a, i.e. that images (or pictures, or paintings: the terminology for these items is still unstable) can be better or worse made. Indeed, Socrates is now explaining what it is for an image to be better or worse made. A fine image must contain *all and only* the 'appropriate' colours and shapes, i.e. colours and shapes like those of its subject matter, without omitting or adding anything and without altering the proportion between the subject's parts.[71] When this condition is not satisfied we still have an image, still an image of the same subject, but a bad one instead of a fine one.

If this much is clear, there remains room for doubt concerning various other issues. To start with, how exactly is Socrates' point about images connected to the argument about false speaking? The transition is signalled by the particle οὐκοῦν and the adverb αὖ (c1). The latter expresses that Socrates is *again* exploiting the analogy between names and pictures, which was crucial to the foregoing argument. The former is more problematic. It may have inferential force (*GP* 434), as in c10, and is sometimes translated so.[72] But since it is unclear how Socrates could derive his present claim from the conclusions about the false distribution of names, verbs and sentences, it seems better to take οὐκοῦν as 'proceeding to a new point, or a new step in the argument' (*GP* 434–5).[73] The discussion about false speaking has been a parenthesis within the discussion of better and worse names, as Schofield 1982: 69 stresses, and what Socrates is now drawing from it is just a renewed emphasis on the close analogy between names and images/pictures/paintings. This analogy was crucial at 424d–425a, in Socrates' project of a perfectly rational language, but at 429ab it was only one among various possible analogies between names and the products of various crafts. Now, since 430ab, it has recovered its special relevance, which depends on the specific conception of names as imitations.

Let us come to the contents of our lines. If we take Socrates' words literally, he is contrasting the *fine* image, where nothing is added or subtracted,

---

[71] So I understand Socrates' elliptical claim that the colours and shapes included may be 'too many and too large' (c8 καὶ πλείω καὶ μείζω). Ficino's translation, 'pluraque et pauciora', suggests that in place of μείζω (which is also the reading of the Plato MS from which he translated, Laurentianus 85.9) he conjectured μείω. But μείων is not used 'in good Att. Prose or Com., nor in Hdt.' (LSJ) – though Xenophon employs it at *Hier.* 1.8 and elsewhere.

[72] E.g. Fowler 'then', Dalimier 'Par conséquent'.

[73] Cf. Reeve: 'Further, …'

with the *bad* image, where something is added or subtracted. This contrast (whose presence is confirmed by what Socrates is going to say about the parallel case of names, see below) seems hardly satisfactory; for it ignores the fact that not all additions or omissions are equally relevant and that we should at least distinguish trifling from serious ones. Furthermore, the contrast may seem to be at odds with Socrates' own use of comparatives at 429a, where he spoke of 'finer' (καλλίω) and 'inferior' (φαυλότερα) paintings, thus sensibly suggesting the existence of *degrees* of fineness and badness. Socrates' actual view is, I surmise, the following. Strictly speaking, only a perfectly accurate image, where nothing is added or omitted, counts as an unqualifiedly fine one, all other images being (for some reason or other) defective and therefore bad. But among bad images some are less bad, hence finer, than others; and the unqualifiedly fine one can be reckoned finer than all the others. This of course is quite independent of the question, which will be raised later on (432ad), whether a perfect and unqualifiedly fine image *can* be realized.

A delicate matter, of a completely different sort, is the meaning of the verb ἀποδίδωμι in its three occurrences (c6, 10, 11). In the argument about false speaking (430c, 431b) this verb referred to someone's assigning or applying a picture or an expression to an object. Is it now being used in the same way? Not at c6 and c10, where (as again at 432bc) it rather refers to the painter's *putting* certain elements *into* a painting:[74] cf. 417b, 419a, b, 431e, where the verb refers to the 'assignment' of letters to names. The occurrence at c11 is more difficult to assess. Here the object of the verb is not the colours and shapes in the pictures, but the pictures themselves. So what is at issue here may again be the assignment of a picture to an object. Only, here the assigned picture would not be an already existing one, as in the argument about false speaking: Socrates is no longer concerning himself with the use of pictures but rather with their *making*. We could argue that from the naturalist standpoint this difference is irrelevant: 'if correctness consists in resemblance, it evidently makes no difference whether the assignment is taking place for a first time or subsequently' (Barney 2001: 114; cf. Williams 1982: 89–90). But we should also consider a completely different possibility, i.e. that καλὰ τὰ γράμματά τε καὶ τὰς εἰκόνας ἀποδίδωσιν means '*renders* the pictures and the images fine'.[75] This interpretation – which I have adopted in my translation – is philosophically unproblematic and accords with the fact that the verb used in the parallel

---

[74] This is rightly seen by Ficino and Dalimier. Contrast Minio-Paluello and Reeve ('present').
[75] Thus Ficino, Stallbaum and Minio-Paluello. See LSJ 1.5.a for this meaning of ἀποδίδωμι.

case of the bad images is the very neutral ἐργάζεται, 'makes' (c12). On the other hand, it requires that the same verb bear two distinct meanings in the very same sentence. This instance of *falsa anaphora*[76] is certainly an unpalatable consequence, but by no means a fatal one: the passage contains another similarly harsh switch, from γράμματα 'pictures' (c10) to γράμματα 'letters' (d2).

Now back to the text. From the case of pictures Socrates moves on to the analogous case of names:

SO. And what about the one who imitates the essence of the objects through syllables and letters [ὁ διὰ τῶν συλλαβῶν τε καὶ γραμμάτων τὴν οὐσίαν τῶν πραγμάτων ἀπομιμούμενος]? By the same token, if he includes[77] all the appropriate elements [ἂν μὲν πάντα ἀποδῷ τὰ προσήκοντα] the image – that is, the name – will be fine, whereas if he sometimes omits or adds a little[78] there will come to be an image, but not a fine one [εἰκὼν μὲν γενήσεται, καλὴ δὲ οὔ], so that some names will be finely made, others badly [τὰ μὲν καλῶς εἰργασμένα ἔσται τῶν ὀνομάτων, τὰ δὲ κακῶς], won't they?
CR. Perhaps.
SO. Perhaps, therefore, one person will be a good craftsman of names and another will be a bad one?
CR. Yes.
SO. But this was named the 'lawgiver'.
CR. Yes.
SO. Perhaps, therefore, by Zeus, as in the other arts, so among lawgivers one will be good and another bad, if we grant those previous assumptions. (431d2–e9)

If the 'previous assumptions' are granted (i.e. if we grant that an image can be fine or bad as an image, and that names, *qua* imitations, are significantly like images, or rather – as Socrates now prefers to put it – are themselves a kind of images), then names too can be finely or badly made. A name is finely made, is a fine image of its referent, if it contains *all and only* the appropriate letters and syllables: that is to say, if every element of the name imitates a part of the referent's nature, and every part of the referent's nature is imitated by an element of the name. If, instead, the name contains elements extraneous to the referent's nature, or there is a part of the nature which no element of the name imitates, then the name is badly made and is a bad image.

This contrast between fine and bad names, according to which even a small fault is sufficient for a name to be reckoned bad, is analogous to the

---

[76] Cf. §2.2.1 on 385b.
[77] Here ἀποδίδωμι is used as at c6, 10: see above. The verb is understood so by Dalimier ('attribue à l'image'), as against Méridier ('attribue aux objets') and others.
[78] More precisely, 'omits or adds *something small*' (σμικρά: 'de menus détails' Méridier).

Naturalism and imperfect resemblance (431c–433b)

contrast we recognized above, in Socrates' previous claims about images, and seems as Manichaean. As above, however, I think this is actually compatible with the view (which Socrates certainly intends to convey, and which was implied by his comparative talk of 'worse' and 'better' names earlier at 429b) that a name can be finer or worse than another and that the fineness and badness of names come in degrees.

But what relation is there between the fineness and the correctness of names? Is it just the same property under two different designations? Then Socrates' contention would amount to the following: a name can be correct or incorrect without therefore ceasing to be a name. This would be a turning point in the dialogue, because thereby Socrates would abandon what I have called the Redundancy Conception of correctness (see §I.1.1). In effect, this is how Socrates' point is understood by Cratylus in his immediate reply, as we shall see in a moment. This was also a possible interpretation of 429b, where Cratylus denied that names can have been set down better or worse, and Socrates replied: 'Therefore all names have been set down correctly?'[79]

However, as I rejected this interpretation with regard to 429b (§7.1.2), so I reject it here too; for 432a–433b will show that Socrates still holds on to Redundancy. Thus when Socrates here says that, if the name is flawed by omissions or additions, 'there will come to be an image, but not a fine one' (d6–7), I think he means the following: there will come to be a name, [hence a *correct* name,] but not a fine one. In my view, here Socrates is introducing a *new* criterion according to which a name can be assessed: once we have ascertained that a certain string of letters or sounds is a (correct) name of something, we can go on to ask whether it is a fine or a bad name of that thing, i.e. whether it is a perfectly accurate imitation or contains flaws. (In fact we shall see in §8.1.5 that Socrates' final solution of the nature/convention debate will precisely involve a crucial distinction between what it is for a name to be correct and what it is for a name to be fine.) And as in the parallel case of pictures, it is natural to assume that these flaws can be more or less numerous or relevant, making the name not only fine or bad, but also *finer or worse* than another name.

Thus Socrates' argument to the effect that names can be fine or bad, once again based on the analogy between names and pictures, is complete. What will Cratylus reply? Given that so far he has expressed agreement

---

[79] See 388c for a place where Socrates probably does use the adverb καλῶς, 'finely', as equivalent to ὀρθῶς, 'correctly' (cf. §3.3.1).

with Socrates at every step, at this point we might expect him to declare himself convinced. But this is not what he is going to do.

7.3.2 Second round: Cratylus' argument from spelling (431e–432a)

After another, purely formal expression of agreement, Cratylus comes out with a fresh argument for his position, thereby starting the second round of the discussion about imperfect resemblance:

> CR. It is so. But look, Socrates: when with the art of literacy we assign to names [τοῖς ὀνόμασιν ἀποδιδῶμεν] these letters, α and β and each of the elements of the alphabet, if we subtract or add or transpose something, it is not the case that we have written the name, though not correctly. Rather, we have not written it at all: it is immediately a different name if it undergoes one of these changes [<οὐ>⁸⁰ γέγραπται μὲν ἡμῖν τὸ ὄνομα, οὐ μέντοι ὀρθῶς, ἀλλὰ τὸ παράπαν οὐδὲ γέγραπται, ἀλλ' εὐθὺς ἕτερόν ἐστιν ἐάν τι τούτων πάθῃ]. (431e9–432a4)

Cratylus does not directly address the making of names by means of the lawgiver's art. Rather, he makes a point about a different (if closely related) activity, that of *spelling* an existent name, performed by means of the art of literacy.⁸¹ He plainly assumes that the same point applies to the former activity as well, but he does not take the trouble to make the analogy explicit: he leaves it to Socrates (and us) to complete the argument. In what follows I shall first comment on the explicit point about spelling, then discuss the implicit analogy with name-making.

Let us begin with spelling. Here an example will be helpful. Suppose that someone has to spell the name 'Cleon' in writing and, instead of correctly writing 'CLEON', mistakenly writes 'CREON', substituting 'R' for 'L'. Then, Cratylus contends, we should not describe the situation saying that the name 'Cleon' has been written, albeit incorrectly; we should rather say that it has not been written at all and another (ἕτερον) name has been written in its place, i.e. 'Creon'.⁸²

---

⁸⁰ οὐ (a2) is Bekker's elegant and almost universally accepted insertion. Those who keep the transmitted text, like Stallbaum and Méridier, have to understand ἀλλ(ά) as 'indeed' – which does not seem to be possible.

⁸¹ Cf. *Tht.* 207a–208b for another philosophical argument which turns on spelling and ascribes it to the competence of the 'literate' (γραμματικός). Elsewhere Plato mentions other competences which fall within the scope of γραμματική: being able to recognize each letter in every different syllabic context in which it may occur (*R.* 402ab), knowing the various kinds of letters (*Phlb.* 17b, 18bd), knowing which letters combine with each other and which do not (*Sph.* 253a). On spelling cf. also *Plt.* 285cd and X. *Mem.* 4.4.7.

⁸² More precisely, *at best* another name has been written in its place. For what gets written might also be the name of nothing, and hence no name at all. Cratylus seems to consider only the

Naturalism and imperfect resemblance (431c–433b)

Is Cratylus' contention true? This is a slippery question; and since, as we are going to see, Socrates will not concern himself with spelling in his reply, we have to cope with it on our own. To my mind, the answer is 'Yes', if the spelling of a name is viewed merely as the production of a token of a certain type-sequence of letters; for 'CLEON' and 'CREON' are obviously different type-sequences of letters. We may have some sympathy for this stance. After all, we usually say that two names may differ from each other by just one letter, or in the arrangement of the very same letters (cf. §7.3.3 on *Dissoi Logoi* 90.5.12 DK). That said, however, the answer to the above question is instead 'No', if we take – as I think we should do – a more complex view of the spelling of a name. According to this view, for a token sequence of letters (or sounds) to constitute the spelling of a name, it must have an appropriate historical or causal connection with a token of that name. For example, there is such a connection between a teacher's uttering the name 'Cleon' in the course of subjecting her pupils to a spelling exercise and the pupils' writing 'CLEON' or 'CREON' or whatever in their exercise books. Crucial to this historical connection is one's *intention* to perform the spelling of a certain name. Thus writing 'CREON' with the intention to spell the name 'Cleon' is not the same as writing 'CREON' with the intention to spell the name 'Creon'. Whenever the former act takes place we should say that the name 'Cleon' has been written incorrectly or badly or faultily, not that the name has not been written at all and the name 'Creon' has been correctly written instead. From this point of view, therefore, Cratylus' contention is false.[83]

We must now turn to Cratylus' implicit analogy between spelling and name-making. The analogy consists in the fact that in making a name the lawgiver performs a spelling of a sort. Of course he does not spell a name; rather, *with* a name he spells, as it were, the nature of something. The implicit conclusion seems to be the following: if the lawgiver, in making a name for something, does not perfectly 'spell' its nature, but omits or adds or transposes some letter, then it is not the case that he has made a name for that thing, albeit incorrectly; he has rather made a name *for something else*.

---

most favourable possibility: cf. 429c, where he claimed that 'Hermogenes' is the name not of Hermogenes but of someone else, i.e. of the person who has the appropriate nature. To bring this out I have chosen an example where two *real* Greek names differ from one another by one letter.

[83] It is no accident that the viewpoint from which Cratylus' contention turns out to be false is based on the notion of the speller's intentions; for this notion is somehow connected with those of convention and arbitrary decision. Cf. §7.2.1, where I argued that the distinction between speaker's reference (i.e. what the speaker *intends* to refer to) and semantic reference entails that names are conventional.

This implicit conclusion is meant to contradict the conclusion of Socrates' own previous argument, which was based on the analogy between names and pictures (431ce). There is, however, a difference between what Socrates previously affirmed and what Cratylus is now implicitly denying. Socrates claimed that a name can be *finely* (καλῶς) or *badly* (κακῶς) made and a namegiver can be good (ἀγαθός) or bad (κακός). Cratylus, instead, is now implicitly denying that a name can be *incorrectly* (οὐ ... ὀρθῶς 432a2) made while still being the name of a given thing. But this is unlikely to be what Socrates meant with his previous claims about fine and bad names; indeed, Socrates presumably shares Cratylus' denial. For, as I anticipated above, his reply (432a–433b) will show that he still holds to the Redundancy Conception of correctness, according to which an incorrect name of something is not a name of that thing (§I.1.1). Thus Cratylus, whether deliberately or not, is misrepresenting Socrates' position as a departure from the Redundancy Conception and at the same time is presenting his own position as a defence of that conception.

In any case, let us now concentrate on the *positive* part of Cratylus' implicit conclusion, according to which any minimal mistake in the making of a name is already sufficient to turn it into the name of something else. This does actually contradict Socrates' thesis that a name can be made finely or badly, and elaborates on Cratylus' point-blank rejection of that thesis at 429b.

This may also seem to have some plausibility within the naturalist framework. As Barney (2001: 116) puts it, 'names which differ even by one letter should be considered different names, since, after all, they are correctly adapted to distinguish objects which differ in just that way'. Nevertheless, the conclusion must be rejected. We shall shortly see Socrates reply from the very inside of the naturalist framework; before looking at that reply, let us consider another one that comes from the outside. Suppose that someone paints a portrait of Cleon and this turns out to resemble much more closely (indeed, as closely as possible) Creon, whom the painter knows nothing about. Should we then say that the painter has not painted a bad portrait of Cleon, but rather a fine portrait of Creon? Surely not. For the portrait has a historical connection with Cleon which it does not have with Creon; and it is Cleon, not Creon, whom the painter *intended* to paint. Therefore the presence of flaws or mistakes does not stop a picture being a picture of a given object. And the same must hold of names, if names are basically akin to pictures.

Note also that, as Méridier 124 n.1 points out, Cratylus' positive conclusion seems to be at odds with his own earlier approval (428c) of Socrates'

Naturalism and imperfect resemblance (431c–433b) 359

etymologies. For the etymologies – at least those of the secondary names – worked precisely by supposing that the name's original form has been altered by additions, omissions and transpositions of letters, due partly to the action of time and the speakers' love for embellishments (414cd), partly to the namegiver himself (404c).

7.3.3 Second round: Socrates' reply and the 'Two Cratyluses' (432ad)

Socrates is unperturbed by Cratylus' argument from spelling:

SO. Your point doesn't affect our previous conclusions.[84] For this is not, I fear, a good way of looking at the matter.
CR. What do you mean? (432a5–7)

Socrates goes on to argue that Cratylus' point does apply to a certain sort of objects, like numbers, but not to the relevant sort of objects, i.e. images. Here is the former, positive part of this reply:

SO. Perhaps the things that must necessarily be composed of a certain number of elements or not be at all [ὅσα ἔκ τινος ἀριθμοῦ ἀναγκαῖον εἶναι ἢ μὴ εἶναι] might be in the condition you're describing: as ten itself [ὥσπερ καὶ αὐτὰ τὰ δέκα], or whatever other number you like, if you subtract or add something to it, is immediately a different number. (432a8–b1)

Some things are such that their identity and existence depend on their being composed of a certain number of elements or parts. Thus it is essential for a string quintet to be composed of five elements, neither more nor less; the subtraction or addition of just one element is sufficient to turn the quintet into a different sort of ensemble.

Socrates seems to regard *numbers* themselves as an instance – presumably the limiting case – of these 'things necessarily composed of a certain number of elements'.[85] This ought not to disconcert us. For there is a very close parallel at *Tht.* 204d, where almost the same expression (ὅσα ἐξ ἀριθμοῦ ἐστι, 'the things which are composed of a number of elements')

---

[84] This sentence is not in the Greek; but something of this sort is implied by the following γάρ (432a5). Cf. *Phd.* 69a, quoted with our passage in *GP* 76.
[85] In Reeve's translation ('numbers, which have to be a certain number or not be at all') numbers seem to be all that Socrates is speaking of. Barney 2001: 116–17, instead, implies that numbers are not themselves included among the things which depend on number: she translates ὥσπερ καὶ αὐτὰ τὰ δέκα (a9) as 'just as *also* in the case of the number ten itself' and speaks of the class constituted by 'numbers *and* things which depend on number for their existence' (my italics). However, the καί need not mean 'also' (see *GP* 296); and the hypothesis that Socrates introduces numbers as a limiting case enables us to account for his talk of 'ten *itself*'. (In any case, here αὐτά does not convey a reference to a Platonic form.)

covers both numbers and numerable objects such as a mile and an army. Furthermore, we must bear in mind that, on the ancient Greek conception of numbers, a number is a collection of abstract units which are absolutely identical to each other and of which there is an infinite stock (*R.* 526a, *Phlb.* 56de; Arist. *Cat.* 6.4b22–31; Euc. *Elementa* 7 Def. 2 'a number is a plurality composed of units'). So the number 10 is conceived of as a collection of ten such units,[86] and of course subtracting or adding one unit to the collection turns it into a different collection and a different number. Therefore it makes sense to include numbers, such as 10, as a special case among the 'things which must necessarily be composed of a certain number of elements or not be at all'.

There are at least two interesting parallels for Socrates' point about numbers. First, *Dissoi Logoi* 90.5 DK, where the author, after claiming that things may change in virtue of a simple transposition of letters (as with ὄνος/νόος, 'ass'/'mind'), goes on as follows: 'Since, then, there is such a difference without anything being subtracted, what if one adds or subtracts something? I'll show what this consists in too. *If someone subtracted one from ten* [αἴ τις ἀπὸ τῶν δέκα ἓν ἀφέλοι], there would no longer be one or ten; similarly with the other cases' (90.5.12–14 DK). Thus one and the same passage of the *Dissoi Logoi* constitutes a parallel – unlikely to be accidental – both for Cratylus' argument from spelling and for the first part of Socrates' reply to it, including the example of the number 10.[87] The second parallel is a fragment ascribed to the comic poet Epicharmus, reckoned among the spurious ones in *PCG* 1 fr. 276, where the speaker remarks that numbers and measures of length (and hence human beings as well!) do not stay the same if one unit or part is added to or subtracted from them.[88]

We must now see how Socrates draws the contrast between the things whose nature is essentially tied up with number, to which Cratylus' point does apply, and those to which the point does *not* apply.

(so.) But I fear that this is not the correctness of what is qualified somehow, and of an image in general [τοῦ δὲ ποιοῦ τινος καὶ συμπάσης εἰκόνος μὴ οὐχ αὕτη <ᾖ> ἡ ὀρθότης],[89] and that, on the contrary, one must not assign to it

---

[86] Indeed, strictly speaking there is no such thing as *the* number 10, for we can form as many collections of ten units as we want. See Arist. *Cat.* 6, quoted in the text: 10, i.e. any collection of ten abstract units, is composed of two 5's, i.e. two collections of five abstract units. (On the Greek conception of numbers cf. Pritchard 1995: 9–32, 63–83; Burnyeat 2000a: 30–3.)

[87] See Robinson 1979: 207 (whose text I am following; DK have 'If someone subtracted one from ten <or added one to ten>') for a different interpretation of the *Dissoi Logoi* passage.

[88] Cf. also Arist. *Metaph.* 1043b36–1044a2, and see Ademollo (in preparation-3) on the pseudo-Epicharmus fragment.

[89] Along with Fowler, Méridier and Reeve I interpret συμπάσης εἰκόνος (b1–2) as 'an image in general' rather than 'une image considérée dans son ensemble' (Dalimier).

features which are all such as what one is representing is [οὐδὲ τὸ παράπαν δέῃ πάντα ἀποδοῦναι οἷόν ἐστιν ὃ εἰκάζει], if it is to be an image. (432b1–4)

Leaving aside for the moment the reference to 'what is qualified somehow', the gist of these lines seems to be the following. The implied conclusion of Cratylus' argument from spelling (431e–432a) was that the conditions for a sequence of letters to be the name – hence the *correct* name – of a given thing are very severe: any minimal discrepancy between a name and the nature of its intended referent turns the name into the name of something else. But this is not how images (of which names are a kind) work. Indeed, it rather lies in the very nature of an image that it *cannot* possibly have all the same features as its object.

This thesis, which here is just stated, is going to be elaborated and defended with an argument in the next lines. The present, bare statement, however, is already worthy of some comments.

I start out with a remark on the notion of correctness. Socrates' first claim ('this is *not* the correctness ... of an image in general', b1–2) makes it clear that he is rejecting the Manichaean view of the correctness of names contained in the implicit conclusion of Cratylus' argument. Hence it is reasonable to suppose that Socrates' second claim ('*on the contrary* ...' etc., b2–4) positively specifies his alternative view of correctness. More precisely, it is reasonable to suppose that this alternative view is that for an image/name to be correct it need not, indeed cannot, be completely like its object and may, indeed must, contain some omissions or additions. Thus I suppose that 'if it is to be an image' is actually equivalent to 'if it is to be a *correct* image' – as 422e 'if they are to be names' (εἴπερ μέλλει ὀνόματα εἶναι) was doubtless equivalent to 'if they are to be *correct* names'. Socrates is not abandoning the Redundancy Conception of correctness and arguing that incorrect images/names must be included among images/names, correct ones being only identified with perfect ones, or that correctness admits of degrees. Indeed, if this were what Socrates is arguing for, then, it seems, he should conclude that no name is correct (or *maximally* correct, if correctness were a matter of degrees), because none is perfect! Rather, Socrates is sticking to the Redundancy Conception. The ensuing argument will confirm this interpretation, as we shall see in due course.

Now, the notion of 'being like', which I have just referred to, raises an important question. Socrates talks about the image's having 'features all *such as* what one is representing *is*', or more literally 'features all *as is* what one is representing' (b3).[90] Taken by itself, this can be interpreted in two

[90] The subject of εἰκάζει (b3) cannot be the image, as most interpreters assume, and must rather be the image-maker, as Stallbaum saw: see LSJ εἰκάζω.

different ways. Socrates might be claiming only (a) that the features of an image cannot all be *the same as* the features of the represented object; or he might be making a stronger claim, i.e. (b) that the features of an image cannot all be *similar to* the features of the object. In effect, it will shortly become clear that (a) is what Socrates is claiming here; but it will be helpful to keep (b) too in mind as the argument goes on.

We can finally turn to 'what is qualified somehow' (τοῦ δὲ ποιοῦ τινος b1).[91] What role does this play here? The expression τὸ ποιόν τι must refer to a kind of items whose nature is essentially *qualitative*, which here are contrasted with those items (referred to at a8–b1) whose nature has an essential connection with *number*. In this connection we should bear in mind that Aristotle uses the expression ποιόν τι precisely to characterize an item as possessing a feature from the category of *quality* (e.g. *Cat.* 8.8b25) rather than from some other category, such as *quantity*.[92] Socrates' point is that what holds of numbers etc., i.e. that any small subtraction or addition turns the item in question into a completely different one, does not hold of 'what is qualified somehow'. If you add a further unit to a number, it becomes a different number. But a certain amount of a hot liquid does not, as a rule, cease to be hot if you add to it a minimum of the same liquid at a lower temperature: it just becomes less hot than before. In short, qualified items seem to admit of *degrees*, whereas numbers etc. do not; as Aristotle would put it, qualified items admit of the more and the less (*Cat.* 8.10b26–11a14), whereas quantified items like numbers do not (6.6a19–25).[93] The notion of degrees, however, must be handled with care. For, as I argued above, Socrates' view is not that a name can be more *correct* than another, but rather that a name, i.e. a correct name, can be more or less *similar* than another to a given thing.

But what exactly is the relationship between 'what is qualified somehow' and 'an image in general'? I suggest that Socrates is presenting images in

---

[91] In ποιόν τι the τι qualifies ποιόν. Cf. *R.* 438d–439a, *Tht.* 182ab, *Sph.* 262e (Barney 2001: 117 and n.8), and Arist. *Cat.* 8, quoted below.

[92] Barney 2001: 117–18 makes the further claim that in our passage τὸ ποιόν τι 'seems to pick out ordinary sensible particulars as the bearers of qualities' (cf. Reeve's 'things with sensory qualities'). This, however, seems an unwarranted guess. No doubt the expression does apply to sensible particulars *qua* bearers of qualities; but I see no indication in the text that it applies *only* to them and does not cover universal or non-sensible items as well. So its import is likely to be very generic.

[93] More precisely, for Aristotle most but *not all* qualified items admit of the more and the less: geometrical figures do not. Besides Aristotle, Barney 2001: 118 n.9 aptly compares the distinction at *Phlb.* 23c–27c between the 'unlimited' things like hot and cold, which admit of 'the more and the less', and those things which, being the mixture of the unlimited with the 'limit', i.e. with number and proportion, have a definite quantity.

general as a *particular case* of 'what is qualified somehow', and that this should be understood along the following lines. Socrates assumes that an image must be *similar*, ὅμοιον, to what it represents (see 433c, 434ab). Now one may see a close connection between similarity and quality. So, at least, does Aristotle, who tells us that the proprium of the category of quality is that things are said to be similar to each other in respect of their qualities (*Cat.* 8.11a15–19) and that 'similar are said to be the things whose quality is one' (*Metaph.* Δ15.1021a11–12). Thus the notion of similarity is the missing link between 'what is qualified somehow' and images. In general things are similar to each other, and in particular images are similar to their objects, insofar as they share certain qualities.[94]

Socrates, however, does not just mention 'what is qualified somehow' while discussing the relation between images and their objects. He goes so far as to talk about 'the correctness *of* what is qualified somehow *and of* an image in general', thus apparently extending the scope of the notion of correctness, which was originally limited to names, not only to images but also to qualified items in general. This extension is problematic; for it makes little sense to speak of the correctness of such qualified items as a white thing or a just person or a sweet taste. But perhaps Socrates is speaking loosely and his talk of the correctness of 'what is qualified somehow' is not to be understood at face value, but is rather due to the influence of the adjacent case of images, which is clearly what he is really interested in. After all, Socrates did *not* seek to apply the notion of correctness to number and related entities, which 'what is qualified somehow' is here being contrasted with. So what Socrates actually means at b2–4 is: 'This does not hold of what is qualified somehow, and this is not the correctness of an image in general.'

So much for Socrates' statement of his thesis that images are necessarily different from the objects they represent. We can now move on to Socrates' argument for this thesis, known as the 'argument of the Two Cratyluses'. The argument occupies the passage 432b4–d3 and can be divided into two parts. First (b4–c6) Socrates describes a particular hypothetical situation and leads Cratylus to take a certain view of it; then (c7–d3) he draws a general conclusion about the relation between images and objects, stressing that he is thereby proving the thesis stated at a8–b4.

---

[94] For a different view see Barney 2001: 118, who apparently holds that Socrates is *generalizing* from ordinary sensible particulars (her construal of τὸ ποιόν τι, see n.92), which are images of the forms, to 'a broader category, presumably also including names, works of art and so on'. I cannot accept this interpretation, also because it involves a cryptic reference to the forms which seems out of place in the present context.

Here is the first part:

(SO.) Look if I've got a point. Would there be two such objects as Cratylus and an image of Cratylus, if some god did not only represent your colour and shape as painters do, but made also all the internal features and parts such as yours are [καὶ τὰ ἐντὸς πάντα τοιαῦτα ποιήσειεν οἷάπερ τὰ σά],⁹⁵ and provided the same softnesses and warmths [καὶ μαλακότητας καὶ θερμότητας τὰς αὐτὰς ἀποδοίη], and put into them motion and soul and reason such as are in you [καὶ κίνησιν καὶ ψυχὴν καὶ φρόνησιν οἷάπερ ἡ παρὰ σοὶ ἐνθείη αὐτοῖς], and in a word, for all the features and parts you have, brought beside you other suchlike features or parts [πάντα ἅπερ σὺ ἔχεις, τοιαῦτα ἕτερα καταστήσειεν πλησίον σου]? Should then we have, as the upshot of such a process, Cratylus and an image of Cratylus, or two Cratyluses?
CR. Two Cratyluses, Socrates, it seems to me. (432b4–c6)

Suppose that someone wants to produce an image of Cratylus which is as like the original as possible. The easiest option is to depict Cratylus on a suitable surface, e.g. a wooden panel. This, however, is not satisfactory for the purposes in question. The portrait may perfectly reproduce the colour and shape of Cratylus' body (b6–7) as seen from a certain point of view; but even the most accurate life-size portrait is very different from the real Cratylus in many respects. For it is a two-dimensional object, whereas Cratylus has three dimensions; it is wooden, whereas Cratylus is flesh and blood; it is inanimate, whereas Cratylus is a living being. Then one might consider making a statue. But that would obviate only the first of the just mentioned inconveniences, leaving the others untouched; the image would still be very different from Cratylus. Now suppose the would-be image-maker is an omnipotent god. He could put together flesh, blood, bones and all sorts of organic materials to make a three-dimensional image, provided, even internally, with bodily organs and tissues exactly like those belonging to Cratylus (b7–8). He could cause the statue's organs and tissues to have the very same properties as Cratylus' own organs and tissues have, and in the very same degree: what is warm or soft in Cratylus' body could be as warm and as soft in the statue's body (b8–c1).⁹⁶ Indeed, the divine image-maker could provide the statue with 'motion, soul and reason' that are exactly like Cratylus' own (c1–2). In short, let the god make the statue into an *exact duplicate* of Cratylus in all possible respects (c2–4). Would it still be possible, in such a situation, to regard the final

---

⁹⁵ 'Features and parts' (b7–8): here, as at c3 and d2 below, the Greek has a bare neuter, 'items', whose very generic force I have attempted to capture.
⁹⁶ The plural 'softnesses and warmths' refers to different *degrees* of softness and temperature, each belonging to a distinct bodily part.

Naturalism and imperfect resemblance (431c–433b)

product as an *image* of Cratylus? Wouldn't it rather be *another Cratylus*? Cratylus – the dialogue's character – agrees it would rather be another Cratylus (c4–6).[97]

The present argument is designed to back up the thesis, stated at b2–4, that an image's features cannot all be 'such as is' (οἷόν ἐστιν) the original. That formulation, which we found somewhat ambiguous, is taken over here, where Socrates repeatedly refers to the image's features being rendered 'such as' the object's features are (b8, c2, c3). Here, however, it is very clear what Socrates has in mind. He describes the god striving to provide the image with features that are all *the same as* those of the represented object (see especially c1, and cf. d2 below), and therefore striving to make the image *exactly similar*, or *qualitatively identical*, to the object.[98] This goal, according to the argument, cannot be achieved. For the god ends up making not an *image* of Cratylus, but rather another Cratylus, i.e. a *perfect duplicate* of Cratylus.[99]

Here several pressing questions arise. Is the existence of two Cratyluses any more acceptable than the existence of an exactly similar image of Cratylus? And, in any case, is this discussion of exact similarity what we really need to counter Cratylus' extreme views on names? Before addressing such questions, however, it will be best to read the argument's general conclusions.

SO. Do you see then, my friend, that we must search for a different sort of correctness of an image and of the things we were talking about just now [ἄλλην χρὴ εἰκόνος ὀρθότητα ζητεῖν καὶ ὧν νυνδὴ ἐλέγομεν], and we must not contend that it can no longer be an image if something is missing or added? Or don't you realize how much images fall short of having the same features and parts as those things of which they're images [ὅσου ἐνδέουσιν αἱ εἰκόνες τὰ αὐτὰ ἔχειν ἐκείνοις ὧν εἰκόνες εἰσίν]?

CR. I do. (432c7–d4)

---

[97] Sedley 2003: 46 n.44 compares the story, told by Stesichorus and Euripides, that Hera made a duplicate of Helen, who went to Troy in place of the real Helen. Euripides, however, insists that the duplicate is made of air (*Hel.* 33–4, 584, 704–5). So it is not, after all, *exactly* like the original, although it is externally indistinguishable from it.

[98] *X* is exactly similar (or qualitatively identical) to *Y* if and only if, whatever property *X* has, *Y* also has, and vice versa. The properties in question are only non-relational ones (e.g. being red), as opposed to relational ones (e.g. being north of Athens): having different relational properties does not prevent two things from being exactly alike.

[99] Strictly speaking the idea of there being *two Cratyluses* is intrinsically absurd. For there cannot be two tokens, as it were, of the same particular; and a perfect duplicate of Cratylus would not be another Cratylus, but a wholly distinct individual, who after his coming to be would have a different history from Cratylus'. Yet it is rather natural to speak loosely of Cratylus' perfect duplicate as 'another Cratylus'.

From the example of the two Cratyluses Socrates draws a general conclusion about images, whose formulation is very close to that of a8–b4, where he first stated the thesis to be proved. We need, he says, a different sort of correctness of images and of 'the things we were talking about just now' – a periphrasis referring both to names and to the whole category (mentioned at b1) of 'what is qualified somehow'.[100] That is to say (c8 καί₂ is explanatory), we must not maintain that any omission or addition stops an image being an image of a given thing. For an image is in any case far from being qualitatively identical to the object it represents, as we have just seen in the two Cratyluses case.

Socrates thus takes himself to have established *two* theses, of which one – which he states as second – entails the other. Let me set them out in their natural logical order: (i) an image is necessarily different from its object (d1–3, cf. b2–4); *therefore* (ii) the correctness of images and other related items is not the one advocated by Cratylus, *that is to say*, it is not the case that any omission or addition stops an image being an image of a given thing (c7–d1, cf. a8–b2). We shall discuss the two theses separately.

(i) has, I think, been successfully proved. For it does seem to be part of the very nature of an image that in some respects it is different from the object it represents. We might put the point as follows: a perfect duplicate of *X* is not an image of *X*.

Here a question arises: *may* there be a perfect duplicate of something? Is it *possible* at all for two things to be exactly alike (qualitatively identical) down to the smallest details? Socrates and Cratylus seem to assume that it is at least possible.[101] This assumption commits them to rejecting one version of the principle of the Identity of Indiscernibles,[102] according to which, *necessarily*, if *X* and *Y* have all the same intrinsic (non-relational) properties, then they are one and the same thing.[103] It must be mentioned

---

[100] καὶ ὧν νυνδὴ ἐλέγομεν (a8) has been found troublesome. Schanz, followed by Dalimier, excised it; Minio-Paluello translates the whole sentence 'per la imagine bisogna cercare un'altra giustezza da quella che or ora dicevamo'. This, however, would require transposing the καί to obtain a connection ἄλλην ... ὧν, e.g. writing ὧν καὶ νυνδὴ ἐλέγομεν, and in any case would not be completely satisfactory, because Socrates should not refer to Cratylus' peculiar views as 'what *we* were saying just now'. In fact there is no need to alter the transmitted text. For the periphrasis sounds awkward only if we assume (as is usually done) that it can only refer to names. But it is instead perfectly justified, if Socrates is also picking up the mention of 'what is qualified somehow' from b1–2.

[101] Cf. Sedley 2003: 46 n.44.

[102] But cf. *Tht.* 209bc, where Socrates seems to talk as if Theaetetus' peculiar snubnosedness were qualitatively different from any other instance of snubnosedness.

[103] This version of the principle is the strongest one, endorsed by the Stoics (see below) and Leibniz. Weaker versions allow one to take into account relational properties, or take the principle to state only a contingent truth. See Armstrong 1978: 91–7 for discussion.

Naturalism and imperfect resemblance (431c–433b) 367

that the denial of the Identity of Indiscernibles, which here is at most implied with reference to a counterfactual situation, was explicitly taken over by the Academics, with reference to the *actual* world, in the course of a controversy with the Stoics, where the Academics produced examples concerning exactly similar twins, hairs, grains of wheat etc. to counter the Stoic claim that no two things may be exactly alike (Cic. *Ac.* 2.54–8, 85; Plu. *Comm. not.* 1077c).

So far so good. Now from (i), the thesis that an image is necessarily different from its object, Socrates at c7–d1 infers (ii). This can be further divided into two theses: (ii.a) the correctness of images is different from the one advocated by Cratylus; (ii.b) it is not the case that any omission or addition stops an image being an image of a given thing. The link between the latter two theses is provided by the second καί at c8, which presents (ii.b) as an *explanation* of (ii.a).

As could only be expected, Socrates' point here seems to be the same as at a8–b2, where the present conclusions were first announced: Cratylus' severe criterion of correctness, expressed in his argument from spelling (431e–432a), must be relaxed to include among naturally correct names also names where some letter is missing or added. Once again, on the most natural way of reading the text Socrates is *not* giving up the Redundancy Conception of correctness and arguing that names include also incorrect names, or that names may be more or less correct. Rather, he is sticking to Redundancy but advocating a more democratic application of it.

Does (i) really entail (ii), and more precisely (ii.b), as Socrates assumes? Instead of passively accepting Socrates' conclusions, Cratylus might try to argue as follows: 'Dear Socrates, your argument misfires; for you are confusing two quite different ways in which an image may fail to be exactly similar to its object. Consider again the example of a portrait of mine painted on a wooden panel. Granted, the portrait is two-dimensional rather than three-dimensional, wooden rather than flesh and blood, inanimate rather than alive, etc. These facts follow of necessity from the portrait being an image and from it being the very sort of image it is. They don't depend on the artist's ability; even a divine painter, brought before a wooden panel, wouldn't be able to overcome all of these limitations. But there is also another kind of flaw which may prevent the image from being exactly like me. I may be depicted as having different features from those I do have: my nose may be depicted as aquiline, whereas it's actually straight; my left cheek may be depicted as smooth, whereas there is actually a wart on it; etc. Unlike the former flaws, these latter don't follow of necessity from the portrait being an image, or from it being the very sort of image it is; their presence and number depends solely on the artist's ability, i.e. they would be completely absent in an image made by a sufficiently skilled artist; and they are what people usually reckon as relevant for judging how closely an image resembles its object. So I grant that an image in general, or a name in particular, is very far from being exactly like the object it represents. But the factors which necessitate it being such are of the former, not of the latter kind; whereas those I was thinking of when I claimed that any omission or addition prevents a name from being a name of a given thing are of the latter, not of the former kind.'

It may well seem that thereby Cratylus would have a point. After all, it would be odd if someone complained that David's portrait of Napoleon does not resemble its original on the grounds that the real Napoleon was not made of canvas. As Sedley 2003: 137–8 remarks, the Two Cratyluses argument is essentially analogical: if Cratylus acknowledges the former kind of shortcoming, which involves major differences from the original, then he should *a fortiori* acknowledge the possibility of the latter kind of shortcoming, which involves minor differences. But this does not seem to amount to a formal refutation of Cratylus' view.

And yet I do believe that Socrates has the better of the argument. For, although there may be a sound intuition behind our defence of Cratylus, as it is this intuition is not embedded in a suitable theoretical framework. More precisely, the problem is the unqualified view – never called into question in *Cra.* or elsewhere in Plato – that an image *resembles* or is *similar to* the object it represents. As long as we stick to this unqualified view, we seem to preclude the possibility of distinguishing between features or parts of an image that are relevant to the assessment of its similarity to the object and features or parts that must be discounted as irrelevant. We should refine the unqualified view by specifying exactly *how and in which respect* an image of a certain sort is similar to the object it represents.[104] Thereby we would achieve the required distinction and would be able to block Socrates' argument.

We can now resume our reading of the text and see that Socrates' next move is to return to names:

---

[104] For such a sophisticated account of depiction see Peacocke 1987: a silhouette of Salisbury Cathedral 'is presented in an area of the perceiver's visual field which is experienced as similar in shape to the region of the visual field in which Salisbury Cathedral itself is presented when seen from a certain angle'. Here the relation is not similarity, but *experienced* similarity, and it does not hold between the image and the object themselves, but between two *regions* of the perceiver's *visual field*.

Naturalism and imperfect resemblance (431c–433b)

SO. Then names would have a ridiculous effect on those things of which they're names, if they became completely similar to them in every respect [εἰ πάντα πανταχῇ αὐτοῖς ὁμοιωθείη]. For everything would, it seems, be duplicated, and neither of two identical things could say which of the two was the real one and which was the name.[105]
CR. What you say is true. (432d5–10)

The function of these lines is not crystal clear. It depends on the exact force of γοῦν (d5). If, as most interpreters assume, γοῦν here means 'at any rate', then Socrates is claiming that his conclusions hold at least of that particular kind of image which is constituted by names: whatever may be true of images in general, at any rate names cannot be exactly similar to their referents. Alternatively, γοῦν may be inferential, as I have translated it, and be 'marking the conclusion of what is almost a formal syllogism' (so *GP* 456); to wit, Socrates may be just applying his general conclusion about images to the particular case of names. Either way, the basic point is the same. Names have many features which most things named do not have; and most things named have countless features which names themselves could never have, even granting that they might come to represent all such features.

Thus Socrates has finally disposed of Cratylus' argument from spelling, arguing that it commits Cratylus to the 'ridiculous' (d5) view that a name ought to be exactly similar to its referent. Socrates can now state his *positive* conclusions about names.

7.3.4 Conclusions on fine and bad names (432d–433b)

Here is what Socrates says:

SO. So, my excellent friend, don't be afraid, and admit that one name may have been set down well and another not [ἔα καὶ ὄνομα τὸ μὲν εὖ κεῖσθαι, τὸ δὲ μή], and don't contend that a name must necessarily have all the letters, so as to be exactly like the thing whose name it is [καὶ μὴ ἀνάγκαζε πάντ' ἔχειν τὰ γράμματα, ἵνα κομιδῇ ᾖ τοιοῦτον οἷόνπερ οὗ ὄνομά ἐστιν], but admit that one may also apply[106] an inappropriate letter [ἀλλ' ἔα καὶ τὸ μὴ προσῆκον

---

[105] This is the only possible meaning of the MSS text οὐκ ἂν ἔχοι αὐτῶν εἰπεῖν οὐδέτερον ὁπότερόν ἐστι τὸ μὲν αὐτό, τὸ δὲ ὄνομα (d8–9), preserved in the OCT: αὐτῶν ... οὐδέτερον must be the subject of ἔχοι. Many have found this personification hard to swallow and have corrected the text: ἔχοι<ς> Heindorf (+ Stallbaum, Méridier, Dalimier); εἰπεῖν <οὐδεὶς> Burnet (+ Fowler, Minio-Paluello, Reeve). It is difficult to take a stand; among textual interventions the best course seems to me to write οὐδεὶς in place of οὐδέτερον.

[106] I take ἐπιφέρειν (e3) and ἐπιφέρεσθαι (e5) to refer to the *application* of a linguistic item to an object: cf. 424de, 435b, and 430e ἐπιφοράν. For most interpreters, instead, the verb here refers to

γράμμα ἐπιφέρειν]. And if a letter, then also a name in a sentence; and if a name, then admit that also a phrase in a sentence may be applied to the objects without being appropriate [εἰ δὲ γράμμα, καὶ ὄνομα ἐν λόγῳ· εἰ δὲ ὄνομα, καὶ λόγον ἐν λόγῳ μὴ προσήκοντα τοῖς πράγμασιν ἐπιφέρεσθαι],[107] and that the object may nonetheless be named and spoken of, as long as the character of the object we're talking about[108] is present [καὶ μηδὲν ἧττον ὀνομάζεσθαι τὸ πρᾶγμα καὶ λέγεσθαι, ἕως ἂν ὁ τύπος ἐνῇ τοῦ πράγματος περὶ οὗ ἂν ὁ λόγος ᾖ], as in the names of letters, if you remember what I and Hermogenes were saying just now.

CR. I do remember. (432d11–433a3)

In this very difficult passage Socrates considers three successive cases where a smaller linguistic unit is contained in a larger one: (i) a letter in a name, (ii) a name in a λόγος, (iii) a λόγος in another λόγος. Socrates claims that, in each of these cases, an object can be named, or spoken of, by the larger unit even if this contains one or more inappropriate tokens of the smaller unit. We shall examine the three cases one by one.

With case (i) Socrates goes back to the very point which the discussion had reached when, at 431d, Cratylus' argument from spelling got in the way. There Socrates held that those names which contain all (and only) the appropriate (προσήκοντα) letters and syllables are 'finely' (καλῶς) made, whereas those where something is omitted or added are 'badly' (κακῶς) made. Here at d11–e3 he seems to make exactly the same point: a name has been imposed 'well' if it contains all and only the appropriate letters, whereas it has been imposed 'not well' if it contains one inappropriate letter (or more). In any case, Socrates adds at e5–7, if an inappropriate letter is contained in a name, this does not stop a given object being named by the name (ὀνομάζεσθαι τὸ πρᾶγμα), provided that the object's τύπος is present in it.

Thus Socrates identifies a condition, a minimal threshold of resemblance, which any name, well or badly made, must necessarily meet if it is to name a given object. It is of utmost importance to bear in mind that, here as elsewhere, talk of the name's naming something is equivalent to talk of the name's naming that thing *correctly* (or, as Socrates prefers to

---

the *inclusion* of a smaller linguistic item into a larger one, like ἀποδίδωμι at 431d (see n.77 above). But on this construal at e4 we should expect (twice) λόγῳ, not ἐν λόγῳ.

[107] I take it that τοῖς πράγμασιν (e5) goes ἀπὸ κοινοῦ with both μὴ προσήκοντα and ἐπιφέρεσθαι (on which see n.106) and that the plural here is a non-significant variant on the singular πρᾶγμα, which occurs at e6, 7 (cf. 433c1).

[108] τοῦ πράγματος περὶ οὗ ἂν ὁ λόγος ᾖ (e7) is ambiguous as between 'of the object we're talking about' and 'of the object which the λόγος is about'. Here also *names* are in question, so the former, more generic interpretation is required. But I shall freely switch to the latter when Socrates comes to discuss λόγοι: see below.

express himself here, *appropriately*):[109] the Redundancy Conception of correctness appeared to be in force at 432ad (see §7.3.3), will still be in force at 433ab (see below), and must be in force here too, as further evidence will shortly confirm. Therefore we should not assume (as e.g. Barney 2001: 122–3 does) that here 'well' is equivalent to 'correctly' and that Socrates is drawing a distinction between naming something and naming it correctly, between names and correct names. Rather, Socrates' point at e5–7 could be rephrased as follows: if an inappropriate letter is contained in a name, this does not stop the object being *correctly/appropriately* named by the name, provided that the object's τύπος is present in it.

The minimal threshold of resemblance Socrates identifies consists in the name's containing the τύπος of the object named. But what does τύπος mean here? From the term's basic meaning 'imprint' some draw a specific meaning like 'intrinsic quality' (Fowler) or 'caractère distinctif' (Méridier). Thus Socrates would be saying that a name, however imperfectly made, names a certain thing as long as its letters resemble some distinctive or peculiar character of that thing.[110] But if a name lacks some appropriate letters, or even contains only few of them (cf. 433a6), it is unlikely to resemble any *distinctive* character of the referent at all. Thus τύπος is more likely to mean something like 'outline', 'general character' (McDowell 1973: 236, Guthrie v.13; LSJ VIII.1; Sedley 2003: 138), as e.g. at *R.* 403de, 414a, Arist. *Pol.* 1341b29–32. So the condition which Socrates is stating for a name to name a given thing is very weak: the name's sounds/letters must express *at least something* of the thing's essence (423d–424a). Of course this is not only a weak condition; it is also a vague one. How little of a thing's essence need a name resemble to be a name of that thing, albeit an imperfect one? Apparently even a faint and very generic resemblance will suffice.

At e7–a2 Socrates illustrates his present claims about names in general by recalling what he said at 393de about one particular kind of names, i.e. those for the letters of the alphabet. A close comparison between the two

---

[109] For the equivalence between correct (ὀρθόν) and appropriate (προσῆκον) cf. 430c, 431b.
[110] Barney (2001: 122 and n.15) views the τύπος-condition 'as consisting in the notion that even a sloppy name or *logos* may function so long as I can *recognize* it … as being the name or *logos* of the object it is'. She compares the use of τύπος at *Tht.* 192a, 194b, where the soul is being compared to a wax block imprinted with the memories of past perceptions (cf. 191d 'whatever gets impressed one remembers and knows *as long as its image is present*', ἕως ἂν ἐνῇ τὸ εἴδωλον αὐτοῦ), and comments that 'in both cases a *tupos* is a likeness derived from some object in the world … making possible acts of identification, albeit of different kinds. A *logos* of Cratylus counts as such if his *tupos* is present in it: that is, I suppose, if it "resembles" Cratylus sufficiently for me to pick him out as the object it is about.'

passages, however, reveals a small but possibly significant difference. In the earlier passage Socrates said that the same signification can be obtained by means of different syllables, and a name can have some letters added or subtracted, 'as long as the object's being, indicated in the name, is *dominant* [ἐγκρατής]'. Here at 432e, instead, the referent's 'outline' need only be *present* (ἕως ἂν ... ἐνῇ). Again Socrates seems to be lowering the minimal threshold of resemblance which a name must necessarily meet.

Note how the principles set forth in the present passage apply to, and in turn receive elucidation from, the etymologies of actual Greek primary names, of which Socrates offered a sample at 426c–427d. First, those names appeared to contain several intrusive letters and only a few appropriate ones; therefore by the present criterion they were 'bad' names. They were nevertheless deemed correct (425d–426a, 427d), in line with the Redundancy Conception of correctness and with my interpretation of the present passage.[111] Secondly, the few appropriate letters those names did contain often did not resemble more than a generic feature of their nominatum, as in the case of the names containing the letter ρ (see §6.4.4). This confirms the interpretation of τύπος as 'general character' in our passage.

We must now come to cases (ii) and (iii), which are dealt with at e4–7. A preliminary point first. From the conclusion of the defence of false speaking (431c) to these very lines Socrates has been speaking of the *imposition* of names, more precisely of the way names are made, not of their use; but now he is suddenly adding some considerations about the *use* of names and other larger linguistic items. This switch, however, is not unjustified. For there really is a certain continuity between name imposition and name use, as long as resemblance between name and thing constitutes a *necessary* condition for naming in any sense of the term, so that complete lack of resemblance prevents a name from naming a given thing at all (cf. Barney 2001: 114, quoted in §7.3.1).

It is crucial to decide how we should translate the term λόγος at e4: 'sentence' or 'phrase'?[112] I shall discuss λόγον when dealing with case (iii). But it seems clear that the two occurrences of ἐν λόγῳ had better be translated

---

[111] This also holds of the names of letters at 393de. There, however, the context was the analysis of *secondary* names, and Socrates had not yet identified imitation as a criterion of correctness. As a consequence, intrusive letters were no problem for him; he could even extol how 'finely' (καλῶς) a name like βῆτα is made.

[112] λόγος as 'phrase': 396ab, 410de; *Lg.* 10.895e. We should not regard 'phrase' and 'sentence' as two alternative *meanings* of λόγος here; it may well be that the term means something generic and neutral between the two and that it is the context that decides whether a phrase or a sentence is at stake. It is just so in Aristotle, *Int.* 16b26–17a12, *Po.* 1457a23–7: cf. ch. 6 n.65.

in the same way[113] and that this way is '*in a sentence*'; for it would be odd if in case (iii) Socrates spoke of a phrase or sentence contained *in a phrase*. Thus case (ii) concerns an inappropriate name contained in a sentence, e.g. 'Callias is a *dog*'. Let us see how it works.

Here is a first paraphrase of the relevant portions of e4–7: if an inappropriate name is contained in a sentence (ἐν λόγῳ), this does not stop the object which the sentence is about[114] being spoken of (λέγεσθαι), provided that the object's outline is present in the sentence. Said otherwise: an object can be spoken of by a sentence which contains one or more inappropriate names, provided that the object's outline is present in the sentence. Now, it is reasonable to assume that a sentence which contains one or more inappropriate names is a *false* sentence. Therefore Socrates is here trying to explain how a sentence can speak of something and yet be false, contrary to those sophistic arguments according to which, if a sentence speaks of something, it is *ipso facto* true (see §7.2.2).

These things being so, it might be tempting to construe Socrates' claim about case (ii) as follows: a thing can be spoken of by a sentence which contains one or more inappropriate names, and hence is false, provided that the sentence's *subject-term* refers to that thing. For example, the false sentence 'Callias is a dog' contains the inappropriate name 'dog', and hence is false; but, insofar as its subject-term refers to Callias, it speaks of Callias, is about Callias, exactly like the true sentence 'Callias is a man'. In other words, the distinction between a sentence's speaking of something and its being true or false would presuppose the distinction between a sentence's subject and its predicate, exactly as at *Sph.* 261d–263d.

This is what Socrates *ought* to say. The temptation to assume that it is also what he does say should, however, be resisted, for at least two reasons. First, Socrates seems to claim that what need be present in the sentence is just the thing's outline or general character (τύπος), whereas for a sentence to speak of X its subject-term must *exactly* refer to X. Secondly, Socrates appears to posit an analogy between a name containing an inappropriate letter and a sentence containing an inappropriate name. This suggests that he views a sentence as a sort of *noun phrase*, where each term refers to some

---

[113] *Pace* Reeve, who renders e4–5 as 'an inappropriate name may be included in a phrase. And if an inappropriate name may be included in a phrase, a phrase which is inappropriate to the things may be employed in a statement.'

[114] τοῦ πράγματος περὶ οὗ ἂν ὁ λόγος ᾖ (e7): cf. *Euthd.* 283e τὸ πρᾶγμα περὶ οὗ ἂν ὁ λόγος ᾖ, most significantly in the context of an argument against false speaking. As I see it, the notion of a subject matter which the sentence is about is, by itself, quite generic and does not entail a correct conception of sentence structure, contrary to what Burnyeat 2002: 53 seems to assume. (Denyer 1991: 81 takes πρᾶγμα here to refer to a *fact*, which I find hardly plausible.)

feature of the thing described, just as each letter of a name refers (on the naturalist view) to some feature of the referent. Such a phrase, like a name, has the function of referring to something by describing it, and all its component names, like the letters in a name, contribute to the fulfilment of that function. It cannot perform the twofold function of referring to something and saying something about it; it cannot have subject-predicate structure. Thus case (ii) seems to boil down to the following: a thing can be spoken of by a sentence which, containing some inappropriate names, is neither so accurate as to be a true sentence about it nor so inaccurate as not to be a sentence about it at all. That is, on Socrates' present view, what it is for a sentence about something to be false (McDowell 1973: 236–7, Denyer 1991: 81).[115]

If this interpretation is correct, then Socrates is out to draw a sound distinction between a sentence's speaking of something and its being true or false, but he is drawing the distinction in the wrong way. More precisely, he is committing no less than two serious mistakes – of which the latter partially counteracts the former. On the one hand, he still adheres to the mistaken assumption that sentences are a sort of noun phrases;[116] on the other, he adopts a mistaken conception of noun phrases themselves. For a noun phrase – unlike what Socrates here says of a sentence – refers to a thing only if *all* the terms it comprises refer to, or are true of, that thing; if one term fails to refer to, or be true of, the thing, then so does the whole phrase. For example, 'Callias the dog' does not refer to Callias, the rich Athenian nobleman.

This interestingly confirms and supplements the conclusions we reached about the two previous passages, 385bd and 431bc, which also dealt with the problem of falsity and the relation between sentences and names. For one thing, already in those passages we had reason to suspect that Socrates was not adopting a correct conception of sentence structure and was treating sentences as if they were a sort of noun phrases (§§2.2.3, 7.2.4). So the

---

[115] Would Socrates see any difference between such a false sentence and the phrase 'Athenian foreigner, son of Smicrion, Hermogenes', which was falsely addressed to Cratylus in the 429e example? Note that there the reference to a subject matter was in any case secured by the interlocutor seizing Cratylus' hand.

[116] Denyer 1991: 81–2 levels another criticism at case (ii)'s conception of sentences, focusing on two points which Socrates leaves aside: true sentences and the omission of appropriate names (as opposed to the inclusion of inappropriate ones). Here is a slightly modified version of his criticism. Sometimes the omission of an appropriate name does not make a true sentence into a false one (e.g. both 'Callias is a rich Athenian' and 'Callias is rich' are true), but sometimes it does (e.g. 'Callias is a bad cobbler' is true, 'Callias is bad' false); Socrates, however, does not seem to have the means to draw a distinction between those names which can be omitted from a true sentence without affecting its truth and those which cannot.

same misconception is independently suggested by no less than three passages of *Cra.*; and it seems, at long last, reasonable of a commentator to return a guilty verdict on this issue.

Now on to case (iii), the crux of the whole passage. We must now confront the expression λόγον ... μὴ προσήκοντα. In the translation given above I rendered this as 'an inappropriate *phrase*' though rendering ἐν λόγῳ twice as 'in a sentence'. On this construal, while (ii) concerns an inappropriate name contained in a sentence, e.g. 'Callias is a *dog*', (iii) concerns an inappropriate phrase contained in a sentence, e.g. 'Callias is a *black dog*'. This is, however, not the standard construal of e4–5. Most interpreters rather hold that λόγος should be translated uniformly as 'sentence' and that while case (ii) concerns a name contained in a simple sentence, (iii) concerns a simple sentence contained in a compound one.[117]

Let me set aside for a moment my own construal and examine the standard one first. There are at least two reasons for endorsing it. First, Socrates' talk of an 'inappropriate' λόγος echoes 431bc, where he spoke of the distribution of inappropriate names, verbs and λόγοι, 'sentences'; this suggests that case (iii) concerns a *sentence* contained in another, larger sentence. Secondly, it seems just natural to assume that all the e4 occurrences of λόγος refer to linguistic items of the same kind (albeit of different size); and if so, since these items are unlikely to be all phrases, they are rather likely to be all sentences.

Here is a first paraphrase of the relevant portions of lines e4–7 on this standard construal: an inappropriate sentence (λόγον ... μὴ προσήκοντα) may be contained in a larger sentence (ἐν λόγῳ) without the thing which the larger sentence is about failing to be spoken of, provided that the thing's general character is present in the larger sentence. In other words: a thing can be spoken of by a sentence which contains an inappropriate smaller sentence, provided that the thing's general character is present in the larger sentence. Socrates is presumably thinking of a compound sentence composed of several simple sentences. But (a) what is it for one of the component sentences to be 'inappropriate'? And (b) what sort of compound sentence does Socrates have in mind?

Here is a tentative answer to (a): an 'inappropriate' sentence is simply an ordinary *false* sentence. And here is a tentative answer to (b): Socrates is thinking of a *conjunctive* sentence – more precisely, a conjunctive

---

[117] E.g. Fowler translates ὄνομα ἐν λόγῳ as 'a noun in a clause' and λόγον ἐν λόγῳ as 'a clause in a sentence'; Dalimier translates the former expression as 'un nom dans l'énoncé', the latter as 'un énoncé ... dans le discours' (cf. her 270 n.409).

sentence where all the conjuncts have the same subject: e.g. 'Callias is rich and Callias is Athenian and *Callias is a dog*'. If we join them together, the two tentative answers amount to the following: Socrates is thinking of a conjunctive sentence where all the conjuncts have the same subject and one of them (or more) is false. Upon reflection, however, this does not seem to be satisfactory. For a false sentence like 'Callias is a dog' is a sentence where some names but not all are inappropriate or incorrect, and which therefore is an instance of case (ii); as such it speaks of Callias, while at the same time being false, independently of its being included in a larger sentence about Callias. Thus our tentative answer to (a) collapses the distinction between cases (ii) and (iii) and makes Socrates' talk of the inappropriate sentence's being 'in a sentence' (ἐν λόγῳ) appear superfluous; talk of an 'inappropriate sentence' would suffice. By contrast, no such superfluity could be recognized in cases (i) and (ii), whose point was precisely that, when an inappropriate element (a letter, a name) is contained in a larger unit (a name, a sentence), the remainder of the larger unit can nevertheless ensure that the whole refers to a certain thing.

So it seems that, if case (iii) is not to collapse on (ii), an 'inappropriate' sentence must be something even worse, as it were, than a 'normal' false sentence. Here our suspicion that Socrates is mistakenly assimilating sentences to noun phrases might be helpful. Case (ii) sentences seemed to be like *partially* misfiring noun phrases, i.e. noun phrases where only some names fail to refer to, or be true of, a given thing (e.g. 'Callias the dog', where 'dog' is not true of Callias). Therefore we may guess that the 'inappropriate' sentences of case (iii) are somehow like *totally* misfiring noun phrases, i.e. noun phrases where all names fail to refer to, or be true of, a given thing (e.g. 'Coriscus the dog', where no name is true of Callias). To understand what this might concretely amount to, consider the following example. Callias is laughing fit to bust; someone who is watching the scene at a distance forms the false belief that the person she is seeing is Coriscus and that what he is doing is crying. So the observer points to Callias and says to her neighbour 'Look – Coriscus is crying.'[118] Here we have a false sentence which both misidentifies and misdescribes an independently given subject matter, i.e. Callias. A sentence of this sort I call a *totally misfiring sentence,* and I venture the hypothesis that this might be the right answer to question (a): Socrates has such a sentence

---

[118] To make things easier you may add the further assumption that the real Coriscus is not crying either.

in mind when he speaks of an 'inappropriate' sentence as distinct from a sentence which just contains an 'inappropriate' name. Now in such cases it is of course necessary that a subject matter be identified independently of the sentence itself. In the above example this function was performed by the observer's pointing; but it might also be performed by a full-blown sentence which makes it clear what one is talking about. Consider a variant of the above example, in which the observer, rather than pointing, just says to her neighbour 'The man over there is doing something funny: Coriscus is crying.' Here the phrase 'The man over there' refers to Callias, who is in a sense the subject matter of the whole sentence, and relative to whom 'Coriscus is crying' is totally misfiring. So perhaps this might be the right answer to question (b): Socrates has something along these lines in mind when, at 432e4–7, he says that a thing can be spoken of by a sentence which contains a smaller 'inappropriate' sentence, provided that the larger sentence captures the thing's 'general character'.

Now note that, on this construal of case (iii) as involving totally misfiring sentences, our passage bears a special relevance to its two predecessors on false speaking. At 385bd Socrates seemed to say, or implicate, that *all* the names of a true sentence are true and *all* those of a false sentence are false (§2.2.3); and a sentence all of whose names are false can be described as a totally misfiring one like those we have been considering thus far. As for 431bc, recall that there from the possibility of distributing inappropriate (μὴ προσήκοντα) names and verbs[119] Socrates inferred the possibility of doing the same with whole sentences. At first blush it seemed natural to take an inappropriate sentence to be simply a false sentence which contains *at least one* inappropriate name or verb. Now, however, after reading the present passage, we may rather be led to suspect that for Socrates, already at 431bc, an 'inappropriate' sentence was not simply a false sentence, but – much more specifically – a totally misfiring sentence, and that he was actually reasoning as follows: if we can distribute inappropriate names and verbs, then we can distribute inappropriate sentences, i.e. sentences entirely consisting of inappropriate names and verbs. If we can inappropriately distribute to Callias both the noun 'Coriscus' and the verb 'flies', we can also inappropriately distribute to him the sentence 'Coriscus flies.'

[119] Or: of distributing names and verbs *incorrectly* (μὴ ὀρθῶς). I assume that 'correct' and 'appropriate' are perfectly equivalent, and that distributing a name or verb correctly (appropriately) is the same as distributing a correct (appropriate) name or verb.

This hypothesis has the advantage that it enables us to give a unitary account of Socrates' various treatments of false sentences throughout the dialogue. In particular, if we suppose that 431bc was concerned with *ordinary* false sentences, not totally misfiring ones, then here we have to identify them with case (ii) sentences, which contain one or more inappropriate names. Thus we have to say that Socrates offers *two* irreconcilable explanations of how an ordinary false sentence can manage to be about something (cf. Denyer 1991: 76–82). According to the *first* explanation, offered at 431bc, a false sentence is about something by being distributed to an independently given subject matter. According to the *second* explanation, offered in our case (ii), a false sentence is about something by containing enough appropriate names to preserve its 'general character', though not enough appropriate names to be true. These two explanations are incompatible with each other; for the reference to the sentence's subject matter is located outside the sentence itself by the first one, but inside the sentence by the second one. By contrast, if we accept the hypothesis that at 431bc Socrates was thinking of totally misfiring sentences, then these are *different* from 432e's case (ii) sentences, and are rather identical with case (iii) inappropriate sentences. This identification is unproblematic. For as a 431bc sentence was inappropriately distributed to an independently given subject matter, so on the present interpretation a case (iii) sentence is inappropriate to something which is referred to only in a larger sentence; in both cases the reference to the relevant subject matter is *external* to the inappropriate sentence itself.

That said, the hypothesis that totally misfiring sentences play such a role in Socrates' arguments remains hard to swallow. For they constitute an outlandish case of falsity, whose presence in actual linguistic practice is extremely marginal; and it is difficult to see why Plato should be so interested in them.

So, if we do not like where the analysis of the passage has brought us, we had better reconsider the beginning of our discussion of case (iii). Our present troubles ultimately stem from the decision to interpret λόγον ... μὴ προσήκοντα (e4) as 'an inappropriate sentence', in keeping with the other two occurrences of λόγος. Hence we can try an alternative course, as in my translation above, and understand the expression as 'an inappropriate *phrase*', severing the link between it and the inappropriate λόγοι of 431bc. On this construal, to repeat, while case (ii) concerns an inappropriate name contained in a sentence ('Callias is a *dog*'), case (iii) concerns an inappropriate phrase contained in a sentence

Naturalism and imperfect resemblance (431c–433b)

('Callias is a *black dog*'). Both are quite ordinary kinds of false sentence, and totally misfiring sentences do not come into question at all, either here or at 431bc.[120]

Of course this welcome philosophical simplification is achieved at a price. For it goes against our respectable reasons for taking all three e4 occurrences of λόγος as 'sentence'; and it gives Socrates two irreconcilable accounts of ordinary false sentences here and at 431bc. But the price is, on balance, one that I am willing to pay. This is partly because I am far from sure that Plato would regard Socrates' offering two competing accounts of ordinary false sentences as a shortcoming of the dialogue rather than an advantage.

We finally leave our struggle against 432d11–433a3 and move on to the immediately following passage, where Socrates forcefully reasserts his conclusions:

SO. Very well, then. For when this is present, even though it doesn't have all the appropriate elements [κἂν μὴ πάντα τὰ προσήκοντα ἔχῃ], the object will be spoken of, finely when it has all the appropriate elements, badly when it has a few [λέξεταί γε τὸ πρᾶγμα, καλῶς ὅταν πάντα, κακῶς δὲ ὅταν ὀλίγα]. But that it does get spoken of, my dear friend, we must admit, lest we incur a penalty, like those who at Aegina go about in the streets late at night [ἵνα μὴ ὄφλωμεν ὥσπερ οἱ ἐν Αἰγίνῃ νύκτωρ περιιόντες ὀψὲ ὁδοῦ], and truly seem in our turn, much in the same way, to have arrived at the objects [ἐπὶ τὰ πράγματα] later than we should. Otherwise, search for some other sort of correctness of names [ζήτει τινὰ ἄλλην ὀνόματος ὀρθότητα], and don't acknowledge that a name is a means to indicate an object with syllables and letters [δήλωμα συλλαβαῖς καὶ γράμμασι πράγματος ὄνομα εἶναι]. For if you'll maintain both of these views you won't be able to be in agreement with yourself.

CR. Well, Socrates, you seem to me to be speaking reasonably, and I take this to be so. (433a4–b7)

The part of this passage which is pronounced by Socrates (a4–b5) can be divided into three smaller parts.

(1) In the *first* part (a4–6) Socrates states a sort of generalization from, or compendium of, the three cases distinguished at 432de. He says that a

---

[120] But perhaps there might come into question totally misfiring *phrases*. When in case (iii) Socrates talks about a thing being spoken of by a sentence which contains an inappropriate phrase, clearly this phrase itself is meant to be such as not to refer to the thing at all. But when in case (ii) Socrates admitted that a thing can be spoken of by a sentence which contains an inappropriate name, above we ascribed to him the view that a thing can be referred to by a partially misfiring phrase, i.e. a phrase where only some terms fail to refer to, or be true of, the thing (e.g. 'white *dog*' relative to Callias). Therefore it seems that, if in case (iii) λόγου ... μὴ προσήκοντα means 'inappropriate phrase', this must be a totally misfiring phrase ('black dog').

linguistic expression (whose kind he does not specify) speaks of an object as long as the object's general character is present in it (a4 τοῦτο refers loosely to the τύπος of 432e6); it speaks of that object 'finely' if it contains all (and, we should add, only) the appropriate elements (whose nature he again leaves unspecified), whereas it speaks of that object 'badly' if it contains (not all or even) a few appropriate elements.

What kind of linguistic expression and elements thereof is Socrates talking about? Since the noun to which τὰ προσήκοντα is attached and the subject of ἔχῃ (a3) are not expressed, apparently the point may apply to any of the three cases of 432de. But while in this context the repeated use of the verb λέγεσθαι (a5–6) suggests a reference to cases (ii) and (iii), which concerned λόγοι, the adverbs 'finely' and 'badly' instead convey a special reference to case (i), which concerned names and their relation to letters. Socrates takes pains to argue that names may be finely or badly set down, depending on the letters they are composed of (see 431ce, 432de, and especially 433bc, where he is going to sum up the results achieved so far); and in the third part of this very passage (b1–7) it is clearly names and letters he is concerning himself with. By contrast, nowhere else in the dialogue, apart from a passage at 435cd which is clearly parallel to ours but is as unclear and in any event very generic (§8.1.5), does Socrates talk about 'fine' and 'bad' sentences, or about a sentence's speaking of something 'finely' or 'badly'.[121]

(ii) In the *second* part (a6–b1) Socrates says that he and Cratylus ought to accept the conclusion he has just restated in order to avoid a certain unwelcome consequence, which he illustrates by means of a comparison. Unfortunately both the first and the second term of comparison – respectively, the unwelcome consequence and the situation it is compared to – are rather obscure.

The second term, which comes first in the text (a7–8), is very problematic. All the available interpretations are, to my mind, unsatisfactory; I shall discuss two of them, which correctly grasp the overall point that Socrates is referring to a situation where Aegina was placed under curfew and offenders incurred some sort of penalty. (a) Some take ὄφλωμεν to mean 'be convicted', with ὀψὲ ὁδοῦ as *genetivus criminis*, 'for being too late in the streets' (cf. *Lg.* 874b, And. 1.74).[122] But it is very doubtful whether an expression like ὀψὲ ὁδός, lit. 'late [adv.], street', may function

---

[121] Some translations (Fowler, Minio-Paluello, Reeve) take these lines to be concerned *only* with names and their relation to letters.
[122] So LSJ (ὀφλισκάνω I.4) and Dalimier. On curfew in Greek cities cf. Aen. Tact. 10.10, 14–15; 22.23–4.

Naturalism and imperfect resemblance (431c–433b)

as the name of a *crime*. (b) Méridier takes ὄφλωμεν to have absolute construction, meaning 'incur a penalty', 'be condemned' (*Lg.* 745a, 754e, etc.), and takes ὀψὲ ὁδοῦ to mean 'late *in* the street'. I have adopted this rendering in my translation above; but in fact ὁδοῦ can hardly mean 'in the street'.[123] So I suspect that the text is corrupt. This view is already implied by Q, where in place of ὀψὲ ὁδοῦ we find ἐφ' ὁδοῖς, certainly a conjecture, which should presumably mean 'on the streets' and accommodate the text to interpretation (b), but in fact is – as far as I know – not Greek. Burnet considered correcting ὀψὲ ὁδοῦ into ὀψισμοῦ ('of belatedness') or ὀψοδίου ('of being late in the street'); both conjectures would accommodate the text to interpretation (a), but the former would make it difficult to explain the corruption, while the latter would be a *hapax*. Perhaps we should resign ourselves to the *cruces*.

The first term of comparison (a8–b1) is at least literally clear: Socrates and Cratylus risk incurring a penalty for arriving at 'the objects' too late. The point of comparison with the second term consists of course in the notion of *arriving too late at a destination* – which in the second term is presumably one's house, whereas it is 'the objects' in the first term. But what does 'arriving at the objects too late' mean? Since the term πρᾶγμα in all its occurrences throughout 432d–433b refers to the object named or referred to (e5–7, a5, b3), this must be the case here too. So I think that 'to arrive at the objects too late' means 'to impose unnecessarily demanding conditions for a name to name something' – exactly what Cratylus was doing with his all-or-nothing stance on perfection in names.

(III) In the passage's *third* part (b1–7) Socrates claims that, if Cratylus does not accept the conclusions summarized in the first part, then he should adopt a different view on the correctness of names; that is to say (b2 καί is explanatory), he should abandon the view that a name indicates an object with syllables and letters. For, Socrates says, maintaining 'both of these views' (i.e. *both* that, contrary to Socrates' conclusions, any omitted or added letter stops a name naming a given object *and* that a name indicates an object with syllables and letters) is an inconsistent stance. The reason why it is inconsistent is of course that the latter view (which must be equivalent to the naturalist thesis) entails something incompatible with the former, i.e. that names, *qua* images, admit of degrees of resemblance and perfection, as Socrates has been arguing at length.

---

[123] The genitive may have local sense: see KG 1.384–5. But this is extremely rare in prose, and KG mention no Platonic example. Furthermore, in those examples which might be most relevant to our passage the local sense is *figurative*: see Hdt. 4.12.3, 7.124, 9.89.4, Ar. *R.* 174 τῆς ὁδοῦ; Aesch. *Ch.* 711 μακρᾶς κελεύθου, where ὁδός and κέλευθος mean 'journey', not 'road' or 'street'.

Now the fact that in this context the sentence 'a name is a means to indicate an object with syllables and letters' (b3) must count as a formulation of the naturalist thesis poses a problem. For it may seem that the sentence, as I have translated it, rather makes an innocuous and non-committal claim, which even a conventionalist could endorse. So we should find out what it is about this sentence that makes it fit to characterize the naturalist position as opposed to the conventionalist one. Many scholars would contend that this element is to be identified with the term δήλωμα, that my 'means to indicate' (or 'indicator') is altogether too neutral a translation of this term, and that something more loaded like 'representation' (Fowler, Méridier) or 'revelation' (Robinson 1956: 132) would be more appropriate. As I have already remarked time and again, however, the verb δηλόω in our dialogue is usually just equivalent to σημαίνω, 'signify' (see §§4.2.4, 4.2.6); and as 433d–434a is going to confirm (see §8.1.1), there is every reason to keep it and cognate terms as neutral as possible in the dispute between naturalism and conventionalism. So I suggest that the naturalist element might instead be located in the phrase 'with syllables and letters' (συλλαβαῖς καὶ γράμμασι). Of course this phrase too may be neutral and non-committal, if it means just that a name, unlike other devices for indicating something, is *made up of* syllables and letters; this is how the phrase γράμμασί τε καὶ συλλαβαῖς was used at 423ae. Nevertheless, in our passage 'with syllables and letters' also admits of a different, stronger interpretation: the *particular* syllables and letters which make up a name *determine* what it indicates. This is, as required, a formulation of the naturalist thesis.

A final remark on a crucial question which has accompanied us throughout the discussion between Socrates and Cratylus. Here Socrates clearly holds that (on the view which is presently in force) the correctness of a name consists in its performing the function of a name by indicating something with its syllables and letters. Clearly, therefore, he holds that there is no difference between correct names and names *simpliciter* – i.e. he sticks, as he did at 432ad (cf. §7.3.3, and more generally §I.1.1), to the Redundancy Conception of correctness – and presents the distinction between those names which name 'finely' or 'well' and those which name 'badly' as a distinction *internal* to the set of correct names or names *simpliciter*.

CHAPTER 8

Naturalism refuted and conventionalism defended (433b–439b)

In the section of the dialogue which we are going to explore in this chapter, Socrates finally engages in a complex and powerful criticism of the very core of naturalism. The section can be divided into two parts. In the first part (433b–435d), to be dealt with in §8.1, Socrates, after rehearsing some previous conclusions, criticizes the naturalist view that names are naturally correct and that their natural correctness consists in their being similar to their referents. In the second part (435d–439b), to be dealt with in §8.2, Socrates turns to the related view that knowledge of names yields knowledge of their referents.

8.1 RESEMBLANCE AND CONVENTION IN NAMES (433B–435D)

8.1.1 Preliminaries (433b–434b)

Cratylus' answer at 433b6–7 seemed to show that he was meekly yielding to the arguments of Socrates. This latter then hammers his point home:

SO. So, since we're agreed on these points, let us then examine the following question. If the name is, as we say, to have been imposed finely, must it contain the appropriate letters?
CR. Yes.
SO. But those letters are appropriate which are similar to the objects? [προσήκει δὲ τὰ ὅμοια τοῖς πράγμασιν;]
CR. Of course.
SO. Therefore those that have been set down finely have been set down so [Τὰ μὲν ἄρα καλῶς κείμενα οὕτω κεῖται]. But if some has not been imposed finely, for the most part it might perhaps be composed of appropriate and similar letters, if it is to be an image, but it would also contain something inappropriate, because of which the name would not be fine or finely made [εἰ δὲ μή τι καλῶς ἐτέθη, τὸ μὲν ἂν πολὺ ἴσως ἐκ προσηκόντων εἴη γραμμάτων καὶ ὁμοίων, εἴπερ ἔσται εἰκών, ἔχοι δ' ἂν τι καὶ οὐ προσῆκον, δι' ὃ οὐκ ἂν καλὸν

εἴη οὐδὲ καλῶς εἰργασμένον τὸ ὄνομα]. Are we saying this or something different? (433b8–c7)

This passage is at first puzzling. For although Socrates opens it with a typical formula whose purpose is to claim that a section of the discussion is over and a new one is beginning (b8–9), he next goes on to offer what is almost a recapitulation of the conclusions of 431c–432b: a 'finely' imposed name must contain (all and only) the appropriate letters, i.e. letters similar to (the nature of) the thing named, whereas a name that contains some inappropriate letters (or lacks some appropriate ones), even if most of its letters are appropriate, has not been finely made and is itself not fine, i.e. is bad.[1] Thus the new subject announced at b8–9 is still to be introduced, and indeed will not be until 434c. The fact that Socrates approaches it in this roundabout way is a signal both of its importance and of the relevant role which the earlier conclusions he is recapitulating are going to play.

It becomes clear, however, that Cratylus, despite his assent of b6–7, has not really swallowed the conclusions about fine and bad names:

CR. I think I must not keep on arguing, Socrates; yet[2] I don't like to say that something is a name but has not been imposed finely. (433c8–10)

Unperturbed by Cratylus' lack of persuasion, Socrates goes on to recall and submit to Cratylus two points from his earlier discussion with Hermogenes:

SO. What about the view that the name is a means to indicate the object [δήλωμα τοῦ πράγματος]? Don't you like this idea?
CR. I do.
SO. But that among names some are composed of prior ones, while others are first, doesn't seem to you a fine thing to say?
CR. It does. (433d1–6)

The second point (d4–5) is the familiar distinction between primary and secondary names, i.e. between those names which are etymologically simple and those which are analysable – directly or indirectly – into simple ones (421c–422b).[3] The first point (d1–2) is that a name is a 'means to indicate', literally an 'indicator of', the thing it names. We have been familiar

---

[1] 433a has made it clear that a bad name may contain only a few (ὀλίγα) appropriate letters. Hence a name composed mostly of appropriate letters (c4–5) can only be the *most favourable* case among non-fine names, not the only possible case, and ἴσως (c4) must mean 'perhaps' rather than 'sans doute', as Méridier translates it.
[2] Where I have 'yet' the Greek has an elliptical ἐπεί: '[but I'm not really convinced,] *because* ...' (cf. §8.1.5 on 435c).
[3] On the expression '*prior* names' (d4) cf. 422d8 and §6.2.1.

Resemblance and convention in names (433b–435d)

with this idea at least since 422e–423b, where Socrates, in developing his theory of the primary names, talked about our 'indicating the objects', δηλοῦν … τὰ πράγματα, by means of mimetic gestures or sounds, and where the term δήλωμα occurred first. Of course the term's translation is as controversial here as elsewhere in *Cra.*;[4] but the text itself is about to remind us which translations are acceptable and which are not.

SO. But if the first ones are to become means to indicate something [δηλώματά τινων], do you know any finer way [τρόπον] of them becoming means to indicate than making them as like those things which they must indicate as possible [ὅτι μάλιστα τοιαῦτα οἷα ἐκεῖνα ἃ δεῖ δηλοῦν αὐτά;]? Or do you prefer this other way, advocated by Hermogenes and many others, i.e. that names are conventional tokens [συνθήματα] and indicate to those who have made the convention and know the objects beforehand [δηλοῦν τοῖς συνθεμένοις προειδόσι δὲ τὰ πράγματα], and that this, I mean convention [συνθήκην], is the correctness of names, and that it makes no difference whether one makes a convention like the one which is presently in force or, quite the contrary, one makes the convention to call 'large' what is presently called 'small' and 'small' what is presently called 'large' [ἐπὶ μὲν ᾧ νῦν σμικρόν, μέγα καλεῖν, ἐπὶ δὲ ᾧ μέγα, σμικρόν]? Which of these two ways do you like?

CR. Indicating whatever one indicates with a likeness [τὸ ὁμοιώματι δηλοῦν ὅτι ἄν τις δηλοῖ], Socrates, is absolutely and completely superior to indicating it with any chance means [τῷ ἐπιτυχόντι]. (433d7–434a2)

What is most interesting in this passage is not so much the two theoretical options that are being contrasted as the manner in which they are contrasted, which presents the dialogue's whole issue in an importantly new light. Here for the first time Socrates identifies a minimal *common ground* between the naturalist and the conventionalist view of names and distinguishes it sharply from what they disagree upon. On his present account, the two views agree that names bear to their referents a certain *relation*, signified by the verb δηλόω and the cognate noun δήλωμα (which I have translated 'indicate' and 'means to indicate' respectively). But they disagree upon the *way* (τρόπος d8, e3, e9) in which names bear this relation to their referents.[5] It is also clear, on the basis of what Socrates says both here (e5–6) and elsewhere, what the place of the concept of correctness is in this picture. '*X*' is a correct name of *X* if and only if it bears the relevant relation to *X* (i.e. indicates *X*). '*X*' is a *naturally* correct name of *X* if and

---

[4] 'Declaratio' Ficino, 'representation' Fowler and Méridier, 'revelation' Robinson (1956: 132), 'modo di manifestare' Minio-Paluello, 'way of expressing' Reeve, 'moyen de faire voir' Dalimier.

[5] The passage's gist is partially obscured by mistranslations of τρόπος as 'theory' (Fowler on e3 and e9), 'explication' (Méridier on e3) or 'façon de raisonner' (Dalimier on e3 and e9).

only if it bears the relevant relation to X (indicates X) in the natural way; it is *conventionally* correct if and only if it bears the relevant relation to X (indicates X) in the conventional way.

Let us first investigate more closely the common ground between naturalism and conventionalism. Since Socrates here presents the name-object relation signified by δηλόω and δήλωμα as an uncontroversial issue, on which both parties are at one, we should reject any interpretation of those terms suggesting a privileged connection with the naturalist side. Socrates cannot be plausibly construed as claiming that both Cratylus and Hermogenes hold that names 'represent' (Fowler, Méridier), or 'disclose' (Schofield 1982: 71, Barney 2001: 123–4, 128), or are 'revelations' of (Robinson 1956: 132–3), their referents. The meaning of these terms must be neutral, as indeed it turns out to be in other contexts as well (394bc, see §4.2.6; 422e–423b, see §6.2.2; 435ab, see §8.1.3). Hence my translations 'indicate' and 'means to indicate'.[6]

This neutral, non-committal account of the function of names is interestingly at variance with another account, advanced elsewhere in the dialogue, which instead is strongly biased towards naturalism and says that the function of names is (or is also) to *teach* – which in the dialogue is taken to mean that knowledge of names yields knowledge of their referents.[7] The biased account was introduced at 388bc, in the course of Socrates' arguments for naturalism, and picked up at 428e, at the outset of his conversation with Cratylus; what is more, it will be strikingly reinstated at 435d, immediately after the end of a cluster of arguments against naturalism for which Socrates is presently setting the stage. To explain the compresence of these two mutually conflicting conceptions one could speculate that the historical Cratylus actually held one of the two, i.e. the biased one, which is also the one he is made to state with his own words, whereas the other, the neutral and more sensible one, which is being presented in these lines, was Plato's own contribution.

Let us now come to Socrates' account of the conflict between naturalism and conventionalism, i.e. to the two alternative ways in which names can be thought to indicate objects. The account of the naturalist way, proposed by Socrates at d8–e2 and endorsed by Cratylus at

---

[6] Rijlaarsdam's (1978: 97) rendering of the verb as 'bezeichnen' I find unobjectionable. Reeve's 'express' for δηλόω, and 'way of expressing' for δήλωμα, are also acceptable; but see ch. 4 n.49).
[7] When I say that the two accounts are at variance I do not mean that they are irreconcilable: a third account which embraced them both would be conceivable. What I mean is that as they are presented in the text they cannot be true together; for each purports to be not a partial but an exhaustive account of the function of names.

434a1–2, is very succinct: a name indicates an object by being similar to it. The account of the conventionalist way (e2–9) is more interesting. I shall not dwell upon the propositions that names are conventional tokens (συνθήματα)[8] and that the correctness of names consists in convention, to focus instead on the two remaining propositions in Socrates' account.

(1) 'Names ... indicate [sc. objects][9] to those who have made the convention and know the objects beforehand' (e4–5). A tricky sentence, despite its innocuous appearance. Compare Fowler's translation, which seems representative of the opinion of several scholars: names indicate objects 'to those who established the convention and knew the objects beforehand'.[10] This translation seems to rest upon the twofold assumption that τοῖς συνθεμένοις means 'to those who established the convention' and that προειδόσι ... τὰ πράγματα means 'to those ... who knew the objects before establishing the convention', where 'knew the objects' should presumably be equivalent to 'knew the objects' nature'. Both assumptions seem questionable, for the following reasons.

(a) In the present context τοῖς συνθεμένοις cannot refer only to those who *established* a hypothetical original convention whereby a name was first bestowed on its referent. Here the notion of 'making a convention' must also apply to all those who subsequently *agree to* the convention, even if they live centuries after it has been established. Socrates is assuming that there is no substantial difference, from the speaker's point of view, between establishing a new convention and agreeing to an already existing one. This was precisely the philosophical ground for Hermogenes' equation of convention and custom at 384d, as we saw in §2.1.1.

(b) Socrates should not ascribe to Hermogenes the view that those who established the convention – or, for that matter, those who subsequently agree to it – have prior knowledge of the things to be named. This idea has nothing to do with the conventionalist thesis, according to which naming is an entirely democratic matter, such that *anyone* can establish a new convention or agree to an existing one. In fact, Fowler's construal makes

---

[8] σύνθημα: 'agreement' (Hdt. 5.74.2, Th. 4.67.4, Pl. *Grg.* 492c, X. *HG* 5.4.6), 'agreed sign' (Hdt. 8.7.2, Th. 4.112.1), 'password' (Hdt. 9.98.3, Th. 7.44.4). Cf. *Suda* Σ 1590, 2622–3 Adler.
[9] Schofield's view that, on Socrates' account of the conventionalist view, names should not indicate things but rather 'their utterers' thoughts or meanings' (1982: 72, cf. 77; he renders δηλόω as 'disclose') is unfounded. Socrates is clearly contrasting naturalism and conventionalism in terms of the *way* names are supposed to indicate things, not of *what* they are supposed to indicate.
[10] Cf. Ficino ('iis qui ita constituerunt ac res ipsas praecognovere'), Dalimier and Reeve.

Socrates inappropriately anticipate the much later discussion (435d–438c) of Cratylus' view that names are the only source of knowledge of the objects named. More precisely, it makes Socrates anticipate, and ascribe to Hermogenes, his own objection that Cratylus cannot explain where the first namegivers got their knowledge from at a time when no name had yet been imposed (437e–438b).

So we should look for a different construal. I would start off with the suggestion that 'knowing the objects' here means knowing *what object* a name '*X*' indicates. This suggestion entails the following interpretation of the whole clause δηλοῦν ... τὰ πράγματα. On Hermogenes' view, '*X*' indicates X only to those who agree to a convention to that effect, which enables them to recognize any token of '*X*' they may subsequently come across as indicating X. When adherents of the convention come across a token of '*X*', this does not indicate X to them in virtue of the mimetic force of its letters; rather, they 'know beforehand', in virtue of having agreed to the convention, that tokens of '*X*' indicate X.

If this interpretation (whose core seems to be already held by Barney 2001: 124, 129–30) is correct, then Socrates' present characterization of Hermogenes' view incorporates three important assumptions. First, if '*X*' indicates X to a speaker, then the speaker understands that '*X*' indicates X. This epistemic dimension to the signification of names will be explicitly introduced by Socrates at 434e–435a, in the course of the ensuing argument. Secondly, if '*X*' indicates X by likeness, and not by convention or habit, then any token of '*X*' does, hence (in virtue of the first assumption) any token of '*X*' gets understood by likeness, and not by convention or habit. Thirdly, if a speaker understands that a token of '*X*' indicates X solely on the basis of previous knowledge that tokens of '*X*' indicate X, this is a case of '*X*' indicating X not by likeness, but rather by convention or habit.

(11) 'It makes no difference whether one makes a convention like the one which is presently in force or, quite the contrary, one makes the convention to call "large" what is presently called "small" and "small" what is presently called "large"' (433e6–8). Here Socrates is making on Hermogenes' behalf the point that, if names are conventional, any particular convention is as good as any other, so that a convention in which the names 'large' and 'small' refer respectively to what is small and what is large is as good as the present one. At the same time he also suggests that it would be possible to *substitute* such a convention for the present one by inverting the reference of 'large' and 'small'. Thereby he is of course recalling the 385ab discussion of the possibility of interchanging the referents of 'human' and 'horse'.

Resemblance and convention in names (433b–435d)

In his reply (434a1–2) Cratylus says that indicating something with a likeness is far superior to indicating it 'with any chance means',[11] i.e. with an arbitrary sign. This reply need not and should not be understood as if Cratylus believed that there are *two* genuinely possible ways of indicating something, one of which is superior to the other (cf. §1.1.2). Rather, Cratylus means that there is only one possible way of indicating something, i.e. 'with a likeness', and that this is how names indicate their referents. His reply must be understood in the light of Socrates' question, which of the two alternative ways is 'better' or preferable, whereby Socrates was clearly asking which is the one Cratylus believes in.

We can now go back to the text, where Socrates resumes and finally concludes his recapitulation:

SO. Fine. Then, if the name is to be similar to the object [εἴπερ ἔσται τὸ ὄνομα ὅμοιον τῷ πράγματι], the elements out of which one is to compose the first names must of necessity be naturally similar to the objects [ἀναγκαῖον πεφυκέναι τὰ στοιχεῖα ὅμοια τοῖς πράγμασιν]? What I mean is this. Could one ever compose what we were speaking of just now, a painting similar to any of the beings, if there weren't already dyes, of which the painted items[12] are composed, naturally similar to those things which the art of painting imitates? Wouldn't that be impossible?
CR. Impossible.
SO. Then, likewise, there could never come to be names similar to anything, unless those items of which names are composed already bear in the first place some similarity to those things of which names are imitations [εἰ μὴ ὑπάρξει ἐκεῖνα πρῶτον ὁμοιότητά τινα ἔχοντα, ἐξ ὧν συντίθεται τὰ ὀνόματα, ἐκείνοις ὧν ἐστι τὰ ὀνόματα μιμήματα]? And the items of which names must be composed are the elements, aren't they?
CR. Yes. (434a3–b9)

Socrates has already recalled the distinction between secondary and primary names (433d) and has contrasted the naturalist view that the primary names indicate things by resembling them with the rival view that names are mere conventional signs (433d–434a). Now he goes into greater detail: names can only be similar to things in virtue of the fact that their letters or sounds are such (more precisely, that their letters or sounds resemble some features of their referents). Socrates is thereby summarizing 423e–425a. There, however, the transition from the primary names to their

---

[11] Cf. 390d, where Socrates, concluding his defence of naturalism, told Hermogenes that namegiving is not a matter 'for any chance person' (τῶν ἐπιτυχόντων).
[12] With Minio-Paluello I take τὰ ζωγραφούμενα (b1–2) to be not the paintings (usually called ζωγραφήματα, cf. here a7, or ζῷα or γράμματα) but the painted items, i.e. the images *inside* the paintings.

letters was natural and seamless, whereas here he stresses it, making his point twice, first at a3–6 and then again at a6–b8 by means of the familiar comparison between names and letters, on the one hand, and paintings and dyes, on the other.[13]

Socrates has now collected the premises he needs. The ensuing part of the discussion (434b–435d) will contain a cluster of arguments to the eventual conclusion that convention, agreement and habit 'have some authority concerning the correctness of names'. In §§8.1.2–7 we shall strive to understand how Socrates arrives at this conclusion and what it means exactly.

8.1.2 *The* sklerotes *argument: conflicting letters in the same name (434bd)*

Socrates starts off by picking up his earlier survey of the mimetic force of the Greek letters:

SO. Well, then, this is the moment for you to have a share in the discussion I was having with Hermogenes a moment ago. Tell me, do you believe it was a fine thing to say that ρ resembles movement and motion and hardness [τῇ φορᾷ καὶ κινήσει καὶ σκληρότητι προσέοικεν], or not?
CR. I believe it was.
SO. And that λ resembles what is smooth and soft and those things we mentioned just now?
CR. Yes. (434b10–c6)

Socrates is referring back to 426ce and 427b, where he illustrated the mimetic force of ρ and λ respectively. The former back-reference is somewhat problematic, although Cratylus accepts it without objections; for the text of 426ce does not contain a claim to the effect that ρ imitates *hardness* besides movement, although it seems that such a claim, were it present, would explain certain features of the passage (cf. §6.4.2). The latter back-reference is instead all right. At 427b Socrates said that λ is used to imitate what is *smooth*, gliding, oily or gluey 'and all such things'; now we need only suppose that what is soft was included among 'all such things'.

Then Socrates focuses on a particular example, consisting in the very name σκληρότης ('hardness'), i.e. the name for one of the things which ρ has just been agreed to resemble, and points out a difficulty about it:

---

[13] 'Just now' (νυνδή a7) refers back to 424d–425a, where he compared letters and names with dyes and paintings respectively, and to 430b–432d, where he resumed the name/painting analogy.

SO. Now do you know that the same thing is called σκληρότης by us and σκληρότηρ by the Eretrians?
CR. Of course.
SO. Then do ρ and ς both resemble the same thing [ἔοικεν ἀμφότερα τῷ αὐτῷ], and does the name indicate the same thing to them with the final ρ as to us with the final ς [δηλοῖ ἐκείνοις τε τὸ αὐτὸ τελευτῶντος τοῦ ῥῶ καὶ ἡμῖν τοῦ σῖγμα]? Or doesn't the name indicate that to one or other of the two communities [τοῖς ἑτέροις ἡμῶν οὐ δηλοῖ]?
CR. It does indicate that to both [δηλοῖ μὲν οὖν ἀμφοτέροις].
SO. Insofar as ρ and ς happen to be alike or as they are not?
CR. Insofar as they're alike.
SO. Are they alike in all respects?
CR. At least in respect of their equally indicating movement [Πρός γε τὸ ἴσως φορὰν δηλοῦν]. (434c7–d6)

The Greek name for hardness is spelt differently in Attic and in the Ionic dialect of Eretria, a city in southern Euboea: what the Athenians call σκληρότης the Eretrians call σκληρότηρ (c7–9).[14] Socrates is evidently assuming – and Cratylus is granting – that this is a *primary* name, which indicates its referent by resembling it, and resembles it by being composed of sounds which resemble it (433d–434b). More precisely, since it has just been agreed that the mimetic force of ρ consists, among other things, in resembling *hardness* (434c), Socrates is clearly implying that the presence of ρ in σκληρότης/σκληρότηρ is especially relevant to the whole name's indicating hardness. Here some have detected 'a delicate hint by Socrates that the Eretrian form of the word', which contains one additional ρ, 'lives up to naturalist standards of correctness better than the Attic'.[15] Is Socrates' point really this? Read on.

At c10–13 Socrates asks Cratylus whether ρ and ς 'resemble the same thing', so that (c11 καί is consecutive) the whole name indicates the same thing both with the final ρ and with the final ς, or the whole name does not

---

[14] For Eretrian rhotacism cf. Strab. 10.1.10 and Buck 57 (who however remarks that 'there is no inscriptional example of ρ for final ς except once ὅπωρ ἄν'; and there 'final ς may be treated as intervocalic', 83). There is no agreement among MSS and scholars about the Eretrian word's accent. BW read σκληροτήρ (printed by Burnet and the OCT) and T σκληροτηρ with no accent, while Méridier reports that Par. 1808 reads σκληρότηρ (accepted by LSJ and most editors). Matters seems to stand as follows. The abstract nouns like σκληρότης, which end in -της in Attic-Ionic, must have originally been accented on the last syllable (cf. the Homeric ἀνδροτής); but in the classical period Attic and various other dialects withdrew the accent to the penultimate syllable (cf. κακότης, νεότης etc.). So we may either read σκληροτήρ with BW, supposing that in this case the Eretrian dialect preserved the original accent, and reject σκληρότηρ as (perhaps) a piece of trivialization, or follow Par. 1808 and reject σκληροτήρ as the result of a mistaken assimilation to the *nomina agentis* in -τήρ (δοτήρ, σωτήρ etc.). I have adopted the latter, more cautious policy.

[15] Schofield 1982: 74, cf. Barney 2001: 124.

indicate that thing to both.[16] Here Socrates is apparently assuming that, if ς and ρ did not resemble the same thing (i.e., presumably, hardness itself), neither would σκληρότηρ as a whole and σκληρότης as a whole resemble, and hence indicate, the same thing. This assumption in turn can only be correct if *all* the sounds of which a name is composed contribute to determining what the name resembles and indicates. But it may seem that none of this should be endorsed by Socrates at this stage. For he has been at pains to argue that a name may contain inappropriate sounds or lack appropriate ones, and thus fail to be a 'fine' name, while nonetheless successfully indicating its referent (431d–433c). So why should it not be possible that ς and ρ do not resemble the same thing, that the final ς of σκληρότης is an intruder which has ousted the ρ preserved instead in σκληρότηρ, and that, therefore, in this respect the Athenian form is 'worse' than the Eretrian one, although both succeed in indicating hardness?

To answer this question we must perhaps remember that, for all Socrates' efforts to prove that names may represent things imperfectly, at 433c Cratylus appeared still unconvinced by his arguments. Perhaps, therefore, Socrates here is *not* presupposing his own previous conclusions on imperfect images and is instead adopting, for the sake of argument, a view much closer to Cratylus' own (431e–432a) that any change in the letters of which a name is composed turns the name into the name of something else.[17] Cf. Schofield 1982: 74, according to whom at this stage Socrates is still arguing that 'names certified as genuine by the naturalist theory need not (*contra* Cratylus) be perfectly constructed resemblances'.

At d1 Cratylus reassures Socrates with regard to the whole name: it does indicate the same thing both to the Eretrians and to the Athenians.[18] But this is not enough for Socrates, who, in conformity with his previous question, wants Cratylus to grant explicitly that this is because ρ and ς are 'alike' (d2–3). When Cratylus agrees (d4), Socrates goes on to ask whether ρ and ς are alike in *all* respects (d5). They are alike, Cratylus answers, at

[16] Lines c11–d1 present us with two difficulties, concerning both the subject and the object of δηλοῖ. Together with Schofield 1982: 73, Reeve and Sedley 2003: 143, I assume that (i) the *subject* must be understood to be 'the name' throughout, (ii) the *object* is 'the same thing' (τὸ αὐτό) at c11, but then at c13–d1 becomes an understood 'that', referring back to the 'same thing' of c11. An alternative to (i) is proposed by Fowler: 'does the final ρ mean to them just what the sigma means to us ...?' But the genitives absolute τελευτῶντος τοῦ ῥῶ ... τοῦ σῖγμα cannot function as the subject of δηλοῖ. An alternative to (ii) is proposed by those scholars who take δηλοῖ at c13–d1 to be used *absolutely*: 'indicates', i.e. 'is significant'. This, however, would entail that the second horn of Socrates' dilemma (c12–13) means 'Or doesn't the name *indicate anything* to one or other of the two communities?'; and there is no reason why Socrates should present so radical an alternative.

[17] Perhaps Socrates is modifying that Cratylan view only insofar as he assumes that a letter *can* be safely replaced by another one whose mimetic force is the same.

[18] See n.16 on the subject of δηλοῖ.

least insofar as they equally[19] indicate (resemble) movement (d6). Thereby he is right as far as Socrates' earlier mimetic survey was concerned: all that ρ and ς could have in common was the imitation of some sort of movement, since at 427a 5 was mentioned among a few 'breathy' sounds as fit for imitating 'what is blowy'.

Now the problem is, of course, that if ρ and ς are alike in that they both indicate movement, this has nothing to do with the matter at issue, which is the indication of *hardness*. Thus Socrates could argue that, if the Eretrian final ρ and the Attic final ς really indicate movement, then the final letter of both forms is inappropriate, and that hence Cratylus must admit that names may be imperfect while still indicating their referents. Indeed, then Socrates could go further and argue that actually, if names may after all be imperfect, we have no reason to keep holding that the final ρ of σκληρότηρ is equivalent to the final ς of σκληρότης. We can more simply say that only σκληρότης is really imperfect, at least as far as the final letter is concerned; that the final ρ of σκληρότηρ does indicate hardness, as it was natural to think from the start; and that hence the Eretrian form is better than the Attic one.[20]

This may well be how we are supposed to develop the argument. It is not, however, how Socrates goes on. He rather decides to focus on another problematic aspect of the example, an aspect which is common to the Athenian and the Eretrian form. He could point out that the name contains another ς, the initial one, which is presumably as extraneous to the whole name's signification as the Attic final one. Or he could inquire about the role of the two η's and the ο, which should indicate length and roundness respectively (427c). He could also ask for what reason the internal ρ indicates hardness instead of movement (as is pointed out by Schofield 1982: 75, in whose view the argument is already 'supplying pointers to outright rejection of naturalism'). But Socrates asks none of these questions and just focuses on λ:

SO. Does this also hold of the λ included in it? Doesn't it indicate the contrary [τὸ ἐναντίον] of hardness?

---

[19] The position of the adverb ἴσως suggests that this, not (as some interpreters think) 'perhaps', is its meaning here.

[20] Sedley 2003: 143–4 supposes that the very point of the discussion of the Eretrian form is to show that its final ρ indicates something other than hardness and hence that it too, like the Attic form, contains only one ρ for hardness and one λ for softness. Thereby, according to Sedley, Socrates prevents Cratylus from invoking 'the Eretrian form, with its additional R, to show that hardness is after all dominant in the word, outnumbering softness sounds ... he made his preemptive move about the Eretrian form in order to ensure that this level score would not be challenged'. We should not, however, overestimate the relevance of the numerical equality of ρ and λ in σκληρότης, a feature which Socrates does not as much as mention: see below and n.39.

CR. Yes; for perhaps it isn't correctly included, Socrates. It's as in the cases you were mentioning to Hermogenes just now, when you removed and added letters wherever this was necessary. You seemed to me to do this correctly; and now perhaps we must say ρ in place of λ. (434d7–12)

What is special about λ – which has been agreed to indicate what is smooth and what is soft – is that it does not simply indicate something *different* from what the whole name does, as other letters (at least the final ς of σκληρότης, and presumably others too) seem to; it even indicates something *contrary* to what the whole name and its internal ρ indicate. For softness is the contrary of hardness.

This is too blatant a flaw to be ignored or explained away. Cratylus immediately realizes this and grants that in this context the λ is incorrect and should be replaced by another ρ (d9, 12). Though he does not avow it in so many words, as a matter of fact he is admitting that a name may contain inappropriate letters and thus be imperfect or 'bad'. He also compares how Socrates in the etymologies freely removed and added letters in order to recover the original form of names (d10–11). Thereby he must be referring to Socrates' etymologies of *secondary* names and to his own approval of them at 428c – a reference which, however, is only indirectly appropriate to the present context.

There is a further reason why the λ in σκληρότης/σκληρότηρ is especially interesting: at least in the Attic form, λ occurs exactly *as frequently as* ρ. This fact is not pointed out by Socrates, but has been stressed by modern scholars. Thus Schofield (1982: 75) comments that 'The presence of λ is not very plausibly taken as an isolated flaw in an otherwise satisfactory representation of hardness. After all, the only phoneme in the word which has been alleged to resemble hardness is ρ, which in the Attic form appears no more nor less frequently than λ. One might think it more reasonable to hold that the two liquids just cancel each other out, leaving a set of phonemes with no particular tendency to indicate hardness or its opposite.'

A final point before reading on. In the light of the troubles into which Socrates' example is getting Cratylus, we may well wonder why he does not try to disarm it. He might contend that in fact σκληρότης is not a primary but a secondary name, composed of two primary names, one containing λ and the other containing ρ, such that λ no more conflicts with the whole name's signification. Or he might try to reject σκληρότης altogether as a pseudo-name, a mere piece of noise like 'Hermogenes'.[21]

---

[21] Note that the latter defensive move is no more open to Cratylus once he has conceded that a name may be imperfectly made and contain only a few appropriate letters: according to this

Resemblance and convention in names (433b–435d) 395

Probably, however, Plato thinks that neither move would take Cratylus very far, because Socrates could adduce names which, while posing the same difficulties, are uncontroversially primary and are too many for Cratylus to dismiss them all as pseudo-names. As Sedley (2003: 139 n.22) says, the value of the discussion of σκληρότης 'should be taken as no more than illustrative'.

8.1.3 *The* sklerotes *argument: understanding, indication, correctness (434e–435b)*

Socrates is satisfied with Cratylus' admission. But this does not block his attack:

SO. Good. What about it? As we *now* speak [νῦν ὡς λέγομεν], don't we understand each other at all [οὐδὲν μανθάνομεν ἀλλήλων] when one says σκληρόν, and don't you now know what I'm saying?
CR. I do, because of habit [διά γε τὸ ἔθος], my dear friend.
SO. But by saying 'habit' do you think you're saying anything different from 'convention'? (434e1–4)

These lines open the decisive argument about the σκληρότης example, which stretches to 435a10, and already encapsulate its essentials. Before entering into a discussion of substantive matters, however, we must observe that here Socrates is having recourse to a slightly different (if cognate) example from σκληρότης, i.e. the adjective σκληρόν, 'hard' (e2). This seldom noticed fact, if it is not a mere quirk, calls for an explanation. The explanation, I take it, must have something to do with the fact that the new example has no final ρ or ς and no alternative Eretrian form: Socrates wants to make it clear that he is now leaving the discussion about σκληρότης/σκληρότηρ behind. Perhaps he also wants a word where ρ for hardness and λ for softness clearly and uncontroversially occur in equal numbers.[22]

Let us now turn to the substance of the argument that Socrates begins to put forward in these lines by means of the new example. We can distinguish several crucial points.

First, Socrates forces Cratylus to give an account of the name σκληρόν in its altered *present* shape (e1), even if it contains an inappropriate letter.

---

relaxed standard σκληρότης, which in virtue of its ρ does resemble hardness, however poorly, surely counts as a genuine name. It is unclear, however, whether Cratylus has made the relevant concession at 433c or is making it only now, as a result of the present argument: see above.

[22] If this is so, then Socrates is at least considering the possibility that the final ρ of σκληρότηρ may, after all, indicate hardness and not movement (cf. §8.1.2).

The reason Cratylus cannot avoid doing this is clearly that the matter at issue is the signification and correctness of names, i.e. of *all* names, not just of the incorrupted ones.

Secondly, Socrates focuses on an aspect of the signification of names which, for all its importance, so far had not been explicitly touched upon.[23] This is the speakers' *understanding* of the names in use. Socrates asks Cratylus whether speakers do not understand utterances of σκληρόν (e1–3). The question is a rhetorical one; it amounts to a statement that speakers *do* understand such utterances and challenges Cratylus to give an account of this fact. Cratylus can only answer that he does understand σκληρόν and that his understanding is due to *habit* (e4). For the conflict between the mimetic power of λ and ρ – which, as we saw in §8.1.2, seem to cancel each other out, especially since they occur in equal numbers – prevents us from understanding the name in any natural or immediate way.

Then Socrates immediately points out that habit is no different from Cratylus' *bête noire*, convention (e5). Thereby he agrees with Hermogenes, who also appeared, in the initial statement of his views (384cd), to identify 'convention and agreement' with 'custom and habit'. They are both right, at least for the purposes of the present discussion (cf. §2.1.1).

We must be clear about Socrates' overall strategy. He introduces the issue of the understanding of names because he realizes that there is a very close connection – which he is going to spell out in the next lines – between (a) the fact that a competent speaker understands utterances of 'X' and (b) the fact that 'X' indicates X (to a competent speaker). Furthermore, he has been assuming since 433de that names indicate objects and that this is what, generally speaking, their correctness consists in. So he identifies (b) the fact that 'X' indicates X with (c) the fact that 'X' is a correct name of X. Thus he realizes that a question concerning (c), i.e. whether 'X' is correct by nature or by convention, can be transformed into a question concerning (b), i.e. whether 'X' indicates X by nature or by convention, and that this in its turn can be transformed into a question concerning (a), i.e. whether 'X' is understood by nature or by convention. This last question is raised and answered in our lines with regard to the example σκληρόν. In the sequel Socrates will move on, more or less explicitly, to the other two questions, until he reaches the conclusion that σκληρόν is correct by convention (435a7–10).

Let us, then, see how Socrates continues:

---

[23] According to my interpretation of 433e the idea was already implicit in that passage: see §8.1.1.

(SO.) Or is the habit you're speaking of anything but [ἢ ἄλλο τι λέγεις τὸ ἔθος ἤ] the fact that, when I utter *this*, I think of *that*, and you recognize that I think of *that* [ὅτι ἐγώ, ὅταν τοῦτο φθέγγωμαι, διανοοῦμαι ἐκεῖνο, σὺ δὲ γιγνώσκεις ὅτι ἐκεῖνο διανοοῦμαι]? Isn't this what you're speaking of?
CR. Yes.
SO. Then if you recognize this when I make my utterance, you receive from me a means to indicate [εἰ γιγνώσκεις ἐμοῦ φθεγγομένου, δήλωμά σοι γίγνεται παρ' ἐμοῦ]?
CR. Yes.
SO. Thanks to what is dissimilar from the thing thinking of which I make my utterance [Ἀπὸ τοῦ ἀνομοίου γε ἢ ὃ διανοούμενος φθέγγομαι], since λ is dissimilar from the hardness you're speaking of. (434e6–435a7)

Here Socrates first turns to explaining his previous talk of our 'understanding' (e6–a1), then spells out the connection between our understanding and the name's 'indicating' something (a2–3), and finally makes a point about the way in which σκληρόν indicates what it does (a5–7).

Socrates' very first words here (a6) already deserve some comment. At first glance it might seem natural to translate them as 'Or *do you mean by "habit"* anything but ...' This is, in effect, what most existing translations do; but it cannot be right. For the following clause (e6–8), which suggests an answer to Cratylus, cannot be an attempt to specify the *meaning* of the term 'habit'. Rather, it must be an attempt to describe in more detail the fact which has just been agreed to occur by habit (and which can surely be said to constitute itself *a* habit), i.e. the fact that we understand something when σκληρόν is uttered. Hence we need a different translation, like the one I have proposed above.[24]

Now we come to the following analysis of our understanding something when σκληρόν is uttered: 'when I utter *this*, I think of *that*, and you recognize that I think of *that*' (e6–8). This means primarily 'when I utter σκληρόν, I think of hardness';[25] Socrates is still speaking of the σκληρόν example, as lines a5–7 make clear.[26] The mechanism of mutual understanding among speakers which Socrates is describing, however, apart from the question of its being effective in virtue of habit, should presumably be the same in the case of any meaningful word. Hence we

---

[24] Cf. Schofield (1982: 75): 'Do you not call it "habit" when ...' and Sedley 2003: 139–40 and n.23, who however sticks to the standard translation.
[25] For the sake of simplicity, and conforming to what Socrates himself does at a5–7, here and in what follows I express myself as if the referent of σκληρόν were hard*ness*. It could also be the hard or what is hard.
[26] *Pace* Schofield 1982: 76, who apparently holds that at 435a1 Cratylus allows 'that mutual understanding of *any* word is a matter of habit or convention'.

can also, in the second place, construe Socrates' description as having generic import: 'when I utter "X", I think of X, and you recognize that I think of X'.

The clause 'I think of *that*' (διανοοῦμαι ἐκεῖνο) calls for some special comment. What I have been saying so far presupposes that ἐκεῖνο stands for the *referent* of the term σκληρόν, or more generally of 'X', here presented as the *extramental* object of the speaker's act of thinking. Some scholars seem, instead, to interpret ἐκεῖνο as standing for some *mental* item which is the internal object of the speaker's thinking, or in any case for the meaning or sense of 'X'. But this latter interpretation is disproved, and the former is confirmed, by lines a2–7, especially a5–7, where the verb's object is what λ is dissimilar from and is hence identified with hardness – surely an extramental feature which is the term's referent. Further confirmation comes from 435b6, as we shall see in §8.1.4.[27]

At a2–3 Socrates spells out the connection between understanding and indication. This is of course in order, given that he wants to cash his result about how σκληρόν gets understood in terms of a result about how σκληρόν indicates something. The connection is the following: if, when the speaker utters σκληρόν, the hearer achieves the sort of recognition that has just been described, then the hearer receives from the speaker a 'means to indicate' (δήλωμα).[28] But in the present context it is fairly clear that what a 'means to indicate' indicates is a πρᾶγμα, an object in the world (cf. especially 433de and the use of the verb δηλόω 'indicate' at 434d6–8) – in this case, the very same thing as the speaker is thinking of.[29] Therefore what Socrates is saying at a2–3 actually amounts to the following: if, when the speaker utters σκληρόν, the speaker thinks of hardness and the hearer recognizes that the speaker is thinking of hardness, then σκληρόν *indicates hardness* to the hearer. Generally speaking:

---

[27] For διανοοῦμαι with extramental object cf. *Phd.* 65e, *R.* 526a. The construal I reject is held by Méridier 129 n.1 ('ἐκεῖνο: la notion représentée par le nom') and Barney 2001: 131; cf. Schofield and Sedley cited in n.29.

[28] Two remarks on δήλωμα. First, the present lines, as well as the following ones, make it clear once more (cf. §§4.2.6, 6.2.2, 8.1.1) that δηλόω and cognate terms have *no* privileged connection with the naturalist view of names (*pace* Barney 2001: 128, who sticks to her translations 'disclose' and 'disclosure' throughout). Second, one might be tempted to take δήλωμα here at a2–3 as an abstract noun, 'indica*tion*' (thus Fowler), despite the parallels quoted in §6.2.2 for the concrete rendering 'means to indicate'. But the concrete rendering will be clearly correct at 435b2, whereas the term for 'indication' is δήλωσις (435b5). So the relation between δήλωμα and δήλωσις seems to be like that between, e.g., the concrete πρᾶγμα and the abstract πρᾶξις.

[29] *Pace* Schofield 1982: 77, who holds that what is indicated (he has 'disclosed') here is the speaker's 'thought or meaning', and Sedley 2003: 139–40, who speaks of 'communication (*deloma*) of the associated concept'.

If, when the speaker utters 'X', the speaker thinks of X and the hearer recognizes that the speaker is thinking of X, then the speaker's utterance of 'X' indicates X to the hearer.

Indeed, it is reasonable to guess that Socrates is giving not only a *sufficient*, but also a *necessary* condition for a speaker's utterance of 'X' to indicate X to a hearer; and in that case the 'If' of the previous formulation must be replaced by 'if and only if'.

An important feature of Socrates' account is that it assigns the speaker's and hearer's thought a crucial role in a name's indicating its referent. But *what* exactly is this role? Here we must be very careful. Consider *De interpretatione* 1.16a3–8, where it is claimed that 'the first items' of which utterances are signs are 'affections of the soul' (παθήματα τῆς ψυχῆς) and that the items of which the affections of the soul are 'likenesses' (ὁμοιώματα) are 'objects' (πράγματα). On a standard interpretation of that famous and controversial passage, Aristotle is saying that utterances signify primarily and directly 'affections of the soul' (i.e. 'thoughts', νοήματα, as the passage's sequel suggests and 14.23a32–3, 24b1–2 confirm), and is thereby implying that utterances signify secondarily and indirectly objects, via thoughts being likenesses of objects.[30] Now it has been suggested that this Aristotelian account of the relations between utterances, thoughts and objects is already essentially anticipated in our *Cra.* passage.[31] This suggestion, however, is dubious. In our passage Socrates does not say that a name, prior to or besides indicating an object, also indicates a mental item comparable to Aristotle's 'affections of the soul' or 'thoughts'. Indeed, he does not mention any such item at all. He mentions only the speaker's *act* of 'thinking of' the object indicated; and even if this commits him, strictly speaking, to the view that there is, after all, in the speaker's mind an item corresponding to the object indicated, it certainly does not commit him to the stronger Aristotelian view that this mental item is itself *indicated* or signified by the name.[32]

---

[30] See e.g. Amm. *in Int.* 17.24–6, 24.5–12, and Weidemann 2002: 134–51.
[31] Weidemann 2002: 148. Barney 2001: 131 n.25 too holds that our passage 'points towards' *Int.* 1.
[32] Cf. Robinson 1955: 106–7. At 393a–394e, in his discussion of 'Hector' and 'Astyanax', Socrates spoke of names as 'signifying' or 'indicating' something which appeared to be distinct from their referent and rather seemed to be their (etymological) sense (see §4.2.6). But he did *not* say that the item so signified was anything *mental*. In the etymologies Socrates referred to the (etymological) sense of names as their διάνοια (see §5.4, (C)); but, again, he did not describe this διάνοια as a mental item proper. Cf. the discussion of the Stoic theory of signification offered by Barnes 1993, who argues that the references to thought in our testimonies do not entail that the Stoics believed ordinary linguistic expressions to signify any mental items.

Back to the text. At 435a5–7 Socrates stresses that, if when he utters the name σκληρόν Cratylus receives from him a 'means to indicate' hardness, this is 'thanks to [ἀπό] what is dissimilar from the thing thinking of which I make my utterance, since λ is dissimilar from the hardness you're speaking of'. This means just that one of the letters which make up the name and thus constitute the material basis, as it were, for its indicating hardness, i.e. λ, is dissimilar from hardness. Thereby Socrates is of course recalling what was said above (434d7–8) about λ indicating the contrary of hardness.[33]

Socrates can now complete the transition from the idea that σκληρόν is *understood* by habit, which is the same as convention (434e1–5), via the idea that σκληρόν *indicates* what it does by habit and convention, to the idea that σκληρόν is *correct* by habit and convention:

(SO.) But if this is so, isn't it true that you made a convention with yourself [αὐτὸς σαυτῷ συνέθου] and the correctness of the name becomes a matter of convention for you [καί σοι γίγνεται ἡ ὀρθότης τοῦ ὀνόματος συνθήκη], since both the similar and the dissimilar letters indicate, meeting with habit and convention [ἔθους τε καὶ συνθήκης τυχόντα]? (435a7–10)

The pith of the conclusion is that 'if this is so', i.e. if Socrates' utterance of σκληρόν conveys to Cratylus (a competent Greek speaker) what Socrates is thinking of, and hence indicates its referent to Cratylus, despite its containing a dissimilar letter, then the name turns out to be correct by convention.[34] For only by 'meeting with' (a10), i.e. by receiving the sanction of, habit and convention can a string of letters succeed in indicating something to which some of them are similar and some are dissimilar.

It is important to be aware that the argument yields the conclusion that the correctness of σκληρόν is a matter of convention only in virtue of the fact that at 433de Socrates has introduced the idea that names are 'means to indicate' things and that this is what, generally speaking, their correctness consists in. If Socrates had not introduced this idea, and instead had stuck to his earlier thesis that the function of names is to teach (388bc, 428e, cf. 435d), now he could of course argue from the fact that σκληρόν is

---

[33] 'What is dissimilar' (a5) is the dissimilar λ contained in the name, which Socrates immediately goes on to mention, not the name itself as Reeve thinks (cf. n.37). Why Socrates says that λ is dissimilar from 'the hardness *you're speaking of*' (a6–7) is not very clear. The interpretation of Schofield 1982: 77 and Reeve, 'to revert to your example', is mistaken: the example was Socrates', not Cratylus'. Sedley 2003: 140 translates 'L is dissimilar to hardness according to you', which is unfaithful to the Greek.

[34] Socrates is not speaking of names in general, *pace* Schofield 1982: 77 and Reeve, who translate τοῦ ὀνόματος (a8) respectively as 'of a name' and 'of names'.

understood by convention to the fact that σκληρόν indicates what it does by convention; but he could not proceed further to the conclusion that σκληρόν is *correct* by convention.

Let us take a closer look at a7–8, where Socrates says that Cratylus 'made a convention with himself', so that (consecutive καί) the correctness of the name 'becomes a matter of convention for him'. Both claims call for some comment. The former may sound puzzling: we might expect Socrates to say that Cratylus made (or adhered to) a convention with the other Greek speakers, or at least with his interlocutor. But Socrates apparently thinks that Cratylus' adherence to the public convention according to which σκληρόν indicates hardness is *grounded* in his private convention with himself. His point seems to be that, since utterances of σκληρόν do not have a meaning which depends on their intrinsic features and which a hearer is somehow naturally forced to recognize, Cratylus had to decide, as it were, that he would interpret utterances of σκληρόν as indicating hardness.[35] Thereby Socrates seems to view the collective convention as the sum of a plurality of individual decisions. This (quite plausible) stance reminds us of 384d–385a, where Hermogenes put a convention among a plurality of speakers on a par with the arbitrary decision of a single speaker (see §§2.1.1–2; cf. Barney 1997: 155, 2001: 136 n.34).

In Socrates' latter claim, 'the correctness of the name becomes a matter of convention for you' (a8), I take it that 'becomes' means 'turns out to be'. What about 'for you' (σοι)? Maybe this is simply an ethical dative: Cratylus *has to admit that* the correctness of the name turns out to be convention. But 'for you' might also have something to do with a2–3, where Socrates literally said 'from me there comes into being *for you* [σοι] a means to indicate', and also with the previous clause's reference to Cratylus' convention *with himself*. In this case, Socrates would be concluding that σκληρόν is conventionally correct for Cratylus and for anyone who understands the name by habit and convention; but he would be leaving formally open the possibility that the name might be naturally correct for someone who understood it in a natural and immediate way. I say 'formally' because as a matter of fact we have no reason to expect anyone to be able to achieve such a natural understanding of σκληρόν. Socrates himself will implicitly rule this possibility out of court when he says it is habit that 'indicates both with something similar and with something dissimilar' (b2–3).

---

[35] Of course Cratylus also had to decide that he would himself *use* utterances of σκληρόν to indicate hardness; but this is, strictly speaking, irrelevant to the argument. Indeed, he actually made no decision at all; he rather engaged in an unconscious process which for present purposes can be conveniently represented as the conscious making of a decision.

We can now chance a very rough attempt at summarizing Socrates' argument:

(P1) σκληρόν contains a letter dissimilar and contrary to hardness. (434d7–12, 435a5–7, 9)
(P2) The hearer recognizes by habit that the speaker, in uttering σκληρόν, is thinking of hardness. (434e1–4, e6–435a1; from (P1))
(P3) Habit is the same as convention. (434e5)
(P4) If the hearer recognizes that the speaker, in uttering σκληρόν, is thinking of hardness, then σκληρόν indicates hardness to the hearer. (435a2–4)
(P5) σκληρόν indicates hardness while containing also a letter dissimilar and contrary to it. (435a5–7, 9; from (P1), (P2) and (P4))
(P6) σκληρόν indicates hardness by habit/convention. (435a9–10; from (P2) – (P5))
(P7) 'X' is a conventionally correct name of X if and only if it indicates X conventionally. (433de)
(C) Therefore σκληρόν is a conventionally correct name of hardness. (435e7–8; from (P6) and (P7))

This sketch is pretty crude and lacking in logical precision; but it should bring out the structure of the argument as set forth in the text. You will perhaps detect a tinge of redundancy as far as the derivation of (P6) is concerned: Socrates seems first (434d7–435a4) to suggest that the presence of conflicting letters entails that σκληρόν is understood by habit and convention, and that this in turn entails that σκληρόν indicates hardness by habit and convention; but then (a5–10) he stresses again the presence of conflicting letters and speaks as if this directly entailed that σκληρόν indicates hardness by habit and convention. I will not dwell upon such details; the argument is essentially sound.

Socrates has claimed at 434e5, and presupposed in these lines, that habit is the same as convention. But he has not proved that this identification is correct; and Cratylus might perhaps deny that it is. In order to forestall any such objection, Socrates argues that it would make little difference:

(SO.) And even if habit were not convention [εἰ δ' ὅτι μάλιστα μή ἐστι τὸ ἔθος συνθήκη],[36] still it would no longer be right to say that similarity is a means

---

[36] In Plato and other authors εἰ ὅτι μάλιστα is a typical way of introducing a hypothesis which the speaker puts forward for the sake of argument, without endorsing it and sometimes even regarding it as false. See especially 439b, *Chrm.* 160c, 169b, *Euthphr.* 4d, Arist. *Metaph.* 1008b31 (with indicative); *Men.* 80d, *R.* 450c, 505a, *Prm.* 135a (with optative). Cf. εἰ τὰ μάλιστα in Xenoph. 21 B34.3 DK

to indicate, but that habit is [οὐκ ἂν καλῶς ἔτι ἔχοι λέγειν τὴν ὁμοιότητα δήλωμα εἶναι, ἀλλὰ τὸ ἔθος]; for that, it seems, indicates both with something similar and with something dissimilar [καὶ ὁμοίῳ καὶ ἀνομοίῳ δηλοῖ]. (435a10–b3)

Here is an approximate paraphrase of this passage. Even granting that habit is *not* the same as convention (i.e. denying (P3) in the above sketch), and hence refraining from the conclusion that correctness is a matter of convention, still we are left with the conclusion that σκληρόν indicates its referent, and hence is correct, in virtue of habit and not of similarity. For habit can, whereas similarity cannot, explain how a name can indicate its referent when only some of its letters are similar to it, while others are dissimilar.[37] Therefore Cratylus' thesis stands refuted in any case, and one of Hermogenes' initial claims, i.e. that 'no name belongs by nature to anything, but in virtue of the custom and habit of those who made names into habits and those who call things by them' (384d5–7), has finally been vindicated, at least as far as the present example is concerned.

The claim that habit 'indicates both with something similar and with something dissimilar' (b2–3) seems clearly meant to pick up the previous claim that in the name σκληρόν 'both the similar and the dissimilar letters indicate'. Its function is clearly to confirm that, even if habit and convention were two different concepts, in any case σκληρόν would indicate hardness in virtue of habit, not of similarity. But it is not very clear what the *scope* of the b2–3 claim is. According to Sedley 2003: 140, even here Socrates is speaking only of the σκληρόν example, as he has been doing so far, most notably at a9–10. If so, then the present claim could mean that only habit can explain how σκληρόν can indicate hardness despite its containing letters similar to hardness (i.e. ρ) as well as letters dissimilar from it (i.e. λ and presumably others too: see §8.1.2).

However, I prefer to take the b2–3 claim as a *general* one. In order to support the thesis that σκληρόν indicates hardness in virtue of habit Socrates may make a general point about the power of habit: if '*X*' indicates *X* and is such that some of its letters are similar to *X* while others are dissimilar (as in the case of σκληρόν), then '*X*' indicates *X* by habit. A snippet of evidence in favour of this possibility is the lack of the article before ὁμοίῳ and ἀνομοίῳ, which is naturally taken as a sign of generality; contrast a5

---

and Dem. 18.95, and the Latin *si maxime*. In our passage the expression is misunderstood by many interpreters, who translate ὅτι μάλιστα as 'entirely', 'completely' *vel sim.*

[37] In this context 'something similar' and 'something dissimilar' can only be *letters*, not names as Reeve thinks (cf. n.33).

Ἀπὸ τοῦ ἀνομοίου, where 'what is dissimilar', with the article, referred to a particular dissimilar letter (i.e. the λ in σκληρόν).[38]

On this interpretation, Socrates says nothing about the ratio of similar to dissimilar letters and thus seems to take their balance, or lack of balance, to be irrelevant in this context. That is to say, we are entitled to ascribe to Socrates the view that '*X*' indicates *X* by habit both if '*X*' contains only few similar letters, outnumbered by a majority of dissimilar ones, and if vice versa '*X*' contains only few dissimilar letters, outnumbered by a majority of similar ones. In fact, this is just as it should be. For Socrates has already argued, at 431c–433c, that a name may fail to be 'finely' made by containing one or more inappropriate (i.e. dissimilar) letters, and may even contain just 'a few' (ὀλίγα 433a6) appropriate letters. So if you take a name where only a minority of letters is similar to *X*, while most are dissimilar (such, in effect, seemed to be the case of σκληρόν), then whatever the other letters may resemble, even if most consistently resemble another thing *Y*, in any case it is possible for the name to latch on to *X* and indicate *X* (if only very 'badly') thanks to the similar letters it does contain. But clearly only a convention or habit can decide which letters must prevail, whether the name is a very bad name of *X* or a less bad name of *Y*, etc. So from Socrates' previous conclusions it does follow that, if '*X*' contains both letters similar to and letters dissimilar from *X*, whatever the ratio of the former to the latter, then '*X*' indicates *X* by convention or habit. And hence this may well be the (admittedly compressed) meaning of Socrates' b2–3 claim.[39]

---

[38] Barney 2001: 128 n.21, 138 draws an interesting comparison between, on the one hand, Socrates' reformulation of conventionalism at 433e and the argument about σκληρόν, and, on the other hand, his account of recollection at *Phd.* 73c–76e. There Socrates says that being reminded consists in perceiving something and 'coming to think of' something else, or 'getting' something else 'in one's thought' (73d ἐν τῇ διανοίᾳ ἔλαβον, cf. *Cra.* 434e διανοούμεθα); that one is reminded of something one must 'know beforehand' (74e προειδέναι, cf. *Cra.* 433e προειδόσι); that – most important for our present concerns – recollection may be either '*from something similar*' or '*from something dissimilar*' (74a ἀφ' ὁμοίων ... ἀπὸ ἀνομοίων). Socrates also suggests that, in this latter case, reminiscence takes place in virtue of a habitual association of reminder and object (73d εἴωθε).

[39] My interpretation of the whole argument is at variance with that of Sedley, who maintains that 'The *limiting case* of successful imitation, the one which gave rise to a deadlock that only an appeal to linguistic custom could break, was the *sklerotes* example, where there was a 50–50 split between positively appropriate and positively inappropriate sounds. We may infer that if the balance had tipped, however marginally, in favour of the inappropriate sounds, the word would have had to be disqualified from being the thing's name' (2003: 145) and that 'the most problematic case Socrates could raise against the imitation theory was a name with *one* appropriate element and *one* inappropriate element ... A primary name may contain all or only some appropriate components ... but cannot have a preponderance of positively *in*appropriate components' (149). Here are my reasons for disagreeing with him. (i) Socrates *never* says that a name like σκληρότης represents the most problematic case against the imitation theory; nor does he make *any* reference

8.1.4 Convention 'contributes' to correctness (435bc)

At this point Socrates takes his leave from σκληρόν by drawing a general conclusion about the role of convention and habit in the correctness of names:

(SO.) And since we grant these conclusions, Cratylus – for I'll take your silence as a sign of consent – then necessarily, I think, convention and habit contribute something to the indication of the items thinking of which we speak [ἀναγκαῖόν που καὶ συνθήκην τι καὶ ἔθος συμβάλλεσθαι πρὸς δήλωσιν ὧν διανοούμενοι λέγομεν]. (435b3–6)

Do not miss the irony conveyed by Socrates' incidental remark 'I'll take your silence as a sign of consent' (b4). In the conversation which took place before the opening of the dialogue, Cratylus' silence in the face of Hermogenes' questions was part of his enigmatic and superior attitude, similar to that of the Heracliteans described at *Tht.* 179d–180c. But now that he has been exposed to Socrates' arguments, his silence can be taken as a mere sign of acquiescence.

We must now consider the claim that 'convention and habit contribute something to the indication of the items thinking of which we speak' (b5–6). This is the *first general conclusion* Socrates reaches in the argument.[40] I start with a remark about what convention and habit are said to contribute to. In the Greek text πρὸς δήλωσιν ὧν [= ἐκείνων ἅ]

---

whatsoever to the fact that λ and ρ occur in equal numbers. So I am disinclined to regard this fact as crucial to the present argument, let alone to the whole cluster of arguments set out at 434b–435d. (ii) Sedley can hold that λ is the only 'inappropriate' sound/letter in σκληρότης because he assumes that the 'inappropriate' sounds are those 'that actually conflict with the nature of the object, like the L in *sklerotes*, not those which are merely irrelevant to it. The presence of irrelevant sounds is never treated as problematic' (148). This assumption too is questionable. Socrates never draws a distinction between inappropriate letters and irrelevant ones (not even at 393de, which Sedley seems to cite as evidence at 148 n.6). The notion of an 'inappropriate' letter was introduced without explanation at 431c–433c, well *before* the σκληρότης example made us think of anything as specific as the ρ–λ contrariety, and in a context where Socrates also talked about 'inappropriate' names, verbs and λόγοι (431bc, 432e) – hence in a context where 'inappropriate' had to hold of any linguistic unit that does not fit, does not apply to, is not true of its subject matter, not only of units contrary to their subject matter. Indeed, Socrates says that an 'appropriate' letter is one that is 'similar' to the name's referent (433c, 435c), which strongly suggests that an 'inappropriate' letter is just one that is *dissimilar* from the referent and need not be altogether contrary to it. In any case, bear in mind that in the σκληρότης argument Socrates only speaks of 'dissimilar' letters, *not* of 'inappropriate' ones! Finally, note that even a letter which is merely different from the name's referent will in a sense conflict with its nature: in the example σκληρότης η, which resembles length, or σ/ς, which resembles movement, do conflict with hardness insofar as the name's referent cannot be simultaneously hardness and length, or hardness and movement.

[40] It is certainly not, as Schofield 1982: 78 thinks, the beginning of 'Socrates' summary of what he and Cratylus have agreed'.

διανοούμενοι λέγομεν, the object of the δήλωσις[41] is the same as that of the participle διανοούμενοι. That is to say, the items indicated by the names are the same as the items thought (of). And since names indicate extramental *objects*, πράγματα (433de, 434d6–8), i.e. their referents, it follows that the items thought (of) are extramental objects too, as we already supposed while commenting on 434e6–8 (see §8.1.3).

Once this point has been clarified we can turn to another part of Socrates' conclusion, i.e. the claim that convention and habit *'contribute something'* to the indication of the things we think of in speaking. This cautious formulation has no less than two parallels in the following lines (b8–c2, c5–7), as we shall see in due course; hence it should be taken seriously, at least prima facie, and not explained away as a mere understatement. Here are three possible ways of interpreting it:[42]

(1) Some names indicate their referents by convention
(2) All names indicate their referents partly by convention
(3) Some names indicate their referents partly by convention.

According to (1), the particular quantification in 'contribute something' ranges over names: 'some names' (possibly not all). According to (2), the quantification ranges over the features of each name: 'partly' (possibly not completely). According to (3), the quantification ranges both over names and over their features. But remember that our conclusion is a generalization from the σκληρόν case, where Socrates argued that the name is correct and indicates its referent by habit and convention, not in virtue of similarity, without adding any qualification. Therefore only (1), not (2) or (3), is likely to represent what he is saying now.[43]

Thus Socrates generalizes from the view that σκληρόν indicates by habit and convention to the view that some names do. The inference would be sound even if σκληρόν were the only name which indicates so; but Socrates is probably confident that, as a matter of fact, many a name is in the same condition as σκληρόν, i.e. contains letters which do not resemble its referent or are altogether contrary to it.

---

[41] This is the only place in *Cra.* where this abstract noun occurs. Cf. *Plt.* 287a, *Lg.* 942bc, Arist. *HA* 618b16–17, etc.

[42] Here and in the following lines, for simplicity I omit to add 'and habit' after each occurrence of 'by convention'.

[43] This should also be Proclus and Ammonius' view: see §8.1.7. The interpretation of Sedley (2003: 141, 145) is only compatible with (3): 'For *any* name, its success as a tool for communication depends, at least largely, on its imitative powers, but may also depend on a degree of convention.' It is not clear to me how Sedley can square this with his recognition that 'In the special case of *sklerotes*, the name's "correctness" does … come down to mere agreement' (145).

Actually it seems that Socrates would be in a position to reach a stronger conclusion:

(4) All names indicate their referents by convention.

He could just point out that it is reasonable, on grounds of philosophical economy, to assume that all names indicate their referents in the same way, and that hence, if σκληρόν indicates its referent by convention, all names are likely to do so. Or he could try to argue along the following lines. Necessarily, any name 'X' is such that either some of its letters resemble its referent X while others do not, or all its letters resemble X, or none of them does.[44] In the first case, the σκληρόν argument shows that 'X' indicates X by convention. In the third case, it is obvious that 'X' can indicate X only by convention. In the second case, 'X' *might* also be a (very imperfect) name of something else, Y, which has some features in common with X and which only some (possibly only one) of the name's letters resemble. But then 'X' would indicate Y by convention, as the σκληρόν argument shows. Therefore, if it does *not* indicate Y, but X instead, this too must be by convention. So in any case 'X' indicates X by convention.

Socrates, however, avails himself of neither argument; he is content with (and will in the sequel insist on) his weaker conclusion that convention and habit 'contribute something' to indication. Of course Plato may just fail to realize that either argument is available; but he may also deliberately keep Socrates from employing them. In the latter and more interesting case, what is the reason for Plato's doing so? Does he think that something is wrong with the arguments' premises or their conclusion? These questions will stay with us almost until the end of Socrates' speech.

For the moment we go on and witness Socrates advancing a fresh argument:

(SO.) For, my excellent friend, if you're willing to turn to the case of number, where do you think you'll be able to find similar names to apply to each single one of the numbers [πόθεν οἴει ἕξειν ὀνόματα ὅμοια ἑνὶ ἑκάστῳ τῶν ἀριθμῶν ἐπενεγκεῖν], if you don't allow your agreement and convention to have some authority concerning the correctness of names [ἐὰν μὴ ἐᾷς τι τὴν σὴν ὁμολογίαν καὶ συνθήκην κῦρος ἔχειν τῶν ὀνομάτων ὀρθότητος πέρι]? (435b6–c2)

As the initial 'For' (ἐπεί) makes clear, this argument is designed to bring further support to the b5–6 conclusion that convention and habit 'contribute

---

[44] Socrates does not as yet show himself alive to anything like the third case. But cf. below the 'Non-resemblance Interpretation' of the argument about number-names (b6–c2).

something' to the indication of their referents, and the present thesis that agreement and conclusion 'have some authority concerning the correctness of names' (b8–c2) is a reformulation of that conclusion. We shall return to the b8–c2 thesis after we have tried to figure out how the argument works. In this connection a few preliminary points must be made.

(i) It is important to recognize the modal component in the argument: if you do not grant convention any role, then – Socrates argues – it will not be *possible* to get names similar to each (natural) number. Thus the argument does not turn on a particular example from a particular language; it is not about the existing Greek number-names, but about number-names in any possible language, including a perfectly rational language like the one envisaged by Socrates at 424b–425a. In this respect it is different from, and stronger than, the σκληρόν argument.

(ii) The question 'where do you think you'll be able to find similar names to apply to *each single one* of the numbers?' may suggest that the argument somehow turns on the difficulty of providing names similar to *all* numbers, as opposed to just *some* numbers. In other words: if you do not have recourse to convention, you can provide names similar to some numbers, but not to all. We must, however, be careful: Socrates might also mean that, if you do not have recourse to convention, you cannot provide names similar to all numbers, *nor indeed to any number at all*. In effect, we shall see that both possible interpretations of the argument allow for (or indeed require) the latter construal.

(iii) We should bear in mind that in Greek, as in the other Indo-European languages, the names of natural numbers fall into two groups. On the one hand there is a basic set of numbers whose names are simple or, as Socrates would put it, *primary*, i.e. not composed of other names. Such are in the first place the names of the numbers 1–10: ἕν, δύο, τρία … δέκα (cf. 'one', 'two', 'three' … 'ten'). On the other hand, the names of most numbers are complex or *secondary*, i.e. composed of the names of the numbers into which the number named must be analysed: ἕν-δεκα, δώ-δεκα, τρισ-καί-δεκα etc. (cf. 'thir-teen', 'four-teen' etc.). Some such distinction is a necessary feature of any language which is to provide its speakers with a comparatively easy way of naming every conceivable number.[45]

---

[45] It stands to reason that by mentioning the 'names' of numbers Socrates refers to expressions which can be spoken, like the Greek ἕν, δύο, τρία etc. or the English 'one', 'two', 'three' etc. *Pace* Bestor 1980: 324–5 and Reeve xxxix–xl, he is not referring to written numerical symbols, like the Greek α, β, γ etc. ('alphabetic' notation) or I, II, III etc. ('acrophonic' notation, more common in classical Attica), or the Arabic 'o', '1', '2' etc. On Greek numerical notations see *OCD* s.v. *numbers, Greek*.

We are now ready to come to grips with the argument. It can be understood in at least two very different ways.

One possible interpretation, which I dub the 'Resemblance Interpretation', essentially consists in taking 'if you don't allow' (ἐὰν μὴ ἐᾷς b8) as equivalent to '*unless* you allow' – as Fowler and Dalimier actually translate. Then Socrates' words amount to the following: *only if* you somehow have recourse to convention can you provide each number with a similar name. As Sedley 2003: 142 puts it, 'an element of convention must be permitted *in order to ensure that the names of the numbers resemble them*'. But how exactly could the names of the numbers manage to resemble them? And what role would convention have to play exactly? Here is Schofield's (1982: 79) answer: 'we can disclose the differences between 1, 2 and 3 through their names only by some purely conventional device such as giving the name of 1 one syllable, that of 2 two syllables, that of 3 three; and it will have to be agreed by convention that they are designed to signify *numbers* in the first place. This is the one place in the dialogue where we glimpse the idea that representation is not a natural relationship, but is itself subject to convention.' For most numbers, however, this proposal is out of the question: it would be absurd to think that the name of the number 1,000 should be composed of one thousand syllables. Here the distinction between primary and secondary number-names comes in. Schofield's account may hold good for a small set of primary names; but, as Sedley 2003: 143 argues, 'the length of a large number has to be captured through the devices of multiplication and addition; and it is the established conventions for the formation of compound number-names that provide this vital short-cut … convention may be needed to establish the rules by which descriptive *economy* is attained, but for all that the system remains fundamentally imitative, and the conventions are strictly subservient to the goal of successful imitation'. Note, however, that secondary, descriptive number-names can be thought to resemble their referents only on a very weak conception of resemblance – which Socrates admittedly seems to adopt elsewhere (427cd, 438d, 439ab; see §6.4.3). Note also that, on the Resemblance Interpretation, Socrates' position should be that, unless you have recourse to convention somehow or other, you cannot provide names similar to *any* number (see (ii) above).

The Resemblance Interpretation is confronted with several difficulties. Let us review them one by one.

First, the notion of convention contributing to resemblance seems problematic. Socrates might well hold that if a name, whether primary or secondary, resembles its referent at all, this is because they have some common feature, and that this sharing of features is a perfectly objective matter. The resemblance between an *n*-syllabic name and the number *n* is not conventional, but perfectly objective; and so is the resemblance between a secondary number-name and its referent, to the extent that they resemble each other at all. Socrates could then regard as conventional something else: e.g. the speakers' *recognition* that one particular *n*-syllabic name, in virtue of its being *n*-syllabic, resembles the number *n* and is therefore meant, unlike all other *n*-syllabic names, to indicate it.[46] But this is not what he says here.

Secondly, the notion of convention contributing to resemblance does not sit well with the fact that in the following lines (c2–7) Socrates will once again *contrast* resemblance with convention (cf. the resemblance/habit contrast at b1–2).

Thirdly, it is doubtful whether Socrates would believe that primary number-names of the sort envisaged by Schofield would resemble their referents *in a way that met the requirements of the naturalist thesis*. There is clearly something very extrinsic about the sort of resemblance Schofield advocates: it is arbitrary whether we decide that the relevant items are syllables or letters or tokens of one particular letter or whatever; it is also arbitrary which of the many names composed of *n* syllables (or letters, etc.) is chosen to indicate the number *n*. In fact, much of what Socrates said of primary names does *not* apply to Schofield primary number-names. When he established that primary names imitate the essence of things 'with letters and syllables' (423e, cf. 424ab etc.), he was clearly referring to the movements and positions of the phonatory apparatus in pronouncing each letter; he was not allowing for the interpretation 'with *the number of* their letters and syllables'. Further, at 431c–433c Socrates took pains to argue (and a few lines below, at c7–d1, he is even going to remind us) that the omission of some appropriate letters, or the addition of some inappropriate ones, need not turn the name of something into the name of something else, but just into a better or worse name of the same thing. This is *not* how Schofield number-names work; they rather behave like – indeed, are among – the 'things that must necessarily be composed of a certain number of elements or not be at all', which at 432ad were distinguished from primary names and images in general. For a Schofield number-name resembles one and only one number (i.e. the number of its syllables, or letters, or whatever is chosen as the relevant unit), and cannot resemble it more or less; if the name acquires or loses any unit of the relevant kind, it immediately resembles another number instead.

---

[46] Cf. Barney 2001: 132 and n.26.

Fourthly, so far Socrates has never made the point that the composition of secondary names, whether of numbers or of anything else, involves an element of convention. Hence it is not very plausible that such a crucial point is now simply understood, as Sedley assumes.

These difficulties make the 'Resemblance Interpretation' appear rather unpalatable and should induce us to consider a completely different interpretation, according to which the argument goes as follows (cf. Robinson 1956: 117, Ackrill 1994: 47). If Cratylus allowed convention to play some role, then he would be in a position to recognize that a name may completely *fail* to resemble its referent. If Cratylus, instead, does not grant convention any 'authority' concerning correctness (b8–c2 ἐὰν μὴ – πέρι), then he is committed to the view that every name resembles its referent. But in fact there *cannot* be names similar to each single one of the numbers (b7–8 πόθεν – ἐπενεγκεῖν). Therefore convention does have some 'authority' concerning correctness.

This interpretation – which I call the 'Non-resemblance Interpretation' – is perfectly compatible with the text, if we only postulate a modicum of ellipse. According to it, Socrates does *not* hold that there may be (if only by convention) a name similar to each number; quite the contrary, he implies that this is *not* possible. If this is what he is implying, he is presumably considering that, as I argued above, Schofield *primary* number-names would not resemble their referents in a way relevant to the present concerns; this in its turn seems to entail that *secondary* number-names composed of Schofield primary ones would not be similar to their referents either. Thus Socrates might actually hold that you cannot provide names similar to *any* number at all (see my preliminary remark (ii) above).

In any case, even the view that *some* numbers are such that it is impossible to provide them with similar names is a novelty of great moment, because so far Socrates had not explicitly abandoned the assumption that a necessary (though not sufficient) condition of a name is that it be similar to its referent.[47] Note, however, that Socrates is likely to be dropping that assumption – or to have already dropped it – on *any* interpretation of the argument. For it should be uncontroversial that at least the *present* Greek names of the numbers 1–10 do not resemble their referents.[48]

---

[47] *Pace* Sedley (2003: 149, cf. 145): 'Nowhere in the dialogue does Socrates acknowledge a case where a name bears no resemblance at all to its object.'
[48] Cf. Leibniz, *Dialogus* (1677), 1923:–, A VI, 4A, 23.9–14: 'what similarity do you think there is between ten and the character "10"? ... what similarity do the primary elements themselves have with things, for example, "o" with nothing, or "a" with a line? You are forced to admit, at very least, that no similarity is necessary in these elements' (Ariew/Garber's translation, 1989: 271).

It is now time to look more closely at the conclusion that agreement and convention[49] 'have some authority' (τι ... κῦρος ἔχειν) concerning the correctness of names. As we saw above, this is a reformulation of the previous general conclusion, drawn at b5–6, that convention and habit 'contribute something' (τι ... συμβάλλεσθαι) to the indication of their referents. The main formal difference is that b5–6 apparently turned on indication, whereas b8–c2 is couched in terms of correctness; but this is irrelevant, given that these two concepts are being taken to be equivalent (see 433de and (P7) in §8.1.3).[50] Now, the b5–6 conclusion seemed to amount to (1), i.e. to the thesis that *some names* indicate their referents by convention and habit. Hence the present conclusion should presumably mean something equivalent. Socrates says that convention and agreement have 'some authority' concerning the correctness of names; but he actually means that convention and agreement have authority – i.e. *complete* authority – concerning the correctness of *some* names (cf. Minio-Paluello's translation: 'in qualche caso ... abbiano autorità'). The particular quantifier 'some' (τι), which in the Greek text is attached to 'authority', actually ranges over names. In short:

(1*) Some names are correct by convention,

which is equivalent to (1). But while the b5–6 conclusion only rested upon the σκληρότης example, now our stock of conventional names has expanded to include the names of at least some numbers – and perhaps of all.

As with b5–6, of course, so here too we may ask why Socrates does not conclude that convention and agreement govern the correctness of *all* names, as he would actually be in a position to do (especially, though not only, if the Non-resemblance Interpretation is right). Indeed, some interpreters do take the present conclusion as an understatement and deny the qualifying force of 'some' any substance, instead of transferring it from 'authority' to 'names' as I would rather do. Thus τι ... κῦρος ἔχειν τῶν ὀνομάτων ὀρθότητος πέρι is translated by Fowler as 'to control the

---

[49] Socrates actually speaks of '*your* agreement and convention'. Thereby he stresses (as already at 434e–435a) that Cratylus, as a speaker, is personally engaged in the process of communication, and that therefore, if this process is partly based on convention, Cratylus himself must partake in this convention. Schofield 1982: 78–80 and Reeve translate the phrase as 'this agreement and convention of yours', which Schofield thinks has a ring of mockery to it; but 'this', which should presumably be crucial to the mockery, is not in the text.

[50] Socrates substitutes the phrase 'agreement and convention' for the earlier 'convention and habit' (435a10, b5). But such terms as 'convention', 'agreement', 'custom' and 'habit' have already been treated as substantially equivalent both by Hermogenes (384d) and by Socrates himself (434e5; see §8.1.3, also on 435a10–b1).

Resemblance and convention in names (433b–435d) 413

correctness of names', while Méridier speaks of 'une autorité décisive en ce qui concerne la justesse des noms'.[51] As we saw above, however, Socrates' insistence on expressing himself so cautiously, which will emerge for the third time in the following lines (c2–7), should be taken more seriously. Commenting on those lines in §8.1.5 we shall see what the reason for his cautiousness might be.

8.1.5 Conclusions on resemblance and convention in names (435cd)

We are approaching the end of Socrates' speech, where he states his final conclusions on the part played by resemblance and convention in the correctness of names. But if you expect that these lines will yield the key to Socrates' and Plato's ultimate views on the subject and cast light on the previous claims, you are likely to be put off: the text is going to prove as difficult and obscure as it can be.

(SO.) Well, I myself too like the idea that names are, as far as possible, similar to the objects [ἐμοὶ μὲν οὖν καὶ αὐτῷ ἀρέσκει μὲν κατὰ τὸ δυνατὸν ὅμοια εἶναι τὰ ὀνόματα τοῖς πράγμασιν]. But I fear that this power of similarity is actually 'poor' [ἀλλὰ μὴ ὡς ἀληθῶς ... γλίσχρα ᾖ ἡ ὁλκὴ αὕτη τῆς ὁμοιότητος], to use Hermogenes' expression, and that it is necessary to make use also of this vulgar means, convention, for the correctness of names [ἀναγκαῖον δὲ ᾖ καὶ τῷ φορτικῷ τούτῳ προσχρῆσθαι, τῇ συνθήκῃ, εἰς ὀνομάτων ὀρθότητα]. (435c2–7)

This pericope is divided into two parts. (I) The first part coincides with the first clause, 'I myself ... to the objects' (c2–3), which seems to contain some sort of concession to the naturalist side. This clause is introduced by the particle group μὲν οὖν, composed of a retrospective and transitional οὖν plus a prospective μέν which is then picked up by the following ἀρέσκει μέν; both μέν's are then answered by c4 ἀλλά 'but', which opens the pericope's second part.[52] (II) The second part is composed of two clauses, linked together by c5 δέ: (II.a) 'I fear that ... expression', which seems to voice a reservation about the previous concession; (II.b) 'it is necessary ... of names', which acknowledges a role for convention. Needless to say, at first glance it is far from clear what the concession, the reservation or the acknowledgement consists in.

---

[51] Cf. Schofield 1982: 79, who invites us to 'construe "contribute something" [b5] as an understatement for "govern entirely", and "a certain authority" as saying in effect "all authority"'; Robinson 1956: 122; Williams 1982: 90–1.

[52] See *GP* 470–3 (μὲν οὖν) and 386 (duplicated μέν).

Let us embark on a detailed analysis of these crucial lines, beginning with (1). The first question to be asked is: What does the verb ἀρέσκει mean here? Generally speaking, 'X ἀρέσκει Y' ('X' the grammatical subject, 'Y' in the dative or accusative) may mean that X 'pleases' Y in the sense that Y finds X fine or good or convenient. Thus many construe this clause as expressing Socrates' *preference* for those names that are similar to the things named or his *wish* – whether confident or not – that names were so: e.g. Méridier 'j'aime que les noms soient … semblables'; Schofield 1982: 81 'I am happy with the idea that names should resemble things so far as is possible'.[53] But 'X ἀρέσκει Y', like 'X placet Y' in Latin, may also mean that Y *believes* X, where 'X' stands in for a proposition. On this latter construal, Socrates is saying he *believes* that names actually *are*, 'as far as possible', similar to the objects named; thus Fowler, followed by Dalimier, translates 'I myself prefer the theory that names are …'

Now, the former construal may seem to be supported by a comparison with c7–8, where Socrates says that 'perhaps, as far as possible, one would speak most finely when one spoke with all or as many as possible similar elements'. Since 'as far as possible' there clearly picks up 'as far as possible' here, it may be tempting to suppose that also 'most finely' there picks up – and thus explains – ἐμοί … ἀρέσκει here. Nevertheless, I believe that this temptation is misleading and that the latter construal of ἀρέσκειν is the right one. For all the other occurrences of the verb in *Cra.* (391c, 400a, 427e, 433ce), and all the Platonic occurrences where its grammatical subject is, as here, a clause with the accusative and infinitive, are instances of this use or can be somehow traced to it.[54]

Thus Socrates is claiming he *believes* that names are 'as far as possible' similar to their referents. Our next step must of course be to grasp the purport of the proposition believed. In my opinion, Socrates cannot mean that *all possible names* resemble their referents (i.e. that, necessarily, any name resembles its referent); nor can he mean that *all actual Greek names* resemble their referents.[55] For, as we saw in §8.1.4, on any interpretation of the number-names argument at least the actual Greek names

---

[53] Schofield (1982: 67) warns us that we should read this 'as nothing more than an expression of vain regret'. Grote, instead, took Socrates' words, which he construed similarly (1888: III.318), much more seriously, and went on to compare Plato's views on the knowledgeable statesman in the *Politicus* and on the ideal state in the *Republic* (1888: III.328–30).

[54] For this construal of ἐμοί … ἀρέσκει cf. Ademollo 2009: 59 and Sedley 2003: 147–8.

[55] What about actual languages different from Greek, such as Persian or Egyptian? Obviously Greek is what Socrates is primarily thinking of; but he would, I surmise, be ready to grant that also in other existing languages 'names are, as far possible, similar to the objects' (provided that those languages use different sounds/letters from the Greek ones: see §6.3.6).

of the numbers 1–10 do not resemble their referents; indeed, if the Non-resemblance Interpretation of that argument is right, then Socrates holds that some (if not all) numbers *cannot* bear names that resemble them. In this connection the phrase 'as far as possible' is especially important. As Sedley 2003: 147 n.2 aptly remarks, the same phrase occurred at 422de in Socrates' question how the primary names can 'make the beings as manifest as possible to us'. At this stage of the discussion, however, the phrase has become pregnant and serves two additional purposes. First, it incorporates the outcome of the Two Cratyluses argument: a name cannot resemble its referent *perfectly*. Second – and more important for our present concerns – it precisely leaves room for objects that cannot bear names that resemble them.

So what Socrates claims he believes is essentially the following:

(5) Most names resemble their referents

(where 'resemble' does not mean 'resemble perfectly' or 'resemble completely' – just 'bear some degree of resemblance to'). Now you will remember that Socrates' interim conclusions in favour of convention at b5–6 and b8–c2 seemed (§8.1.4) to boil down to this:

(1) Some names indicate their referents by convention.

There is no contradiction between (5) and (1) or (1*); indeed, they can even (and presumably do) turn on the same names. For from the fact that most names resemble their referents it does not follow that they indicate their referents *in virtue* of this resemblance or *because* they resemble them. A name may resemble its referent as a matter of fact, and yet indicate it by convention; this was precisely the case of σκληρότης, which did resemble hardness by containing one ρ, but nevertheless indicated hardness, and was a correct name thereof, only conventionally.[56]

We now turn our attention to part (II) of our pericope, where Socrates says he fears that (II.a) the ὁλκή of resemblance may be γλίσχρα and (II.b) it may be necessary to make use also of vulgar convention for the correctness of names. The terminology in (II.a) is very unusual and requires detailed comment.

ὁλκή, from the same root as the verb ἕλκω, can have various material and figurative senses. Among the former we may mention 'pull, haul, drag' (*Plt.* 282e, Aesch. *Supp.* 884, [Arist.] *Mech.* 853b1), 'attraction' (*Ti.*

---

[56] This crucial distinction is, I suspect, not generally appreciated.

80c), 'weight' (Men. *Aspis* 84; Thphr. *HP* 9.16.8.5). For the latter see *Phlb.* 57d (a 'strain' put on the meaning of linguistic expressions), *Lg.* 659d (the activity of 'drawing' children towards the teachings of law).[57] The term is glossed by Hsch. ο 582 Latte as 'power' (δύναμις),[58] 'strength' (ἰσχύς), 'weight' (ῥοπή, βάρος, σταθμός) and 'rein' (ῥυτήρ).

γλίσχρος basically means 'viscous' (427b; *Ti.* 74d, 82d, 84a; Arist. *Mete.* 385b5, 387a11–12, and cf. 382b13–16).[59] Thence the adjective acquires various figurative uses; those that may be of any interest to us are 'niggardly' (Arist. *EN* 1121b22), 'mean, rudimentary' (buildings, Dem. 23.208; an organ, Arist. *PA* 660b14). The cognate adverb γλίσχρως may mean 'greedily' (*R.* 553c; Arist. *Pol.* 1314b3) and 'poorly, with difficulty, hardly' (X. *Cyr.* 8.3.37; Arist. *Pol.* 1266b26, 1275a37–8; Dem. 37.38).[60] Now in our passage Socrates explicitly presents γλίσχρα as a back-reference to 414bc, where the question whether the name τέχνη ('art') 'signifies "possession of mind" [ἕξιν νοῦ σημαίνει] to one who takes away the τ and inserts an ο between χ and ν and between ν and η' (i.e. whether τέχνη < ἐχονόη) was answered by Hermogenes with the words Καὶ μάλα γε γλίσχρως, which apparently had to mean 'It does so *with great difficulty*'[61] and prompted Socrates to explain that the original names have acquired and lost letters through time (see §5.5.1).

What should we conclude from this evidence? Some take *both* terms in a pejorative sense. So e.g. Méridier translates 'je crains qu' … il ne faille ici … tirer laborieusement sur la ressemblance'; Schofield 1982: 81 'this dragging in of resemblance is a niggardly business'; *DGE* γλίσχρος II.1 'temo que sea forzado el arrastrar la semejanza'. This will not do. The phrase ἡ ὁλκὴ αὕτη, '*this* ὁλκή', conveys a reference to part (1), where Socrates has just maintained – to my mind seriously – that names do resemble objects; so this reference cannot be cast in disparaging terms.

Others construe Socrates' words more plausibly as a *single* metaphor to the effect that, for some reason, resemblance plays only a limited role. So Williams 1982: 93 takes 'the γλίσχρα ὁλκή as, straightforwardly, a "sticky haul", like getting a ship to move over a gummy slip-way: one has to work

---

[57] Cf. the adjective ὁλκός, which at *R.* 521d, 524e, 527b means 'tending to draw' the soul towards truth.

[58] Cf. ο 75 ὁλκά· δυνατά.

[59] Aristotle mentions oil, pitch and birdlime as examples of γλίσχρα materials. He offers the following definition: 'something is γλίσχρον when it is moist, or soft, and tensile [ἑλκτόν]'.

[60] Cf. the English 'sticky' in its informal meaning 'problematic'.

[61] Or 'It does so very stickily'. *Pace* Williams 1982: 93, strictly speaking at 414c γλίσχρως is not attached to ἀφελόντι and ἐμβαλόντι (c1), but rather to σημαίνει (b10).

Resemblance and convention in names (433b–435d) 417

hard to try to keep the resemblance theory moving';[62] and Sedley 2003: 141 translates the text as 'this is … a "sticky" trail that resemblance has to travel'. I believe that this is on the right track. Only, the back-reference to 414bc, where γλίσχρως did *not* have its literal meaning 'viscously' or 'stickily' (in the literal sense of the English), suggests that γλίσχρα and ὁλκή, instead of forming a single figurative expression, might have figurative meaning independently of each other: γλίσχρα would then mean something like 'poor' or 'little', while the ὁλκή of resemblance would be its 'weight' or 'power'.[63] Actually, I suspect that the phrase is designed to admit of both construals.

However that may be, I understand Socrates' point as follows. (II.a) must be read in close connection with (II.b), where Socrates says he also fears that 'it is necessary to make use also of this vulgar means, convention, for the correctness of names' (c5–7). In particular, the phrase 'for the correctness of names' (εἰς ὀνομάτων ὀρθότητα), which formally closes (II.b), is also relevant to (II.a) – indeed, grammatically it might even be part of both clauses – because it specifies the respect in which the 'power' of resemblance is 'little', or its 'haul' is 'sticky'. Thus, although Socrates holds that names do 'as far as possible' resemble their referents, he now remarks that this resemblance *carries little weight with regard to the correctness of names*. That is to say, it is difficult to hold also that names *indicate* their referents *because* they resemble them: witness again the name σκληρότης, which does as a matter of fact resemble hardness, but indicates it and is a correct name thereof by convention. This remark is complementary to the acknowledgement, conveyed by (II.b), that convention must play a part in the correctness of names. It is, therefore, a plausible guess that the back-reference to 414c is an indirect means to recognize that Hermogenes' conventionalist views were at least partly right.

By now we have already started to engage in the interpretation of (II.b). Here the conundrum is the phrase 'make use *also* [καί] of … convention'.[64] For the third time, after saying that convention and habit 'contribute something' to the indication of what we think of in speaking (b5–6) and

---

[62] The reference to the ship and the slip-way (which has passed to Reeve's very translation, not only here but even at 414c3) is presumably meant to suggest a connection with the noun ὁλκός, which denotes a machine for hauling ships on land (Th. 3.15.1 etc.).
[63] Cf. at least the second part of Fowler's translation: 'this attractive force of likeness is … a poor thing'.
[64] The verb προσχράομαι could by itself mean 'use in addition', as it perhaps does in Arist. *Rh.* 1358b19. But it need not do so, because it often means simply 'use' (*Ap.* 23a, *Phd.* 79c, 99b, *R.* 510d, *Phlb.* 44cd, *Plt.* 293d; Arist. *Pol.* 1263a20). Both interpretations are possible also at *Criti.* 115a and Arist. *Ph.* 200b19.

that agreement and convention 'have some authority' concerning the correctness of names (b8–c2), Socrates expresses himself in very cautious terms, limiting the role of convention. It seems reasonable to assume that the purport of this statement is the same as that of b5–6 and of b8–c2; that, in other words, we have before us another version of (1)/(1*), the thesis that *some names* are correct by convention. But why does Socrates say that we must make use *also* of convention, or mean that *some* names are conventional, if he could actually argue that we must make use *only* of convention, or that *all* names are conventional ((4), see §8.1.4)? This is, at long last, the place to try to answer this question, which we left pending on both previous occasions.

I would start by observing that, in view of the immediately preceding (11.a), 'make use also of ... convention' seems to be elliptical for 'make use *not only of resemblance*, but also of convention'. This expanded version of (11.b) should, in its turn, be interpreted in a way analogous to that in which we interpreted the shorter version we have in the text. So if 'it is necessary to make use also of convention for the correctness of names' means that some names are correct by convention, then apparently 'it is necessary to make use [not only of resemblance] ... for the correctness of names' ought to imply that *some other names are correct by resemblance – and hence by nature*. Socrates' words in (11.b) seem to imply that some names resemble their referents in such a way that they indicate them, and are correct names thereof, in virtue of this resemblance, and hence naturally rather than conventionally:

(6) Some (not all) names are correct by resemblance and hence by nature.[65]

Of course (6) is false: no name can indicate its referent simply by resembling it, however great this resemblance may be. But Socrates may be presently failing to realize that this is so; or he may have some reason not to disclose his views fully. Either way, I submit that throughout his speech Socrates has been assuming (6), and that this is the reason why he has repeatedly restricted his endorsement of convention. Indeed, already the ancient commentators took Socrates to hold both (1)/(1*) and (6): see §8.1.7.[66]

---

[65] Socrates might hold that such naturally correct names do not actually exist but *could* exist; to wit, that their absence from actual languages is basically accidental, and that they would feature in a perfect language like the one envisaged at 424b–425a. If this were his view, then 'Some' in (6) (and hence also in (1)/(1*)) should be taken to range over a domain including *possible* names.

[66] Cf. Grote 1888: III.318 and Keller 2000: 301–2. Socrates, Grote holds, 'admits that non-natural names also, significant only by convention, are available as a make-shift – and that such names

Now what about Plato? My hypothesis is that, whether or not Socrates, the character, is aware that (6) is false, Plato, the dialogue's author, *is*; that nevertheless he has some reason for making Socrates endorse (6); and that the very reticent way in which Socrates endorses (6) is presumably designed to minimize Plato's (if not also Socrates') involvement with it.

We can find evidence that positively supports this possibility, and at the same time understand what Plato's reasons for doing so might be, if we consider the structure of Socrates' discussion with Cratylus. At 428e Socrates obtained Cratylus' assent to two theses: (i) 'the correctness of a name ... consists in showing what the object is like', (ii) 'names are said for the sake of teaching'. It is (i) that he has been discussing since.[67] But at 435d1, as soon as he has finished with it, he will uninterruptedly ask Cratylus what power or function names have and what fine result they achieve; and as Cratylus answers that names 'teach', and that 'he who has knowledge of names has also knowledge of the objects', thus confirming his adherence to (ii), Socrates will start examining this latter thesis from scratch. The ensuing discussion (435d–439b), wholly independent of the previous one, will lead to the conclusion that names do not yield knowledge of objects and give access only to the *opinions* of their makers, which may well be *false* (as with the many names whose etymology presupposes the flux theory and also most proper names of heroes and men, which Socrates dealt with way back at 397ac), so that one who took names as guides in an inquiry into the nature of things would risk being 'deceived'. Thereby that discussion will also have implications which are relevant to our appraisal of (i) and which can hardly escape Plato's attention. For if a name may convey false information about its referent, then clearly it can only indicate its referent by convention.

Thus the sequel of the dialogue contains evidence that Plato knows that (6) is false. At the same time, the sequel also suggests a possible reason

---

are in frequent use. Still however he contends, that natural names, significant by likeness, are the best, so far as they can be obtained: but inasmuch as that principle will not afford sufficiently extensive holding-ground, recourse must be had by way of supplement to the less perfect rectitude (of names) presented by customary or conventional significance.' I disagree with Grote on the following points. First, he ascribes (1)/(1*) + (6) not only to Socrates but also to Plato (cf. n.53 above); *contra* see below. Second, he does not see that (5) and (1)/(1*) may turn on the same names (1888: III.319). Third, he thinks that the correctness of the conventional names is inferior to that of the natural ones (cf. III.324–5, 329–30); this goes against the text, where σκληρόν is declared unqualifiedly correct (a8; see below on c7–d1).

[67] This is true even though in the course of the discussion (433de) 'showing what the object is like' has been downgraded from the function of names to the *way* in which names accomplish their function, redefined as *indicating* the object.

why Plato should make Socrates endorse (6). Plato evidently wants him to discuss theses (i) and (ii) separately from each other. But if the discussion of (i) ended in *total* rejection of naturalism, then discussion of (ii) might seem to be superfluous or uninteresting. If, instead, at the end of the discussion of (i) Socrates still holds that nature plays a part in the correctness of names, i.e. that some names are naturally correct, this may help keep the readers' interest in (ii) alive, or at least provide a dramatic justification for Socrates' moving on to (ii).

More generally, I think that Socrates' endorsement of (6) can be regarded as another instance of the sort of authorial strategy we have already supposed to operate in Socrates' arguments for naturalism at 387a–390e: Plato expects us, the readers, to engage actively in the argument and to subject what we read to a critical scrutiny, also in the light of the subsequent stages of the discussion. So it should come as no surprise that the present passage does not contain Plato's last word on the correctness of names.

Above we left pending the question why convention is termed 'vulgar' (435c6). The answer, however, is evident: convention is vulgar because it is arbitrary and changeable. In particular, conventional names bear no intrinsic relation to their referents, and hence can be created and imposed on anything by anyone: conventional namemaking is a 'democratic' business in that it does not require any special expertise and thus is within any layman's reach. Contrast the words with which Socrates at 390d declared that names are naturally correct: 'the imposition of names seems not to be a trivial matter, as you believe, nor a thing for trivial men, nor for any chance person'. This negative appraisal of convention is, I think, Plato's own. Generally speaking, the author of the dictum that God, not any human being, is the measure of all things (*Lg.* 716c) cannot feel an instinctive attraction to the concept of convention, even though here he is in fact recognizing its authority over the particular sphere of names.

This brings us to the following lines, the last which Socrates devotes to the direct discussion of thesis (i) for the time being:

(SO.) Yet perhaps, as far as possible, one would speak most finely when one spoke with elements all of which, or as many as possible, were similar, i.e. appropriate, and one would speak most poorly in the opposite case [ἐπεὶ ἴσως κατά γε τὸ δυνατὸν κάλλιστ' ἂν λέγοιτο ὅταν ἢ πᾶσιν ἢ ὡς πλείστοις ὁμοίοις λέγηται, τοῦτο δ' ἐστὶ προσήκουσιν, αἴσχιστα δὲ τοὐναντίον]. (435c7–d1)

As this sentence is opened by ἐπεί ('for, because', c7), it should apparently give a reason or explanation for something which precedes it. At first glance it is not clear what the explanandum is; but ἐπεί can be used elliptically, the explanandum being understood, as we saw at 433c (see n.2).[68] Thus in our passage Socrates, who has just said that, although names are similar to their referents, we must necessarily have recourse also to convention, goes on as follows: '[*and that's a pity,*], because ... etc.' In a translation we can also avoid supplying the missing words and just render the elliptical ἐπεί as 'yet', as I have done above.

Now that we have elucidated the logical connection between this sentence and what precedes it we can turn to its content. The word 'elements' in my translation (like 'elementi' in Minio-Paluello's) is an attempt to capture the ambiguity of the Greek text, where the noun qualified by 'similar' and 'appropriate' is not specified. So what are the 'elements' in question? Most scholars assume that they are *names*; on this interpretation, Socrates says that one would speak most finely (i.e., as Fowler has it, that 'language would be ... most excellent') when one spoke with names all of which, or as many as possible, were similar or appropriate to their referents, whereas one would speak most poorly in the opposite case. Schofield 1982: 81 and Sedley 2003: 141, instead, think that Socrates is talking about similar *letters*. On their interpretation, Socrates rather says that one would speak most finely (i.e. a name would be finest) when one spoke with (i.e. when the name were composed of) letters which were all, or as many as possible, similar or appropriate to the name's referent, whereas one would speak most poorly (i.e. a name would be poorest) in the opposite case.

Which of these two interpretations is right? We faced a similar problem while commenting on a passage which seems clearly parallel to the present one, i.e. 433a, where Socrates said that, as long as an (unspecified) linguistic unit contains something's 'outline', 'even though it doesn't have all the appropriate [προσήκοντα] elements, the object will be spoken of, finely when it has all the appropriate elements, badly when it has a few [λέξεταί γε τὸ πρᾶγμα, καλῶς ὅταν πάντα, κακῶς δὲ ὅταν ὀλίγα]'. Here, however, the stakes are higher. For here the main difference between the two interpretations is that according to the former, but not to the latter, Socrates is acknowledging the possibility of *names not similar to their referents*, like the present Greek number-names – indeed, like *any* possible number-

---

[68] *Prt.* 335c provides two neat examples: ἐγὼ δὲ τὰ μακρὰ ταῦτα ἀδύνατος, ἐπεὶ ἐβουλόμην ἂν οἷός τ' εἶναι ('I'm incapable of making these long speeches, [*and I am sorry,*] because I wish I were able to') ... εἶμι· ἐπεὶ καὶ ταῦτ' ἂν ἴσως οὐκ ἀηδῶς σου ἤκουον ('I'm leaving; [*and that's a pity,*] because I think it would have been nice to hear these things from you'). Cf. also *Euthphr.* 4c, 9b; *Ap.* 19e; *Prt.* 317a, 333c (and see LSJ B.4 and Burnet 1924: 24). In some of the examples the word immediately after ἐπεί is followed by γε, as in our passage.

name (see §8.1.4), on one version of the Non-resemblance Interpretation of the number-names argument.

Now, the fact that the adjective 'similar' in its last two occurrences (b8, c3) was applied to names invites us to understand 'names' as the missing noun and thus supports the former interpretation. But, on the other hand, Socrates' talk of speaking 'finely' and 'poorly' points instead to the latter interpretation, according to which the missing noun is 'letters'. For, as I remarked in §7.3.4, names are the *sole* linguistic units of which Socrates uncontroversially says that they can be fine or poor/bad (431ce, 432de, 433bc, 439a), and he goes out of his way to show that this is so. In particular, on the latter interpretation the present passage has another striking parallel at 433bc, where Socrates sums up the following points (see §8.1.1): a name that has been finely set down contains the appropriate letters; the appropriate letters are those similar to the objects; a name that has not been finely set down can at best be composed for the most part of appropriate, i.e. similar, letters. So I conclude that the text is certainly meant to admit of the latter interpretation, but possibly also of the former. Socrates' point might be the very generic one that, when a linguistic unit (a name in the first place, but also a sentence or even a whole language) is composed of simpler elements (letters in the first place, but also names), then the more the elements that are similar (sc. to the extralinguistic entities they are applied to), the finer the whole unit is.[69]

So far I have not spelt out the exact import of Socrates' expression 'and one would speak most poorly *in the opposite case*'. But the parallel with 433a makes it clear that 'in the opposite case' here means 'when one spoke with elements none of which, or as few as possible, were similar, i.e. appropriate'. This in its turn seems clearly equivalent to 'when one spoke with elements all of which, or as many as possible, were dissimilar, i.e. inappropriate'.[70] Either way, names like σκληρότης, or the sample names which Socrates examined in his survey at 426c–427c, or the number-names (whether actual or possible), all seem to count as instances of the 'opposite case' and hence to be (more or less) poor.

Several commentators (e.g. Sedley 2003: 149–50) assume that in these lines the words 'most finely ... most poorly' are equivalent to 'most

---

[69] Once again, Leibniz's stance in the 1677 *Dialogus* is strikingly similar. Read 1923–: A VI, 4A, 24.3–5: 'if characters can be employed for reasoning, there is in them some complex arrangement, some order which agrees with things, an order, if not in individual words (*though that would be better*), then at least in their conjunction and inflection' (tr. after Ariew/Garber 1989: 271; my italics).

[70] Sedley 2003: 148–50 would modify the first formulation by eliminating the 'none' case and deny the equivalence with the second: cf. nn.39, 43.

correctly ... least correctly', and hence that Socrates (insofar as he is talking about names and their relation to their component letters) is actually saying that a name is *more or less correct* depending on how many of its letters are similar to its referent. Here as elsewhere, I oppose this interpretation, which is not adequately supported by the evidence and indeed runs foul of some evidence to the contrary. At 431c–433c Socrates has been defending the view that names may be better or worse by employing a number of synonymous expressions: a name may or may not be 'fine', may be 'finely made' or 'badly made', may or may not be 'set down well' or 'finely', may be used to speak of something 'finely' or 'badly'. But so far in the course of his conversation with Cratylus Socrates has *never* said that a name may be more or less correct, or that a name may be an incorrect name of something while still being a name of that thing. Quite the contrary, in some of those very passages (432a–433b: see §§7.3.3–4) he appeared to be sticking to the Redundancy Conception of correctness, according to which 'being a name of X' means the same as 'being a correct name of X' – which entails that correctness does not come in degrees and that a word cannot be an incorrect name of something while still being a name of that thing.[71] So I hold on to the view that the distinction between fine and poor names has been introduced by Socrates, and is being reaffirmed here, as a distinction internal to the set of correct names (i.e. of names *simpliciter*) – a distinction whose function is to accommodate the naturalist view that a name which resembles its referent is somehow superior to one which does not, while leaving untouched the theoretical framework (i.e. the Redundancy Conception) within which the debate began and that view was first advanced.

We are almost finished. But we still have to face Barney's (2001: 135–6) severe judgement: 'To suppose that conventionalism is now proven correct after all involves supposing that the earlier argument against it was wrong, and that Plato is aware of this but cannot be bothered to note or diagnose the error, or to give us any clues as to how it is to be corrected ... the conventionalist reading has no option but to deny the unity of the dialogue and read the *Cratylus* as an incoherent parade of disconnected

---

[71] At 429b Socrates asked Cratylus whether all names are correct; this however does not imply that he believes that some names might fail to be correct: see §7.1.2. At 432a Cratylus seemed to ascribe this view to Socrates; but this suggestion was disproved by the sequel, where Socrates appeared to hold on to Redundancy, and was not repeated any more. Virtually the only place in the dialogue where Socrates says a name is 'more correct' than another is 392ad, in the course of the discussion of Homer on names; cf. 437a, in the second series of etymologies of secondary names. In both cases I am inclined to believe that Socrates is speaking loosely; cf. §4.1.

arguments, some good and some bad, from which we are left to choose our favourites.'

To my mind this picture does not apply to my interpretation, for several reasons. To start with, I suppose some weight should be carried by the fact that the dialogue follows a certain course, i.e. that Socrates first argues in favour of naturalism, then argues against it, *and eventually exits from the dialogue as a conventionalist*. Secondly, as I have been arguing throughout ch. 3, the conclusions of the arguments for naturalism at 387a–390e were designed to admit of a reinterpretation which would make them compatible with conventionalism. Thirdly, it is not completely true that Socrates does not criticize his own earlier arguments for naturalism. He has not done so as yet; but in the sequel the discussion of Cratylus' thesis that names 'teach' (435d–439b) has an evident bearing on Socrates' earlier claim that 'A name is an instrument for *teaching* and discriminating the essence' (388bc).

8.1.6 Convention elsewhere in the Platonic corpus

The interpretation of Plato's own stance which I have been advocating so far fits well with Socrates' characteristic claim – which occurs repeatedly in the corpus – that it becomes a philosopher to care little for terminological exactitude: as he says at *Tht.* 184c,

being careless in the use of names and expressions, and omitting to subject them to a strict examination, is in most cases not base, but rather the contrary is unworthy of a free man.

Other passages along the same lines are *R.* 533de, *Tht.* 199a, *Sph.* 227bc, *Plt.* 261e.

A text containing, more relevantly, a genuine conventionalist profession, albeit limited to a particular case, is *Chrm.* 163d, which we encountered in §2.1.2. But our conclusions should be especially compared with a famous passage from the *Seventh Letter*, more precisely from the section where the author illustrates the four stages through which knowledge of each form is to be attained and explains that their faultiness makes it impossible to write a philosophical treatise. Here is what he has to say about the first stage, which is the form's *name* (343b):

And we say that none of them has any stable name [ὄνομά τε αὐτῶν φαμεν οὐδὲν οὐδενὶ βέβαιον εἶναι], and nothing prevents the things now called 'circular' from bearing the name 'straight', and those now called 'straight' from bearing the name 'circular', and from being no less stable than before for those who changed the names and call things in reverse [καὶ οὐδὲν ἧττον βεβαίως ἕξειν τοῖς μετατεθεμένοις καὶ ἐναντίως καλοῦσιν].

It is perfectly possible, the author says, to interchange the reference of the names we use without thereby affecting the nature of things. This claim is clearly reminiscent of Hermogenes' conventionalism, especially as developed at 385ab and then joined with rejection of Protagorean relativism (386a). The claim also harmonizes with my interpretation, according to which Plato conceives of correctness as completely conventional.[72] Note, however, that the *Letter* acknowledges the changeability of names *but complains about it*.[73] For it says that because names are unstable they are an unsound starting point for acquiring knowledge of anything. This hardly makes any sense as a philosophical view; and it is one of the reasons which make me (like other scholars) suspect that the *Letter* – or, at the very least, its philosophical section – is inauthentic.[74] Nor does the *Letter*'s view of names really harmonize with *Cra.*, where Socrates will not display the slightest regret in arguing, at 435d–439b, that names are unreliable and therefore we had better look for some other source of knowledge. But, nevertheless, the *Letter* might be taking (misguided) inspiration from the regret that Socrates does voice at 435bc about the necessity of giving convention a role in the correctness of names. If this hypothesis is sound, the *Letter*'s author construes – rightly, as I see it – Plato as a conventionalist; recognizes that Socrates regrets that convention plays such a role; and misunderstands this regret as arising out of epistemological concerns.

8.1.7 *The ancient commentators*

As I mentioned above, the ancient commentators ascribe to Socrates both (1)/(1*) and (6). Here is e.g. Proclus, x, 4.6–16 (cf. 18–23, and also I, 1.1–9; XIX, 8.21–3; XXVII, 10.10–11; XXX, 11.1–4; LI, 18.20–6):

The characters are Cratylus the Heraclitean, of whom Plato too was a student, who said that names are all by nature … ; Hermogenes the Socratic, who on the contrary said that no name is by nature, but all are by imposition; and thirdly Socrates, who judged and showed that *some are by nature and others are by*

---

[72] Cf. Robinson 1956: 120–1.
[73] This is rightly emphasized by Barney 2001: 167, although I do not agree with what she makes of it.
[74] For a powerful (if at times excessive) attack on the *Letter*'s authenticity, and a denouncement of its philosophical absurdities, see Karsten 1864. Karsten too thought that the *Letter* misunderstands *Cra.*, but on completely different (and, I think, mistaken) grounds; for he took Plato in *Cra.* to be averse to conventionalism (1864: 195).

imposition, i.e. arisen by chance [τὰ μὲν αὐτῶν εἶναι φύσει, τὰ δὲ καὶ θέσει, οἷον τύχῃ γεγονότα]. For the names for the eternal things partake more of being by nature, while those for the perishable ones partake more of being by chance. For he who calls his son Athanasius [= 'Immortal'] shows the faultiness of names with regard to these things.[75]

To understand these lines we must bear in mind that Proclus is using the expression 'by imposition' (θέσει) to mean 'by *mere* imposition' and hence as equivalent to 'by convention'. Thus Proclus ascribes to Socrates the view that some names are by nature whereas others are conventional and arbitrary ('arisen by chance': cf. *Cra*. 397a, 402b, 434a). On Proclus' interpretation, this distinction coincides with that between names of eternal things and names of perishable things. He is clearly thinking of 397ac. As we saw in §5.2.1, there Socrates was actually signalling a serious difficulty for naturalism, which consists in the fact that the etymologies of many secondary proper names give *false* descriptions of their referents. Thus Proclus is right in believing that proper names of perishable particulars must be conventional. In our passage, however, such names are entirely out of the question; and the names that are in question, i.e. σκληρότης/σκληρόν and the number-names, should presumably be reckoned by Proclus among those of 'eternal things'. Thus Proclus is wrong in believing that proper names of perishable particulars are the only conventional names. You might perhaps doubt whether his interpretation relates to Socrates' present arguments at all; but this is confirmed by Ammonius, *in Int*. 37.1–13, who in expounding the same interpretation says that for Socrates 'most of the names imposed on particulars are by imposition even in this vulgar [φορτικόν] sense of "by imposition" employed by Hermogenes' – with a clear reference to 435c5–7.

Proclus' and Ammonius' interpretation is complicated by the fact that they ascribe to Socrates the view that those very names which are 'by nature', and not 'by imposition' in Hermogenes' sense, are at the same time 'by imposition' in a *different* sense, i.e. in that they did not arise naturally (as Epicurus thought), but were imposed (more precisely, were imposed by a wise namegiver who knew the nature of things and described it via their etymology). See how the passage just quoted from Proclus goes on (X, 4.16–18; and cf. XII, 5.1–4; XVII, 8.11–14; LI, 18.15–17; Amm. *in Int*. 34.10–37.18):

Further, since names have both form and matter, in respect of their form they partake more of being by nature, whereas in respect of their matter they partake more of being by imposition.

[75] Tr. partly after Blank 1996: 150 n.169.

Here Proclus is, of course, speaking only of the 'names for the eternal things'.

8.2 NAMES AND KNOWLEDGE (435D–439B)

8.2.1 Cratylus' view that names 'teach' (435d–436a)

As soon as Socrates has finished setting forth his conclusions about the correctness of names he goes on without a break[76] to ask Cratylus a closely related question:

SO. But tell me this further thing: what power [δύναμιν] do names have for us and what fine result shall we say they achieve?
CR. For my part, Socrates, I believe that their power is to teach [διδάσκειν], and that this is perfectly straightforward, that he who has knowledge of the names has also knowledge of the objects [ὃς ἂν τὰ ὀνόματα ἐπίστηται, ἐπίστασθαι καὶ τὰ πράγματα]. (435d1–6)

In substance, Socrates asks, and Cratylus in his answer explains, what the *function* of names is. (Do not confuse this use, at d2, of the term δύναμις as the 'power' of names with the distinct use of the same term at 394ac.) As I anticipated in §8.1.5, both question and answer pick up the thesis, which Cratylus accepted at 428e, that 'names are said for the sake of teaching'. That thesis in its turn echoed the first part of Socrates' early claim that names are tools for 'teaching something to each other and separating the objects as they stand' (388b). So far, however, the thesis had never been explicitly spelt out, and it had been left to us to gather from the dialogue's development in what sense a name (or a speaker in uttering a name) can be thought to 'teach' something. Now, at long last, Cratylus explains what he means (d4 καί is explanatory): if you have knowledge of a name, then you also have knowledge of the object named. That is to say: the etymology of names encapsulates the truth (or at least some relevant truth) about the nature of their referents; if you know what the etymology of a name is, you thereby know (some relevant truth about) the nature of its referent; and the function of a name is precisely to be such a receptacle of information about its referent.

Two comments are in order here. First, remember that, as we saw in §8.1.1, there is some reason to conjecture that the view that the function of names is to 'teach' was actually held by the historical Cratylus. Secondly,

[76] In an edition or translation we might consider indenting these words to signal the change of subject.

note that the present view of the function of names fits secondary names better than primary ones; for only secondary names seem to convey, by means of their etymology, genuine new information about their referent. If you etymologize the primary name γογγύλον you discover how the two o's it contains make it imitatively fit to name what is round (427c); but thereby you do not learn anything about the nature of what is round. By contrast, if you etymologize the secondary name ἄνθρωπος you discover that it derives from ἀναθρῶν ἃ ὄπωπεν, 'he who examines what he has seen' (399c), and thereby you do learn something new and important about the nature of the human being. This latter point is consistent with the former; for it is likely that Cratylus, like any other representative of the Greek etymological tradition before Plato, concerned himself only with secondary names, and that Plato's Socrates was the first to focus on primary names and argue that a naturalist account can and should be given of them (§6.4.2).

We can now check our interpretation of Cratylus' 435d4–6 answer against Socrates', which receives Cratylus' own approval:

SO. Perhaps, Cratylus, you're saying something like this, that whenever one knows what the name is like – and it is like the object – then one will also know the object [ἐπειδάν τις εἰδῇ τὸ ὄνομα οἷόν ἐστιν – ἔστι δὲ οἷόνπερ τὸ πρᾶγμα – εἴσεται δὴ καὶ τὸ πρᾶγμα], since it happens to be similar to the name, and there is one and the same art for all the items that are similar to each other. It is, I think, in this sense[77] that you're saying he who knows the names will also know the objects.
CR. What you say is perfectly true. (435d7–e5)

In quoting and interpreting Cratylus' words Socrates makes no less than four moves, among which the third and fourth are the relevant ones. (i) At d8–e1 he interprets the syntactical structure of Cratylus' claim, 'he who ... also ...', as 'whenever one ..., one also ...', which I take to be equivalent to 'if one ..., then one also ...' (ii) He replaces the verb ἐπίσταμαι with οἶδα; to mirror this replacement somehow, while at the same time conveying that it does not seem to have any philosophical significance, I have translated ἐπίσταμαι as 'have knowledge of' and οἶδα as 'know'.[78] (iii) At d8 he

---

[77] What does κατὰ τοῦτο (e3) mean exactly? Several interpreters take it as causal (cf. *Phdr.* 229d, Aesch. *Pr.* 226, and LSJ κατὰ IV), evidently taking it to refer to the argument just constructed by Socrates on Cratylus' behalf: e.g. 'hac ratione inductus' Ficino, 'on this ground' Fowler. Following Minio-Paluello and Méridier, instead, I understand the phrase more generically as 'in this sense', because e3–4 is meant to pick up also d7–e1, with κατὰ τοῦτο answering anaphorically the cataphoric τὸ τοιόνδε: 'Perhaps you're saying something *like this* ... It is, I think, in *this* sense that you're saying ...'

[78] For οἶδα replacing ἐπίσταμαι cf. e.g. *Tht.* 163b (and Lyons 1963: 177–9, along with the ensuing detailed analyses).

expands 'know the name' into, literally, 'know the name, *what it is like*', i.e. 'know *what the name is like*', which in turn clearly means 'know what the name's etymology is' (as distinct, perhaps, from knowing the name in the trivial sense of knowing, e.g., that someone's name is 'Callias'[79]). There is, apparently, no corresponding expansion of 'know the object' (ει) into 'know what the object is like'; but this may well be understood, and in any case it is what Socrates ultimately means.[80] (iv) He brings in the notion of the name's being similar to the object and a general principle according to which items similar to each other are the province of the same art.[81] Thus he hints at the following syllogism:

> Items similar to each other fall under the same art;
> Name and object are similar to each other;
> Therefore name and object fall under the same art

and he takes its conclusion to entail that, if one knows 'what the name is like', then one also knows the object – i.e. knows what the object is, or what it is like.

Socrates goes on to ask three further questions about Cratylus' view that the power of names is to teach:

SO. Now, let us see what on earth this way of teaching about the beings which you're now talking about could be, and whether there is also another way, but this is better, or there is none other than this at all. What do you think?
CR. I think the latter, that there is none other at all, and that this is both the only and the best [τοῦτον δὲ καὶ μόνον καὶ βέλτιστον].
SO. Do you also think that the method for making discoveries about the beings is this same one, and that as soon as one discovers about the names one has also discovered about those things which the names belong to; or do you think that one must search and discover in another way, but learn in this way?
CR. One must certainly search and discover likewise and in this same way. (435e6–436a8)

---

[79] Cf. *Ap.* 18cd, *Tht.* 144c, *Lg.* 964a.
[80] Cf. 422d: the correctness of names consists in their 'indicating *what* each of the beings is *like*' (δηλοῦν οἷον ἕκαστόν ἐστι τῶν ὄντων).
[81] Cf. Arist. *Rh.* 1355a14–15 'seeing the truth and what is similar to the truth belong to the same capacity' (the formulation is also reminiscent of the Aristotelian commonplace that 'there is one science of contraries'). The principle, if it is to make any sense at all, must actually mean that, if *X* and *Y* are similar with respect to *Z*, a property which they share, then they fall under the same craft or science with respect to *Z*, or *qua* bearers of *Z*. If a cloud resembles a camel in shape, both will be studied by the branch of geometry concerned with cameliform objects; but *qua* cloud and camel they remain objects of meteorology and zoology respectively.

The first question, 'what on earth this way of teaching about the beings[82] ... could be' (e6–7), is not addressed for the moment; nor is its purport particularly clear. Perhaps we should read it as an embryo of the objection which Socrates advances at 436ab: names encapsulate no more than the namegiver's beliefs about their referents, which may well be false. If so, then the question is, in the last analysis, equivalent to something like: 'How can names possibly teach us anything at all?'

With the second question (e7–9) Socrates asks whether names are only the *best* or also the *sole* source of knowledge available to us. Both alternatives are compatible with the view that the function of names is to teach (cf. *R.* 352e–353a: the function of each thing is what can be performed either only or best by it); Cratylus, unsurprisingly, espouses the latter (a1–2). So his 435d5–6 claim, 'he who has knowledge of the names has also knowledge of the objects', did not simply mean that, if you know a name's etymology, then you know its referent (i.e. you know what its referent is, or what it is like), as Socrates interpreted it at d8–e1. Cratylus is now accepting a stronger interpretation, according to which you know something (i.e. you know what it is, or what it is like) if *and only if* you know the etymology of its name.

With his third question (a3–6) Socrates fastens on Cratylus' d4–6 answer and interprets it, not as containing the claim that names teach (i.e. convey information about their referents) and that this is their function, but rather as containing the somewhat different claim that names are the *means* by which *someone* teaches someone else (cf. 388bc). That is to say, he construes the teaching at issue as effected not by names themselves but by speakers through names. This enables him to draw a contrast between, on the one hand, being taught and hence learning (from someone else) the etymology of names and the nature of things, and, on the other, discovering them after inquiring by oneself. The contrast of being taught and learning *vs* inquiring and discovering is a stock one.[83] Here it could

---

[82] 'Of teaching about the beings': τῆς διδασκαλίας τῶν ὄντων, literally 'of the teaching *of* the beings', as though the beings were what is taught. Likewise at a3 εὕρεσιν τῶν ὄντων literally means 'discovery *of* the beings', whereas the actual meaning is 'discovery *about* the beings'; and at a4–5 τὸν τὰ ὀνόματα εὑρόντα καὶ ἐκεῖνα ηὑρηκέναι κτλ. means 'as soon as one discovers [*about*] the names one has also discovered [*about*] those things etc.' The verbs εὑρίσκω, μανθάνω and ζητέω take this construction also at 438ab, e, 439ab; cf. the use of δοξάζω 'judge' at *Tht.* 190d and elsewhere (on which see Burnyeat 1990: 70 n.4).

[83] It is attested as early as Sophocles, *TrGF* 843: 'What can be taught I learn; what can be discovered I inquire into; what can be prayed for I begged of the gods' (τὰ μὲν διδακτὰ μανθάνω, τὰ δ' εὑρετὰ / ζητῶ, τὰ δ' εὐκτὰ παρὰ θεῶν ᾐτησάμην). Then we find it in Archytas, 47 B3 DK, and in a host of Platonic passages (e.g. *Phd.* 99cd, *Alc. I* 106de, *R.* 618c).

perhaps have the specific purpose to stress that, in Cratylus' view, the *only* way in which *anyone* can obtain knowledge of things is through the etymology of their names; perhaps also to start us thinking of the case, on which Socrates' objection at 437d–438b will focus, of someone who is the *first* to discover the nature of something and to baptize it accordingly. This latter guess accords with the fact that in advancing that objection Socrates will again make use of the contrast introduced here.

8.2.2 Names might express false beliefs (436a–437d)

Socrates is now ready to launch a devastating criticism of Cratylus' views on names and knowledge. He starts off by objecting that knowledge of the etymology of names does *not* yield knowledge of their referents, because names might encapsulate *false* beliefs about their referents:

SO. Come on, Cratylus, let's reflect. If one, inquiring into the objects, followed the guidance of their names, examining what each means [σκοπῶν οἷον ἕκαστον βούλεται εἶναι],[84] don't you reflect that there would be no small danger of being deceived [ἐξαπατηθῆναι]?
CR. How come?
SO. It is clear that, as we say, he who first imposed the names imposed them such as he believed the objects to be, didn't he?
CR. Yes.
SO. Hence, if his beliefs were incorrect, but he imposed the names in accordance with his beliefs, what do you think will happen to us who follow his guidance? Won't we be deceived? (436a9–b11)

Socrates' point is too neat to require any explanation; but there is room for a couple of comments. First, the claim that taking etymology as our guide in the inquiry into the nature of things we are in danger of being 'deceived' significantly picks up something Socrates said earlier and anticipates something he will say later on. At 397ab, near the outset of the etymologies, he observed that the proper names of heroes and human beings 'might perhaps *deceive* us' (ἴσως ἂν ἡμᾶς ἐξαπατήσειεν) and hence must be left out of the etymological enterprise. At 411bc, introducing those names whose etymology presupposes the flux theory, he presented this theory in a very unfavourable light by saying that the namegivers projected their own

---

[84] This phrase would be more literally translated 'what each means *to be like*', or even more literally 'what each *wants to be like*' (for this use of βούλομαι cf. §5.4), where 'be like' echoes 435d8–e1 and makes it clear that *etymological* meaning is here at stake.

internal state of dizziness on to the objects outside them. Then at 428d, at the beginning of his conversation with Cratylus, Socrates expressed cautious reservations about his own etymological prowess and warned against the danger of *self-deceit* (τὸ γὰρ ἐξαπατᾶσθαι αὐτὸν ὑφ' αὑτοῦ). The present claim that names might deceive us picks up those earlier passages; and it will be picked up in its turn by 439bc, where Socrates explicitly voices the suspicion – which he subsequently strengthens with arguments – that the flux theory is in fact wrong and that, therefore, the names which presuppose it may *deceive* (ἐξαπατᾷ) us. This web of intratextual connections can hardly be fortuitous: Plato has been warning us all along against the temptation to assume that the etymology of names conveys true information about their referents; and at the end of the day he will make Socrates positively argue that in a great many cases it does *not* do so.

Secondly, the problem for Cratylus is not just that the namegiver might have had false beliefs about the nature of the things on which he imposed names, but also that he might have had *true beliefs* about it and yet failed to have knowledge of it. If, e.g., the namegiver had simply hit, by sheer luck, on the nature of the things on which he was imposing names, then our etymological reconstruction of his views, however successful, could not give us *knowledge* of those things, and names would not 'teach' us anything about them. But, although Plato is perfectly aware (at least since *Men.* 97a–98a; and cf. *Tht.* 200d–201c) of the distinction between knowledge and true belief, Socrates does not make this point here; and in the sequel too there will be no clear distinction between the question of whether the namegiver knew the nature of the things named and the question of whether he was right about it.

Now for Cratylus' response to the objection:

> CR. But I think that it is not so, Socrates, and that necessarily he who imposed the names imposed them with knowledge [εἰδότα]; otherwise, as I was saying a while ago,[85] they wouldn't be names at all. Take this as the greatest evidence that the imposer did not miss the truth: otherwise his names would never be so universally concordant [σύμφωνα]. Or didn't you yourself reflect, while you were speaking,[86] that all names turned out to be made in the same way and to point in the same direction? (436b12–c6)

---

[85] ὅπερ πάλαι ἐγὼ ἔλεγον (c2): not 'as I've been saying all along' (e.g. Fowler, Reeve), which would require λέγω in place of ἔλεγον.
[86] λέγων (c5) is *participium imperfecti* (see KG 1.200), 'while you were speaking', referring back to 411ac ff.; the following ὡς πάντα κτλ. is governed by ἐνενόεις.

At first (c1–2) Cratylus simply asserts that names must have been imposed by someone who had knowledge of the things named, because otherwise they would be no names at all. That is to say, he invokes a general thesis like the following:

(K) If '*X*' is a name of *X*, then the maker of '*X*' knows *X*

(where 'knows *X*' means, as usual, 'knows the nature of *X*', i.e. 'knows what *X* is, or what it is like'). Thus Cratylus sees that, if names are to 'teach', i.e. to impart *knowledge* of their referents, it is necessary for them to have been imposed on the basis of such knowledge. At the same time, however, he seems to make a back-reference to 429bc, where he said that, if 'Hermogenes' does not contain a true description of Hermogenes, then it is not a name of Hermogenes at all; and that seems an instance of the following general thesis:

(T) If '*X*' is a name of *X*, then '*X*' contains a true description of *X*.

Now, while there is an innocuously loose sense in which (K) can be said to entail (T),[87] in no way can (T) be said to entail (K); the two theses are not equivalent and Cratylus' back-reference is imprecise. We can surmise that this imprecision is the symptom that he is not really clear about the difference between knowledge and true belief. This supposition is confirmed by the second part of Cratylus' response (c3–6), where he offers an argument as evidence, not that the namegiver had knowledge, but just that he 'did not miss the truth'!

The argument, which Cratylus regards as very powerful, is that names are all 'concordant' (σύμφωνα) with each other.[88] What does 'concordant' mean here? Fowler and Reeve translate the Greek adjective as 'consistent'; but Cratylus has something stronger than mere (logical) consistency in mind, as Sedley 2003: 125 and n.6 sees. Cratylus is more specifically referring to the fact that the views expressed in a great number of etymologies (though not really in *all*) agree or fit well with each other insofar as they naturally integrate with each other to form a single homogeneous philosophical theory, i.e. a particular variety of flux theory. Cf. 402c, where after detecting a reference to flux in the names of Rhea and Cronus, and quoting Homer and Orpheus on Ocean as the gods' ancestor, he commented

---

[87] Strictly speaking, to derive (T) from (K) you need – among other things – the extra premiss that the maker of '*X*' embodied in it his knowledge of *X*.

[88] αὐτῷ (c5) is an ethical dative and does not go with σύμφωνα: cf. ε1 (and *Phd.* 101d σοι) and contrast d1.

'Look how these things *are concordant with each other* [ἀλλήλοις συμφωνεῖ] and all point to Heraclitus' views.'[89]

Cratylus' 'greatest evidence' is a dud. But it gives Socrates the opportunity for a lesson in method:

SO. But this, my good Cratylus, is no defence. For if the imposer made a mistake in the first place and then forced the other steps to conform to this and compelled them to be concordant with himself [εἰ γὰρ τὸ πρῶτον σφαλεὶς ὁ τιθέμενος τἆλλα ἤδη πρὸς τοῦτ' ἐβιάζετο καὶ αὐτῷ συμφωνεῖν ἠνάγκαζεν], it wouldn't be absurd at all, as in mathematical propositions sometimes, once the first small and inconspicuous falsehood has occurred [ὥσπερ τῶν διαγραμμάτων ἐνίοτε τοῦ πρώτου σμικροῦ καὶ ἀδήλου ψεύδους γενομένου], the very numerous remaining steps follow in agreement with each other [τὰ λοιπὰ πάμπολλα ἤδη ὄντα ἑπόμενα ὁμολογεῖν ἀλλήλοις].[90] So it is about the starting point [περὶ τῆς ἀρχῆς] of every matter that every man must make his big discussion and his big inquiry, to see whether or not it has been correctly laid down [εἴτε ὀρθῶς εἴτε μὴ ὑπόκειται]; and when that has been adequately examined, the remaining steps must appear to follow from it [ἐκείνης δὲ ἐξετασθείσης ἱκανῶς, τὰ λοιπὰ φαίνεσθαι ἐκείνῃ ἑπόμενα]. (436c7–d8)

Concordance is no guarantee of truth: if the namegiver systematically embodied in all names the same mistaken theory (or different bits thereof), then the views expressed by the etymologies would just be concordantly mistaken.[91] Socrates illustrates this point with an example drawn from mathematics (d2–4), which requires careful scrutiny.

The basic question is: what does τῶν διαγραμμάτων (d2) mean? The term διάγραμμα here may mean either (a) 'mathematical diagram' (*Phd.*

---

[89] Does 'concordant' then mean something as strong as 'logically equivalent', i.e. mutually entailing? Granted, sometimes Plato seems to stretch the metaphor of 'concordance' or 'agreement' to cover what is actually a case of entailment (see *Grg.* 480b, 480e, and perhaps also *R.* 510d, 533c); but here this seems an unnecessary supposition, also because the views expressed by the flux etymologies do not all entail each other. Cf. the construal of Socrates' talk of 'concordance' at *Phd.* 100a, 101d advocated by Mueller 1992: 181–3 and Kahn 1996: 315–17.

[90] It may seem that the infinitive ὁμολογεῖν (d4) is governed by οὐδὲν ἄτοπον (d2), 'it wouldn't be absurd at all *that* … the remaining steps should follow', and that the comparison with mathematics is, strictly speaking, limited to ὥσπερ … γενομένου (d2–3). But τὰ λοιπὰ … ἀλλήλοις (d3–4) must clearly still be part of the ὥσπερ-clause: note especially the difference between d1 τἆλλα and d3, d7 τὰ λοιπά. The use of ὁμολογεῖν in place of ὁμολογεῖ may be a slight anacoluthon; or οὐδὲν ἄτοπον is again understood after ὥσπερ (so Stallbaum 211).

[91] The namegiver's original mistake (c8–d1) may just be his endorsement of a mistaken theory; if this is so, then τἆλλα is very generic – as I have tried to convey by translating it 'the other steps' – and refers to the subsequent imposition of names in accordance with the mistaken theory. Alternatively, the original mistake may be the embodiment of a mistaken theory in a primitive set of names; in this case τἆλλα means 'the other [*names*]', as it is usually translated. Cf. n.95 and text below for a parallel problem in the mathematical comparison.

73b) or (b) 'mathematical proposition' (*Tht.* 169a, Arist. *Cat.* 14a38–b1, *A. Pr.* 41b14, *Metaph.* 998a25–7, 1014a35–b2;[92] since a 'proposition' is comprehensive of a proof,[93] 'mathematical proof' may sometimes seem a more appropriate rendering). Meaning (b) derives from (a) by metonymy; for the propositions of Greek mathematics are regularly accompanied by diagrams, which indeed form an integral part of the propositions they illustrate.[94] Now if (a) is the meaning here, as most translators seem to assume, then the genitive τῶν διαγραμμάτων expresses belonging and Socrates is saying that the drawing of a geometrical figure may contain a small initial error such that the subsequent steps, i.e. the figure's remaining parts, though mutually consistent, are affected by it.[95] Here a difficulty arises. For this interpretation requires that ψεῦδος (d3) does not mean 'falsehood' but 'error'; and I doubt whether this is linguistically possible. So I opt for (b), following Vlastos 1966: 376 n.2 and Dalimier, 272–3 n.423. The genitive I still take to express belonging, and I understand Socrates' claim as follows: in a mathematical proof a false premiss, accepted because its falsity is 'small and inconspicuous' (i.e. depending on some sort of detail), may, in virtue of a valid deduction, give rise to many false but mutually consistent consequences.

Thereby Socrates is probably not thinking simply of a situation in which a mathematician inadvertently fouls up a demonstration. I submit that we should understand what he has in mind in the light of the following Aristotelian passage (*Top.* 101a5–17):

Further, besides all the aforesaid kinds of deduction there are the paralogisms that start from the premisses appropriate to particular sciences, as happens in the case of geometry and of the sciences akin to it. For this type of reasoning seems to differ from the aforesaid deductions: for the proponent of the false proof does not deduce from true and primary premisses, nor from reputable ones ... but he effects his deduction from assumptions which are appropriate to the science in question, on the one hand, and not true, on the other. For he effects his paralogism either by describing the semicircles as he should not or by drawing certain lines as they cannot be drawn.

---

[92] See also Ascl. *in Metaph.* 174.9–10 'διαγράμματα, i.e. theorems in geometry', and Papp. *Collectio* 7.670.2, 672.16, 682.22 'theorems or διαγράμματα'.

[93] In studies of Greek mathematics it is customary to use the term 'proposition' to refer to the sum of an enunciation and the following proof, as I am doing.

[94] The close connection between (a) and (b) is particularly evident in Arist. *Cael.* 279b32–280a11. See Netz 1999: 19–43 on the mutual dependence of text and diagram in Greek mathematics and on the term διάγραμμα.

[95] Some adherents of (a), e.g. Stallbaum and Méridier, take the genitive τῶν διαγραμμάτων as partitive, 'among diagrams', and then understand τὰ λοιπά (d3) as 'the remaining [diagrams]'. This is hardly plausible; see below for an analogous possibility within (b).

Here, and in other related texts,[96] Aristotle shows himself familiar with a kind of deceitful reasoning that works by assuming *false* geometrical premisses in order to deduce the desired conclusion (e.g. a conclusion contradicting an established truth of geometry). Of course these false premisses must have a specious appearance of truth if they are to be accepted: the falsehood must be 'small and inconspicuous', as Socrates says; and this specious appearance can be provided by incorrectly drawn diagrams. In the final sentence of the quotation Aristotle seems to hint at two examples of such reasonings; and Alexander of Aphrodisias, *in Top.* 23.25–25.9, actually reports two arguments which purport to refute the theorem that 'in any triangle two sides taken together in any manner are greater than the remaining one' (Euc. 1.20, trans. Heath 1926) by constructing an (actually impossible) triangle where one side is equal to, or even greater than, the sum of the other two.[97]

Now the fact that Socrates speaks of 'very numerous' (d4) concordant consequences that follow from the 'first falsehood' may seem not to sit well with this picture: surely a single paralogism has only *one* conclusion? This might invite us to suppose that Socrates has in mind something more complex than a single paralogism, i.e. is viewing the 'first falsehood' as generating a whole *system* of false propositions. We might then imagine a situation where the proponent of a false proof like those mentioned by Aristotle and reported by Alexander is not content with deducing the conclusion, but goes on to build upon it further proofs without falling into selfcontradiction.[98]

This interpretation, however, would probably be incorrect. For it would require that we reconsider both the genitive τῶν διαγραμμάτων, construing it as partitive, '*among* propositions', and the phrase τὰ λοιπά, construing it as 'the remaining [*propositions*]'.[99] But the fact that τὰ λοιπά reoccurs at d7 as a self-standing expression meaning 'the remaining *steps*' of the proposition (cf. also *R.* 510d, on which see below) strongly suggests that

---

[96] *Top.* 132a32–3, 157a1–3, 160b33–7; *SE* 171b34–172a7 (collected by Heath 1949: 76–8); cf. *APo.* 77b19–21.
[97] Suchlike arguments were probably discussed in Euclid's no longer extant *Pseudaria*, which might even be the source of Alexander's very examples: see Acerbi 2008. (NB: In Acerbi's article the translations of *Cra.* 436c7–d8 and Arist. *Top.* 101a5–17, as well as the very idea of a connection between the two passages, are taken from a partial draft of the present chapter which Acerbi read in March 2005.)
[98] It may then be natural for a modern reader to think of the development of non-Euclidean geometries from the rejection of Postulate 5. But Socrates' 'first falsehood' need not be anything as fundamental as a postulate.
[99] Cf. Dalimier's translation: 'comme dans une suite de démonstrations géométriques, malgré une erreur initiale ..., toutes les démonstrations qui suivent s'accordent etc.'

this is its meaning here already at d3, and that hence τῶν διαγραμμάτων is not partitive but expresses belonging, as I have been assuming so far. As for Socrates' reference to the consequences being 'very numerous', it is not necessary to suppose that he is thinking of a system of propositions. It is sufficient to consider that a mathematical proposition like those in the *Elements* usually contains several intermediate conclusions which precede the conclusion proper (the συμπέρασμα) and are needed to establish it. Just by way of example, *Elem.* 1.47 (Pythagoras' Theorem) contains no less than ten conclusions including the συμπέρασμα; the first of Alexander's two examples has four.[100] Therefore Socrates may be just speaking of a plurality of conclusions *internal* to a proposition.

At 436d4–8 Socrates draws from his comparison with mathematics a general, positive conclusion about what a methodical procedure should consist in. Although these lines do not contain the term ὑπόθεσις, they must be read alongside other passages (*Men.* 86e–87c; *Phd.* 100a, 101de, 107b; *R.* 510b–511d, 533be) where Plato discusses the role of 'hypotheses' in philosophy.[101] This is made clear by Socrates' use of the term ἀρχή ('starting-point', d5), which designates a hypothesis at *Phd.* 101e, *R.* 511bc, 533c, together with the verb ὑπόκειται ('has been laid down', d6–7), which does duty for the passive of ὑποτίθεμαι 'hypothesize, lay down as a hypothesis'. Note also the expression τὰ λοιπά ('the remaining steps', d3, 7), which here as at *R.* 510d refers to the consequences drawn from the hypothesis.[102]

Thus Socrates' recipe goes as follows: (i) first investigate whether the starting point of your reasoning, the hypothesis on which it ultimately depends, is 'correct', i.e. true; (ii) then make sure that the consequences you deduce from the hypothesis do follow therefrom, i.e. are validly deduced.[103] (NB: He says nothing about the truth of the consequences: he is clearly aware that whatever is validly deduced from true premisses is

---

[100] See Netz 1999: 198–216 on the structure of Greek mathematical proofs.
[101] Although some of his claims have been challenged by subsequent scholars, Robinson 1953: 93–179 remains unrivalled as an overall account of Plato's views on hypotheses.
[102] *R.* 510d1–3 is worth quoting in full: the mathematicians, 'starting from these [= the hypotheses], go through the remaining steps until at the end they consistently reach that for the investigation of which they set out'. In the Greek 'starting' is ἀρχόμενοι: a further parallel for ἀρχή as a hypothesis in our passage.
[103] Some interpreters (Fowler, Rose 1964: 115, Reeve) take Socrates to be saying that, once the hypothesis has been adequately examined, 'the remaining steps *will* appear to follow from it'. As Rose explains, this means that the consequences 'can be drawn out without much difficulty ... it is always perfectly obvious what follows from a hypothesis'. But the infinitive φαίνεσθαι (d7–8) is still governed by δεῖ (d4): 'the remaining steps *must* appear to follow from it'. Socrates does not say that the deduction of the consequences is trifling (and it is just as well he does not say so); he only says that it must take place after the assessment of the hypothesis.

itself true.) It may be tempting to read this as a prescription about how to *carry out* a fresh philosophical reasoning; but what it is primarily meant to be is a recipe for the *assessment* of an already finished reasoning, because what Socrates is presently engaged in is the assessment of the namegiver's work.

Socrates does not say how, exactly, stage (i) ought to be pursued, i.e. how the hypothesis should be examined. In particular, he does not say that we should see whether it can be positively supported by recourse to another 'higher' hypothesis which there are independent reasons to assume, as at *Phd.* 101d; still less does he refer to the more ambitious version of this procedure outlined in *R.* 510b–511d, 533be, where he says that dialectic reasons 'upwards' from the mathematical hypotheses to an 'unhypothetical starting point' and then again 'downwards' from this, demonstrating the hypotheses and their consequences. But we can suppose at least that the examination would involve seeing whether the hypothesis, or some of its consequences, conflicts with other hypotheses you assume, or with some of their consequences. For Socrates will employ this procedure – which is standardly used in the dialogues to test a thesis – to reject the flux theory later on (439b–440c), when he shows that it is incompatible with the existence and knowability of forms; and here he is viewing the flux theory precisely as the hypothesis on which names were imposed by the namegivers. In any event, note that, if the examination of the hypothesis involves deduction of consequences from it, this deduction is not meant to be exhaustive; otherwise stage (ii) could not be distinct from (i).

Thus far Socrates has explained to Cratylus that, if names (i.e. their etymologies) are 'concordant' with each other, i.e. concordantly presuppose the theory of flux, this is no evidence that the theory is true. Now he goes on to make a further point: in fact names are *not* concordant with each other. To do so he produces a short new series of etymologies which appear to presuppose the contrary doctrine that things are not in flux but are stable. It goes without saying that the names in question are all secondary ones: primary names have no place in this discussion.

(so.) And yet I would be surprised if names are really concordant with each other. For let us re-examine the things we went through before. We say that names signify being for us [σημαίνειν ἡμῖν τὴν οὐσίαν] on the assumption that everything moves and is carried about and flows [ὡς τοῦ παντὸς ἰόντος τε καὶ φερομένου καὶ ῥέοντός].[104] Don't they seem to you to indicate so?

---

[104] 'Names signify being' (436e3–4) may mean either (a) 'names signify the being [*of their referents*]' (οὐσία used as at 388c, 393d, 423e), as Ficino, Minio-Paluello and Reeve believe, or (b) 'names

Names and knowledge (435d–439b)

CR. Absolutely, and they signify correctly.
SO. Then let us see, taking up among them this name first, ἐπιστήμη ['knowledge']: it is ambiguous and seems to signify that it arrests [ἵστησι] our soul at the objects rather than that it is carried about together with them, and it is more correct to pronounce its beginning as we do now than as ἐπιστήμην, inserting the h, and to make the insertion on the ι instead of that on the ε.[105] Again, βέβαιον ['certain'][106] is an imitation of some sort of basis [βάσις] and rest, not of movement. Again, ἱστορία ['information'] signifies by itself, I think, that it stops the flow [ἵστησι τὸν ῥοῦν];[107] and πιστόν ['convincing'] definitely signifies 'arresting' [ἱστάν]. Again, μνήμη ['memory'] expresses to anyone, I think, that it is permanence [μονή] in the soul, not movement. On the other hand, if you like, ἁμαρτία ['error'] and συμφορά ['misfortune'], if one will pursue them according to their name, will appear to be the same as this σύνεσις ['understanding'] and ἐπιστήμη ['knowledge'] and to all the other names for things good.[108] Further, ἀμαθία ['ignorance'] and

---

signify *the beings*' (οὐσία as a collective noun = τὰ ὄντα: cf. ch. 3 n.34), as Méridier and Dalimier's 'la realité' apparently implies. Some support for (b) comes from 437c5–8, where Socrates eventually concludes that 'he who imposed the names did not *signify the objects as* moving or being carried along'.

[105] The MS text of a7 is ἐμβάλλοντας τὸ εἶ ἐπιστήμην, which cannot stand. Schmidt's conjecture ἐμβάλλοντας τὸ ⊢ hεπιστήμην (a7, cf. 412a4), printed in the OCT, is far superior to the unsatisfactory attempts accepted by the other editors and translators (some of whom falsely believe that at a6 B reads ἐκβάλλοντας). It cannot, however, represent exactly what Plato wrote. For as a sign for aspiration Attic script did not use ⊢ (the ancestor of our '), which 'is attested mainly on south Italian vases, after the fifth century ... its place of origin may have been Taras ..., for most of the early examples are from that area' (*LSAG* 29). The sign used in Attica was H, and when in the course of the fifth century, with the introduction of the Eastern Ionic alphabet (see §5.5.3 n.142), it came to indicate long open *e*, the Athenians did not substitute another sign, but simply stopped marking the initial aspiration – except in some fixed contexts, i.e. in the words ὅρος and, less frequently, ἱερόν on boundary stones up to the mid fourth century BC (Threatte I.24–5). In such contexts H = h could be used even in compresence with H = η: a stone of the late fifth century BC reads ΗΟΡΟΣ ΗΙΕΡΟ ΝΥΜΦΗΣ = hόρος hιερō [i.e. ὅρος ἱεροῦ] Νύμφης (*SEG* XVII.10, cf. Guarducci IV.58; in other regions of Greece it was normal to use the same sign for h and η, see *LSAG* 28, 289, 294, 345). Another use in which H = h survived was as the sign for ἑκατόν, '100', in acrophonic numeral notation. So I surmise that, in a context where it was necessary to write a sign for aspiration, even in the absence of a fixed formula, Plato would have defied ambiguity and written H for h. That is to say, he wrote ΕΜΒΑΛΛΟΝΤΑΣ ΤΟ Η ΗΕΠΙΣΤΗΜΗ, which *we* should print as ἐμβάλλοντας τὸ h ἐπιστήμην. The form which Socrates is thinking of as the correct one, with the aspiration inserted 'on the ι' (a7–8), is manifestly ἑπιστήμην, from ἵστημι.

[106] βέβαιον here is usually translated as 'stable'; but the context rather requires the epistemic meaning 'certain', as Reeve sees (cf. Hdt. 7.50.2).

[107] 'Signifies by itself ... that ...' (b1) is Méridier's and Dalimier's construal of the Greek αὐτό που σημαίνει ὅτι κτλ. (for the neuter αὐτό in connection with the feminine ἱστορία cf. *Prt.* 360e, *R.* 363a, 612b, *Tht.* 146e). Socrates' point is that ἱστορία *completely* encapsulates the phrase ἵστησι τὸν ῥοῦν: contrast e.g. ἐπιστήμη, which is explained as ἵστησιν ἡμῶν ἐπὶ τοῖς πράγμασι τὴν ψυχήν but in fact seems to contain only the word ἵστησιν. Others instead take αὐτό as the object of σημαίνει: 'signifies this very thing, that ...'

[108] Socrates is deriving ἁμαρτία from ὁμαρτέω 'to accompany' and συμφορά from συμφέρομαι 'to be carried together' (cf. the etymology of συμφέρον 'advantageous' at 417a). The former derivation is made easier by the existence of ἁμαρτέω (Bacch. 18.46 etc.), an alternative form of

ἀκολασία ['intemperance'] appear to be close to these: for the former, i.e. ἀμαθία, appears to be the progress of the one who goes together with God [ἅμα θεῷ ἰόντος], while ἀκολασία definitely appears to be a following of the objects [ἀκολουθία τοῖς πράγμασι]. And so those names which we take to belong to the worst things could appear to be very similar to those belonging to the finest ones. But I believe that one could find many others, if one took the trouble, on whose basis one could form the opposite belief that he who imposed the names did not signify the objects as moving or being carried about but as being at rest. (436d8–437c8)

These names all belong to the ethical and epistemological sphere and hence should have been included among those 'concerning virtue', etymologized at 411a–420e. Most of them, however, were *not* considered there, with the explicit exception of ἐπιστήμη, of which Socrates here offers an etymology alternative and allegedly superior to the one given at 412a, which derived the name from ἕπομαι 'follow' (sc. the things in flux).[109] This means that Socrates is not recanting his earlier etymologies: as Sedley (2003: 159–61) points out, 'the contradiction which Socrates claims to have revealed is not an exegetical but a *philosophical* one'. This also has some bearing on the text's interpretation: πάλιν ... ἐπισκεψώμεθα ἃ τὸ πρότερον διήλθομεν (e1–2) should mean 'let us re-examine the *things* [i.e. the subject matters, ethical and epistemological] we went through before', not 'let us re-examine the *names* etc.'; ἐξ αὐτῶν (a2) should be equivalent to 'among names' in general (τὰ ὀνόματα e4), not 'among those names we went through before'; and ἀναλαβόντες (a2) should mean just 'taking up' for consideration, as at *Men.* 87e, not 'taking up *again*', as it is often translated.

Socrates here employs the same kind of analysis as in the previous 'virtue' section – only he obtains results *specular* to the previous ones: now the etymologies of names which have a positive connotation ('knowledge', 'information' etc.) somehow involve the notion of rest, whereas the etymologies of names whose connotation is negative ('error', 'ignorance' etc.) involve the notion of movement. For example (as Socrates says, rather obscurely, at b5–7), if earlier such positive names as ἐπιστήμη 'knowledge' and σύνεσις 'understanding' were derived from expressions which connoted the soul's 'following' or 'going together with' the objects in movement, now the same sort of analysis applies to negative names like

---

ὁμαρτέω, and of the adverb ἁμαρτή, 'together' (*Il.* 5.656 etc.). Both etymologies remind him of those of ἐπιστήμη and σύνεσις offered at 412a.

[109] Another, not explicitly acknowledged, exception might consist in the fact that at 420d Socrates seemed to hint at a connection between ἀμαθία 'ignorance' and ἁμαρτία 'error' (see §5.3.3), whereas here at b4–c1 he etymologizes both independently of each other.

ἁμαρτία 'error' and συμφορά 'misfortune'. Thus Socrates can claim that all the names of the new series presuppose the view that – contrary to the flux theory – reality is stable and unchanging (sc. at least in some important respects).

At this point Cratylus makes an attempt – which Socrates immediately blocks – to get out of trouble by invoking the fact that the names whose etymology presupposes the flux theory were much more than the rival ones:

CR. But, Socrates, you see that most names had the former sort of signification.
SO. So what, Cratylus? Shall we count names like votes, and will their correctness depend on this? The true views will be those which the greater number of names turn out to signify?[110]
CR. That is not reasonable.
SO. Not in the least, my friend. (437d1–8)

Socrates' riposte is a variant of his typical contention that in a philosophical dispute it is immaterial how many people support one or other of the rival views: see e.g. *La.* 184ce, *Grg.* 471e–472c.

8.2.3 Names and the namegiver's knowledge (437d–438d)

Next Socrates advances an argument showing that Cratylus' two theses, that knowledge can only be obtained from names and that the namegiver had knowledge, are incompatible with each other. The argument (which runs from 437d8 to 438b8)[111] is plain and straightforward; but it poses a major textual difficulty because it is transmitted by the MSS in two alternative versions. Trying to make things easier for the reader, here I will, without further ado, translate and comment on the text which the OCT editors print as 'Versio B' of the passage, reserving a thorough discussion of the textual issue for Appendix 1.

(SO.) And let us leave these things alone and go back to the point where we started this digression. A while ago in our previous discussion, if you remember, you said that he who imposed the names necessarily imposed them with knowledge of the things on which he was imposing them [εἰδότα τίθεσθαι οἷς ἐτίθετο]. Do you still believe so or not?
CR. I still do.

---

[110] At d5 ταῦτα picks up ὁπότερα, which is the *object* of σημαίνοντα. Hence ταῦτα does not refer to *names* (as several interpreters assume), but rather to the contents they signify.
[111] NB: For reasons to be explained in Appendix 1, at 438b4–c10 I use Burnet's line numbers, not the OCT's.

SO. Do you also say that he who imposed the first names imposed them with knowledge? ["Η καὶ τὸν τὰ πρῶτα τιθέμενον εἰδότα φῂς τίθεσθαι;]
CR. Yes, with knowledge.
SO. Then from what sort of names had he learnt or discovered about the objects, if the first ones had not yet been set down, and on the other hand we say it is impossible to learn and discover about the objects other than by learning or discovering by ourselves what their names are like? (437d8–438b3)

Here Socrates explicitly picks up Cratylus' 436c claim, which he quotes almost literally, that 'necessarily he who imposed the names imposed them with knowledge'; and once Cratylus has confirmed that he still endorses that earlier claim, Socrates goes on to ask him whether, in particular, the giver of the 'first' (i.e. most ancient) names gave them with knowledge. Again Cratylus answers in the affirmative (d8–a10). Then (a11–b4) Socrates apparently draws his conclusion, in the form of a rhetorical question: if (as Cratylus maintained at 435e–436a) one can acquire knowledge about something *only* by coming to know the etymology of its name (Socrates actually picks up the learning/discovering distinction employed in the earlier passage), then from what names did he who imposed the very first names acquire knowledge of their referents?

Here is Cratylus' response:

CR. In my view, Socrates, the truest account of these matters is that it was some more than human power [μείζω τινὰ δύναμιν εἶναι ἢ ἀνθρωπείαν] that imposed the first names on the objects, so that they are necessarily correct. (438c1–4)

Earlier at 397c, near the beginning of the etymologies, Socrates voiced the suspicion that some names 'were imposed by a force *more divine* than the human one'. At 425d, however, he warned Cratylus not to find shelter from discussion in any such *deus ex machina* as the thesis that the first names were imposed by the gods and therefore are correct. Thus Cratylus is now doing precisely what Socrates advised him not to do. According to some scholars, this is because he has been holding from the start that there is a 'Créateur divin des noms' (Goldschmidt 1940: 159–60).[112] But it seems unlikely that Cratylus should state this thesis only now, at this late stage of the discussion, if it had been part of his original stock of views. More probably, he is feeling cornered by Socrates' arguments and is trying to cop out; and thus, ironically, he realizes a possibility that Socrates had already criticized in advance.

---

[112] Cf. Rijlaarsdam 1978: 3, 20, 33–4, 104 etc.

An interesting point to be made is that the phrase 'the first names', both here at c3 and in Socrates' question at a8 (or 437e6 in what the OCT editors call 'Versio A' of the passage), must refer to the *chronologically* first names (i.e. the earliest ones), as at 421d, whereas it seemed to refer to the *logically* first names (i.e. the primary or elementary ones) at 422cd, 425b–426b (including the parallel passage 425d, quoted above), 431c, 433d, 434a. In §6.1.1, reflecting upon the relation between these two meanings, we considered the possibility that Socrates might be assuming that most (if not all) of the earliest names were elementary names and vice versa, and hence that the phrase's two meanings might be broadly (if not completely) equivalent in extension. But now Socrates' ensuing reply to Cratylus seems to reveal that he does *not* make that assumption.

SO. Then you think that the imposer would have contradicted himself in imposing them, though he was a daimon or a god? Or did we seem to you just now to be talking nonsense?
CR. But I suspect that those which made up one of the two groups were not really names.
SO. Which of the two, my excellent friend: those which pointed to rest or those which pointed to movement? As we said just now, this matter won't be decided by majority, I think.
CR. That wouldn't be right, Socrates. (438c5–d1)

The contradiction evoked at c5–6 is of course that, discovered at 436d–437c, between the names whose etymon presupposes the flux theory and those whose etymon presupposes the rival rest theory (let us call them 'flux-names' and 'rest-names' respectively). Cratylus, however, despite what Socrates says, is not committing himself to the view that the superhuman giver of the first (i.e. earliest) names contradicted himself in this sense; for he is not committed to the view that the first (i.e. earliest) names included both some flux-names and some rest-names. Therefore Socrates' criticism is unfair. Apart from this, note that neither flux-names nor rest-names include any *logically* first (i.e. elementary) names. This suggests that, for Socrates, logically first names do not substantially coincide with chronologically first names, i.e. with the names of which he is (unfairly) assuming that they included both some flux-names and some rest-names.

At c7 Cratylus, instead of pointing out the weakness of Socrates' objection, takes shelter in his old thesis that a name whose etymon misdescribes something is no name of that thing – and pro tanto is no name at all (cf. 429bc, 436bc). We might expect Socrates to retort that this thesis has already been refuted by the argument (434b–435d) which established that convention plays a part in the correctness of names. But the present discussion of Cratylus' claim that names have the power to 'teach' has been introduced at 435d as a fresh start and has hitherto been wholly independent of the previous discussion. So here too Socrates takes a different route (c8–10). Assuming for the sake of argument that Cratylus is right, he remarks that it is not evident whether the fake names are the rest-names or the flux-names; nor can this be decided on a purely numerical basis, as was said at 437d.

8.2.4 Knowledge 'without names' (438d–439b)

Thus the conversation has returned to the topic of the conflict between rest-names and flux-names. Indeed, the reason why at c5–6 Socrates unfairly charged that Cratylus made the superhuman namegiver contradict himself is precisely (I suspect) that Plato wanted him to revert to this point, which is going to prove decisive.

> SO. Then, if names are in conflict, and some of them claim that they are those similar to the truth [τὰ ὅμοια τῇ ἀληθείᾳ], whereas others claim that *they* are such, on what further basis shall we decide, or turning to what? We cannot turn to other names different from these, because there are none. Rather, we must evidently search for some items other than names, which will reveal to us without names which of these claims are the true ones, evidently by showing the truth about the beings [ἃ ἡμῖν ἐμφανιεῖ ἄνευ ὀνομάτων ὁπότερα τούτων ἐστὶ τἀληθῆ, δείξαντα δῆλον ὅτι τὴν ἀλήθειαν τῶν ὄντων].[113]
>
> CR. It seems so.
>
> SO. Therefore, Cratylus, it is possible, as it seems, to learn about the beings without names, if these things are so.
>
> CR. So it seems. (438d2–e4)

Since both the rest-names and the flux-names irreconcilably claim to be 'similar to the truth', i.e. to convey the true ontological theory, we must find a method to assess their claims and determine which of the two rival

---

[113] Two notes on d6–7. First, ὁπότερα τούτων is usually understood as 'which of these two groups of names'. This is certainly possible; but remember that at 437d, in a verbally very similar sentence, ὁπότερα referred to the *contents* expressed by the two groups of names (see n.110). Hence my translation. Secondly, among those who take ὁπότερα to refer to names, some also construe δείξαντα ... ὄντων as a gloss on τἀληθῆ: e.g. Reeve 'the true ones – that is to say, the ones that express the truth about the things that are'. Although this construal is imprecise (for the text says δείξαντα, not τὰ δείξαντα, and δῆλον ὅτι means 'evidently', not 'that is to say'), its proponents could reformulate it by linking δείξαντα with ὁπότερα. But in any case the gloss would be quite superfluous. The repetition of δῆλον ὅτι from d5 and Socrates' following inference (e2–3) prove that δείξαντα rather goes with ἃ and explains *how* the 'items other than names' will 'reveal to us without names etc.'

theories is the true one. This method will evidently (δῆλον ὅτι d5, 7–8) have two features: it will involve no recourse to names and will give us access to the ontological truth. Therefore it must be possible, *contra* Cratylus, to acquire knowledge of the beings independently of names.

The phrase 'similar to the truth' (d3)[114] is interesting, because it constitutes (along with 426cd and 439ab) one of Socrates' few attempts to present secondary names as imitating or resembling their referents, and thus to assimilate them to primary names. These attempts are hardly convincing; for Socrates never explains in what sense a description can count as an imitation of what it describes.

When Socrates says it is possible to 'learn about the beings without names' he is not speaking of a sort of intuitive knowledge reached without recourse to discursive thought (διάνοια, defined as the soul's silent conversation with itself at *Tht.* 189e–190a, *Sph.* 263e) and not expressible in words. All he needs to say here, and all he does say, is that the investigation of reality is independent of the (etymological) *investigation* of names – not of their *use*.[115]

So the route to knowledge of reality is not the indirect one of looking at names first. More generally, no indirect route will do. Reality must be investigated directly:

SO. Then through what else do you expect that you could learn about them?[116] Do you expect that you could do so through anything else than that through which it is reasonable and most legitimate to do so, i.e. through each other, if they are akin in some respect, and through themselves [δι' ἀλλήλων γε, εἴ πῃ συγγενῆ ἐστιν, καὶ αὐτὰ δι' αὑτῶν]? For, I think, what is other and different from them would signify something other and different but not them.
CR. What you say appears to me to be true. (438e5–10)

What is the difference between acquiring knowledge of the beings 'through each other, if they are akin in some respect' and 'through themselves'? For a start, I take it that you learn about X 'through' Y if you infer that X is Z on the grounds that Y is Z and that X is similar to Y in some relevant respect. This case must be prominent in Socrates' mind. For similarity is precisely the relation which, according to Cratylus, obtains between names and their referents; therefore Socrates is probably contrasting the

---

[114] Or 'in accordance with the truth'. For ὅμοιος + dat. = 'in accordance with' see *R.* 549e, Ar. *Th.* 167.
[115] *Pace* Silverman 2001: 25–6. In rejecting his view I am siding with Sedley 2003: 162.
[116] At e5 I read αὐτά (W) instead of ταῦτα (βTQ, adopted by Burnet and the OCT).

illegitimate name-to-object similarity inference with the legitimate object-to-object similarity inference. But different sorts of cases, and of 'kinship' between X and Y, would no doubt also fit the bill: e.g. cases where X and Y are relative or even contrary to each other. Generally speaking, I take it that by 'kinship' Socrates here means any relation, logical or other, which allows you to derive truths about X from truths about Y. Cf. *Men.* 81cd: 'Since *all nature is akin* [τῆς φύσεως ἁπάσης συγγενοῦς οὔσης], and soul has learned everything, nothing prevents one, once he has recollected just one thing ..., from rediscovering all the others by himself, if he is brave and does not weary of searching.' By contrast, I suppose that you 'learn about' X 'through itself' when you derive truths about X from other truths about X – or perhaps also, by induction, from truths about *instances* of X, if there are any.

At e8–9 Socrates explains why it is impossible to acquire knowledge of reality other than by means of a direct inquiry. To understand what he says we must apparently suppose that 'signify' here does not have its usual meaning but is rather equivalent to something like 'make one learn about', hence 'provide knowledge of'. Then Socrates' explanation goes as follows: an area of inquiry completely distinct from reality (i.e. from the extralinguistic and extramental reality) cannot provide us with knowledge of reality, but only of something completely distinct. In the case at hand, names only provide us with knowledge of the namegivers' opinions.

Next comes a fresh argument:

SO. Stop, by Zeus: didn't we often agree that the names that have been finely set down are like those things of which they have been set down as names, and are images of the objects [τὰ ὀνόματα ... τὰ καλῶς κείμενα ἐοικότα εἶναι ἐκείνοις ὧν ὀνόματα κεῖται, καὶ εἶναι εἰκόνας τῶν πραγμάτων;]?
CR. Yes.
SO. Then, even if it were possible [Εἰ ... ἔστι ... ὅτι μάλιστα] to learn about the objects through names, while on the other hand it is also possible through themselves, which way of learning would be finer and more exact? To learn from the image both about itself, whether it has been finely made as an image, and about the truth it is an image of, or rather to learn from the truth both about the truth itself and about its image, whether it has been produced properly?
CR. Necessarily to learn from the truth, I think. (439a1–b3)

At a1–4 Socrates states the premiss that, if a name has been 'finely' set down, then it is 'like' its referent and is an 'image' thereof. On this ground at a6–b2 he shows that Cratylus is refuted even if we, for the sake of argument, assume something weaker than the conclusion we have just reached.

More precisely, *even if* (a6 εἰ ... ὅτι μάλιστα, where ὅτι μάλιστα is usually mistranslated as 'inprimis', 'really', 'au mieux' etc.: cf. 435a10 with n.36 above) it were possible to learn about the objects through their names, in any case it would be obviously better to learn about them 'through themselves' (this formulation here covers also the case of learning about the objects 'through each other', distinguished at 438e from learning about them 'through themselves' in a narrower sense). But the a1–4 premiss would license a stronger conclusion. The alternative which Socrates here seems to present as inferior is in fact altogether impossible; for you cannot assess the accuracy of an image solely on the basis of the image itself, without relying on any prior knowledge of the thing it is an image of.[117]

Let us say something more about the premiss itself. Socrates says it has been 'often' agreed upon; thereby he must be referring to 431ce, 432de, 433ac, 435cd. But those passages were concerned with *primary* names, whereas now we are speaking first and foremost of *secondary* names. Once again, Socrates is extending to secondary names notions (fineness, similarity, being an image) which were originally introduced to account for primary ones, without explaining how this extension can be justified.

To make the extension possible, Socrates has to make at least some adjustments. The aforementioned passages focused on the issue of the sounds/letters which make up primary names; there Socrates held that a name 'finely set down' contains all and only the letters that are similar to its referent, and that any name which falls short of this standard, even if it consists for the most part of similar letters, has been set down not finely, i.e. 'badly'. Here, instead, Socrates says nothing about the name's letters; and this is just as well, given that letters are not directly relevant to secondary names.

Socrates can finally state his conclusions about names and knowledge:

SO. Well, to know in what way one must learn or discover about the beings is perhaps something that exceeds my capacities and yours; but we should be content to agree upon this limited point: that one must learn and search about them not from names but from themselves rather than from their names.
CR. So it seems, Socrates. (439b4–9)

---

[117] As Barney 2001: 146 remarks, 'In the *Phaedo*, this is the essence of Socrates' argument for recollection: since we *do* judge sensible particulars, and find them wanting, in relation to the Forms, we must already be independently acquainted with the originals (73e–5e).' For the point that the assessment of an imitation presupposes knowledge of the thing imitated she also cites *Lg.* 667b–669b.

'In what way' ("Ὄντινα ... τρόπον b4) is a back-reference to 435e–436a, where Cratylus contended that the best and only way (τρόπος) of teaching, searching and discovering about the objects is through the etymology of their names. That contention has now been eventually disposed of.

Apart from these lines, there are at least two other passages in *Cra.* where Socrates declares himself unable to solve a major philosophical problem: 429d (the paradox of false speaking) and 440cd (the conflict between the theory of forms and the flux theory). It is always difficult to decide whether such disclaimers are merely subservient to the dialogue's economy (Socrates cannot embark on a detailed discussion of every subject he touches upon) or they constitute a genuine admission of perplexity on Plato's part. At all events, note that, while in both of the other cases Socrates does take at least some steps towards a solution to the problem at hand, here he seems to give absolutely no indication. In this case it is rather, I submit, the whole dialogue that conveys (though it does not expressly state) several scattered suggestions about how we could achieve knowledge of reality: e.g. that knowledge has something to do with the question-and-answer method of inquiry (390c) and with the method of division (424b–425b); or that knowledge of a complex presupposes knowledge of its elements (426ab, see §6.4.1).

CHAPTER 9

Flux and forms (439b–440e)

Now, less than two Stephanus pages from the end, comes a turning point: Socrates turns to an explicit – if still provisional – assessment of the flux theory. His arguments, and the final parting of the ways between him and Cratylus, are the subjects of this final chapter.

9.1 THE ARGUMENTS (439B–440D)

9.1.1 *The lawgivers in a whirl (439bc)*

SO. Again, let us investigate this further point, in order that these many names which point in the same direction do not deceive [ἐξαπατᾷ] us, if those that imposed them did impose them believing that all things are always moving and flowing – for it does seem to me that they too had this belief [φαίνονται γάρ ἔμοιγε καὶ αὐτοὶ οὕτω διανοηθῆναι][1] – whereas this is perhaps not so, and it is rather that they, having fallen into a sort of vortex [εἴς τινα δίνην], are themselves whirled around and, dragging us to them, try to make us too fall inside. (439b10–c6)

This passage is crucial in several respects, all of which bear on the interpretation and structure of the whole dialogue.

First, Socrates expressly confirms that, as he said at 411bc, he believes that the first namegivers held the flux theory (c1–4). There seems no reason why we should not assume that Socrates is being sincere. But if this is so, then it follows (as we saw in §5.5.1; cf. Grote 1888: III.319 n.2, Sedley 2003: 165) that the flux etymologies he is referring to, and indeed the whole etymological enterprise, were put forward in a spirit of seriousness – at least in some relevant sense – and not as a parody or joke.

---

[1] At 439c3 καὶ αὐτοί, 'they *too*' (sc. like the later flux theorists, Heraclitus etc.: cf. text below), is the reading of βTQ, accepted by Stallbaum, Méridier and Dalimier. It was unnecessarily corrected into καὶ αὐτῷ (ἔμοιγε καὶ αὐτῷ = 'even to me') by Heindorf, followed by Burnet and Fowler. W reads simply αὐτοί, printed in the OCT, whose force in context, however, is not very clear.

Secondly, Socrates' explicit suspicion that the flux-names may 'deceive' us and that the namegivers may have fallen prey to a state of giddiness and mental confusion recalls several earlier passages (as I partially anticipated in §8.2.2). At 428d and 439bc he pointed out that names *might* 'deceive' us by encapsulating false beliefs. Far more significantly, way back at 411bc he introduced the etymologies of the 'virtue' names by expressing the opinion that

> the very ancient men who imposed names were absolutely like most present-day wise men who, by dint of turning around and around searching how the beings are, get dizzy, and then things seem to them to be moving around and moving in all ways. And they don't hold responsible for this opinion what has happened inside them, but allege the things themselves to have such a nature.

It is evident that both in our passage and at 411bc Socrates says that the namegivers came to hold the flux theory out of a state of giddiness which led them to think that the things outside them were whirling around, whereas in reality the whirl was in their heads. It is perhaps less evident that in our passage he is hinting at something he asserted at 411bc, i.e. that the namegivers anticipated the views of later flux theorists. The hint is conveyed both by 439c4 'they *too*' (see n.1) and by the very image of the vortex, clearly a reference to those Presocratic theories which posit a rotation or vortex at some stage of the cosmic development.[2]

Thirdly, it is noteworthy that our lines, which introduce the examination of the flux theory, immediately follow upon the conclusion that reality must be investigated directly and 'without names' (438b–439b). The examination of the flux theory is still, in a way, part of the discussion about names which constitutes the dialogue's main topic; for it shows us how to decide the dispute between flux-names and rest-names (438d) and helps us understand to what extent names *can* deceive us by showing that perhaps the flux-names *do* deceive us.[3] But at the same time Socrates is also, as it were, putting the 438b–439b conclusion into practice by offering a sample of inquiry 'without names' into the nature of reality.[4] And since this shift of focus from names to things occurs, of all places, right at the end of the dialogue, it becomes a feature of the whole dialogue's structure (cf. §5.2.3). It is the whole *Cra.* that, after a long discussion of names and their relation to their referents, in whose course it has come out that

---

[2] Empedocles: 31 B35 DK, Arist. *Cael.* 295a29–b1. Anaxagoras: 59 B9, B12–13 DK. Leucippus and Democritus: 4.1, 72.3, 80.1 Leszl (= D. L. 9.44–5, Simpl. *in Ph.* 327.24–6, D. L. 9.31–2 = 68 A1, 68 B167, 67 A1 DK).
[3] Cf. Kahn 1973a: 157, 165, 167.
[4] Cf. Barney 2001: 143, 157.

the etymon of many names implies the flux theory, ends by giving us a glimpse of how that theory is to be examined for its own sake.

9.1.2 Flux and forms: the arguments previewed

The section that follows (439c6–440d7) is a nest of difficulties, which concern both the structure of the whole and the interpretation of individual claims or arguments. The last OCT editors have even been led to suspect some serious textual corruption: in their apparatus on d8–a5 they remark that those are 'argumenta mire elliptica' and express their fear that what our MSS report might be 'disiecta fragmenta longioris horum argumentorum versionis'. I believe, however, that it is possible to resist this fear and make sense of the text as it stands.

It will be helpful to start by taking an aerial view of the section's structure and purpose and raising a few general questions. Subsequently (§§9.1.3–9) I shall comment on each bit separately. Some of the claims which I make here will be justified there.

At 439c6–d2 Socrates obtains Cratylus' assent to a first assumption: (i) the beautiful itself, the good itself and all the forms exist. Then (d3–4) he announces that he is not going to address the question whether the flux theory is true of sensible particulars, but will focus on the forms instead. And here comes (d5–7) a second assumption about the forms: (ii) the beautiful itself – and by extension any other form – is unchanging. It is important to bear in mind that both assumptions, precisely insofar they are *assumptions* or hypotheses and thus have not been demonstrated, are presented by Socrates as something provisional or revisable. He expresses this by describing them both, figuratively, as part of a 'dream' he often dreams.

Then, from 439d8 to 440b4, Socrates sets out four arguments that explore the consequences of a certain general thesis, the flux theory's main tenet, which can be phrased so:

(1) Everything is always changing,

but which he appears to understand as 'Everything is always changing *in every respect.*' In a nutshell, Socrates argues that, if (1) is true, then certain consequences follow. The consequences are unpalatable or even absurd, but Socrates does not explicitly point this out along the way. At 440b4–c1 he adds that, if some of the consequences don't hold, then (1) is false. Then, somewhat surprisingly, at c1–d7 he winds up saying that it is difficult to investigate how matters really stand, i.e. whether (1) is true or false, and leaves it at that.

Now let us focus more closely on Socrates' four arguments from (1) to its consequences. They can be regarded as proving – or aiming to prove – in the final analysis, that:

if anything is always changing, then
- nothing true can ever be said of it (439d),
- it is not anything (439e),
- it cannot be known (439e–440a);

if everything is always changing, then
- no one ever knows anything (440ab).

'In the final analysis', because strictly speaking the first argument is concerned only with an instance of (1) – and a special instance at that: it proves that, if *the beautiful itself* is always changing, then nothing true can be said of *it*. But this instance is obviously intended as the basis for a generalization.

So the first three arguments can be regarded as ultimately proving something of the form

(2) $\forall x$ (x is always changing $\rightarrow \neg \varphi x$),

while the fourth can be regarded as proving only something of the form

(3) $\forall x$ (x is always changing) $\rightarrow \forall x$ ($\neg \varphi x$).

The special instance through which Socrates routes the first argument brings us to a first set of problems. In accordance with his decision to leave sensible particulars out of consideration (439d3–4), in all four arguments (even though the first clearly invites a generalization, and the second and third seem to be formulated in perfectly general terms) Socrates appears to be interested primarily, if not exclusively, in *what would happen to the forms* – or to *some* forms – if (1) were true. From the point of view of someone who believes in the forms, the expression 'everything' in (1) includes the forms within its range: if everything is always changing, then, amongst other things, every form is always changing; and so it is legitimate to ask what would happen to a form, if it were always changing.

But at 439d5–7 Socrates assumes that the forms are unchanging. Why do this and immediately after (d8 ff.) go on to ask what would happen to a form if it were always changing? We might be tempted to give the following answer: 'Socrates ... pursues some of the counterfactual implications of supposing that even such stable things might change' (Kahn 2002: 116). But this cannot be exactly so. Throughout the arguments (1) is never presented as false. Consider in particular the conditionals which Socrates uses to formulate the first and fourth argument (439d8–9 'is it possible, if it is always slipping away, …?', 440a6–7 'it is not reasonable …, if all things are changing'): both the protasis and the apodosis are in the present indicative. This means that Socrates is not explicitly committing himself to the falsity of the protasis and hence of (1).[5] And this is just as well, given that he emphasized the provisional character of the assumption that the forms are unchanging, and given also that he will wrap up the arguments with a profession of uncertainty. Therefore Socrates' strategy here rather seems to be this. First he makes it clear that he, for his part, assumes that the forms are unchanging; then he sets aside this assumption, which plays no active role in the sequel, and considers what follows from the rival assumption that everything – hence, from Socrates' point of view, also the forms – is in flux.

But what about the even more basic fact that Socrates explores the consequences of the flux theory with regard to the forms, when the theory countenances no forms at all? In this respect, Socrates' arguments may seem pointless. Surely the flux theorist could reply that, since he does not grant the existence of the forms, he need not bother himself with the arguments? If I believe that goblins exist while you do not, and I want to argue you out of a thesis which you hold, it will be no good alerting you to the implausible consequences which your thesis entails about the nature of goblins.

This charge can, however, be rebutted. To start with, at present Socrates is *not* really arguing with a flux theorist; his interlocutor is Cratylus, who has just conceded the existence of the forms and is not yet a committed Heraclitean, but is beginning to adhere to the flux theory only in the course of our dialogue (436e–437a, 440de; see §9.2). Hence Socrates is entitled to submit to *him* an argument that adverts to the forms. Think of those occasions when Aristotle – who is perfectly alive to the rules of a dialectical debate – derives the absurd consequences of a rival view from his own theoretical standpoint (e.g. *Metaph.* 990b22–991a2, 1007a20–b18).

There might be a further reason for rebutting the charge; but the matter is controversial, and depends on how we construe Socrates' refusal to speak of sensible particulars (see §9.1.3). If a genuine flux theorist were present at the conversation and dismissed the arguments on the grounds that he rejects the forms, perhaps Socrates would still retort: 'That won't let you off the hook. True, in setting forth the arguments I was mainly

---

[5] See KG II.466–8. In a counterfactual conditional both the protasis and the apodosis would be in a historical tense of the indicative, accompanied in the apodosis by ἄν.

interested in the forms. But in fact at least some of them apply to *anything* whatsoever that may supposed to be in flux and draw consequences from your theory which are as unpalatable for sensible particulars as they are for the forms.' Actually, he will do exactly this in the *Theaetetus*: he will apply the first argument to sensible particulars and use it to build up an explicit refutation of the flux theory.

We can now leave behind us the question of the forms' role in the arguments and move on to something else. All four arguments are plainly meant to show that (1) entails unpalatable or absurd consequences and to be potentially subservient to a refutation of (1). Consider in particular the second argument (439e). Here 'If anything is always changing, then it is not anything' is equivalent to 'If anything is always changing, then *it does not exist*.' Hence, if Socrates combined the argument with the initial assumption that each of the forms exists, he would already be in a position to conclude that each of the forms is not always changing and therefore (1) is false.

It is, however, not completely clear whether Socrates really does anything of that sort. What he does, at 440b4–c1, is to add something that can be paraphrased so:

if it is always the case that someone knows something and each of the forms exists, then it is not the case that everything is always changing.

Of the two conjuncts that make up the antecedent here, the former ('it is always the case that someone knows something') conflicts with the consequence drawn from (1) in the fourth argument. The latter conjunct ('each of the forms exists'), as it is stated in the text, repeats almost literally the 439c8–d1 assumption that the forms exist: it is as if Socrates were saying 'if, *as we were saying above*, each of the forms exists'. And as we saw above, this could be combined with the second argument to yield the conclusion that (1) is false.

To get a sense of what Socrates is doing here it is helpful (though not completely accurate)[6] to abbreviate (1) as 'p' and regard the four arguments as deriving from p four consequences $\neg q_1$, $\neg q_2$, $\neg q_3$, $\neg q_4$, thus jointly proving that

(4) $(p \to \neg q_1)$ & $(p \to \neg q_2)$ & $(p \to \neg q_3)$ & $(p \to \neg q_4)$,

---

[6] Because the first three arguments, insofar as they prove something of the form (2), cannot be formulated in the language of propositional logic. To do so we must regard them as proving something weaker, which has the form (3), as the fourth does. Thus, e.g., we shall regard the third argument not as proving that, if *anything* is always changing, then *it* cannot be known, but rather as proving that, if *everything* is always changing (p), then *nothing* can be known ($\neg q_3$).

i.e. that

(4*) $p \to (\neg q_1 \,\&\, \neg q_2 \,\&\, \neg q_3 \,\&\, \neg q_4)$.

Here at 440b4–c1 we could, with some simplification, regard Socrates as inferring that

(5) $(q_4 \,\&\, q_2) \to \neg p$.[7]

Only for the sake of brevity, I take it, does he not add in the antecedent two further clauses to the effect that each of the forms can be known and is such that something true can be said of it. If he did, we could expand '$q_4 \,\&\, q_2$' into '$q_1 \,\&\, q_2 \,\&\, q_3 \,\&\, q_4$'.

But there is an alternative, more interesting construal of these lines. Socrates might mean: 'But if [*we supplement the previous four arguments with the assumptions that*] it is always the case that there is something that knows and something that is known, and that the forms exist, then [*it follows that*] it is not the case that everything is always changing.' That is to say, in these lines Socrates, instead of just inferring (5) from (4*), might be cautiously hinting at an argument along the following lines:

(4*) $p \to (\neg q_1 \,\&\, \neg q_2 \,\&\, \neg q_3 \,\&\, \neg q_4)$
(6) $q_4 \,\&\, q_2$
―――――――――――――――――――
(7) $\neg p$.

And this would, at long last, be a fully fledged refutation of (1).

The refutation, however, is only hinted at. As I anticipated above, in the sequel (440c1–d7) Socrates ends by professing uncertainty as to whether (1) is true or false; and although it is as clear as day that he does believe (1) to be false, we shall not hear anything more definite from him about this issue in *Cra.*

Why does Socrates not administer the *coup de grâce* to the flux theory? I can think of at least two explanations. One is this: Socrates has emphasized the provisional and hypothetical status of the initial assumptions that the forms exist and are unchanging; he has presumably the same attitude to the assumption that it is always the case that something knows something (q_4 in the above outline), or to any other assumption he could use as a premiss to build up a refutation of (1); and for this reason he now feels (or acts as if he felt) unable to take a stand.

---

[7] 'With some simplification', because, if '$\neg q_2$' = 'nothing is anything' ≡ 'nothing exists' (cf. n.6), then 'each of the forms exists' is not the contradictory of $\neg q_2$, but is just inconsistent with it. Hence it should not be abbreviated as 'q_2', though it entails q_2.

I suspect that this is the explanation which Socrates is implicitly inviting us to adopt – the one he would give as an answer if we asked him. But, at the same time, I doubt whether it can be the ultimate explanation. For why did he emphasize the provisional and hypothetical status of the initial assumptions in the first place? I submit that the ultimate explanation has rather to do with a matter of authorial design, i.e. with Plato's view of the dialogue's structure and unity. We have been travelling a long way since, back at 383a, Hermogenes involved Socrates in his discussion with Cratylus; it is now time to stop. The discussion of flux here, along with Socrates' eventual profession of uncertainty, can be read as an overture to other dialogues – especially the *Theaetetus* – that will confront this issue more directly and effectively.

9.1.3 Enter the forms, exeunt particulars (439cd)

Equipped with the map which we have just drawn, we can resume our reading of the text and watch Socrates begin his discussion of the flux theory:

(SO.) Examine, my wonderful Cratylus, what I for my part often dream of [ὃ ἔγωγε πολλάκις ὀνειρώττω]. Shall we say that there is a beautiful itself, and a good itself, and likewise each single one of the beings [φῶμέν τι εἶναι αὐτὸ καλὸν καὶ ἀγαθὸν καὶ ἓν ἕκαστον τῶν ὄντων οὕτω], or not?
CR. To me it seems that there is, Socrates. (439c6–d2)

Socrates introduces the ensuing arguments as a 'dream' he often makes. What is the significance of this metaphor?

Plato typically uses the dream image to characterize the cognitive state of someone who lacks proper knowledge about a given subject matter. Sometimes this involves some sort of confusion or misapprehension (*R.* 476c, 520c, 534cd; *Plt.* 277d; *Ti.* 52b; *Lg.* 656b); sometimes, instead, it is just the state of someone who has merely true beliefs about the subject matter, or is considering a tentative suggestion, or is reasoning on the basis of hypotheses that have not yet been adequately examined (*Chrm.* 173a; *Men.* 85c; *R.* 443b, 533bc; *Tht.* 201d). Since Socrates will close his discussion of flux with an emphatic admission of uncertainty, here the latter variety of dream must be at stake. This accords with the fact that Socrates' dream crucially includes the existence of the forms, which he elsewhere describes precisely as a hypothesis requiring further investigation (*Phd.* 92d, 100b, 107b).[8]

---

[8] Cf. Burnyeat 1970: 104–5, Barney 2001: 149–51, Sedley 2003: 165 and n.30. Probably Socrates' dream does not include only the existence of the forms, which is the subject of the following

The arguments (439b–440d)

We can now focus on the clause 'there is a beautiful itself, and a good itself, and likewise each one of the beings' (c8–d1). Here the phrase 'a beautiful itself' (τι ... αὐτὸ καλόν) is, I take it, simply derived from the more familiar 'the beautiful itself' (αὐτὸ ... τὸ καλόν, d5) by suppression of the article and introduction of the indefinite τι; hence it is roughly equivalent to 'some such thing as the beautiful itself'.[9]

The way Socrates expresses himself here is strongly reminiscent of some passages in the *Phaedo* and elsewhere. Read *Phd.* 65d:

Do we say that there is a just itself or that there is none? [φαμέν τι εἶναι δίκαιον αὐτὸ ἢ οὐδέν;] ... And also a beautiful and a good itself? [Καὶ αὖ καλόν γέ τι καὶ ἀγαθόν;]

Again, *Phd.* 74a 'We say ... that there is an equal' (φαμέν ... τι εἶναι ἴσον); 76d 'If there are those things we always keep talking about, a beautiful and a good [καλόν τέ τι καὶ ἀγαθόν] and all this sort of being'; 100b 'there is a beautiful itself by itself and a good and a large [εἶναί τι καλὸν αὐτὸ καθ' αὑτὸ καὶ ἀγαθὸν καὶ μέγα] and all the rest'; *R.* 476c 'he who believes in a beautiful itself' (ὁ ... ἡγούμενός ... τι αὐτὸ καλόν).

It is instructive to compare the existence questions which Socrates asks in our passage and at *Phd.* 65d with certain passages from the 'Socratic' dialogues where Socrates asks his interlocutor whether he concedes the existence of an item which is or is going to be the subject of Socrates' remarks. See especially *Prt.* 332c ('is there something beautiful [ἔστιν τι καλόν]? ... Is there something good [ἔστιν τι ἀγαθόν]? Is there something high in sound?'); cf. *Prt.* 330cd, 332a, 358a; *Men.* 75e–76a; etc. These existence claims do not really commit the speakers to a Platonist ontology; at least for the most part they 'serve merely to fix the topic on which

---

question; the ensuing arguments too fall within its scope. This is suggested both by d3 σκεψώμεθα, which picks up Socrates' present invitation to Cratylus to 'examine' (σκέψαι) his dream, and by Socrates' eventual profession of uncertainty. As a matter of fact, though, Socrates' dreamlike state is to be blamed on the initial assumption of the forms. He is (or pretends to be) uncertain about how to assess his arguments, not because they seem inconclusive to him, but because they make use of an undemonstrated assumption. (Plato's authorial reasons for making Socrates feel uncertain are quite another matter: see §9.1.2).

[9] The view that τι ... αὐτὸ καλόν is a unitary phrase is shared by most scholars; I endorse Reeve's translation and Sedley's (2003: 167 n.35) defence. Some, instead, take τι as the complement of εἶναι: 'the beautiful itself is something' etc. εἶναί τι is indeed a Platonic expression for existence, and it occurs at e1. Here, however, the lack of the article before καλόν tells in favour of the former construal. Contrast *Hp. Ma.* 288a εἴ τι ἔστιν αὐτὸ τὸ καλόν, with the article; and note that our text does feature, at d5, the phrase αὐτὸ τὸ καλόν for '*the* beautiful itself'. Similar considerations also hold for the parallel passages *Phd.* 74a, 100b; *R.* 476bc; *Ti.* 51bc. What is more, they are confirmed by the unequivocal use of τι in *Phd.* 65d, 76d; *Smp.* 210e; *Prm.* 130bc; cf. Aristotle's *De ideis*, e.g. 79.11 (τις).

comment is to be made'.[10] But in our passage and in *Phd.* 65d matters are different in a number of respects. To start with, formulation. Both passages introduce the subject matter of the existential question very abruptly as 'a beautiful itself' and 'a just itself' respectively. This has no parallel in the 'Socratic' dialogues, where instead: (i) there are no exact parallels for the very unusual expression τι ... αὐτὸ καλόν; (ii) an expression like 'the *F* itself' is used to refer to a subject of inquiry only in a context in which it has been prepared by some previous relevant occurrence of the term '*F*';[11] (iii) the aforementioned topic-fixing existential questions never contain 'itself' expressions – they never have the form 'Is there some such thing as the *F itself*?'. In our passage and in *Phd.* 65d, therefore, Socrates' questions are phrased in quasi-technical language and do not invite a naïve, non-committal interpretation. This suggests that the items Socrates is talking about are Platonic forms; and the suggestion is confirmed by further evidence. As regards our passage, this further evidence is both internal and external. Inside the passage there is the expression 'and likewise each single one *of the beings*' (καὶ ἓν ἕκαστον τῶν ὄντων οὕτω), which seems to contain an instance of the characteristic use of τὰ ὄντα to refer to the forms as the beings *par excellence*, the things that (really) are.[12] Outside the passage there is the fact that Socrates already introduced the forms at 389a–390e, in the course of his conversation with Hermogenes; indeed, there he availed himself freely of the ὅ ἐστιν terminology, whose technical status he elsewhere underlines.[13] As for *Phd.* 65d, in the sequel Socrates goes on to ask Simmias whether he has ever perceived any such items or whether thought is the proper means to know 'each thing itself' which one is inquiring into; Simmias promptly rejects the former alternative and

---

[10] Dancy 2004: 75. See the whole of his 65–79, and Woodruff 1982: 163–5.
[11] Typically, in the context of a contrast with particular or specific *F*s; see *Euthphr.* 5c–6e, *Hp. Ma.* 286ce.
[12] Cf. especially τὸ ὂν ἕκαστον at *R.* 484c, d, 486d. Cf. also *R.* 500bc, 597a; *Phdr.* 247d–248b, 249e; and perhaps *Phd.* 66a. This was not the use of τὰ ὄντα in its previous occurrences in the dialogue. Mostly, and as recently as 438d–439b, the phrase rather meant 'the beings' or 'the things that are' quite generally, with no special reference to the forms; it will again do so at 440c. Cf. the similar contrast between *Phdr.* 247d–248b, 249e (narrow use) and 262a, 263d (broad use); between *Phd.* 66a (narrow?) and 74de, 79a (broad), or between *Ti.* 27d–28a (narrow) and 35a (broad use of οὐσία).

There is an alternative construal of ἓν ἕκαστον τῶν ὄντων οὕτω (Calvert 1970: 36): 'each one *of the things that are thus*', i.e. 'each one of the things of this sort'. But this is no Platonic idiom; and the standard construal is proved correct by the reprise without οὕτω at 440b6–7.

[13] See *Phd.* 75d, 92de; *R.* 507b. Luce 1965: 24–32 and Irwin 1977: 2 maintain that here 'Plato is not concerned with *separated* Forms', as he is, by contrast, in *Phaedo* and *Republic*. This is groundless: the passage does not contain any evidence for or against the separateness of forms, whatever that may be.

espouses the latter. This goes beyond anything in the 'Socratic' dialogues and confirms that the items in question are the forms.

Thus it seems clear that Socrates is talking about Platonic forms. There is, however, a problem. In our lines Socrates does not assert outright the existence of a beautiful itself, a good itself etc. Rather, he *asks* Cratylus whether they shall say that there are such things; Cratylus assents and says he believes so (d2). Yet Cratylus is no member of the Socratic circle; indeed, he has recently implied that the flux theory is true (437a) and will shortly endorse it (440de). Surely it would be dramatically implausible to portray him as a believer in Platonic forms? To escape this difficulty it has been supposed that Socrates' question is deliberately ambiguous: 'While to Platonically attuned readers the reference is unmistakably to the intelligible world postulated by Platonic ontology, to Cratylus Socrates' question need mean no more than whether, in addition to the beautiful things in the world, there is also such a thing as what it is for them to be beautiful' (Sedley 2003: 167).[14]

What I have been arguing so far about the peculiarities of our passage and of *Phd.* 65d shows that this suggestion cannot be right. Socrates' question is not ambiguous; to suppose that Cratylus understands it as Sedley suggests is to suppose that he misunderstands it.[15] This is hardly progress to my mind. Therefore I acknowledge the problem of dramatic plausibility, but I put it down as an imperfection in the dialogue's texture, and I unqualifiedly hold on to the view that both Socrates and Cratylus are talking about Platonic forms. After all, the fact that the forms were already introduced in the conversation between Socrates and Hermogenes, and that Cratylus endorsed the contents of that conversation (428c), goes some way towards justifying Cratylus' assent. And as for his Heraclitean sympathies, a careful reading of 440de suggests that he is beginning to conceive them only now, in the course of the present conversation. Furthermore, if we assume – as it is reasonable to do – that here Plato wants to set up a clash between the theory of flux and the theory of forms, and that it is important to him that Cratylus be Socrates' interlocutor during this clash,[16] then we only have to suppose that for Plato the intention to put this plan into effect overrides any concern with dramatic plausibility.[17]

---

[14] See already Barney 2001: 151.
[15] 'We may fairly suppose that Cratylus has no very determinate notion of what he has accepted – what, for example, the *auto* ... contributes to its meaning' (Barney 2001: 151).
[16] See §I.2.1 on Cratylus' role in Plato's intellectual biography.
[17] At *Phd.* 65d too some have denied that the forms are already explicitly in play: see Rowe 1993: 141, Dancy 2004: 246–50. Dancy tries to explain away the claim that the just itself, the beautiful itself etc. are not perceived through the body; his explanation I find far-fetched.

Socrates next puts 'the beautiful itself' at the centre of his argument:

SO. Now let us examine that thing itself[18] – not whether some face, or some of such things, is beautiful and all these things seem to flow [μὴ εἰ πρόσωπόν τί ἐστιν καλὸν ἤ τι τῶν τοιούτων, καὶ δοκεῖ ταῦτα πάντα ῥεῖν], but rather: isn't the beautiful *itself* always such as it is [ἀλλ' αὐτό ... τὸ καλὸν οὐ τοιοῦτον ἀεί ἐστιν οἷόν ἐστιν]? What shall we say?
CR. Necessarily. (439d3–7)

In these lines Socrates puts one question aside (d3 'not whether ...') and asks another one instead (d5 'but rather ...').

The latter question, the one Socrates does ask, is the question whether the beautiful itself, i.e. the form of beautiful, is 'always such as it is'. It is a recurrent theme of the dialogues that the forms are absolutely immutable, 'always constant and in the same state' (*Smp.* 211ab; *Phd.* 78d; *R.* 479a, e; *Ti.* 28a; etc.); and it seems clear that here we have one of its occurrences.[19]

The former question is more problematic. What exactly is its extent? Some scholars have held that the question ends with the words τῶν τοιούτων (d4) and that the immediately following words καὶ δοκεῖ ταῦτα πάντα ῥεῖν fall outside it and *assert* that all sensible particulars 'seem to flow'. But this cannot be so, as most have seen, unless Socrates is speaking quite carelessly. The d4 καί can only coordinate the clause δοκεῖ ... ῥεῖν with what precedes it and thus bring it under the scope of the d3 εἰ.[20] So the question Socrates puts aside is actually *twofold*: it is the question

---

[18] Αὐτό ... ἐκεῖνο (d3) is (perhaps deliberately) ambiguous. On the most natural construal, ἐκεῖνο is proleptic and anticipates the ensuing question. But it might also be anaphoric; then the phrase would refer to the beautiful itself.

[19] According to Sedley 2003: 168–9, if this were what Socrates means, then at d8–9 Socrates would ask an inconsequential question: 'If ... [in d5–7] Cratylus already agrees that the Beautiful itself is unchanging, why does Socrates follow up with ... [d8–9] "*Then* is it possible to speak of it correctly, if it is always slipping away?", as if he still had to prove that it is unchanging?' This worry should be adequately answered by my account of Socrates' line of reasoning in §9.1.2. Note that d8 οὖν need not mean 'then' as Sedley translates it, because ἆρ' οὖν can introduce a question that simply adds a new point, without presenting it as a consequence of what has been said before: see e.g. 385b, 387b, 390c, 430c; *Phd.* 73c; *Tht.* 152c; *R.* 335c, 352e.

Sedley's worry results in the supposition that at d5–6 Socrates is asking, not whether the beautiful itself is unchanging, but whether it is always *beautiful* (so already Jowett; cf. *Hp. Ma.* 292e). But it is hardly credible that here Socrates should be using so generic a phrase to say something so specific. There is, to my knowledge, no parallel for that in any of the passages where 'self-predication' is at stake. (Some such worry is probably also the source of Stokes's suspicion – recorded in the OCT's apparatus – that there is a lacuna in the text before d8.)

[20] *Pace* Ficino, who translated 'quippe haec omnia fluunt', and Jowett, 'for all such things appear to be in a flux'; cf. Grote 1888: III.320, Gulley 1962: 72, and Minio-Paluello. Heindorf too thought that this was what the text had to mean, but he saw that this required a supplement: καὶ <γὰρ> δοκεῖ etc. Schanz, followed by Luce 1965: 32–3, excised the clause – the cure that kills the patient.

whether *both* (i) a particular face 'or something else of that sort' is beautiful *and* (ii) all these things 'seem to flow'.

(i) parallels the question asked in c7–d1, i.e. whether 'there is a beautiful itself, and a good itself, and likewise each one of the beings'. The parallel would be more evident if we took d5 ἐστιν as existential, like c8 εἶναι, and construed (i) as the question 'whether *there is a beautiful face*[21] or something else of that sort'. As for (ii), I understand it as the question whether all sensible particulars *can be plausibly regarded as being in flux*.

Thus Socrates, in order to examine the flux theory, decides to exclude sensible particulars from consideration and concentrate on the forms instead. What is the rationale for this decision? Someone might be inclined to the following answer (which accepts the view of the scholars cited in n.20, though not their construal of the text): the rationale is that Plato rejects the flux theory as far as the forms are concerned, but accepts it and its consequences as *true of sensible particulars*. The main ground for this answer would be that Plato's dialogues often tell us that sensible particulars, in contrast to the immutable forms, are subject to all sorts of change (*Phd.* 78de, *Ti.* 48e–52d, *Phlb.* 59ab etc.).[22] The answer would also agree with Aristotle's report that Plato, 'when he was young, became familiar first with Cratylus and the Heraclitean doctrines that all sensible things are always in flux and there is no knowledge of them. This he believed later too' (*Metaph.* 987a32–b1, cf. 1078b12–17, 1086a35–b2).[23]

Yet this answer would be unconvincing, for several reasons.[24] First, why should Socrates cast his belief that sensible particulars are in flux as a refusal to address the question whether they are in flux? Secondly, in the following arguments Socrates will construe the flux theory as an *extreme* theory, according to which everything is always changing *in every respect*; and I (along with many scholars) am reluctant to believe that Plato would really take (or want Socrates to take) such a hallucinatory view of the world we live in. Indeed, in the *Theaetetus* we shall precisely see him reject such a theory in relation to sensible particulars, on the basis of an argument closely parallel to the first of those offered here. Thirdly, at 411bc Socrates presented the flux theorists, ancient and modern, in an entirely unfavourable light, without suggesting that they might be partly right. He did not say 'They believe that all things are in flux because they see that sensible

---

[21] The face example is reminiscent of *Smp.* 211a.
[22] On Plato's conception of the change of sensible particulars see Vlastos 1991: 70–1 and Ademollo (in preparation-3).
[23] See §I.2.1.
[24] The remainder of this section is especially consonant with Ackrill's (1997: 52) succinct remarks.

things are'; he rather said 'They believe that all things are in flux because they are dizzy.'

Why, then, put sensible particulars aside? Here is an alternative conjecture. Plato does, I take it, believe that the flux theory which is in question here is false also with regard to the sensible world. Perhaps, however, he is unwilling to point this out without at the same time explaining that he agrees with the theory on some counts though not on others. Unquestionably, sensible particulars are always changing in *some* respect or other; and (though I won't argue this here)[25] that is enough to deprive them of identity through time. Indeed, it might even be that some of the consequences which the first three arguments draw from (1) are true for sensible particulars, though not for the forms. That is to say, for some φ, Plato might believe that (a) anything of which the flux theory is true is not φ, (b) sensible particulars are not φ, even though the flux theory is not true of them, (c) forms are φ and therefore the flux theory is not true of them. (We shall explore this possibility in more detail as we discuss each single argument.) Thus to take account of sensible particulars Socrates would have to complicate his line of reasoning and confront complex issues which here he does not want (or is not able) to go into; and for this reason, I submit, he prefers to steer clear of the whole matter.

9.1.4 *The first argument (439d)*

Let us turn to the argument without further demur:

SO. Now is it possible, if it always slipping away, to say of it correctly, first that it is *that*, and then that it is *such* [προσειπεῖν αὐτὸ ὀρθῶς, εἰ ἀεὶ ὑπεξέρχεται, πρῶτον μὲν ὅτι ἐκεῖνό ἐστιν, ἔπειτα ὅτι τοιοῦτον]? Or is it rather necessary for it, while we're speaking [ἅμα ἡμῶν λεγόντων], to become immediately another thing and withdraw and no longer stand in this state [ἄλλο αὐτὸ εὐθὺς γίγνεσθαι καὶ ὑπεξιέναι καὶ μηκέτι οὕτως ἔχειν]?
CR. Necessarily. (439d8–12)

Here Socrates takes an arbitrary example of a form, the beautiful itself (d8 αὐτό, here simply an anaphoric pronoun referring back to d5), and explores a consequence of supposing that it 'is always slipping away' (d8–9). For our present purposes we can regard 'slipping away'[26] as a metaphorical

---

[25] See Ademollo (in preparation-3).
[26] ὑπεξέρχομαι: 'leave, go away, emigrate' (Hdt. 1.73.3, 8.36.2; Th. 4.74.2; And. 1.15; Dem. 59.103; Arist. *Ath. Pol.* 15.2, 20.3; the prefix ὑπο- may sometimes express that one is leaving *secretly*); 'withdraw' (R. 557a, Th. 8.70.1); 'escape from' someone (Th. 3.34.2). For the crucial parallel at *Tht.* 182d see §9.1.5.

expression for change in general[27] and mentally complete it as follows: the beautiful is always slipping away *from its previous condition* (cf. 439e, where 'without departing [ἐξιστάμενον] from its own form' = 'without changing at all').[28] We should, however, also be aware that the use of 'slipping away' here harmonizes with the fact that throughout the etymologies Socrates has been formulating the flux theory in terms of *spatial* movement. Those expressions were *not* metaphorical; I explained the rationale behind them in §5.3.1.

So we are supposing that Socrates' premiss,

(8) The beautiful is always slipping away,

can be paraphrased as

(8*) The beautiful is always changing

and hence can be viewed as an instance of

(1) Everything is always changing,

the flux theory's main tenet.[29] Now consider these:

(9)   Everything is always changing in *some* respect
(10) Everything is always changing in *every* respect

and their respective instances,

(11) The beautiful is always changing in some respect
(12) The beautiful is always changing in every respect.

On the one hand, (1) is logically equivalent to (9), as (8*) to (11). For if X is changing, then there must be some respect in which it is changing; and conversely, if X is changing in some respect, then we can say that it is changing, full stop. On the other hand, (1) does not entail (10), but is entailed by it; and the same relation holds between (8*) and (12). But what is the flux theorist committed to, in Socrates' view? Does his endorsement of (1) commit him to (9) and hence (11), or rather to (10) and hence (12)?

---

[27] *Pace* Fowler and Reeve, who translate εἰ ἀεὶ ὑπεξέρχεται as 'if it is always passing away'. Cf. the premiss of the fourth argument: 'if all things *change* [μεταπίπτει] and nothing is at rest' (440a).

[28] An alternative completion would be: the beautiful is always slipping away *from us* (Owen 1953: 72 n.39), i.e. from our attempts to identify or describe it. If this were right, then Socrates would be loosely anticipating what he goes on to say at d10–11. That is, he would be conflating a statement of the flux hypothesis with a statement of some of its consequences.

[29] The instance reads somewhat awkwardly; for it seems to implicate something which is not implicated by (1) and which Socrates' argument will deny, i.e. that the changing object remains identical through time and change.

We might, in a spirit of charity and parsimony, suppose that (9) and its instance (11) are all that Socrates wants to introduce into the argument. We might be encouraged to suppose so by the fact that the theory set forth in the etymologies (which should, after all, be what we are presently discussing) did *not* at all claim that everything is changing in every respect, as (10) would have it. For example, that theory posited a quick and thin element which 'governs all the other things by going through them' (412e) and clearly assumed it to possess these features permanently.

But this supposition cannot be right; for the bewildering consequences which Socrates goes on to derive can only be derived from (12). Therefore (10) and (12) must somehow enter into Socrates' argument.[30] He must, I take it, have some sort of subsidiary argument from (1) to (10) up his sleeve; that is to say, he must be tacitly assuming that supporters of the view that everything is changing are, for some reason, committed to the extreme view that everything is changing *in every respect*. But how does the tacit subsidiary argument work? I won't try to confront this difficult question here; in §9.1.5 a parallel argument in the *Theaetetus* will suggest an answer.

According to Socrates' main argument, if the beautiful is always changing, then (in the final analysis) it is impossible 'to say of it correctly, first that it is *that*, and then that it is *such*' (d8–9 προσειπεῖν αὐτὸ ὀρθῶς ... πρῶτον μὲν ὅτι ἐκεῖνό ἐστιν, ἔπειτα ὅτι τοιοῦτον). In order to understand this it is obviously crucial to be clear about the meaning of the phrase between quotes. Here Socrates does not seem to be primarily concerning himself with the use of the *pronouns* ἐκεῖνο and τοιοῦτον.[31] Rather, in the present context it is natural to think that ἐκεῖνο, '*that*', stands in for the very phrase 'the beautiful itself' (and presumably for any other coreferential expression), while τοιοῦτον, '*such*', stands in for any predicate that can be truly ascribed to the beautiful itself. This idea can be made more precise in two different ways.

On one possible construal (see Vlastos 1991: 70 n.111), Socrates is essentially talking about two kinds of statement. To say correctly of the beautiful 'that it is *that*' is to make a true *identity* statement about it, i.e. to say truly that it is the beautiful (or the good, or whatever else the beautiful

---

[30] (10), by the way, seems to be the view the historical Cratylus eventually came to hold, according to Aristotle's report: see §1.2.1.

[31] Contrast *Tht.* 157b and *Ti.* 49d–50a, where the appropriateness or inappropriateness of applying pronouns to an object in flux is unequivocally part of what is at issue.

may be truly identified with; any definition of the beautiful will be a case in point). To say correctly of the beautiful 'that it is *such*' is to make a true *predicative* statement about it – e.g. to say that it is pleasant or appropriate. On this construal, the adverbs 'first … then …' do not have their literal, temporal meaning; they rather emphasize the distinction and express that identity statements are, for some reason (e.g. because they are in a sense simpler), logically prior to predicative ones.

Instead of our being able to say correctly of the beautiful that it is *that* and *such*, Socrates claims, something else is the case (d10 'Or is it rather necessary …'). Socrates' description of this something else is, at the same time, his explanation of why it is impossible to say correctly of the beautiful that it is *that* and *such*.

The clause at d10–11 contains three expressions that refer to change: 'to become … another thing and withdraw and no longer stand in this state' (ἄλλο … γίγνεσθαι καὶ ὑπεξιέναι καὶ μηκέτι οὕτως ἔχειν). A glance at the Greek reveals that the second expression is a very close counterpart of d9 ὑπεξέρχεται and is presumably as generic.[32] This generic talk of change is unpacked by the other two expressions: the beautiful 'becomes another thing' and 'no longer stands in this state'. The former of these backs the previous claim that it is impossible to say truly of the beautiful that it is '*that*'. Becoming another thing entails passing away: if X becomes Y at time t, and X ≠ Y, then X ceases to exist at t. As for the latter expression, 'no longer stand in this state',[33] this backs the previous claim that it is impossible to say truly of the beautiful that it is '*such*'. The meaning is, I take it, roughly that if you are describing X as being F, then while you are doing so X ceases to be F. And this means that the beautiful is constantly changing *all* of its features.

The time is ripe for an overall paraphrase:

If the beautiful is always changing, then you cannot make a true identity or predicative statement about it, because while you are still speaking it suddenly becomes another thing, endowed with other features.

Of course it does not matter how fast you speak. However short the duration of your utterance may be, by the end of that lapse of time the beautiful has turned into another object, endowed with other features; and these continuous transformations prevent you from ever saying anything true of it. Whatever you say of it is inevitably out of date.

---

[32] ὑπέξειμι: *Phd.* 103d, 106a; Hdt. 4.120.1, 7.211.1; Arist. *Pol.* 1276a39.
[33] On οὕτως ἔχειν = '*stand* in this state' see n.45.

Now for a few comments.

(i) Strictly speaking, Socrates' ban applies only to *present-tense* statements and not also to past-tense ones: in principle, nothing prevents you from making a perfectly true statement if after time *t* you say 'It *was X* at *t*' or 'It *was F* at *t*' (Calvert 1970: 38).[34] From the fact that the world cannot be described live it does not follow that it cannot be described at all; the fastest succession of events is immutable once it is past. In practice, though, denizens of a world in continuous flux could hardly manage to keep track of every transformation of the objects around them. So, after all, Socrates does have a point also in the case of past-tense statements.

(ii) If through (8), 'The beautiful is always slipping away', Socrates were not assuming anything stronger than (11), 'The beautiful is always changing *in some respect*', the argument would be that, if the beautiful is always changing in some respect, then you cannot make any true statement about it. It is very hard to see how that could be supposed to work. Therefore, as I anticipated above, we should rather take it that via (8) Socrates is somehow introducing (12), 'The beautiful is always changing *in every respect*.'

(iii) Although the argument is about the beautiful, and by extension about any form, it seems clear that it could be further extended to anything whatsoever, including sensible particulars like Aspasia or the Parthenon; for nothing in it hinges on the fact that the beautiful is a form. Therefore Socrates is clearly committed to holding that, if Aspasia 'is always slipping away', and hence is always changing in every respect, then it is impossible to say truly of her that she is *that* or *such*. And I do not see how he could fail to realize that he is thus committed or how he could regard this impossibility as something the least bit acceptable.[35]

My remarks (ii) and (iii) will be confirmed, and matters will become a little clearer, when we turn to the parallel argument in the *Theaetetus*.[36]

---

[34] Cf. Bostock 1988: 105–6, Dancy 2004: 17–18.
[35] Note, in particular, that our argument has nothing to do with the contrast between *being* and *becoming*, which Plato introduces elsewhere (*Ti*. 37e–38b; cf. *Tht*. 152de, 157ab). That is to say, here Socrates cannot mean that, if *X* is always changing (in every respect), then it is always impossible to say truly of *X* that it *is* that or such, but it is instead possible to say truly that it *becomes* that or such. Socrates cannot mean this for three reasons. First, it would be strange if the being/becoming contrast, so explicit in *Tht*. and *Ti*., were left implicit here (as well as in the rest of the dialogue). Secondly, since utterances with 'to become' too take time, no less than those with 'to be', the argument could be easily reformulated to yield the conclusion that, if *X* is always changing (in every respect), then it is always impossible to say truly of *X* that it is *becoming* that or such (cf. *Tht*. 183a). Thirdly, at 438d–439b and 440c Socrates does not hesitate to use the phrase τὰ ὄντα in the broad sense in which it applies also to sensible particulars (see n.12).
[36] See instead §I.2.1, (6), for the relationship between our argument and the views of the historical Cratylus.

The arguments (439b–440d)

Before doing so, however, we still have to address a question which has been left pending. I mentioned above that another construal of Socrates' *'that'*–*'such'* distinction is possible. On this alternative construal (advanced by Kahn 1973a: 170) Socrates is not distinguishing between identity and predicative statements, but rather between the act of *referring* to the beautiful and the act of *describing* it truly as such-and-such by ascribing a predicate to it. Indeed, Reeve (xlv, 94 n.159) suggests that the distinction is between these two acts as they occur successively in the making of a *single* predicative statement like 'The beautiful is pleasant.'[37] On this suggestion, the adverbs 'first … then …' can retain their temporal meaning.

Let (a) be the construal of the *'that'*–*'such'* distinction in terms of identity *vs* predicative statements and (b) the construal in terms of reference *vs* predication. To my mind, (a) has the edge over (b) on two counts. First, Socrates' actual words fit more naturally with (a): the expressions 'to say of it … that it is *that*' and '[to say of it] that it is *such*' are very naturally taken to represent two kinds of statement. Secondly, (b) gives Socrates a dubious point. We usually assume that, if '*X*' refers to *X*, then it continues to do so when *X* is no longer in existence (e.g. 'Aspasia' still refers to Aspasia, although she is no more); and it is irrelevant to this assumption whether *X* is a comparatively long-lived item that endures through time, like the objects which populate our commonsensical world-picture, or a very short-lived item that stays in existence only for an instant, like the objects which – on Socrates' argument – the flux theory is committed to recognizing. But if (b) is right, then Socrates is implicitly rejecting this assumption with regard to the short-lived items; for he is arguing that the fact that *X* 'becomes another thing' prevents us from subsequently referring to it.[38]

The *'that'*–*'such'* distinction might have implications on a major issue which we have been discussing time and again; and the option between (a) and (b) is important in this respect. If (b) were right, or at least captured part of what Socrates has in mind here, then Socrates would turn out to

---

[37] Barney 2001: 153 and Sedley 2003: 169 maintain that Socrates is talking about something even more specific, i.e. the self-predicative statement that the beautiful itself is beautiful. Of course this sits well with the view (on which see n.19) that at d5–6 Socrates was actually claiming that the beautiful itself is always *beautiful*.
  Kahn 2002: 116 holds that (a) and (b) are equivalent to each other and apparently also that Plato wants the text to admit of both construals. Granted, there is a very close connection between the notions of identity and reference (on which the (a) and the (b) construal of 'to say of it correctly … that it is *that*' respectively centre): *X* = *Y* if and only if '*X*' refers to *Y*. But (a) and (b) are not really equivalent: see main text below.

[38] Cf. the above remark that Socrates' argument does not prove it impossible to make true past-tense statements – e.g. '*X was F*' – about an object in flux.

be alive to the distinction between referring to something and predicating something of it, and hence to have a sound conception of the structure of predicative statements. Elsewhere in the dialogue he did *not* seem to be clear on this issue; he got closer and closer to the right conception without ever quite attaining it (see §§2.2.3, 7.2.4, 7.3.4). Now (b) gives us a last-minute chance to let Socrates finally purge himself of all confusion; and some of us may well think that such a chance should not get lost. According to (a), instead, Socrates is mentioning two kinds of statement without explicitly committing himself to an analysis of their internal structure. So, if (a) is right and (b) is not, as I incline to believe, the ascription of a sound conception of statement structure to Socrates remains no more than a guess.

Now for the promised excursion into the *Theaetetus*.

9.1.5 *The first argument and the* Theaetetus

Our excursion starts from the Secret Doctrine which Socrates ascribes to Protagoras and almost all Greek thinkers at *Tht.* 152ce (see §5.3.4). According to the Doctrine, as Socrates initially reports it,

> Nothing is one thing just by itself [ἓν μὲν αὐτὸ καθ' αὑτὸ οὐδέν ἐστιν], nor could you correctly speak of anything either as *something* or as *qualified somehow* [οὐδ' ἄν τι προσείποις ὀρθῶς οὐδ' ὁποιονοῦν τι], but if you speak of it as large, it will also appear small, if as heavy, light, and so on with everything, in that nothing is one, either *something* or *qualified somehow*; and it is from movement and motion and mixture with each other that there come to be all the things which we say 'are' [ἐκ δὲ δὴ φορᾶς τε καὶ κινήσεως καὶ κράσεως πρὸς ἄλληλα γίγνεται πάντα ἃ δή φαμεν εἶναι] – thereby speaking of them incorrectly, because nothing ever is, but everything always comes to be [ἔστι μὲν γὰρ οὐδέποτ' οὐδέν, ἀεὶ δὲ γίγνεται].

Lines 152d3–4 seem to mean that you cannot say truly of anything either *what* it is or what it is *like*: you cannot say either what Aspasia is (e.g. that she is a human being; perhaps also that she is Aspasia) or what she is like (e.g. that she is beautiful). And in the light of what Socrates goes on to say at d7–e1 about everything coming to be from motion, at least part of the meaning of this seems to be that nothing has any stable feature, whether essential or non-essential – nor perhaps any stable identity. The consonance with our argument is evident. But there is a difference: whereas in our argument (as well as in its counterpart at *Tht.* 181c–183b, on which see below) the impossibility of speaking correctly of an object in flux seems to be an unexpected and unpalatable consequence which Socrates draws from the flux theory, here it is rather introduced as an outrageous *tenet* of the Secret Doctrine itself, such as might have been advanced by the historical Cratylus in the final phase of his career (see §I.2.1). Caution, however, is required: another part of the meaning of 152d3–4, and indeed the main one in context, is that nothing has any intrinsic or *subject-independent* feature. The Secret Doctrine's opening claim is primarily a denial of objectivity and only secondarily a denial of stability.[39]

At *Tht.* 153d–157c the Secret Doctrine unfolds into a very sophisticated account of perception. I summarized this account in §5.3.4; there I also pointed out that in several respects it is indebted to the views of Leucippus and Democritus (whom Socrates never mentions among flux theorists). This is an analogy with *Cra.*, where the flux theory expounded in the etymologies contains several allusions to atomist views (§§5.3.1–3). Of course the two theories are different, though not incompatible; on either occasion Plato borrows from the atomists (as well as from his other sources) only what suits his present purposes.

One important point to remark – and another analogy between the two dialogues – is this. The world depicted by the Secret Doctrine is certainly in the grip of very radical change. According to the Doctrine's most advanced stage (159e–160a), whenever a perceiver and a perceived object enter into a perceptual transaction with each other, they are *ipso facto* turned into two items qualitatively and numerically different from before. Yet it seems that this world, like the one depicted by the flux theory of the *Cra.* etymologies, is *not totally unstable*; for there are at least some transformations it does not allow for. In particular, it does not seem possible for a 'slow' motion to become a quick one or vice versa: e.g. an eye cannot become a stream of whiteness, nor can a stream of seeing become a stone.

At *Tht.* 181c–183b the Secret Doctrine is refuted. Socrates starts off by drawing a distinction between spatial change, or movement, and qualitative change, or alteration, and arguing that the flux theorists must hold that everything is constantly undergoing *both* kinds of change – more generally, *every* kind of change (181c–182a). Then he briefly recapitulates the Secret Doctrine's account of perception and argues that, if the twin offspring are constantly subject to qualitative as well as to spatial change, they cannot be correctly said to be respectively (e.g.) an instance of whiteness and an instance of seeing (182ae). In the final analysis, the thesis that perception is knowledge, and more generally any statement whatsoever, is as right and as wrong as its negation (182e–183b).

[39] See Lee 2005: 93.

We can now look in more detail at the section about the flux of whiteness (182ce):

SO. Now, if things were only moving through space and not altering, we should presumably be able to say with what qualities the moving items flow ... But since not even this stands still, that the flowing item flows white, but it changes, so that there is flux of this very thing, whiteness, and change into another colour, lest it be convicted of standing still in this respect [ἵνα μὴ ἁλῷ ταύτῃ μένον], is it ever possible to speak of any colour in such a way as to speak of it correctly?

THEODORUS. And how could one do so, Socrates, either with it or with anything else of that sort, if, while one is speaking, it is always slipping away from him because it is in flux?

The verbal parallels between *Tht.* 182d4–7 and *Cra.* 439d8–11 are striking. 'Is it ever possible to speak of any colour in such a way as to speak of it correctly?' (ἆρά ποτε οἷόν τέ τι προσειπεῖν χρῶμα[40] ὥστε καὶ ὀρθῶς προσαγορεύειν;) corresponds to our 'is it possible ... to say of it correctly ...?' (Ἆρ' οὖν οἷόν τε προσειπεῖν αὐτὸ ὀρθῶς ... ;). 'If it is always slipping away while one is speaking' (εἴπερ ἀεὶ λέγοντος ὑπεξέρχεται) corresponds to our 'if it is always slipping away ... while we're speaking' (εἰ ἀεὶ ὑπεξέρχεται ... ἅμα ἡμῶν λεγόντων).[41]

So the *Tht.* argument turns out to be a more complex and sophisticated version of that in *Cra.* This relationship resembles the one between the argument against Protagoras at *Cra.* 386ad and its refinement in *Tht.* (see §2.4.2). It also accords with the various connections between the two flux theories that are at stake in either dialogue. But *Cra.* and *Tht.* share also a puzzling feature, as we have seen: both expound first one flux theory and then apparently criticize another, more extreme one. Hence both dialogues raise the same question: how do we get from the moderate theory that is expounded to the extreme theory that is refuted?

Now *Tht.* does seem to provide at least some sort of answer to this question; and it is reasonable to expect that a version of the same answer will hold good of *Cra.* as well. To see what the answer of *Tht.* is we must shift the spotlight back to the refutation's first section (181c–182a). Socrates kicks off as follows (181c):

[40] At *Tht.* 182d4 I remove the comma which most editors print after χρῶμα.
[41] At *Tht.* 182d7 I take λέγοντος as a genitive absolute corresponding to *Cra.* 439d10 ἅμα ἡμῶν λεγόντων (cf. Levett/Burnyeat 1990, McDowell 1973, Sedley 2004b: 95; see KG II.81 on the lack of an explicit subject, and add *R.* 604e to their examples). Some instead take the genitive to be governed by ὑπεξέρχεται: 'slipping away from someone who is speaking' (cf. Cornford 1935, Chappell 2004). This would be a parallel for Owen's construal of *Cra.* 439d8–9 ὑπεξέρχεται as 'is slipping away *from us*' (see n.28).

The arguments (439b–440d)

It seems to me that the starting point of our inquiry is about motion, i.e. what sort of thing they mean when they assert that all things are in motion [ποῖόν τί ποτε ἄρα λέγοντές φασι τὰ πάντα κινεῖσθαι].

He characterizes the flux theorists as holding that 'all things are in motion' (i.e., of course, *always* in motion). This chimes with the formulation of the Secret Doctrine: cf. 156a 'everything is motion [τὸ πᾶν κίνησις ἦν] and nothing else', 156c 'all these things ... are in motion' (ταῦτα πάντα ... κινεῖται).⁴² It also chimes with the formulations to be found in *Cra.*, i.e. (1) (e.g. 412d, 436e, 439c) and a variant of it, which can be compendiously phrased as

(1*) Everything is always changing and nothing is ever at rest

and occurs (with 'ever' invariably understood) at 401d–402a (very first mention of the theory, with reference to Heraclitus), 411bc, 440a (the only occurrence within the arguments themselves).

Thus Socrates announces that we must find out what the flux theorists mean when they hold that all things are in motion. Then he distinguishes between movement and alteration; and then comes the following exchange (181d–182a):

SO. Well now, having thus drawn this distinction let us talk to those who assert that all things are in motion [τοῖς τὰ πάντα φάσκουσιν κινεῖσθαι] and ask them: 'Do you say that everything is in motion in both ways, both moving through space and undergoing alteration, or that something is in motion in both ways and something in just one way?'
THEO. By Zeus, I can't say; but I think they'd answer 'in both ways'.
SO. Otherwise, my friend, they'll find that things turn out to be both in motion and standing still [κινούμενά τε αὐτοῖς καὶ ἑστῶτα φανεῖται], and it won't be any more correct to say that all things are in motion than to say that they stand still [οὐδὲν μᾶλλον ὀρθῶς ἕξει εἰπεῖν ὅτι κινεῖται τὰ πάντα ἢ ὅτι ἕστηκεν] ... Therefore, since they must be in motion [ἐπειδὴ κινεῖσθαι αὐτὰ δεῖ], and there must not be absence of motion in anything, all things are always in every kind of motion [πάντα δὴ πᾶσαν κίνησιν ἀεὶ κινεῖται].

The argument seems to go as follows. If by the claim that everything is (always) changing, i.e. (1), the flux theorists meant nothing more than that

(9) Everything is always changing in some respect,

---

⁴² Strictly speaking, the claim that everything *is* motion (156a) is very different from the claim that everything is *in* motion (156c, 180d, 181c). But on any interpretation it is hard to give a strictly literal construal of the former claim. For an analogous looseness cf. *Sph.* 247e 'the beings *are nothing other than* capacity.'

then they should at the same time accept that

(13) Everything is always at rest in some respect.

That is to say, they should accept

(14) Everything is always changing *in some respect* and is always at rest *in some other respect*.

But this is not – or should not be – the *spirit* in which the original claim was put forward; all the emphasis on the universality of change would be pointless, if supporters of (1) were in fact ready to stay content with anything as modest as (14). The original spirit is rather captured by a stronger claim:

(10) Everything is always changing in every respect.

That is to say, (10) is what supporters of (1) really mean by it. A version of this argument might well underlie Socrates' tacit move, in *Cra.*, from (1) to (10); and I submit that this is so.

Of course the argument is thoroughly unsatisfactory. As far as *Tht.* is concerned, it is unclear why the flux theorist could not stay content with (9) and (14), which in fact are all that the Secret Doctrine's account of perception appears to require – and also all that even the most biased of readers might ascribe to the authors (Homer etc.) on whom the Secret Doctrine was fathered. It is natural to suspect that the argument is *ad hominem*: Plato is attacking someone who endorses the bare slogan 'everything is (always) in motion', i.e. (1), but as a matter of fact seems unwilling to impose any restriction on flux. His target might be the fanatic Heracliteans humorously portrayed at 179d–180c, who

take most care not to allow anything to be stable either in their words or in their own souls, believing, as it seems to me, that this would be something stationary – which they are totally at war with and try to banish from everywhere as far as they can.

But if this is so, then the argument leaves the Secret Doctrine's account of perception to stand essentially unimpaired.[43]

Unsatisfactory as it may be, this is the only argument offered in *Tht.* to explain why supporters of (1) should be committed to (10).[44] Only in virtue

---

[43] My interpretation is partly consonant with Lee's (2005: 111–17).
[44] An influential interpretation ascribes to Socrates a different, more interesting argument, according to which extreme flux is a consequence of Theaetetus' definition of knowledge as perception, i.e. is the price Theaetetus has to pay in order to guarantee the total incorrigibility of perceptual judgements. 'If a thing is stable, or stable in some respect ..., that means there is an objective

of this argument can Socrates, at 183a, eventually wind up his refutation by claiming that the original, bare slogan that everything is (always) changing entails, in the final analysis, the collapse of language:

if all things are in motion [εἰ πάντα κινεῖται], then every answer, about any subject, is equally correct, both to say 'it is so' and 'it is not so'.

We can regard *Cra.* 439d8–9 as an instance of this general, summary statement. In place of the general antecedent 'all things are in motion' *Cra.* has 'the beautiful is always slipping away' (where 'always' makes explicit what was just understood in *Tht.*, and 'is slipping away' is, we are assuming, equivalent to 'is in motion', i.e. 'is changing'). In place of the consequent 'every answer, about any subject, is equally correct, etc.' *Cra.* has a consequent to the effect that it is impossible to say of the beautiful itself that is *that* and *such*.

From our present perspective, one of the most interesting things about the *Tht.* refutation is that it is entirely devoted to showing how absurd it would be to suppose that anything *in this world* is always changing in every respect. This corroborates the suspicion (see (ii) in §9.1.4) that, although the argument of *Cra.* is formulated with reference to the forms, Socrates cannot but see that it could be extended to sensible particulars.

9.1.6 *The second argument (439e)*

Somehow or other, we have finally got out of the first argument. We can now turn to the second – to discover that it is no easier read:

so. How, then, could that which never stands in the same state be something [Πῶς οὖν ἂν εἴη τὶ ἐκεῖνο ὃ μηδέποτε ὡσαύτως ἔχει];[45] For if it ever stands in the same state, during that time it clearly is not changing at all [εἰ γάρ ποτε ὡσαύτως ἴσχει, ἔν γ' ἐκείνῳ τῷ χρόνῳ δῆλον ὅτι οὐδὲν μεταβαίνει]; and if

---

basis for correcting or confirming someone's judgement as to how it is, or how it is in that respect' (Burnyeat 1990: 49; see the whole of his 42–52, and cf. Denyer 1991: 100–3, Sedley 2004b: 90–2). This is a subtle argument (though it is not clear whether it is valid); but it is not the one that is offered in the text. A further drawback of this interpretation is that it cannot be extended to *Cra.*, where no deep connection between Protagorean relativism and flux is stated or suggested; nor does it fit well with Aristotle's reference to extreme flux at *Metaph.* Γ5.1010a7–9 (in a chapter thick with echoes of *Tht.*). Yet another drawback is that, on this interpretation, *Tht.* does not argue against flux in its own right, but only against flux insofar as Protagorean relativism and Theaetetus' definition of knowledge as perception are (allegedly) committed to it. We should rather expect a 'standalone' argument, something that can be abstracted from its context; and the argument in the text, however flimsy, is precisely of this sort.

[45] I render ὡσαύτως ἔχειν/ἴσχειν as 'to *stand* in the same state', instead of 'to *be* in the same state', in order to mirror the fact that the Greek expression does not contain 'to be'. This may prove important in an argument where *being* is at stake.

it always stands in the same state and is always the same [εἰ δὲ ἀεὶ ὡσαύτως ἔχει καὶ τὸ αὐτό ἐστι], how could this thing change or be in motion, given that it does not depart at all from its own form [πῶς ἂν τοῦτό γε μεταβάλλοι ἢ κινοῖτο, μηδὲν ἐξιστάμενον τῆς αὑτοῦ ἰδέας;]?

CR. There's no way it could. (439e1–6)

In the first sentence (e1–2) Socrates states another consequence of the flux theory. More precisely, he seems to be stating a *corollary* or development of the first argument; this is suggested by the particle οὖν, 'then', which introduces the sentence.[46] Then, at e2–5, he adds some sort of justification, introduced by e2 γάρ.

The grammatical subject of e1–2 is 'that which never stands in the same state'. Here we may, following Sedley 2003: 170, take 'that' (ἐκεῖνο) to refer back to the beautiful, which was the subject matter of the preceding lines (and was referred to by the αὐτό's at d8 and d10). But then the relative clause would have to mean, not very naturally, '*if* it never stands in the same state' or 'which – *on the hypothesis we are presently examining* – never stands in the same state'; otherwise Socrates would be implying that, *actually*, the beautiful never stands in the same state. An alternative, safer construal is available (and seems in fact to have been adopted by most interpreters): 'that' may be not anaphoric but proleptic and be just the antecedent of a general relative clause: 'that which' = 'whatever'.[47]

Thus Socrates may be talking about the beautiful, characterizing it as never in the same state on the flux hypothesis; or he may be talking generally about what never stands in the same state, sc. like the beautiful on the flux hypothesis. Henceforth I will assume that the latter is the case; and I will paraphrase e1–2 thus:

(15) X never stands in the same state $\rightarrow \neg$ (X is something).

On this construal, the argument is expressly meant to be valid for *anything* – not just any *form* – that is supposed to be in flux. It may seem that thereby Socrates fails to comply with the intention, stated at d3–4, to leave

---

[46] Cf. Calvert 1970: 37.
[47] Sedley 2003: 170 objects that 'that which never stands in the same state' cannot continue as the subject of e2–3. But at e2–3 Socrates may well be using 'it' loosely, as though the previous question had not read 'that which never stands in the same state' but rather '*if something* never stands in the same state, …' The same sort of looseness occurs at *Tht.* 152e: ἔστι μὲν … οὐδέποτ' οὐδέν, ἀεὶ δὲ γίγνεται, 'nothing ever is, but [*everything*] always comes to be'.

Smith 1917 doubted (in connection with *R.* 596a) whether a relative clause which is introduced by the pronoun ὅς and has the verb in the indicative can be general. His doubts were unfounded: see the replies of Mair and Sonnenschein 1918, and to their examples add 440a ὃ γιγνώσκει, *Chrm.* 172d, *Phd.* 65a, *R.* 477d, *Lg.* 667de.

aside sensible particulars and focus on the forms instead. But he does not put forward specific examples of particulars; and 440b will confirm that the forms remain prominent in his mind.[48]

Let us examine (15) in more detail, beginning with its left side. Where does this notion of *never standing in the same state* come from? Clearly Socrates is picking up d11 'no longer stand in this state', the last expression used to refer to any sort of change. Now, the flux theory claims (1), 'Everything is always changing'; the first argument assumed an instance of this, i.e. (8*) 'The beautiful is always changing', as a premiss; and thence it takes but a trivial step to introduce our notion:

(16) X is always changing ↔ X never stands in the same state.

But while at d11 the notion of a 'state' in which X stands at time t seemed to coincide with the notion of a feature which X has at t, here it rather seems that the 'state' in which X is at t is best understood as the *collection* of X's features at t – something we might prefer to call its *total* state.[49]

Actually, in discussing the first argument we saw (§9.1.4) that, although the only premiss explicitly stated was (8*), Socrates was actually assuming the extreme (12), 'The beautiful is always changing in every respect.' So here too it is reasonable to suspect that by (15) Socrates actually wants to introduce

(17) X never stands in the same state *in any respect* → ¬ (X is something),

and that he is not assuming (16) but rather

(18) X is always changing *in every respect* ↔ X never stands in the same state *in any respect*.

Let us come to the right side of (15) and (17). What does 'to be something', εἶναί τι, mean here? I take it that 'X is something' means just 'For some Y, X is Y' and that, therefore, 'It is not the case that X is something,' i.e. 'X is not *any*thing,' means 'For any Y, X is not Y.' I mean this formulation to cover both the case where 'X is Y' has the form of an identity sentence and the case where 'X is Y' has the form of a predicative sentence; that is to say, 'X is something' picks up both of the kinds of statement

---

[48] Alternatively, it could be suggested that in (15) the range of 'X' is implicitly *restricted* to forms. But I am sceptical: clearly there is no restriction at 440a (where Socrates states as his premiss a version of (1*), 'All things [πάντα χρήματα] change and nothing is at rest') or 440cd.
[49] Cf. the use of the expression ὡσαύτως/κατὰ ταὐτὰ ἔχειν at *Phd.* 78c–80b.

which Socrates distinguished at d9 (§9.1.4).⁵⁰ At the same time, we should also bear in mind that 'to be something' is also a Platonic expression for existence (e.g. *Hp. Ma.* 288a, *Prm.* 130b). Therefore (17) can be read as saying also that, if *X* never stands in the same state in any respect, then *X does not exist*.⁵¹ (This construal will be confirmed by 440b: see §9.1.9.)

Anyway, (17), and indeed (15) too, seem to be obviously false. Surely, if *X* stands in (total) state *Σ* at *t*, and *Y* is a feature that is part of *Σ*, then *X exists* and *is Y* at *t*, even if one instant later *X* is replaced by another object, *X**, which is not in *Σ* but in a completely different state?

To assess the force of this objection we must investigate the rationale for (17). We might expect the following γάρ-sentence (e2–5) to come to our aid. But these lines contain no reference whatsoever to *(not) being anything*. They do not explain the connection between never standing in the same state and not being anything;⁵² they are rather concerned with the connection between being always changing and never standing in the same state. Hence their function cannot be to justify (17); it must rather be – less interestingly – to justify the introduction of 'that which never stands in the same state' in place of 'that which is always changing'. We shall see the details of this in due course; for the moment we have to try to reconstruct the justification for (17) which Socrates leaves unexpressed (if it has not dropped out of the text, as is supposed by Strachan, who in the OCT's apparatus suspects a lacuna after e2 ἔχει).⁵³

In doing so we should take into account the fact that εἰ οὖν seems to present the second argument as a corollary of the first.⁵⁴ One conjecture that satisfies this desideratum and fits well with the paucity of what Socrates says consists in supposing that he is implicitly relying on some such principle as this:

(19) *X* is *Y* → Some utterances of '*X* is *Y*' are true.

---

⁵⁰ For a comparably generic use of εἶναί τι see Arist. *APo.* 90a2–14, *SE* 166b37–167a6, 180a32–8. According to Sedley 2003: 170, instead, 'be something' here means 'be beautiful': Socrates is once again, as already at d9, talking about the self-predication 'The beautiful itself is beautiful.' This is implausible (cf. n.19). Why should Socrates be so cryptical?
⁵¹ Cf. Jowett's translation of εἰ Πῶς ... ἂν εἴη τι as 'how can that be a real thing' and Fine 1993: 136.
⁵² *Pace* Sedley 2003: 170, who takes the gist of e2–5 to be that '*any* degree of being brings with it a corresponding absence of change'.
⁵³ The same apparatus records also David Robinson's suspicion that the whole of e1–5 should be transposed somewhere else. But where? And would this help us understand (17)?
⁵⁴ There is another possibility: οὖν 'Proceeding to a new point, or a new stage in the march of thought' (*GP* 426, see 385c7). But the inferential οὖν seems better, because it gives the reader a clue about the grounds for (17). Furthermore, I doubt whether Plato or Aristotle ever use οὖν to introduce a new item in a series of *arguments*, as here.

The first argument can be regarded as showing that, if X is always changing in every respect, then the right side of (19) is false: no utterance of 'X is Y', however short its duration, can come out true. In the second argument, Socrates goes on to point out that, if this is so, *then* (οὖν), if X (is always changing in every respect, and hence, equivalently,) never stands in the same state in any respect, then the left side of (19) too must be false: X is not Y, for any Y. That is to say, X is not anything – and so does not exist either.[55]

Now, when X is a form, its not being anything – i.e. the right side of (17) – is undoubtedly inconsistent with the assumption that the forms exist, which was advanced at 439cd and will be picked up at 440b (see §9.1.2). But if I am right about the very close connection between the present argument and the previous one, and if I was right in §9.1.4 that, even when X is a sensible particular, Socrates cannot accept the impossibility of saying truly that it is *that* or *such*, then it follows that he must regard the right side of (17) as false even when X is a sensible particular.

Now we come to e2–5, the γάρ-sentence. As I anticipated above, the function of these lines seems to be to justify the introduction of the notion of 'that which never stands in the same state'. More precisely, the lines seem to prove

(20) ¬ (X never stands in the same state) → ¬ (X is always changing).

and thus to prove by contraposition

(21) X is always changing → X never stands in the same state,

which is the left-to-right half of (16) and is presumably meant to entail

(22) X is always changing *in every respect* → X never stands in the same state *in any respect*,

which is the left-to-right half of (18).

Strictly speaking, thereby Socrates does nothing to prove the *right-to-left* halves of (16) and (18), which are essential to the argument's validity. Perhaps he regards the matter as trifling – as it actually is.

---

[55] On this interpretation the argument, just like the previous one (see n.35), has nothing to do with the being/becoming contrast: Socrates cannot mean that X *is* not anything but *becomes* something. The contrast might perhaps play a role in a completely different reconstruction, which is suggested by Fine (1993: 136): 'if forms change, they cannot be "things" (*ti*); for an object to exist, it must be minimally stable and endure for more than an instant'. But both this suggestion and its possible expansion in terms of being and becoming seem to me less economic and straightforward than my interpretation.

In his proof of (20) Socrates distinguishes between two possible situations in which it is not the case that X never stands in the same state: either X stands in the same state only *for some time* (ποτε) or X stands in the same state *always* (ἀεί). In the former situation, there is some time during which X is not changing; in the latter, X is always not changing. Either way, it is not the case that X is always changing; (20), and hence (21), and hence (22), turn out to be true.

The formulation of e2–5 contains a couple of asymmetries which so far I have ignored. At e3–4 Socrates says 'and if it always stands in the same state *and is always the same*'. The addition of 'is always the same' (i.e. the same thing) enables Socrates to pick up the distinction, introduced in the first argument (d10–11), between 'becoming another thing' and 'no longer standing in this state', i.e. between numerical and qualitative (non)identity. The addition has no parallel within the second argument. But in fact Socrates is presumably just taking it for granted that, if X never stands in the same state (in any respect), then neither does X stay identical through time.[56] The reason why he adds an explicit reference to identity here is the same as the reason why at e4–5 he concludes the sentence with another addition, i.e. 'given that it does not depart at all from its own form' (or 'without departing ...': μηδὲν ἐξιστάμενον τῆς αὑτοῦ ἰδέας), which is but a variant formulation for 'if it always stands in the same state (and is always the same)'. Both additions are emphatic; for e3–5 describe what in fact is the *real* condition of the beautiful itself, our original subject matter and still the centre of Socrates' interest, which at d5–6 was agreed to be 'always such as it is'.

9.1.7 *The third argument (439e–440a)*

Socrates goes on:

SO. But neither could it come to be known by anyone [οὐδ' ἂν γνωσθείη γε ὑπ' οὐδενός]. For while that which[57] was going to know it was approaching, it would become another thing and otherwise qualified [ἅμα γὰρ ἂν ἐπιόντος τοῦ γνωσομένου ἄλλο καὶ ἀλλοῖον γίγνοιτο], so that it could no longer come to be known what sort of thing it is or what state it stands in [ὥστε οὐκ ἂν γνωσθείη ἔτι ὁποῖόν γέ τί ἐστιν ἢ πῶς ἔχον]; and no knowledge, I

---

[56] On qualitative and numerical nonidentity through time in Plato see Ademollo (in preparation-3).
[57] 440b4–5 strongly suggest that τοῦ γνωσομένου is the genitive of the *neuter* participle.

think, knows what it knows as being in no state [γνῶσις δὲ δήπου οὐδεμία γιγνώσκει ὃ γιγνώσκει μηδαμῶς ἔχον].
CR. It's as you say. (439e7–440a5)

Socrates deploys an argument closely parallel to the first to draw a new unpalatable consequence from the flux theory: it destroys the possibility of knowledge. As he puts it in the argument's initial sentence (e7), what never stands in the same state (the grammatical subject of e1–2, which is naturally taken to continue as the subject here and in the following lines until a3 γνῶσις),[58] besides not being anything as the second argument has shown, cannot be known either. The reason for this is explained in the sequel (e7–a4). Acquiring knowledge of something is a process that takes time; but from (1), or rather (10), it follows that, before this process can be completed, the thing to be known becomes another thing, endowed with other features (ἄλλο καὶ ἀλλοῖον, a1–2: again the distinction between numerical and qualitative nonidentity, as in the previous two arguments); and then it is no longer possible to know anything about the former thing (a2–3); indeed, it is no longer possible to know it at all (a3–4).

This was a long shot view of the argument. Now for a close-up of some details.

I start with e7–a1 ἅμα … ἐπιόντος τοῦ γνωσομένου (which of course is meant to be parallel to 439d10 ἅμα ἡμῶν λεγόντων). Taken at face value, this reference to the knower-to-be 'approaching' or 'going towards' the object suggests a situation where the object is a sensible particular: I see something at a distance and want to know what it is; I 'approach' it to find out; but before I reach it, it transmogrifies into something completely different, leaving me with no way to discover what the former object was. This sort of situation, however, is too specific to allow an interesting generalization, even within the realm of sensible particulars. Moreover, we know that throughout these arguments Socrates is mainly interested in the forms, not in sensible particulars. So his talk of 'approaching' the object is primarily metaphorical for a process of rumination which aims at knowledge of a form.[59]

On the other hand, insofar as the argument does, after all, apply to sensible particulars – or to some situations in which sensible particulars are involved – the consequence that the object is unknowable need not be

---

[58] Cf. Calvert 1970: 39. Sedley (2003: 170 and n.45) instead takes the subject to be 'the beautiful' throughout; see §9.1.6 on e1–2. In any event, the subject is certainly not 'what always stands in the same state and is always the same' (cf. e3–5) as Mackenzie 1986: 138 and n.34 claims.
[59] Cf. the use of ἐπάνειμι, 'ascend', at Smp. 211bc; and also Arist. Ph. 186a4 τὸν … τρόπον τοῦτον ἐπιοῦσιν, 'if … we *approach the thesis* in this way' (tr. Barnes 1984, my italics).

regarded by Socrates as absurd. For Plato often denies that sensible particulars can be known at all.[60]

The next detail to focus on is 'what sort of thing it is or what state it stands in' (ὁποῖόν ... τί ἐστιν ἢ πῶς ἔχον [sc. ἐστίν], a2–3). Thereby Socrates seems to be referring to a distinction between two kinds of things we may wish to know about X. This is presumably equivalent to a distinction between two kinds of substitutions for 'Y' in 'Z knows that X is Y.' Now, in the light of a1 and the previous two arguments, what we should expect is a distinction between (a) the case in which 'X is Y' is an identity sentence and (b) the case in which 'X is Y' is a predicative sentence. And if Socrates' distinction coincides with the expected one, then ὁποῖόν ... τί ἐστιν corresponds to (a) and πῶς ἔχον to (b), as in Ficino's bold translation 'quid sit aut quale'.[61] Admittedly, the former correspondence would read somewhat oddly; for elsewhere (*Men.* 71b, 87b; cf. *Chrm.* 159a) Socrates rather distinguishes between knowing ὁποῖόν τί ἐστιν X and knowing τί ἐστιν X, i.e. knowing X's definition – which will presumably take the form of an identity sentence. Plato's terminology, however, is notoriously fluid. Compare the vicissitudes of the related formula ποῖόν τί ἐστιν, which at *Men.* 86e–87b is equivalent to ὁποῖόν τί ἐστιν and contrasted with ὅτι ἐστίν (= τί ἐστιν), but at *Euthphr.* 5cd is instead equivalent to τί ἐστιν.

As for πῶς ἔχον, note that here the notion of a 'state' in which X stands seems to coincide again with that of a single feature of X, as in the first argument (d11, see §9.1.4), and not with that of the collection of X's features, as it rather seemed to do in the second argument (§9.1.6).

Bear this in mind as we come to the argument's final sentence (a3–4). Virtually all interpreters here translate as though the force of the phrase μηδαμῶς ἔχον were conditional, 'if it stands in no state'. Thereby, however, Socrates' train of thought is spoiled. So far the object in flux had rather been referred to as 'that which never stands in the same state' (e1–2), and this seemed to be the understood subject of the argument's opening sentence (e7), which anticipated the conclusion by claiming that, if X never stands in the same state, then X cannot be known.[62] Socrates went on to say that, if X never stands in the same state, then X is always becoming something numerically and qualitatively different while you are trying to know it (e7 ἅμα ... a2 γίγνοιτο), and that if this is so, then it cannot be

---

[60] He does so in *Phaedo*, *Republic* and *Timaeus*. But sometimes he seems to take a milder stance: see *Phd.* 73cd (on which see Dancy 2004: 262), *R.* 520c, *Tht.* 201bc (on which see McDowell 1973: 227–8).
[61] Cf. Kahn 2002: 116.
[62] Cf. Calvert 1970: 40.

known either what sort of thing *X* is or what state *X* stands in (a2 ὥστε ... a3 ἔχον). Now he needs a further premiss to the effect that, *if this is so* (i.e. if it cannot be known either what sort of thing *X* is or what state it stands in), *then* X *cannot be known full stop*. This will enable him to justify the opening claim that, if *X* never stands in the same state, then *X* cannot be known full stop. He does not need a further premiss to the effect that, if *X* stands in *no* state, then *X* cannot be known full stop.

These considerations lead me to follow Ficino[63] in construing μηδαμῶς ἔχον as predicative: 'no knowledge knows what it knows *as standing in no state*'; and to regard this as a loose way of making the following point:

(23) *Z* knows *X* → for some state *S*, *Z* knows *X* as standing in *S*.

To know *X* is to know *X* as standing in some specific state or other; therefore, if for some reason (e.g. because *X* never stands in the same state in any respect) it is impossible to know *X* as standing in any specific state, then it is impossible to know *X* tout court.

The context makes it clear that (23) in its turn is meant to be equivalent to

(24) *Z* knows *X* → for some feature *Y*, *Z* knows that *X* is *Y*.

This is an important principle. It ties together two kinds of knowledge (knowing an *object* and knowing *that* something is the case) which most philosophers nowadays take to be distinct; and scholars have suspected that it – or something close to it – is operating in other Platonic discussions, most notably in the *Theaetetus*.[64]

Let me add a brief afterthought. It may seem that in (23) Socrates disregards his own distinction between knowing what sort of thing *X* is and knowing what state *X* stands in, and that therefore (23) ought to be emended as follows (assuming the above construal of the distinction):

(23*) *Z* knows *X* → (for some *W*, *Z* knows *X* as being identical with *W*) ∨ (for some state *S*, *Z* knows *X* as standing in *S*),

Perhaps, however, Socrates believes that the former variety of knowledge involves the latter: you cannot know of something that it is identical with *X* if you do not know of some feature that it belongs to *X*. And if this is what Socrates believes, then (23) is a concise and correct way of expressing it.

---

[63] 'Cognitio nulla ita rem percipit, ut nullo modo se habentem percipiat.' Cf. Barney 2001: 156.
[64] On *Tht.* see e.g. Bostock 1988: 37–8 and Burnyeat 1990: 129–34, esp. 132.

9.1.8 The fourth argument (440ab)

SO. But it is not even reasonable to say that there is knowledge [οὐδὲ γνῶσιν εἶναι φάναι εἰκός], Cratylus, if all things change and nothing is at rest. For if this thing itself, knowledge [αὐτὸ τοῦτο, ἡ γνῶσις], does not change from being knowledge, then knowledge would always be at rest and there would be knowledge. On the other hand, if the form itself of knowledge changes [εἰ δὲ καὶ αὐτὸ τὸ εἶδος μεταπίπτει τῆς γνώσεως], then at the same time as it changed into a form other than knowledge there would be no knowledge [ἅμα τ' ἂν μεταπίπτοι εἰς ἄλλο εἶδος γνώσεως καὶ οὐκ ἂν εἴη γνῶσις]; and if it is always changing, there would always be no knowledge, and according to this reasoning there would be neither that which is to know nor that which is to be known [ἐκ τούτου τοῦ λόγου οὔτε τὸ γνωσόμενον οὔτε τὸ γνωσθησόμενον ἂν εἴη]. (440a6–b4)

If *everything* is always changing (in every respect), then, among other things, the *form of knowledge* itself is. But as the form of knowledge turns into some other form,[65] there is no form of knowledge – and hence no knowledge – any more.[66] And if there is no knowledge, then there is nothing that knows and nothing that gets known.[67] More precisely, if there is *never* any knowledge, then there is *never* anything that knows or is known:

(25) $\forall x \, \forall y \, \neg \exists t$ (x knows y at t).

Someone might perhaps suppose that at b4 the phrases τὸ γνωσόμενον and τὸ γνωσθησόμενον are meant to refer to a pair of forms, closely connected with the form of knowledge but distinct from it, i.e. respectively

---

[65] εἰς ἄλλο εἶδος γνώσεως (b1–2): 'into a form *other than knowledge*', not 'into another form of knowledge' as some have it, which makes no sense in context. The hyperbaton ἄλλο … γνώσεως is indeed remarkable; some have interpreted analogously Arist. *De An.* 431a6 ἄλλο εἶδος τοῦτο κινήσεως. See Riddell 1867: §289.b for other (less outrageous, because unambiguous) Platonic hyperbata.
  Anyway, why does Socrates assume that knowledge would turn into another *form*? Since the hypothesis under scrutiny is that of change in *every* respect, it should be possible for knowledge to turn into anything whatsoever – even a coconut. But the assumption that it turns into another form is sufficient for the argument's purposes.

[66] The occurrences of εἴη at a9 (εἴη γνῶσις) and b2–3 (οὐκ ἂν εἴη γνῶσις) are existential, as the parallel with a6 and b4 proves. Those who instead translate 'it would/would not be knowledge' unnecessarily blur Socrates' train of thought.

[67] According to Sedley 2003: 171, the argument is closely parallel to *Tht.* 182de, where it is argued that, on the flux hypothesis, the definition of knowledge as perception 'becomes unstatable, since the very thing that has been identified as knowledge will as we speak be changing into something that is *not* knowledge'. That may be so. But I am not sure that the *Tht.* argument need be interpreted as involving a reference to the flux of perception or knowledge (as distinct from *individual instances* of perception or knowledge).

a form of Knower and a form of Thing Known. But then it would be hard to make sense of the participles' future tense; and the ideal triad comprising Knowledge, Knower and Thing Known would look pretty redundant. The phrases are rather equivalent to, respectively, 'anything that knows' and 'anything that gets known'; and the force of the future is consecutive.[68]

The more balanced triad consisting of Knowledge, knower and thing known is worthy of some consideration. For it comes – perhaps unwittingly – closer than most of what we find elsewhere in Plato or Aristotle[69] to the notion of a dyadic *relation* (here, knowledge) instantiated by pairs of items (here, a knower and a thing known). Contrast Aristotle's treatment, in *Cat.* 7 and *Metaph.* Δ15, of ἐπιστήμη, 'knowledge', not as a relation between two items but as itself a relative item, the correlative of τὸ ἐπιστητόν, 'the knowable'.

9.1.9 Flux rejected? (440bc)

(so.) But if there is always that which knows, and there is that which is known [εἰ δὲ ἔστι μὲν ἀεὶ τὸ γιγνῶσκον, ἔστι δὲ τὸ γιγνωσκόμενον], and there is the beautiful, and there is the good, and there is each single one of the beings [ἔστι δὲ τὸ καλόν, ἔστι δὲ τὸ ἀγαθόν, ἔστι δὲ ἓν ἕκαστον τῶν ὄντων], then these things we are now saying don't seem to me to resemble flux or movement at all. (440b4–c1)

I anticipated the essentials of the interpretation of these lines in §9.1.2, where I pointed out that there may be some uncertainty as to their purpose. Socrates might be just inferring from (1) entailing certain consequences that, *if* some of those consequences do not hold, then neither does (1).[70] Or perhaps Socrates is cautiously suggesting a full-blown refutation of (1), to the effect that, *because* some of the consequences are ruled out by our assumptions and hence do not hold, (1) is false.

The lines are occupied by a single conditional sentence. The protasis (b4–7) consists of a series of clauses linked together by an initial μέν and four successive δέ's, but can in fact be regarded as the conjunction of two compound sentences: (i) 'there is always that which knows and there is that which is known', (ii) 'there is the beautiful, and there is the good,

---

[68] Cf. Antiph. 6.4 μή ἐστιν ὁ τιμωρήσων, 'there is not anyone to take vengeance'; S. *El.* 1197, οὐδ' οὑπαρήξων οὐδ' ὁ κωλύσων πάρα; 'isn't there anyone to come to your aid or stop this?'
[69] See Mignucci 1986: 101–5 and Ademollo 2007.
[70] So perhaps Thornton 1970: 589.

and there is each single one of the beings'.[71] The second of these repeats almost word for word the 439c8–d1 assumption that the forms exist. The other initial assumption, made at 439d5–6, according to which the forms are unchanging, is *not* being picked up here, despite what several scholars seem to think.

What does (i), the first conjunct, mean exactly?[72] It does not speak of two *forms*, the form of Knower and the form of Thing Known, and assert that they always exist. Like τὸ γνωσόμενον and τὸ γνωσθησόμενον in the fourth argument, τὸ γιγνῶσκον and τὸ γιγνωσκόμενον here mean simply 'something that knows' and 'something that is known'. The meaning might be supposed to be that there is something (an eternal knower) that always knows something or other and there is something (an eternal object of knowledge) that is always known by something or other:

(26) $\exists x \, \forall t \, \exists y \, (x \text{ knows } y \text{ at } t) \, \& \, \exists w \, \forall t \, \exists z \, (z \text{ knows } w \text{ at } t)$.

It would not be impossible for Plato to endorse (26): x might be something like the Demiurge of the *Timaeus* (or perhaps any human soul), while w could be any form. But Socrates' words would, I think, be too compressed and obscure a way of conveying this. More probably, Socrates is just saying that it is always the case that something or other knows something or other:

(27) $\forall t \, \exists x \, \exists y \, (x \text{ knows } y \text{ at } t)$.

This leaves it open whether y can only be a form or also a sensible particular. In any case, it is presumably meant to entail that the form of knowledge always exists.

(27) is, like (26), inconsistent with (25), the conclusion of the fourth argument. Therefore, once the fourth argument were combined with our first conjunct, the conclusion would follow that it is not the case that everything is always changing (in every respect).

The conflict between (i), the *first* conjunct of Socrates' protasis, and the conclusion of the fourth argument strongly suggests that a similar relation holds between (ii), the *second* conjunct, and the conclusion of one of the previous three arguments. Now, the second argument proved that, if

---

[71] Dalimier 279 n.453 would parse the protasis differently: she thinks that the first δέ clause is explained by the following ones and that the forms are mentioned as *examples* of 'that which is known' (cf. already Fowler's translation). But this construal of the δέ's strikes me as unnatural; nor did I find support for it in *GP*.

[72] The distinction between the alternative construals I go on to discuss in the text is briefly suggested by Kahn 1973a: 171.

something never stands in the same state (in any respect), i.e. is always changing (in every respect), then it *is not anything* – where the italicized words can, and indeed by now should, be interpreted as equivalent to 'does not exist' (§9.1.6). Once that argument were combined with our proposition that the forms exist, the conclusion would follow that *it is not the case that the forms are always changing (in every respect)*, and hence, again, that it is not the case that everything is always changing (in every respect).[73] At the same time, the present reference to the forms confirms that, although the second argument was formulated in general terms, Socrates there had primarily the forms in mind.

As for the apodosis (b7–c1), 'these things we are now saying' (ταῦτα ... ἃ νῦν ἡμεῖς λέγομεν) is a way of referring back to the contents of the apodosis, i.e. means 'the existence of the forms and of something that knows and something that's known';[74] and the claim that these 'things' do not 'resemble flux or movement at all' means that they are *inconsistent* with the thesis that everything is always changing (in every respect). Whether the existence of the forms, and of subjects and objects of knowledge, is being assumed as a genuine *premiss* of the argument is not completely clear, as we have seen.

9.1.10 Conclusion (440cd)

Socrates has said what he had to say and wraps it up by refusing to go any further:

(s o.) Now I'm afraid that it may be not easy to investigate whether these things are so or rather as Heraclitus and his followers say, along with many others. Nor is it worthy of a person completely in his sense to commit the care of himself and his own soul to names, trusting them and those who imposed them, and thus make confident assertions as if he knew anything and say in condemnation of himself and the beings that there's nothing sound in anything but all things flow like pots, and believe that the objects are in the very same condition as the people who suffer from catarrh – that all things are in the grip of flux and catarrh. Perhaps it is so, Cratylus, and perhaps not. So you must inquire bravely and thoroughly, and not accept anything

---

[73] Sedley 2003: 171 claims that (i) 'presupposes' (ii): the existence of subjects and objects of knowledge presupposes that of the forms. This is probably so; but it is unnecessary to suppose that this connection is being *stated* here.

[74] The translations of Jowett, 'I do not think that *they* can resemble a process or flux, *as we were just now supposing*' (taken over by Reeve), and Barney 2001: 158, 'it does not seem to me that these *beings* are, *as you now say*, anything like flowing or motion', are mistaken. (My italics throughout.)

easily (for you're still young and in your prime); and once you've inquired, if you find out how matters stand, share your findings with me. (440c1–d7)

In these lines Socrates interlaces *two* points which it is very important to keep distinct.

On the one hand, he suspends judgement over the question whether the flux theory is true, and urges Cratylus to pursue the further inquiry that is necessary to discover the truth. In fact, the derisive way in which he refers to the theory – by comparing, at c8–d3, the state of things allegedly in flux to that of leaking pots or people with runny noses[75]– would by itself be sufficient, if we knew nothing else, to show that he has no sympathy for it.

On the other hand, Socrates claims (c3 ff.) that it is unwise to think that knowledge about such a matter can be attained through etymology. In particular, since the etymologies revealed that the ancient namegivers were mostly supporters of the Catarrh Theory (see 439c), it is unwise to believe anything that radical on the grounds of etymology.

It is important to be clear that Socrates' professed uncertainty and his exhortation to investigate further (c1–3, d3–7) concern *only* the truth or falsity of the flux theory, *not* the silliness of believing it (or anything else) on the grounds of etymology. As regards the latter question, he is not weakening, but merely restating, the conclusion he reached at 439b (at the end of a discussion begun at 435d), i.e. that we must 'learn and search about' the nature of things 'not from names but from themselves'. And with that conclusion, the whole of Socrates' rejection of naturalism about names is being allowed to stand as a permanent result of the dialogue.

These lines also give us a piece of factual information about Cratylus, namely that he, unlike Socrates, is 'still young and in his prime' (or 'still young and of fit age', sc. for inquiring: d5–6 ἔτι ... νέος εἶ καὶ ἡλικίαν ἔχεις).[76] This agrees with 429de, where Socrates claimed that Cratylus' sophism was 'too clever' for him and for his age.

---

[75] This twofold comparison is a virtuoso piece of satire, trading on the ambiguity of the verb ῥέω and its derivatives. (i) Besides meaning 'flow', ῥέω also means 'leak' and thus can be said of a pot (Plu. *Ad principem ineruditum* 782EF); hence πάντα ὥσπερ κεράμια ῥεῖ (c8) = 'all things flow like [leaking] pots'. The pun is made more complex by the fact that immediately before Socrates ascribed to flux theorists the view that οὐδὲν ὑγιὲς οὐδενός, 'nothing is sound in anything': a well-established idiom (see LSJ ὑγιής II.3; cf. esp. the parallel of *Phd.* 89e + 90c, which was relevant also to 411bc), where however the adjective ὑγιής could also be applied to *pots* (*Grg.* 493e, *Tht.* 179d). Apelt's correction of κεράμια into χείμαρροα, 'torrents', would spoil everything. (ii) The noun κατάρρους, 'catarrh', recognizably derives from ῥέω; what is more, the noun ῥεῦμα can mean either 'stream' or 'bodily discharge, rheum' (see Hp. *VM* 18 for the latter use).

[76] For ἡλικίαν ἔχειν = 'to be in one's prime' see *Euthd.* 306d; cf. *Men.* 89b (ἀφικέσθαι εἰς τὴν ἡλικίαν), *Tht.* 142d (εἰς ἡλικίαν ἐλθεῖν). For the alternative meaning 'to be of fit age [for doing something]' see *Tht.* 146b (and cf. *Grg.* 484c), Hdt. 1.209.2.

9.2 EPILOGUE (440DE)

Cratylus' response to Socrates' exhortation to inquire further is an endorsement of the flux theory:

CR. I'll do so. But be assured, Socrates, that even now my view of the matter is not unconsidered [οὐδὲ νυνὶ ἀσκέπτως ἔχω], and as I consider it and take trouble over it [μοι σκοπουμένῳ καὶ πράγματα ἔχοντι], I am much more inclined to think that things are as Heraclitus says. (440d8–e2)

Already at 436e–437a, by claiming that the flux-names are correct (i.e. *naturally* correct), Cratylus committed himself to the truth of the flux theory. Here, however, the present tense of the participles σκοπουμένῳ and ἔχοντι seems to indicate that 'Cratylus is ... referring to the active consideration which he has been devoting to the problem *during the dialogue itself*' (Kirk 1951: 236, my italics;[77] as Sedley 2003: 18 n.40 notes, this is confirmed by a comparison with 391a σκοπουμένοις ἡμῖν ... φαίνεται). That is to say, Cratylus is not represented as already a convinced Heraclitean, as many scholars have thought,[78] but – quite the contrary – as first coming to believe in the flux theory in the course of this dialogue, when he is still young, as a result of being exposed to Socrates' etymologies.

If Aristotle's testimony about the further development of Cratylus' career is reliable (see §1.2.1), then these lines depict a fatal turn: we are actually watching Cratylus ignore Socrates' warnings and take his first steps along the path that will, in due course, make him into the extremist Heraclitean who decided to give up speech.[79]

Socrates' reply is a valediction:

SO. You'll teach me on another occasion, when you come back. Now go to the countryside, as you've prepared for doing; and Hermogenes here will accompany you [προπέμψει δέ σε καὶ Ἑρμογένης ὅδε]. (440e3–5)

Socrates' last words contain a subtle, delightful allusion to the old controversy about Hermogenes' name, which Cratylus alleged to be incorrect by his natural standards, as Hermogenes himself told Socrates at the very outset (383b–384a). In the course of the dialogue two explanations of this

---

[77] See already Méridier's translation.
[78] See e.g. Stallbaum 225, Allan 1954: 279–80, Cherniss 1955: 185, and Reeve: 'I have already investigated them and have taken a lot of trouble over the matter.'
[79] Cf. Adomėnas 2006: 32–3 and Sedley 2003: 19, 171–2. As Sedley remarks, Plato makes use of these 'prescient historical ironies' elsewhere too, e.g. in his portrayal of Critias and Charmides in the *Charmides*. A case that is especially relevant to our passage is Socrates' prophecy about Isocrates' future philosophical achievements at *Phdr.* 278e–279a (on which see de Vries 1969: 15–18, Rowe 1986: 215–16).

Cratylan riddle were considered: according to the first, the feature whose lack barred Hermogenes from qualifying as a true 'offspring of Hermes' was that of being good at making money (384c); according to the second, it was rather eloquence (408b). But now that Hermogenes will accompany (προπέμψει) Cratylus to the countryside, he will (as Barney 2001: 160 has pointed out) act as a true descendant of Hermes πομπαῖος, the 'accompanier' who guides travellers and escorts the souls of the dead to Hades.[80] The deictic pronoun ὅδε emphasizes Hermogenes' right to his name. Thus Socrates – in no more than five words – has a dig at Cratylus, as if he had, after all, been wrong about Hermogenes' name even by his own standards; pays a final oblique tribute to Hermogenes, whose views were eventually vindicated; and makes the dialogue end where it began.

And yet Plato gives Cratylus the last word. So shall we too:

CR. It will be so, Socrates; but you too now try to reflect further upon these matters. (440e6–7)

[80] Hermes πομπαῖος/πομπός: Hom. *Il.* 24.153, Aesch. *Eum.* 91, Soph. *Aj.* 832, etc. The attribute is precisely προπομπός in Alexis fr. 93 *PCG*; and see *IG* 14.769 for Hermes and προπέμπω. NB: The moral Barney draws from Socrates' allusion is different from (and, to my mind, less persuasive than) the one I go on to state in the text. I rather side with Reeve liii: 'Cratylus is thus as wrong about the correctness of Hermogenes' name as he is about things and names.'

Appendix 1: *The text of 437d10–438b8*

As announced in §8.2.3, this Appendix is devoted to the textual issue of 437d10–438b8, the passage transmitted by the MSS in two different versions. To get a clearer view of the matter it will be helpful to start by translating a text that is roughly identical with the one reported by W and with the one printed by Stallbaum and Hirschig, with line spaces added to highlight some relevant joints and a couple of further changes (I also translate the first words of c1–4):[1]

(so.) And let us leave these things alone (437d8–9)

 and examine these others [τάδε δὲ ἐπισκεψώμεθα], to see whether or not you agree with us on this point too. Come on, those who impose the names in the cities, both in the Greek and in the barbarian ones, on any given occasion, didn't we agree a while ago that they are lawgivers and that the art which has this power is the lawgiving [νομοθετικήν] art?

cr. Of course.

so. And tell me, did the first lawgivers impose the first names with knowledge of the objects on which they were imposing them or in ignorance of them? [οἱ πρῶτοι νομοθέται τὰ πρῶτα ὀνόματα πότερον γιγνώσκοντες τὰ πράγματα, οἷς ἐτίθεντο, ἐτίθεντο ἢ ἀγνοοῦντες;]

cr. I think with knowledge, Socrates.

so. Yes; for presumably they did not do so in ignorance, my friend Cratylus.

cr. I don't think so. (d10–438a2)

(so.) And go back to the point where we started this digression [ἐπανέλθωμεν δὲ πάλιν ὅθεν δεῦρο μετέβημεν]. A while ago in our previous discussion, if you remember, you said that he who imposed the names necessarily imposed them with knowledge of the things on which he was imposing them [εἰδότα τίθεσθαι οἷς ἐτίθετο]. Do you still believe so or not?

cr. I still do.

---

[1] NB: For reasons that will soon become clear, at 438b4–c10 I do not use the OCT's line numbers but Burnet's.

490   *Appendix 1*

SO. Do you also say that he who imposed the first names imposed them with knowledge? ["Ἦ καὶ τὸν τὰ πρῶτα τιθέμενον εἰδότα φῂς τίθεσθαι;]

CR. Yes, with knowledge. (a3–10)

SO. Then from what sort of names ['Ἐκ ποίων οὖν ὀνομάτων] had he learnt or discovered about the objects, if the first ones had not yet been set down, and on the other hand we say it is impossible to learn and discover about the objects other than by learning or discovering by ourselves what their names are like? (a11–b3)

CR. I think you've got a point there, Socrates. (b4)

SO. Then how shall we say that they imposed them with knowledge or were lawgivers, before any name whatsoever had been set down and they had knowledge of it, if it is not possible to learn about the objects other than from their names? (438b5–8)

CR. In my view, Socrates, the truest account of these matters is that … (c1ff.)

As I said above, the text of W goes basically as I have translated, with two differences. After a2 Οὔ μοι δοκεῖ 'I don't think' W adds the words ἐκ ποίων δὲ 'But from what sort', which suggest that readers should skip over the following lines a3–10 and resume reading at a11 Ἐκ ποίων οὖν ὀνομάτων 'Then from what sort of names' (strictly speaking the added words contain themselves a variant, i.e. δέ for οὖν).[2] W also omits δέ after a3 ἐπανέλθωμεν 'let us go back' (while Stallbaum and Hirschig print δή). The other primary MSS omit d10–a2 and after d9 go immediately on to a3 ἐπανέλθωμεν δέ: 'let us leave these things alone … and go back to the point where we started this digression'. Thus W contains some lines, d10–a2, which are omitted by the other primary MSS and which in their turn end by inviting us to ignore the immediately following a3–11. In other words, the MS tradition itself somehow suggests that d10–a2 and a3–10 are alternative variants. That they are so is confirmed by an examination of their content.

In d10–a2 Socrates, after putting a stop to the discussion of the alleged consistency of names, explicitly collects the premises for a new argument. First he recalls an earlier agreement to the effect that those who impose names, whether in Greek or in barbarian cities, are lawgivers and possess the lawgiving art. Then he goes on to ask Cratylus whether 'the first lawgivers' had knowledge of the objects on which they imposed 'the first names' (i.e. the most ancient ones).[3] Cratylus obviously answers the question in the affirmative, apparently meeting with Socrates' approval.

---

[2] Cf. Valenti 1998: 782–8.
[3] On 'the first names' at 437e6, 438a8 and c3 see §8.2.3.

These lines pose four difficulties. (a) Socrates' back-reference is imprecise. Since at e3 it is natural to understand 'didn't we agree' as 'didn't *I and you* agree', Socrates should be referring back to 428e–429a, where Cratylus agreed that namegiving is an art, whose practitioners are the lawgivers. But that passage said nothing of Greeks, barbarians and their cities. Greek and barbarian lawgivers and their art were the subject of 388d–390a, where Socrates' interlocutor was not Cratylus but Hermogenes; the cities were mentioned at 385e, a passage which has nothing to do with the present topic. (b) The claim that the namegivers' art had been previously agreed to be the 'lawgiving' art is strictly speaking false, because the term νομοθετική (τέχνη) is never used in *Cra.*, but only at *Grg.* 464b–465c, 520b, and *Plt.* 294a, in completely different contexts. Proclus, LI 18.28, 19.15, however, does use it with reference to namegiving. (c) The function of d10–e5 (i.e. of the characterization of the namegivers as *law*givers, and of the reference to their possessing an art) in the argument is unclear. (d) The e6–8 question seems not to consider that at 436c Cratylus had already claimed that 'necessarily he who imposed the names imposed them with knowledge'.

Perhaps we can dismiss (a), (b) and (d) as minor inaccuracies and solve (c) by supposing that the function of d10–e5 is to prepare the e6–8 question, although this connection is not explicit in the text. In any case, bear all of (a) – (d) in mind as we turn, or turn again, to a3–10, which I analysed in §8.2.3. It is evident that, as Jachmann 1941: 322 saw and all subsequent scholars have recognized,[4] these lines make essentially the same point as the previous ones and cannot coexist with them in the text as they do in W: before us we have two alternative versions of the same passage. Furthermore, these lines are free from the difficulties of d10–a2; in particular, they do not drag in the lawgivers and the lawgiving art, and they appropriately open with an explicit reference to Cratylus' 436c claim. Hence they are unquestionably genuine.

What, then, of d10–a2? Jachmann and most editors regarded them as an interpolation; but the OCT editors (following an unpublished suggestion by Ernst Kapp, and followed in their turn by Dalimier) hold that they were written by Plato just like a3–10 and constitute an 'author's variant'. This proposal is made more precise by Sedley (2003: 9 and n.17): 'the variant version could not belong to the *Cratylus* as we now have it, and must in fact belong to an earlier, superseded edition', where it was not preceded

---

[4] The lines had already been excised by Schanz 1874: 38–9; but it was Jachmann who first recognized their nature as an 'Ersatz' and pointed (d) out. For a history of the scholarly views on our passage see Valenti 1998: 771–7.

by Cratylus' 436c claim that the namegiver had knowledge of the objects, and was instead preceded by an explicit characterization of the lawgivers' art as νομοθετική.[5]

The authorship of d10–a2 is a very important question. At the present stage, however, I broach it only to set it aside for later, when we have dealt with another, more basic question, which concerns the *extension* of either variant. To confront this latter question we must move on from the whole of 437d10–438a10 to 438a11–b8, where, according to the implicit indication conveyed by the words ἐκ ποίων δέ, added by W after a2, we might expect that the two variants reunite into the common text.

At a11–b3, which I also discussed in §8.2.3, Socrates draws his conclusion: if one can learn or discover about something *only* by learning or discovering about the etymology of its name (as Cratylus maintained at 435e–436a), then from what names did he who imposed the very first names learn or discover about their referents? At b4 Cratylus seems to admit that Socrates is right. But at b5–8 Socrates asks another question: if it is impossible to acquire knowledge of the objects other than from their names, then how can the first namegivers have imposed names with knowledge, at a time when there wasn't yet any name for them to know?[6]

These lines are no less problematic than the previous ones, for two reasons which point in the same direction. (i) At a11–b3 Socrates speaks of an *individual* namegiver, as in the immediately preceding a3–10, whereas at b5–8 he speaks of a *plurality* of namegivers and also characterizes them as *lawgivers*, as at d10–a2. (ii) b5–8 looks like a doublet

---

[5] Cf. §2.2.5 for a parallel proposal concerning 385bd. On author's variants see Pasquali 1952: 395–465 and Dorandi 2000: 155–77, who discuss many examples; a plausible one from a classical Greek text is at Ar. *Ran.* 1435–66 (on which see Dover 1993: 373–6). Note that author's variants need not derive from a revised *edition* of the work in question (like those attested, e.g., for Aristophanes' *Clouds*, Apollonius' *Argonautica* or Cicero's *Academica*; see Dorandi 2000: 129–54); in principle, they may just derive from the author's unpublished drafts. As far as Plato is concerned, the evidence is scanty. The ancient sources (D. H. *Comp.* 25, Quint. *Inst.* 8.6.64, D. L. 3.37: see Riginos 1976: 185–6) report that after his death a writing tablet was found containing the *Republic*'s initial words arranged in various orders; but none of those variant word orders has survived. The anonymous *Theaetetus* commentator (III.28–37) says that in his days a variant proem to the dialogue 'circulated' and quotes its first words, but regards it as spurious. Finally, Wilamowitz 1920: II.344 thought he had spotted an author's variant at *Cri.* 52b, where βδ omit the words ὅτι μὴ ἅπαξ εἰς Ἰσθμόν; but it is far from certain that he was right.

[6] Two notes on b5–8. (I) 'That they imposed names with knowledge or were lawgivers' (b5–6): being a lawgiver is here taken to be equivalent to imposing names with knowledge. This is unobjectionable from Cratylus' viewpoint: cf. 428e–429b. Still, the disjunction seems somewhat awkward. Anyway, for ἤ = 'or in other words' cf. *Cri.* 50e, *R.* 349e, *Phdr.* 249a. (II) 'There wasn't yet any name for them to know' (b6–7): the object of εἰδέναι is ὄνομα.

of a11–b3, exactly as d10–a2 looked like a doublet of a3–10. These two difficulties, especially if they are taken together, strongly suggest that (as Kapp, followed again by the OCT, saw) the two variants have *not* yet reunited into the common text: *a11–b3 is the continuation of a3–10, while b5–8 is the continuation of d10–a2*. This is somewhat surprising, because W's solitary addition ends at a2, and the whole of a11–b8 is unanimously reported by all MSS. Indeed, there is a further, disconcerting consequence: if the two variants consist respectively of d10–a2 + b5–8 and a3–b3, then it is unclear what we should make of b4 ('I think you've got a point there, Socrates'). For b4 is now immediately followed by another answer spoken by Cratylus, i.e. c1–4 ('In my view, Socrates, the truest account of these matters is that …'), to which it is by no means equivalent.

Kapp's and the OCT's solution is to call d10–a2 + b5–8 'Versio A', call a3–b3 'Versio B', and *delete* b4 (indeed, the OCT editors relegate it to the apparatus and even deprive it of its line number, thus causing an inconvenient shift of numbers which I have ignored). This conjecture seems to require the following hypothetical reconstruction. At some early stage of the history of our text, when the three MS families βTδ had not yet separated from each other, two alternative versions of the same passage (whether Plato was the author of both or of one only) were available: (A) d10–a2 + b5–8, (B) a3–b3. Part of (A), i.e. b5–8, was mistakenly inserted after (B) by someone who failed to see that it was an alternative version of (B)'s final part, a11–b3. Perhaps the insertion was facilitated by the plurals μαθόντας … ἐξευρόντας at b3, which could be taken to refer to the lawgivers of b5–6 (whereas their reference is in fact indefinite). But since Socrates thus appeared to ask two consecutive questions, someone (perhaps the same person who made the insertion) added a line spoken by Cratylus, i.e. b4, to divide a11–b3 from b5–8. Lines b4–8 were thus present in the common source of βTδ and were copied into each of them. Some time later, the scribe of W (or of some of its sources) incorporated into the text the rest of (A), i.e. d10–a2.

A very complicated story. Perhaps too complicated; you may well have misgivings about the complex series of accidents it assumes to have affected the passage's transmission. But the story is not unparalleled;[7] and as long as we take seriously difficulties (i) and (ii), as I for one think we should, there is no evidently better way of accounting for the text's present

---

[7] See n.10.

shape.[8] As Paul Maas said, 'No error is as impossible as a reading can be necessary.'

Now that we have established the extension of the disputed textual territory it is time to return to the authorship question. Shall we endorse the view that version (A) of our passage, although it fits in awkwardly with the rest of *Cra.* as we now read it and is inferior to (B), was nevertheless written by Plato? Granted, there is nothing suspect about the style of these lines or their content (provided that they are taken in isolation from the rest of the dialogue, as Sedley thinks we should), and the interpolation's length would be quite unusual for Plato's text.[9] But caution is in order. Generally speaking, we must bear in mind that our MSS contain many certain interpolations[10] and few likely author's variants. In our particular case, moreover, the only major MS to report d10–a2 is W, the main representative of the δ family; and the text of *Cra.* offered by δ suffers from a number of interpolations and non-mechanical errors (some of which are shared with the other two families). Some of the most significant examples are collected in Appendix 2. Note that several of these variants and additions are linguistically irreproachable; note also that at 384d the right reading and its doublet coexist in βδ as our passage's two versions do in W. So, although in our passage the author's variant view cannot be disproved, it cannot be established with any certainty either.[11]

---

[8] To limit the variants' extension it will not do to suppose with Robinson (in the OCT's apparatus *ad* b3; cf. Valenti 1998: 781–6) that in (A) the plurals in d10–a2 were once answered in a11–b1 by a now no longer extant variant μεμαθηκότες ἢ ηὑρηκότες ἦσαν in place of μεμαθηκὼς ἢ ηὑρηκὼς ἦν. This would smooth the progress from d10–a2 to a11–b3 in (A), but would not solve (ii): the compresence of a11–b3 and b5–8 in the same text would remain redundant. Sedley's (2003: 8 and n.16) proposal that (A) consists of d10–a2 and (B) of a3–b4 is also unsatisfactory; for it leaves both (i) and (ii) untouched in the text of (B). Sedley grants that the use of the plural at b5–8 'goes more smoothly with the variant version than with our mainstream text', but takes that 'to be a vestige of the imperfect editorial process whereby Plato supplanted the former with the latter'. That is to say, Plato did not arrive at a final, consistent text of this passage – a view which I find hardly plausible.

[9] The only comparable case would be *Alc. I* 133c8–17 (if that really is an interpolation, as scholars are inclined to think).

[10] See Renehan 1969: 28–34, 38–41 for paradigmatic examples, especially D.L. 10.50–1, a spectacular case of multiple corruption also involving an interpolated doublet (even larger than Renehan thinks: cf. von der Mühll 1922). For another instance of interpolated doublet see Arist. *Top.* 113a20–3, where the interpolation is older than Alexander of Aphrodisias (cf. Brunschwig 1967: cxxv). For an instance of twofold, possibly two-stage interpolation (without doublets) see *Tht.* 190c, where after the words τὸ ῥῆμα two distinct glosses have penetrated into the text of βW, whereas T has one in the text and the other in the margin. Other instructive examples of how complex a textual corruption can be are provided by Arist. *Metaph.* Θ6.1048b18–35, on which see Burnyeat 2008 (who argues that the interpolated passage is Aristotelian).

[11] Valenti 1998: 795–7 advances the following argument for Platonic authorship. ὦ ἑταῖρε Κρατύλε (438a1) is an instance of a rare pattern (ὦ ἑταῖρε + proper noun) which occurs only in four other

It is as possible – indeed more likely – that (A) was created by someone who thought that a reference to the lawgivers and their art would be appropriate here, perhaps because he wanted Socrates to recall and take stock of the previous discussion as a whole (cf. Carlini 1996: 374–5, Murphy 1997).

passages of the Platonic corpus (*Cri.* 54d; *Phd.* 82c; *Men.* 94e, 98a), and it is therefore likely to be authentic: 'il diascheuasta è generalmente portato a non discostarsi dall'*usus*; ogni allontanamento può tradursi in spia di interpolazione e rischia di mettere a nudo l'intervento'. A naïve argument; for few interpolations are meant as forgeries, and few interpolators are so diabolic.

Appendix 2: Some interpolations and non-mechanical errors in W and δ

383b3	After ὁμολογεῖ **δ** adds αὐτῷ γε τούτῳ [WB²: αὐτό γε τοῦτο Q: the intended reading is αὐτῷ γε τοῦτο] ὄνομα εἶναι, 'agrees that this is his name'.
384d5	After μετατιθέμεθα **βδ** add οὐδὲν ἧττον τοῦτ᾽ εἶναι ὀρθὸν τὸ μετατεθὲν τοῦ προτέρου [i.e. πρότερον] κειμένου, 'this, i.e. the substituted one, is no less correct than the previous one', clearly a doublet of d4–5 οὐδὲν ἧττον τὸ ὕστερον ὀρθῶς ἔχειν τοῦ προτέρου.[1]
384d7	In place of ἐθισάντων W has μεθιστάντων, 'of those who make the change' (but reports the right reading in the margin).
385b1	After Ἔμοιγε δοκεῖ **δ** adds τί γὰρ ἂν ἄλλο τις φαίη;, 'For what else could one say?'.
385c4–5	In place of τὰ δὲ σμικρὰ οὔ **δ** has τὰ δὲ σμικρότερα οὐκ ἀληθῆ, 'whereas the smaller ones are not true'.
389c10–11	In place of εἰς ξύλον **δ** has εἰς τὸ ξύλον δεῖ τιθέναι, 'one must put into wood'.
389d9	In place of ὁ νομοθέτης **δ** has ὀνοματοθέτης.
410b5	After 'ἀητόρρουν' **βΤδ** add ὅθεν δὴ βούλεται αὐτὸν οὕτως εἰπεῖν, ὅτι ἐστὶν ἀήρ, 'this is why he [= Plato?] wants him [= the namegiver?] to say in this sense that it is air' (a sentence I don't understand).
415d4	After καλεῖν **βΤδ** add ἴσως δὲ αἱρετὴν λέγει, ὡς οὔσης ταύτης τῆς ἕξεως αἱρετωτάτης, 'but perhaps he says αἱρετή, on the assumption that this is the state most worth pursuing', a new etymology of ἀρετή.
429b4–5	In place of οἱ μὲν βελτίους, οἱ δὲ φαυλότεροι **δ** has οἱ μὲν χείρους, οἱ δὲ βελτίους, 'some worse, some better'.

[1] The addition is (absurdly) considered genuine by Stallbaum, Méridier, Reeve and Dalimier.

References

Acerbi, F. (2008) 'Euclid's *Pseudaria*', *Archive for History of Exact Sciences* 62.5: 511–51.
Ackrill, J. L. (trans. and comm.) (1963) *Aristotle: Categories and De Interpretatione*. Oxford.
  (1966) 'Plato on False Belief: *Theaetetus* 187–200', *The Monist* 50: 383–402. Reprinted in Ackrill 1997: 53–71 (page numbers are cited from the latter).
  (1970) 'In Defence of Platonic Division'. In *Ryle*, eds. O. P. Wood and G. Pitcher. New York: 373–92. Reprinted in Ackrill 1997: 93–109 (page numbers are cited from the latter).
  (1994) 'Language and Reality in Plato's *Cratylus*'. In *Realtà e ragione. Studi di filosofia antica*, ed. A. Alberti. Florence: 9–28. Reprinted in Ackrill 1997: 33–52 (page numbers are cited from the latter).
  (1997) *Essays on Plato and Aristotle*. Oxford.
Ademollo, F. (2001) 'Platone, *Cratilo* 395c, 408b: due presunte interpolazioni', *Rivista di Filologia e di Istruzione Classica* 129: 129–33.
  (2003) 'Democritus B26, on Names'. In *Etymologia. Studies in Ancient Etymology*, ed. C. Nifadopoulos. Münster: 33–42.
  (2007) 'The Equals, the Equals Themselves, Equality, and the Equal Itself', *Documenti e Studi sulla Tradizione Filosofica Medievale* 18: 1–20.
  (2009) 'Un'interpretazione del *Cratilo* di Platone'. In *La logica nel pensiero antico*, eds. M. Alessandrelli and M. Nasti de Vincentis. Naples: 15–73.
  (in preparation-1) '*Cratylus* 393c and the Prehistory of Plato's Text'.
  (in preparation-2) 'The γυνή < γονή Etymology in Democritus, Plato and the Ancient *Etymologica*'.
  (in preparation-3) 'Plato's Conception of Change'.
  (in preparation-4) 'Plato's Conception of the Forms: Some Remarks', in *Universals in Ancient Philosophy*, eds. R. Chiaradonna and G. Galluzzo.
  (in preparation-5) 'The Platonic Origins of Stoic Theology'.
Adomėnas, M. (2006) 'Discipleship Theme in Plato's *Cratylus*', *Literatūra* 48: 22–33.
Allan, D. J. (1954) 'The Problem of Cratylus', *American Journal of Philology* 75: 271–87.
Anceschi, B. (2007) *Die Götternamen in Platons* Kratylos. Frankfurt a. M.

Annas, J. (1982) 'Knowledge and Language: the *Theaetetus* and the *Cratylus*'. In Nussbaum/Schofield 1982: 95–114.
Ariew, R., and Garber, D. (1989) *G.W. Leibniz: Philosophical Essays*. Indianapolis, IN, and Cambridge.
Armstrong, D. M. (1978) *Universals and Scientific Realism*, vol. 1: *Nominalism and Realism*. Cambridge.
Ax, W. (1986) *Laut, Stimme und Sprache. Studien zu drei Grundbegriffen der antiken Sprachtheorie*. Göttingen.
Barber, E. J. W. (1991) *Prehistoric Textiles. The Development of Cloth in the Neolithic and Bronze Ages*. Princeton, NJ.
Barnes, J. (1982) *The Presocratic Philosophers*, 2nd edn. London and New York.
  (ed.) (1984) *The Complete Works of Aristotle. The Revised Oxford Translation* (2 vols.). Princeton, NJ.
  (1993) 'Meaning, Saying and Thinking'. In *Dialektiker und Stoiker*, eds. K. Döring and Th. Ebert. Stuttgart: 47–61.
  (2007) *Truth, etc. Six Lectures on Ancient Logic*. Oxford.
Barney, R. (1997) 'Plato on Conventionalism', *Phronesis* 42: 143–62.
  (1998) 'Socrates Agonistes: the Case of the *Cratylus* Etymologies', *Oxford Studies in Ancient Philosophy* 16: 63–98.
  (2001) *Names and Nature in Plato's* Cratylus. New York and London.
Barrett, W. S. (ed. and comm.) (1964) *Euripides: Hippolytos*. Oxford.
Baxter, T. M. S. (1992) *The* Cratylus. *Plato's Critique of Naming*. Leiden, New York and Cologne.
Belardi, W. (1985) 'Platone e Aristotele e la dottrina sulle lettere e la sillaba'. In his *Filosofia grammatica e retorica nel pensiero antico*. Rome, 21–89.
Bernabé, A. (1995) 'Una etimología platónica: ΣΩΜΑ-ΣΗΜΑ', *Philologus* 139: 204–37.
Bestor, T. W. (1980) 'Plato's Semantics and Plato's "Cratylus"', *Phronesis* 25: 306–30.
Binder, G., and Liesenborghs, L. (1976) 'Eine Zuweisung der Sentenz οὐκ ἔστιν ἀντιλέγειν an Prodikos von Keos'. In *Sophistik*, ed. C. J. Classen. Darmstadt: 452–62.
Blank, D. L. (trans. and comm.) (1996) *Ammonius: On Aristotle On Interpretation 1–8*. London.
  (trans. and comm.) (1998) *Sextus Empiricus: Against the Grammarians*. Oxford.
Bolelli, T. (1953) 'Origine e sviluppo delle formazioni greche in *MEN / MON*', *Annali della Scuola Normale Superiore di Pisa* 22: 5–74.
Bonitz, H. (1870) *Index Aristotelicus* (*Aristotelis Opera* vol. v). Berlin (reprint Graz 1955).
Bostock, D. (1988) *Plato's* Theaetetus. Oxford.
von Bothmer, D. (1985) *The Amasis Painter and His World*, with an intr. by A. L. Boegehold. Malibu, CA, New York and London.
Boyancé, P. (1941) 'La "Doctrine d'Euthyphron" dans le *Cratyle*', *Revue des Etudes Grecques* 54: 141–75.
Brancacci, A. (1996) 'Protagora e la critica letteraria'. In Funghi 1996: 109–19.

Brown, L. (1993) 'Understanding the *Theaetetus*', *Oxford Studies in Ancient Philosophy* 11: 199–224.
  (1994) 'The Verb "To Be" in Greek Philosophy: Some Remarks'. In Everson 1994: 212–36.
  (1999) 'Being in the *Sophist*: a Syntactical Enquiry'. In *Plato 1. Metaphysics and Epistemology*, ed. G. Fine. Oxford: 455–78.
Brunschwig, J. (ed., trans. and comm.) (1967) *Aristote: Topiques. Livres I–IV*. Paris.
Burge, T. (2005) *Truth, Thought, Reason. Essays on Frege*. Oxford.
Burkert, W. (1959) 'Στοιχεῖον. Eine semasiologische Studie', *Philologus* 103: 167–97.
Burnet, J. (ed.), (1924) *Plato's* Euthyphro, Apology of Socrates *and* Crito, with comm. Oxford.
Burnyeat, M. F. (1970) 'The Material and Sources of Plato's Dream', *Phronesis* 15: 101–22.
  (1979) 'Conflicting Appearances', *Proceedings of the British Academy* 65: 184–97.
  (1982) 'Idealism and Greek Philosophy: What Descartes Saw and Berkeley Missed', *Philosophical Review* 91: 3–40.
  (1990) *The Theaetetus of Plato*, with a translation of Plato's *Theaetetus* by M. J. Levett, rev. by M. B. Indianapolis, IN, and Cambridge.
  (1999) 'Culture and Society in Plato's *Republic*', *The Tanner Lectures on Human Values* 20: 217–324.
  (2000a) 'Plato on Why Mathematics is Good for the Soul'. In *Mathematics and Necessity*, ed. T. Smiley. Oxford: 1–81.
  (2000b) 'Plato', *Proceedings of the British Academy* 111: 1–22.
  (2001a) *A Map of* Metaphysics Zeta. Pittsburgh.
  (2001b) 'What Was The "Common Arrangement"? An Inquiry into John Stuart Mill's Boyhood Reading of Plato', *Philologus* 145: 158–86.
  (2002) 'Plato on How Not to Speak of What Is Not: *Euthydemus* 283a–288a'. In Canto-Sperber/Pellegrin 2002: 40–66.
  (2003) '*Apology* 30b 2–4: Socrates, Money, and The Grammar of γίγνεσθαι', *Journal of Hellenic Studies* 123: 1–25.
  (2008) '*Kinēsis* vs. *Energeia*: A Much-Read Passage in (but not of) Aristotle's *Metaphysics*', *Oxford Studies in Ancient Philosophy* 34: 219–92.
Calvert, B. (1970) 'Forms and Flux in Plato's *Cratylus*', *Phronesis* 15: 26–47.
Cambiano, G. (1991) *Platone e le tecniche*, 2nd edn. Rome and Bari.
Campbell, L. (ed. and comm.) (1867) *The Sophistes and Politicus of Plato*. Oxford.
Canto-Sperber, M., and Pellegrin, P. (eds.) (2002) *Le style de la pensée. Recueil de textes en hommage à J. Brunschwig*. Paris.
Carlini, A. (1996) 'Il nuovo Platone di Oxford', *Rivista di Filologia e di Istruzione Classica* 124: 366–75.
  (1999) 'Marsilio Ficino e il testo di Platone', *Rinascimento* 39: 3–36.
Chantraine, P. (1933) *La formation des noms en Grec ancien*. Paris.
Chappell, T. (2004) *Reading Plato's* Theaetetus. Sankt Augustin.

Cherniss, H. (1955) 'Aristotle, *Metaphysics* 987 A32–B7', *American Journal of Philology* 76: 184–6.
Conti, C. (1977–8) 'Storia di una parola greca: ῥῆμα', Università di Firenze (unpublished thesis).
Cooper, J. M. (ed.) (1997) *Plato: Complete Works*. Indianapolis, IN, and Cambridge.
Cornford, F. M. (trans. and comm.) (1935) *Plato's Theory of Knowledge: The Theaetetus and the Sophist*. London.
 (1937) (trans. and comm.) *Plato's Cosmology: The Timaeus of Plato*. London.
Crivelli, P. (2004) *Aristotle on Truth*. Cambridge.
 (2008) 'Plato's Philosophy of Language'. In *The Oxford Handbook of Plato*, ed. G. Fine. New York: 217–42.
 (forthcoming) *Plato's Account of Falsehood: A Study of the Sophist*. Cambridge.
Crombie, I. M. (1963) *An Examination of Plato's Doctrines* (2 vols.). London and New York.
Crowfoot, G. M. (1936–7) 'Of the Warp-Weighted Loom', *Annual of the British School at Athens* 37: 36–47.
Dancy, R. M. (1986) 'Aristotle on Existence'. In *The Logic of Being*, eds. S. Knuuttila and J. Hintikka. Dordrecht: 49–80.
 (1987) 'Theaetetus' First Baby: *Theaetetus* 151e–160e', *Philosophical Topics* 15: 61–108.
 (1999) 'The Categories of Being in Plato's *Sophist* 255c–e', *Ancient Philosophy* 19: 45–72.
 (2004) *Plato's Introduction of Forms*. Cambridge.
Decleva Caizzi, F. (trans. and comm.) (1996) *Platone: Eutidemo*. Milan.
Denyer, N. (1991) *Language, Thought and Falsehood in Ancient Greek Philosophy*. London.
Derbolav, J. (1972) *Platons Sprachphilosophie im Kratylos und in den späteren Schriften*. Darmstadt.
Dodds, E. R. (ed. and comm.) (1959) *Plato: Gorgias*. Oxford.
Donnellan, K. (1966) 'Reference and Definite Descriptions', *Philosophical Review* 75: 281–304.
Dorandi, T. (2000) *Le stylet et la tablette*. Paris.
Dover, K. J. (ed. and comm.) (1980) *Plato: Symposium*. Cambridge.
 (ed. and comm.) (1993) *Aristophanes: Frogs*. Oxford.
Dummett, M. (1991) *The Logical Basis of Metaphysics*. London and New York.
Duvick, B. (trans. and comm.) (2007) *Proclus: On Plato Cratylus*. London.
Everson, S. (ed.) (1994) *Companions to Ancient Thought 3: Language*. Cambridge.
Falcon, A. (2001) *Corpi e movimenti. Il De caelo di Aristotele e la sua fortuna nel mondo antico*. Naples.
 (2005) *Aristotle and the Science of Nature. Unity Without Uniformity*. Cambridge.
Fehling, D. (1965) 'Zwei Untersuchungen zur griechischen Sprachphilosophie', *Rheinisches Museum* 108: 212–29.

Fine, G. (1977) 'Plato on Naming', *Philosophical Quarterly* 27: 289–301.
  (1979) 'Knowledge and *Logos* in the *Theaetetus*', *Philosophical Review* 88: 366–97.
  (trans. and comm.) (1993) *On Ideas. Aristotle's Criticism of Plato's Theory of Forms*. Oxford.
Frede, M. (1967) *Prädikation und Existenzaussage: Platons Gebrauch von '… ist …' und '… ist nicht …' im Sophistes*. Göttingen.
  (1978) 'Principles of Stoic Grammar'. In *The Stoics*, ed. J. M. Rist. Berkeley, CA, and Los Angeles: 27–75. Reprinted in Frede 1987: 301–37 (page numbers cited from the latter).
  (1981) 'Categories in Aristotle'. In *Studies in Aristotle*, ed. D. J. O'Meara, Washington: 1–24. Reprinted in Frede 1987: 29–48 (page numbers cited from the latter).
  (1987) *Essays in Ancient Philosophy*. Minneapolis, MN.
  (1992a) 'Plato's Arguments and the Dialogue Form'. In *Methods of Interpreting Plato and His Dialogues*, eds. J. C. Klagge and N. D. Smith. Oxford: 201–19.
  (1992b) 'The *Sophist* on False Statements'. In Kraut 1992: 397–424.
  (2007) 'On the Unity and Aim of the Derveni Text', *Rhizai* 4: 9–33.
Funghi, M. S. (ed.) (1996) *ΟΔΟΙ ΔΙΖΗΣΙΟΣ – Le vie della ricerca. Studi in onore di Francesco Adorno*. Florence.
Gaiser, K. (1974) *Name und Sache in Platons 'Kratylos'*. Heidelberg.
Garlan, Y. (1988) *Slavery in Ancient Greece*, 2nd edn. Ithaca, NY.
Geach, P. T. (1962) *Reference and Generality*. Ithaca, NY.
Gensini, S. (1991) *Il naturale e il simbolico. Saggio su Leibniz*. Rome.
Gill, C., and McCabe, M. M. (eds.) (1996) *Form and Argument in Late Plato*. Oxford.
Gold, J. B. (1978) 'The Ambiguity of "Name" in Plato's "Cratylus"', *Philosophical Studies* 34: 223–51.
Goldschmidt, V. (1940) *Essai sur le 'Cratyle'*. Paris.
Grote, G. (1888) *Plato and the Other Companions of Sokrates*, 2nd edn (4 vols.). London.
Gulley, N. (1962) *Plato's Theory of Knowledge*. London.
Guthrie, W. K. C. (1962–81) *A History of Greek Philosophy* (6 vols.). Cambridge.
Hackforth, R. (trans. and comm.) (1952) *Plato's Phaedrus*. Cambridge.
Heath, Sir T. (trans. and comm.) (1926) *The Thirteen Books of Euclid's Elements*, 2nd edn (3 vols.). Cambridge.
  (1949) *Mathematics in Aristotle*. Oxford.
Heitsch, E. (1985) 'Platons Sprachphilosophie im "Kratylos"', *Hermes* 113: 44–62.
Hoekstra, M., and Scheppers, Fr. (2003) 'Ὄνομα, ῥῆμα et λόγος dans le *Cratyle* et le *Sophiste* de Platon. Analyse du lexique et analyse du discours', *L'Antiquité Classique* 72: 55–73.
Horn, F. (1904) *Platonstudien*, neue Folge. Vienna.
Huffman, C. A. (1993) *Philolaus of Croton*. Cambridge.
Irwin, T. (1977) 'Plato's Heracleiteanism', *Philosophical Quarterly* 27: 1–13.

Jachmann, G. (1941) 'Der Platontext', *Nachrichten von der Gesellschaft der Wissenschaften zu Göttingen*, Phil. Hist. Kl., 11: 225–389. Reprinted in *Günther Jachmann: Textgeschichtliche Studien*, ed. C. Gnilka, Königstein/Ts. 1982: 581–745 (page numbers are cited from the latter).
Jackson, B. D. (comm.) and Pinborg, J. (ed. and trans.) (1975) *Augustine: De Dialectica*. Dordrecht.
Jacquinod, B. (2000) 'Le *Cratyle* et l'origine des noms. L'aspect dans les verbes de dénomination'. In *Etudes sur l'aspect verbal chez Platon*, ed. B. Jacquinod. St.-Etienne: 317–38.
Jones, F. (1996) *Nominum Ratio. Aspects of the Use of Personal Names in Greek and Latin*. Liverpool.
Jones, W. H. S. (ed. and trans.) (1931) *Hippocrates (vol. IV): Nature of Man. Regimen in Health. Humours. Aphorisms. Regimen 1–3. Dreams. Heracleitus: On the Universe*. Cambridge, MA, and London.
Jori, A. (1996) *Medicina e medici nell'antica Grecia. Saggio sul* Perì téchnes *ippocratico*. Naples.
Jouanna, J. (ed., trans. and comm.) (1988) *Hippocrate* v.1: *Des vents. De l'art*. Paris.
Jowett, B., and Campbell, L. (ed. and comm.) (1894) *Plato's* Republic (3 vols.). Oxford.
Kahn, C. H. (1960) *Anaximander and The Origins of Greek Cosmology*. New York.
  (1966) 'The Greek Verb "To Be" and the Concept of Being', *Foundations of Language* 2: 245–65.
  (1973a) 'Language and Ontology in the *Cratylus*'. In Lee/Mourelatos/Rorty 1973: 152–76.
  (1973b) *The Verb 'Be' in Ancient Greek*. Dordrecht.
  (1978) 'Questions and Categories'. In *Questions*, ed. H. Hiz. Dordrecht: 227–78.
  (1979) *The Art and Thought of Heraclitus*. Cambridge.
  (1981a) 'Some Philosophical Uses of "To Be" in Plato', *Phronesis* 26: 105–34.
  (1981b) 'The Origins of Social Contract Theory'. In *The Sophists and Their Legacy*, ed. G. B. Kerferd. Wiesbaden: 92–108.
  (1986a) 'Les mots et les formes dans le "Cratyle" de Platon', in *Philosophie du langage et grammaire dans l'antiquité*, Brussels and Grenoble: 91–103.
  (1986b) 'Retrospect on the Verb "To Be" and the Concept of Being'. In *The Logic of Being*, eds. S. Knuuttila and J. Hintikka. Dordrecht: 1–28.
  (1996) *Plato and the Socratic Dialogue*. Cambridge.
  (2002) 'Flux and Forms in the *Timaeus*'. In Canto-Sperber/Pellegrin 2002: 113–31.
Karsten, H. T. (1864) *Commentatio Critica de Platonis Quae Feruntur Epistolis*. Utrecht.
Kassel, R. (1991) *Kleine Schriften*. Berlin and New York.
Keller, S. (2000) 'An Interpretation of Plato's *Cratylus*', *Phronesis* 45, 284–305.
Ketchum, R. J. (1979) 'Names, Forms and Conventionalism: *Cratylus*, 383–395', *Phronesis* 24: 133–47.

Keyser, P. (1992) 'Stylometric Methodology and the Chronology of Plato's Works', *Bryn Mawr Classical Review* 3: 58–73.
Kingsley, P. (1995) *Ancient Philosophy, Mystery and Magic*. Oxford.
Kirk, G. S. (1951) 'The Problem of Cratylus', *Americal Journal of Philology* 72: 225–53.
Kirk, G. S., Edwards, M., Hainsworth, B., Janko R., and Richardson, N. (1985–94) *The Iliad: a Commentary* (6 vols.). Cambridge.
Kneale, W., and Kneale, M. (1962) *The Development of Logic*. Oxford.
Kouremenos, Th., Parássoglou, G. M., and Tsantsanoglou, K. (eds., trans. and comm.) (2006) *The Derveni Papyrus*. Florence.
Kraut, R. (ed.) (1992) *The Cambridge Companion to Plato*. Cambridge.
Kretzmann, N. (1971) 'Plato on the Correctness of Names', *American Philosophical Quarterly* 8: 126–38.
Kripke, S. (1979) 'Speaker's Reference and Semantic Reference'. In *Contemporary Perspectives in the Philosophy of Language*, eds. P. A. French, T. E. Uehling and H. K. Wettstein. Minneapolis, MN: 6–27.
 (1980) *Naming and Necessity*, 2nd edn. Oxford.
Labarbe, J. (1949) *L'Homère de Platon*. Liège.
Landercy, M. (1933) 'La destination de la κερκίς dans le tissage en Grèce au IVe siècle', *L'Antiquité classique* 2: 357–62.
Lane, M. (2006) 'The Evolution of *Eirōneia* in Classical Greek Texts: Why Socratic *Eirōneia* Is Not Socratic Irony', *Oxford Studies in Ancient Philosophy* 31: 49–83.
Lapini, W. (1997) *Commento all'*Athenaion Politeia *dello pseudo-Senofonte*. Florence.
Lee, E. N., Mourelatos, A. P. D., and Rorty, R. M. (eds.) (1973) *Exegesis and Argument: Studies in Greek Philosophy Presented to Gregory Vlastos*. Assen.
Lee, M.-K. (2005) *Epistemology After Protagoras. Responses to Relativism in Plato, Aristotle, and Democritus*. Oxford.
Leibniz, G. W. (1923–) *Sämtliche Schriften und Briefe*. Leipzig and Berlin.
Lejeune, M. (1972), *Phonétique historique du mycénien et du grec ancien*. Paris.
Leroy, M. (1967) 'Sur un emploi de ΦΩΝΗ chez Platon', *Revue des Etudes Grecques* 80: 234–41.
Leszl, W. (1975) *Il "De ideis" di Aristotele e la teoria platonica delle idee*. Florence.
 (trans. and comm.) (2009) *I primi atomisti. I testi in traduzione italiana*. Florence.
 (forthcoming) *I primi atomisti. I testi in greco e latino*.
Levett, M. J., and Burnyeat, M. (1990) See Burnyeat 1990.
Levin, S. B. (2001) *The Ancient Quarrel Between Philosophy and Poetry Revisited. Plato and the Greek Literary Tradition*. Oxford.
Levinson, R. B. (1957) 'Language and the *Cratylus*: Four Questions', *Review of Metaphysics* 11: 28–41.
Lewis, D. K. (1969) *Convention. A Philosophical Study*. Cambridge, MA.
 (1983) 'Languages and Language'. In his *Philosophical Papers*, vol. 1, New York and Oxford: 163–87.

Linguiti, A. (1988) 'Studi recenti sulla vita e l'opera di Simplicio', *Studi classici e orientali* 38: 331–46.
Lohse, G. (1964/1965/1967) 'Untersuchungen über Homerzitate bei Platon', *Helikon* 4: 3–28; 5: 248–95; 7: 223–31.
Long, A. A. (2005) 'Stoic Linguistics, Plato's *Cratylus*, and Augustine's *De dialectica*'. In *Language and Learning: Philosophy of Language in the Hellenistic Age*, eds. D. Frede and B. Inwood. Cambridge: 36–55.
Lorenz, K. and Mittelstrass, J. (1967) 'On Rational Philosophy of Language: the Programme in Plato's Cratylus Reconsidered', *Mind* 76: 1–20.
Lowe, E. J. (1998) *The Possibility of Metaphysics*. Oxford.
Luce, J. V. (1965) 'The Theory of Ideas in the *Cratylus*', *Phronesis* 10: 21–36.
  (1969a) 'Plato on Truth and Falsity in Names', *Classical Quarterly* 19: 222–32.
  (1969b) 'An Argument of Democritus About Language', *Classical Review* 19: 3–4.
Lutoslawski, W. (1897) *The Origin and Growth of Plato's Logic*. London.
Lyons, J. (1963) *Structural Semantics*. Oxford.
Maat, J. (2004) *Philosophical Languages in the Seventeenth Century: Dalgarno, Wilkins, Leibniz*. Dordrecht, Boston, MA and London.
Mackenzie, M. M. (1986) 'Putting the *Cratylus* in its Place', *Classical Quarterly* 36: 124–50.
Mair, A. W. (1918) 'General Relative Clauses in Greek', *Classical Review* 32: 169–70.
Mansfeld, J. (1983) '*Cratylus* 402 A–C: Plato or Hippias?'. In *Atti del Symposium Heracliteum*, ed. L. Rossetti, vol. 1. Rome: 43–55.
Marcovich, M. (ed., trans. and comm.) (1978) *Eraclito: Frammenti*. Florence.
Masson, O. (1973) 'Les noms des esclaves dans la Grèce antique'. In *Actes du Colloque 1971 sur l'Esclavage*. Paris: 9–23.
McDowell, J. (trans. and comm.) (1973) *Plato: Theaetetus*. Oxford.
McGinn, C. (2000) *Logical Properties*. Oxford.
Meillet, A. (1948) *Aperçu d'une histoire de la langue grecque*, 6th edn. Paris.
Mignucci, M. (1986) 'Aristotle's Definitions of Relatives in Cat. 7', *Phronesis* 31: 101–26.
Momigliano, A. (1969) 'Prodico da Ceo e le dottrine sul linguaggio da Democrito ai Cinici'. In his *Quarto contributo alla storia degli studi classici e del mondo antico*. Rome: 155–65.
Mondolfo, R. (with Tarán, L.) (ed., trans. and comm.) (1972) *Eraclito: testimonianze e imitazioni*. Florence.
Morel, P.-M. (2002) 'Le *Timée*, Démocrite et la nécessité'. In *Platon source des Présocratiques: exploration*, eds. M. Dixsaut and A. Brancacci. Paris: 129–50.
Morgan, K. (2000) *Myth and Philosophy. From the Presocratics to Plato*. Cambridge.
Mueller, I. (1992) 'Mathematical Method and Philosophical Truth'. In Kraut 1992: 170–99.
Mühll, P. von der (ed.) (1922) *Epicurus. Epistulae tres et ratae sententiae*. Leipzig.

Murphy, D. J., and Nicoll, W. S. M. (1993) '*Parisinus Graecus* 1813 in Plato's *Cratylus*', *Mnemosyne* 46: 458–72.
  (1997) Review of OCT (see Abbreviations, §1) in *Bryn Mawr Classical Review* 97.1.8.
Murray, G. (1946) 'The Beginnings of Grammar'. In his *Greek Studies*. Oxford: 171–91.
Murray, P. (ed. and comm.) (1996) *Plato on Poetry*. Cambridge.
Netz, R. (1999) *The Shaping of Deduction in Greek Mathematics*. Cambridge.
Norden, E. (1913) *Agnostos theos*. Leipzig and Berlin.
Nussbaum, M., and Schofield, M. (eds.) (1982) *Language and Logos. Studies in Ancient Greek Philosophy Presented to G. E. L. Owen*. Cambridge.
Oehler, K. (1962) *Die Lehre vom noetischen und dianoetischen Denkens bei Platon und Aristoteles*. Munich.
Orenstein, A. (2002) 'Existence, Identity and an Aristotelian Tradition'. In *Individuals, Essence and Identity*, eds. A. Bottani, M. Carrara and P. Giaretta. Dordrecht: 127–49.
Ostwald, M. (1969) *Nomos and the Beginnings of the Athenian Democracy*. Oxford.
Owen, G. E. L. (1953) 'The Place of the *Timaeus* in Plato's Dialogues', *Classical Quarterly* 3: 79–95. Reprinted in Owen 1986: 65–84 (page numbers are cited from the latter).
  (1965) 'Aristotle on the Snares of Ontology'. In *New Essays on Plato and Aristotle*, ed. R. Bambrough. London: 69–95. Reprinted in Owen 1986: 259–78 (page numbers are cited from the latter).
  (1986) *Logic, Science and Dialectic. Collected Papers in Greek Philosophy*. London.
Pasquali, G. (1952) *Storia della tradizione e critica del testo*, 2nd edn. Florence.
Peacocke, C. (1987) 'Depiction', *Philosophical Review* 96: 383–410.
Pfeiffer, R. (1968) *History of Classical Scholarship, from the Beginnings to the End of the Hellenistic Age*. Oxford.
Pfeiffer, W. M. (1972) 'True and False Speech in Plato's *Cratylus* 385 b–c', *Canadian Journal of Philosophy* 2: 87–104.
Pritchard, P. (1995) *Plato's Philosophy of Mathematics*. Sankt Augustin.
Quine, W. V. O. (1960) *Word and Object*. Cambridge, MA.
Renehan, R. (1969) *Greek Textual Criticism*. Boston, MA.
Richardson, M. (1976) 'True and False Names in the "Cratylus"', *Phronesis* 21: 135–45.
Richardson, N. J. (1975) 'Homeric Professors in the Age of the Sophists', *Proceedings of the Cambridge Philological Society* 21: 65–81.
Riddell, J. (ed., trans. and comm.) (1867) *The Apology of Plato*. Oxford. (Quotations by § refer to the Appendix B, *A Digest of Platonic Idioms*, reprinted separately, Amsterdam 1967.)
Riginos, A. S. (1976) *Platonica*. Leiden.
Rijlaarsdam, J. C. (1978) *Platon über die Sprache. Ein Kommentar zum Kratylos*. Utrecht.

Risch, E. (1974) *Wortbildung der homerischen Sprache*, 2nd edn. Berlin and New York.
Robinson, D. B. (1995) 'Κρόνος, Κορόνους and Κρουνός in Plato's *Cratylus*'. In *The Passionate Intellect*, ed. L. Ayres. New Brunswick, NJ and London: 57–66.
Robinson, R. (1953) *Plato's Earlier Dialectic*, 2nd edn. Oxford.
  (1955) 'The Theory of Names in Plato's *Cratylus*', *Revue Internationale de Philosophie*. Reprinted in Robinson 1969: 100–17 (page numbers cited from the latter).
  (1956) 'A Criticism of Plato's *Cratylus*', *Philosophical Review* 65. Reprinted in Robinson 1969: 118–38 (page numbers cited from the latter).
  (1969) *Essays in Greek Philosophy*. Oxford.
Robinson, T. M. (ed. and comm.) (1979) *Contrasting Arguments. An Edition of the Dissoi Logoi*. Salem, NH.
Rose, L. E. (1964) 'On Hypothesis in the *Cratylus* as an Indication of the Place of the Dialogue in the Sequence of Dialogues', *Phronesis* 9: 114–16.
Ross, W. D. (ed. and comm.) (1949) *Aristotle's Prior and Posterior Analytics*. Oxford.
  (1953) *Plato's Theory of Ideas*, 2nd edn. Oxford.
Rowe, C. J. (ed., trans. and comm.) (1986) *Plato: Phaedrus*. Warminster.
  (ed. and comm.) (1993) *Plato: Phaedo*. Cambridge.
  (ed., trans. and comm.) (1995) *Plato: Statesman*. Warminster.
Russell, B. (1956) 'The Philosophy of Logical Atomism'. In his *Logic and Knowledge*, ed. R. C. Marsh. London: 57–281.
Sainsbury, M. (2005) *Reference without Referents*. Oxford.
Sambursky, S. (1959) 'A Democratean [sic] Metaphor in Plato's *Cratylus*', *Phronesis* 4: 1–4.
Schanz, M. (1874) *Studien zur Geschichte des platonischen Textes*. Würzburg.
Schmidt, M. (1976) *Die Erklärungen zum Weltbild Homers und zur Kultur der Heroenzeit in den bT-Scholien zur Ilias*. Munich.
Schofield, M. (1972) 'A Displacement in the Text of the *Cratylus*', *Classical Quarterly* 22: 246–53.
  (1982) 'The Dénouement of the *Cratylus*'. In Nussbaum/Schofield 1982: 61–81.
Sedley, D., (1973) 'Epicurus *On Nature*, Book XXVIII', *Cronache Ercolanesi* 3: 5–84.
  (1996) 'Three Platonist Interpretations of the *Theaetetus*'. In Gill/McCabe 1996: 79–103.
  (1998) 'The Etymologies in Plato's *Cratylus*', *Journal of Hellenic Studies* 118: 140–54.
  (2002) 'The Origins of Stoic God'. In *Traditions of Theology. Studies in Hellenistic Theology, its Background and Aftermath*, eds. D. Frede and A. Laks. Leiden: 41–83.
  (2003) *Plato's* Cratylus. Cambridge.
  (2004a) 'Aristote et la signification', *Philosophie Antique* 4: 5–25.
  (2004b) *The Midwife of Platonism: Text and Subtext in Plato's* Theaetetus. Oxford.

(2007a) 'Equal Sticks and Stones'. In *Maieusis: Essays in Ancient Philosophy in Honour of Myles Burnyeat*, ed. D. Scott. Oxford: 68–86.

(2007b) *Creationism and Its Critics in Antiquity*. Berkeley, CA, Los Angeles and London.

Sellars, W. (1963) 'Abstract Entities', *Review of Metaphysics* 16: 627–71. Reprinted in *In the Space of Reasons. Selected Essays of Wilfrid Sellars*, eds. K. Scharp and R. B. Brandom. Cambridge, MA 2007, 163–205.

Sharples, R. W. (ed., trans. and comm.) (1985) *Plato:* Meno. Warminster.

Shorey, P. (1919) 'On Plato's *Cratylus* 389 D', *Classical Philology* 14: 85.

(ed., trans. and comm.) (1930–5) *Plato: The Republic* (2 vols.). Cambridge, MA.

Silverman, A. (1992) 'Plato's *Cratylus:* The Naming of Nature and the Nature of Naming', *Oxford Studies in Ancient Philosophy* 10: 25–71.

(2001) 'The End of the *Cratylus:* Limning the World', *Ancient Philosophy* 21: 25–43.

Smith, I. (2008) 'False Names, Demonstratives and the Refutation of Linguistic Naturalism in Plato's *Cratylus* 427d1–431c3', *Phronesis* 53: 125–51.

Smith, J. A. (1917) 'General Relative Clauses in Greek', *Classical Review* 31: 69–71.

Snell, B. (1944) 'Die Nachrichten über die Lehren des Thales und die Anfänge der griechischen Philosophie- und Literaturgeschichte', *Philologus* 96: 170–82.

Sonnenschein, E. A. (1918) 'The Indicative in Relative Clauses', *Classical Review* 32: 68–9.

Sprague, R. K. (1962) *Plato's Use of Fallacy*. London.

Stanford, W. B. (1973) 'Onomatopoeic *Mimesis* in Plato, *Republic* 396b–397c', *Journal of Hellenic Studies* 93: 185–91.

Steinthal, H. (1890–1) *Geschichte der Sprachwissenschaft bei den Griechen und Römern*, 2nd edn (2 vols.). Berlin.

Stern, E. M. (2007) 'Ancient Glass in a Philological Context', *Mnemosyne* 60: 341–406.

Stewart, M. A. (1975) 'Plato, *Cratylus* 424c9 sqq.', *Archiv für Geschichte der Philosophie* 57: 167–71.

Szaif, J. (1998) *Platons Begriff der Wahrheit*, 2nd edn. Freiburg and Munich.

Tarán, L. (1999) 'Heraclitus: the River-Fragments and Their Implications', *Elenchos* 20: 9–52. Reprinted in his *Collected Papers (1962–1999)*. Leiden, Boston, MA and Cologne, 2001: 126–67.

Taylor, A. E. (1960) *Plato. The Man and His Works*, 7th edn. London.

Thornton, M. T. (1970) 'Knowledge and Flux in Plato's *Cratylus* (438–40)', *Dialogue* 8: 581–91.

Tod, M. N. (1927) 'The Economic Background of the Fifth Century', in *The Cambridge Ancient History*, eds. J. B. Bury, S. A. Cook, F. E. Adcock, vol. v: *Athens 478–401 B.C.* Cambridge: 1–32.

Valenti, V. (1998) 'Una variante d'autore: Plat. *Crat.* 437D10–438A2', *Studi Classici e Orientali* 46.3: 769–831.

Van den Berg, R. M. (2008) *Proclus'* Commentary on the Cratylus *in Context*. Leiden and Boston, MA.
Vlastos, G. (1966) 'Plato on Knowledge and Reality', *Philosophical Review* 75: 526–30. Reprinted in his *Platonic Studies*, 2nd edn. Princeton, NJ 1981: 374–8 (page numbers cited from the latter).
(1991), *Socrates: Ironist and Moral Philosopher*. Cambridge.
de Vries, G. J. (1955) 'Notes on Some Passages of the *Cratylus*', *Mnemosyne* IV 8: 290–7.
(1969) *A Commentary on the* Phaedrus *of Plato*. Amsterdam.
Warren, J. (2002) *Epicurus and Democritean Ethics*. Cambridge.
Weidemann, H. (trans. and comm.) (2002) *Aristoteles: Peri hermeneias*, 2nd edn. Berlin.
West, M. L. (ed. and comm.) (1966) *Hesiod: Theogony*. Oxford.
(2002) 'Seventeen Distorted Mirrors in Plato', *Classical Quarterly* 52: 380–1.
Whitaker, C. W. A. (1996) *Aristotle's* De Interpretatione: *Contradiction and Dialectic*. Oxford.
Wilamowitz, U. von (1920) *Platon*, 2nd edn (2 vols.). Berlin.
Williams, B. (1982) 'Cratylus' Theory of Names and its Refutation'. In Nussbaum/Schofield 1982: 83–93.
Wilson, J. (1982) '"The Customary Meanings of Words Were Changed" – or Were They? A Note on Thucydides 3.82.4', *Classical Quarterly* 32: 18–20.
Woodruff, P. (trans. and comm.) (1982) *Plato: Hippias Major*. Oxford.
Worthington, I. (1982) 'A Note on Thucydides 3.82.4', *Liverpool Classical Monthly* 7: 124.
Wright, M. R. (ed. and comm.) (1981) *Empedocles: The Extant Fragments*. New Haven, CT.
Young, C. M. (1994) 'Plato and Computer Dating', *Oxford Studies in Ancient Philosophy* 12: 227–50.

I General index

NB: Some very general subjects, which recur almost ubiquitously throughout the book (e.g. *Correctness, Conventionalism, Naturalism*), are not indexed, or are only partially indexed, here. Their most important occurrences can, however, be traced through the list of Contents.

Academics
    on the categories of beings 287–8
    on the Identity of Indiscernibles 367
accent 264–5
actions
    better and worse ways of
        performing *see* degrees of success
    naturalness of 95–106
Aegina 19, 379, 380–1
Aeschylus 34–5
aether 195–7
Ajax 247, 318
alphabet *see* orthography, Attic
ambiguity, *see* 'homonymy'
Ammonius 406
anacoluthon 291, 351, 434
analogy 94
Anaxagoras 192–3, 195, 201–2, 212, 222, 239
    on mind 220, 222
Anaximander the younger 150
Anaximenes 212
Antisthenes 61, 150, 237, 332–5
Archelaus 222
Archinus 283
Aristonicus 196
Aristophanes 34
Aristotle 59, 60, 61, 69
    attacks a rival view from his own theoretical
        standpoint 453
    on the elements, the first body and the
        etymology of 'aether' 195–7
    on essential and accidental features 277
    on etymology 239–40
    on existence 277–8
    on genera and species 130, 292
    on geometrical figures 362

    on kinds of change 211, 212
    on names as instruments 114–15
    on Platonic forms 161
    on sameness 171
    on signification and the role of thought 399
    on substances and accidents 169
    on the Synonymy Principle 160–1, 169
art 117, 125, 127–8, 321–3
artefacts, forms of *see* forms, of artefacts
article 42, 56–7, 60–2, 144, 403–4, 457
articulatory mimesis 309–11
Aspasia 250
aspiration, signs for 439
astronomy 192
Astyanax/Scamandrius 152–9, 172–5
Atomists
    on atoms, void, qualities, change and
        movement 213–15
    in the etymologies' flux theory 213–15,
        216–17, 223–5, 252, 469
    on letters, syllables and rhythms 283
    on perception 223–4
        on vision 227
    in the 'Secret Doctrine' of *Tht.* 226–7, 469
    on soul 216–17
    on verbs 296
author's variants 68–70, 195–7, 489–95

barbarian languages *see* languages, different
being 276–8
    and becoming 466, 477
    see also Index III *s.v.* οὐσία
beings
    categories of 287–8, 292
        old Academic 287–8
    division of 285–90

beliefs
   knowledge and true belief   432–3
   of the namegivers, embedded in the etymon of names and possibly (or even actually) false   419, 431–4, 449–50
Bolus of Mendes   224

Callias (Hermogenes' grandfather)   18
Callias (Hermogenes' half-brother)   18–19, 20, 28–9, 147–8
Carneades   184
catarrh   485–6
categories of beings   see Beings
change
   kinds of   211, 212, 469
   see also flux
Charmides   487
Comenius, J. A.   301
'concordance' among names (according to Cratylus)   433–4
   no 'concordance' (according to Socrates)   438–41
connotation   163–7, 169–77
consonants, kinds of   281–5
convention   37–41, 386–8, 395–424
   and arbitrariness as 'chance'   42
   compatible with names being similar to their referents   415–17
   and habit   40–1, 396, 402–3, 412
   private   401; see also imposition, individual
   in the Seventh Letter   424–5
   is 'vulgar'   420, 425
   see also Index II s.v. συνθήκη
conventional designators   29–31, 324–6
correctness of names   1–6
   consists in the names' indicating the objects   384–6
   conventional   see convention
   degrees of   151–2, 153–4, 423; see also correctness of names, Redundancy Conception of
   and the etymologies of primary names   314–15
   and fineness   300–1, 355, 358, 423
   natural   23–32, 417–20
   natural vs conventional   4–6
   Redundancy Conception of   2–4, 24, 26, 41, 98, 151–2, 198–9, 267, 323, 355, 358, 360–1, 367, 370–1, 372, 382, 423
   the same for primary and secondary names   267
   consists in the name's 'indicating what each of the beings is like'   267–8, 319–20
   two 'manners' of   199–201

and understanding and indication   396, 400–1
see also signification
Cratylus
   the dialogue's character
      on 'bad' or imperfect names   321–3, 356–7, 358
      is becoming a Heraclitean   15, 487
      on 'concordance' among names   433–4
      on falsehood   332–8
      on Hermogenes' name   4, 15, 26–32, 324–8, 433
      on laws/customs (νόμοι)   321–3
      on names and knowledge   430, 441–2
      on Platonic forms   459
      is still young   14, 486
   the historical character   14–18, 190, 209, 309, 318, 319
   and etymology   319, 428
   and flux   15–16, 17–18, 464, 469
   and 'teaching' as the function of names   385–6, 427
Critias   121, 487
Cronus   192, 242–3
custom/law (νόμος)   40–1, 117–21, 123, 412
   cannot be better or worse for Cratylus   321–3
   naturalist conception of in Plato   322–3
   see also Index III s.v. νόμος.
cutting and burning   99–100

Dalgarno, G.   301
Damon   283
date of the Cratylus
   dramatic   20
   relative   20–1, 194–5
   see also stylometry
dative
   ethical   271, 401, 433
   expressing relation or point of view   85, 87
death   21, 193–5
definite descriptions   345
definition   110–11
   see also division
degrees
   of correctness   151–2, 154–5; see also correctness, Redundancy Conception of
   of success, in various sorts of activities   98, 101, 105, 117, 130–1, 135–6, 321–3
Demiurge   123, 484
Democritus   39, 92–4, 150, 217, 252, 469
   Sayings of Democrates   225
   see also Atomists
depiction   368

I General index

dialectic 112–14, 140–4
  and division by kinds 141, 285, 289–90
  and the forms 141–2
  as knowledge of how to ask and answer questions 141
dialectician
  and lawgiver 142–4
  as the user of names 142
  see also dialectic
Diodorus Cronus 39
divination 249–50
divine and human names *see* Homer.
division by kinds 112–14, 129, 285, 289–90, 291–2, 299, 302
  as the function of names 113–14
  of beings 285–90
  of letters 281–5
    correspondence between division of beings and division of letters 290–2
Donnellan, K. 345
dream image 451, 456
drugs 170
Dummett, M. 13
duplicate, perfect 363–9

editions, revised, of ancient works 492
elements 195–7
Empedocles 212
  'conventionalism' 89–90
  doctrine of elements 195, 196–7
  on vision 227–8
Epicurus, on the origin of names 4–5, 426
Eretrian dialect 391
essence 110–11, 276–80
etymologies of primary names 306–9, 312–15
  and the correctness of names 314–15
  likely to be Plato's own creation 309, 428
  parallel with other authors 314
  serious purpose of 312–15
etymologies of secondary names in *Cra.*
  as 'agonistic display' 250–1
  allegedly the product of inspiration 182, 197, 241–6, 250, 252, 313–14, 318
  as chariot race 242, 251
  humorous and playful 246–50, 252, 313–14
  literary, virtuosic character of 252–6, 313–14
    comparable to myths 313–14
  not a parody 237–41, 252, 313–14, 449
  taken seriously throughout antiquity 239
  references to other authors 189–91
  structure of the section 182–9
    systematic character and historical ordering of 189–91, 251–2
  'suicide of naturalism' 199–201, 208, 251–2

etymology
  in Aristotle 239–40
  criticized by few ancient authors 239
  in other Platonic dialogues 239
  popular conception of 33–6
Euripides 247, 365
Euthydemus 84–7
Euthyphro 182, 190, 193, 242–3
  allegedly the source of Socrates' inspiration 241–6, 250, 252, 313, 318
existence 277–8, 333
  existence questions
    about the forms 457–9
    in the 'Socratic' dialogues 457–8

facts 334, 349, 373
falsa anaphora 53, 353–4
false beliefs, may be expressed by names *see* beliefs
falsehood, impossibility of (ISF) 30–1, 36, 48, 61–3, 65, 101–2, 448
  applies both to statements and to acts of naming 336–7
  Cratylus' defence of 332–8
  entailed by Cratylus' theory of names 326–32
  Socrates' refutation 338–50
  see also sentence, structure of
fire
  in the atomist theory of the soul 216–17
  in Heraclitus 221
flux 15–16, 17–18, 27, 183, 201–33, 251–2, 276, 448
  affecting both numerical and qualitative identity through time 464–8, 469, 478, 479
  arguments against 451–86
    role of the forms 451–4
  and the atomists 213–15, 216–17, 223–5, 252, 469
  and 'being something' 473–7, 484–5
  and identity / predicative sentences or statements 464–8, 475, 476–7, 480–1
  and knowledge 478–81, 482–5
  moderate and extreme 451, 461, 462–6, 468–73
  and reference/predication 467–8
  and relativity 233
  and sensible particulars 15–16, 17–18, 453–4, 460–2, 466, 473, 474–5, 477, 479–80
  in some/in every respect *see* moderate and extreme
  and the structure of *Cra.* 209–10, 450–1
  and the 'that'-'such' distinction 464–8
theory

flux (cont.)
  details 210–24
    basic role of movement (spatial change) 210–15, 462–3
    duality of principles 202–3, 211–12, 215–23, 226–32
    Plato's assessment of 206–9, 460–2, 485–6
    widespread in Greek culture 208–9, 450
form(s), Platonic 15–16, 20, 21, 125–38, 161, 188, 276
  of artefacts 128
  assumed to exist and to be unchanging 451–4, 455–60, 478, 483–5
  existence questions about 457–9
  as the beings par excellence 458
  generic and specific 129–34, 137–8
  intelligible, not perceptible 458–9
  'itself' terminology 458
  of knowledge 482–3, 484
    as a relation 483
  'looked to' 125, 127–8
  and matter 131–2
  of name 132–8, 164, 171–2
  as 'parts' of other forms 129
  supposed to be in flux 451–4, 462–3, 474–5, 477, 479–80, 482–3, 484–5
  see also Index III s.v. ὅ ἐστι F
Frege, G. 12, 134, 175, 334

general relative clauses 474
general terms 105–6, 343
  and proper names 162, 172, 175, 177–80, 198
genitive 96–7
  absolute without explicit subject 470
  criminis 380–1
  locative 381
  partitive 96–7
glass 275
god(s)
  as the giver(s) of names 34–5, 303, 442–3
  names of 182–4, 188, 199–201
  unknowable by us 199–201
Gorgias 247

habit 40–1, 396, 402–4, 412
  see also custom/law
Hades 21, 193–5
heavenly bodies, divinity of 184
Hector 152–9, 172–5
Helen 34–5, 365
'Hellenism' 259–60
Heraclides Ponticus 237
Heracliteans 15–16, 17–18, 27, 36, 318, 405, 472
Heraclitus
  on fire 221, 222
  on flux 15, 17, 27, 202, 203–4, 205, 210, 433

on names 36
Hermes 28–9, 487–8
Hermodorus 287, 288
Hermogenes
  the dialogue's character, upholder of conventionalism 37–41, 42–8
  the historical character 18–19, 28–9
  name of 4, 15, 26–32, 324–8, 433, 487–8
Herodotus 352
Hesiod 34, 189, 204–5
Hippias 283
Hipponicus 18–19, 20, 28–9, 147–8
Hobbes, Th. 66, 76
Homer 149–57, 189, 190, 196–7, 208–9, 210, 238, 246–8, 252, 318, 433, 472
  on divine and human names 149–52, 154–5, 254–5
  (mis)quotations from 152–6
Homeric exegesis 150–1, 154, 190
'homonymy' 93
human being 192
humour, in the etymologies 246–50, 252–6
Humpty Dumpty 40, 44
hymns to the gods 200
hyperbaton 482
hypotheses 437–8, 451, 456

ideal language see language, ideal
identity (and nonidentity)
  of Indiscernibles 366–7
  qualitative 365
  and reference 467
  through time 462
  numerical and qualitative 464–8, 469, 478, 479
images
  better and worse 351–4
  contrasted with quantitative items 360–3
  include secondary names see names, secondary
  and knowledge of the objects 446–7
  names compared to, or as a kind of 338–46, 351–82
  and qualitative items 362–3
  similar to their objects 363, 368
  cannot be exactly similar to their objects 359–69
imitation 269–76, 278–80, 311–15, 338–50
  of animal cries 273–4, 279
  carried out also by secondary names see names, secondary
  of the essence 278–80
  by means of letters and syllables 279
  by means of the articulation of each letter/sound 309–11
  as the way of indicating something 269–72

I General index

see also images, similarity
imperfect
  equivalent to timeless present 99
  retrospective 99, 107
imposition, *vs* use, of a name 24, 39, 48, 63, 73, 74, 79, 291, 320–1, 372
  individual 40, 42–8, 74–5
indication *see* signification; *see also* Index III s.v. δηλόω
infinitus imperfecti 205
inspiration, Socrates' *see* etymologies
instruments 107–15
  and forms 125–32
  function of 107
  production and use of 138–40
intention 330, 356–7, 358
interpolations 68–70, 489–95, 496
Ionian philosophers 189
Ionic alphabet *see* orthography, Attic
iron 136–7
irony 27, 151, 246–8, 487
Isocrates 487

knowledge
  and flux 478–81, 482–5
  form of 482–3, 484
  as a relation 483
  'must be based on knowledge' 304–5
  of an object and knowledge of its image(s) 446–7
  of an object and knowledge *that* 481
  of the object named 110, 111–12, 387–8
    provided by the etymology of names 111–12, 419, 427–31, 486
    provided *only* by the etymology of names (according to Cratylus) 430, 441–2, 492
    'without names' 444–8, 450–1
  of sensible particulars 479–80
  and true belief 432–3
Kripke, S. 159, 330

language(s)
  different 25, 75–6, 93–4, 133, 135, 136–7, 257–8, 414, 490–1
  ideal 290–3, 298–301
law *see* custom/law (νόμος)
lawgiver(s) 5, 39, 117–25, 142–4, 236, 320–1, 449–50, 490–2
Leibniz, G. W. 66, 134, 135, 301, 310, 312, 314, 366, 411, 422
letters
  kinds of 281–5
  of a name
    altered through the course of time 230–2, 234, 236, 240, 250

  contrary to each other 393–4, 400
  dissimilar from the object named 400, 402–4, 406–7
  irrelevant 163–4, 169–74, 292, 297–8, 310–11, 372
  as the means to imitate things 279, 382
  similar to the object named 290–2, 389–90, 402–4
  see also name(s), fine and bad (or better and worse)
  names of 164, 166, 292, 297, 371–2 (and syllables,)
  analogy with things 289–90
  the subject matter of literacy (γραμματική) 356
Leucippus *see* Atomists
Lewis, D. 38, 40
likeness *see* image, similarity
literacy (γραμματική) 356
Locke, J. 47, 76
Lysias 250, 251

manuscripts 21–2
  β family 22, 493
  Bodleianus MS E. D. Clarke 39 (B) 22
  common source of βTδ 493
  δ family 22, 493, 494, 496
  Laurentianus 59.1 309
  Laurentianus 85.9 309
  T family 22
  Venetus app. cl. 4.1 (T) 22, 76, 131, 493
  Venetus gr. 185 (D) 22
  Venetus 590 160
  Vindobonensis, Philos. gr. 21 (Y) 160
  Vindobonensis suppl. gr. 7 (W) 22, 489–95, 496
mathematical propositions 434–8
meaning
  lexical and etymological 229–32
  ways of referring to 233–7
  see also sense
metrics, study of 282–3
Mill, J. S. 12, 13, 165
'music' (μουσική) 274–5
myths, Plato's conception of 253–6

name(s) 1
  all 'concordant' with each other, according to Cratylus 433–4
  not 'concordant', according to Socrates 438–41
  change of 42–8, 94, 388
  elementary *see* first (primary)
  etymologized
    'concerning the things that always exist by nature' 182, 188, 198

name(s) (cont.)
  'concerning virtue'   143, 184–7, 188, 210, 438–41
  of the gods   182–4, 188, 199–201
  'greatest and finest' = concerning logic and ontology   187–8
  of heroes and human beings   182
  of the objects of natural science   184
  fine and bad (or better and worse)   4, 116, 321–3, 351–82, 383–4, 391–5, 402–4, 420–3, 446–7
  fineness and correctness   355, 358
  first (primary)   136–7, 181, 257–62, 267–8, 271–81, 296–301, 302–15, 389–90
    imitate the *essence* of things   278–80
    logically *vs* chronologically 'first'   261–2, 443
    relation to secondary names   272–3, 293, 297–8, 304–5, 311–12, 343–4, 427–8, 445, 446–7
  forms of   *see* form(s)
  Greek popular conception of   33–5
  as imitations or images   338–9, 351–82
    compared to paintings   338–46, 389–90
  imposition of   *see* imposition
  'indicate' objects   *see* signification
  as instruments   114–15
  may express false beliefs   419, 431–4, 449–50
  of nonexistent objects   141
  origin of   4–6, 32–3
  proper
    and general terms   *see* General terms
    and naturalism   197–9
  public and private   42–8
  sameness of   169–77
  secondary   181, 384
    presented as being similar to, or images or imitations of, their referents   312, 445, 446–7
    relation to primary names   272–3, 293, 297–8, 304–5, 311–12, 343–4, 427–8, 445, 446–7
  sense of   *see* sense
  spelling of   356–7
  true and false   54–71, 303, 336–7
    true and false *of* something, or correct and incorrect   58–62, 67–8
    truly and falsely distributed or applied to things   338–46
  types and tokens   57
  and verb(s)   54, 55, 59, 60, 61–2, 294–6
  see also Index I s.v. ὄνομα
namegiver(s)   *see* lawgiver(s).
naming   103–6
  and speaking/stating   103–4, 349

natural kinds   160, 167–9, 178
  see also Principle of Synonymical Generation
Niceratus   150–1
nominativus pendens   194
nonexistent objects   141
numbers
  Greek conception of   359–60
  names of   407–13, 414–15, 421–2, 426
  written notation   408, 439

Ocean   204–5, 208–9, 433
onomatopoeia   309–11
opinions   *see* beliefs
Orpheus   124–5, 204–5, 433
orthography, Attic   216, 240, 247, 283, 439

paintings   *see* images
paralogisms, mathematical   435–7
Parmenides   191, 226, 227
  on names   19
  Plato's interpretation of   332
  on 'what is not'   331–2, 333
paronymy   94
participium imperfecti   432
Peacocke, C.   368
Penetrating Principle   *see* flux, theory, details, duality of principles
perfect language   *see* language, ideal
Philip of Opus   195–7
pictures   *see* images
Plato's name   15
play   *see* humour in the etymologies
pluperfect   99
poetry, discussion of   151
'polyonymy'   25, 93–4
'power' (δύναμις)
  of drugs   170
  of names   134–5, 171–7
Principle of Synonymical Generation   159–64, 167–9, 172, 177–80, 276, 287–8
  Restricted   160
  Unrestricted   161–2, 168–9
Proclus   5, 64, 70–2
  inconsistencies in   32–3, 71–2
  interpretation of Socrates' views on names   406, 425–7
  own views on names   198
Prodicus   1, 27–8, 61, 147–8
prosody, study of   282–3
Protagoras   1, 28, 72, 148–9, 219, 236, 250, 251
  grammatical distinctions   283
  linguistic naturalism   36, 148
  relativism   21, 63, 76–88, 226, 276, 470
purification   243–6

I General index

Pythagoreans 190, 225
Pseudo-Pythagorean literature 124

qualitative items
  and images 362–3
  vs quantitative items 362–3
quantitative items
  vs images 360–3
  vs qualitative items 362–3

recollection 404, 447
redundancy at the end of a sentence 289
reference *see* signification
relations in Plato and Aristotle 483
relative clauses
  general 474
  involving transposition of the relative pronoun's antecedent 159–60
relativism 66–7, 72, 76–8, 82, 276, 425, 472–3
  and conventionalism 78–81
  individual *vs* collective 85
  refutation of 81–4
  in the 'Secret Doctrine' of *Tht.* 226
resemblance *see* similarity
rhythms, study of 282–3
ridicule 302–3, 305–6, 315
Russell, B. 334

Sappho 250
Scamandrius *see* Astyanax
Secret Doctrine 219, 225–7, 468–73
  and the atomists 226–7, 469
  on quick and slow motions 226–7
  refutation of 469–73
self-predication 460, 467, 476
Sellars, W. 135
semantic type 133–5
sense, of names 12, 133–5, 155–9, 163–7, 169–77, 399
  see also meaning
sensible particulars 362, 363
  being of 277
  and flux 15–16, 17–18, 453–4, 460–2, 466, 473, 474–5, 477, 479–80
  and forms 15
  not objects of knowledge 479–80
sentence(s)
  declarative 50, 348
  grammatical *vs* ungrammatical 101
  parts of 54–5
  simple and compound 54
  structure of 59–62, 70, 103–4, 294–6, 329, 333–5, 344–5, 348–50, 372–9, 467–8
  true and false 49–71, 336–7, 348–50, 372–9

  see also falsehood, impossibility of
  types and tokens 57
shuttle 108–10
signification (*or* indication) 155–9, 163–7, 169–77, 233–7, 267–8, 269–72, 384–9, 395–407
  Aristotle on 399
  conventional (at least partly) 387–8, 395–424
    compatible with names being similar to their referents 415–17
  of objects as common ground between naturalism and conventionalism 384–6
  of an object *vs* of an object's features 271–2
  the Stoics on 399
  and teaching as two alternative functions of names 385–6, 400–1
  and thought 396–9, 405–6
  and understanding 395–403
  and correctness 396, 400–1
similarity (*or* resemblance) 290–3, 312, 407–11, 413–23, 429, 445–6
  compatible with convention 415–17
  exact 363–9
  the ground of the correctness of only some names 417–20
  holding also between *secondary* names and their referents *see* names, secondary
  'items similar to each other fall under the same art' 429
  minimal threshold of 371–2
  as one 'way' of indicating objects 384–6
  and quality 362–3
  see also correctness, images, imitation
Simonides 250, 251
'sky-watchers' 190, 201–2
slaves' names 39
Smicrion 14, 336, 337–8
Socrates 81–2
Solon 237
'something' as entailing existence 333
Sophists 28, 36, 102, 147–8, 189, 238, 244–5, 246–8
soul 192–5
sound-symbolism 309–11
Sous 223–4
speaker's reference and semantic reference 329–31
  in Plato 331
speaking/stating 56, 100–3
  and naming 103–4, 349
spelling 356–7
stability 87

stage-directions, Plato's 102–3, 162, 300, 313, 319
state, of something 465, 475, 480
  total state 475
Stesichorus 365
Stesimbrotus of Thasos 150
Stoics 69, 221
  on etymology 239
  on the Identity of Indiscernibles 366, 367
  influenced by *Cra.* 218
  on mimetic primary names 259–60, 314
  on signification 399
  on 'something' 333
  theology 218
structure of *Cra.* 145, 209–10, 423–4, 450–1
stylometry 20
subject and predicate 59–62, 70, 294–6, 329, 344–5, 348–50, 372–9, 467–8
  see also sentences, structure of
sun 220
  and moon, divinity of 184
Synonymenwechsel 96
synonymy 28, 155–9, 163–7, 169–77; *see also* 'Polyonymy'
Synonymy Principle *see* Aristotle

teaching, as the (or part of the) function of names 110, 111–12, 141, 320–1, 424, 427–31
  and indicating objects as two alternative functions of names 385–6, 400–1
teleology 113–14, 115, 116, 142
Tethys 204–5, 208–9
Thales 204–5

'that' and 'such' 464–8
thought, role in signification 396–9, 405–6
Thrasymachus 247, 322
Thucydidean 'conventionalism' 90–1
tools *see* instruments
tragedians 34, 189
truth and falsehood
  distinction between truth/falsehood and correctness/incorrectness 346
  of names 54–71, 303, 336–7, 338–46
    truth and falsehood *of* 58–62, 67–8
  of sentences 49–71, 336–7, 348–50, 372–9
  Two Cratyluses argument 363–9, 415

understanding 397–8
  and indication 395–403
  and correctness 396, 400–1
Uranus 192, 242–3

validity, logical 437–8
verb(s) 54, 294–6, 347–8
  see also names and verbs
'virtue is knowledge' 81–2, 85
vortex 450

warp and weft 108–10
weaving 115
Wilkins, J. 301
women and men 153

Zeno of Elea 247
Zeus 157, 244

II Index of ancient texts

Passages from the *Cratylus* have not been indexed.

Aelian
  Varia Historia (*VH*)
    4.17 123–4
Aelius Dionysius
  A *158 244
Aeneas Tacticus (Aen. Tact.)
  10.10 380
  10.14–15 380
  22.23–4 380
Aeschines (Aeschin.)
  1.17 262–3
  2.40 263
  3.72 263–4
  3.166–7 262–3
Aeschines Socraticus
  SSR VI A83 19
  VI A92 18
Aeschylus (Aesch.)
  Agamemnon (*Ag.*)
    681–91 34–5
    699 34–5
    849 99–100
    1080–2 175, 190
    1245 242
    1485–6 190
  Choephori (*Ch.*)
    514 242
    555 38
    711 381
  Eumenides (*Eum.*)
    91 488
  Persians (*Pers.*)
    1003 94
  Prometheus Bound (*Pr.*)
    85–6 35, 64
    226 428
    717 64
    883 242

  Seven Against Thebes (*Th.*)
    658 34–5
    670 64
    829–31 34–5
  Supplices (*Supp.*)
    884 415–16
Aetius
  1.7.33 218
  1.26.2 225
  1.28.1 221
Alcinous
  Didaskalikos
    159.44–5 Hermann 239
    160.4–16 5–6
    160.29–30 111
Alcmaeon
  24 B1a DK 190, 192
Alexander of Aphrodisias (Alex. Aphr.)
  In Aristotelis Metaphysica (*in Metaph.*)
    79.15–80.7 128
    303.31–2 213
    834.5–11 283
  In Aristotelis Topicorum libros octo (*in Top.*)
    23.25–25.9 436, 437
    42.4–8 99
    301.19–25 333
  De Mixtione (*Mixt.*)
    224.32–225.2 218
Alexis
  fr. 93 *PCG* 488
Ammonius (Amm.)
  In Aristotelis Categorias
    11.11–14 39
  In Aristotelis De interpretatione (*in Int.*)
    17.24–6 399
    24.5–12 399
    34.10–37.18 426–7
    34.20–35.23 5–6

Ammonius (Amm.) (cont.)
   34.22–32   5, 32–3
   34.24–30   31
   35.1–12   32–3
   35.13–16   40
   35.21–36.21   148
   36.22–37.13   5–6
   37.1–13   198, 426
   37.28–38.16   93–4
   38.2–17   25
   38.17–20   39
   60.21–3   55
Anaxagoras (Anaxag.)
   59 A42 §8 DK   190
   B9   450
   B11   222
   B12   190, 192–3, 222, 450
   B13   450
   B14   222
   B17   89
Andocides (And.)
   1.15   462
   1.20   235
   1.74   380–1
Anonymus
   In Platonis Theaetetum
      III.28–37   492
   Prolegomena philosophiae Platonicae
      4.4–7   15–16
Anthologia Palatina (*AP*)
   6.174   108
   6.288   108
   7.17   94
Antiphon (Antiph.)
   2.2.9   336
   5.5   262–3
   6.4   483
   fr. 44(a) I.27–II.1 Pendrick   39, 121
      II.30–1   121
Antisthenes
   V A53–4 *SSR*   247
   V A155   332–5
Apollonius Rhodius
   Argonautica   492
Apuleius
   De interpretatione
      4   295
Archilochus (Archil.)
   fr. 109 West   262–3
Archytas
   47 B3 DK   430
Aristarchus
   ap. sch. A *ad Il.* 2.458
      196–7
   ap. sch. A *ad Il.* 14.288   196–7

Aristophanes (Ar.)
   Acharnians (*Ach.*)
      392   258
   Birds (*Av.*)
      227–8   273–4
      237   273–4
      260–2   273–4
   Clouds (*Nu.*)   492
      60–7   33
      228   202
      333   202
      360–1   202
      658–93   148
      1134   237
      1421–4   40
      1421–2   39
      1485   202
   Frogs (*Ran.*)
      97   262–3
      97–102   263
      174   381
      209–68   273–4
      924–9   262–3
      1059   262–3
      1155   262–3
      1316   108
      1435–66   492
   Knights (*Eq.*)
      1059   236
   Pax
      92   202
      361   49–50
      929–31   263
      959   49
   Plutus (*Pl.*)
      290–5   273–4
      842   328
   Thesmophoriazusae (*Th.*)
      167   445
   fr. 113 *PCG*   286
   fr. 349   258
Aristotle (Arist.)
   Prior Analytics (*APr.*)
      41b14   434–5
      49b3–9   176–7
   Posterior Analytics (*APo.*)
      77b19–21   436
      81b30–7   260
      90a2–14   476
      90b25–6   320
   De anima (*De an.*)
      1.2.403b31–404a9
         216–17
      1.2.403b31–404a1   220–1
      1.2.405a5–13   216–17
      3.7.431a6   482

II Index of ancient texts

The Athenian Constitution (Ath. Pol.)
15.2   462
20.3   462
De audibilibus (Aud.)
800a25–9   273–4
De caelo (Cael.)   195–7
270b16–25   195, 239–40
279a22–3   35
279b32–280a11   435
295a29–b1   450
300b8–11   213
313b4–6   223
Categories (Cat.)
4.2a4–10   59
5.3b10–13   173
5.4a10–b19   57
6.4b22–31   360
6.6a19–25   362
7   483
8.8b25   362
8.10a27–b11   94
8.10b26–11a14   362
8.11a15–19   362–3
8.11a32–4   130
12.14a38–b1   434–5
14   212
On Democritus   214
De generatione animalium (GA)
725a26   290
Historia animalium (HA)
504b1–3   279
519a18–20   150
618b16–17   406
De ideis
79.11–15   457
79.15–80.7   128
De interpretatione (Int.)   59, 114
ch. 1   399
chs. 1–3   294
16a3–8   76, 399
16a9–18   59
16a19   25, 47
16a19–29   38
16b6–10   295
16b19–22   55
chs. 4–5   293
16b26–17a12   372
16b33–17a2   114–15
17a1–2   38
18a19–20   47
23a32–3   399
24b1–2   399
Metaphysics (Metaph.)
A3.983b27–33   204–5
A6.987a29–b7   15–16, 36, 318
A6.987a32–b1   461

A6.987a32   15–16
A6.987a34–b1   16
A9.990b22–991a2   453
A9.991b6–7   128
B3.998a25–7   434–5
Γ4.1007a20–b18   453
Γ4.1008b31   402–3
Γ5.1010a7–15   17–18, 31, 36
Γ5.1010a7–9   472–3
Γ5.1010a10–15   203–4, 464, 487
Γ7.1011b26–8   51–2
Δ3.1014a35–b2   434–5
Δ15   483
Δ15.1021a11–12   362–3
Δ25.1023b23–5   292
Δ29.1024b26–1025a1   334–5
Δ29.1024b27–8   58
Z7–9   160, 169
Z8.1033b29–1034a2   160–1, 178
Z8.1033b33–1034a2   178
Z8.1034a2–5   161
Z9.1034a21–3   161
Z9.1034b7–19   169
Z9.1034b16–19   169
Z12.1038a5–6   130
H3.1043b36–1044a2   360
Θ6.1048b18–35   494
Θ10.1051b1–17   57
K5.1062a14–15   173
Λ3.1070a4–5   161
Λ3.1070a4   260
Λ3.1070a18–19   128
Λ6.1071b32–4   213
M4.1078b12–32   15
M4.1078b12–17   461
M9.1086a32–b11   15
M9.1086a35–b2   461
[*Mechanics*] ([*Mech.*])
853b1   415–16
Meteorologica (Mete.)
339b16–30   195, 239–40
382b13–16   416
385b5   416
387a11–12   416
[*De mundo*]
392a5–9   196
Nicomachean Ethics (EN)
1110b30   234
1119b34   234
1121b22   416
1125b33   234
1132a30–2   239–40
1133a29–31   79
1133a29   38
1134b18–1135a5   79
1134b32   38

Aristotle (Arist.) (cont.)
  1134b35 38
  1147a21 299
  1152b7 239–40
  1164b4 93
  De partibus animalium (*PA*)
    660a4–7 284–5
    660a7–8 283
    660a14–b2 279
    660b14 416
  Physics (*Ph.*)
    186a4 479
    200b19 417
    226a32–b1 211
    243a35–40 211
    243b3–9 108–9
    256a29 260
    260b8–15 212
    265b17–32 212
    265b25–9 214
  Poetics (*Po.*)
    1456b15–18 283
    1456b22–37 279
    1456b25–31 284–5
    1456b31–8 283
    1457a10–18 294
    1457a14–18 295
    1457a23–30 293
    1457a23–7 372
    1457b1–10 55
  Politics (*Pol.*)
    1263a20 417
    1266b26 416
    1275a37–8 416
    1276a39 465
    1314b3 416
    1341b29–32 371
  Rhetoric (*Rh.*)
    1355a14–15 429
    1358b19 417
    1373b4–9 118
    1376a33–b31 38
    1379b31–2 27
    ch. 2.23 35
    1400b16–25 35
    1401a27–8 85
    1406b21 51
    1407b7–8 148, 283
    1415b15–17 28
    1417b1–2 18
    1419b7–9 27
  De sensu
    437b23–5 227–8
    438a4–5 227–8
    442a29–b1 223–4
  Sophistici Elenchi (*SE*)
    165b35–8 130–1
    166b37–167a6 476
    ch. 10 236
    170b16–17 236
    171b34–172a7 436
    173b17–22 283
    173b17–174a4 148
    177b12–13 85
    180a32–8 476
  Topics (*Top.*)
    101a5–17 435–6
    ch. 1.7 171
    ch. 1.9 277
    112b21–6 28
    113a20–3 494
    132a32–3 436
    134a25 58
    134b11 58
    157a1–3 436
    160b33–7 436
Asclepius (Ascl.)
  In Aristotelis Metaphysica (*in Metaph.*)
    174.9–10 435
Athenagoras
  Pro Christianis
    18 124
Augustine
  De dialectica
    VI 9 239
    VI 9–10 259–60
    VI 9–12 314
  De magistro
    43 44

Bacchylides (Bacch.)
  18.46 439–40
Bias
  10 ẞ 1 DK 81

Calcidius
  in Platonis Timaeum
    CCXCIV 218
Chaeremon
  fr. 71 F4 *TrGF* 35
Cicero (Cic.)
  Academica (*Ac.*) 492
    1.24–9 218
    1.35 218
    1.39–43 218
    2.54–8 367
    2.85 367
  De natura deorum (*Nat.*)
    2.62–9 239
    3.62–3 239
  Tusculanae Disputationes (*Tusc.*)
    1.62 123–4

Clemens of Alexandria
 Stromateis (*Strom.*)
  6.15   204–5
Critias
 88 B25 DK   39
 B48.17–18   121
 B53–73   121

Democritus
 68 A1 DK = 4.1 Leszl
 A33 DK = 0.6.1 Leszl   150, 283, 296
 A37 = 7.1 Leszl   214
 A49 = 8.3 Leszl   213–14
 A57 = 8.1 Leszl   213–14
 A58 = 19.3 Leszl   190
 A62 = 69.1 Leszl   190, 223
 A66 = 77.1 Leszl   190, 225
 A101 = 102.1 Leszl   190, 216–17
 A119 = 120.1 Leszl   223–4
 A135 = 117.1 Leszl   227
 B9 = 60.1 Leszl   213
 B26 = 129.1 Leszl   39, 92–4
 B83 = 161.1 Leszl   190, 225
 B122a = 191.2 Leszl   190
 B167 = 72.3 Leszl   450
 13.3 Leszl   213
 19.2 Leszl   214
 19.4 Leszl   214
Demosthenes (Dem.)
 14.30   98
 18.95   402–3
 19.13–14   262–3
 19.209   262–3
 23.208   416
 24.1   136
 [25.15–16]   120–1
 37.38   416
 59.103   462
Derveni Papyrus (*PDerv.*)   124–5
 col. x   176–7
 col. xi   176–7
 col. xiv   124–5
 col. xvii   124–5
 col. xviii   124–5
 col. xix   124–5
 col. xxi   124–5
 col. xxii   42, 124–5, 305
 col. xxiii   124–5, 262–3
[Didymus Caecus] ([Did. Caec.])
 De trinitate
  2.5.15   93
Diodorus Siculus (Diod. Sic.)
 1.16.1   35
Diogenes of Apollonia
 64 B5 DK   222
Diogenes of Babylon

fr. 536 *FDS* = Long/Sedley 33M   173
Diogenes Laertius (D. L.)
 1.24   204–5
 1.58   237
 3.6   15–16, 19
 3.37   492
 3.108   288
 3.108–9   287
 6.15   247
 7.58   173
 7.134   218
 9.31–2   450
 9.40   217
 9.44–5   450
 9.47–8   283
 9.48   296
 9.52   236
 10.50   494
Diogenes of Oenoanda
 12.2.11–5.14 Smith   4–5
Dionysius of Halicarnassus (D. H.)
 De compositione verborum (*Comp.*)
  12   167
  25   492
  80   307
  95–6   239
 De Thucydide (*Th.*)
  29   90
[Dionysius Thrax] ([Dion. Thr.])
 Art of Grammar
  3   264
  6   284
  12–13   294
Dioscorides (Dsc.)
 De materia medica
  1 Pr. 1   170
  1.34.1   170
  1.37.1   170
  1.58.3   170
  1.77.3–4   170
Dissoi Logoi
 90.5.3–5 DK   85
 90.5.12   360
 90.5.13–14   360
Divisiones Aristoteleae
 39–41 Mutschmann   287

Empedocles
 31 B8 DK   89–90
 B9   89–90
 B11   89
 B12   89
 B17.1–13   89
 B35   450
 B84   227–8
 B134   222

[Epicharmus]
  PCG I fr. 276 360
Epicurus
  Letter to Herodotus (*Ep. Hdt.*)
    75–6 4–5
Epiphanius
  Ancoratus
    4.5 93
  Panarion
    69.32 93
Erotian
  50.7–8 Klein 93
Etymologicum Gudianum (*Et. Gud.*)
  325.25 de Stefani 224
  326.25–6 224
Euclid (Euc.)
  Elements 437
    Common Notion 7 93–4
    1.20 436
    1.47 437
    7 Def. 2 360
  Pseudaria 436
Eupolis
  fr. 386 *PCG* 202
Euripides (Eur.)
  Bacchae (*Ba.*)
    367 35
    1029 235
  Hecuba (*Hec.*)
    808 192
  Helen (*Hel.*)
    33–4 365
    584 365
    704–5 365
  Medea (*Med.*)
    128 328
  Troades (*Tr.*)
    990 35
  fr. 578 *TrGF* 284–5
Eusebius (Eus.)
  Praeparatio Evangelica (*PE*)
    XV 20.2–3 203–4
Eustathius
  In Homeri Odysseam (*in Od.*)
    1935.9–13 244

Galen (Gal.)
  De elementis ex Hippocrate
    1.2, 3.2–5.9 Helmreich 213–14
  Institutio logica
    2.2.3 295
  De naturalibus facultatibus (*Nat. Fac.*)
    2.9 28
Gellius (Gell.)
  Noctes Atticae (*NA*)
    11.12.2 39

Gorgias
  82 B11a DK 247
Heraclitus (Heracl.)
  22 A8 DK 221
  B12 203–4
  B16 190, 221
  B30 221
  B31 221
  B41 221
  B48 36
  B58 99–100
  B64–6 221
  B66 221
  B90 221
  B91 190, 204
  B108 81
  B114 36
Herodotus (Hdt.)
  1.73.3 462
  1.97 50
  1.209.2 486
  2.30.1 176–7
  2.142.2 328
  2.161.3 130–1
  3.124 194
  3.153.2 262–3
  4.12.3 381
  4.110.1 176–7
  4.120.1 465
  4.192.3 176–7
  5.74.2 387
  6.65.4 262–3
  6.86.γ 328
  6.98.3 176–7
  7.50.2 87, 439
  7.124 381
  7.211.1 465
  8.7.2 387
  8.36.2 462
  9.89.4 381
  9.98.3 387
Hesiod (Hes.)
  Theogony (*Th.*) 241
    195–8 190
    326 190, 240
    337–70 + 383–403 190, 204–5
  Works and Days (*Op.*)
    2–3 190
    154 94
    267–9 220
    361–2 317
Hesychius (Hsch.)
  α 4741 Latte 290
  ε 1750 157
  ε 3395 71

o 75   416
o 582   415–16
Hippias
  86 A2 DK   246–8
  A9   246–8
  B6   204–5
Hippocrates (Hp.)
  De arte
    2   92
    2.3   121–2
  De carnibus
    2   222
  De natura hominis
    5   91–2
  De vetere medicina (*VM*)
    3.4   170
    18   486
    20.4   170
  De victu or Περὶ διαίτης (*Vict.*)
    1   221
    2.39   170
Hippolytus
  Refutatio omnium haeresium (*Haer.*)
    1.12.1   213
    9.10.7–8   221
Hippon
  38 A10 DK   190, 193
Homer (Hom.)
  Iliad (*Il.*)   148
    1.1   148, 283
    1.343   319
    1.403–4   150
    2.458   196–7
    2.813–14   150
    3.109   319
    3.277   220
    5.221–2   242
    5.472–3   157
    5.656   439–40
    5.844–5   193
    6.265   240
    6.401–3   152–6
    8.18–27   209, 220
    9. 442–3   247
    9.644–5   318
    12.70   94
    13.43   190
    14.201 = 302   190, 204–5, 208–9
    14.203–4   194
    14.288   196–7
    14.291   150
    18.250   319
    20.74   150
    21.6   190, 202
    22.505–7   152–6

    23   251
    24.153   488
    24.730   157
  Odyssey (*Od.*)
    1.62   34
    9.364–70   34
    9.407–12   34
    13.239   94
    19.406–9   34
    22.330–1   34
    24.452   319

Iamblichus (Iamb.)
  Vita Pythagorae (*VP*)
    82   123–4
    183   225
Inscriptiones Graecae (*IG*)
  14.769   488
Isocrates (Isocr.)
  3.6   39
  4.176   38
  15.166   262–3

Leucippus
  67 A1 DK = 80.1 Leszl   450
  A10 = 4.4 Leszl   213
  A16 = 64.1 Leszl   213
  A18 = 42.3 Leszl   213
  A28 = 101.1 Leszl   190, 216–17, 220–1
Lucretius
  5.1028–90   4–5
Lysias (Lys.)
  [6.53]   243–4
  10.7   176
  18.15   136
  23.6   237

Martianus Capella (Mart. Cap.)
  4.393   295
Menander (Men.)
  Aspis
    84   415–16

Ocellus
  129.15 Thesleff   202
Olympiodorus (Olymp.)
  Vita Platonis (*Vit. Pl.*)
    192–3 Hermann   15–16
Origenes (Orig.)
  Contra Celsum (*Cels.*)
    1.24   260
Orpheus
  22F *PEG*   190, 204–5
  1141 III *PEG* = fr. 57 Kern = 1 B13 DK   124

Pappus (Papp.)
  Collectio
    7.670.2   435
    7.672.16 435
    7.682.22 435
Parmenides (Parm.)
  28 B1 DK 242
  B1.28–30 331–2
  B2.7–8   333
  B6.1   333
  B8.38   19
  B8.50–2   331–2
  B8.53–4   19
  B9.1   19
  B19   19
Philolaus (Philol.)
  44 B6 DK 202
  B11   202
  B14   190
Philoponus (Philop.)
  In Aristotelis Categorias
    11.34–12.1 39
Philostratus (Philostr.)
  Vitae sophistarum (*VS*)
    1.11.4 247
Phrynichus
  Praeparatio sophistica
    9.12–17 de Borries 244
Pindar (Pi.)
  Isthmian Odes (*I.*)
    2.2   242
    8.61 242
  Nemean Odes (*N.*)
    4.94 262–3
  Olympian Odes (*O.*)
    9.81 242
    10.51 94
  Pythian Odes (*P.*)
    10.65 242
Plato (Pl.)
  Alcibiades I
    106de   430
    133c8–17 494
  Alcibiades II
    108e 80
  Apology (*Ap.*)
    17bc   263–4
    18cd   429
    19e   421
    20a   147–8
    20ac   120
    23a   417
    23d   27, 303
    24d   235
    25ac   120
    26d   184
    29b   269
    38b   28
  Charmides (*Chrm.*) 487
    159a   480
    160c   402–3
    163d   28, 46–7, 424
    168d   78, 275
    169b   402–3
    172d   474
    173a   456
    175b   121
  Critias (*Criti.*) 20
    115a   417
  Crito (*Cri.*)
    47a   81–2
    50e   492
    51d–52b 38
    52b   492
    52d   38
    52de   38
    54c   38
    54d   494–5
  [*Epinomis*]
    981c   195–7
  Euthydemus (*Euthd.*) 84, 102–3, 335
    275d–278b 93
    277e   28
    283e   373
    283e–284a 334–5
    284a   50, 51
    284c   52–3
    285e–286b 334–5
    286c   328
    286e   80
    287c   262–3
    288ab   200–1
    288d–292e 143–4
    290c   140
    293b–296d 86
    294a   86
    296c   86
    296cd   86
    300b   51
    302b   27
    305a   262–3
    306d   486
  Euthyphro (*Euthphr.*) 242
    3bc   242–3
    4c   421
    4d   402–3
    4e–5a   242–3
    5c   242–3
    5c–6e   458
    5cd   480

II Index of ancient texts

5e–6c   242–3
6e   125
8e   150
9b   421
11ab   111
11e–12d   129
15d–16a   242–3
Gorgias (Grg.)
448d   141
455a   49
456b   99–100
461d   317
464b–465c   120, 491
471e–472c   441
476c   99–100
479a   99–100
480b   434
480e   434
482e–483b   118
483e   118
484c   486
489bc   262–3
492c   387
493a   190
493b   73, 193
493e   486
503de   127–8
503e   125
520b   491
Hippias Major (Hp. Ma.)
284b–285b   322–3
285cd   283
286ab   247
286ce   458
288a   457, 476
288d   248
289ac   16
292e   460
299e   125
301b   302
304e   27
Hippias Minor (Hp. Mi.)
368d   283
Ion
536c   262–3
Laches (La.)
180cd   283
184ce   441
186c   28
186c–187a   318
190cd   129
191e   80
192b–199e   81–2
197d   283
198a   129

Laws (Lg.)   20
654a   35, 239
656b   456
659d   415–16
667b–669b   447
667de   474
669b   274
669cd   273–4
681cd   39
684ab   39
714a   239
715ab   322–3
716c   420
730d   235
745a   381
751d   258
754e   381
783c   262–3
792a   269–70
793ad   118
793b   41
793c   289
816b   121, 239
838b   262–3
854b   243–4
874b   380–1
877e   243–4
889e–890a   78–9, 118
895e   372
896a–897b   192–3
898d–899b   184
900b   243–4
908e   27
942bc   406
964a   429
965bc   128
Letters
Seventh   424–5
  7.342de   128
  7.343b   424–5
Lysis (Ly.)
204d   80
219c   260
Menexenus (Menex.)   250–1
236ac   250
236c   250
249e   250
Meno (Men.)
71b   480
72ac   171
72b   111

72c   125, 129
74b   344
74c   344

Plato (Pl.) (cont.)
  75d 140
  75e–76a 457
  76c 227–8
  80d 402–3
  81cd 446
  85c 456
  86c–89c 81–2
  86e–87b 480
  86e–87c 437
  87b 480
  87e 440
  89b 486
  92e–94e 120
  93a–94e 169
  94e 494–5
  96d 28
  97a–98a 432
  98a 494–5
  99bd 120
  [*Minos*] ([*Min.*]) 118
  314c–315a 322–3
  315bd 79
  317c 324
Parmenides (*Prm.*) 20, 102–3
  128b 194
  130b 476
  130bc 457
  130e 106
  132bc 333
  134a 126
  135a 402–3
  135d 202
  137c 51, 320
  138bc, 211
  147de 24–5
  147e 129
  156de 129
Phaedo (*Phd.*) 21, 127, 194–5, 447, 457, 458, 480
  57a 80
  59b 19
  60e–61a 274
  65a 474
  65d 111, 457–9
  65e 398
  66a 458
  68c–69c 81–2
  69a 359
  70c 202
  73b 434–5
  73c–76e 404
  73c 460
  73cd 480
  73d 404
  73e–75e 447

  74a 404, 457
  74d 126
  74de 458
  74e 404
  75b 126, 287
  75cd 142
  75d 21, 126, 458
  76d 287, 457
  78c–80b 475
  78d 126, 142, 460
  78de 461
  78e 106
  79a 277, 458
  79c 207, 417
  80d–81a 21, 194–5
  82c 494–5
  89e 486
  90ab 81
  90be 207
  90c 87, 486
  92d 126, 456
  92de 126, 458
  94d 51
  95c 235
  99b 417
  99cd 430
  99de 96
  100a 434, 437
  100b 456, 457
  101d 433, 434, 438
  101de 437
  101e 437
  102b 106, 262–3
  103d 465
  104d 110
  106a 465
  107b 437, 456
  109a 93
  109bc 196–7
  111b 196–7
  111c–114c 253
  114d 254, 255
Phaedrus (*Phdr.*) 20–1, 112, 140, 246, 250–1
  228d 262–3
  229d 428
  229e 311
  235cd 246, 250
  235d 250
  237c 111
  237d 287
  238a 231
  238b 277
  238cd 246
  241e 246
  242b–243e 246, 250–1
  244bd 249–50, 254

244c6–7   250
245c–246a   192–3
245e   111
247d–248b   458
249a   492
249e   458
251ae   253, 254
251c6–7   254
252b   150, 305–6
252bc   254–5
260bc   331
261bd   246–8
262a   458
262d   246
263d   246, 458
264c   293
265a–266b   246
265bc   255
265d–266c   112
265e–266b   141, 285
265d   112, 141
267c   148
269e–270a   201–2
271a–272a   290–2
273c   200–1
274e   259
277b   285
277bc   290–2
278e–279a   487
Philebus (*Phlb.*)   20, 112, 140
12bc   200
14b   235
16c   324
16c–18d   35, 285, 289
16e   112, 141
17b   356
18a   155
18bc   284–5
18bd   356
18d   24–5
23b   80
23c–27c   362
23d   328
36e   49
38cd   52
44cd   417
56bc   127
56de   360
57d   415–16
59ab   461
61de   125
63b   80
Politicus (*Plt.*)   20, 112, 140, 285, 414
258a   277
261e   113, 424
262a–263d   141

262ab   129
263d   103
264d   113
267a   299
274b   259
277c   291, 293
277d   456
277e–278d   289
281ab   58–9, 68
282bc   108
282e   415–16
283ab   108
283b   155
285cd   356
287a   406
293ce   322–3
293d   417
294a   491
294e–295a   118
299b   202
306e   129, 277
Protagoras (*Prt.*)   250–1, 254
316de   150–1
317a   421
319a–320c   120
321b   80
324a   328
329ab   338
330c   344
330cd   457
332a   457
333c   421
335c   421
336a   262–3
336bc   141
337ac   28
337c   28
338e–339a   250–1
340ab   28
341a   28
341e   262–3
343ab   262–3
347b–348a   151, 250–1
355d   49
355e   42
358a   200–1, 457
360e   439
Republic (*R.*)   20, 120, 127, 128, 140, 414, 458, 480, 492
335c   460
340d–341a   322
349e   492
352e   460
352e–353a   98, 430
358e–359b   39

II Index of ancient texts

Plato (Pl.) (cont.)
  359a 38
  363a 439
  366b 235
  373b 274
  376e 274
  396b 273–4
  397a 273–4
  398b 274
  399c 324
  399e–400c 282, 283
  402ab 356
  402c 159–60
  403b 120
  403de 371
  406d 99–100
  413a 50
  414a 371
  421a 286
  428b 277
  431d 277
  432d 80
  435c 27
  438d–439a 362
  443b 456
  450c 402–3
  452ae 315
  455ce 153
  455e–456a 49
  456b 120
  462c 263
  473c 315
  476bc 457
  476c 456, 457
  477b 52, 53
  477c 159–60
  477d 474
  478a 52, 53
  478bc 333
  479a 460
  479e 460
  books 6–7 140
  484c 125, 287, 458
  484d 458
  486d 458
  488e–489a 202
  489c 202
  497d 27, 120
  500bc 458
  501b 126
  505a 402–3
  507b 126, 458
  507c 275
  510a 128
  510b–511d 437, 438
  510d 417, 434, 436, 437
  511bc 437
  520c 456, 480
  521d 416
  524e 416
  525d 248
  526a 360, 398
  527b 416
  527d–528a 192
  528e–530c 192
  530d 190
  532ab 126
  533b 126
  533bc 127, 456
  533be 437
  533c 434, 437
  533de 424
  534bc 111
  534bd 142
  534cd 456
  538d 118
  544c 231
  549e 445
  553c 416
  557a 462
  560c–561a 91
  book 10 128, 138
  596a 474
  596b 106, 125, 128
  596d 193
  597a 126, 458
  598e 73
  600cd 73
  601a 263–4
  601c–602a 138–9
  601e–602a 142
  604e 470
  612b 439
  616b–617d 253
  618c 430
Sophist (Sph.) 20–1, 60, 61, 70, 112, 140, 285, 293, 335, 349
  219a–221c 113
  220a 113
  220c 73, 113
  221c 312
  222c 113
  223b 113
  224c 113
  226bc 108
  227bc 424
  229e–230e 141
  230a–231b 245
  234b 157
  237bc 333
  237d 263
  239b 78

240d–241a	51–2	152ce	219, 226, 468–9
241d	332	152c	82, 460
251ab	106	152de	208–9, 466
253a	356	152d3–4	468–9
253ae	289–90	152d7–e1	468
253be	112	152e	474
255cd	287–8	153a	220–1
257b	235, 263	153c	311
257c	173	153cd	209, 220
257d	129	153d–157c	226–7, 469
258ab	129	156a	99, 470–1
258ce	332	156c	226–7, 234, 275, 470–1
261c–263d	187–8	156d1	227
261d–262a	55, 269–70	156d3	227
261d–262d	50, 173	157a	97
261d–263d	59, 294–6, 345, 373	157ab	466
261e	25, 110	157b	464
261e–262a	295	159e–160a	469
262a1	295	160c	78
262a4	295	161a	82
262b	348	161c	82, 149
262c	78	161c–162c	21, 84
262c2–3	295	161d	77
262d	56	162a	82
262e–263d	295	163b	428
262e	96, 362	166d–167d	84
263a	52	167ad	77
263b	51–2	167c	82
263bd	341	168b	78
263d	348	168bc	263–4
263e	445	169a	84, 434–5
264a	49	171d–172b	84
265c	262–3	172a	78, 82
267e	113	172b	77, 78
268a	27	175d	201–2

Symposium (Smp.)

197d1–5	264	176b	80
197de	263–4	177c–179c	21, 84
198b	263–4	177cd	78
199b	263–4	178b	50
203d	193	179b	136
210e	457	179d	486
211a	461	179d–180c	27, 209, 405, 472
211ab	460	180bc	318
211bc	479	180d	471
211c	126	181c	470–1
212c	200–9	181cd	211
221e	51, 263–4	181c–182a	469, 470–3

Theaetetus (Tht.) 18, 20–1, 78, 84, 102–3, 123, 305, 453–4, 456, 461, 468–73, 492

		181c–183b	21, 468, 469–73
		181d–182a	471–3
142d	486	182ab	362
144c	429	182ae	469
146b	486	182ce	470
146e	439	182d	462
150d	80	182de	482
151e–179c	76–8	182d4–7	470
		182d4	470

Plato (Pl.) (cont.)
  182d7 470
  182e–183b 469
  183a 466, 472–3
  184b–186e 78
  184c 263–4, 280, 424
  185a 275
  186bc 192
  187c 231
  188d–189b 334–5
  189e–190a 445
  190c 262–3, 494
  190d 430
  191d 371
  192a 371
  194b 371
  195bc 201–2
  199a 424
  200d–201c 432
  201bc 480
  201d 456
  201e 78
  201e–206b 305
  201e–208b 289
  203b 284–5
  204d 359–60
  206d 263–4
  207a–208b 356
  209bc 366
Timaeus (*Ti.*) 20, 123, 196, 218, 225, 253, 480, 484
  27d–28a 458
  28a 125, 460
  28ab 128
  29bc 188
  35a 458
  37e–38b 466
  40a 184
  45bd 227–8
  46e–47e 113–14
  47bc 192
  47cd 113–14
  48e–52d 461
  49d–50a 464
  49e 263
  51bc 457
  52a 106
  52b 456
  52d 324
  55d 235
  56ab 217
  58b 217
  58d 195, 196
  61e 217
  63a 49
  67b 275
  67cd 227–8
  74d 416
  78a 217
  78e 121
  80c 415–16
  81e 98
  82d 416
  84a 416
  90cd 192
  90c 239
Plinius (Plin.)
  Naturalis Historia (*Nat.*)
    34.143–5 137
Plutarch (Plu.)
  Adversus Coloten (*Adv. Col.*)
    1110E5–1111F1 213–14, 227
    1113AB 89
  De communibus notitiis (*Comm. not.*)
    1077C 367
  De E apud Delphos (*De E*)
    392B 203–4
  De Iside et Osiride (*De Is. et Os.*)
    375CD 239
  Lycurgus (*Lyc.*)
    1.4–2.1 223
  Ad principem ineruditum
    782EF 486
  Solon (*Sol.*)
    25.4 237
  Quomodo adulescens poetas audire debeat (*Quomodo adul.*)
    18C 273–4
Pollux
  Onomasticon
    1.33.5 244
    7.129.6 290
Polybius (Plb.)
  10.47.8 167
Proclus (Procl.)
  In Euclidis Elementa
    193.10–14 93
    196.15–26 93
  In Platonis Cratylum
    I, 1.1–9 425–6
    I, 1.7–9 71
    X, 4.6–16 425–6
    X, 4.11–16 198
    X, 4.16–18 426–7
    X, 4.18–23 425–6
    XII, 5.1–4 426–7
    XVI, 5.27–6.19 123–4
    XVI, 6.20–7.6 92–4
    XVI, 7.6–13 93–4
    XVI, 7.10–13 25

II Index of ancient texts

XVII, 7.18–8.14   5
XVII, 7.18–8.4   32–3, 71–2
XVII, 8.11–14   426–7
XIX, 8.21–3   198, 425–6
XXI, 8.26–8   19
XXII, 9   70
XXVII, 10.10–11   425–6
XXX, 10.23–6   39, 94
XXX, 11.1–4   198, 425–6
XXXI, 11.9–10   76
XXXIII, 11   70
XXXIII, 11.15–23   40, 43–4
XXXIII, 11.15–17   71–2
XXXVI, 11.30–12.17   70
XXXVI, 11.30–12.3   57
XXXVI, 12.6–16   71–2
XXXVII, 12.18–23   332–5
XXXVII, 12.21–3   334–5
XXXVII, 12.23   334–5
XXXVIII, 12   70
XXXVIII, 12 24–7   82
XLI, 13.13–18   85
XLV, 14   69
XLV, 14.10–30   103
XLVI, 15.1–26   69, 71–2, 106
XLVIII, 16.5–27   71–2, 111
XLVIII, 16.19–23   71
XLVIII, 16.25–6   106
LI, 18.15–17   426–7
LI, 18.20–6   198, 425–6
LI, 18.28   491
LI, 19.15   491
LIV, 23.26–30   132
LVIII, 25.33–26.3   32–3, 71–2
LXI, 26.27–27.2   142
LXVIII, 29.6–12   151
LXXI, 33.7–11   151
LXXI, 34.13–35.8   150
In Platonis Parmenidem (*in Prm.*)
631–3   250
866.11   71
Protagoras (Prot.)
80 A1 DK   283
A27   283
A28   283
A29   283
B1   51–2
B2   200
Pseudo-Archytas
19 Thesleff   202
23.18   202
24.18   202
26.21   202
27.16   202

Quintilian (Quint.)
Institutio oratoria (*Inst.*)
1.6.32–8   239
8.6.64   492

Sappho (Sapph.)
fr. 180 Voigt   157
Scholia (*sch.*)
in Homeri Iliadem
2.458   196
14.288   196
in Platonem
3 Cufalo   27
23   244
Supplementum Epigraphicum Graecum (*SEG*)
XVII.10   439
Seneca (Sen.)
Letters to Lucilius (*Ep.*)
58.15   333
Sextus Empiricus (S.E.)
Adversus Mathematicos (*M.*)
1.37–8   76
1.142–53   148
1.145–9   76
1.184–90   148
1.199   94
1.216–17   94
1.241–5   259–60
7.135   213
9.75–6   218
9.182–4   184
10.263   288
Outlines of Pyrrhonism (*PH*)
2.214   76
3.135   71
Simonides (Sim.)
fr. 543.19 *PMG*   262–3
Simplicius (Simpl.)
In Aristotelis Categorias (*in Cat.*)
27.19–21   39
63.22–4   287
In Aristotelis De Caelo (*in Cael.*)
12.21–7   195–7
87.20–6   195–7
119.2–4   239–40
294.33–295.20   214
In Aristotelis Physicam (*in Ph.*)
157.7–9   222
164.23–4   222
164.24–5 + 156.13–157.4   222
248.2–5   287, 288
327.24–6   450

1165.33–9   195–7
1318.35–1319.1   224–5
1320.16–19   214
Sophocles (S.)
Ajax (Aj.)
  243   262–3
  430–2   35
  606–7   193
  832   488
Antigone (Ant.)
  404   159–60
Electra (El.)
  1084   94
  1197   483
Oedipus Coloneus (OC)
  873   262–3
  907–8   159–60
Philoctetes (Ph.)
  77   130–1
  fr. 658 *TrGF*   35
  595   108
  843   430
  890   108
Stobaeus (Stob.)
  1 *Prooem. coroll.* 3   202
  1.20.3   202
  1.41.2   190
  2.31.119   225
  4.20.65   28
Strabo (Strab.)
  10.1.10   391
Suda
  Σ 1587 Adler   38
  Σ 1590   387
  Σ 2622–3   387

Theagenes
  8 A2 DK   190, 202
Theophrastus (Thphr.)
De sensu (Sens.)
  7   227–8
  25   192
  50   227
Historia Plantarum (HP)
  9.16.8.5   415–16
  9.19.4   170
Thucydides (Th.)
  1.1.1   42
  2.42.2   93, 235
  2.79.1   97
  3.15.1   417
  3.34.2   462
  3.81.5   231
  3.82.4–5   90–1
  4.3.3   194
  4.67.4   387
  4.74.2   462
  4.87.1   192
  4.112.1   387
  4.126.3   97
  5.111.3   262–3
  6.36.2   328
  6.40.2   328
  6.80.4   149
  7.8.2   50
  7.44.4   387
  8.37.1   38
  8.70.1   462
Timaeus
Lexicon Platonicum
  50 Bonelli   290
  58   244

Varro
De lingua latina (L.)
  8.54   94
  8.57   94
  8.61   94

Xenocrates
  frr. 264–6 Isnardi Parente = 53
    Heinze   195–7
Xenophanes (Xenoph.)
  21 B34.3 DK   402–3
Xenophon (X.)
Anabasis (An.)
  1.5.6   328
  4.4.15–16   51–2
Apology of Socrates (Ap.)
  2.10   19
Cynegeticus (Cyn.)
  6.15   98
Cyropaedia (Cyr.)
  8.3.37   416
  8.7.10   41
Hiero (Hier.)
  1.8   352
Historia Graeca (HG)
  5.4.6   387
Memorabilia (Mem.)
  1.2.42   118
  1.2.48   19
  2.10   19, 28–9
  3.9.10   322–3
  4.4.7   356
  4.4.13   118
  4.8.4–11   19
Oeconomicus (Oec.)
  10.5–6   290
Symposium
  4.6–7   150–1

III Index of Greek expressions

This Index lists Greek expressions discussed in the commentary with regard to matters of meaning or grammar. It does not list words which are etymologized or discussed in the *Cratylus*, for which see instead Index IV.

ἀήρ 196–7
Ἅιδης 193
αἰθήρ 195–7
αἴρω/ἀείρω 195
ἀλλά 356
  ἀλλά … γάρ 249
ἁμαρτέω 439–40
ἁμαρτή 439–40
ἀναθρέω 192
ἀναλαμβάνω 440
ἀναφέρω 287
ἀνδρείκελον 290
ἀποβλέπω (πρός τι) 125
ἀποδείκνυμι 304
ἀποδίδωμι 353–4
(ἀπο)διοπομπέομαι, (ἀπο)-
  διοπόμπησις 243–4
ἄρα 69, 73–4
ἀρέσκω 414
ἆρ' οὖν 110, 460
ἀρχή 437
αὖ 149
αὐτό with feminine nouns 439
αὐτὸ ἐκεῖνο ὅ ἐστι F *see* ὅ ἐστι F.
αὐτὸ τὸ F 458

βέβαιος 87, 439; *see also* Index IV
βεβαιότης *see* βέβαιος.
βούλομαι, βούλησις 233–5

γάρ 39
  presupposing ellipsis 331, 359
γιγνώσκω 127
γλίσχρος, γλίσχρως 416–17
γοῦν, inferential or not 369
γράμμα
  = 'letter' 166, 353–4

  = 'picture' 339, 353–4
γραμματική 356

δέ 484
  used in place of γάρ 76
δεῖ, expressing inevitability or
  prescription 130–1, 135–6
δηλόω 164–7, 172–5, 267–8, 269–70, 304,
  324, 384–6, 398–9
δήλωμα 165, 173, 269–70, 382, 384–6,
  398–9
δήλωσις 398, 406; *see also* Index I *s.v.*
  signification
διάγραμμα 434–5
διαλεκτικός 140
διάνοια 176, 236–7, 399
διανοοῦμαι 398
δοκεῖ, impersonal 194
δοξάζω 430
δύναμαι
  = 'be equivalent to' 328
  = 'mean' 176–7, 328
  = 'entail' 328
δύναμις 167, 171–7

ἐθίζω 41
εἰκών 339
εἰμί 50–3
  relation between copulative and existential
  use 277–8, 320
  εἶναί τι 457, 475, 484–5
  (τὸ) ὄν 281, 332–5
  (τὰ) ὄντα 50–3, 87, 96–7, 207, 214–15,
    287–8, 458, 466
εἶναί τι *see* εἰμί
εἰ ὅτι μάλιστα 402–3, 447
εἰρωνεία, εἰρωνεύομαι 27

533

III Index of Greek expressions

ἐκεῖνο/τοιοῦτον 464–8
ἐντρεπτικός 71
ἐξαπατάω 245
ἐπάνειμι 479
ἐπεί, elliptical use 384, 420–1
ἔπειμι 479–80
ἐπεφύκει 99
ἐπί
  with dative 24–5, 259
  with genitive 206
  ἐπὶ ξενίας 336
ἐπίσταμαι 127, 428–9
ἐπιστήμη 127; see also Index IV
ἐπιφέρω 369–70
εὑρίσκω 430

ζητέω 430
ζῷον = 'picture' 291, 339

ἤ = 'or in other words' 492
ἡλικία 486

θέσις 4–6, 426

ἰδέα 231
ἴθι δή 49–50
ἰσόρροπος 93
ἴσως
  = 'equally' 393
  = 'perhaps' 384

καί 359
  consecutive 391, 401
  explanatory 366, 381, 427
  separated from the word it emphasizes 16
καίω/κάω 219
καλέω 24
  ὄνομα καλεῖν ἐπί τινι 24–5
καλός, καλῶς 116, 140; see also Index IV
κατάδηλος 303
κατὰ τοῦτο 428
κατὰ τρόπον 300–1
κάτοπτρον/κάτροπτον 240
κερκίς, κερκίζω 108–10, 115
κομψός, κομψῶς 248
κύριος 135–6

λανθάνω 157
λέγω 332–5
  = 'state' 56, 100, 103–4
  with accusative = 'speak of something' 51, 100, 333
  = 'mean' (?) 235–6
λεγόμενα 199
λόγος 50, 291, 293, 328, 348, 372–9

τὰ λοιπά 437

-μα, nouns ending in 270
μανθάνω 430
μείων 352
μέν, duplicated 413
  μὲν οὖν 413
οἱ μετεωρολόγοι 201–2
μηνύω 235

νοέω 236–7
νομοθετική (τέχνη) 491
νόμος 118
  νόμῳ 42, 119
  νομοθέτης 118
νώνυμος / νώνυμνος 94

ὃ ἐπεφύκει κερκίζειν 126
ὅ ἐστι F 21, 126–7, 195, 458
οἶδα 428–9
οἷόν ἐστιν 428–9
οἰωνιστική 249–50
ὁλκή 415–17
ὁλκός (adjective) 416
ὁλκός (noun) 417
ὅλως οὐκ 149
ὁμαρτέω 439–40
ὅμοιος, with dative = 'in accordance with' 445
ὁ μέν, understood 49
ὄνομα 1, 55, 60, 61–2, 105–6, 119
ὀνόματα καὶ ῥήματα see ῥῆμα; see also Index IV
(τὰ) ὄντα see εἰμί
ὁποῖόν τι ἐστιν 480
ὀρθοέπεια 148
ὅτι, pleonastic 344
οὐ καθ' ὁδόν 300–1
οὐκοῦν 153, 352
οὖν
  inferential 474, 476–7
  not inferential 476; see also ἆρ' οὖν
οὐ πάνυ 80, 191
οὐ πάνυ τι 80
οὐσία 77–8, 87, 110–11, 166–7, 173, 175, 202–3, 267–8, 276–8, 438–9; see also Index IV
οὗτος + noun, without article 324

πάλαι 432
πέφυκε, personal and impersonal construction 98
ποιόν τι 362
ποῖόν τί ἐστιν 480
ποιότης 123
πολύσημος 93

III Index of Greek expressions

πρᾶγμα, τὰ πράγματα   87, 96–7, 207, 214–15, 381
προσβιβάζω (τι κατά τι)   311
προσῆκον   371, 377, 405
πρόσρησις, πρόσρημα   277
προσχράομαι   417

ῥέω   486
ῥεῦμα   486
ῥῆμα   50, 55, 259, 262–7, 291
  = 'expression' or 'phrase'   262–7
  = 'verb'   266–7, 294–6, 347–8
  ὀνόματα καὶ ῥήματα   263–4

σημαίνω   155–9, 164–7, 169–77, 446
σημεῖον   269–70; see also σημαίνω
σοῦς   223–4
σοφιστής   193, 244–5
στοιχεῖον   166, 259
σύγκειμαι   299
σύμφωνος   433–4
συνείρω   299
συνήθης   15
συνθήκη   38, 39
  σύνθημα   387
  συντίθεμαι   299; see also Index I s.v. convention

τε, postponed   288
τε καί   288
  explanatory   311

τέχνη   127; see also Index IV
  -της, feminine nouns ending in   391
τὶ αὐτὸ καλόν   457
τίθημι   347
  τίθεμαι   24
τις, understood as subject   269
τὸ τί ἦν εἶναι   99
τρόπος   248
τύπος   371–2

ὑγιής   486
ὑπέξειμι   465
ὑπεξέρχομαι   462–3
ὑπόκειμαι   437

φαῦλον   300–1
φέρε δή   49–50, 107
φέρομαι, φορά   211
φημί = 'assert'   337
φθέγγομαι   173, 337
φύσις   4–6, 129
φωνή   24–5, 247, 275

χρηστῶς   302
χωρέω   215

ψεῦδος   435

ὦ ἑταῖρε   494–5
ὡς   50–3

IV Index of words discussed in the Cratylus

Here I list Greek words which are discussed (often, though not always, by being etymologized) in the dialogue. I list them in the form in which they are usually mentioned in the text: thus adjectives and participles in the neuter nominative singular, verbs in the infinitive.

ἀβουλία (ill-advisedness) 186–7
ἀγαθόν (good) 185, 211–12, 215, 229–30, 258–9, 266
Ἀγαμέμνων (Agamemnon) 179
Ἆγις (Agis) 172
ἀδικία (injustice) 185
ἀήρ (air) 184, 195, 197, 205, 208
Ἀθηνᾶ (Athena)/Παλλάς (Pallas) 25, 154, 183
Ἅιδης (Hades) 21, 183, 193–5
αἰθήρ (aether) 184, 195–7, 205
αἰσχρόν (ugly) 185, 231
Ἀκεσίμβροτος (Acesimbrotus) 172
ἀκολασία (intemperance) 439–40
ἀλγεδών (distress) 186
ἀλήθεια (truth) 187–8, 265–6
ἀμαθία (ignorance) 439–40
ἁμαρτία (error) 187, 225, 439, 440
ἀναγκαῖον (compulsory) 187
ἄναξ (lord) 156–7, 159
ἀνδρεία (courage) 158, 185, 228, 235
ἀνήρ (man) 185, 342
ἄνθρωπος (human being) 182, 192, 248, 264–5, 428
ἀνία (sorrow) 186
Ἀπόλλων (Apollo) 175–6, 183, 235
ἀπορία (difficulty) 185
ἀρετή (virtue) 185, 234
Ἄρης (Ares) 183–4
ἄρρεν (male) 185
Ἄρτεμις (Artemis) 183
ἄστρα (stars) 184
ἀστραπή (lightning) 184
Ἀστυάναξ (Astyanax) 152–9, 172–5
Ἀτρεύς (Atreus) 179, 234
Ἀφροδίτη (Aphrodite) 183, 248–9
ἀχθηδών (trouble) 186

βέβαιον (certain) 439
βλαβερόν (harmful) 185–6, 231
βλάπτον (harming) 185–6
βούλεσθαι (to want) 186–7
βουλεύεσθαι (to deliberate) 186–7
βουλή (deliberation) 186–7

γῆ/γαῖα (earth) 184, 195, 205, 234
γλίσχρον (viscous) 308
γλοιῶδες (glutinous) 308
γλυκύ (sweet) 308
γνώμη (judgement) 185, 206
γογγύλον (round) 309, 312–13, 428
γυνή (woman) 185, 224

δαίμων (daimon) 182, 236
δειλία (cowardice) 185
δέον (necessary) 185–6, 230–2
δεσμός (bond) 308, 312–13
Δημήτηρ (Demeter) 183
δίκαιον (just) 185, 215–23, 228, 229–30
δικαιοσύνη (justice) 185, 215
Διόνυσος (Dionysus) 183, 248–9, 256
Δίφιλος (Diphilus) 264–5
δόξα (opinion) 186–7
δοῦν (binding) 257, 259, 260–1, 280

ἑκούσιον (voluntary) 187, 224–5
ἕκτωρ (holder) 156–7, 159
Ἕκτωρ (Hector) 152–9, 172–5
ἔνδον (inside) 309, 312–13
ἐνιαυτός/ἔτος (year) 184, 205
ἐντός (within) 309
ἐπιθυμία (appetite) 186
ἐπιστήμη (knowledge) 185, 206, 235, 439, 440
ἐρείκειν (to rend) 306–8, 312–13
Ἑρμῆς (Hermes) 183–4

IV Index of words discussed in Cratylus

Ἑρμογένης (Hermogenes) 4, 15, 26–32, 324–8, 433, 487–8
ἔρως (love) 186
Ἑστία (Hestia) 183, 202–3, 276–7
Εὐπόλεμος (Eupolemus) 172
εὔπορον (prosperous) 185–6, 231
Εὐτυχίδης (Eutychides) 198
εὐφροσύνη (good cheer) 186

ζέον (seething) 308
Ζεύς, Διός (Zeus) 179, 218
ζημιῶδες (hurtful) 185–6
ζυγόν (yoke) 185–6, 230

ἡδονή (pleasure) 186
ἥλιος (sun) 184, 205
ἡμέρα (day) 185–6, 230
Ἥρα (Hera) 183, 202
ἥρως (hero) 182, 246–8, 252
Ἥφαιστος (Hephaestus) 183

θάλλειν (to flourish) 185
Θεόφιλος (Theophilus) 177–8, 198
θηλή (nipple) 185
θῆλυ (female) 185, 342
θραύειν (to fracture) 306–8
θρύπτειν (to break) 306–8
θυμός (spirit) 186

Ἰατροκλῆς (Iatrocles) 172
ἰέναι (to go) 308, 312–13
ἵεσθαι (to rush) 308
ἵμερος (desire) 186
ἰόν (going) 257, 259, 260–1, 280
Ἶρις (Iris) 183–4
ἱστορία (information) 439

κακία (badness) 185, 234
κακόν (bad) 185
καλόν (beautiful) 185
κάτροπτον (mirror) 185, 240
κερδαλέον (gainful) 185–6, 231
κέρδος (gain) 185–6, 228–30, 232
κερματίζειν (to crumble) 306–8
κίνησις (motion) 306–7
κολλῶδες (gluey) 308
Κρόνος (Cronus) 179, 183, 192, 203–4, 433
κρούειν (to strike) 306–8
κύων (dog) 184

λεῖον (smooth) 308
Λητώ (Leto) 183
λιπαρόν (oily) 308
λύπη (pain) 186

λυσιτελοῦν (profitable) 185–6, 228–30, 231, 232

μέγα (large) 309
μείς (month) 184, 205
μῆκος (length) 309
μηχανή (contrivance) 185
μνήμη (memory) 439
Μνησίθεος (Mnesitheus) 177–8
Μοῦσαι (Muses) 183

νόησις (intellection) 185, 206, 235

ὀδύνη (grief) 186
οἴησις (belief) 186–7
οἶνος (wine) 183
ὀλισθάνειν (to glide) 308
ὄν/οὐκ ὄν (what is / what is not) 187–8, 257
ὄνομα (name) 187–8
Ὀρέστης (Orestes) 179
Οὐρανός (Uranus) 179, 192, 241
οὐσία/ἐσσία/ὠσία (being) 183, 187–8, 202–3, 210, 211, 276–7

Παλλάς (Pallas) 25, 154
Πάν (Pan) 183–4
Πέλοψ (Pelops) 158, 179
πιστόν (convincing) 439
Πλούτων (Pluto) 183, 193
πόθος (longing) 186
Πολέμαρχος (Polemarchus) 172
Ποσειδῶν (Poseidon) 183
πῦρ (fire) 184, 195

Ῥέα (Rhea) 183, 203–4, 433
ῥεῖν (to flow), ῥέον (flowing), ῥοή (stream) 257, 259, 260–1, 280, 306–8, 312–13, 314
ῥυμβεῖν (to whirl) 306–8

σείεσθαι (to be shaken) 308
σεισμός (shock) 308
σελήνη (moon) 184, 237
Σκάμανδριος (Scamandrius) 152–4
σκληρότης/σκληρότηρ, σκληρόν (hardness, hard) 390–407, 415–17, 422, 426
σοφία (intelligence) 185, 223–4
στάσις (rest) 306–7, 308
συμφέρον (advantageous) 185–6, 231
συμφορά (misfortune) 439
σύνεσις (understanding) 185, 236
Σφίγξ (Sphinx) 185, 234, 240
σῶμα (body) 183, 190, 191–2
Σωσίας (Sosias) 198
σωφροσύνη (temperance) 185, 206

Τάνταλος (Tantalus) 179
τερπνόν (delightful) 186
τέρψις (delight) 186
τέχνη (art) 185, 240
Τηθύς (Tethys) 183, 205
τραχύ (?) (harsh) 306–8
τρέχειν (to run) 306–8, 312–13
τρόμος (trembling) 306–8, 312–13

ὕδωρ (water) 184, 195

Φερρέφαττα/Φερσεφόνη (Persephone) 183, 205, 210, 223, 235

φρόνησις (wisdom) 185, 206
φυσῶδες (blowy) 308

χαρά (joy) 186

ψεῦδος (falsehood) 187–8, 234, 265
ψυχή (soul) 183, 191–3
ψυχρόν (cold) 308

ὧραι (seasons) 184, 205
ὠφέλιμον (useful) 185–6, 231

CPSIA information can be obtained
at www.ICGtesting.com
Printed in the USA
LVHW01s0418170418
573666LV00016B/302/P